STEAM BRITISH ISLES

The complete guide to railway preservation, minor and miniature railways

Roger Crombleholme
and
Terry Kirtland

DAVID & CHARLES
Newton Abbot London North Pomfret (Vt)

KEY TO ABBREVIATIONS USED IN THIS BOOK

LOCATIONS

Classification of preservation sites into types:

- **A** Fully-operational for public traffic, offering train rides with steam motive power.
- **B** Fully-operational for public traffic or demonstration purposes using internal combustion, electric, cable or horse motive power.
- **C** Privately-operated railways using any form of motive power.
- **D** Live steam centres where locomotives are steamed and rides given on special open days.
- **E** Museums of preserved locomotives and rolling stock or static public exhibits. Non-operational.
- **F** Preservation sites where stock is gathered for eventual use on a preserved line. Check on public access before visiting.
- **G** Private premises on which locomotives or rolling stock are housed. PLEASE OBTAIN PERMISSION FROM THE OWNER BEFORE VISITING.
- **H** Groups owning rolling stock used on operating lines.
- **I** Industrial steam locations. No public access without permission.

LOCOMOTIVE TYPES

The Whyte notation for wheel arrangement has been used throughout this book to designate steam locomotive types. The same system is also used for electric and internal combustion locomotives with driving wheels coupled by outside rods. Small locomotives with non-coupled wheels are shown as 4W or 6W to indicate four- or six-wheel drive. The following abbreviations are also used to indicate locomotive type:

- T Side tank. Tanks mounted on the frame, usually on each side of the boiler.
- CT Crane tank. Side tank locomotive fitted with a crane.
- PT Pannier tank. Side tanks slung, pannier fashion, either side of the boiler.
- ST Saddle tank. Tank mounted above the boiler.
- WT Well tank. Tank mounted between the frames.
- TG Geared tank. Locomotive drive transmitted by gears and/or chains.
- VB Vertical boiler.
- F Fireless thermal storage steam locomotive.
- DM Diesel locomotive with mechanical transmission.
- DE Diesel locomotive with electric transmission.
- DH Diesel locomotive with hydraulic transmission.
- PM Petrol locomotive with mechanical transmission.
- BE Battery powered electric locomotive.
- PH Petrol locomotive with hydraulic transmission.
- E Electric locomotive.
- R Railcar.

British Library Cataloguing in Publication Data

Crombleholme, Roger
Steam British Isles: the complete guide to railway preservation, minor and miniature railways.
1. Railways – Great Britain – History
I. Title II. Kirtland, Terry
385'.0941 HE3018

ISBN 0-7153-8673-5

Typeset by Typesetters (Birmingham) Ltd, Smethwick, Warley, West Midlands
and printed in Great Britain
by Billings
for David & Charles (Publishers) Limited
Brunel House Newton Abbot Devon

Published in the United States of America
by David & Charles Inc
North Pomfret Vermont 05053 USA

Contents

Introduction

Steam British Isles continues the tradition we have carefully built up over the last 15 years by the *Steam* Yearbook series for complete, reliable and up-to-date coverage of the activities of every railway preservation society, steam centre, and operating railway in the British Isles. From the miniature to the 5ft 3in gauge of Ireland – you will find it all here!

Updated and expanded to include every new development at the time of going to press, this is the 'Bible' for the dedicated expert and for the young newcomer, intrigued by this increasingly popular leisure activity, who is keen to know more and be well-informed. The number of railway projects now exceeds 600, and all are fully described.

Information about each railway or centre is presented in handy area form, with easy-reference numbers contained in an alphabetical list as an index. In addition to descriptive text, each article features a detailed list of locomotives and rolling stock and their historical origins. To help the newcomer, carefully researched details of the location of each railway, how to get there, and the facilities available to visitors are included.

For our part, we are delighted to set before you this comprehensive review of Britain's 'Alternative Railways'. As ever, it has been a pleasure to renew acquaintances with all the dedicated amateurs and professional railwaymen who make today's British steam scene so rich and varied.

As the railway preservation movement rolls on through its fourth decade, growing stronger and ever more confident on its journey, new generations of enthusiasts are being fired to power it on its way. Wherever you live, there is a nearby railway project just waiting to use *your* skills and enthusiasm. Why not get involved? But be warned – railways are an infectious mania which has a habit of taking over your life!

What you read between these covers is largely the result of that infectious mania, a tribute in iron and steel to the unbridled dedication of the British enthusiast when faced with the prospective extinction of that which he loves best. What gives us most pleasure is to reflect their efforts in *Steam British Isles* and produce for the movement as a whole what has become the acknowledged definitive book of reference to which everybody turns for all the facts about preserved railways.

Roger Crombleholme
Terry Kirtland

AREA A

South West

Cornwall
Devon
Somerset
Dorset
Wiltshire
Avon
(Group Nos 1–50)

1 Dart Valley Railway A

Passenger-carrying standard gauge railway, 7 miles in length from Buckfastleigh to Totnes Riverside

Buckfastleigh Station, Devon TQ11 0DZ
Access: Buckfastleigh Station is just off the A38 trunk road, halfway between Exeter and Plymouth
Bus route Nos 188 from Newton Abbot and Plymouth
Tel: Buckfastleigh 2338
OS Ref: SX 747663

Services operate over Easter week, then Sundays, May Day Holiday weekend and daily from mid-May to mid-September.
Facilities for visitors include free car parking, riverside picnic area, restaurant, toilets, transport museum and book and souvenir shops.
The Dart Valley Railway is a portion of the old GWR Totnes–Ashburton branch which was closed by BR in 1962. Services were restored between Totnes and Buckfastleigh in May 1969 by Dart Valley Light Railway Ltd who operate the line on GWR principles but as a commercial company rather than as a preservation organisation.
Passengers can enjoy excursions through the heart of South Devon's wonderful country behind gleaming Great Western steam locomotives and can join trains at Buckfastleigh and Staverton Bridge stations. The railway operates to a point north-eastwards of Ashburton Junction at Totnes where a new station is under construction. Access at Buckfastleigh is recommended, as there is no car park or public transport at Staverton Bridge and no access whatever to trains at the Totnes end of the line.

Stock
[2]GWR 2-6-2T No. 4555 (Class 45XX) built 1924
[3]GWR 0-6-0PT No. 1369 (Class 1366) built 1934
[4]GWR 0-6-0PT No. 1638 *Dartington* (Class 16XX) built 1951
[5]GWR 0-6-0PT No. 6430 (Class 64XX) built 1937
[5]GWR 0-6-0PT No. 6435 (Class 64XX) built 1937
[6]GWR 0-4-2T No. 1420 *Bulliver* (Class 14XX) built 1933
[7]GWR 0-4-2T No. 1450 *Ashburton* (Class 14XX) built 1935
GWR 2-8-0 No. 3803 (Class 28XX) built 1939
[11]GWR 4-6-0 No. 4920 *Dumbleton Hall* built 1929
[1]Peckett 0-4-0ST No. 1 *Ashley* 2031 built 1942
[9]Peckett 0-4-0ST *Lady Angela* 1690 built 1926
[10]Hunslet 0-6-0ST *Glendower* 3810 built 1954
[10]Hunslet 0-6-0ST *Barbara* 2890 built 1943
[10]Bagnall 0-6-0ST 2766 built 1944
Fowler 0-4-0DM 421041 built 1958
GWR auto-trailers Nos 225, 228 & 232 built 1951
GWR auto-trailer No. 240 built 1954
GWR open 3rd coaches Nos 1285 & 1295 built 1937
[1]GWR super saloon No. 9111 'King George' built 1932
GWR dynamometer car No. 7 built 1901
GWR directors saloon No. 249 built 1894
GWR engineers saloon No. 6479 built 1910
BR Mk.1 FO coach No. 3081 built 1957
GWR Hawksworth BCK coach No. 7377 built 1948
BR Mk.1 SK coach No. 18308
BR Mk.1 SK coach No. 25323 built 1957
BR Mk.1 SK coach No. 25355 built 1957
BR Mk.1 SK coach No. 25580 built 1958
BR Mk.1 SK coach No. 25693 built 1958
BR Mk.1 SLF coach No. 2080 built 1959
BR Mk.1 SLS coach No. 2574 built 1959
BR Mk.1 SLS coach No. 2599 built 1960
BR Mk.1 SLS coach No. 2801 built 1959
[1]LMS Stanier bogie parcels van No. M31927 built 1944
GWR 'Toad' 20-ton goods brake van No. 68479 built 1947
[1]GWR 'Toad' 20-ton goods brake van No. 68777 built 1939
SR goods van No. S65495 built 1939
[1]LMS open wagon PLA No. C19 built 1944
[1]GWR fruit van No. 95979
GWR 'Mink B' van No. 125814 built 1939
GWR 'Damo B' van No. 42223 built 1939
GWR breakdown tool van No. DW146 built 1970
GWR banana van No. 105658 (rebuilt for service use)
[1]GWR banana van No. 5576 built 1929 (rebuilt for service use)
GWR shunters truck No. 41873 built 1895
[1]GWR iron 'Mink A' covered van No. 59119 built 1896
GWR 'Mica B' insulated van No. 79740 built 1925
[1]GWR open wagon No. 102776
[1]GWR 'Mink' covered van No. 104700 built 1930
[1]LMS box van built 1923
GWR 'Fruit D' van No. W92067
GWR 'Fruit D' van No. W92091
[1]GWR 4-wheel mess van No. 215 built 1900
SR 'Lowmac' wagon No. 61091
GWR 3-compartment composite coach body built c1850
GWR 30-cwt Traffic Department crane No. 610 built 1893
Ten Wickham petrol rail trolleys

Note: Rolling stock may be interchanged between the Totnes–Buckfastleigh and Paignton–Kingswear sections from time to time as traffic demands.

[1]Property of Dart Valley Railway Association.
[2]Withdrawn from Laira shed, Plymouth in December 1963

and purchased privately for preservation.
[3]Withdrawn from Wadebridge shed in November 1964. A modified version of the 1361 class, six locomotives (1366–71) were built to replace old Cornwall Minerals Railway saddletanks. The class was divided between Swindon and Weymouth depots for much of its existence, those at Weymouth depots for much of its existence, those at Weymouth often being used to hault the boat trains through the street to the quay. In 1962, the three survivors, Nos 1367–9, were sent to Wadebridge to work on the Wenford Bridge branch, for so long the preserve of the LSWR 2-4-0T. No. 1369 worked the last steam-hauled train over the branch and thus became the last steam engine to work on BR in Cornwall.
[4]Withdrawn from Croes Newydd (Wrexham) in August 1966 as BR No. 1638. Although pure GWR in design, the first of the class did not appear until 1949. Many lines being too restricted to allow for workings by the standard 57XX class, something lighter was required and the result was the 16XX class. It was the last class of pannier tank to be designed and built at Swindon.
[5]Withdrawn from Yeovil shed in October 1964 and purchased for preservation.
[6]Withdrawn from Gloucester shed in November 1964 and purchased for the DVR.
[7]Withdrawn from Exmouth Junction shed in May 1965 and purchased for the DVR.
[9]Owned by the Lady Angela Group.
[10]Owned by the Glendower Group.
[11]Owned by the Dumbleton Hall Preservation Society. Withdrawn from Bristol Barrow road in 1965. Sold to Woodham Bros., Barry, for scrap and purchased for preservation in 1973. Moved to Buckfastleigh by road in 1976 and is now undergoing a thorough overhaul which is expected to take several years. When complete, it will enter service on the Torbay and Dartmouth line.
The following locomotives are housed in the Railway Museum at Buckfastleigh:
[1]South Devon Railway 0-4-0VBWT No. 151 *Tiny* built Sara & Co, Penryn, 1868
[2]LSWR 2-4-0T No. 3298 Beyer Peacock 1412 built 1874
[1]Withdrawn in 1883 as GWR No. 2180 and used as a stationary engine at Newton Abbot Works until placed on display in 1927. This is the sole surviving engine representing the GWR Broad Gauge era which came to an end in 1892. On loan from the National Collection
[2]On loan from the National Collection. Formerly BR No. 30587

Dumbleton Hall Preservation Society **H**

Headquarters: Buckfastleigh Station, Dart Valley Railway, Devon
Details from: R. Elliott, 172 Sweetbrier Lane, Exeter, Devon

Restoring and rebuilding former GWR 'Hall' class 4-6-0 No. 4920 *Dumbleton Hall* at Buckfastleigh for eventual use on the Torbay and Dartmouth line.

Dart Valley Railway Association and Torbay & Dartmouth Railway Society **H**

The DVRA is the only Supporters' Society that offers the choice of helping with two separate railways – the original Totnes–Buckfastleigh line and the Paignton–Kingswear section. Membership privileges include unlimited free travel (except on specified peak trains) between Buckfastleigh and Totnes and up to six journeys per year on the Torbay line.
Headquarters: GWR Super Saloon No. 9111 'King George', Buckfastleigh Station, Dart Valley Railway, Devon
Details of DVRA from: F. W. Cooper, 11 Bow Creek, Tuckenhay, Totnes, Devon
Details of T&DRS from: D. Gates, 18 Redbrook Close, Broadsands Park, Paignton

2 Torbay and Dartmouth Railway **A**

Passenger-carrying standard gauge railway, 7 miles in length from Paignton to Kingswear
Paignton Queens Park Station, Paignton, Devon TQ4 6AF
Access: Torbay and Dartmouth line station is next door to BR Paignton station and the bus station. From South Hams area, make for Dartmouth, then take the ferry to Kingswear station. By public transport: rail from Exeter or beyond, Newton Abbot and Torquay to Paignton BR. There are frequent local buses to Paignton from the Torbay area itself.
Tel: Paignton 555872
OS Ref: SX 889606

A full daily steam service is operated at Easter, then Sundays and daily from mid-May to early October. The Torbay line runs through some spectacular scenery offering panoramic views of Torbay and the Dart Estuary, high viaducts and a 492-yard tunnel. Gradients up to 1 in 60 prevail in both directions. DVRA members are able to assist in running the railway in the same way as at Buckfastleigh.
Both lines are run as far as possible with Great Western traditions in mind, with GWR type locomotives. Although some fine specimens of Great Western coaches have been acquired, most of the service trains are formed of former BR Mk.1 coaches, particularly on the Torbay line where summer crowds require the use of high-capacity trains. Most trains are normally steam-operated, but some Saturday trains and evening services may be diesel-hauled.

Stock
[1, 2]GWR 4-6-0 No. 7827 *Lydham Manor* built 1950
[4]GWR 2-6-2T No. 4588 (Class 4575) built 1927
[5]GWR 2-8-0T No. 5239 *Goliath* (Class 52XX) built 1924

[6]BR Co-CoDH No. D1023 *Western Fusilier* built 1963
BR/Drewry 0-6-0DM No. D2192 *Ardent* (Class 03) built 1962
Hudswell Clarke 0-6-0DM *Enterprise* D810 built 1953
BR Class 127 DMU motor coaches Nos M51592 & M51604 built 1959
BR DMU trailers Nos M59003 & 59004 built 1957
GWR super saloon No. 9116 *Duchess of York* built 1932
GWR engineers saloon No. 9035 built 1896
GWR auto-trailer No. 238 built 1954
Pullman observation car No. 13 *Devon Belle* built 1921, rebuilt 1947
BR Mk.1 SK coach No. E24949 built 1956
BR Mk.1 SK coach No. E24985 built 1956
BR Mk.1 SK coach No. E25307 built 1957
BR Mk.1 SK coach No. E25341 built 1957
BR Mk.1 SK coach No. E25454 built 1957
BR Mk.1 SK coach No. E25501 built 1958
BR Mk.1 BSK coach No. M34550 built 1955
BR 2nd class coaches Nos 48006, 48008 & 48009
BR Mk.1 TSO coaches Nos 4046, 4166, 4256, 4275, 4288, 4289, 4317 & 4507 built 1954–57
BR prototype FO coach No. 3084 built 1957, rebuilt 1972 as disco/dancing car, and 1984 as Exhibition car
GWR steam crane No. 2 built Ransomes & Rapier 1908
GWR match truck No. ADW150434
Wickham 4wPMR No. PWM 3773 6652 built 1953
Wickham 4wPMR No. PWM 2210 4127 built 1946
Shell tank wagon built 1924

[1]Property of Dart Valley Railway Association.
[2]Withdrawn in 1965 and sold to Woodham Bros., Barry, for scrap. Purchased by the DVRA and moved to Buckfastleigh in June 1970. Fully restored to working order and transferred to the Torbay line in 1973.
[4]Withdrawn July 1962 and sent to Woodham Bros. scrapyard, Barry. Purchased for preservation and moved to Buckfastleigh in November 1970. After restoration to working order, it was transferred to the Torbay line.
[5]Withdrawn in April 1963 and sent to Woodham Bros scrapyard, Barry. Purchased for preservation and moved to Newton Abbot in May 1973 for restoration. Entered service on the Torbay line in July 1978.
[6]On loan from the National Collection.

3 East Somerset Railway A

Passenger-carrying standard gauge railway, owning 1¼ miles of track with ¾ mile open to passengers at present, and a depot housing the railway's locomotives and stock

East Somerset Railway Co Ltd, Cranmore Station, Shepton Mallet, Somerset BA4 4QP
Access: Cranmore is 3 miles east of Shepton Mallet on A361 Frome road. Bus: 'Crown Tours' Shepton–Frome service
Tel: Cranmore 417
OS Ref: ST 664429

The depot is open daily from April to October inclusive from 10 am to 5.30 pm, and at weekends only from November to March inclusive from 10 am to 4 pm, except for organised parties which are welcomed at any time. Passenger trains run on every Sunday, Bank Holiday and other advertised days from April to the end of October and on Wednesdays in July and August.
Facilities for visitors include free car parking, refreshments, with a full meal service available when trains are running, souvenir shops, toilets, picnic areas and an art gallery in the station signal box.
The development of the East Somerset Railway project has been motivated by railway and wildlife artist David Shepherd. Originally part of the broad gauge East Somerset Railway from Witham to Shepton Mallet, Cranmore station was closed to passenger traffic in 1963, but goods traffic remained, enabling the fledgling project to get established there. In addition to the renovation of the station buildings, a brand new two-road engine shed to authentic Victorian design was built. Since 1973, the collection of locomotives has been steadily growing in number, and Cranmore 'works' is gaining a fine reputation for the engineering standards it sets in restoring them to working order.

Stock
[2]BR 2-10-0 No. 92203 *Black Prince* (Riddles Class 9F) built 1959
[3]BR 4-6-0 No. 75029 *The Green Knight* (Riddles Class 4MT) built 1954
[6]LBSCR 0-6-0T No. 32110 (Stroudley Castle E1) built 1877
[5]GWR 0-6-2T No. 6634 (56XX class) built 1928
[8]LMS 0-6-0T No. 47493 (Fowler Class 3F) Vulcan Foundry 4195 built 1927
[1]RSH 0-6-0ST No. 68005 7169 built 1944
[1]Barclay 0-4-0ST *Lord Fisher* 1398 built 1915
[1]Barclay 0-4-0ST *Glenfield* 1719 built 1920
[1]Dubs 0-4-0CT 4101 built 1901
BR Mk.1 TSO coach No. E4562 built 1956
BR Mk.1 BS coach No. W43264 built 1955
BR Mk.1 BSO coach No. 9241 built 1955
BR Mk.1 brake 2nd coach No. 43289 built 1955
BR Mk.1 2nd class experimental all-fibreglass coach No. 1000 built 1962
BR (LNER design) 2nd class sleeping car No. 1767 built 1951
[7]LMS 1st class saloon coach No. 3322 built 1929 rebuilt 1973
WD 20 ton goods brake van No. 49028 built 1959
LSWR road van No. 12424 built 1900
[1]LSWR box van No. 9128
[1]LSWR flat wagon No. 6095
[1]LNWR 20 ton goods brake van No. 49026
SR PMV 4-wheeled utility vans Nos 1137 & 1396 built 1946
LMS 6 ton flat wagon No. 73039 (painted GWR colours)
LMS box van No. 47760

LSWR box van No. 47754
BR 5-plank open wagons Nos 66014, 66024, 66054, 66056 and 63033
Grafton diesel crane
BR horsebox chassis for use with GWR coach body No. 254
GWR sleeper wagon No. DW100684
GWR 10-ton 'Starfish' wagon No. DW80637
Wickham 4wPMR No. TR38 6643 built 1953
Esso fuel tank wagon No. 1800 built 1939
LMS 7-plank open wagons Nos 72403, 72426, 73178 & 73226
[1]MR match truck No. 82620 built 1916

[1]Owned by Lord Fisher Locomotive Group.
[2]Withdrawn from Birkenhead shed in December 1967 and purchased for preservation by David Shepherd. No. 92203 worked the last steam-hauled John Summers Bilston–Shotwick iron ore train on 6 December 1967. Stored at Longmoor, Liss and Eastleigh before being moved to Cranmore in 1973.
[3]Withdrawn from Stoke-on-Trent shed in August 1967 and purchased for preservation by David Shepherd. Subsequently repainted in BR green livery and named. Stored at Longmoor, Liss and Eastleigh before being moved to Cranmore in 1973.
[5]Withdrawn from Pontypool Road shed in 1964 and sent to Woodham Brothers scrapyard, Barry. Purchased by a group of ESR members and arrived at Cranmore in July 1981.
[6]Built at Brighton Works in 1877 as No. 110 *Burgundy*. Sold in 1927 to Cannock & Rugeley Colliery Company and became No. 9 *Cannock Wood*.
Withdrawn in 1963 and purchased for preservation by the RPS (Chasewater Light Railway). Purchased by Barry Buckfield, Dean Knights and Dick Bellchambers and arrived at Cranmore on 11 September 1978.
[7]Carries its WD number – LMS identity not known. Originally built as an Open 3rd, it was captured by the Germans during the Second World War. Now converted into a video coach.
[8]Withdrawn December 1966 and sent to Woodham Bros. scrapyard, Barry. Purchased for preservation and moved to Radstock in December 1972. Moved by rail to Cranmore in November 1973 and since restored to working order.

East Somerset Railway Society **H**

Details from: Membership Secretary, 24 Lower Street, Merriott, Crewkerne, Somerset TA16 5NL

Lord Fisher Locomotive Group **H**

Details from: B. G. Buckfield, Newton Gardens, Park Road, Paulton, Bristol BS18 5NF

This group is a consortium of owners or part owners of some of the locomotives on the East Somerset Railway.

4 West Somerset Railway A

Passenger-carrying standard gauge railway, 20 miles in length, operating from Minehead to Bishops Lydeard

Minehead Station, Minehead, Somerset TA24 5BG
Access: By road, off the main A39 near the seafront. Bus route No. 218 for Watchet or Minehead. The WSR's own coach meets some trains from Taunton
Tel: Minehead 4996
OS Ref: SS 984464

Diesel multiple-unit trains operate all the year round (except Sundays), whilst steam trains run daily in the summer season. Facilities for visitors include car parking, souvenir and book shops, refreshments and toilets.
The original West Somerset Railway opened as a Broad Gauge branch line from Taunton to Watchet in 1862. It was extended to Minehead in 1874 by a separate Company (The Minehead Railway), and both parts of the line were worked by the Bristol and Exeter Railway until all were absorbed into the Great Western. The whole branch was converted to standard gauge in 1882, ten years before the last Great Western broad gauge train of all. The Minehead branch had an uneventful history thereafter, until final closure by British Railways in 1971.
Shortly after closure, a new West Somerset Railway Company appeared on the scene with the object of purchasing and re-opening the line. Protracted negotiations, which also involved Somerset County Council, took place, followed by the application for a Light Railway Order and bringing the line back up to a standard ready for passenger trains. The official re-opening ceremony took place at Minehead on 28 March 1976 and inaugurated the initial service to Blue Anchor (3½ miles).
In successive seasons, services have been extended further and further along the line, until trains now run through to Bishops Lydeard, making the West Somerset Railway the longest privately owned passenger railway in the British Isles.
Membership details from: Mr. G. Hitchcock, 49 Greenway Crescent, Taunton, Somerset.

Stock
GWR 4-6-0 No. 7820 *Dinmore Manor* built 1950
[10]GWR 2-6-2T No. 4561 (Class 45XX) built 1924
[11]GWR 2-6-2T No. 5542 (Class 4575) built 1928
[1]GWR 0-6-0PT No. 6412 (Class 64XX) built 1934
GWR 2-8-0 No. 3850 (Class 2884) built 1942
[4, 8]S & DJR 2-8-0 No. 88 Stephenson 3894 built 1925
Hudswell Clarke 0-6-0T No. 20 *Jennifer* 1731 built 1942
[3]Bagnall 0-6-0ST *Vulcan* 2994 built 1950
[3]Bagnall 0-6-0ST *Victor* 2996 built 1951
[5, 8]Hawthorn Leslie 0-6-0ST *Isabel* 3437 built 1919
[6, 8]Peckett 0-4-0ST *Kilmersdon* 1788 built 1929
[8]Bagnall 0-4-0F No. 12473 built 1932
[9]BR 0-6-0DH No. D9551 (Class 14) built 1965
[9]BR 0-6-0DH No. D9526 (Class 14) built 1965

[7]BR Bo-BoDH No. D7017 (Hymek Class) Beyer Peacock 7911 built 1962
BR Drewry 0-6-0DM No. D2271 (Class 04) 2615 built 1958
Ruston Hornsby 0-6-0DE No. D2994 *Archibald Lewis* 480695 built 1962
NE London Poly. 4WDMR built 1979 (converted Bristol LH bus)
[13]Ruston Hornsby 4WDM 183062 built 1937
[8]Ruston Hornsby 4WDM No. 24 (Class 80/88HP) 210479 built 1941
[9]PO Rly. 2w-2-2-2wE English Electric 808 built 1930 (2ft. gauge)
BR/Craven dmu coaches Nos E51485 and E56121 built 1959
[9]BR/Park Royal dmu power cars Nos W50413 and W50414 built 1957
[9]BR/Park Royal dmu trailer cars Nos W56168 and W56169 built 1957
BR Mk.1 SK coach No. E24307 built 1951
BR Mk.1 BSO coach No. E9278 built 1956
BR Mk.1 TSO coach No. S4039 built 1955
BR Mk.1 TSO coach No. E4602 built 1956
BR Mk.1 TSO coach No. E4346 built 1956 (cond)
BR Mk.1 TSO coach No. E4493 built 1956 (cond)
BR Mk.1 TSO coach No. E4814 built 1959
BR Mk.1 suburban compartment coach No. E46141 built 1954
BR Mk.1 TSO coach No. 4260 built 1956
BR Mk.1 TSO coach No. 4599 built 1957
BR Mk.1 TSO coach No. 4680 built 1957
BR Mk.1 HST instruction coach FO No. 3058 built 1955
BR Mk.1 restaurant car No. W1909 built 1957
BR Mk.1 buffet car No. SC1804 built 1957
BR Mk.1 BCK coach No. 21174 built 1958
BR Mk.1 TSO coach No. E4660 built 1957
BR Mk.1 SK coach No. E24778 built 1954
BR Mk.1 SK coach No. W24006 built 1951
BR Mk.1 BSK coach No. 35257 built 1959
BR 4-wheel CCT van No. M94917 built 1961
GWR 'Toplight' corridor 3rd coach No. 2573 built 1914
GWR 'Toplight' corridor 3rd coach No. 2578 built 1914
GWR 'Toplight' corridor 3rd coach No. 3639 built 1910
GWR 'Toplight' corridor 3rd coach No. 3668 built 1917
GWR 'Toplight' corridor 3rd coach No. 3885 built 1920
GWR 'Toplight' corridor 3rd coach No. 3980 built 1919
GWR 'Toplight' corridor composite coach No. 7740 built 1911
LMS 2nd class sleeping car No. M615M built 1952
[8]GNR brake/first coach No. 3178 built 1910
[8]LSWR brake/third bogie coach No. S3204 built 1926
GWR Hawksworth coach No. W2180 built 1950
GWR open wagon PBA No. 58176
[8]MR eight-ton open wagons Nos 112 and 1402 (ex-PBA)
[8]LTSR tank wagon (Shell Mex/BP) No. 401 built 1902
[8]GNR six-wheeled goods brake van built *c*1880
[8]NCB six-plank 12-ton open wagon No. 72395 (registered in 1936 as LMS 137495)
[8]NCB five-plank 12-ton open wagon No. 72399 (LMS 239195)
[8]NCB seven-plank 13-ton open wagon No. 72401 (registered as LMS 138934, possibly owned by James More)
Esso four-wheeled oil tank wagons Nos 1326 (built 1918) and 1822 (built 1939)
[8]LMS 'Stove R' 6-wheeled van No. M32994 built 1938
[8]GWR 'Fruit C' van No. W150346 built 1939
[8]GWR 'Fruit D' van No. W3450W built 1955
[8]GWR gunpowder van No. W105493 built 1924
[8]BR (SR) standard van
[8]Two 10-ton open wagons
[8]SR box van No. 48949
[8]LNER 20-ton goods brake van built 1925
LMS CCT van No. M94917 built 1938
GWR 'Siphon G' goods van No. W2980 built 1945
3½-ton hand crane
18-ton sleeper wagon
Seven PBA open wagons
Six PBA flat wagons
Two GWR 'Mink A' vans built *c*1901
LMS 12-ton steel van built *c*1930
Smith Rodley 5-ton steam crane No. 95 built *c*1951
[8]NCB seven-plank 13-ton open wagon No. 72402 (LMS 607324)
[8]NCB seven-plank 13-ton open wagon No. 73031
[8]NCB seven-plank 13-ton open wagon No. 73152
[8]NCB eight-plank 13-ton open wagon No. 79515 (built Cambrian Wagon Works, Cardiff)
[8]Stothert and Pitt steam crane (10-ton capacity) No. 312 built 1908
[8]Wickham 4WPMR Nos 6168 and 6967 built 1932
Wickham 4WPMR No. 8502 built 1960

[1]Withdrawn from Gloucester shed in November 1954 as BR No. 6412 and purchased for preservation. Used on the Dart Valley Railway until 1972 then transferred to the Torbay Steam Railway, from whom it was bought in 1976.
[3]Ex-British Leyland Motor Corporation, Austin-Morris Division, Longbridge, Birmingham, 1973.
[4]Built 1925 by Stephensons as S & DJR No. 88. Renumbered twice by the LMS, firstly as 9678 in 1930 and then as 13808 in 1932. After nationalisation in 1948 it became BR No. 53808. Reboilered in 1953; withdrawn from service in March 1964; saved from Barry scrapyard and moved back to Radstock in 1970 before coming to the West Somerset Railway.
[5]Built 1919, this locomotive worked at Blackley Dyestuffs factory near Manchester for 50 years. Purchased in 1969 by the Keighley and Worth Valley Railway but was unsuitable for the heavy trains there. Bought by three members of the S & D Trust and arrived at Radstock in 1971. First steamed over the Spring Bank Holiday 1972.
[6]Built 1929, this locomotive worked at the nearby Kilmersdon Colliery hauling coal from the pithead to a gravity-operated incline connecting with the GWR Frome to Bristol line. Made redundant when the colliery closed

in October 1973. It is now on permanent loan from the NCB.

[7]The Hymeks were the most numerous of the Western Region hydraulics and were used on both main-line passenger and freight services. They were soundly engineered and soon became popular with management and operating crews alike. Their light weight and rugged reliability also helped in the success of the preservation appeal, it being the first successful appeal in this country for a main-line diesel locomotive. The locomotive was purchased, in working order, in April 1975 and was moved from Old Oak Common to Taunton on 30 July. Locomotive owned and maintained by the Diesel and Electric Group (*q.v.*).

[8]Rolling stock owned and maintained by the Somerset and Dorset Railway Trust (*q.v.*).

[9]Owned by the Diesel and Electric Group (*q.v.*).

[10]Withdrawn May 1962 and sent to Woodham Brothers scrapyard, Barry. Purchased for preservation and moved to Bishops Lydeard in September 1975.

[11]Withdrawn December 1961 and sent to Woodham Brothers scrapyard, Barry. Purchased for preservation and moved to Bishops Lydeard in September 1975.

[13]Ex United Dairies, Chard 1980.

Somerset and Dorset Railway Trust — H

Washford Station, Somerset
Access: By West Somerset Railway train to Washford. On A39 Minehead–Bridgwater road
OS Ref: ST 044411

The Trust started as the S&D Railway Circle in 1966, with the prime aim of collating and circulating information on the S&DJR. In 1969, practical preservation started with the leasing of Radstock North station, engine shed and yard as a base to house a working Railway Museum. During the next few years, various items of rolling stock arrived, and trains were run over the ex-S&D line to Writhington. In 1975, the Trust's lease at Radstock was terminated and the search for a new site led to Washford Station on the West Somerset Railway.

The stock was moved from Radstock and stored at various places along the WSR, until sufficient site clearance, levelling and track laying had been carried out at Washford. In 1977, the Museum re-opened in the station buildings, and work continues on the restoration of stock for eventual display in the former goods yard.

Many of the Trust's extensive collection of S&DJR relics are on display in the Museum. The items are changed at intervals, and illustrate various aspects of Somerset and Dorset Railway History. Relics from other Railway Companies are also displayed and a collection of archival films, still photographs, books and documents is available to Trust members wishing to study particular topics. A permanent display of signalling equipment relating particularly to single line working is mounted in Washford Signal Cabin. The Museum is open most weekends, and at other times by arrangement with the Curator. A small entrance fee is charged to members of the public. Open Sundays and Bank Holidays from Easter to end September and Wednesdays in August 11 am–5 pm.

The original aims of the Circle are maintained with the issue of a Bi-monthly Bulletin (free to members), containing much information on the S&DJR, both historical and anecdotal, with additional articles on modelling and current activities. The Trust publishes several booklets with particular relevance to the S&DJR, as well as an annual calendar and Christmas cards.

Members of the Trust give illustrated talks on the S&DJR, and films and videotapes from the Trust's collection are shown in many parts of the country. For modellers, there is a Model Railway Exhibition held annually at New Year in Edington, near Bridgwater. The Trust is an associate member of the ARPS and a registered charity (No. 265098). Local Area Groups of members of the Trust are active in Bridgwater, Wimborne, Wincanton, London and the Midlands.

Membership details from: R. H. Wood, 35 Stamford Avenue, Syvechale, Coventry CV3 5BW, West Midlands.

Diesel and Electric Group — H

Williton Station, West Somerset Railway
Details from: John M. Crane, 7 Robert Close, Potters Bar, Herts EN6 2DH
Tel: 0707 43568

The Diesel and Electric Group owns three diesel locomotives: two class 35, Hymeks, D7017 & D7018, and Class 14, D9526. Class 14 No. D9551 is also under the Group's care from its owners, Railway Power Services.

D7017, D9526 and D9551 are based at the Group's depot at Williton on the West Somerset Railway, whilst D7018 is at Didcot Railway Centre.

Members receive the bi-monthly magazine 'Inter City Express' which contains articles on the whole range of railway subjects, with contributions from some of the leading photographers of the present day.

5 Lappa Valley Railway — A

Passenger-carrying 15in gauge light railway, 1 mile in length

St Newlyn East, Newquay, Cornwall
Access: Via the A3075 road, 5 miles from Newquay
Tel: Mitchell 317
OS Ref: SW 839564

Daily operation from end of May to October, 11 am to 5 pm.

Also runs during Easter week and Wednesdays and Sundays only from Easter to the end of May from 2 pm to 6 pm.

Facilities for visitors include car parking, shop, refreshments, toilets, picnic area, boating and a nature trail.

The railway is laid along the trackbed of the former GWR Newquay–Chacewater line, commencing from Benny Mill, about 1 mile north of St Newlyn East, and running to East Wheal Rose Mine. The line was opened on 16 June 1974 and it is hoped to extend it at both ends at some future date. At East Wheal Rose there is a characteristic ruined engine house and chimney. Trains negotiate a turning circle at the mine, whilst the locomotive is turned on a 10ft turntable at Benny Mill so that it always works chimney-first.

Stock
Curwen/Berwyn 0-6-0 *Muffin* built 1967
Curwen/Severn-Lamb 0-6-2T *Zebedee* 34 built 1974
Minirail Bo-BoE *Lappa Lady* plus diesel generator trailer built 1965
Lister 4WDM *Pooh* 20698 built 1942
Booth/Villiers 4W–4PM *Dougal* service vehicle built 1975
Five semi-open bogie coaches (built Jays Gates 1974)

6 Swanage Railway A

Passenger-carrying standard gauge steam railway from Swanage to Herston offering 1½-mile train rides

Swanage Railway Co Ltd, Swanage Station, Dorset BH19 1HB
Access: BR Wareham Station, thence Hants and Dorset bus Nos 141 & 142. By bus from Bournemouth and Poole
OS Ref: SZ 026789

The railway operates at Easter, then every Sunday until August, when a daily service runs. The line is being extended progressively towards Corfe Castle. Swanage station is open every weekend of the year from 10 am to 5 pm.
Facilities for visitors include a display of rolling stock, railway shop, refreshments, car parking and toilets.
The project is first concerned with restoring a public amenity service from Swanage to Wareham and the BR network. The secondary object is to form a working railway museum in an authentic setting to recreate the atmosphere of Southern Steam. In this, the Society is supported by a number of rolling-stock owning groups, principally the Southern Steam Trust.

Stock
[1]BR 2-6-4T No. 80104 (Riddles Class 4MT) built 1955
[3]BR 2-6-4T No. 80078 (Riddles Class 4MT) built 1954
[4]GWR 0-6-2T No. 6695 (Class 56XX) Armstrong Whitworth 983 built 1928
Hunslet 0-6-0ST *Cunarder* 1690 built 1931
[5]RSH 0-6-0ST No. 47 *Moorbarrow* 7849 built 1955
[6]Hawthorn Leslie 0-6-0ST No. 16 3837 built 1934
[6]Hawthorn Leslie 0-6-0ST No. 21 *Linda* 3931 built 1938
[2]Peckett 0-6-0ST *Mardy No. 1* (QQ Class) 2150 built 1954
Fowler 0-4-0DM No. 2 *May* 4210132 built 1957
[1]Hibberd 4WPM *Beryl* 2054 built 1938
Ruston Hornsby 4WDM 402812 built 1957
[1]SR Bulleid brake/3rd coach No. 4365 built 1947
SR Maunsell open 3rd coach No. 1381 built 1930
BR Mk.1 restaurant car No. S1908 built 1957
SR passenger brake van No. S13 built 1941
[1]SR scenery van No. 4594 built 1938
[1]SR PMV 4-wheel van No. 1234 built 1935
[1]LSWR coach No. 0695 (body only) built 1885
SR 'Brighton Belle' motor brake/3rd Pullman coach No. 288 built 1932 (ex-Unit 3051)
BR Mk.1 TSO coach No. 4349 built 1956
[1]BR Mk.1 sleeping car No. 2564 built 1958
SR Maunsell brake/3rd coach No. 2768 built 1931
SR Maunsell bogie brake van No. 385 built 1936
SR Goods brake van built for the Army 1942
LMS open 3rd class coach No. 7868 built 1925
Smith Rodley 5-ton rail-mounted diesel crane
ICI ammonia tank wagon
Three LSWR open wagons
Two GWR open wagons
LMS open wagon
[1]SR goods brake van
BR standard open wagon
[1]Three converted flat wagons
[1]Two WD box vans
[1]WD 4-wheel dropside open wagon No. 45020
SR 4-plank dropside open wagon (to LBSCR design) built 1925
Wickham 4WPMR No. 9024 7090 built 1955
[1]SR 'Walrus' 40-ton ballast hopper wagon No. DS 62070
[1]SECR 4-plank open wagon
LNWR covered carriage truck built 1916
[7]LSWR 6-wheel composite coach body No. 49 built *c*1882
[7]LSWR 6-wheel composite coach body built *c*1882

[1]Owned by the Southern Steam Trust.
[2]Ex NCB Mardy Colliery 1979.
[3]Withdrawn July 1965 and sent to Woodham Bros. scrapyard, Barry. Purchased for preservation by the Southern Steam Trust and moved to Swanage in September 1976.
[4]Withdrawn July 1964 and sent to Woodham Bros scrapyard, Barry. Purchased for preservation and moved to Swanage in May 1979.
[5]Ex-North Yorkshire Moors Railway 1982.
[6]Ex-Market Bosworth Light Railway 1982.
[7]Sited on trackbed at Corfe Castle Station.
Details of the Swanage Railway are available from: R. W. Orchard, 33 Grove Road West, Christchurch, Dorset. Tel: 0202-474862

Southern Steam Trust H

Details from: Southern Steam Trust, Swanage Station, Dorset BH19 1HB

The Trust was formed as the Southern Steam Group in 1972. Since then, charitable status has been obtained. The object of the Trust is to preserve locomotives, rolling stock and other apparatus associated with the LSWR, the Southern Railway and the Southern Region of BR for operation on the Swanage–Wareham branch when it is reopened. In this regard, it supports the Swanage Railway Company who plan to restore both vintage steam and amenity services over the branch.

7 Bicton Woodland Railway A

Passenger-carrying 1ft 6in gauge line 1¼ miles in length

Bicton Gardens, East Budleigh Salterton, Devon
Access: On A376 Newton Poppleford–Budleigh Salterton Road, slightly north of St Mary's Church. Nearest BR station Exmouth, thence by No. 334 bus on Exmouth–Sidmouth route
Tel: Colaton Raleigh 68465
OS Ref: SY 074862

Facilities for visitors include car parking, souvenir shop, refreshments, Countryside Museum and Hall of Transport displaying vintage cars and motorcycles.
Open daily from 1 April to 31 October 10 am to 6 pm.
The railway was opened in 1963 and a 537-yard branch to the Hermitage added in 1976. Although a product of the steam preservation age, the Bicton Woodland Railway has much period charm and slips well into its lush surroundings. Bicton Gardens themselves were laid out in 1735 to the designs of André le Nôtre, who was landscape gardener at the Palace of Versailles. Much of the railway's equipment hails from the 18in gauge system at the Woolwich Arsenal and is of First World War vintage; whilst a finishing touch is added by the former LSWR lower-quadrant signals, shortened to dwarf stature to fit the scale of their new surroundings.

Stock

[1]Avonside 0-4-0T No. 1 *Woolwich* 1748 built 1916
[2]Ruston Hornsby 4WDM No. 2 *Bicton* (20DL Class) 213839 built 1942
[3]Hunslet 0-4-4-0D No. 3 *Carnegie* 4524 built 1954
[4]Ruston Hornsby 4WDM No. 4 *Budley* (20DL Class) 235624 built 1945
Four open bogie coaches
Five covered bogie coaches
4-wheeled passenger brake van
Woolwich Arsenal Rly bogie wagon built 1914

[1]Originally built for the Woolwich Arsenal Railway, London. Ex E. L. Pitt & Co (Coventry) Ltd, Brackley, Northants, April 1962.
[2]Ex Woolwich Arsenal Railway, London, via M.E. Engineering Ltd, Cricklewood, May 1963.
[3]Ex Woolwich Arsenal Railway, London, via F. J. Dartnell, Upminster, Essex, February 1966.
[4]Ex Bromyard & Linton Light Railway, June 1974.

8 Longleat Railway A

Passenger-carrying 15in gauge railway 1¼ miles in length

Longleat Park, near Warminster, Wiltshire BA12 7NW
Access: Longleat is about 100 miles west of London, on the A362, between the cities of Bath and Salisbury. Coach tours from all principal towns. Nearest Bus Route runs Bath–Warminster, Nos 253 and 254 (then a beautiful 2½ mile walk!). Fast trains from Paddington and Exeter to Westbury or Warminster – thence by taxi (or bus as above). Details from British Rail Travel Centres of excursions including Waterloo–Salisbury (train/coach).
Tel: Maiden Bradley 579
OS Ref: ST 808432

The railway operates from Easter to the end of October. The railway shop remains open until Christmas.
Other facilities for visitors include car parking, refreshments, toilets, picnic area, amusements and, of course, the famous lions of Longleat and its stately home.
Longleat House, the Safari Park and Pets Corner, as well as the formal Gardens, the Lakes and the Orangery, complemented by a well stocked Garden Centre, are open throughout the year (Longleat House is closed on Christmas Day). During the Summer months there are numerous other attractions appealing to both young and old alike – fishing in season, the world's largest Maze, the Victorian Kitchens, a delightful collection of 19th century Dolls Houses, and Lord Weymouth's unique paintings and murals.
The railway was opened in 1967 and came under the control of Lord Weymouth, the son of the Marquis of Bath, the present owner of Longleat, in 1975. The track was then extended from the original ½-mile run through a cutting, out on to a high embankment, curving back to run through wooded parkland, beside a waterfall, to return to the main station.

Stock

Severn-Lamb Bo-BoDHR No. 1 *Lenka* 7322 built 1973
Severn-Lamb 2-8-0PH No. 2 *Ceawlin* R7 built 1975 (steam outline)
Curwen/Severn-Lamb 0-6-2T No. 3 *Dougal* built 1970
Four enclosed 16-seat bogie coaches built by Severn-Lamb 1975
Four enclosed 16-seat bogie coaches built at Longleat 1977–79
3-ton bogie wagon
4-wheel ballast hopper wagon
Tool van

9 Bitton Railway Centre A

Standard gauge railway preservation centre, featuring steam-hauled train rides on open days

Bristol Suburban Railway Society, Bitton Station, Bristol, Avon

Access: Bitton Station is on the A431 near Willsbridge
OS Ref: ST 670705
Bus route No. 332 Bristol–Bath. Nearest BR station: Keynsham (1½ miles)

Facilities for visitors include car parking, museum of railway relics and souvenir shop.
The Bristol Suburban Railway Society has relaid all the track within station limits at Bitton on the former Midland Railway Bristol–Bath line and has now extended its running line some two-thirds of a mile to Cherry Garden Lane. Permission has been granted for a further extension southwards towards Kelston.
Bitton station is open every weekend with steam trains operating on Sundays and Bank Holidays from Easter to the end of September and also during each weekend in December. Services between Bitton and School Road Halt, Oldland commenced on August 27 1983.

Stock
[1]LMS 4-6-0 No. 45379 (Stanier Class 5MT) Armstrong
[2]Whitworth 1434 built 1937
[3]Avonside 0-6-0ST No. 2 *Edwin Hulse* 1798 built 1918
[6]Peckett 0-6-0ST *Fonmon* 1636 built 1924
[3]Fox Walker 0-6-0ST No. 3242 built 1874
[8]Manning Wardle 0-6-0ST *Littleton No. 5* 2018 built 1922
[9]RSH 0-6-0T No. 9 7151 built 1944
[4]Ruston Hornsby 4WDM (Class 48DS) 235519 built 1945
Baguley-Drewry 0-4-0DM 2158 built 1941
GWR corridor 3rd class coach No. 5856 built 1934
BR Mk.1 BSK coach No. E35255 built 1958
BR Mk.1 SK coach No. E25040 built 1956
BR Mk.1 SK coach No. E25299 built 1958
BR Mk.1 CK coach 15447 built 1953
BR Mk.1 restaurant/buffet car No. W1933 built 1959
LMS 12-ton covered vans Nos 26 & 29
MR open wagon
GWR hand crane + LNER runner wagon
LBSCR open wagon
LNWR box van
LMS refrigerated box van
LNER refrigerated box van
GWR refrigerated box van
LMS goods brake van No. 294176 built 1928
LSWR wooden-wheeled box van built *c*1900
[5]GWR steel ballast wagon built *c*1900
Smith Rodley 5-ton steam crane 24080 built 1955
[5]GWR open wagons Nos 10931 and 86582 built 1912
[5]GWR 'Fruit C' van
Two GER wagon underframes (ex-Army)
Wickham 4WPMR No. PWM 3769 6648 built 1953

[1]Withdrawn from service in July 1965 and sold to Woodham Brothers, Barry, for scrap. Purchased for preservation 1974 and undergoing restoration by the Bristol Black 5 Society.
[2]Ex Imperial Smelting Corporation Ltd, Avonmouth 1971.
[3]Owned by Bristol Industrial Museum (Group No. 21).
[4]Ex Keynsham Paper Mills Ltd, Bristol (at one time BR No. DS1169).
[5]Owned by GWR 813 Preservation Fund.
[6]Ex Aberthaw & Bristol Channel Portland Cement Co Ltd, Rhoose, Glamorgan, September 1974.
[7]Ex RAF Chilmark, December 1978.
[8]Ex Great Central Railway 1980.
[9]Ex CEGB, Hams Hall Power Station 1980.
Society details from: E. H. Amos, 32 Milford Avenue, Wick, Bristol BS15 5PJ.

10 Crowlas Woodland Railway A

Passenger-carrying 10¼in gauge railway over 1½ miles in length

'Age of Steam', Rospeath Lane, Crowlas, near Penzance, Cornwall TR20 8DU
Access: By road and rail to Penzance or St Erth, thence various buses
Tel: Cockwells 631 (STD 0736 74)
OS Ref: SW 5233

The railway operates from Easter to October inclusive. First trains run at 10.30 am.
Facilities for visitors include car parking, picnic areas, refreshments, model railways and model displays, children's paddle-boats, croquet lawn, gift shop, picture gallery, games room, crazy golf, self-drive cars, and toilets. Excellent toilets are also provided for disabled visitors who in any event are always admitted free.
'Age of Steam' is a comprehensive project which sets out to echo the qualities of pleasure and elegance, leisure and learning that were the hallmarks of the historic and great age of steam. Within its rural surroundings, visitors can not only ride behind live steam locomotives, but can also study five models, see working model railways, view rare prints and paintings, and even drive their own model trains and model steam paddleboats. The Crowlas Woodland Railway was opened in the spring of 1977 and makes little pretence at hiding its similarity in livery and initials to the famous Great Western Railway. The CWR's special claim to fame is that it is both the first and last steam railway in England – being only some 12 miles from Land's End!

Stock
Curwen 4WDM No. 1 *Kingsley* built 1954
Guest Bo-BoPM No. 2 *Sir Humphry Davy*
Minimum Gauge Railways 0-6-2T No. 3 *Trevithick* built 1975
Curwen 2-6-0 No. 4 *Isambard Kingdom Brunel* built 1977
Six saloon bogie coaches built 1976–77

11 Forest Railroad Park A

Passenger-carrying 7¼in gauge railway, featuring intensive steam operation on two routes, each about a mile long. Both routes return passengers to their starting place

Dobwalls, Liskeard, Cornwall

Access: Nearest BR station, Liskeard
Tel: Dobwalls (0579) 20325
OS Ref: SX 216650

Operator: John Southern.
The railway operates from April to September daily between 10 am and 6 pm. Last admission 5 pm.
Facilities for visitors include car parking, picnic areas, cafe, museum, model railway, souvenir shop, radio-controlled model boats, forest walk, children's playground, waiting room and toilets.
A special feature is the Thorburn Museum and Gallery, commemorating Britain's greatest wildlife artist, Archibald Thorburn. Opening times the same as for the railroad.
This is the most arduous and spectacular 7¼in gauge railway in the country. It has severe gradients, high embankments, deep cuttings and five tunnels ranging from 60 to 85ft in length. The track layout is in the form of continuous, intertwined ovals and up to four trains can use each circuit at once. Operation is protected by automatic, four-aspect colour-light signalling installed by BR signal engineers and follows North American practice. In concept and in fact, the Forest Railroad is a spectacular railway entertainment for its visitors – plenty of moving trains to watch and ride, complete with all the atmosphere conjured up by steam, hot oil and chime whistles. But don't just take our word for it; go and see John Southern's achievements for yourselves. As if all these distinctions weren't enough, the Forest Railroad's principal claim to fame lies in the most massive of its steam locomotives – the Union Pacific *Big Boy* No. 4008. This is, quite simply, the largest and most powerful 7¼in gauge steam locomotive anywhere in the world.

Stock
Union Pacific 4-8-8-4 No. 4008 *William Jeffers* built Severn-Lamb 1978
Union Pacific 4-8-4 No. 818 *Queen of Wyoming* built Curwen/Severn-Lamb 1974
Union Pacific 4-8-4 No. 836 *Queen of Nebraska* built 1981
Rio Grande 2-8-2 No. 488 *General Palmer* K36 class built Curwen 1971
Rio Grande 2-8-2 No. 478 *Otto Mears* K27 class built Curwen 1980
Hudswell Clarke 2-6-2 No. 8 *David Curwen* built Curwen 1972
Rio Grande Bo-BoDH No. 3008 *Mathias Baldwin* built Severn-Lamb 1980
Union Pacific Do-DoDH 'Centennial' class built Severn-Lamb 1979
Rio Grande Bo-BoPM No. 108 built Curwen 1971
50 Cromar White 'sit-astride' bogie coaches

You can support the future of steam on the Forest Railroad by becoming a member of the Forest Railroad Circle. Membership entitles you to a concessionary rate of Park admission and a twice yearly newsletter, etc.
For details, send s.a.e. to Forest Railroad Park, Dobwalls, Cornwall.

12 Beer Heights Light Railway — A

Passenger-carrying 7¼in gauge railway built to narrow gauge proportions, approx ⅔ mile in length

Beer Modelrama, Beer, near Seaton, Devon
Tel: Seaton 21542 Ext 36
OS Ref: SY 230892

High on the hillside at the back of the village of Beer is Modelrama. The very attractive grounds contain a passenger carrying 7¼in gauge railway to narrow gauge proportions which runs from the terminus station of 'Muchnatter', past 'Upsan Downs Junction', 'White Falls' and then enters the tunnel – 183ft long which passes under the car park and emerges in the field beyond forming a reverse loop. Since this field has been raised some 25ft in height to get a level terrain, it was christened 'Mount De-Light' when the tunnel was opened on 1 August 1982 by Lord Gretton. The length of the journey is now half a mile; the tunnel is traversed twice in the round trip. This is believed to be the longest and deepest tunnel on any 7¼in gauge railway open to the public.
Modelrama has much to offer, in the grounds there is a Putting Green and Children's Play Corner while indoors in addition to the Light Railway there is an Exhibition containing twelve Model Railways each in a location around the house or garden with a separate outdoor extensive O Gauge layout. Refreshments are available either at the Station Buffet or in the 'Orion' preserved Golden Arrow Pullman Car where full meals are served. Car parking is free and there are ample toilets. There are two shops, one specialising in model railways and books and the other in souvenirs. By way of interest H.M. Queen Elizabeth II rode in 'Orion' on 24 October 1956. The Beer Heights Light Railway was officially opened by Rev. Awdry of 'Thomas the Tank' fame on 14 July 1975.
Indoor exhibition open all year. Outside activities: the week following Easter, then Spring Bank Holiday to approximately early October. Sunday opening during school holiday period.

Stock
Curwen 0-4-2 No. 3 *Dickie* built 1977
Marsh 0-4-2 STT No. 4 *Thomas II built 1979*
Cromar White 4WBE No. 1 Little Nell built 1975
Eight Cromar White 4-seat open bogie coaches built 1975–80 (The 'East Devonian' set)
Six PECO sit-astride bogie coaches (The 'Beer Belle' set)
2 PECO open wagons
Standard gauge static exhibit:
BR Pullman car 'Orion' built 1951

13 Oakhill Manor Miniature Railway AE

Passenger-carrying 10¼in gauge railway 1 mile in length

'The World of Models', Oakhill Manor Museum, Oakhill, near Bath, Somerset BA3 5AW
Access: Off A37 road, 4 miles north of Shepton Mallet. Turn at The Mendip Inn
Tel: Oakhill 840210
OS Ref: ST 641474

Operates daily from 12 noon to 6 pm Easter to October. Facilities for visitors include car parking, refreshments, toilets, souvenir shop, picnic area and railway walk, historic country house featuring displays of fine models, N gauge model railway and gardens.
The home of Mr and Mrs Walter Harper, Oakhill Manor is a pleasing example of England's smaller country estates of about 45 acres. In this beautiful environment, high in the Mendip Hills, has been created an unusual and fascinating project incorporating a superb collection of models and pictures relating to transport, a furnished mansion house set in landscaped gardens and a very fine miniature railway. The railway itself is an outstanding feature with close-to-scale track, locomotives and rolling stock and pretty stations in Mendip stone. It has an air of authenticity reminiscent of a cross-country main line in the days of steam.

Stock
SR 4-6-0 No. 772 *Sir Percivale* N15 class built 1979
GWR 2-8-0 (47XX Class) built 1981
Hunslet 0-4-0STT *Nelly* built Richards Engineering 1977
Curwen 4-6-2 No. 2647 *Robin Hood* built 1947
Five SR-styled saloon bogie coaches including one full brake
NER brick and sulphate bogie wagons
Ten articulated open bogie coaches

14 New Cornish Riviera Lido A

Passenger-carrying 10¼ in. gauge line 1,000ft in length operated by Mr Lovett. The railway was opened in 1974

Carlyon Bay, Par, Cornwall

Stock
LMS 4-4-2 No. 1 built 1949
Dove Bo-BoPM *Texas Ranger*
[1]Hunt Bo-BoPE No. 50 A451
Cromar White bogie coaches

[1]Ex Drayton Manor Miniature Railway.

15 Little Western Railway A

Passenger-carrying 7¼in gauge line in the form of a 300-yard circuit

Trenance Park, Newquay, Cornwall

Stock
[1]LMS 4-6-0 No. 6100 *Royal Scot* built Maldon SME
Freelance 0-4-0T *Midge*-type
Cromar White Bo-BoP built *c*1969
Open bogie coaches

Ex-Jersey Miniature Railway

16 Seaton and Colyford Electric Tramway B

Passenger-carrying 2ft 9in gauge electric tramway, operating along the trackbed of the former LSWR Seaton branch

Riverside Depot, Harbour Road, Seaton, Devon EX12 2NQ
Access: Axminster BR Station, thence by bus No. 213
Tel: Seaton 21702
OS Ref: SY 252904

12-minute interval service of trams at peak periods from Seaton to Colyton throughout the holiday season.
This 3-mile line was opened on 28 August 1970 using trams from the former Modern Electric Tramways line at the Crumbles, Eastbourne.

Stock
MET-type bogie double-deck tramcar No. 2 built 1964
Blackpool 'Boat'-type bogie single-deck tramcar No. 4 built 1961
Bournemouth-type bogie double-deck tramcar No. 6 built 1956
Bournemouth-type bogie double-deck tramcar No. 7 built 1958
Bournemouth-type bogie double-deck tramcar No. 8 built 1968
Open-top streamlined bogie double-deck tramcar No. 12 rebuilt 1979
MET bogie single-deck tramcar No. 14 built 1905, rebuilt 1984
[1]Ruston Hornsby 4WDM (48DL Class) 435398 built 1959
Mobile tram shop car No. 01 built 1954
Engineering car No. 02 built 1968, rebuilt 1981

[1]Ex North Devon clay Co Ltd, Peters Marland, September 1972.

17 Launceston Steam Railway A

Passenger-carrying 60cm gauge railway 2 miles long on former LSWR trackbed between Launceston and Egloskerry

Launceston, Cornwall
Services operate over ¾ mile of this route from Spring Bank Holiday to mid-October 11 am–6 pm

Stock
Hudswell Clarke 0-4-2ST *San Justo* 639 built 1903
Hunslet 0-4-0ST *Covertcoat* 679 built 1898

Hunslet 0-4-0ST *Lilian* 317 built 1883
Motor Rail 4wDM 5646 built 1933
Two open bogie coaches
Twenty-seven open wagons built Cravens and Pickerings

18 Morwellham Open Air Museum B

Passenger-carrying 2ft gauge railway, nearly ½-mile in length

Dartington Amenity Research Trust, Morwellham Quay, near Tavistock, Devon PL19 8JL
Access: Off the A390 between Tavistock and Gunnislake, close to the Dartmoor National Park
Tel: Tavistock 832766
OS Ref: SX 446697

Operates daily throughout the year, except Christmas Day, from 10 am to 6 pm or during November–March from 10 am to dusk.
Trains run at 15-minute intervals or as required.
Facilities for visitors include car parking and subterranean floodlit display of mine interior.
The railway was brought into operation in August 1978 to give visitors to the Mining Museum the chance to ride into the old George and Charlotte copper mine, closed for over 100 years. Trains start from the Old Quay, running through the woods for over ¼ mile along a ledge cut in the hillside above the River Tamar and into the mine for a further 150 yards. At the end of the journey into the adit, the working face of the mine is floodlit to show working conditions and mining equipment of 100 years ago.

Stock
Wingrove & Rogers 4WBE No. 2 (W227 Class) 6298 built 1960
Wingrove & Rogers 4WBE No. 3 (W227 Class) G7124 built 1967
Wingrove & Rogers 4WBE 5665 built 1957
Wingrove & Rogers 4WBE 6800 built 1964
Wingrove & Rogers 0-4-0BE
Wingrove & Rogers 4WBE No. 1 (W227 Class) H7197 built 1968
Nine passenger coaches

19 Somerset Railway Museum E

Static display of steam locomotives and railway equipment. In the station building there is a display of relics, including locomotive chimneys, signalling equipment, signs, etc

Bleadon and Uphill Station, near Weston-super-Mare, Avon
Access: Situated on the main A370 Highbridge road approximately three miles from Weston-super-Mare
OS Ref: ST 325578

Open on Saturday afternoons only, between 2 pm and 6 pm, June to October.

Details from: B. K. Kinsey, 15 Brookland Road, Weston-super-Mare, Avon

Stock
[1]Cardiff Rly 0-4-0ST No. 5 (Preserved as GWR 1338) Kitson 3799 built 1898
[2]Hunslet 0-4-0T 1684 built 1931
[3]Sentinel 4WVBTG No. 19374 built 1947
[4]Hibberd 4WDM 3057 built 1946
[5]BR 4WDM Railbus No. W 79976 built by AC Cars Ltd 1958

[1]Withdrawn from Swansea East dock shed as BR No. 1338 in 1963. This locomotive spent most of its working life shunting in the Docks owned by the GWR and its constituents, having served at Cardiff, Bridgwater and Swansea. It was the last of the pre-grouping GWR engines in BR service and the ultimate surviving GWR 0-4-0ST. Owned by the 1338 Preservation Fund.
[2]Ex NCB Kilmersdon colliery, Somerset. Owned by the 1338 Preservation Fund.
[3]Ex Roads Reconstruction (Quarries) Ltd, Frome, Somerset.
[4]Ex Plymouth Tar Distillery.
[5]Ex British Railways, Bristol, June 1973.
Details of the 1338 Preservation Fund may be obtained from John B. True, 119 The Avenue, Kennington, Oxford.

20 Great Western Railway Museum E

Static steam locomotive exhibits as well as other relics and displays of GWR items. All the locomotives are part of the National collection

Thamesdown Borough Council, Museums Division, Faringdon Road, Swindon, Wilts SN1 5BQ
Access: Swindon BR station
Tel: Swindon 26161 Ex. 3131
OS Ref: SU 145846

The Museum is open Monday–Saturday 10 am–5 pm and Sundays 2 pm–5 pm throughout the year. Closed Christmas Day, Boxing Day, New Year's Day and Good Friday. Facilities for visitors include museum shop, toilets and parking nearby.

Stock
[1]GWR 0-6-0 No. 2516 (Class 2301) built 1887
[3]GWR 4-6-0 No. 4003 *Lode Star* built 1907
[4]GWR 0-6-0PT No. 9400 (Class 94XX) built 1947
[5]GWR 2-2-2 (replica) *North Star* built 1837 (broad gauge)
GWR Bo-BoDM Railcar No. 4 built AEC 1934

[1]William Dean's standard goods engine for the GWR totalling 260 engines built 1883–99. Large numbers of the class were sent overseas during both world wars and many were destroyed in action. They were to be found at home working throughout the entire GWR system.
[3]Withdrawn from Landore (Swansea) shed in July 1951 as BR No. 4003. The 'Stars' were the first four-cylinder loco-

motives built in this country. When new, some were constructed as 4-4-2s and all locomotives were designed for easy conversion to and from 4-6-0. The 4-6-0 type proved itself and modifications were incorporated into successive batches until 1922. Built for express passenger work, the class remained so employed virtually until the end of its existence.

[4]Withdrawn from Old Oak Common (Paddington) shed in December 1959 as BR No. 9400. The largest pannier tanks and final GWR class appearing prior to nationalisation, the class is virtually a tank version of the 2251 Class 0-6-0 but with smaller wheels. Originally designed as carriage pilots and trip goods and shunting locomotives, the type was never as popular as the more numerous 57XX Class. Orders for 200 of the type were placed by the GWR and the last engine was not in traffic until 1956.

[5]Replica incorporating parts of the original locomotive which was withdrawn in 1871 and preserved at Swindon Works until scrapped in February 1906. Replica built for GWR Centenary celebrations and then preserved in Swindon Erecting Shop until placed in the Museum in 1962.

21 Bristol Industrial Museum AE

The Museum houses machinery and vehicles associated with Bristol's industrial past. At intervals throughout the summer season, a standard gauge steam railway operates in conjunction with the Museum, offering a ⅛ mile ride as far as the Great Western drydock where Brunel's famous ship, the SS 'Great Britain' is on display

Princes Wharf, Bristol, Avon BS1 4RN
Access: 5 minutes walk from the centre of Bristol. Nearest BR station, Bristol Temple Meads. Car parking adjacent to site in Wapping Road.
Tel: Bristol (0272) 299771 Ext 290
OS Ref: ST 583722

The Museum is open Saturdays–Wednesdays throughout the year from 10 am–12 noon and 1–5 pm. Admission free.
Facilities for visitors include a museum shop, car parking and toilets.
Bristol Industrial Museum was opened in March 1978, in what was once a transit warehouse in the heart of the City Docks. The exhibits on display are only a part of the technology collection, and are chosen for their particular connections with the Bristol region. Outstanding amongst these is the 1880 Grenville steam carriage – the world's oldest self-propelled passenger vehicle still in working order.

Stock
[4]Peckett 0-6-0ST No. S9 *Henbury* 1940 built 1937
[4]Avonside 0-6-0ST No. S3 *Portbury* 1764 built 1917
[1]Fox Walker 0-6-0ST No. 3242 built 1874
[2]GWR 6-wheel tri-composite coach No. 820 built 1886
Esso prototype bogie LPG tank wagon No. 78000 built 1967
GWR 'Toad' goods brake van No. DW17391 built 1941
[3]GWR 'Mogo' motor car van No. DW65814 built 1946
Various sections of GWR broad gauge coach bodies

[1]Located at Bitton, Bristol Suburban Railway.
[2]In store pending restoration. On loan from the National Collection.
[3]On loan from the National collection.
[4]Ex Port of Bristol Authority, 1964.

22 St Austell China Clay Museum E

Static steam locomotive exhibits plus display of machinery and equipment representing the history of the china clay mining industry in Cornwall

Wheal Martyn, Trenance Valley, St Austell, Cornwall PL26 8XG
Access: Bus route No. 529 St Austell to Bodmin. Nearest BR station: St Austell (2 miles)
Tel: St Austell 850362
OS Ref: SX 009549

The Museum is open daily from 1 April to 31 October between 10 am and 5 pm.
Facilities for visitors include car parking and a museum shop. A long-term aspiration of the Museum is to restore and operate about one mile of the adjacent ex-GWR Trenance Valley branch.

Stock
[1]Bagnall 0-4-0ST *Judy* 2572 built 1937
[2]Peckett 0-4-0ST *Lee Moor No. 1* 783 built 1899 (4ft 6in gauge)
Ruston Hornsby 4WDM 244558 built 1946 (2ft 6in gauge)
Wooden clay wagons (2ft gauge)
Peerless lorry built 1916
Lee Moor Mineral Railway signal box

[1]Ex English Clays Company, Par, 1978.
[2]Withdrawn November 1945. Ex English Clays Lovering Pochin & Co Ltd, May 1964.

23 Bird Paradise Railway B

Passenger-carrying 15in gauge railway, 440 yards in length in the form of a continuous circuit

Bird Paradise, Paradise Park, Hayle, Cornwall
Tel: Hayle 753365
OS Ref: SW 555365

Operates daily throughout the summer season 11 am to 5.30 pm.
Trains start from, and return to, Cockatoo Halt – a ride comprising two circuits of the track.

Stock
Barlow 4-6-0+Bo-BoDE *Princess Anne* built 1959 (Steam outline)

Lister 4WDM *Zebedee* 101 80 built 1938
Six articulated bogie coaches

24 Foster Yeoman Quarries Ltd G

Industrial railway location featuring ex-BR 'Western' class diesel locomotive

Merehead Stone Terminal, Torr Works, Shepton Mallet, Somerset

Stock
[1]BR Co-CoDH No. 1035 *Western Yeoman* built 1962
[1]Loco is actually No. 1010 *Western Campaigner*

25 Poldark Mine E

Standard gauge static steam locomotive exhibit in newly-opened museum of rural machinery. Also features underground tin mine

Wendron Forge, Wendron, near Helston, Cornwall
Access: 3 miles north of Helston on B3297 road. Bus routes: Falmouth–Penzance and Helston–Redruth at hourly frequencies
Tel: Helston 3173 and 3531

The museum is open from 1 April to 31 October between 10 am and 6 pm.
Facilities for visitors include car parking, museum, shop, refreshments and toilets.
Wendron's main claim to fame is its tin mine which extends for a considerable distance below the site. This facility is supported by a large collection of steam, gas and oil engines restored to working order and running daily. In addition, there are nine museum chambers containing thousands of interesting 19th century artifacts. The whole complex at Wendron stretches over 3 acres and includes a 40ft high beam engine which runs daily in the summer. The licensed restaurant contains a 5-ton working waterwheel.

Stock
Peckett 0-4-0ST No. 6 *Poldark Mining Co* 1530 built 1919
Ex Falmouth Docks & Engineering Co 1978. Restored to exhibition finish (non-operational)

26 Plymouth Railway Circle E

4ft 6in gauge static exhibits from the former Lee Moor Tramway

Saltram House, Plympton, Plymouth, Devon
OS Ref: SX 521556

Saltram House is open on Sundays from 1 April to October between 11 am and 6 pm.
The Lee Moor Tramway was the last of the privately-owned mineral railways built to the 'Dartmoor' gauge of 4ft 6in. It was built to carry china clay and other produce from the pits and works on the southern slopes of Dartmoor to the quays of Plymouth. From 1899 to 1947 three different forms of traction – steam, gravity and horse – were needed to convey a train the full length of the line. From 1947 until final closure in 1960 only the lower part of the line remained open, where horses were used and which thus outlasted the other forms of motive power.

Stock
Peckett 0-4-0ST *Lee Moor No. 2* 784 built 1899
Lee Moor Tramway china clay wagon

Locomotive withdrawn in 1945. Purchased for preservation in 1964 and kept in original shed leased from English Clays Limited. Now restored to exhibition condition for display at Saltram House.

27 Tiverton Museum E

Static steam locomotive exhibit

St Andrew Street, Tiverton, Devon EX16 6PH
Access: Near centre of town, on St Andrew Street (near Town Hall)
Entrance from public car park in Phoenix Lane
Nearest BR station: Tiverton Junction (6 miles). Open all year except Bank Holidays, Monday–Saturday 10.30 am to 1 pm and 2 pm to 4.30 pm. Admission free.
Tel: Tiverton 256295 (Curator 2446)
OS Ref: SS 955124

Other small exhibits include a large model of a GWR broad-gauge 4-4-0T *Lalla Rookh* which was built *c*1870. Proudly dominating this large collection of railway relics is the Museum's most popular exhibit, the GWR locomotive No. 1442. Known affectionately as the 'Tivvy Bumper', it plied up and down the Exe Valley and Culm Valley lines. Its technical records from the Swindon Works are mounted on panels for easy inspection, together with many other documents and ephemera to delight the enthusiast.
The split-level design of the gallery permits the locomotive to be inspected at all angles and the privilege of going into the driver's cab is appreciated, particularly by young people. An explanatory key to the controls is provided.
The display area on the mezzanine floor includes pictures of the 'Tivvy Bumper' under steam, a case containing a miscellany of railway exhibits and another devoted to the versatile genius, Roger Langdon, who was the first stationmaster at nearby Silverton.

Stock
GWR 0-4-2T No. 1442 (Class 14XX) built 1935

Withdrawn from service in 1965 and purchased by Lord Amory who presented it for display.
The Museum's activities are supported by the Tiverton Museum Society.

Details from: Tiverton Museum Society, St Andrew Street, Tiverton, Devon EX16 6PH.

28 Dawlish Warren Railway Museum and Model Railway E

A museum of small railway relics open daily between 10 am and 5 pm from mid-May to mid-September

Dawlish Warren Station, Dawlish, Devon
Access: Dawlish Warren BR station
Tel: Dawlish (0626) 862131
OS Ref: SX 979787

A fascinating collection of the often neglected smaller items of railway history including locomotive name and number plates, signs, tickets, books, documents, etc. in the ideal setting of a former station building. The booking office has been restored as near as practicable to its original condition and there is an operating 'OO' model railway with a sequence of over twenty different trains, both old and new.
The museum shop has a fine selection of railway books by leading publishers and a range of model railway items by major manufacturers. We also sell railway records, photographs, colour slides, souvenirs, and the 'Dawlish Warren Railway Museum' series of colour postcards.

29 Mendip District Council E

Standard gauge steam locomotive on static display

Welshmill Adventure Playground, Frome, Somerset
OS Ref: ST 778486

Stock
Sentinel 4WVBTG *ARC* 9387 built 1948
Ex Roads Reconstruction (Quarries) Ltd, Vallis Vale, Frome, 1971.

30 New Farm Sawmills Railway I

1ft 9in gauge light railway serving a working sawmill

Mr P. S. Weaver, New Farm, Lacock, near Corsham, Wilts
OS Ref: ST 899691
No public admittance without prior permission

Stock
Weaver 0-4-0VBTG built 1978
Side-tipping wagons

31 Bugle Steam Railway D

Standard gauge railway preservation centre featuring steam operation over a short demonstration line on open days

Cornish Steam Locomotive Preservation Society Ltd, Imperial Sidings, Bugle, near St Austell, Cornwall
Access: British Rail | Bugle station. Alongside A391 Bodmin–St Austell road. Turn up lane by telephone box
Tel: St Austell 5194 for information
OS Ref: SX 013583

The depot is open on the last Sunday in June, the last two Sundays in July, and the first Sunday in September, plus every Sunday during August and Bank Holiday Mondays, Easter, May Day, Spring and August between 11 am and 5.30 pm.
Facilities for visitors include train rides, railway shop, refreshments, car parking, toilets and picnic area.
The Society was formed in 1973 and leases sidings from English Clays Ltd which once joined the Goonbarrow mineral branch. Although the branch was lifted in March 1979, it is hoped eventually to relay part of it. On the closure of the GW Society depot at Bodmin in October 1977, much of the stock there was moved to Bugle to form the nucleus of the Society's collection.
Passengers are given short rides in a brake-van along the sidings which are situated amongst old clay drying kilns. Future projects include the provision of a new platform at the end of the line and a new shed where locomotive restoration can be carried out.

Stock
[1]Bagnall 0-4-0ST *Alfred* 3058 built 1953
[2]Bagnall 0-4-0ST No. 19 2962 built 1950
[3]Peckett 0-4-0ST *Progress* 1611 built 1923
[4]Bagnall 0-4-0F 3121 built 1957
[5]GWR Churchward 'Toplight' 3rd class coach No. 2434 built 1910
LMS 20-ton goods brake van No. 294315 built 1930
LNER 12-ton fruit van No. 222814 built 1938
GWR 12-ton ventilated van No. 103999 built 1926
Taylor Hubbard 10-ton steam crane built 1948
LMS 12-ton box van built 1935
GWR 12-ton meat van built 1925
Two LNER 12-ton vans built *c*1938
Esso tank wagon
Shell tank wagon
Two GWR coach bodies built 1880s
Two MR 3-plank open wagons
[6]LSWR 4-wheel velocipede *Camel* built 1875
An item of particular interest is the outer fire box wrapper of Liskeard and Caradon Railway locomotive *Caradon* which had been in use at Moorswater as a toilet until rescue in 1971.

[1]Ex English Clays Ltd, Par Docks 1978.
[2]Ex Devonport Dockyard, February 1969.
[3]Ex Albright & Wilson Ltd, Portishead 1978.
[4]Ex English Clays Ltd, Marsh Mills, Plymouth.
[5]Converted to mess vehicles 1956. Now used as Mess, sales and refreshments.
[6]Ex Wenford Mineral branch.
Society details from: M. Orme, 24 Margaret Gardens, Eglashayle, Wadebridge, Cornwall. Tel: 2335.

32 Gorse Blossom Miniature Railway Park A

Passenger-carrying 7¼in gauge railway, 1100 yards long in 8 acres of woodland and gardens

Situated near Liverton, Newton Abbot, Devon
Tel: Bickington (062 682) 361
Access: Just off old A38 road between Drumbridges roundabout, Liverton, and Bickington, halfway between Exeter and Plymouth
OS Ref: SX 815745

The railway operates at Easter, and daily from early May Bank Holiday to end of September from 10 am to 5 pm. Facilities include car and coach park, refreshment and souvenir kiosk, toilets, picnic areas, children's play areas, woodland and adventure walks. The railway is set in undulating woodland giving high banks and deep cuttings and some stiff climbs. This is the first stage, opened in July 1984, of the park which will include an outdoor model railway.
The line is operated by G.&P. Kichenside Ltd. Rolling stock transferred from the Riverside Miniature Railway, Buckfastleigh, 1983.

Stock
Lynton & Barnstaple Railway 2-6-2T *Yeo* Milner Eng 107 built 1979
[1]Freelance B-B DH *Little Bear* built Willbro Precision 1973 as petrol loco
Four-car articulated set of coaches
Four bench seat bogie coaches

[1]Rebuilt 1976 with Petter diesel engine and new body. Formerly ran on the Kingsbridge Miniature Railway.

33 Somerset County Council E

Standard gauge diesel locomotive on static display. Children's playground, Wansbrow, Somerset

Stock
BR 0-6-0DE No. D3003 *Merehead* built 1952

34 Lynton and Barnstaple Railway Association F

The Association is dedicated to the re-establishment of at least part of the former Lynton and Barnstaple Railway on its original trackbed

Lynton Station, Lynton, Devon
Tel: Lynton 2381
OS Ref: SS 719489
Details from: Colin Rainsbury, 50 Cumbrian Avenue, Barnehurst, Kent DA7 6SL

⅓ mile of trackbed has been purchased at Parracombe and this may well be the site of a small-scale revival of railway operation.

Stock
Kerr Stuart 0-6-0T ('Joffre' Class) 2451 built 1915
[1]Ruston Hornsby 4WDM No. 3 *Brunel* (30DL Class) 179880 built 1936
Two sections of L&BR bogie coaches
Flat wagon
Frames of Kerr Stuart 0-4-0ST 2395 built 1917

[1]Ex Crockway Light Railway, Dorset 1979

35 Swindon and Cricklade Railway F

Standard gauge railway society seeking to re-open the former Midland & South Western Junction railway line between Moredon and Cricklade. Almost ½-mile of track has been laid at Blunsdon so far

Blunsdon Station site, Wiltshire
Access: Off the A419, two miles north of Swindon
Tel: Swindon 693029
Details from: Mrs A. R. Palk, 5 Bradene Close, Wootton Bassett, Swindon, Wiltshire SN4 8DG

Stock
SR 4-6-2 No. 34072 *257 Squadron* (Bulleid BB Class) built 1948
SR 4-6-2 No. 35027 *Port Line* (Bulleid MN Class) built 1948
[2]GWR 0-6-2T No. 5637 (56XX Class) built 1925
[1]GWR 4-6-0 No. 7903 *Foremarke Hall* (6959 Class) built 1949
Barclay 0-4-0ST *Richard Trevithick* 2354 built 1954
Kerr Stuart 0-4-0WT 3063 built 1918
Fowler 0-4-0DM No. 2 4210082 built 1953
Fowler 0-4-0DM 4210137 built 1958
Fowler 0-4-0DM No. SBL1 4210105 built 1955
Fowler 0-4-0DM 21442 built 1936
BR/Drewry 0-6-0DM No. D 2022 (Class 03) built 1958
BR Mk.1 brake/3rd coach No. E43140 built 1954
Smith Rodley 20-ton steam crane and match truck built 1940
GWR 'Toplight' brake tricomposite coach No. KDW 7545 built 1907
MOD open wagons Nos 46062, 46092, 46094 & 46259
Six open wagons
PBA covered vans Nos 27 & 60
Esso tank wagon built for LMS 1938
Wickham 4wPMRs WD Nos 9031 & 8089
GWR packing van No. ADW 150309
GWR riding van No. ADW 150307
PBA 5-plank open wagons Nos 59251, 59567, 61047 & 61062
GWR clerestory coach body
Brecon & Merthyr Railway van body
Body of Swindon Electric Tramcar No. 13 (3ft 6in gauge)

[1]Withdrawn June 1964 and sent to Woodham Bros scrapyard, Barry. Purchased for preservation in June 1981 and moved to Blunsdon.

[2]Withdrawn June 1964 and sent to Woodham Bros scrapyard, Barry. Purchased for preservation by Birmingham Railway Museum and moved to Tyseley in August 1974. Resold to the Swindon & Cricklade Railway in 1982.

36 Old Delabole Slate Co. Ltd — E

1ft 11½in gauge rolling stock restored for static display in a small museum devoted to the Cornish slate industry

Lower Pengelly, Delabole, Cornwall
Tel: Camelford 2242
OS Ref: SX 075836

The museum is adjacent to an ancient slate quarry worked continuously since 1555. Over 500ft deep and 1⅝ miles round, it is claimed to be the largest man-made hole in England (possibly Europe).
Open at Easter, then Monday–Friday May to September 10 am–6 pm.

Stock
Motor Rail 4WDM 3739 built 1925
Various narrow gauge slate wagons

37 Falmouth Shiprepair Ltd — I

Industrial steam location featuring occasional steam working

Falmouth Docks, Cornwall
OS Ref: SW 822324

No public access.

Stock
Hawthorn Leslie 0-4-0ST No. 3 3597 built 1926
Hudswell Clarke 0-4-0ST No. 5 1632 built 1929

38 British Rail Engineering, Swindon — G

Standard gauge diesel locomotives on static display outside the works, grouped round the turntable and visible from passing trains

BREL, Swindon Works, Wilts
OS Ref: SU 140846

No public access.

Stock
[1]BR Bo-BoDH No. D818 *Glory* built 1960
[2]BR Co-BoDE No. D5705 built Metrovick 1958
[2]BR Co-CoDH No. D1015 *Western Champion* built 1963

[1]Owned by BR Research and Development Division.
[2]Owned by the Diesel Traction Group.
Details of the DTG may be obtained from A. Bennett, 125 Hythe Avenue, Bexleyheath, Kent.

39 Westonzoyland Engine Group — E

2ft gauge rolling stock on static display

Westonzoyland Pumping Station, near Bridgwater, Somerset
OS Ref: SS 339329

Stock
Motor Rail 4wDM 40s310 built 1968
Ransomes winch wagon
Lister generator wagon
Two skip wagons

40 Inny Valley Railway — C

Private 1ft 10¾in gauge light railway ½ mile in length owned by Mr J. J. A. Evans of Launceston, Cornwall

This line is not open to the general public and any interest in it is actively discouraged. Under no circumstances will casual visitors be shown round, therefore readers are recommended to note its existence, respect the owner's wishes and leave it well alone.

Stock
[1]Hunslet 0-4-0ST *Velinheli* 409 built 1886
[1]Bagnall 0-4-0ST *Sybil* 1760 built 1906
Hibberd 4WDM No. 2 1896 built 1935
[2]Motor Rail 4WDM No. 3 9546 built 1950
Three 4-wheel verandah-end coaches based on Lister truck chassis and incorporating seats built from pews from a church at Probus

[1]Ex Dinorwic Slate Quarries, Llanberis, Caernarfonshire, 1969.
[2]Ex ECC Quarries Ltd, Pitts Cleave Quarry, Devon, September 1970.

41 Poole Miniature Railway — B

Passenger-carrying 10¼in gauge line, ¾ mile in length

Poole Park, Poole, Dorset

Stock
Freelance 4-6-2 GasH (steam outline)
Longfleet Co-BoP No. D1007
Southern Min. Rlys Bo-BoP No. D7000 built 1965
Six open bogie coaches

42 Tucktonia — AE

Tucktonia is a 21-acre leisure park with a model railway layout which is claimed to be the country's largest 2½in gauge railway. The ½-mile line has over 75 items of rolling stock and runs around a 1⁄24th scale exhibition of model buildings which are illuminated and animated. Tucktonia also features a ½-mile long 7¼in gauge passenger-carrying steam railway encircling the park

Tuckton Park Leisure Complex, Stour Road, Christchurch, Dorset BH23 1JW
Tel: 0202-482710

Open 10 am to dusk, April to October.

Stock
Marsh 0-4-2T *Tinkerbell* built 1968
Marsh 0-4-2T *Talos* built 1981
Marsh 2-6-2WT No. 6 *Medea*
Freelance 2-4-0TT *Sir Goss* built 1982
Marsh 4-6-0TT *Sapper* built 1982
Freelance 4wPM *The Bog*
Closed bogie coaches built J. Haylock
Sit-astride bogie coaches
There is also a standard gauge steam locomotive on static display in Tucktonia Leisure Complex

Stock
Bagnall 0-4-0ST No. 2 *Hampshire* 2842 built 1946
On loan from the Mid-Hants Railway (Group No. 55)

43 Bowleaze Cove Railway B

A 7¼in gauge passenger-carrying line 150 yards long operated by Mr Pat Henshaw

Bowleaze Cove, Weymouth, Dorset

The railway operates daily during the summer season.
The line is arranged as a continuous circuit with a two-road engine shed adjoining the main station, access to which is via a footbridge.
Earthworks include a 4ft deep cutting and a tunnel. The railway was opened in May 1975.

Stock
Henshaw 4WPM built 1970
Smith Bo-BoBE built 1975
Two covered bridge bogie coaches built by T. Smith 1975

44 Blaise Castle Miniature Railway B

A 15in gauge passenger-carrying line in the grounds of an 18th century mansion, now a folk museum

Blaise Castle, Henbury, near Bristol, Avon
Access: 4 miles North-West of City, off B4957
OS Ref: ST 559786

Open Monday–Saturday throughout the year (except Bank Holidays) from 2 pm to 5 pm. Museum admission free.

Stock
Hayne/Cromar White Bo-BoBER No. 1 built 1977
Hayne 0-4-2BE No. 2 *Foxglove* built 1977 (steam outline)
Hayne 2w-2-4BER built 1983

45 Cornwall Railway Museum F

Standard gauge railway preservation project based on the trackbed of the former GWR Chacewater–Newquay branch

Zelah, Cornwall
OS Ref: SW 806537

Stock
Hunslet 0-4-0DM 3133 built 1949
Hibberd 4WDM 3776 built 1956
Shell oil tank wagon
Esso oil tank wagon
GWR 4-wheel coach body built 1883

46 Kingsbridge Miniature Railway B

Passenger-carrying 7¼in gauge line running round three sides of the quay car park alongside the estuary at Kingsbridge and giving an out-and-back ride of about ½-mile

The Quay, Kingsbridge, Devon
Operated by G. & P. Kichenside Ltd, Gorse Blossom Farm, Liverton, Newton Abbot, Devon, Tel: Bickington (062 682) 361, to whom all communications should be addressed as there are no facilities for receiving mail at Kingsbridge Quay
Access: Totnes British Rail, then bus (four times a day); or Kingswear (Torbay and Dartmouth Railway), ferry to Dartmouth, then bus. Adjoins quay car park of local authority
OS Ref: SX 735439

The railway operates for Easter week and daily from mid-May to mid-September, 11 am to 5 pm.
The line was built in stages from 1969 and was originally steam-worked with a GWR 0-6-0ST.

Stock
Cromar-White 4WBE No. 2 *Heidi* E7050 built 1976
Bench-type passenger coach
Bogie coach as tank wagon with six seats and handles

47 Butlins, Minehead B

Passenger-carrying 2ft gauge line

Butlins Ltd, Minehead Holiday Camp, Somerset
Adjacent to Minehead Station, West Somerset Railway
OS Ref: SS 984464

Stock
Chance 4-2-4DH No. 30 *C. P. Huntington* 64–5031–24 built 1964 (steam outline)
BR Bo-BoDM 'Western' type
Open bogie coaches

48 Weston-super-Mare Miniature Railway B

Passenger-carrying 7¼in gauge line over ½ mile in length

Marine Parade, Weston-super-Mare, Avon

Open Easter week, then Sundays until Spring Bank Holiday, then daily until September

Stock
American outline Bo-BoDH
Open bogie coaches
Steam locos may work occasionally

49 Plym Valley Railway F

Standard gauge preservation project dedicated to restoring services over the former GWR Marsh Mills to Yelverton line, a distance of 7½ miles. The initial project involves relaying 1¼ miles of track from Marsh Mills to Plym Bridge Halt

Marsh Mills, Plymouth, Devon
Tel: 0752-44804 or 665764

Stock
GWR 2-8-0 No. 3802 (2884 Class) built 1938
[1]GWR 2-6-2T No. 4160 (41XX Class) built 1948
GWR 2-8-2T No. 7229 (72XX Class) built 1935
[2]SR 4-6-2 No. 34007 *Wadebridge* (Bulleid 'West Country' Class) built 1945
BR 4-6-0 No. 75079 *City of Plymouth* (Riddles 4MT Class) built 1956
SAR 4-8-2+2-8-4T No. 4112 (Class GMAM) Beyer Peacock 7827 built 1957 (3ft 6in gauge)
[4]BR Co-CoDH No. D1048 *Western Lady* built 1963
BR 0-6-0DE No. D3002 *Dulcote* built 1952
GWR 'Crocodile' 60ft well wagon No. 334
Twenty-five goods wagons ex-Devonport Dockyard
BR Mk.1 BSK coach
GWR bogie tool van
Two 4-wheel anti-aircraft gun chassis
Smith Rodley steam crane ex-Falmouth Docks
4-wheel hand crane and match truck
Five Wickham 4w PMR rail inspection trollies

[1]Withdrawn June 1965 and sent to Woodham Bros scrapyard, Barry. Purchased for preservation by Birmingham Railway Museum, Tyseley in August 1974. Resold to the Plym Valley Railway in May 1981.
[2]Withdrawn October 1965 and sent to Woodham Bros scrapyard, Barry. Purchased for preservation May 1981.
[3]Withdrawn November 1966 and sent to Woodham Bros scrapyard, Barry. Purchased for preservation December 1981.
[4]Stored at Steamport, Southport (Group No. 253).

50 Callington Light Railway C

Private 2ft gauge railway under construction

Mr D. Preece, Pengally Farm, Callington, Cornwall
Tel: Callington 3419
OS Ref: SX 364698

No public access, but visitors can be accommodated by prior arrangement (telephone preferred).
This 150-yard line was opened in Summer 1977 and operates on an irregular basis on Mr Preece's private property.

Stock
Hibberd 4WDM No. 1 *Samson* 1887 built 1934
Ruston Hornsby 4WDM 186318 built 1937
Baguley 0-4-0DM 3235 built 1947

AREA B

South East

Kent
Surrey
Sussex
Hampshire
Isle of Wight
(Group Nos 51–100)

51 Sittingbourne and Kemsley Light Railway A

Passenger-carrying 2ft 6in gauge light railway, 2 miles in length running from Sittingbourne to Kemsley Down

Access: The entrance to the Sittingbourne Terminal is from a lane off Milton Road, only five minutes from the British Rail station and bus stops. For motorists a free car park is available by courtesy of Bowaters. The route from London is via the A2 and M2 to junction 5, thence A249 to Key Street traffic lights and right into Sittingbourne. From Maidstone or the Isle of Sheppey the route is along the A249 to Key Street traffic lights, thence as above; and from the Kent Coast the route is Thanet Way and the A2 to Sittingbourne. Once in Sittingbourne the direction is signposted along Chalkwell Road B2005 and St Paul's Street B2006.
There is no public road access to Kemsley Down.
Tel: Sittingbourne 24899 (weekends) or 0634 32320 (other times)
OS Ref: TQ 905643

The railway operates passenger services on Saturdays, Sundays and Bank Holidays from Easter to mid-October, also Tuesdays, Wednesdays and Thursdays in August and certain days over the Christmas period.
Facilities for visitors include a sales kiosk at Sittingbourne; refreshment room and picnic area at Kemsley Down. Special facilities for parties by prior arrangement, including set meals and guide, etc. Large free car park at Sittingbourne SKLR station in Milton Road (close to Sittingbourne BR station and A2 road).
Running between Sittingbourne and Kemsley in Kent, the railway was built by Edward Lloyd Ltd to a gauge of 2ft 6in and was used by them to transport paper and other material (also employees) between their mills and Ridham Dock on the banks of the Swale. In 1948, Edward Lloyd Ltd was taken over by the Bowater Group.
The railway is now leased from Bowaters and is operated as a tourist attraction by a Limited Company. Passenger trains are normally steam-hauled and are formed of a varied selection of open and covered coaching stock, including coaches from the former Chattenden and Upnor Railway. The journey to Kemsley covers a distance of almost two miles and is by way of Milton, Church Marshes and Kemsley Marshes, with distant views of the fine parish church at Milton and of the Swale.
A number of examples of former Bowater freight rolling stock is also on display together with a set of Post Office lineside exchange equipment.
Parties are welcome, although prior notification is requested. During the mid-week openings in July and August, accompanied school, scout, girl guide and cub parties are also welcome midweek (10 am to 3.30 pm) during May and June. Special trains can be run if previously booked, operating restrictions permitting, including times in the evenings and mid-week. Set meals (teas and lunches) can be served and a guide provided by prior arrangement.
Further details, Christmas and party bookings from Mr W. E. Fuge, 48 Taverners Road, Rainham, Gillingham, Kent. Telephone Medway 32320.
Details of membership can be obtained at Sittingbourne ticket office on request, or from (s.a.e. please): The joint Secretaries, Mr and Mrs G. A. Stickler, Lite Hjem, Woodlands Estate, Blean, Canterbury, Kent.

Stock
Bagnall 0-6-2T *Alpha* 2472 built 1932
Bagnall 0-6-2T *Triumph* 2511 built 1934
Bagnall 0-6-2T *Superb* 2624 built 1940
Bagnall 2-4-0F *Unique* 2216 built 1924
Kerr Stuart 0-4-2ST *Premier* 886 built 1905
Kerr Stuart 0-4-2ST *Leader* 926 built 1905
Kerr Stuart 0-4-2ST *Melior* 4219 built 1924
Ruston Hornsby 0-4-0DH *Edward Lloyd* (LH Class) 435403 built 1961
Hunslet 4WDM *Victor* 4182 built 1953
Chattenden and Upnor Light Railway bogie coach No. 196 *Chattenden*
Chattenden and Upnor Light Railway bogie coach No. 199 *Upnor*
Chattenden and Upnor Light Railway bogie coach No. 200 *Lodge Hill*
Chattenden and Upnor Light Railway bogie coach No. 204 *Four Elms*
Saloon bogie coaches Nos 1, 2, 3, 4, 5 and 647, converted from Butterley pulp wagons built 1953
Standee passenger coaches Nos 7 and 8 converted from Butterley pulp wagons built 1951
Open coach No. 6 converted from Butterley pulp wagon built 1953
Twenty-eight 14-ton bogie pulp trucks built Butterley 1951 & 1953
Bagnall 10-ton rubbish box bogie wagons Nos 530 and 576
Bagnall high-capacity bogie wagon No. 580
Bagnall 10-ton wooden pulp wagons Nos 412, 494 and 495

Bagnall 8-ton bogie wooden pulp wagon No. 306
Bagnall 20-ton coal box bogie wagons Nos 1 and 2
Kerr Stuart 8-ton bogie pulp wagon No. 126 built *c*1910
Two clay hopper wagons
Four tipper wagons
Nine flat bogie wagons
Breakdown wagon No. 627
The railway also has on display the following standard gauge steam locomotives:
Hawthorn Leslie 0-4-0ST *Swanscombe No. 4* 3719 built 1928
Peckett 0-4-0ST *Bear* 614 built 1896
Barclay 0-4-0F No. 1 1876 built 1925

52 Bluebell Railway A

The Bluebell Railway is a standard-gauge passenger-carrying line operating services at weekends throughout the year and weekdays in the summer between Sheffield Park and Horsted Keynes (five miles)

Sheffield Park Station, Uckfield, West Sussex TN22 3QL
Access: Sheffield Park station is exactly nine miles from both Lewes and East Grinstead on the A275 road, 2 miles north of its junction with the A272.
Horsted Keynes station is situated at the foot of the hill which leads from the West Hoathly to Horsted Keynes road at Great Oddynes turning. Car parking facilities are available at both stations, also buffets and shops.
Frequent trains operate to Haywards Heath. Services also operate to Lewes, Uckfield and East Grinstead. Southdown express bus service 769 departing from Haywards Heath Bus Station. BR run through rail/bus link in summer.
Tel: Newick 2370
OS Ref: TQ 403238

The railway operates during Easter week, on Sundays in January, February and December, on weekends in March, April and November, on weekends and Wednesdays in May and October, daily June–September inclusive and on Bank Holidays.
Facilities for visitors include buffet, souvenir shops, car parking and toilets at both stations. Picnic area at Horsted Keynes. Established in 1960 as a living museum for the steam train in a rural branch-line setting, it has become one of the major attractions of South-Eastern England. From small beginnings with two locomotives and two coaches, the Bluebell Railway is now the home of the largest and most comprehensive collection of Vintage Railway Locomotives, Carriages, and Wagons, that operated in the South of England. Situated in the heart of the Sussex Weald and running for 5 miles through some of its most beautiful countryside, the line offers the ideal setting for the operation of vintage steam trains.

Stock

[1]LBSCR 0-6-0T No. 55 *Stepney* (Stroudley AIX Class) built 1875
[2]LBSCR 0-6-0T No. 72 *Fenchurch* (Stroudley AIX Class) built 1872
[3]LBSCR 0-6-2T No. 473 *Birch Grove* (Billinton E4 Class built 1898
[19]SECR 0-6-0T No. 27 (Wainwright P Class) built 1910
SECR 0-6-0T No. 323 *Bluebell* (Wainwright P Class) built 1910
[27]SR 4-4-0 No. 928 *Stowe* (Maunsell V Class) built 1934
[23]SR 2-6-0 No. 31638 (Maunsell U Class) built 1931
[21]SECR 0-6-0T No. 1178 (Wainwright P Class) built 1910
[4]LSWR 4-4-2T No. 488 (Adams 0415 Class) Neilson 3209 built 1885
[9, 18]LSWR 0-4-0T No. 96 *Normandy* (Adams B4 Class) built 1893
[10]NLR 0-6-0T No. 2650 built 1880
[7, 14]SECR 0-4-4T No. 263 (Wainwright 'H' Class) constructed at Ashford Works in 1905
[8, 15]SECR 0-6-0 No. 592 (Wainwright 'C' Class) (BR No. 31592) built 1901
[9, 16]SR 4-6-2 No. 21C123 *Blackmoor Vale* (Bulleid WC Class) built 1946
[17]SR 0-6-0 No. 33001 (Bulleid Q1 Class) built 1942
[5, 12]SR 2-6-0 No. 1618 (Maunsell U Class) built 1928
[13]SR 0-6-0T No. 30064 (USA Class) built 1943
[5]SR 4-6-0 No. 30847 (Maunsell S15 Class) built 1936
[5]SR 0-6-0 No. 541 (Maunsell Q Class) built 1939
[25]SR 4-6-2 No. 34059 *Sir Archibald Sinclair* (Bulleid rebuilt BB Class) built 1947
[22]BR 4-6-0 No. 73082 *Camelot* (Riddles 5MT Class) built 1955
[26]BR 2-10-0 No. 92240 (Riddles 9F Class) built 1958
[24]BR 2-6-4T No. 80100 (Riddles 4MT Class) built 1955
BR 2-6-4T No. 80064 (Riddles 4MT Class) built 1953
BR 2-6-0 No. 78059 (Riddles 2MT Class) built 1956 (for possible conversion to 84XXX tank)
[26]BR 4-6-0 No. 75027 (Riddles 4MT Class) built 1954
[30]Fletcher Jennings 0-4-0T *Baxter* 158 built 1877
[28]Avonside 0-6-0ST No. 24 *Stamford* 1972 built 1927
[29]Aveling Porter 2-2-0TG *Blue Circle* 9449 built 1926
Manning Wardle 0-6-0ST *Sharpthorn* 641 built 1877
[31]Howard 4w PM *Britannia* 957 built 1926
LBSCR directors' saloon No. 60 built 1913
LSWR third-class coach No. 320 built 1900, rebuilt SR 1935
GNR saloon coach No. 706E built 1897
LNWR observation car No. 1503 built 1913
SR Bulleid open third-class bogie coach No. 1481 built 1951
Metropolitan Railway bogie coaches Nos 512, 515, 516 and 518 built 1898–1900
SECR bogie coach No. 971 built 1923
SR third-class bogie coach No. 1050 rebuilt 1927
SECR brake composite coach No. 1061 built 1909
SECR third-class bogie coach No. 1098 built 1923
LSWR third-class corridor coach No. 494 rebuilt as camping coach No. S39S in 1953
SR Maunsell third-class open coach No. 1365 built 1927

BR 3rd-class sleeping coach No. M623M built 1952 to LMS design
SR Maunsell TPO van No. S4922 built 1939
SR Bulleid open 3rd coach No. 1464 built 1946
[6]SR Bulleid open 3rd coach No. 1456 built 1947
LCDR six-wheel brake/third-class coach (SECR No. 2781) built 1894
SR Bulleid brake/third-class bogie coach No. 4279 built 1948
SR Maunsell BCK bogie coach No. 6575 built 1927
SR Maunsell buffet bogie coach No. 7864 built 1927
BR composite compartment coach No. E43010 built 1954
BR brake/second No. E43172 built 1954
BR open second-class coach No. E48015 built 1955
SR Maunsell BSO bogie coach No. 4441 built 1933
SR Maunsell 'Nondescript' brake coach No. 4444 built 1933
SR Pullman 1st class car *Fingal* built 1924
SR Maunsell 3rd class corridor coach No. 2356 built 1931
SR Maunsell third-class saloon coach No. 1309 built 1930
SR Bulleid third-class saloon coach No. 1482 built 1946
SR Bulleid BTK semi-open coach No. 2515 built 1946
[9]SR Bulleid CK bogie coach No. 5768 built 1947
SR Maunsell BCK coach No. 6686 built 1935
SR Pullman kitchen composite No. 278 *Bertha* built 1932
SECR 'Birdcage' brake van No. 1170 built 1912
LCDR 6-wheel coach No. 48
LSWR lavatory brake/3rd coach No. 1520 built 1910
LMS 2nd class sleeping car No. 603 built 1951
[32]LMS dormitory coach No. DM395584 built 1924
LMS 12-wheeled first-class sleeping coach No. M398M built 1952
LBSCR 6-wheel 1st class coach body built 1880
SR CCT 4-wheel van No. S2531 built 1955
SECR 10-ton high-roofed van No. 15750 built 1920
SECR six-wheeled passenger brake van No. 719 built 1905
LSWR four-wheeled express luggage van No. 5498 built 1920
GWR 'Toad' 20-ton goods brake van No. 17908 built 1913
LNER Wickham petrol rail trolley built 1932
[9]BR goods brake van No. 49027 built 1959 for Army use
SR eight-plank open goods wagon PBA No. 58164 built *c*1923
SECR eight-plank open goods wagon PBA No. 58162
SR five-plank open goods wagon No. 59425 built 1931
'Cory' 12/13-ton mineral wagons Nos 67 and 68 (BR Nos P91344 and P383095)
SR 'Borail' SA wagon SR No. 57949S built 1944
SR BY parcels brake van No. 653 built 1937
SR BY parcels brake van No. 442 built 1937
SR 'Covcar' four-wheeled utility van No. 2276 built 1929
LBSCR milk van No. 270 built 1908
SECR four-wheeled utility van No. 153 built 1922
GWR flat wagon PLA No. E2 built *c*1890
SR 25-ton goods brake van No. DS55993
[5]SR passenger luggage van No. S2186 built 1934
SR 10-ton van No. 44611 built 1931
SR 12-ton six-wheeled hand crane No. DS1748 built 1943
SR match truck No. 1748SM built 1943
Shell petrol tank wagon No. 4497 built 1930
LSWR covered van No. 8112 built 1912
LSWR 20-ton road van No. 5706 built 1898
LMS open wagon No. 474558 built 1937
LMS banana van No. 570027 built 1946
BR Palvans Nos B761349, 772970 and 772972 built 1954–6
[9]LSWR tool van No. 47773 built 1912
[5]GWR tool van No. 92 built 1920
SR BY parcels brake van No. 404 built 1937
LMS 12-ton van built 1945
GWR 'Monster' GUV No. W600 built 1951
SR bogie elephant van No. 4601 built 1949
LMS 'Stove R' 6-wheeled passenger brake van No. M32975
SR ambulance car rebuilt 1959
Two Chaldron wagons built 1869
LMS 'Medfit' open wagon No. 480222 built 1948
BR 'Medfit' open wagon No. DB458525 built 1951
BR 'Medfit' open wagon No. DB461224 built 1955
LBSCR eight-ton open wagon No. 3346 built 1914
CPR *Sylvester* 4WPM permanent way trolley 14384
BR Wickham 4WPMR No. PWM 3959 6944 built 1955
BR Wickham 4WPMR No. PWM 3962 6947 built 1955
BR Wickham 4WPMR 7581 built 1956
BR Wickham 4WPMR 7441
SR covered van No. 47588 built 1931
BR 'Lowmac' wagon No. B904134 built 1957
Esso tank wagon No. 1921 built 1942
SR ventilated meat van No. 51202 built 1931
GWR 'Lowflat' sleeper wagon No. 100067
SR bogie luggage van No. 2462 built 1931
GWR 5-plank wagon
Two LMS 5-plank wagons
Two SR 5-plank wagons
Two SR 8-plank wagons
Two SECR 7-plank wagons
SR 6-wheel milk tank wagon No. 4430 ('Unigate')
LNER 45-ton steam crane built Ransomes & Rapier 1942
LNER match truck

Historical notes

[1]Built at Brighton in December 1875. Renumbered 655, it became SR No. B655 and was withdrawn from traffic in 1925, being placed in store. Reinstated in 1927, it eventually became SR No. 2655 and was ultimately withdrawn from Eastleigh shed in May 1960 as BR No. 32655. Purchased for preservation by the Bluebell Railway and restored to Stroudley yellow livery.

[2]Built at Brighton in September 1872, this was the first of William Stroudley's 'Terriers'. The engine was built at a cost of £500 and was sold to the Newhaven Harbour Company in 1898 for the same sum. The Stroudley livery and name were retained until 1902, when it was repainted black with two red lines. The Wellinghouse brake, removed when the engine was sold, was refitted in 1913, when *Fenchurch* was rebuilt to A1X Class at Brighton. In

1925, the Newhaven Harbour Company was taken over by the SR and the engine was taken into stock as No. B636, later No. 2636. Finally withdrawn from Eastleigh shed in November 1963 as BR No. 32636 and sold to the Bluebell Railway. The engine is restored in lined black livery.

[3]Built at Brighton in July 1898 and withdrawn from Nine Elms in October 1962 as BR No. 32473. Seventy-five locomotives of this class were constructed for mixed traffic work and in their early days they did a fair amount of passenger work, but were gradually displaced, spending the latter part of their lives on shunting and cross-London freight workings. Purchased by the Bluebell Railway and restored in the umber livery used by that company in its latter years.

[4]Withdrawn from Exmouth Junction shed in July 1961 as BR No. 30583. This is the sole survivor of a class of 71 engines built for suburban passenger work between 1883 and 1885, but most of the class were withdrawn and broken up between 1921 and 1928. It is appropriate that No. 488 should be the survivor, since it has quite a remarkable history. It was sold out of service by the LSWR in September 1917 and bought by the Ministry of Munitions for £2,104. After a repaint at Eastleigh it was sent to work at Ridham Salvage Depot, Sittingbourne, where it remained until April 1919, when it was again sold, this time to the East Kent Railway for £900, becoming EKR No. 5. The engine worked on the EKR until 1939, when it was laid aside at Shepherdswell and, like many a Colonel Stephens engine, started to slowly decay in open storage. Its slumbers were awakened in 1946, however, when it was sold to the Southern Railway for £800 and thoroughly overhauled for use on the tortuous Lyme Regis branch alongside the two other survivors of its class. The trio continued to work this line until 1960, when replaced by LMS 2-6-2 tanks, and, happily, the Bluebell Railway intervened and saved this elegant and historic engine from the scrapheap in the following year.

[5]Owned by the Maunsell Locomotive Society (*q.v.*).

[6]On loan from the National Railway Museum.

[7]Owned by the 'H' Class Trust (*q.v.*).

[8]Owned by the Wainwright 'C' Class Preservation Society (*q.v.*).

[9]Owned by the Bulleid Society Ltd. (*q.v.*).

[10]Outside-cylinder goods and shunting locomotive built at Bow Works in 1880 as North London Railway No. 116. On absorption by the LNWR in 1909 it became No. 2650, and, after the Grouping, LMS No. 7505. A few of this class migrated to Rowsley during their career for working the mountainous Cromford and High Peak line, where they were often employed in pairs and made a stirring sight belching out masses of smoke as they stormed the banks, their exhaust beats echoing across the valleys. No. 2650 was one of these exiles, and apart from receiving a LNWR-pattern chimney, has remained in original condition. Withdrawn from Rowsley in 1960 as BR No. 58850.

[12]Withdrawn from Guildford shed in 1964 as BR No. 31618 and sold to Woodham Brothers, Barry, for scrap. Purchased for preservation in 1969 and stored at New Hythe, Kent, until moved to Tenterden in 1972.
Originally ordered as 'K' Class 2-6-4T locomotives, the 20 'U' Class engines numbered 1610–1629 were being assembled when No. A800 *River Cray* was involved in the Sevenoaks disaster. As a result of this mishap all the 'K' Class tanks were rebuilt as 2-6-0 tender locomotives and instructions were given for Nos 1610–1629 to be similarly completed. Had No. 1618 been built as a tank engine it would have been named *River Hamble*.
As tender engines, the class resembled the existing 'N' Class moguls with the exception of larger cylinders and driving wheels and greater overall weight. The 2-6-0s were at the time of their construction a new generation of locomotives, capable of working the heaviest goods trains over the whole Southern system, whilst at the same time being able to assist with express passenger work when necessary.

[13]This locomotive was built by the Vulcan Ironworks, Wilkes-Barre, Pennsylvania, USA, in 1943 (Works No. 4432) for use in Europe by the US Transportation Corps. At the end of the war, several European railways acquired some of this class, in particular the SNCF. Of those which remained in England, most were stored at Newbury Racecourse until 1946 when the Southern Railway purchased 14 of them for use in Southampton Docks. No. 30064 remained active until the end of steam on the Southern Region in July 1967, when it was withdrawn from Eastleigh shed and taken to Salisbury for disposal. Happily, the Southern Locomotive Preservation Co Ltd intervened at this point and purchased the engine for preservation. The engine appeared in the film *Young Winston* and immediately afterwards was moved to Sheffield Park to take up regular duties on the Bluebell Railway.

[14]Withdrawn from Three Bridges shed as BR No. 31263 in 1964 and purchased for preservation and restoration to SECR livery. Returned to steam in summer 1967 and has since attended BR and other open days and been featured on TV. The 66 Wainwright 'H' Class engines were a highly successful design and were used on branch line and secondary duties throughout the Eastern and Central Sections of the SR. They were also one of the most handsome of Edwardian tank engine designs.

[15]Withdrawn as BR Departmental Locomotive No. DS239 in 1966 and purchased for preservation in 1967. Altogether 109 engines of this class were built between 1900 and 1908 and remained the backbone of the SECR fleet of freight engines until the 'N' Class 2-6-0s appeared. Like most 0-6-0s, they were more powerful than their appearance suggests, in addition to which they were very speedy machines when occasion demanded, taking almost anything into their stride, including the 'Night Ferry' and 'Thanet Belle', besides numerous hop-pickers' specials. This locomotive is notable as being the only Longhedge-built engine in existence.

[16]Bulleid 'West Country' class light Pacific built at Brighton Works. Withdrawn from Nine Elms shed in 1967

as BR No. 34023. One-hundred-and-ten of these engines (including the identical 'Battle of Britain' class) were built, making this the largest class of Pacific locomotives ever built in this country. Originally built with many of Oliver Bulleid's unorthodox features, such as 'air-smoothed' casting, chain-driven valve gear and BFB cast steel wheel centres, many were reconstructed by BR on more orthodox lines during the late 1950s. 34023 was the final unrebuilt engine in traffic and worked a special 'Farewell to Southern Steam' railtour on 18 June 1967. Moved to Sheffield Park in 1971.

[17]Bulleid Q1 Class 'Austerity' goods engine built for war-time work but lasting until the mid-60s hauling heavy goods, engineer's trains and occasional passenger trains. Like *Blackmore Vale* No. C1 was built at Brighton, and for about the last ten years it has been in store at Preston Park Pullman shed, Brighton. It is part of the National Collection and is on loan to the Bulleid Society and Bluebell Railways as custodians.

[18]Adams dock tank, formerly LSWR No. 96. Sold to Corrals Ltd, Dibbles Wharf, Southampton, and renamed *Corrall Queen*, the locomotive was purchased by the B4 Group of the Bulleid Society and moved to the Bluebell Railway in 1972.

[19]Withdrawn from Dover shed March 1961 as BR No. 31027 and purchased immediately for preservation. Has been restored to fully lined SECR passenger livery.

[20]Withdrawn from Carnforth shed in August 1968 and purchased immediately for preservation by the Bluebell Railway, moving to Sheffield Park in January 1969.

[21]Withdrawn in June 1958 as BR No. 31178 and sold to Bowaters United Kingdom Pulp and Paper Mills Ltd, Ridham Dock, Kent. Purchased for preservation in October 1969.

[22]Withdrawn in June 1966 and sent to Woodham Bros scrapyard, Barry. Purchased for preservation and moved to the Bluebell Railway in December 1979. Owned by the Camelot Locomotive Society (*q.v.*).

[23]Withdrawn in January 1964 and sent to Woodham Bros scrapyard, Barry. Purchased for preservation and moved to the Bluebell Railway in 1980.

[24]Withdrawn in July 1965 and sent to Woodham Bros scrapyard, Barry. No. 80100 was delivered new to Plaistow depot and subsequently transferred to Tilbury. When the LT & S line was electrified, it was moved to Stratford and then Shrewsbury, where it worked the Cambrian and Severn Valley lines. Purchased by the Brighton Standard 4 Tank Fund and moved to the Bluebell Railway in October 1978.

[25]Withdrawn in May 1966 and sent to Woodham Bros scrapyard, Barry. Purchased by the Battle of Britain Loco Group and moved to the Bluebell Railway in October 1979.

[26]Withdrawn in September 1965 after a working life of less than seven years and sent to Woodham Bros scrapyard, Barry. Purchased by the BR Class 9 Preservation Group and moved to the Bluebell Railway in October 1978.

[27]Withdrawn from Brighton shed in November 1962 as BR No. 30928. Purchased by Lord Montagu for static display at the head of three Pullman cars in the grounds of Beaulieu (the Montagu Motor Museum). In 1973 the locomotive was transferred to Eastleigh works for restoration in SR green livery and subsequently moved to Cranmore. It is now jointly owned by Montagu Ventures Ltd and came to the Bluebell Railway on loan in 1980 and entered service in 1981.

[28]Ex Staveley Minerals Ltd, Pilton Ironstone Quarries, Rutland, October 1969.

[29]Restored and presented by APCM, Snodland, Kent, April 1964.

[30]Ex Dorking Greystone Lime Co Ltd, Betchworth, Surrey, September 1960.

[31]Presented by Britannia Iron & Steel Works Ltd, Bedford, March 1965.

[32]Originally built as a Corridor 3rd No. 1272.

[33]Owned by the Camelot Locomotive Society.

The Bulleid Society Ltd — H

The Society was formed in 1966 by a group of railwaymen at Nine Elms (London) locomotive depot, who wanted to see one of the famous Bulleid Pacifics preserved in full working order. The designer O. V. S. Bulleid agreed to become President.

It took nine long years for 'Blackmore Vale' to emerge as 21C123 pristine in her original Southern Railway livery, with six restored Southern coaches to haul. However, the long wait was justified on 15 May 1976, when replica 'Atlantic Coast Express' trains drew crowds of thousands to the Bluebell Railway. The following year the scene was repeated, when the Bulleid and Bluebell Societies were presented with the SR Q1 Class on loan from the National Collection.

Details from: Mrs S. Noel, 19 Bramble Twitten, Estcots Oaks, East Grinstead, West Sussex.

Maunsell Locomotive Society — H

The Society incorporates the interests of the Southern Mogul Preservation Society, the 847 Locomotive Preservation Fund, and the Q Class Locomotive fund, each of whom have secured a locomotive for use on the Bluebell Railway.

The Society owns three locomotives; of these 1618 is in regular service on the Bluebell Railway while restoration work proceeds on Q Class 541 and S15847. Our efforts are concentrated on 541 and funds permitting this engine should be back in working order in 1982. New members are always welcome and details of membership can be obtained from Mr M. Allen, General Secretary, 51 Friar Crescent, Brighton, Sussex BN1 6NL.

'H' Class Trust — H

The Trust owns and maintains SECR 'H' Class 0-4-4T No. 263.

Details from: E. R. C. Oades, 5 Senlac Way, St Leonards-on-Sea, Sussex.

Wainwright 'C' Class Preservation Society **H**

The Society was formed in 1962 to preserve an example of Wainwright's SECR goods locos which became the last class of steam engine used in Kent. The chosen locomotive (ex BR No. 31592) was withdrawn from Capital Stock and transferred to Ashford Works as DS 239. Final withdrawal came in December 1966 and the engine was purchased through a package deal arranged by ARPS. 592 was kept at Ashford running shed until 1970 when it was transferred to the Bluebell Railway. Working parties have continued restoration to full SECR condition and livery.
Details from: I. H. De Maid, 69 Bromley Gardens, Bromley, Kent BR2 0ES.

The Bluebell Railway Preservation Society

The Society exists to support the Railway, to operate and maintain it, to restore its vehicles and often purchase them. The Society elects Trustees who are the Directors of the Bluebell Railway Limited, the owning and operating company of the Railway.
Society members can assist in operating the Railway by joining:
(*a*) the Traffic department which covers Signalmen, Guards and Shunters as well as the staffing of the stations (including shops and car parks).
(*b*) the Carriage and Wagon department, working on restoration and maintenance of the Railway's fleet of some sixty vehicles.
(*c*) the Locomotive department which provides the Engine Crews and Cleaners and assists with locomotive maintenance and restoration now carried on in the new works.
(*d*) the Signal and Telegraph department which provides staff for the enormous tasks of maintenance, repair and extension of this unsung area of the railway.
(*e*) the Engineering department maintaining track and bridges, etc.
Full details of membership are available by post, please send a stamped self-addressed envelope, from The Membership Secretary, Bluebell Railway Preservation Society, 33 The Hollow, Lindfield, Haywards Heath, West Sussex. Or from either station book office.

Camelot Locomotive Society **H**

Owners of locomotive No. 73082 *Camelot*.
Details from: P. W. Gibbs, 71 Broadstone Road, Harpenden, Herts AL5 1RE.

53 Kent and East Sussex Railway A

Standard gauge passenger-carrying light railway, four miles in length from Tenterden Town to Wittersham Road. The line is being reopened in stages to Bodiam (10 miles)

Tenterden Town Station, Tenterden, Kent TN30 6HE
Access: Headcorn and Ashford BR stations, then by Maidstone and District bus services Nos 12 and 400
Tel: Tenterden 2943
OS Ref: TQ 882336

Rolling stock located at Bodiam, Tenterden Town and Rolvenden Stations.
Facilities for visitors include refreshments, souvenir shop, museum, toilets and car parks at Tenterden and Wittersham Road. The 'Wealden Pullman' dining car service operates on Saturday evenings. Advance booking is essential for this train.
Operating days: Weekends and Bank Holidays, March–October; Sunday afternoons in November and December: Wednesdays in June and July; daily from the end of July to the end of August; Sundays only in November. Special steam events take place in mid-September and around Christmas.
The Kent and East Sussex Railway is perhaps the most famous of all British standard-gauge light railways, being the first such line to be built under the Light Railways Act 1896 and now is almost the last survivor. Its principal claim to fame lies in its being engineered and operated by the late Colonel Holman F. Stephens, the uncrowned king of British light railways. Opened in stages from 1900 from Robertsbridge on the Hastings line, through Tenterden to Headcorn on the Tonbridge–Ashford main line. Closures and track-lifting by British Railways have left ten miles intact between Tenterden and Bodiam. The preservation organisation was set up in 1961 immediately following the closure for all traffic of the Tenterden–Robertsbridge section and has faced many severe obstacles since then in its struggle to reinstate services over all or part of this portion of the line. Sheer dogged perseverance and enthusiasm finally won the day and the K & ESR jubilantly reopened for passenger traffic on 3 February 1974, almost exactly 20 years after the last BR passenger train over the line. An official reopening ceremony was performed on 1 June by the Rt Hon William Deeds, MC, DL, MP, and by the end of the year over 37,000 passengers had travelled over the operating section to Morghew Crossing, half-a-mile west of Rolvenden. On 22 March 1975 a special ceremony was held at Rolvenden to celebrate the 75th anniversary of the opening of the original Rother Valley Railway from Robertsbridge, when No. 3 *Bodiam* hauled two 'birdcage' coaches conveying guests in period costume. Dixter Halt opened 23rd May 1981.

Stock
[2]LBSCR 0-6-0T No. 3 *Bodiam* (Stroudley A1X Class) built 1872
[3]LBSCR 0-6-0T No. 10 *Sutton* (Stroudley A1X Class) built 1876
[4]SECR 0-6-0T No. 11 *Pride of Sussex* (Wainwright P Class) built 1909
[8]Peckett 0-4-0T No. 12 *Marcia* 1631 built 1923

Manning Wardle 0-6-0ST No. 14 *Charwelton* 1955 built 1917
Manning Wardle 0-6-0ST No. 15 *Rhyl* 2009 built 1921
Manning Wardle 0-6-0ST No. 16 *Dolobran* 1762 built 1910
Manning Wardle 0-6-0ST No. 17 *Arthur* 1601 built 1903
Peckett 0-6-0ST No. 18 *Westminster* 1378 built 1914
NSB 2-6-0 No. 19 (NSB No. 376) Nohab 1163 built 1919
GWR/AEC Bo-Bo DM railcar No. 20 built 1940
[5]SR 0-6-0T No. 21 *Wainwright* (USA Class) built 1943
[5]SR 0-6-0T No. 22 *Maunsell* (USA Class) built 1943
Hunslet 0-6-0ST No. 23 *Holman F. Stephens* 3791 built 1952
Hunslet 0-6-0ST No. 24 *William H. Austen* 3800 built 1953
Hunslet 0-6-0ST No. 25 *Northiam* 3797 built 1953
Hunslet 0-6-0ST No. 26 *Linda* 3781 built 1952
RSH 0-6-0ST No. 27 *Rolvenden* 7086 built 1943
RSH 0-6-0ST No. 29 7667 built 1950
[9]BTH Bo-Bo DE No. 40 built 1932
RSH 0-4-0DH No. 41 *Baglan* 8377 built 1962
Hunslet 0-6-0DM No. 42 *Dahlech* 4208 built 1958
Fowler 4wDH No. 43 4220031 built 1964
BR 0-6-0DM No. 44 (BR No. D2023) built 1958
BR 0-6-0DM No. 45 (BR No. D2024) built 1958
BR 0-6-0DM No. 46 (BR No. D2205) built 1958
[7]Manning Wardle 0-4-0TG *Gervase* 1472 built 1900
Ford 4wPMR twin 'back-to-back' railbus set under construction 1984
Motor Rail 4WDM 9019 built 1950
North London Poly 4WPM built 1979
Ruston Hornsby 4wDM (48DS Class) 252823 built 1947
Ruston Hornsby 4wDM 210481 built 1942
SR Maunsell BSO R1 bogie coaches Nos 53 and 54 built 1930 (formerly SR Nos 4432 and 4443)
SR Maunsell CK R1 bogie coaches Nos 55 and 56 built 1930 (formerly SR Nos 5153 and 5618)
SR Maunsell SK RO coach No. 59 built 1931 (formerly SR No. 1020)
SR Maunsell SO R1 coach No. 58 built 1931 (formerly SR No. 7798)
SR Maunsell FK RO coach No. 57 built 1931 (formerly SR No. 7400)
LSWR tricomposite coach No. 62 built *c*1900 (formerly SR No. 318)
SR Maunsell SO R4 bogie coach No. 1346 built 1933
SR Maunsell BSO coach No. 4438 (KESR No. 73) built 1933, rebuilt as Ambulance car 1939
BR Mk.1 BSO invalid coach No. 9254 *Petros* built 1956
BR Mk.1 BSO coach No. 9269 built 1956
BR restaurant-kitchen car No. E 1955 *Diana* (KESR No. 69) built 1960
BR Mk.1 SK coach No. M25446 built 1957
BR Mk.1 TSO coach No. E3753 built 1953
BR Mk.1 TSO coach No. S4037 built 1955
SR Maunsell 'Nondescript' Boat Train brake coach No. 4473 built 1933
SECR 'Birdcage' lavatory brake coach No. 1084 built 1910
LCDR brake/2nd coach No. 49 built 1889 (body only)
District Railway 1st class 4-wheel coach No. 100
LSWR 4-wheel coach body
GER Pullman Car *Cambria* built 1920 as kitchen car 119
SECR 'Birdcage' brake/third bogie coaches Nos 60 and 61
SR Pullman coaches Nos 184 *Barbara* and 185 *Theodora* built 1926
LNWR four-wheeled brake/third coach No. 101 built 1910
Shell-Mex oil tank wagon No. 7522 built 1943
Smith Rodley diesel crane No. 12019 built 1935
Five eight-ton open wagons
Two covered goods vans
SR 25-ton goods brake van No. 103 built 1941
SECR six-wheeled goods brake van No. 102
LNWR 20-ton goods brake van No. 104
SR BY parcels/brake van No. S440 built 1937
LNER 20-ton brake van (KESR No. 119) built *c*1925
LMS 12-ton goods van No. M515184 built 1940
LNER 25-ton hopper wagon
BR (ex SNCF) 16-ton mineral wagon NCB No. 54
LSWR 10-ton goods van No. 2780 built 1906
Two flat wagons Nos 115 and 116 (converted from tank wagons)
A 12 cu yd bogie tipper wagon No. 117 built in USA
SR bogie corridor PMV parcels van No. S2339 built 1930
SR PMV 4-wheel van No. S1808 built 1942 (KESR No. 74)
SR CCT 4-wheel van No. S1745 built 1938
LNER 12-ton van (KESR No. 131) built 1920s
LBSCR 8-ton ventilated van (KESR No. 125)
LNWR 20-ton well wagon (KESR No. 121)
Barry Railway 10-ton 'Iron Mink' van (KESR No. 120)
Esso tank wagon No. 2338 built Pickering 1941
GER 6-wheel coach
Wickham 4wPMR No. TR1 6872 built 1954
KESR Wickham trolley built 1920
Wickham 4WPMR No. 900312 built 1931
Wickham 4WPMR No. 900393 400 built 1931
Wickham 4WPMR No. 5 6965 built 1955
Wickham 4WPMR 7438 built 1956
Wickham 4WPMR 6950 built 1955
4wVB steam crane

[2]Built at Brighton as No. 70 *Poplar* in November 1872. Sold to the Rother Valley Railway, becoming their No. 3 *Bodiam* in 1901. Absorbed by BR in 1948 as No. 32670, it was finally withdrawn from Eastleigh in November 1963. Purchased privately for use on the K & ESR, *Bodiam* has returned to the Rother Valley and hauled the reopening special train on 3 February 1974.

[3]Built at Brighton as No. 50 *Whitechapel* in December 1876. Renumbered 650 by the LBSCR, becoming Southern No. B650, it went to the Isle of Wight in 1930 as W9 *Fishbourne*. When returned to the mainland in 1937 the name was removed and it entered service stock as 515S for shunting at Lancing Carriage Works. Converted for oil burning in 1946 and reconverted to coal firing in 1947, it returned to ordinary service in October 1953 as BR No. 32650. Withdrawn from Eastleigh in November 1963,

the locomotive was sold to Sutton Borough Council, who have loaned it to the K & ESR.

[4]Built at Ashford as SECR No. 753 and renumbered A556 by the Southern Railway in 1925. Became BR No. 31556 and was withdrawn in June 1961 and sold to James Hodson (Millers) Ltd of Robertsbridge who named the engine *Pride of Sussex*. Purchased for the K & ESR in 1969 and has since been overhauled and repainted.

[5]Both locomotives built by the Vulcan Ironworks, Wilkes-Barre, Pennsylvania, USA, in 1943 for the US Army Transportation Corps. They were taken into SR stock in December 1946 and on nationalisation became BR Nos 30070 and 30065 respectively. Both were withdrawn in October 1962 and transferred to SR service stock as DS238 and DS237 when they acquired their present names. Final withdrawal came in September 1967 and they were purchased for preservation a year later.

[8]Presented by Hardman & Holden Ltd, Agecroft, Manchester, July 1963.

[9]Ex Ford Motor Co Ltd, Dagenham, Essex, July 1966. On permanent loan from AEI Ltd.

54 Romney, Hythe and Dymchurch Railway — A

Passenger-carrying 15in gauge railway 13¾ miles long

Headquarters: New Romney Station, Kent
Access: The RH & DR is easily reached by road along the A259. Folkestone Central BR Station, thence by East Kent bus to Hythe RH & DR Station
Tel: New Romney (06783) 2353
OS Ref: TR 074249

The railway operates daily from Easter to the end of September, also on Saturdays and Sundays in March, October and November.
Details from: Mr J. B. Snell, RH & DR, New Romney Station, Kent.
Facilities: Car parks and refreshments at main stations. Model exhibition with large working 'O' gauge model railway at New Romney. Cheap return fares available on Friday mornings. Parties catered for.
The RH & DR is the only miniature railway in the British Isles to be authorised by a Light Railway Order. The railway was built by the late Captain J. E. P. Howey to serve a hitherto untapped part of the Kent coast and was opened to all traffic in stages between 1927 and 1929. At first, passenger and goods services operated all the year round, but the winter service did not pay and was withdrawn in 1948, whilst goods traffic ceased in 1951. During the war the railway was taken over by the military and after hostilities ceased the New Romney to Dungeness section was singled. Captain Howey died in 1963, but operation of the railway was continued by local business interests until arrears of maintenance forced them to contemplate closure in 1971. Happily this was forestalled by sale to a new consortium headed by Bill McAlpine and Brian Hollingsworth in February 1972. The RH & DR Association is a subscriber to the consortium and assists in publicising the railway and supplying volunteer labour.
RH & DRA details from: Mr R. L. Smith, 200 Great West Road, Hounslow, Middlesex.

Stock
Davey Paxman 4-6-2 No. 1 *Green Goddess* 21499 built 1925
Davey Paxman 4-6-2 No. 2 *Northern Chief* 21500 built 1925
Davey Paxman 4-6-2 No. 3 *Southern Maid* 22070 built 1926
Krauss 0-4-0 No. 4 *The Bug* 8378 built 1926
Davey Paxman 4-8-2 No. 5 *Hercules* 22071 built 1926
Davey Paxman 4-8-2 No. 6 *Samson* 22072 built 1926
Davey Paxman 4-6-2 No. 7 *Typhoon* 22073 built 1926
Davey Paxman 4-6-2 No. 8 *Hurricane* 22074 built 1926
Yorkshire Engine Co 4-6-2 No. 9 *Winston Churchill* 2294 built 1931
Yorkshire Engine Co 4-6-2 No. 10 *Doctor Syn* 2995 built 1931
Krupp 4-6-2 No. 11 *Black Prince* 1664 built 1937
TMA Engineering Bo-BoDH No. 12 built 1983
Keef 4wPM *Redgauntlet* built 1977
Motor Rail 4WDM 7059 built 1938
RH & DR 4WPM No. PW2 built 1949
Forty-five bogie saloon coaches
Three semi-open bogie coaches
Fourteen open bogie coaches
Three saloon coaches for disabled passengers
Driving trailer coach built 1982
Various works stock, approximately 40 units

55 Mid-Hants Railway — A

Passenger-carrying standard gauge railway, 6¼ miles in length from Alresford to Medstead

(The 'Watercress' Line)
Alresford Station, Alresford, Hampshire SO24 9JG
Access: Close to the main A31 Guildford to Winchester Road, or by Alder Valley buses from Alton, Winchester or Southampton. Bus service Nos 214 and X14 (weekdays) or 452 (Sundays)
Tel: Alresford 3810, during operating days only
OS Ref: SU 588325

The railway operates on Saturday afternoons, Sundays and Bank holidays from the end of March to the end of October.
Facilities for visitors include car parking (at Alresford only), souvenir shop, refreshments and toilets.
The original Mid-Hants 'Watercress' line from Alton to Winchester Junction (17 miles) was closed by British Rail in 1973. Efforts to save the line started at once with Winchester and Alton Railway Ltd being successful in raising sufficient capital in 1975 to secure the land from

Alton to Alresford (10 miles) and the track from Alresford to Ropley (3 miles). Valuable support is given by the Mid-Hants Railway Preservation Society whose membership is growing steadily. Opening of the Alresford–Ropley section took place on 30 April 1977, and since then the railway has become one of the fastest growing lines in the country. The locomotive shed at Ropley was constructed during 1979 and services have now been reinstated from Ropley to Medstead.

Stock

[1]SR 2-6-0 No. 31806 (Maunsell 'U' Class) rebuilt 1928 from 'K' Class 2-6-4T No. A806 *River Torridge* built 1926
[2]SR 2-6-0 No. 31874 (Maunsell 'N' Class) built 1925
[8]SR 2-6-0 No. 31625 (Maunsell 'U' Class) built 1929
[11]SR 4-6-2 No. 35018 *British India Line* (Bulleid MN Class) built 1945
[3]SR 4-6-2 No. 34016 *Bodmin* (Bulleid 'West Country' Class) built 1945, rebuilt 1958
[4]SR 4-6-2 No. 34105 *Swanage* (Bulleid 'West Country' Class) built 1950
[10]SR 4-6-2 No. 34067 *Tangmere* (Bulleid BB Class) built 1947
[5]LSWR 4-6-0 No. 30499 (Urie S15 Class) built 1920
[5]LSWR 4-6-0 No. 506 (Urie S15 Class) built 1920
SR 4-6-0 No. 30825 (Maunsell S15 Class) built 1927 (for spares)
[13]LSWR 4-4-0 No. 30120 (Drummond T9 Class) built 1899
[12]LMS 0-6-0T No. 47324 (Fowler 3F Class) North British Loco Co 23403 built 1926
[14]LMS 0-6-0 No 44123 (Fowler 4F Class) built 1925
USATC 2-8-0 No. 575 Baldwin 70340 built 1944
WD 2-10-0 No. 90775 NB Loco 25438 built 1943
BR 2-6-0 No. 76017 (Riddles 4MT Class) built 1953
[6]Hunslet 0-6-0ST No. 196 *Errol Lonsdale* 3796 built 1953
[7]Hudswell Clarke 0-6-0ST *Slough Estates No. 3* 1544 built 1924
BR Bo-BoDE No. 25219 built 1963
BR 0-6-0DE No. 08.288 (Class 08) built 1956
North British 0-4-0DH 27078 built 1953
[9]Fowler 4WDM No. 4 22889 built 1939, rebuilt 1958
BR Mk.1 TSO coaches Nos E4549 and E4600 built 1956
BR Mk.1 CK coach No. W15798 built 1955
BR Mk.1 BCK coach No. E21077 built 1955
BR Mk.1 FO coach No. 3043 built 1954
BR Mk.1 FK coach No. 13088 built 1954
BR Mk.1 BSK coach No. 34618 built 1955
BR Mk.1 BCK coach No. E21092 built 1956
BR Mk.1 buffet car No. 1668 built 1960
BR Mk.1 buffet car No. W1851 built 1960
BR Mk.1 SK coach No. E25451 built 1957
BR Mk.1 TSO coach No. E3906 built 1954
BR Mk.1 TSO coach No. E4656 built 1957
BR Mk.1 TSO coach No. E4489 built 1956
BR Mk.1 TSO coach No. E4606 built 1957
BR Mk.1 TSO coach No. E4423 built 1956
BR Mk.1 TSO coach No. E4712 built 1957
BR Mk.1 SK coach No. E24458 built 1954
BR Mk.1 SK coach No. E25347 built 1957
BR Mk.1 FO coach No. S3065 built 1955
BR Mk.1 FO coach No. S3067 built 1955
BR Mk.1 FO coach No. S3070 built 1955
BR Mk.1 CK coach No. E15959 built 1957
BR Mk.1 BCK coach No. 21252 built 1963
BR lavatory composite coach No. 43012 built 1954
BR brake/second coach No. 43161 built 1955
BR brake/second coach No. 43190 built 1954
BR second class coach No. 46069 built 1954 (office)
BR second class coach No. 46116 built 1954
SR Bulleid brake/3rd corridor coach No. 2850 built 1945
SR brake/3rd corridor coach No. 3190 built 1923
SR Maunsell brake/2nd open coach No. 4449 built 1933 (being converted to a handicapped persons saloon)
SR Maunsell Post Office stowage van No. 4958 built 1939 (used as a workshop/stores van)
SR Bulleid corridor composite coach No. 5761 built 1947
SR Maunsell brake composite corridor coach No. 6601 built 1930
SR Maunsell SO coach No. S1323 built 1933
LSWR 'Ironclad' BTK coach No. 3187 built 1923
Six BR 'Dolphin' ballast wagons
LMS open wagon No. 66052
LNER open wagons Nos 63022 & 63033
GWR open wagon No. 63018
SR open wagons Nos 59408 & 60046
GWR 'Crocodile' sleeper wagon No. DW100713 built 1942
BR Plasser & Theurer aligning machine No. DB965476
BR Taylor & Hubbard 10-ton steam crane No. DS414 built 1948
BR Taylor & Hubbard 10-ton steam crane No. DRT 80132 built 1956
SR Bulleid brake third-class coach No. 4211 built 1947
SR Maunsell brake third-class coach No. 3719 built 1930
LSWR dining car No. 64 built 1905
LSWR dining car No. 76 built 1908
SR dining car No. 7851 built 1923
LSWR brake/3rd corridor coach No. 1282 built 1921
[12]LMS 3rd corridor coach No. 1501 built 1930
SR CCT van No. 1768 built 1938
SR parcels van No. 2188 built 1934
SR parcels vans Nos 1851 built 1940 and 2196 built 1934
SR parcels brake van No. 765 built 1939
SECR parcels van No. 1995 built 1922
Coal wagon No. P82993 built *c*1930 (has Cambrian Wagon Co axle boxes)
Plassermatic lifting, levelling and tamping machine No. 74108 (DB 965318) built Plasser & Theurer, Austria 1964
LMS 'Stove R' 6-wheel van No. 32990 built 1938
BR (to LNER design) 6-wheel brake van No. 70692 built 1950
GWR 'Toad' 20-ton goods brake van No. 35907 built 1944
Tar tank wagon No. 95 (ex South Western Tar Distilleries) built 1939
LMS flat wagon No. 202 built 1935

SR box van No. 46011 built 1939
LSWR open wagon No. 46102
MR open wagon No. 46270 built *c*1920
Hurst Nelson open wagon No. 47081 built *c*1920
Woolwich Arsenal open wagon No. 47096 built *c*1920
NER box van No. 47764
SR box van No. 47777 built 1940
SR 25-ton brake van No. 55506 built 1926 (SECR type)
Woolwich Arsenal open wagon No. 55858 built *c*1920
Threlkeld Granite Co. open wagon No. 57117 built *c*1920
SR 30-ton bogie flat wagon No. 57849 built 1924 (LSWR type)
LMS box van No. 91395 built 1933
LNER box van No. 110504 built 1928
LMS box van No. 513212 built 1940
SR box van (for LMS) No. 514791 built 1942
LMS box van No. 517317 built 1942
LMS box van No. 523671 built 1945
[12]LMS box van No. 524430 built 1945
BR pallet van No. 776446 built 1957
Wickham 4WPMR No. 1 8267 built 1934
Wickham 4WPMR No. DS3 6642 built 1953
Wickham 4WPMR No. AD9023 8087 built 1958
Isles, Stanningley self-propelled steam crane No. 41215 built 1886

[1]Originally built at Brighton in 1926 as a 'K' Class tank locomotive named *River Torridge*, it was rebuilt two years later as a 'U' Class tender engine. After World War II, No. 31806 was based at Faversham, Kent, but moved to Nine Elms, London, in October 1954 and on to Basingstoke in June 1955. For nearly eight years this locomotive worked mainly semi-fast passenger services to and from the south coast until in March 1963 it was transferred back to Guildford, where it had been sent when new. Ten months later it was withdrawn and sent to Woodham Brothers scrapyard until purchased by two MHRPS directors in July 1975.

[2]Mixed-traffic locomotive built from parts made at Woolwich Arsenal to relieve unemployment after World War I. The boiler came from the North British Locomotive Company in Glasgow and assembly of the complete locomotive took place at Ashford, Kent, in September 1925. For 28 years the locomotive worked between London and the Kent coast, but when the lines in Kent were electrified, No. 31874 was sent to Exmouth Junction in Devon. From February 1961 it was frequently used on the North Cornwall line from Exeter to Padstow until withdrawn in April 1964. The journey to Woodham Brothers scrapyard at Barry then followed, but on 28 April 1973, No. 31874 was purchased by Mr John Bunch, a director of the Mid-Hants Railway Preservation Society. The locomotive was named *Anzar Line* from 1973 to 1979.

[3]One of 110 Pacific locomotives built to Southern Railway design after the last war which received 'West Country' and 'Battle of Britain' names. No. 34016 was built at Brighton and entered traffic at Exmouth Junction, near Exeter, in November 1945. The locomotive was rebuilt to its current form in February 1958 and transferred to Ramsgate. During the summer of 1959 the first stage of railway electrification in East Kent was introduced, and *Bodmin* was transferred to Bricklayers Arms depot in South-East London. A further move took place in May 1961 when No. 34016 became based at Eastleigh, but in June 1964 it was withdrawn from traffic and used for safety-valve setting at Eastleigh until despatched to Woodham Brothers scrapyard. Mr John Bunch saved No. 34016 from destruction in 1971, and on 29 July 1972 the locomotive completed a move by road from the scrapyard to Quainton Road Station, near Aylesbury, where restoration work commenced. Now owned by John Bunch and Richard Heather.

[4]After being built at Brighton in February 1950, *Swanage* was based at Bournemouth for all its comparatively short working life, and regularly handled express workings on the Waterloo–Southampton–Bournemouth route. Unlike many similar locomotives, including *Bodmin* (above), *Swanage* remained in its original form until withdrawn in October 1964. Four months later it was towed to South Wales for cutting up at Woodham Brothers scrapyard, and in April 1976 was purchased by a group of 'Watercress' line supporters. The tender bought to run with this engine was last used with 'Merchant Navy' Class locomotive No. 35018 *British India Line*.

[5]Withdrawn in 1964 and sold to Woodham Brothers, Barry, for scrap. No. 30506 was purchased for preservation in April 1973 and No. 30499 in 1980.

The Urie S15 Class represented an important landmark in locomotive development. Nos 30499 and 30506 are the only preserved locomotives to represent the work of Robert Wallace Urie, the Chief Mechanical Engineer of the LSWR between 1912 and 1922. Twenty of these 4-6-0 engines were built to Urie's design at Eastleigh during 1920–21, and with their 5ft 7in driving wheels provided the main source of power for fast freight duties from Feltham and later throughout the Southern Railway system. At busy periods they were also to be found on passenger duties, being able to produce speeds of 65–70 mph if occasion demanded.

These locomotives are owned by the Urie S15 Preservation Group (*q.v.*).

[6]A fine example of a popular class of 0-6-0 saddletank locomotive built in large quantities during and after World War II. Constructed by the Hunslet Engine Company of Leeds in 1953, No. 196 was included in a batch of 14 destined for the War Reserve. Our locomotive is believed to have been stored near here, at Liphook, until September 1955, when it was transferred to Honeybourne in Worcestershire, arriving on 16 September. Further transfers took place on 26 July 1957 to nearby Long Marston, and on 7 November 1960, when it was sent for general overhaul to the Central Workshops at Bicester. In November 1964 it returned to Hampshire, destined for the 16th Railway Regiment, Royal Engineers, at Longmoor.

Shortly afterwards, on 22 January 1965, No. 196 entered service on the Longmoor Military Railway and worked regularly until the line closed at the end of October 1969. Whilst there, on 8 January 1968, No. 196 was named *Errol Lonsdale* after the Transport Officer-in-Chief, Major General Lonsdale.

[7]This locomotive worked for 49 years at the Slough Trading Estate hauling freight around the extensive system there. In 1973 the last two locomotives were withdrawn and the one in the best condition was offered to Winchester and Alton Railway Limited on free permanent loan, together with a large quantity of spares, by Slough Estates Limited. It became the second locomotive to appear at Alresford for our project, arriving on 18 August 1973.

[8]After emerging in March 1929 from Ashford Works, Kent, A625 went to Nine Elms, London, where it was employed on a number of secondary passenger services including those to Portsmouth, Salisbury, Reading and, most interestingly, Southampton Terminus via Alton and Alresford.

With locomotive coal in short supply after the war, 1625 was converted to oil-firing during 1947, being sent to Exmouth Junction after conversion on 19 October 1947 where it worked well on local services. The plan to convert over 100 Southern locomotives did not materialise and by October the following year it was stored at Fratton to await re-conversion to coal-firing at Ashford.

After further work from Guildford, 31625 was condemned with several others in January 1964 and was stored at Fratton with 31806 until both were taken to Woodham Bros for scrap on 16 June 1964.

Early in 1980, 31625 was purchased by John Bunch, Wayne Thompson and David Warwick, and moved back to Hampshire, sponsored by the Allthread Group.

[9]This useful locomotive was built in Leeds during 1939, and was one of many used by the War Department. In 1958 it was completely modernised and received a new Maclaren six-cylinder 150-hp engine. When renumbering of Army locomotives took place in 1968, the number 242 was allotted in place of 852, but 224 was applied in error and the number was never amended. Latterly No. 224 was used at HM Victualling Depot at Botley, near Southampton, but it was bought in working order by G. A. Day Limited who presented it on permanent loan to Winchester and Alton Railway.

[10]Having been completed at Brighton works by September 1947 *Tangmere* was sent to Ramsgate until transferred to Battersea shed, otherwise known as Stewarts Lane, in November 1949. Here it stayed, working passenger services between London Victoria, Sussex and Kent until the completion of the Kent electrification in June 1961. *Tangmere* was then transferred to Salisbury until September 1963, when it was moved to Exmouth Junction, by now in Western Region hands, for only two months before being set aside in November. After being stored unserviceable at Eastleigh it was sold to Woodham Bros. arriving in the scrapyard at Barry during March 1965.

During the spring of 1980 *Tangmere* was purchased with the Mid-Hants extension to Alton in mind. It will now be paired with a 5,000 gallon tender previously attached to a Merchant Navy class locomotive.

[11]When built in May 1945 the locomotive was painted black but within a few months had been repainted malachite green prior to being named in December that year. Apart from the periods following visits to Eastleigh for attention, and two months towards the end of 1960 when it worked from Bournemouth, 35018 was always based at Nine Elms, London. It had been called upon to work the *Bournemouth Belle* when this all-Pullman express was first re-introduced after the Second World War on 7 October 1946, and subsequently hauled the 'Belle' on many occasions. However, with the onset of main-line diesel locomotives, members of the class started to be condemned in February 1964 and in August *British India Line* was taken out of service having covered a grand total of 956,544 miles. In March 1965 it was towed to Woodhams yard until being bought at the end of 1979 by Richard Heather and John Bunch. It will be paired with the 6,000 gallon tender latterly used with similar locomotive 35025 *Brocklebank Line*.

[12]Owned by the Fowler 3F Society (*q.v.*).

Details of the Mid-Hants Railway Preservation Society Ltd may be obtained from the Membership Secretary at Alresford Station.

[13]On loan from the National Collection.

[13]Withdrawn June 1965 and sent to Woodham Bros. scrapyard, Barry. Purchased for preservation and moved to the Mid-Hants Railway in 1982.

Urie S15 Locomotive Preservation Group **H**

Membership and shares: Hon. Treasurer, Flat 4, 'Lingfield', Elvetham Road, Fleet, Hampshire GU13 8QW

Fowler 3F Society

Details from: John Graham, Esq., 22 Corringway, Fleet, Aldershot, Hampshire

The Society also owns the following locomotive, on loan to Tucktonia, Dorset (Group No. 42):

Bagnall 0-4-0ST No. 2 2842 built 1946

56 Isle of Wight Steam Railway A

Passenger-carrying standard gauge steam railway, 1¾ miles in length, from Haven Street to Wootton

Haven Street Station, near Ryde, Isle of Wight PO33 4DS

Access: Service 3 or 43 Southern Vectis bus operates from Ryde Esplanade or Newport and stops outside Haven Street Station. Inclusive through 'Awayday' tickets available from Portsmouth Harbour, Ryde Pier Head

(rebook facilities for mainland ticket holders), Sandown and Shanklin
Tel: Wootton Bridge 882204
OS Ref: SZ 556898

The railway operates on Easter Sunday and Monday, on Sundays from May to September, on Thursdays in July and August and on Spring and Summer Bank Holidays. Also daily during the week prior to the late Summer Bank Holiday.
Facilities for visitors include car parking, museum, souvenir shop, refreshments and toilets.
The Wight Locomotive Society was formed in 1966 to preserve a selection of Isle of Wight rolling stock, together with the locomotive *Calbourne*. After several years storage at Newport, the stock was moved over the closed line to Haven Street in January 1971 and, following negotiations with the IWCC, the Haven Street–Wootton section of single line was leased. The Society subsequently formed the Isle of Wight Railway Company Limited to operate and administer the steam railway, which has become a popular tourist attraction with holidaymakers and day visitors alike. Haven Street Station, rebuilt by the SR in 1926, was a former passing place on the Ryde–Newport line. The original station at Wootton was closed in 1953 and demolished soon after and, although it was hoped to reopen the former station, an extensive earthslip on the site made this impossible. Consequently, a new terminal station is being built at Wootton. A workshop has been built at Haven Street to speed the process of restoring the growing collection of historic rolling stock. The Isle of Wight Steam Railway is alone amongst the standard gauge preserved railways in the British Isles in using exclusively pre-grouping carriages to form its trains.

Stock
[1]LBSCR 0-6-0T No. W8 *Freshwater* (Stroudley Class A1X) built 1876
[2]LBSCR 0-6-0T No. W11 *Newport* (Stroudley Class A1X) built 1878 (restored as IWCR No. 11)
[3]LSWR 0-4-4T No. W24 *Calbourne* (Adams Class 02) built 1891
[4]Hawthorn Leslie 0-4-0ST No. 37 *Invincible* 3135 built 1915
[5]Barclay 0-6-0T No. 38 *Ajax* 1605 built 1918
[6]Ruston Hornsby 4WDM No. 39 *Spitfire* 242868 built 1946
BR 0-6-0DM No. D2554 Hunslet 4870 built 1955
North British 0-4-0DH *Tiger* 27415 built 1954
LBSCR nine-compartment third-class coach No. 2416 built 1916
SECR four-compartment brake/third coaches Nos 4145 and 4149 built 1911
LBSCR five-compartment brake/third coach No. 4168 built 1922 on an underframe constructed in 1905
SR to LBSCR design eight-compartment composite coach No. 6349 built 1924
SECR composite saloon coach No. 6375 built 1911
LSWR 'Road Van' No. 56046 built 1898
LBSCR 10-ton open wagons Nos 27834 and 28346 built 1924–25
LBSCR 10-ton rebuilt BR dropside open wagons Nos 27766 and 28345 built *c*1924 and rebuilt to ballast wagons in 1966
SR 13-ton high-sided open wagons Nos 27910, 27926, 27936 and 27937 built 1927 (acquired from Messrs Corralls in 1975 and some to be rebuilt for Engineering Department use)
LBSCR 10-ton machinery wagon No. 60579 built 1923
LBSCR single-bolster wagons Nos 59038, 59049 and 59050 built 1909–10
IWCR (originally Midland Railway) six-wheeled crane No. 429S built *c*1860
IWCR (originally LSWR) four-wheeled match wagon No. 429SM built *c*1890
IWCR eight-ton goods van (body only) built *c*1880 at Newport, Isle of Wight
SR PMV parcels van No. 1052 built 1943
[7]LBSCR cattle truck No. 46924 built 1922
BR single bolster wagons Nos DB450157, DB451289, DB451924, DB452018, DB452715, DB453374 built 1950–59
BR Wickham 4WPMR No. DS3320 6645 built 1953
BR Matisa tamping unit No. DS72 built 1955
Underframe of Drewry Railcar No. 2 (Ryde Pier Tramway) built 1927
NLR 4-compartment, first-class coach body IWR No. 46 built 1864
IWR 3-compartment, first-class coach body built 1864
LCDR brake/3rd coach No. 4112 (body only) built 1898
IWR 3-compartment composite coach body No. 38 built 1882
LCDR 7-compartment 3rd class coach No. 2418 (half body only) built 1895
LCDR compartment 3rd class coach (half body only)
IWR four-compartment second No. 39 (body only) built 1882
LCDR five-compartment brake/third No. 4115 (body only) built 1898
SR PMV 4-wheel vans Nos 1497, 1533, 1566, 1603 & 1669 built 1947–1951
SR PMV 4-wheel vans Nos 1783, 1803 & 1930 built 1938–1942
SR CCT 4-wheel van No. 1750 built 1938
LCDR 3rd class coach No. 2515 (body only) built 1894
Esso tank wagons Nos. 1231 & 1343 built 1916–18
BR 13-ton single bolster wagons Nos DB 450665 & DB 451341 built 1950–59
BR 13-ton dropside ballast wagons Nos DB 483700, DB 483701, DB 483725 & DB 483733 built 1949
SECR ballast wagon No. DS 62888 built 1899
A number of the above passenger and goods vehicles are privately owned and are on loan to the Wight Locomotive Society.

[1]Stroudley 'Terrier' sold to the LSWR in 1903 as their No. 734. Resold to Freshwater, Yarmouth and Newport Railway, becoming their No. 2 in 1913. Became SR No. W8 *Freshwater* and returned to the mainland in 1949 as BR No. 32646. Sold to Sadler Rail Coach Ltd in 1964 and resold to Brickwoods Ltd, who restored it to LBSCR yellow livery for use as a 'pub' sign in 1966. Returned to the Isle of Wight in 1979.
[2]Originally LBSCR No. 40 *Brighton*, sold to Isle of Wight Central Railway in 1902, becoming their No. 11, later SR No. W11 *Newport*. Returned to mainland in 1947 as SR No. 2640. Withdrawn as BR No. 32640 in 1963 and restored to LBSCR livery at Eastleigh Works in 1964 for sale to Butlins Ltd for display at their Pwllheli holiday camp. Placed on loan to the Wight Locomotive Society in 1973 and purchased outright in 1976. Restored externally to IWCR lined black livery with replica Hurst and Wheeler chimney and being restored mechanically by 1978.
[3]Originally LSWR No. 209. Rebuilt with enlarged bunker and Westinghouse brake and transferred to the Isle of Wight in 1925 as SR No. W24. Withdrawn in 1967 and purchased for preservation. Moved to Haven Street with remainder of WLS stock in 1971. Now the sole survivor of this once numerous class.
[4]Built for use at Woolwich Arsenal during World War I. Transferred in 1959 to the RAE, Farnborough, to haul coal and stores from the BR goods yard through the streets of the town to the RAE some miles away. Purchased by a Southampton businessman in 1968 and placed on loan to the WLS in 1971. This locomotive has been fitted with Westinghouse brake equipment at Haven Street for the operation of passenger trains. Now owned by the WLS.
[5]Latterly worked at British Steel Corporation works at Harlaxton, near Grantham. Purchased by a private owner and placed on loan to the WLS in 1972. *Ajax* is believed to have been the heaviest single load to cross the Solent on the Portsmouth–Fishbourne car ferry.
[6]This locomotive entered service with the Gas Light and Coke Co at Southall Gas Works in 1946. Made redundant in 1965, it was purchased privately for possible use in the Meon Valley when attempts were being made to reopen this line. Placed on loan to the WLS and transferred to Haven Street in June 1972.
[7]On loan from the National Collection.

Wight Locomotive Society

Full details from: The Secretary, Wight Locomotive Society, Haven Street Station, Ryde, Isle of Wight PO33 4DS

57 Hollycombe Steam Collection A

A 2ft gauge passenger-carrying line, 1½ miles long plus a short standard-gauge line and other steam attractions in the grounds of Hollycombe House

Hollycombe House, near Liphook, Hampshire GU30 7LP

Operated by: Mr J. M. Baldock
Access: A3 and Liphook BR station 1½ miles
Tel: Liphook 723233
OS Ref: SU 852295

The Woodland Railway and Steam Collection are open every Sunday and Bank Holiday from Easter to September from 12 noon onwards. Car park and gardens open at noon.
In an attractive wooded setting of azaleas, rhododendrons and trees planted at the turn of the century, a unique collection of steam-driven equipment has been assembled. It includes a 2ft gauge and a standard gauge railway and other items. Traction engine rides are available.
Facilities for visitors include car parking, museum, souvenir shop, refreshments and toilets.

Stock
[1]Barclay 0-4-0WT No. 1 *Caledonia* 1995 built 1931
[2]Hunslet 0-4-0ST *Jerry D* 638 built 1895
[3]Motor Rail 4WDM 8979 built 1946
Ruston Hornsby 4WDM (44/48HP Class) 203016 built 1941
Three ex-Ramsgate Tunnel Railway bogie coaches built 1936
Open-sided bogie coach
The railway runs for 1¾ miles, past a quarry where there is a vantage point from which extensive views of the South Downs are commanded.
Also a 600-yard standard gauge line on which the following locomotive hauls 2 flat wagons and an LNER Brake Van adapted for passenger-carrying:
[4]Aveling Porter 0-4-0TG *Sir Vincent* 8800 built 1917

[1]Formerly at Dinorwic Slate Quarries, Llanberis, Caernarfonshire, until 1962 when it was preserved by the Hampshire Narrow Gauge Railway Society (Group No. 63). Re-sold to John Baldock in 1967.
[2]Ex Dinorwic Slate Quarries Co Ltd, Llanberis, Caernarfonshire, 1967.
[3]Ex Sir Robert McAlpine and Sons Ltd, Hayes, Middlesex, 1968.
[4]Ex BOCM Ltd, Erith, Kent, 1966. *Sir Vincent* is a standard gauge tramway or shunting locomotive built by Aveling and Porter, the famous makers of steam rollers, in 1917. There are only six of these strange locomotives with flywheels left. They are a cross between a ploughing engine (top half) and a railway locomotive (below). They are slow but very powerful. All Aveling and Porter engines carried the Kent horse Invicta on their smoke-box doors as they were built at Rochester.
Standard gauge static exhibits
[5]Hawthorn Leslie 0-4-0ST *Albert* 2450 built 1899
SR steam crane
[5]Ex J. W. Hardwick, Sons and Co Ltd, dealers, West Ewell, Surrey.
3ft gauge static exhibit:
Aveling Porter 2-2-0WTG *Excelsior* 1607 built 1880

Stone handling and crushing. At the railheads of the quarry railway and the tramway a Grafton crane can be seen grabbing stone from a bank formed by the tipping trucks, representing the transfer from narrow to standard gauge line. The crane is especially interesting as it was probably the last steam-propelled vehicle to operate on British Rail track in London, where it was working as a shunting engine at Nine Elms in 1967. The stone crusher is driven by a large Marshall 12nhp portable engine, No. 72531, new to Henry Sykes Ltd of London in 1920 for pumping service.
Hayling Island station canopy now erected at Quarry Railway terminus.

58 Birchley Railway A

Passenger-carrying 10¼in gauge railway, 750ft in length in the private grounds of Mr D. M. Randall at Birchley House

Biddenden, Kent
Access: Nearest Stations, Headcorn BR or Tenterden Town K&ESR. Bus to Biddenden, thence on foot (1½ miles)
Tel: 0580 291413
OS Ref: TQ 845372

The railway may be visited by prior arrangement only. Please write or telephone beforehand to make firm arrangements. Casual visitors will not be well received, though helpers for construction work on most Sunday mornings will be much appreciated.
Facilities for visitors: plenty of hard work – bring your own spade and wellies!
The Birchley Railway was opened as recently as 1976 and will ultimately offer a ¾-mile run over a figure of eight track. To date, over 700ft of track has been laid, a bridge and tunnel are to be built, and another 500ft of track laid to complete the first loop. Trains are operated over this part of the layout whilst construction work is in progress. Regular operation of the railway has not yet commenced, though operating days are held from time to time.
Mr Randall claims the Birchley Railway must be one of the slowest railways in the country – having progressed 750ft in eight years!

Stock
LBSCR 0-6-0T No. 84 *Crowborough* (AIX Class)
LBSCR 0-6-0T (AIX Class) in SR Isle of Wight livery
Two battery electric locomotives
Petrol hydraulic locomotive under construction
Four sit astride coaches
Two open wagons

59 Littlehampton Miniature Railway A

Passenger-carrying 12¼in gauge railway 900 yards in length

Mewsbrook Park, Littlehampton, Sussex
Access: Littlehampton BR Station
OS Ref: TQ 036014

The railway operates at Easter, then at weekends until Spring Bank Holiday, after which operation is daily until the middle of September.
The railway was opened in 1948 from the eastern end of the Common at Littlehampton, close to the junction of Norfolk and Sea Roads, to Mewsbrook Park, on the eastern fringe of town. The track is single throughout, with two roads at each terminus serving an island platform. The journey time, outwards and return is about 12 minutes.

Stock
Cookson/Bullock 4-6-4 No. 1005 built *c*1933 rebuilt 1939
Cookson/Bullock 4-6-4 No. 2010 built *c*1933 rebuilt 1939
Bognor Pier Railway 0-4-2P No. 3015 built *c*1966 (steam outline)
Bognor Pier Railway 2-4-2BE No. 4020 built 1969 (steam outline)
Ten vacuum-braked bogie open coaches
Both steam locomotives converted from 10¼in gauge tank engines designed by H. C. S. Bullock for the Surrey Border and Camberley Railway and can each haul eight coaches up the maximum gradient of 1 in 70.

60 Hastings Miniature Railway A

Passenger-carrying 10¼in gauge line, 600 yards in length running from Marine Parade to Rock-a-Nore

Rock-a-Nore Road, Hastings, Sussex
Access: Hastings BR Station

The railway operates during Easter week, then at Spring Bank Holiday daily until the end of September.
The railway has operated on this site since 1948 with equipment from Lord Downshire's line at Easthampstead Park. The line at first consisted of 250 yards of straight track but was extended to its present length in 1959.
The railway is single track throughout with a midway passing loop.

Stock
Bullock 0-6-0 No. 3007 *Firefly* built 1934
SR 4-6-0 ('King Arthur' Class) under construction
Shepperton 2-4-2D *Meteor V* built 1970
Shepperton Bo-BoD built 1968
Seven open bogie coaches
Air compressor wagon

61 Great Cockcrow Railway A

Passenger-carrying 7¼in gauge railway offering two runs each of ⅞ mile

Hardwick Lane, Lyne, Chertsey, Surrey
Access: Alder Valley bus from Chertsey or Woking to

Holloway Hill (½ mile walk). Chertsey BR station
OS Ref: TQ 027662

The railway operates on Sundays from the first Sunday in May to the last Sunday in October between 2.45 pm and 5.45 pm. Much of the system of the Great Cockcrow Railway was material from the former Greywood Central Railway, established by the late Sir John Samuel in Burwood Park, Weybridge. This was bought by Ian Allan in 1965 and services began at Great Cockcrow in 1968. The railway consists of a double track main line with single track loop lines, affording a total run of ⅞ mile. Intensive operation is a feature of this railway; an extremely comprehensive signalling installation allowing as many as six trains to run on the circuit at once. Trains are normally three coaches long accommodating twelve passengers and 55 to 60 are worked on most Sundays in the three-hour operating period. The line is fully signalled with semaphores and colour lights controlled from three signal boxes which are linked by block instruments and bells as in full size practice. Further interest is added by the varied gradients, some of them as steep as 1 in 50. A branch line, 306 yards in length, engineering works for which include a 45ft viaduct, was opened for the 1980 season. A friendly welcome awaits all steam enthusiasts on this fascinating little railway.

Stock
Freelance GCR 4-6-2 No. 1947 *Eureka* built 1937
NER 4-4-0 No. 1912 (Class R1) built 1913
SR 4-6-0 No. 837 (Class S15) built 1947
LNER 2-6-0 No. 206 (Class K5) built 1956
LNER 2-6-0 No. 1935 (Class K3) built 1975
GWR 4-6-0 No. 7915 *Mere Hall* built 1952
[1]SR 2-6-0 No. 1803 *River Itchen* built 1938
LMS 4-6-0 No. 6100 *The Royal Scot* built 1947
GWR 2-6-0 No. 6309 built 1966
BR Bo-BoBE ('Hymek' outline) built 1982
LMS 0-6-0DM No. 11 *Winifred* built 1958
Seventeen bogie coaches, including four 'Pullmans'
Eighteen wagons of various kinds

[1]Rebuilt from GWR-type 2-6-0 *Maid of Kent*, formerly owned by Mr Alex Schwab of the Saltwood Miniature Railway (Group No. 80). Purchased by Mr J. Davis 1976.
The railway is operated by a consortium of enthusiasts on behalf of Ian Allan Ltd.
Details from: The Secretary, Terminal House, Shepperton, Middlesex TW17 8AS.

62 Stonecot Miniature Railway — A

Passenger-carrying 10¼in gauge railway. This line is on private property, but opens to the public quite frequently

Queen Mary's Hospital for Children, Carshalton, Surrey

Stock
LMS 4-6-0 No. 6100 *The Royal Scot* built Wilmot
Cromar White Bo-BoDM No. D7022
Four open bogie coaches

63 Hampshire Narrow Gauge Railway Society — C

A short 2ft gauge passenger-carrying private line laid out in the form of a 770ft continuous oval

'Four Winds', Durley, Hants
Tel: Durley 331
OS Ref: SU 512167

The Hampshire Narrow Gauge Railway Society was formed in 1961 to promote the construction of a public narrow gauge railway in Hampshire following the precedent set by the Welsh lines, but over the years has modified these original aims and has now become a group of people building and operating a railway simply for their own pleasure without regard to maintaining a regular public service.
The railway operates on average once a month between 1 pm and 5 pm for the benefit of invited groups such as Railway and Model Engineering Clubs.
Details from: John G. Davis, 57 Alresford Road, Winchester, Hants. Tel: Winchester 3277.

Stock
[6]Hanomag 0-8-0T No. 6 *The Feldbahn* 8310 built 1918
[6,1]Hunslet 0-4-2ST No. 2 *Josephine* 1842 built 1936
[2]Hunslet 0-4-0ST *Cloister* 542 built 1891
[3]Bagnall 0-4-0ST No. 1 *Wendy* 2091 built 1919
[5]Motor Rail 4WDM *Agwi Pet* 4724 built 1929
[4]Motor Rail 4WPM *Brambridge Hall* 5226 built 1935
Motor Rail 4WDM No. 2 *Lord George* 8998 built 1946
[6]Orenstein and Koppel 0-4-0DM *Norden* 20777 built 1936
[6]Orenstein and Koppel 0-4-0DM 21160 built 1938
[6]Orenstein and Koppel 4WDM 4013 built 1930
[6]Orenstein and Koppel 4WDM 5125 built 1935
Ruston Hornsby 4WDM 392117 (48DL Class) built 1956
[6]Two bogie coaches (ex Cotswold Light Railway)
Two bogie toastrack semi-open coaches built by English Electric in 1936 (ex Ramsgate Tunnel Railway)
Three hopper wagons

[1]Ex British Aluminium Co Ltd, Lochaber Works, Fort William, Inverness-shire, 1969. Rebuilt from 3ft gauge.
[2]Ex Dinorwic Slate Quarries Co Ltd, Llanberis, Caernarfonshire, 1962.
[3]Ex Dorothea Slate Quarry Co Ltd, Nantile, Caernarfonshire, 1962.
[4]Ex Hall & Co Ltd, Highbridge Gravel pit, Brambridge, near Eastleigh, 1965.
[5]Presented by Esso Petroleum Co Ltd, Fawley, Hants, 1961.
[6]Owned by Mr & Mrs B. J. Curl, the owners of the site.

Mention should also be made of one of the Society's more unlikely possessions – the carriage portion of Dugald Drummond's 1899 LSWR 4-2-4T inspection saloon (originally No. 733, Class F9, and nicknamed *The Bug*). Latterly this saw service as a hut at Eastleigh Carriage Works but has now been mounted on a concrete plinth at Durley and is in use as a souvenir shop.

64 Chalk Pits Museum — A E

A 2ft gauge industrial demonstration line nearly ⅓ mile in length situated in an open-air industrial museum

Southern Industrial History Centre Trust, Amberley, near Arundel, West Sussex BN18 9LT
Access: On B2139 road near Amberley BR station
Tel: Bury (079881) 370
OS Ref: TQ 030123

The Chalk Pits Museum, opened in May 1979, is the new industrial history centre for the region. Set in a former chalk quarry, this 36-acre open-air museum acts as a working centre where the industrial past of the South-East may be studied and preserved.

The previous occupants of the site, Pepper & Sons, were limeburners, and had a considerable standard gauge railway system linking the kilns and the main line. This system was closed, and the track lifted and sold for scrap in the 1960s. As part of the redevelopment of the site the Trustees are keen to see both narrow and standard gauge industrial railways portrayed in their correct context, i.e. serving industry. The Chalk Pits will become the home of the industrial locomotive, in steam, electric and internal combustion engined form, the wagons, cranes and trackside miscellania.

Railway operation commenced at Easter 1980. Museum open from 11 am to 5 pm Wednesday to Sunday and Bank Holidays from April to October.

At the end of 1981, the Brockham Museum near Dorking closed and its large and varied collection of narrow gauge locomotives and rolling stock has been transferred to Amberley.

Facilities for visitors include car parking, museum shop and toilets.

Members of the Rail Group are drawn from the Museum's own volunteer support organisation. The tasks are many and varied and can range from civil engineering, through tracklaying, to locomotive driving, and suit all tastes and ages. Regular informal working parties are held throughout the summer and on alternate weekends in winter. Major tasks completed to date include the installation of the basic 2ft gauge line, the complete removal of the rail system at Thakeham Tiles for use at the museum, the removal of a 'Peter Pan' funfair railway track from Littlehampton to provide much-needed heavyweight rails, and the restoration of the original standard gauge locomotive shed.

Stock (All 2ft gauge unless otherwise stated)
Decauville 0-4-0T *Progres* 1126 built 1950
Bagnall 0-4-0ST *Peter* 2067 built 1918
Bagnall 2-4-0T *Polar Bear* 1781 built 1905
Ransomes & Rapier 4WDM 80 built 1937
Ruston Hornsby 4WDM No. 2 (16HP Class) 166024 built 1933
Motor Rail 4WPM 872 built 1918
Orenstein & Koppel 4WDM *The Major* 7741 built 1937
Hibberd 4WDM 1980 built 1936
Orenstein and Koppel 4WDM No. 10 5926 built 1935
Motor Rail 4WDM 5297 built 1931
Lister 4WDM 33937 built 1945 (1ft 8in gauge)
Hudson-Hunslet 4WDM 2536 built 1941
Hudson-Hunslet 4WDM *Thakeham Tiles* No. 3 2208 built 1941
Hudson-Hunslet 4WDM *Thakeham Tiles* No. 4 3653 built 1948
Ruston Hornsby 4WDM 187081 built 1937
Lister 4wDM 34521 built 1949
Ruston Hornsby 4wDM 172892 built 1934
Motor Rail 4wDM 11001 built 1951
Hudswell Clarke 0-4-0DM DM686 built 1948
Wingrove & Rogers 0-4-0BE (Type W217) T8033 built 1979
Wingrove & Rogers 4wBE (Type W417) 5034 built 1954
Wingrove & Rogers 4wBE (Type W417) 4998 built 1953
Motor Rail 4WDM 5863 built 1934
Orenstein & Koppel 4WDM *Redland* 6193 built 1937
Hudson-Hunslet 4WDM 3097 built 1944
Fowler 4WDM *Peldon* 21295 built 1936
Wickham 4WPMR No. WD 904 3403 1943
Motor Rail 4WDM No. LR3041 1320 built 1918
Lister 4WPM 29890 built 1946
Wingrove & Rogers 4WBE No. 2 5031 built 1953
Wickham 4-wheeled 12-seat coach No. 3404
Rye and Camber Tramway bogie coach built 1895 (3ft gauge)
RAF Fauld Railway Hudson bogie coach No. 275 built 1940
Groudle Glen railway coach
Oakeley incline man-rider car
Colne Valley/Hudson man-rider car
Two brick drying cars
Flat wagon
Dropside wagon
Four Hudson skip wagons
Spence Converter bogie No. 4 built 1919 (5ft 3in gauge)
Dorking Greystone Lime side tipping wagon No. 3 built 1930 (3ft 2¼in gauge)
Dorking Greystone Lime end tipping wagon No. 10 (3ft 2¼in gauge)
Staveley Minerals wooden side tipping wagon (3ft gauge)
NCB high-capacity mines tub
Sussex & Dorking United Brick cable-hauled side tipping wagon No. 19 (2ft 6in gauge)
Two Alpha cement side-tipping wagons built by Allens of

Tipton (2ft gauge)
Robert Brett side discharge wagon (2ft gauge)
Robert Hudson braked 'V' hopper wagon built 1940 (2ft gauge)
South Durham Iron & Steel Incline 'Breakaway' wagon (2ft gauge)
London Brick Co cable-hauled side-tipping wagon No. 167E (2ft 6in gauge)
Penrhyn Quarrymen's coaches 'F' & 'J' (1ft 10¾in gauge)
Dinorwic Quarries coal wagon (1ft 10¾in gauge)
Dinorwic Quarries incline slab wagon No. 115 (1ft 10¾in gauge)
Oakeley Quarries slate rubbish wagon (1ft 11½in gauge)
Llechwedd 2-ton slate wagon built LNWR in 1887 (1ft 11½in gauge)
Maen Offeren 2-ton slate wagon built GWR in 1889 (1ft 11½in gauge)
Ball clay mine wagon (1ft 10in gauge)
Fireclay mining tub No. 12 (1ft 10in gauge)
Penrhyn Quarries slate wagon No. 205 (1ft 10¾in gauge)
Penrhyn Quarries Fullersite wagon No. 46 (1ft 10¾in gauge)
Penrhyn Quarries coal wagon No. 2 (1ft 10¾in gauge)
Chain-hauled clay tub (fllangeless plateway type) (1ft 6in gauge)
London Brick Co side-discharge clay wagon No. 26 (2ft 11in gauge)
Robert Hudson end-tipping 'V'-hopper wagon (2ft gauge)
Colne Valley inside-framed flat wagon (2ft gauge)
Alpha cement outside-framed flat wagon (2ft gauge)
Cornish china clay metal-framed rotary tipping wagon (2ft gauge)
Cornish china clay wooden-framed rotary tipping wagon (2ft gauge)
Nine Robert Hudson 'V'-hopper wagons
Other narrow gauge locomotives:
Peckett 0-6-0ST *Scaldwell* 1316 built 1913 (3ft gauge)
Fletcher Jennings 0-4-0T *Townsend Hook* 172 built 1880 (3ft 2¼in gauge)
Spence 0-4-0T No. 23 built 1920 (1ft 10in gauge)
Orenstein & Koppel 4WDM *Monty* 7269 built 1936 (3ft 2¼in gauge)
Motor Rail 4WDM 10161 built 1950 (2ft 11in gauge)
Fletcher Jennings 0-4-0T *William Finlay* 173 built 1880 (3ft 2¼in gauge)
The Museum has a 'Member of the Museum' organisation and details are available from the Museum Office.

65 Alderney Railway — A

A passenger-carrying standard-gauge railway two miles long running from Braye to Mannez Quarry

Petit Val, Alderney, Channel Islands
Access: By air from Southampton, Shoreham (Aurigny Air Lines), Hurn (AAF) and Inter-Island
Tel: Alderney 3180

Originally opened in 1847, the Alderney Railway was the first in the Channel Islands and is now the only one, having outlived the lines on Jersey and Guernsey. Furthermore, the Alderney Railway ran its first regular passenger trains as recently as 1980! Further claims to fame are that it was the only railway in the British Isles to be occupied by the Germans during World War II and as a result lost all its steam locomotives by enemy action!
The Alderney Railway Society was formed in 1978 to try to achieve the return of steam to the island. What's happened so far is that a regular service was inaugurated using Wickham petrol railcars running as multiple units and in 1982 the Society obtained a steam locomotive to take over passenger-haulage.
The Society's trains run at weekends between Easter and October; off-season by arrangement.
During the week, the Department of the Environment runs stone-haulage trains over the entire 3-mile length of the line (including the length of the Breakwater).

Stock
Bagnall 0-4-0ST *J. T. Daly* 2450 built 1931
Vulcan Foundry 0-4-0DM *Elizabeth* D100 built 1949
Wickham 4wPMR No. 9022 8086 built 1958
Wickham 4wPMR No. 9028 7094 built 1955
Wickham 4WPMR No. 1 *George* (WD No. 9025) 7091 built 1955
Wickham 4WPMR No. 2 *Shirley* (WD No. 9029) 7095 built 1955
Wickham 4WPMR No. 3 *Mary Lou* (BR No. PWM 3954) 6939 built 1955
Wickham 4WPMR *Cadenza* 6655 built 1953 (BR No. PWM 3776)
Wickham 4WPMR 7092 built 1955 (WD No. 9026)
Wickham 4WPMR 7098 built 1955 (WD No. 9032)
Wickham 4WPMR 7587 built 1957
[1]Ruston Hornsby 4WDM *Molly 2* (88DS Class) 425481 built 1958

[1]Cowans Sheldon steam crane
[1]Hudson hydraulic tipper-truck
[1]Adapted chassis of Sentinel 4WVBTG *Molly* 6909 built 1927
[1]Adapted chassis of several dump-trucks
Seventeen American dump-trucks built 1942 (derelict at Mannez Quarry)
Quarry truck built *c*1880
Two American dump-trucks built 1942

[1]Operated by Property Services Agency of the D.o.E. Mondays–Fridays.

66 Hythe Pier Electric Railway — B

Passenger-carrying 2ft gauge electric railway, 700 yards in length operated by the General Estates Co Ltd, Hotspur House, Hythe, Hampshire, in conjunction with the Hythe–Southampton ferry

Hythe, near Southampton, Hampshire
Access: By ferryboat from Southampton
Tel: 0703-843203
OS Ref: SU 423801

The ferry service and pier railway operate each weekday throughout the year from 7 am to 8 pm. The train fare is now included in the ferry fare. The railway was operated in the early 1900s and converted to electrical operation in July 1922 using a raised outside third rail energised at 240 volts 80 amps. The pier itself dates back to 1880. Trains run in connection with the ferry boat service which generally operates half hourly.

Stock
Brush 4WE 16302 built 1917
Brush 4WE 16307 built 1917
Four bogie saloon passenger coaches
Tank wagon
Baggage wagon

67 Drusilla's Zoo Park — B

Passenger-carrying 2ft gauge railway, ¼ mile in length

Alfriston, East Sussex
Access: Berwick BR Station or Southdown Bus 126. Just off the B2108 between Berwick and Alfriston
Tel: 0323-870234
OS Ref: TQ 524050

Open from 1 April to end of September on a daily basis 11–5.30 pm. Open at weekends in October.
Facilities for visitors include car parking, refreshments, toilets, souvenir shop, pottery and leather worker, antique shop, art gallery, garden centre and zoo.
The present railway at Drusilla's was opened in 1948 and reconstructed on a circular route in 1951. However, in pre-war years, a 9½in gauge steam-operated line conveyed passengers for about a mile from Drusilla's to the River Cuckmere on which boats could be hired. Motive power was provided by a Stroudley LBSCR steam locomotive built by R. H. Morse, of Henfield. Unfortunately, this early line became a war victim, being used by the Canadian Army as a target for tanks. Nowadays, the ride takes passengers past several paddocks and skirts the playground before passing through part of the zoo park. Here the animal paddocks adjoin the track and wallabies and flamingoes, llamas and monkeys may be seen before arriving back at the station. In 1979, both zoo and railway celebrated their Golden Jubilee.

Stock
Hibberd 4WPM (Y type) 3116 built 1946 (now static exhibit)
Motor Rail 4WDM *Nellie* 9409 built 1948
[1]Motor Rail 4WDM 8882
Ruston Hornsby 4WDM *Emily* 226294 built 1943 (steam outline)
Five 4-seat, 4-wheeled open coaches

[1]On loan from Alan Keef

68 Volks Electric Railway — B

Passenger-carrying 2ft 8½in gauge electric railway, 1¼ miles in length operated by the Borough of Brighton, Royal York Buildings, Brighton BN1 1NP

Madeira Drive, Brighton, East Sussex
Access: All buses to Pool Valley and Old Steine pass the Aquarium terminus of the railway, 100 yards off Palace Pier
Tel: Brighton 681061
OS Ref: TQ 3103

The railway operates from Easter to the end of September between 9.45 am and 6.15 pm approx. Also runs later on Bank Holidays and Sundays.
The Volks Electric Railway was the first electrically-powered railway in Great Britain, being opened in 1883, and has thus achieved its operating centenary. The track is single throughout and fenced to keep pedestrians off the 'live' third rail. There are three stations and two passing loops allowing a five minute frequency service to operate. There are warning signals at pedestrian crossings, whilst trains are despatched from the stations by means of a bell signal supported by a flashing light indication controlled from the headquarters at Paston Place. After experiments in 1964, all the cars have now been fitted for multiple working in units of two in order to cope with heavy traffic periods.

Stock
Roofed cross-bench cars Nos 1 and 2
Semi-saloon cars Nos 3, 4, 5, 6 and 7
Ex Southend Pier Railway crossbench cars Nos 8 and 9
Since 1980, the railway has been able to offer an additional free attraction for passengers – it traverses Brighton's famous nude bathing beach.

69 The British Engineerium — E

Industrial Museum housed in former steam Pumping Station

Off Nevill Road, Hove, East Sussex BN3 7QA
Access: Adjacent to Brighton and Hove greyhound stadium. Bus routes No. 16 from Brighton station to Nevill Road or No. 33 from Old Steine to Nevill Road. (Approx. 30 minute frequency)
Nearest BR station: Hove (¾ mile) or Brighton (2 miles)
Tel: Brighton (0273) 559583

Opening times: Daily throughout the year 10 am to 5 pm. Closed Christmas Day but reopens on the afternoon of

Boxing Day. Beam engine in steam every weekend and Bank Holiday.
The Engineerium tells the story of our engineering heritage within the fabric of Goldstone Pumping Station, which itself contains two magnificent beam pumping engines. One of these, built in 1875/6, has been fully restored to original condition and is run in steam every Saturday, Sunday and Bank Holiday. To make this possible, the boiler house and associated equipment has also been restored to original condition. The Exhibition Hall contains over 1,000 exhibits telling the story of the development of steam power on land, sea, rail and road and also covers fire fighting, hot air engines, machine and hand tools, early domestic equipment, etc. The collection includes works by Watt, Trevithick, Hackworth, both Stephensons, Maudslay, Faraday and many more. The larger engines are run in steam with the main engine and special exhibitions are held from time to time throughout the year.
7¼in gauge steam locomotives on static display.

Stock
LSWR 4-6-0 No. 486 H15 Class built 1926
Stephenson 0-4-0 *Locomotion*
Netherlands Railway 2-2-2 built 1864
There is also on display a very fine half-full size model of a Burrell traction engine *The Devonshire*
The activities of the Engineerium are supported by the Friends of the British Engineerium. Membership details available from the above address.

70 Canterbury City Museum G

Standard gauge steam locomotive in store. Special permission is needed to view it

Poor Priests Hospital, Stour Street, Canterbury, Kent

Stock
Canterbury & Whitstable Railway 0-4-0 *Invicta* (Robert Stephenson 24 built 1830)
Withdrawn 1839 and presented for preservation in Darlington in 1850. Later removed and displayed at various exhibitions until presented to the City of Canterbury and placed on display in 1906. Restored by the Transport Trust and York Railway Circle in association with the National Railway Museum, York 1978–80.

71 Ministry of Defence I

Industrial steam location with locomotive in occasional use. No public admittance

Army Department, Marchwood, Hants

Stock
Hunslet 0-6-0ST No. 92 *Waggoner* 3792 built 1953
This locomotive has now been placed in the care of the Army Transport Museum (Group No. 177).

72 Brighton Locomotive Works Association G

Rolling stock in store at Preston Park Works, Brighton pending conversion of the former Pullman Car Co workshops and car shed into a steam locomotive restoration centre

No public access

Stock
SR 4-6-2 No. 34073 *249 Squadron* built 1948
SR 4-6-2 No. 35009 *Shaw Savill* built 1942
BR 0-6-0DE No. 15224 (Class 12) built 1949
SR 2-BIL EMU set No. 2090 built 1937
SR 4-SUB EMU set No. 4732 built 1949
SR Pullman motor brake/2nd coach No. 92 built 1932
SR Pullman motor brake/2nd coach No. 93 built 1932
Two BR CCT vehicles
Esso petrol tank wagon

73 Brooklands Miniature Railway B

Passenger-carrying 10¼in gauge line, ¾-mile in length built on the site of an earlier 9½in gauge steam-operated line

Brookland Pleasure Park, East Worthing, Sussex
The railway operates daily during the holiday season

Stock
Severn-Lamb Co-CoPH *Western Comet* built 1967

74 Kent Country Nurseries Railroad B

Passenger-carrying 10¼in gauge railway, ¼ mile in length laid out round a garden centre

Kent Country Nurseries, Challock, near Ashford, Kent
Tel: Challock 256
Access: On A252 road

This attractive little line includes a timber viaduct over a lake and a tunnel. The line operates at weekends according to demand.

Stock
BR-style freelance Bo-Bo *Trailblazer* built 1970
Open bogie coaches

75 National Coal Board I

Industrial steam location with locomotives out of use. No public admittance

Snowdown Colliery, Nonnington, Kent
OS Ref: TR 246512

Stock
Avonside 0-6-0ST *St Thomas* 1971 built 1927
Avonside 0-6-0ST *St Dunstan* 2004 built 1927

76 Bredgar and Wormshill Light Railway C

Private 2ft gauge railway 500 yards in length and collection of narrow gauge locomotives

D., W. & S. Best, 'The Warren', Bredgar, near Sittingbourne, Kent
Tel: Headcorn 890099
OS Ref: TQ 873585

This is a strictly private small railway collection which can be viewed by appointment only. No casual visitors are seen but, almost without exception, arrangements to visit the site can be made by contacting Mr D. Best on the above telephone number. A telephone call after 7 pm is most likely to find Mr Best at home and he always appreciates a few days notice of a proposed visit.

Stock
[2]Schwartzkopf 0-4-0WT *Bronhilde* 9124 built 1927
Jung 0-6-0WT *Katie* 3872 built 1931
Ruston Hornsby 4wDM No. 6 *Sturry* 349061 built 1953
[3]Wingrove & Rogers 0-4-0BE F7116 built 1966
[3]Wingrove & Rogers 0-4-0BE F7117 built 1966
[3]Riordan 4wBE No. E1 T6664 built 1967
[2]Ex-Bressingham Steam Museum 1979
[3]1ft 6in gauge

77 Ministry of Defence I

Industrial steam location with locomotive in store out of use. No public admittance

Navy Department, Chatham Dockyard, Kent
OS Ref: TQ 764703

Stock
RSH 0-4-0ST No. 361 *Ajax* 7042 built 1941

78 Payton Heights Railway C

Private passenger-carrying 10¼in gauge railway, 900ft in length, running round the private grounds of Mr Pay

Mr A. Pay, Green Lane, East Northdown, Margate, Kent CT9 3UG
Tel: Thanet (0843) 63484
OS Ref: TR 3869

Despite its short length, the railway features a 20ft tunnel, 1 in 27 gradients and 20ft radius curves, a level crossing and a 3-road loco shed. The railway consists mainly of the complete Margate Pier Railway, moved to the present site in 1975 and opened in 1976.
The line operates one Sunday per month, May to October.

Stock
Minimum Gauge Railways 0-6-0 *Marie* 69 built 1975
Curwen & Newbury C–CDH *Lady Sonia* built 1964
Freelance 4-4-0D *General Shirley* built 1969 (American steam outline)
Five 12-seat bogie coaches ex Margate Pier Railway
Bogie flat wagon
The railway is private but is opened to the public about once a month as circumstances allow. Enquiries by phone only please.

79 The Southfleet Collection F

A major railway preservation scheme based on the 2½ mile section of track between Fawkham Junction and the site of the former Southfleet Station: all that remains of the old LC&DR Gravesend West Street branch

Resco (Railways) Ltd, Southfleet Station, Kent
OS Ref: TQ 716726

The Company aims to restore the line to working condition and operate steam trains in due course. A general transport museum at Southfleet is planned to house buses, trolley buses, trams, cars, lorries and other transport exhibits.

Stock
LBSCR 0-6-0T No. 678 *Knowle* (Stroudley A1X Class) built 1880
Also involved on the Southfleet site are the North Downs Steam Railway Preservation Society who were originally intending to run the line themselves.
Details from: Greg Smith, NDSR Publicity Officer, 29 New Road, Cliffe, near Rochester, Kent. Tel: 0634 220587

Stock
[1]Fowler 0-4-0DH 4220008 built 1959
SR 4-6-2 No. 35010 *Blue Star* built 1942
RSH 0-6-0T No. 13 7846 built 1955
[1]Ruston Hornsby 4wDM 412427 built 1957
[1]Motor Rail 4wDM 9019 built 1950
LC&DR 3rd Class 4-wheel coach body built *c*1875
[1]Stored at Wm. Cory, Rochester

80 Saltwood Miniature Railway B

Passenger-carrying 7¼in gauge miniature railway, 610ft in length situated in the private grounds of Mr Alex Schwab

Brockhill Road, Saltwood, Hythe, Kent
Access: Entrance from Brockhill Road, on bus route
Tel: Hythe (0303) 66350

The railway was first opened in 1924 as a private line, but occasional public open days were held each year from 1931 onwards, using steam motive power. Following the demise of both steam locomotives in 1970, the line was reconstructed and reopened in 1975 as an electric railway. The line is laid out as a continuous oval and a ride consists of three circuits of the track.
As it predates the opening of the Romney, Hythe and

Dymchurch Railway, the Saltwood line lays claim to being the World's oldest purpose-built miniature railway.

Stock
Smith BoBoBE No. 5060 *Earl of Berkeley* built 1974
Smith BoBoBE No. 7007 *Great Western* built 1976
Smith enclosed saloon bogie coach (former battery electric rail car)
Smith GWR 'Centenary'-style bogie coach built 1977
4-car articulated bogie open set
Two 6-seat 'children's' carriages
The railway operates on the Saturday preceding Easter, Easter Monday, the Wednesday following Easter, May Day Holiday, Spring Bank Holiday and Wednesdays only from the last Wednesday in July to the first in September.

81 Great Bush Railway C

Private 2ft gauge passenger-carrying line situated in a private showground. No public admittance except during Traction Engine Rallies and Autojumbles

John de Havilland, Tinkers Park, Hadlow Down, near Uckfield, Sussex
OS Ref: TQ 538241

The railway first operated during World War II and trains currently run over a distance of 200 metres. Operation takes place during the May and September Traction Engine Rallies and at Autojumbles as advertised during the summer season.
Volunteers wishing to assist the operation of the Great Bush Railway should contact John de Havilland on Tonbridge 356486.

Stock
Motor Rail 4WDM No. 1 *Aminal* built 1931
Avonside 0-4-0T *Sezela No. 2* 1720 built 1915
Motor Rail 4WDM No. 4 *Mild* 8687 built 1941
Ruston Hornsby 4WDM No. 5 *Alpha* 183744 built 1937
Avonside 0-4-0T *Sezela No. 6* 1928 built 1923
Hibberd 4WDM No. 8 *Tuesday* 2586 built 1941
Hibberd 4WDM No. 12 2163 built 1938
Ruston Hornsby 4WDM No. 14 *Albany* 213840 built 1941
Hibberd 4WDM No. 19 2163 built 1938
Wingrove & Rogers 4WBE No. 20 5033 built 1954
Wingrove & Rogers 4WBE No. 21 *Lama* 5035 built 1954
Wingrove & Rogers 0-4-0BE No. 23 M7534 built 1972
Wingrove & Rogers 0-4-0BE No. 24 *Titch* M7535 built 1972
Two bogie coaches ex Yaxham Park Light Railway

82 The Old Kiln Light Railway B

2ft gauge passenger-carrying light railway in the grounds of the museum

The Old Kiln Agricultural Museum, The Reeds, Reeds Road, Tilford, near Farnham, Surrey
OS Ref: SU 858434

Stock
Hibberd 4wDM 2528 built 1941
Hibberd 4wPM 1767 built 1931
Thakeham 4wPM built 1950
Motor Rail 4wDM 5713 built 1936
Bredonvale 4wPM built *c*1950
Wickham 4wPMR 3031 built 1941
Wickham 4wPMR 3287 built 1943

83 Collection 'X' G

A private collection of narrow gauge locomotives and rolling stock owned by P. J. Rampton and others kept in locked storage and not available for public inspection. All are 600mm gauge unless otherwise stated

Stock
[1]Couillet 0-6-0T No. 1 *Sabero* 1140 built 1895
[1]Couillet 0-6-0T No. 2 *Sahelices* 1209 built 1898
[1]Couillet 0-6-0T No. 3 *Olleros* 1318 built 1900
[1]Sabero 0-6-0T No. 6 *La Herrera* built 1937
[1]Borsig 0-6-2T No. 7 *Sotillos* 6022 built 1906
[1]Henschel 0-4-2T No. 101 16073 built 1918
[1]Henschel 0-4-2T No. 102 16043 built 1918
[1]Henschel 0-4-2T No. 103 16045 built 1918
[4]Avonside 0-4-4-0TG *Renishaw 4* 2057 built 1931
[4]Bagnall 0-4-4-0T *Renishaw 5* 2545 built 1936
Hanomag 2-6-2 + 2-6-2T No. 82 (SAR Class NGG13 Garratt) 10634 built 1928 (2ft gauge)
Bagnall 0-4-2T 2895 built 1948
Hudswell Clarke 0-4-2ST *Santa Ana* 640 built 1902 (550mm gauge)
[2]Dick Kerr 4WDE No. 18 built *c*1918
[1]Sabero Colliery Railway 4-wheeled 'Presidents Coach'
Isle of Man Railway bogie coaches Nos F6, F37 & F38 (3ft gauge)

[1]Ex Hulleras de Sabero y Anexas SA, Sabero, near Cisitierna, Leon, Spain, 1968.
[2]Ex Compagnie Industrielle des Sables de Némours, Seine et Marne, France, 1968.
[4]Ex Crookes Bros Ltd, Renishaw, South Africa, 1969.

84 Ripley, Surrey G

Private collection of narrow gauge locomotives. The site is on private property and casual visitors are most actively discouraged

J. Butler and Frank Jux, 5 Heath Rise, Grove Heath, Surrey
OS Ref: TQ 046557

Stock
Deutz 0-4-0DM 19531 (600mm gauge)
Motor Rail 4WDM *Archer* 4709 built 1936 (2ft gauge)
Motor Rail 4WDM *Bargee* 8540 built 1940 (2ft gauge)
Motor Rail 4WDM *Mac* 8994 built 1946 (2ft gauge)

85 L. J. Searle & Sons G

Steam locomotive undergoing restoration. Viewing by appointment only

Horsham, Sussex

Stock
Peckett 0-4-0ST 1893 built 1936

86 Chessington Zoo Miniature Railway B

Passenger-carrying 12in gauge line, 925 yards in length. The railway operates as required by demand throughout the year when the zoo is open

Chessington Zoo, Surrey KT9 2NE
Access: On the A243, Surbiton to Leatherhead. Free parking. Regular trains to Chessington South station. Ask about combined rail/zoo admission tickets. Routes 65, 72 (Sundays), 265 London Transport, 714 Green Line, 468 London Country
Tel: Epsom 27227

The line was opened in 1937 and still operates with its original equipment.
The locomotives are vacuum-braked and drum brakes are fitted to the rolling stock.
Other attractions include all the fun of the fair and circus, slides and swings, paddle boats and peaceful gardens.
Don't miss the enthralling sights and sounds of the new World of Mechanical Music exhibition!

Stock
Barnard 4-4-0PM No. 1 *Princess Margaret* built 1937
Barnard 4-4-0PM No. 2 *Queen Elizabeth* built 1937
Six open bogie carriages
The locomotives are both steam outline, based on GWR 'Dukedogs'.

87 Mr G. W. Smith G

1ft 6in gauge steam locomotive privately preserved. No public access

Wayland House, 31 Manor Road South, Woolston, Southampton, Hants
OS Ref: SU 440113

Stock
GNR 2-2-2 No. 1 built *c*1863

88 Southsea Miniature Railway B

Passenger-carrying 1ft 5in gauge railway built on the site of the former Southern Miniature Railway's 10¼in gauge line

Southsea, Hampshire
OS Ref: SZ 641982
Railway closed 1984 and rolling stock sold.

89 Eastleigh Railway Preservation Society G

Steam locomotive undergoing restoration. No public admittance

BREL, Eastleigh Works, Eastleigh, Hampshire
OS Ref: SU 457185

Stock
SR 4-6-0 No. 30828 (Maunsell S15 Class) built 1927

Withdrawn January 1964 and sent to Woodham Bros scrapyard, Barry. Purchased for preservation and moved to Eastleigh in March 1981

90 J. Lemon-Burton C

Private passenger-carrying 15in gauge railway situated in the grounds of Mr J. Lemon-Burton. No casual visitors please

'Paynesfield', Aldbourn Green, West Sussex
OS Ref: TQ 243179

Stock
Lister Blackstone 4WPM 51721 built 1960
Morse 0-4-0 No. 212/82 built 1939
J. Lemon-Burton 0-6-0 built *c*1960

91 Surrey Light Railway C

Private 2ft gauge light railway operating at an undisclosed location – 'somewhere in deepest Surrey'.

Casual visitors are strictly not allowed

Stock
Hunslet 0-4-0ST No. 1 *Lady Joan* 1429 built 1922
Orenstein & Koppel 4wDM 3685 built 1931
Ruston Hornsby 4wDM No. 69 264252 built
Wingrove & Rogers 2-4wBE 887 built 1935
Wingrove & Rogers 4WBE D6912 *Amene*
Hunslet 4WDM No. 22 3621 built 1947
Lister 4WDM 37911 built 1952
Ruston Hornsby 4WDM 174535 built 1936
Lister 4WDM 35811 built 1950
Ruston Hornsby 4WDM 177642 built 1936
Ruston Hornsby 4WDM 226302 built 1944
Rhiwbach 4WPM
Passenger coach No. H305B rebuilt from Vallins 4WPM loco
Dick Kerr side tipping skip wagons

92 Mr T. W. Smith G

Private collection of locomotives in store

The Bungalow, Whitworth Crescent, Bitterne, Southampton, Hants
OS Ref: SU 439140

No casual visitors please.

Stock
Bagnall 4-2-2 1425 built 1893 (1ft 6in gauge)
Motor Rail 4WPM 5355 built 1931 (Standard gauge)

93 Sandham Castle Mini-Railway B

Passenger-carrying 10¼in gauge line 250 yards in length, arranged as a continuous circuit

Sandham Grounds, Culver Parade, Sandown, Isle of Wight

The railway operates daily during the summer season.

Stock
Shepperton 2-4-2DM *Sandham Castle* built 1969 (Meteor Class)
Southern Min Railways Co-BoPM No. D108 *Vanguard*
Southern Min Railways Bo-BoPM No. 608
Six open bogie coaches

94 Esmond Lewis-Evans G

Standard gauge locomotives and rolling stock housed at various secret locations in Kent

Stock
[1]SECR 0-6-0 No. 65 (Stirling 01 Class) built 1896
SECR Birdcage family saloon coach No. 950 built 1907
SECR Pullman car *Sapphire* built 1910
SR Pullman Kitchen car *Phyllis* built 1928
SR Pullman Parlour car *Lucille* built 1928
SECR six-wheeled carriage truck No. DS 1450 built 1905
SR four-wheeled box vans Nos 081969 and DS44551 built 1931

[1]Withdrawn from Dover shed in 1961 as BR No. 31065. The original 'O' Class locomotive designed by James Stirling dates from 1878, and when new was typical of the Stirling domeless round-cab locomotives so familiar on the Great Northern Railway. Between 1903 and 1917 a number of the class were rebuilt by Harry Wainwright along the lines of his large 'C' Class (see Group No. 52), the 01s being distinguished by their older-style tenders with springs above running plate level, giving them an appearance of great antiquity. No. 65 was intercepted at the last moment after being prepared for its final journey to the scrapyard in 1965 and saved for preservation. Now located at a private site near Maidstone.

95 Carron Row Farm Museum F

"The Strawberry Line". A 2ft gauge passenger-carrying railway under construction. Operated by Mr H. Frampton-Jones

Titchfield, near Fareham, Hants

Stock
Motor Rail 4wDM 22070 built 1960
Motor Rail 4wDM 20073 built 1950
Ruston Hornsby 4wDM 277265 built 1949
Orenstein & Koppel 4wDM 6504 built 1936
Crockway Light Railway bogie coach
Sheppey Light Railway 4-wheel coach

96 Manston Preservation Group G

Standard gauge steam locomotive undergoing restoration

CEGB, Richborough, Kent

No public access.

Stock
SR 4-6-2 No. 34070 *Manston* built 1947

97 M. Hayter G

Private collection of 2ft gauge locomotives

Tilford, near Farnham, Surrey
OS Ref: SU 843423

Stock
Wickham 4wPMR 2981 built 1941
Wickham 4wPMR 3032 built 1941

Both ex-Wey Valley Light Rly 1982.

98 Dover Transport Museum E

Standard gauge locomotive on static display

Dover Pumping Station, Connaught Road, Dover, Kent

Stock
Fox Walker 0-6-0ST *Minnie* No. 385 built 1878

99 Sea Containers Ltd H

Fully restored Pullman cars and other coaches used on the "Venice Simplon–Orient Express"

Stewarts Lane Depot, London

Stock
Pullman parlour 1st No. 301 *Perseus* built 1951
Pullman parlour 1st *Phoenix* built 1952
Pullman parlour 1st No. 308 *Cygnus* built 1951
Pullman parlour 1st *Zena* built 1928

Pullman kitchen 1st *Ibis* built 1925
Pullman kitchen 1st *Minerva* built 1927
Pullman kitchen 1st No. 280 *Audrey* built 1932
Pullman kitchen 1st *Ione* built 1928
LNER Gresley passenger brake van No. 70741 built 1942
BR Mk.1 BSK coach No. S34991 built 1957

100 Isfield Station C

Private standard gauge railway based on the former LBSCR station at Isfield ('The Lavender Line')

Mr D. Milham, Isfield, near Uckfield, Sussex
OS Ref: TQ 452171

The owner intends to operate a mobile restaurant service on the line, when extended along the former trackbed.

Stock
RSH 0-6-0ST No. 62 7673 built 1950
Barclay 0-4-0ST *Annie* 945 built 1904
WD 2-10-0 No. 960 NB Loco Co 25458 built 1944
SECR Pullman Car 'Sapphire' built 1910
SR Grafton 4-wheel 2-ton steam crane 'Horace' 2671 built 1928

AREA C

Eastern Counties

Norfolk
Suffolk
Essex
Cambridgeshire
Lincolnshire
South Humberside
(Group Nos 101–150)

101 Bressingham Steam Museum and Gardens AE

The site incorporates the 1ft 11½in gauge Nursery Railway (2 miles in length), the 15in gauge Waveney Line (2½ miles in length), a short 9½in gauge line, as well as a museum of steam road and rail locomotives and a 500-yard standard gauge demonstration line

Bressingham Hall, Diss, Norfolk IP22 2AB
Access: Two miles west of Diss on the A1066 road
Tel: Bressingham 386
OS Ref: TM 080806

Museum open Thursdays, Sundays and Bank Holidays, May–September, also at Easter and on Wednesdays during August only. Opening time 1.30 pm.
Facilities for visitors include car parking, museum of over forty railway, road and stationary steam engines, model railway, souvenir shop, steam roundabouts and organs, six acres of gardens, refreshments and toilets.
The Bressingham Steam Museum is the result of the enthusiasm of one man, Alan Bloom, and his love for steam engines, great and small. The collection is housed on the 450-acre nursery surrounding Bressingham Hall and grew steadily from a nucleus of traction engines and steam agricultural machinery to embrace first a 9½in gauge garden line, then a 2ft line using former Welsh slate quarry locomotives. Major expansion occurred in 1968 when standard gauge locomotives from the official BR collection began to arrive. These are housed in the specially constructed museum building and have now been joined by others formerly on display at Butlins holiday camps. A 500-yard demonstration line has been built for the use of these engines, one or more of which may be seen in steam and giving footplate rides on Bressingham open days. With some justification, Bressingham claims to be the most comprehensive live steam museum in the British Isles. Its extensive collection is safely housed under cover in a purpose-built Exhibition Hall.
Details from: Alan Bloom, Bressingham Hall, Bressingham, Diss, Norfolk IP22 2AB.

Stock
Bressingham Hall Miniature Railway (750 yards long, opened in 1965) 9½in gauge
4-6-2 *Princess* built by Motor Gear and Engineering Co, 1947
2 open bogie coaches
3 open articulated coaches

Waveney Valley Railway (two-and-a-half miles in length, opened in 1973) 15in gauge
Krupp 4-6-2 *Rosenkavalier* 1662 built 1937
Krupp 4-6-2 *Mannertreu* 1663 built 1937
LNER 4-6-2 No. 4472 *Flying Scotsman* built Stewart 1976
Bressingham 4wPM *Ivor* built 1979
Nineteen Toastrack bogie coaches built 1937

Nursery Railway (two miles long, opened in 1966) 1ft 11½in gauge
[9]Hunslet 0-4-0ST *Gwynedd* 316 built 1883
[10]Hunslet 0-4-0ST *George Sholto* 994 built 1909
[11]Hudswell Clarke 0-6-0WT *Bronllwyd* 1643 built 1930
[12]Orenstein and Koppel 0-4-0WT *Eigiau* 5668 built 1912
Motor Rail 4WDM (40HP Class) 22210 built 1964

Standard Gauge
[1,2]BR 4-6-2 No. 70013 *Oliver Cromwell* (Riddles Class 7 MT) built 1951
[3]LMS 4-6-2 No. 6233 *Duchess of Sutherland* (Stanier Class 8P) built 1938
[4]LMS 4-6-0 No. 6100 *Royal Scot* (Stanier Class 7P) built 1927
[6]LMS 2-6-4T No. 2500 (Stanier Class 4MT) built 1934
[1]LTSR 4-4-2T No. 80 *Thundersley* (Whitelegg 79 Class) built 1909
[5]LBSCR 0-6-0T No. 662 *Martello* (Stroudley Class AIX) built 1875
[7]LSWR 0-4-0T No. 102 *Granville* (Adams Class B4) built 1893
[1]GER 0-6-0 No. 1217E (Holden Class G58) built 1905 (BR No. 65567)
NSB 2-10-0 No. 5865 *Peer Gynt* (Class 52) Schichau, built 1944
NSB 2-6-0 No. 377 *King Haakon VII* Nohab 1164 built 1919
SNCF 2-8-2 No. 141R73 (Class 141R) Lima 8939, built 1945
[8]Beyer Peacock 0-4-4-0T *William Francis* 6841 built 1937
Neilson 0-4-0WT No. 1 4444 built 1892
Neilson 0-4-0ST No. 25 5087 built 1896
RSH 0-4-0CT *Millfield* 7070 built 1942
Barclay 0-4-0F *Bluebottle* 1472 built 1916
[1]ECJS Royal Saloon Coach No. 396 built 1908
[1]Eastern Counties Railway four-wheeled coach built 1851
LMS open wagon

[1]On loan from the National Collection.
[2]Built at Crewe in May 1951. Withdrawn from Carnforth shed on 11 August 1968 after hauling the Manchester–Carlisle section of the last BR steam train. No. 70013 was the final steam locomotive to be overhauled by British Railways and as such was selected as the official repre-

sentative of the 'Britannia' Pacifics for preservation. Appropriately, for an engine that spent much of its life in East Anglia, it was sent to Bressingham immediately on withdrawal.

[3]LMS 'Coronation' Class Pacific withdrawn from Liverpool (Edge Hill) in February 1964 as BR No. 46233. One of a batch of five engines (Nos 6230–34) built without steamlined casings for performance comparisons with the streamlined members of the class. *Duchess of Sutherland* was purchased by Butlins Ltd and restored to LMS maroon livery for display at Ayr holiday camp in Scotland. It was transferred to Bressingham in 1971.

[4]Three-cylinder 'Royal Scot' Class locomotive built by the North British Locomotive Co Ltd (Works No. 23595) in August 1927. Completely rebuilt with new frames and boiler at Crewe in 1950 and withdrawn from Nottingham shed in 1962 as BR No. 46100. When new the 'Royal Scots' were the largest passenger engines on the LMS. The design was based on the Southern 'Lord Nelson' Class and 50 were built in 1927 as a matter of great urgency to cope with the Anglo-Scottish expresses. Twenty more were delivered in 1930, whilst in 1935 the experimental high-pressure engine *Fury* was rebuilt with a Stanier taper boiler and formed the prototype for the eventual rebuilding of all the 'Royal Scots'. Rebuilding commenced in 1943 at a time when, owing to wartime conditions, materials were in short supply. Unrebuilt engines in sound condition were overhauled where possible, and it was 1955 before the whole class had been rebuilt. Displaced from their normal work by diesels, many of the class migrated to the old Great Central line and to the southern sections of the Midland. Here they were gradually relegated to goods and parcels traffic, finally being withdrawn as they became due for major repairs. As befitted such a famous locomotive, *Royal Scot* was selected for preservation by Butlins Ltd and was displayed at Skegness holiday camp until moved to Bressingham in 1971.

[5]Withdrawn from Eastleigh shed in November 1963 as BR No. 32662. *Martello* led a fairly commonplace existence compared with most Stroudley 'Terriers', spending its entire working life on the former LBSCR system. It was restored to original yellow livery when bought by Butlins for display at their Ayr holiday camp and was moved to Bressingham in 1971.

[6]Three-cylinder passenger tank locomotive built at Derby for the London, Tilbury and Southend line services. Withdrawn from Shoeburyness shed as BR No. 42500 in July 1962. Whilst identical in outward appearance to the other Stanier 2-6-4 tanks, the small batch numbered 2500–36 were built with three cylinders. The whole class spent virtually all its working life on the LT & S line, replacing the older 'Tilbury' 4-4-2 tanks. On the last day of steam haulage on the LT & S, all the remaining Stanier engines were written off without ceremony, many being sent to Doncaster for cutting-up. Selected as typical of a modern suburban passenger tank engine for official preservation, No. 2500 spent several years in store before going to Bressingham in 1968. On loan from the National Collection.

[7]Withdrawn from Eastleigh shed in September 1963 as BR No. 30102. For many years locomotives of this class were a familiar sight at Southampton Docks, where their only readily visible identity was a name painted on their tanksides, numbers being only in evidence on the motion or a small plate at the back of the cab. No. 102 sported the name *Granville*. These names were painted out when the engines moved away from the docks in 1946 on being replaced by the larger USA 0-6-0 tanks. No. 102 was restored to LSWR livery at Eastleigh when purchased by Butlins Ltd for display at their Skegness holiday camp. It was moved to Bressingham in 1971.

[8]Ex NCB, South Midlands Area, Baddesley Colliery, Warwickshire, July 1968. Since restored to an attractive golden-brown livery.

[9]Ex Penrhyn Quarries, Bethesda, Caernarfonshire, 1964. Bought by Alan Bloom 1966.

[10]Ex Penrhyn Quarries, Bethesda, Caernarfonshire, February 1966.

[11]Ex Penrhyn Quarries, Bethesda, Caernarfonshire, January 1966. Rebuilt 1969 with boiler from Kerr Stuart 0-4-2ST *Stanhope*.

[12]Ex Penrhyn Quarries, Bethesda, Caernarfonshire, February 1963.

102 North Norfolk Railway A

Passenger-carrying standard gauge railway from Sheringham to Weybourne, 3 miles in length

Sheringham Station, Sheringham, Norfolk NR26 8RA
Access: BR trains from Norwich and Wroxham. Eastern Counties buses from Norwich, Yarmouth and Kings Lynn (change at Cromer). Adjacent to A149 Hunstanton to Cromer road
Tel: Sheringham (0263) 822045
OS Ref: TG 157431

Sheringham Station is open daily from April to October between 10 am and 5 pm. Steam train services operate from June to the end of September on Saturdays, on Sundays from April to October and on selected weekdays from April to September.

Facilities for visitors include car parking (adjacent to Sheringham Station), museum, souvenir shop, refreshments and the engine shed at Weybourne.

The North Norfolk Railway is part of the former Midland and Great Northern Joint Railway and runs for three miles along unspoilt coastline in an area designated as being of outstanding natural beauty. Despite the general impression that East Anglia is largely flat, the line is steeply graded and the run to Weybourne is largely 'uphill' along two gradients of 1 in 97 and 1 in 80. Although this is, at present, one of the shortest of the preserved standard gauge lines, we intend to extend over the delightful Kelling Heath and perhaps on to the market town of Holt. The railway project can perhaps be seen in some perspective when it is realised that when the line was acquired from British Rail it had already been reduced to a very basic railway with only one single line at Sheringham and no railway at all at Weybourne! Many years of endeavour by our volunteer members have restored the railway to operating condition and after a gap of over ten years the line is again echoing to the sound of steam as trains pound the gradients to Weybourne. From the start of the 1984 season a diesel railbus service runs from Weybourne to Kelling.

Stock

[9]LNER 4-6-0 No. 61572 (Class B12) Beyer Peacock 6488 built 1928
Barclay 0-4-0ST No. ED4 *Edmundsons* 2168 built 1943
[10]GER 0-6-0 No. 564 (LNER Class J15) built 1912
[1]RSH 0-6-0T No. 12 7845 built 1955
[2]Kitson 0-6-0ST No. 45 *Colwyn* 5470 built 1933
[3]Peckett 0-6-0ST No. 5 *John D. Hammer* 1970 built 1939
[4]Hunslet 0-6-0ST *Ring Haw* 1982 built 1940
[5]Hawthorn Leslie 0-4-0ST *Pony* 2918 built 1912
Hudswell Clarke 0-6-0ST *Wissington* 1700 built 1938
[6]Barclay 0-6-0T *Harlaxton* 2107 built 1941
[7]Bagnall 0-6-0ST *Birchenwood* 2680 built 1944
Bagnall 0-6-0F 2370 built 1929
Ruston Hornsby 4WDM 466629 built 1962
Fowler 0-4-0DM No. 3 4210080 built 1953
English Electric 0-4-0DH No. 10 8431 built 1963
LMS 0-6-0DE No. 12131 (BR Class 11) built 1952
BR four-wheeled diesel railbuses Nos 79960 and 79963 built 1958 by Wagon und Maschinenbau AG
LNER quad-art set No. 74 built 1924
LNWR directors saloon No. 5318 built 1913
L & YR directors saloon No. 1 built 1906
GER brake/third coach No. 295 built 1907
BR Mk.1 TSO coach No. E3868 built 1953
LNER passenger brake van No. E040923 built 1929
BR CL bogie coaches Nos E43034 and E43041 built 1954
BR Mk.1 TSO No. E3836 built 1953
BR Mk.1 TSO No. 4651 built 1957
BR SLO bogie coach No. E48026 built 1954
LNER Gresley TK bogie coach No. 3395 built 1930
LNER Gresley buffet car No. 51769 built 1937
LNER bogie passenger brake van No. 70621 built 1945
LMS sleeping car No. 624 built 1951
BR brake 2nd compartment coach No. 43357 built 1954
BR compartment 2nd class coach No. 46147 built 1954
BR brake 2nd compartment coach No. 43359 built 1955
BR Mk.1 BCK coach No. 21103 built 1956
BR Mk.1 TSO bogie coach No. E4521 built 1956
SR 'Brighton Belle' Pullman cars Nos 87 and 91 built 1932
Two GER six-wheeled coach bodies
GER flat wagon (converted from a Colman's mustard van) built 1901
SR 25-ton brake van No. S55169 built 1949
GWR five-plank wagon No. 124148 built 1936
BR 'Vanfit' covered van No. 756939 built 1949
SR 12-ton crane and match truck No. DS1749 built 1943
LMS covered van No. 755094 built 1950
Shell Mex and BP oil tank wagon No. 164686 built 1944
LNER covered carriage truck No. E94464
LNER Grafton 10-ton steam crane and match truck
GER 'Colman's Mustard' van No. 4807 built 1908
GWR 'Pasfruit' van No. W92097 built 1936
L & YR flat wagon built 1890
Six GER box vans
Two NER drop-floor hopper wagons
Wickham 4WPMR M&GN No. 1 1521 built 1934
Wickham 4WPMR *The Bug* 1642 built 1934
Carrick & Wardale steam crane No. 12 built 1919
Esso tank wagon No. 163058 built 1942
BR Lowmac wagon No. 904093 built 1953
BR CCT parcels van

[1]Ex Hams Hall Power Station, Birmingham, 1974.
[2]Ex Stewarts and Lloyds Minerals Ltd, Gretton Brook, Corby, Northants, 1971.
[3]Ex NCB Ashington Colliery, Northumberland, 1969.
[4]Ex Nassington Barrowden Mining Co, Nassington, Peterborough, Cambs, 1971.
[5]Ex Blyth Harbour Commission, Blyth Docks, 1971. After a short stay on the Yorkshire Dales Railway, arrived at Sheringham, 1972.
[6]Ex Stewarts and Lloyds Minerals Ltd, Harlaxton Quarry, Northants, 1969. On Keighley & Worth Valley Railway until 1973 when sold to Buckminster Trust Estate, Sewstern, Lincs. In 1974 re-sold and arrived at Sheringham in same year.
[7]Ex Market Overton (High Dyke), Northants, 1976.
[9]Built as LNER No. 8572 and withdrawn from Norwich shed in 1961, this locomotive is the only inside-cylinder 4-6-0 in existence in Great Britain, sole survivor of a once-numerous collection of such classes.
[10]GER Class Y14 locomotive (LNER Class J15) withdrawn from Stratford shed in 1962 as BR No. 65462. At the time of the 1923 grouping, the 289 J15s were the most numerous class of LNER locomotives and accounted for over 20 per cent of the former GER locomotive stock. Whilst primarily freight engines, many worked passenger services on branch lines at various times. No. 930 of this class made history in 1891 by being erected at Stratford works in just 9¾ hours! Forty-two of them served overseas during World War I.

Midland and Great Northern Joint Railway Society

Secretary: Paul J. Cooper, 11 Blenheim Close, Sprowston, Norwich, Norfolk NR7 8AN.

The Society was formed in 1959 to preserve part of the former M & GN Joint Railway. This truly Norfolk Railway was an independent system with its own rural main line from the Norfolk coast to the Midlands. Although only three miles (so far) have been saved, the emphasis is on

recreating the spirit of the old days. The M & GNJRS supports the railway (which is operated by the North Norfolk Railway Company Ltd) in many varied ways: for example it owns nearly half the rolling stock assembled on the line, including the J15 and B12 locomotives, and operates an extensive programme of rail tours to raise funds (it is, in fact, the largest operator of rail tours engaged in railway preservation).
New members are always welcome to join the ever-increasing ranks at any of the preservation sites.

103 Nene Valley Railway A

Passenger-carrying standard gauge steam railway from Wansford to Orton Mere, a distance of 5½ miles

Wansford Station, Stibbington, near Peterborough, Cambs PE8 6LR
Access: Adjacent to Main A1 road, 1 mile south of junction with A47. Bus routes Nos 265, 266, 312, 316 and 323 from Peterborough to Orton Mere. (Frequency approx 40 minutes). DMU service from Peterborough (BR) to Orton Mere on Sundays and Bank Holidays
Tel: Stamford 782854
OS Ref: TL 903979

The railway is in operation at weekends and Bank Holidays from April to October, and on Tuesdays, Wednesdays and Thursdays in June, July and August. Facilities for visitors include car parking, museum, souvenir shop, refreshments and toilets.
The first passenger train ran on the Nene Valley Railway line on 2 June 1845. After a tremendous amount of hard work, the Peterborough Railway Society were able to reopen the line for all traffic on 1 June 1977. Since then, it has established itself in a unique position amongst preserved railways in Great Britain by specialising in operating locomotives and rolling stock from all over Europe.

Stock
[6]BR 4-6-2 No. 70000 *Britannia* (Riddles Class 7MT) built 1951
[4]BR 4-6-0 No. 73050 *City of Peterborough* (Riddles Class 5MT) built 1954
Swedish State Railways 2-6-4T No. 1928 (Class S1) Nohab 2229 built 1953
Swedish State Railways 2-6-2T No. 1178 (Class S) built Motala 1914
SWBJ 4-6-0 No. 101 (Class B) Nohab 2082 built 1944
Danish State Railways 2-6-4T No. 740 *DFDS Danish Seaways* (Class S) Frichs 86 built 1928
Danish State Railways 0-6-0T No. 656 (Class F) Frichs 360 built 1949
[1]Nord 4-6-0 No. 3628 (SNCF Class 230D) Henschel 10745 built 1911
DB 2-6-2T No. 64–305 (Class 64) Krupp 1308 built 1934
[2]SR 4-6-2 No. 34081 *92 Squadron* (Bulleid 'BB' Class) built 1948
DB 0-6-0T No. 80–014 (Class 80) Wolf 1228 built 1927
[8]Hudswell Clarke 0-6-0ST *Derek Crouch* 1539 built 1924
[10]Hudswell Clarke 0-6-0T No. 1 *Thomas* 1800 built 1947
Hunslet 0-6-0ST No. 75006 2855 built 1943
Peckett 0-6-0ST 2000 built 1942
[11]Hunslet 0-6-0ST *Jacks Green* 1953 built 1939
[13]Avonside 0-6-0ST 1945 built 1926
SJ Bo-BoDMR No. 1212 built 1958
[9]Barclay 0-4-0ST No. 90432 2248 built 1948
Hibberd 4WPM *Percy* 2894 built 1944
Hibberd 4WDM *Frank* 2896 built 1944, rebuilt Perkins 1976
RSH 0-4-0DH *Horsa* 8368 built 1962
Ruston Hornsby 4WDM 294268 built 1951
Ruston Hornsby 4WDM (88DS Class) 321734 built 1952
BR Co-CoDE No. D9000 *Royal Scots Grey* (Class 55) English Electric 2905 built 1961
BR Co-CoDE No. 55.016 *Gordon Highlander* (Class 55) English Electric 2921 built 1961
English Electric 0-4-0DH D1123 built 1966
Nord Corridor 2nd class coach No. 7122 type B9yf
BR Mk.1 TSO coach No. 4615 built 1956
BR Mk.1 TSO coach No. 4627 built 1956
BR Mk.1 TSO coach No. 4635 (body as office) built 1957
BR Mk.1 TSO coach No. 4667 built 1957
BR Mk.1 TSO coach No. 4686 built 1957
BR Mk.1 SK coach No. 24997 built 1957
BR Mk.1 SK coach No. 26193 built 1957
BR Mk.1 SK coach No. 25639 built 1966
BR Mk.1 BSK coach No. E35248 built 1956
BR Mk.1 BSK coach No. M35239 built 1955 (Greene King Bar)
BR Mk.1 TSO coach No. E4200 built 1956
BR 'Mackerel' 17-ton ballast wagon No. AB 992358 built Metro-Cammell 1951
GWR Smith Rodley 3-ton steam crane 14923 built 1943
GNR 'Lowmac' wagon No. ADE 414130 built 1909
SR 4-wheel PMV van No. 1218 built 1936
LNER bogie flat wagon No. DE 320882
LMS mess coach No. ADM395758
[3]SR motor brake third coach No. 11187 built 1933 (ex-4COR Unit No. 3135)
[3]SR corridor third coach No. 10096 built 1937 (ex-4COR Unit No. 3142)
[3]SR motor brake third coach No. 11161 built 1937 (ex-4COR Unit No. 3142)
[3]SR motor brake third coach No. 11201 built 1937 (ex-4COR Unit No. 3142)
[3]SR corridor composite coach No. 11773 built 1933 (ex-4COR Unit No. 3159)
[3]SR corridor composite coach No. 11825 built 1937 (ex-4COR Unit No. 3135)
DSB brake/second saloon coach No. 479 built 1961
DSB 3rd class open driving trailer coach No. 23219 built 1960
DSB 3rd class open coaches Nos 23913 and 23914 built 1962
DSB corridor composite coach No. 21261 built 1939

LMS CCT vans Nos M37011, M37066, M37071, M37096, M37141 built Metro Cammell 1938
BR 'Trout' 25-ton ballast hopper wagon No. DB992164 built Metro Cammell 1951
BR SPV van No. E87537 built 1959
BR CCT van No. M947796 built 1960
LMS 40-ton steam breakdown crane No. MP3 built Ransomes and Rapier 1930
LMS crane runner wagon No. ADM299850 built 1931
BR 10-ton steam crane No. 274 Taylor and Hubbard 1576 built 1950
[7]SR buffet car No. S12529S built 1937 (ex-4BUF Unit No. 3084)
[7]SR Travelling Post Office No. 4920 built 1939
SR 'Brighton Belle' Pullman motor brake/2nd No. S290 built 1932
BR Pullman 2nd class kitchen car No. E337 built Metro-Cammell 1960
Wagons-Lits International sleeping car No. 3916 built 1949
Wagons-Lits dining car No. 2975 built 1927
NSB balcony-end suburban bogie coach No. 601 built 1925
GWR Hawksworth BG van No. W316W built 1948
GNR six-wheeled parcels van No. D940400 built *c*1888
LNWR six-wheeled parcels van
LMS six-wheeled van No. M40284 built Wolverton 1949
BR 20-ton brake van chassis No. B953944
DSB flat wagon No. 20 06 225 159–4 built Scandia 1927
Esso tank wagon No. 1914 built Hurst Nelson 1941
LMS 20-ton hopper wagon built 1938
LNER open wagon built 1942
BR cattle wagon No. B953944 built 1950
BR BSK Coach No. M35239 built 1958
Two LNWR wooden-bodied open wagons built 1920
LNWR gunpowder van No. 11023 built 1910
MR five-plank wooden-bodied wagon
Wickham 4WPMR No. 01044 built 1944
GER pump trolley built 1907
LMS 20-ton goods brake van No. M730302 built 1937
LNER 20-ton goods brake van No. E108064 built 1928

[1]Owned by the Science Museum.
[2]Owned by the Battle of Britain Locomotive Preservation Society (*q.v.*).
[3]Owned by the Southern Electric Group (*q.v.*).
[4]Withdrawn from Patricroft shed in 1968 and purchased for preservation. One of a class of 172 locomotives built between 1951 and 1957 to a design that was basically a modified LMS Stanier Class 5.
[6]*Britannia* was the prototype British Railways 'Pacific' and the first of the 999 BR standard locomotives to be built between 1951 and 1960. It was also a milestone in British locomotive practice, since it was the first two-cylinder 'Pacific' built for use in this country. The idea of standard designs was to facilitate a reduction in the amount of spare parts required, whilst at the same time producing a range of locomotives capable of working without restriction over the whole British Railways system. Had it not been for the introduction of diesels, there is little doubt that several hundred 'Britannias' would have been built. As it was, only 55 locomotives of the class were constructed and they suffered the fate of other steam engines, the first withdrawal taking place in 1965 after a ridiculously short life of only 14 years. All the survivors had been withdrawn by the end of 1967, with the exception of No. 70013, which was the last steam locomotive to be overhauled by BR at Crewe Works earlier that year. *Britannia* was laid aside after withdrawal for official preservation, but was replaced at the last minute by *Oliver Cromwell*, and it was left to a group of amateur enthusiasts to save this historic engine for posterity. Owned by the Britannia Locomotive Society (*q.v.*).
[7]On loan from the National Collection.
[8]Bought new by McAlpine Construction Co for construction of Wissington Sugar Factory, Norfolk. Bought by the sugar company and worked on the Wissington Light Railway until 1955. Sold to Derek Crouch (Contractors) to work at a Northumberland open-cast coal site. Presented on permanent loan in 1972.
[9]Formerly worked at Wissington and Kidderminster sugar factories. Purchased for preservation in 1972. Numbered 90432 after the WD 2-8-0 from Boston shed which was the last steam locomotive driven by the present owner's father.
[10]Ex British Sugar Corporation, Peterborough, 1973. Officially named *Thomas* by the Rev W. Awdry, creator of the 'Thomas the Tank Engine' railway books.
[11]Ex Nassington Ironstone Quarry 1970. Together with sister locomotive *Ring Haw* (now on the North Norfolk Railway) worked at Nassington Quarry for its entire working life.
[13]Ex British Sugar Corporation, Kings Lynn, 1971.

Battle of Britain Locomotive Preservation Society **H**

Details from: Mr R. J. Tanner, 157 Harrowden Road, Bedford MK42 0RM

No. 34081 *92 Squadron* was built at Brighton Works in 1948 to the design of Mr O. V. S. Bulleid, last chief mechanical engineer of the Southern Railway. For the first ten years of her working life she was based at Ramsgate and worked Kent coast expresses and continental boat trains, including such trains as the 'Golden Arrow' and 'Night Ferry'. In 1958, following electrification of the South Eastern area, the locomotive was transferred to Exmouth Junction shed at Exeter, from where she worked all over the West Country on such trains as the 'Atlantic Coast Express'. Withdrawal came in 1964 and *92 Squadron* was sold for scrap to Woodham Brothers of Barry, South Wales, where she joined over 200 other locomotives awaiting the breaker's torch. However, fate, in the form of the Battle of Britain Locomotive Society, intervened. In 1973 BBLS purchased *92 Squadron* and

since then have concentrated on raising funds to cover the costs of restoration to working order.
Following discussions with several organisations it was decided that *92 Squadron* should come to the Nene Valley Railway and the move took place during the first week of November 1976.
During its sojourn in the scrapyard all of the non-ferrous parts of the locomotive and many of the easily accessible high quality steel components were removed, including the main axle bearings, couplings, rods and valve gear. These removals, plus the deterioration following 12 years lying in a scrapyard, have meant that it was impossible to move *92 Squadron* by rail and the move was, therefore, carried out by road. This move marked the commencement of a restoration programme which is likely to take five years and cost several thousands of pounds. Peterborough Railway Society Limited is pleased and proud to be associated with this project and looks forward to the time when *92 Squadron* will be seen again in steam, hauling trains on the Nene Valley Railway.

Britannia Locomotive Society **H**

Secretary: R. L. Kingston, 'Lysander', Merchant Lane, Cranfield, Bedfordshire MK43 0DA.

Southern Electric Group **H**

Aims: To promote and further interest in the electric railway system of the former Southern Railway Company, its predecessors and its successors.
Activities: The Group organises regular meetings in Central London, Croydon, Surbiton, Eastleigh and Worthing, and at least one visit per month to a railway installation. Special events, such as rail-tours and day trips, are also promoted. Members receive the Group's bi-monthly, litho-printed magazine, 'Live Rail', which is packed with useful information about the Southern – past, present and future.
The major achievement of the Group's twelve years has been the preservation of a Southern Railway built, 1938 Portsmouth 4-car corridor electric unit (designated '4-Cor'). No. 3142 is currently in use, steam hauled, on the Nene Valley Railway, but a major project is underway to restore all the electrical equipment, so that eventually she will again be self propelled. This work should be completed in 1983.

Peterborough Railway Society Limited

Membership details from: J. H. Maddocks, 36 Sallows Road, Peterborough, Cambs.

104 Stour Valley Railway Preservation Society D

Standard gauge railway preservation centre offering short steam-hauled rides on periodic open days throughout the year

Chappel and Wakes Colne Station, Essex CO6 2DS
Access: Chappel and Wakes Colne BR Station, 7 miles North West of Colchester, off A604. Bus route: Eastern National No. 88 or Hedingham & District Omnibus services from Colchester to Halstead. BR Paytrain from Colchester and Sudbury
Tel: Earls Colne 2571
OS Ref: TL 898289

The site is open every weekend with Steam Days on the first Sunday of each month from April to October and on Bank Holidays. The site will be open from 11 am to 6 pm each day. Refreshments, car park, model shop, bookshop available.
At least one locomotive will be in steam each day and coach rides will be available within the steam centre.
The Steam Centre at Chappel was established by the Stour Valley Railway Preservation Society in order to provide a means of building up reserves of equipment and rolling stock so that it can eventually fulfil its aims of running a steam operated railway. At present the Centre operates as a live steam museum.
Visitors to the Centre will find that they are not restricted to inspecting a few beautifully preserved locomotives and coaches, but can see every aspect of railway preservation right down to the last little detail. Operating and repairing steam railway engines and equipment can be a dirty occupation – maybe that is why it has such an attraction! However, there are lots of things to see without the need to don a pair of overalls, but visitors are reminded that, in certain areas, care is needed to avoid coming into contact with oil, soot or grease.
Society details may be obtained from: Margaret Booth, P.O. Box 30, Rickmansworth, Herts.

Stock
[10]BR 2-6-4T No. 80151 (Riddles 4MT Class) built 1956
[1]GER 0-6-2T No. 999 (Hill N7 Class) built 1924
[2]Peckett 0-4-0ST 2039 built 1943
[5]Peckett 0-4-0ST 1438 built 1916 (carries BR No. 1151)
[3]RSH 0-6-0ST No. 54 *Penn Green* 7031 built 1941
Hunslet 0-6-0ST No. 68067 *Gunby* 2413 built 1941
RSH 0-6-0ST *Jupiter* 7671 built 1950
Barclay 0-6-0ST *Belvoir* 2350 built 1954
Barclay 0-4-0ST *Storefield* 1047 built 1905
[9]Bagnall 0-4-0ST *Jubilee* 2542 built 1936
BR/Drewry 0-6-0DM No. D2279 2656 built 1960
Fowler 0-4-0DH No. 23 4220039 built 1965
Barclay 0-4-0DM AMW No. 144 *Paxman* 333 built 1938
Metrovick 4WE No. 2 built 1941
Motor Rail 4WPM 2029 built 1920
Wickham 4WPMR No. TR37 6896 built 1954
BR Mk.1 FO coach No. E3125 built 1962
BR Mk.1 TSO coach No. E3779 built 1953
BR Mk.1 brake/2nd coach No. E43147 built 1954
BR prototype bar car No. E1883 built 1968
LNER Gresley BSO coach No. E16631 built 1938

BR Mk.1 BCK coach No. M21027 built 1954
[4]BR Mk.1 brake/2nd coach No. M43157 built 1954
LNER Gresley buffet car No. E9118E built 1936
LMS sleeping car No. M379 built 1951
GER four-wheeled first-class coach No. 19 built 1878
MSLR six-wheeled coach No. 373 built 1889
GWR 'Toad' 20-ton goods brake van No. 17898 built 1914
GER four-wheeled *Pooley* van No. 3 built 1911
[7]GER four-wheeled ventilated van No. 32518 built Bristol Carriage and Wagon Co 1921
[7]PO (Wm. Cory & Son) four-wheeled coal wagon No. 18973 built Midland Carriage and Wagon Co 1923
[6]GER four-wheeled third-class family saloon coach No. 37 built 1897 (formerly six-wheeled)
[8]GER six-wheeled passenger brake van No. 553 built 1890
[8]LNER fish van No. 15139 built 1925
GER four-wheeled gas tank wagon No. 055 built *c*1902 underframe only
William Cory coal wagon No. 61 built 1921
BR 6-wheeled special cattle van No. E765 built 1953
Grafton four-ton steam crane
PO flat wagon built G. R. Turner 1940
Wickham 4WPMR 1583 built 1934
[4]SR four-wheeled PMV vehicle No. 1152 built 1937

[1]Hill Class L77 locomotive which was the last of a batch ordered just prior to the grouping by the GER. Withdrawn from Stratford shed in 1962 as BR No. 69621 and purchased for preservation. The engine was stored at Neville Hill shed, Leeds, for eleven years prior to moving to Chappel and Wakes Colne. The Class N7 (LNER designation) was highly successful on the tightly-timed Liverpool Street suburban 'Jazz' service and 134 examples were built. No. 999 was in fact the last GER locomotive ever built at Stratford Works.
[2]Owned jointly with the Bishop's Stortford Railway Society.
[3]Ex Stewarts and Lloyds Minerals Ltd, Gretton Brook, Corby, Northants, 1969.
[4]On loan from Mr D. C. Petterson.
[5]On loan from Mr C. Dore.
[6]Owned by Saffron Walden Model Railway Club.
[7]Owned by Railway Vehicle Preservations.
[8]Owned by the Great Eastern Railway Group (*q.v.*).
[9]Ex Bowaters UK Pulp & Paper Mills Ltd, Sittingbourne 1971.
[10]Withdrawn May 1967 and sent to Woodham Bros scrapyard, Barry. Purchased for preservation and moved to Chappel and Wakes Colne in March 1975.

Great Eastern Railway Group **H**

Details from: J. Watling, 22 Manor Way, Chingford, London E4 6NW
A small group of enthusiasts dedicated to saving items of GER interest, including the two vehicles maintained at Chappel and Wakes Colne.

105 Colne Valley Railway A

Standard gauge steam railway one mile in length on the site of the former Colne Valley and Halstead Railway

Colne Valley Railway Co Ltd, Castle Hedingham Station, near Halstead, Essex CO9 3DZ
Access: On the A604, ½ mile north of Castle Hedingham
Tel: Hedingham 61174 (24 hour phone number for information, school visits, party visits etc)
OS Ref: TL 774362

The site is open daily for static display between 10 am and 5 pm. Operation takes place on first and third Sunday each month from Easter to October plus Bank Holiday Sundays and Mondays when short steam hauled rides are available between 11 am and 5 pm.
Facilities for visitors include free car park, railway shop, excellent full meal service in specially converted BR Mk.1 coaches, light refreshments, museum, toilets. Admission charge includes all free rides and free car park.
The late and much lamented Colne Valley and Halstead Railway opened in 1858 (to Halstead) and was closed to passengers on 31 December 1961.
Ten years later, the idea was born to recreate a small portion of the railway on its former trackbed, incorporating as much as possible of the original material. Since then, what has been achieved on a 'Greenfield' trackbed by sheer determination and hard work is little short of amazing. Richard Hymas and his fellow enthusiasts have re-erected the former Sible and Castle Hedingham Station brick by brick including two 200ft platforms as well as relaying all the necessary track and pointwork. The old crossing-keepers hut from White Colne has also been erected on site together with the ex-BR Cressing (Braintree–Witham Line) Signal Box (20 lever). With a bridge now replaced over the River Colne a further ½ mile of track can now be relaid. Very definitely a little line with a big future.

Stock
Hunslet 0-6-0ST No. 190 *Castle Hedingham* 3790 built 1952
Vulcan Foundry 0-6-0ST No. 72 5309 built 1945
RSH 0-6-0T No. 40 7765 built 1954
[1]Hawthorn Leslie 0-4-0ST No. 1 3715 built 1928
Barclay 0-4-0ST *Victory* 2199 built 1945
[2]Avonside 0-4-0ST *Barrington* 1875 built 1921
BR 0-6-0DM No. D2041 built 1959
Ruston Hornsby 4WDM (48DS Class) 221639 built 1943
Lake & Elliott 4WPM built *c*1924
Barclay 0-4-0DM 2349 built 1941
Hibberd 4WDM 3147 built 1947
BR/AC cars 4WDMR No. E79978 built 1958
BR Mk.1 TSO coach No. E4628 built 1957
BR Mk.1 TSO coach No. 4810 built 1959
BR Mk.1 BSK coach No. E35169 built 1958
BR Mk.1 SK coach No. E25697 built 1958
BR Mk.1 RMB coach No. 1809 built 1957

SR kitchen/1st Pullman car *Gwen* built 1932
NSB balcony-end coach No. 18803 built 1926
Three bogie wagons
LNWR open-wagon No. DM202440 built 1911
LNER goods brake van No. 2 (ex Bowes Railway) built 1935
BR goods van
BR Grafton 10-ton steam crane No. DRG80103 + runner No. DE32078
Esso oil tank wagon No. 1855 built 1940
MOD box van No. 47700
LMS Stanier bogie parcels brake van
Four BR CCT vans
Wickham 4WPMR

[1]This was the first of six similar locomotives supplied to APCM, Swanscombe Works. In her active life she moved 8½ million tons of chalk from the quarry to the cement works. She was withdrawn from service in 1970, presented to the Gravesend Railway Enthusiasts' Society (*q.v.*) in 1972 and stored at the South Eastern Steam Centre until 1976.
[2]Owned by the Avonside Steam Preservation Society (*q.v.*).

Gravesend Railway Enthusiasts' Society **H**

Other Society activities centred on Gravesend include modelling, meetings and tours. For full details please contact Mr I. G. Rushforth, 74 Main Road, Longfield, Dartford, Kent.

Avonside Steam Preservation Society **H**

Details from: Mr K. Rogers, 58 Castle Street, Cambridge CB3 0AP

Colne Valley Railway Preservation Society

Details from: Mr P. Clark, 14 Endway, Steeple Bumpstead, Haverhill, Suffolk.

106 Lincolnshire Coast Light Railway A

A one-mile long 60cm gauge passenger-carrying line opened in 1960

North Sea Lane Station, St Anthony's Bank, Humberston, Grimsby, Humberside
OS Ref: TA 326059

Operates daily during Spring Bank Holiday week, then weekends only to mid-July, then daily from mid-July to mid-September from 10 am to 5 pm. Steam trains by previous arrangement only.
Facilities for visitors include car parking, souvenir shop, refreshments and toilets.
In April 1960 a group of Lincolnshire railway enthusiasts formed a company to build and operate a passenger-carrying railway that would also fill a real transport need. A site at Humberston, near Grimsby, was chosen and half-a-mile of 2ft gauge line opened between North Sea Lane and Humberston Beach on 27 August 1960. The line has been relaid on a new alignment and extended a further half-mile to South Sea Lane, near the centre of the Humberston Fitties Holiday Camp. The headquarters of the railway and the locomotive shed are at North Sea Lane Station, where there is a run-round loop and sidings. Miniature signals formerly in use on the GN and L & Y railways have been installed. The original track and rolling stock, including several goods vehicles, came from Smith's Potato Estates agricultural railway at Nocton, Lincolnshire, and had also been used in France in the 1914–18 war. For passenger traffic there is an open bogie coach and also two former Ashover Light Railway coaches, now restored and fitted with leather upholstered seats from Glasgow, Leeds and Liverpool tramcars.
This interesting line can be reached via the A16, A18 and A46 roads. It is also served by Grimsby–Cleethorpes Transport buses from the Market Place, Cleethorpes.
Further information can be obtained from the General Manager, Lincolnshire Coast Light Railway Company Limited, North Sea Lane Station, Humberston, Grimsby, Humberside.

Stock
Motor Rail 4WDM No. 1 *Paul* 3995 built 1927
Peckett 0-6-0ST No. 2 *Jurassic* 1008 built 1903
Hunslet 0-4-0ST No. 3 *Elin* 705 built 1899
Motor Rail 4WDM No. 4 *Wilton* 7481 built 1940
Motor Rail 4WDM No. 5 8622 built 1941
Motor Rail 4WDM No. 6 8874 built 1944
Motor Rail 4WDM No. 7 *Nocton* 1935 built 1920
Two bogie coaches ex-Ashover Light Railway built 1925
Bogie coach ex-Sand Hutton Railway built 1924
Bogie coach ex-Nocton Estates Railway
Bogie open coach
Bogie van No. 8
Four-wheeled open wagons Nos 10–12
Bogie open wagons Nos 17 & 18

107 Audley End Miniature Railway A

Passenger-carrying 10¼in gauge line, 1½ miles in length, in the grounds of Audley End House, near Saffron Walden, Essex

Access: Off the A11 adjacent to Audley End House. Nearest station, Audley End (1 mile)
Tel: Saffron Walden 22354
OS Ref: TL 530366

The railway is in operation on Sundays and Bank Holidays from Easter to October, plus Tuesdays, Wednesdays, Thursdays and Saturdays in the school summer holidays. Facilities offered to visitors include car parking, refreshments and souvenir shop.
The railway was opened in 1964, the ceremony being performed by Stirling Moss. Originally just under one mile in length, a half-mile extension was added in 1979. Trains

run through attractive woodlands and cross the River Cam twice before returning to Audley End station, adjacent to the coach park. The railway is noteworthy for its attention to line-side detail, incorporating scale-sized signal boxes, signals and gradient posts which add considerably to its overall effect.

Stock
Rio Grande 2-8-2 built Curwen 1979
Curwen 2-6-2 No. 3548 *Lord Braybrooke* built 1948 (rebuilt 1980 from 4-4-2)
LNER 4-4-2 No. 4433 built Curwen 1965
LMS 4-6-0 No. 6100 *Royal Scot* built Winkler Engineering
Curwen Co-CoDM No. D7011 *Western Thunderer* built 1964
Freelance 0-6-0DM *Doris* built 1982
12 articulated open bogie coaches
2 open bogie coaches

108 Southend Miniature Steam Railway A

Passenger-carrying 10¼in gauge railway, 365 yards in length operating daily during the holiday season

Southend-on-Sea, Essex
OS Ref: TQ 886850

The line was opened in 1977.

Stock
Viking 2-4-2 No. 100 built 1977 (LNER V2 Class style)
Freelance Bo-BoPM No. D3152 (BR Mainline Diesel style)
Freelance 4WBE
Six Cromar White/Viking bogie coaches

109 Felixstowe Miniature Railway A

A 7¼in gauge line located between Sea Road and the Promenade and is laid out in the shape of an irregular oval. The railway is equipped with semaphore signals, an engine shed, turntable, sidings and a signalbox. Trains make three circuits of the track, commencing and finishing at Felixstowe Lawn Station.
Open weekends, Easter to Spring Bank Holiday, then daily until mid-September.

Stock
Freelance 2-6-0 *Rupert* rebuilt 1960 (GWR type)
Cromar White Bo-BoPM built 1974
Articulated open bogie coaches

110 Ingoldmells Miniature Railway A

Passenger-carrying 7¼in gauge railway, 100 yards in length, arranged in a continuous circuit

Ingoldmells Point, Skegness, Lincolnshire

Operates daily during the holiday season

Stock
LMS 4-6-2 *Ingoldmells Flyer* ('Princess Royal' type) built 1969
Cromar White Bo-BoPM No. D7017 built 1969
'Sit-astride' bogie coaches

111 Somerleyton Miniature Railway A

Passenger-carrying 7¼in gauge railway, 449 yards in length, arranged in a circular layout round the estate of Lord and Lady Somerleyton

Somerleyton Hall, near Lowestoft, Suffolk
Access: 5 miles north west of Lowestoft, off B1074 or off A143 from Great Yarmouth
Tel: Lowestoft 730224

Facilities for visitors include car parking, refreshments, 16th-century mansion and grounds, with a famous maze and gardens.
The railway operates on Thursday and Sunday afternoons and Bank Holidays. Also on Tuesdays and Wednesdays in July and August.

Stock
Wright 0-4-0T *Hugh* built *c*1972 ('Hercules' type)
Cromar White Bo-BoPM No. D7026 *Somerleyton* built *c*1971
BR Bo-BoDM (Class 20) built 1981
'Sit-astride' bogie coaches
There is a display of enamel signs around the track.

112 The Thursford Museum AE

Museum of steam road locomotives including showman's, traction and ploughing engines. Steam wagons and barn oil engines. Mechanical musical organs, Wurlitzer theatre organ, unique Savages Venetian Gondola Ride, narrow gauge steam railway

Thursford Green, near Fakenham, Norfolk NR21 0AS
Access: Off the A148 Fakenham–Cromer road
Tel: Fakenham 3839
OS Ref: TF 983342

Live concerts on the Wurlitzer from mid-June to October. Picnic and children's play area. Refreshment and souvenir shop. Ample free car parking. Special events throughout the year.
Opening times: April, May & October – Sundays only. June – Sundays, Tuesdays & Thursdays. July & September – Sundays, Tuesdays, Wednesdays and Thursdays. August – Every day except Saturdays 2 pm–5 pm.
George Cushing has brought together at Laurel Farm a unique collection of steam traction engines and fairground organs. These are displayed in modern exhibition buildings and steaming demonstrations and organ concerts are regular features.
On 20 August 1978, a ¾-mile, passenger-carrying, 1ft

10¾in gauge steam railway was opened running through Norfolk farmland from a terminal station behind the organ museum.

Stock
[1]Hunslet 0-4-0ST *Cackler* 671 built 1898
Two covered bogie coaches

[1]Ex Dinorwic Slate Quarries, Llanberis, Caernarfonshire, March 1966.

113 Wells Harbour Railway B

Passenger-carrying 10¼in gauge railway, 7/10 mile in length, connecting Wells Town with the beach and Pinewoods caravan site

Beach Road, Wells-next-the-Sea, Norfolk
Access: Eastern Counties bus to Wells-next-the-Sea
Tel: Fakenham 710439

This line claims a major distinction in that it supplies a local transport need previously performed by a now-discontinued bus service.
The railway operates during Easter week, then on weekends only until Spring Bank Holiday when a timetable service is run daily until 30 September.
Timetable services commence at 10.30 am and operate at hourly intervals until 8 pm – surely one of the longest operating days of any miniature railway in the British Isles. In August, evening trains run until 11 pm for late customers in town on Saturdays and Sundays.
The Wells Harbour Railway was built during 1975 and 1976, finally opening for public traffic on 1 July of that year. During its first two seasons it carried the dramatic total of 80,000 passengers – a major achievement for so small a line. However, disaster struck on 11 January 1978, when severe storms washed away ½-mile of track and ballast when waves swept over the sea defence banks and the sea-front road. But an energetic rebuilding campaign allowed services to be restored on 1 July 1978.

Stock
Freelance 4WPM
Five 12-seat open coaches

114 Belton House Miniature Railway A

Passenger-carrying 7¼in gauge railway, ½ mile in length at present, running from the Adventure Playground to Suttons Bridge

Belton House, Grantham, Lincolnshire
The Belton House railway opened on 7 April 1979, using stock and track from the former line at Wyndham Park, Grantham.
Access: On A607 north of Grantham. Main entrance in Belton village
Tel: Grantham (0476) 66116
OS Ref: SK 9438

Open from the end of March to early October, daily from 11 am to 5.30 pm and at other times when required for events, school parties, etc.

Stock
LNER 4-6-2 No. 4472 *Flying Scotsman* built Broadfield 1949
Barnes & Thomas 2-6-2 *Mountaineer* built 1974
BR *Deltic* Co-CoPE built 1981
BR *Western* Co-CoPE built 1981
5 bogie coaches
Another 'Pacific' locomotive is under construction
Belton House is attributed to Wren and has been the home of Lord Brownlow's family since built in 1685. Facilities for visitors include fine gardens and 700-acre deer park, children's adventureland, Museum of Horse and nature trails. Special events on most Sundays.

115 Barton House Railway AE

Passenger-carrying 3½in gauge line laid out as an 80-yard oval

Barton House, Hartwell Road, The Avenue, Wroxham, Norfolk NOR 03Z
Access: By road – off A1151; by rail – 15 minutes from BR Wroxham station; by river – adjacent to the River Bure
Tel: Wroxham 2470
OS Ref: TG 302178

Most of the railway's other equipment comprises full-size railway items. There is a complete M & GNJR signal box with 26-lever frame and instruments, M & GN signals from Guestwick and Melton Constable, a gradient post, two Tyers No. 1 tablet instruments and other items mainly from the M & GNJR.
Additionally, a 150-yard long 7¼in gauge passenger-carrying line has been laid, operated with a battery electric loco.
The railway is open on the third Sunday of each month from April to October between 2.30 pm and 5.30 pm.
Facilities for visitors include refreshments, toilets, railway shop and car parking nearby.
Work on the Barton House Railway began in 1960 and continued steadily until the official opening on 28 April 1963. Until 1970, all money raised was in aid of Wroxham Church Restoration Fund, a total of £600 having been reached. From 1971 receipts have been in aid of charities.

Stock
GNR 4-4-2 No. 251 built *c*1920, rebuilt 1960
GNR 4-4-2 No. 1442 built Elsden *c*1939, rebuilt 1964
Way 0-4-0BE (used as standby loco only)
'Sit-astride' bogie trolleys

116 Strumpshaw Hall Steam Museum AE

Passenger-carrying 2ft gauge railway one mile in length in the grounds of Strumpshaw Hall

Strumpshaw Hall, near Brundall, Norwich, Norfolk
The line is in operation on Sundays in the summer
Access: 6 miles east of Norwich, 2 miles south of A47 at Blofield
OS Ref: TF 345065

Also 15in gauge steam locomotive on static display in museum of steam road vehicles.
The museum is open from 2 pm to 5 pm daily except Saturdays from Easter until 30 September.

Stock
Jung 0-4-0WT *Cyclops* 7509 built 1937
Motor Rail 4WDM No. 1 7192 built 1937
Open-sided bogie coach
[1]McGarigle Machine Co 4-4-0 *Cagney* built 1902 (15in gauge)

[1]This historic American-built 4-4-0 is of the classic Cagney type and formerly worked on the Blakesley Hall Railway. Strumpshaw has also acquired an 1893 beam engine and a compound engine with 14ft flywheel.

117 Ferry Meadows Miniature Railway A

Passenger-carrying 10¼in gauge railway, ½ mile in length opened in May 1979 running from Ham Lane to Lynch station

Nene Valley Park, Peterborough, Cambs
Access: Ferry Meadows Station, Nene Valley Railway. Off the A605 between the A1 and Peterborough
Bus services (Nos 265, 268, 312, 316 and 323) stop on Oundle Road close to footpaths which lead into Ferry Meadows. A special bus service runs every Sunday from the first week in May until September, from Peterborough Bus Station to Ferry Meadows. Tel: Peterborough 54571 for details.
Footpaths lead from Bretton, Longthorpe (Bluebell Bridge) and the Ortons (Ham Lane and Goldie Lane) into Ferry Meadows. From the city centre follow the Nene Way (signposted) via Hill's Yard off Bridge Street.
Tel: 0205-64352
OS Ref: TL 1495

The railway operates daily from April to October. Its owners, Chesselgrove Ltd, of Broadfield Lane, Boston, Lincs PE21 8DR, say it's an example of a hobby that got out of hand! Ferry Meadows is the centrepiece of the Nene Park, a Country Park created by Peterborough Development Corporation, with help from the Countryside Commission and the Sports Council, as part of Peterborough's expansion.
It has 500 acres of grassland, woodland and lakes with facilities for sailing, fishing, boating and riding. Miles of footpaths and horse-routes and lots of space for picnics, play and special events. Camping and caravan sites and the preserved foundations of Roman buildings. Something for all the family to enjoy.
Regularly changing displays in the Information Centre illustrate some of the animals, birds and plants which can be seen in Ferry Meadows.
Refreshments are available from the cafés at the Information Centre and the Watersports Centre.
Entry to the park is free, but there is a small charge for car parking at weekends and on Bank Holidays.

Stock
Dove 4-6-2 built 1950, rebuilt 1981
Mills 0-4-0ST *Alice* built 1977
Air-braked open bogie coaches

118 Cleethorpes Miniature Railway B

A 14½in gauge double-track railway located at the south end of the town. The line is four-fifths of a mile long, passing along the length of the boating lake and miniature golf course with a panoramic view of the Humber estuary and shipping

Marine Embankment, Cleethorpes, Humberside

Opened as a steam railway in 1948, it changed hands and became electrically powered in 1954 and was purchased by Cleethorpes Corporation five years later. The system was remodelled and extended in 1972 and now operates with two terminal stations at the bathing pool and zoo, with one intermediate halt at Thrunscoe.
The gauge of the line is unusual, as is the choice of fuel for the locomotives, for the engines have large propane gas tanks mounted in their tenders. Further unusual features are to be found in the operation of the line, which is double track throughout, as two parallel single independent tracks.
The railway operates at Easter, then on Sundays only until Spring Bank Holiday, thence daily until the second half of September.

Stock
Severn-Lamb 2-8-0GasH No. 278 built 1972 (Steam outline)
Severn-Lamb 2-8-0GasH No. 800 built 1978 (Steam outline)
LNER 4-6-2GasH No. 4472 *Flying Scotsman* built Cook
Ten bogie coaches, some of them roofed

119 Suffolk Country and Wildlife Park A

Passenger-carrying 10¼in gauge railway 1¾ miles in length, running through this large country park which contains many wildlife attractions

Kessingland, near Lowestoft, Suffolk
Tel: Lowestoft 69876
OS Ref: TM 5285

The Park is open daily from Good Friday until 30 September from 10 am until one hour before dusk or 6 pm whichever is the earlier.

Suffolk Miniature Light Railway

Located at the top end of the Country Park is the 10¼in gauge miniature railway which operates daily throughout the season from 11 am until 5.30 pm.
Trains, both steam and diesel hauled, depart at regular intervals from the Central Station. This building contains departure and arrival platforms, a passing loop and a display of old enamelled advertisement signs together with a display of pre-war slot machines.
Opened in April 1980, the line is still being extended and developed. When completed, it will offer passengers a choice of routes running for approximately a mile and a half through wood and pastureland and incorporating cuttings, an elevated section with a long embankment, bridge and tunnel. Additional sidings, complete with turntable, signal box and other line side effects, are also planned in order to present a complete and living railway in miniature.
This is thought to be the only railway with a Wurlitzer cinema organ in the station!
Owner & operator: Brian Nicholson, 31 Mount Pleasant, Lowestoft, Suffolk.

Stock
Coleby-Simkins 2-6-4T *E. R. Calthrop* built 1974
[1]Marsh 2-6-4T *Lady of the Isles* built 1981
LMS 4-6-0 ('Royal Scot' Class) built 1982
LMS 4-6-0 No. 6100 *Royal Scot* built Foden 1976
Fenlow Bo-BoDH No. 10 *Conway Castle* built 1972
Fenlow Bo-BoDH No. 11 *Rhuddlan Castle* built *c*1972
Twelve articulated bogie coaches
Five covered bogie coaches

[1]On loan from the Mull & West Highland N.G. Rly.

120 Caister Castle Motor Museum E

Standard gauge steam locomotive on static display in motor museum

Caister Castle, Caister-on-Sea, Norfolk
Access: Four miles north of Great Yarmouth off A1064
Tel: 057-284-251
OS Ref: TG 504123

The Museum is open from mid-May to the end of September from 10.30 am to 5 pm daily except Saturdays.
Facilities for visitors include car parking, museum shop, refreshments, toilets, woodland walk and moated castle ruins. The Museum specialises in unique vehicles of all types, principally steam cars, having examples of Locomobile, White, Stanley and Doble on display. An added attraction is the original Festival of Britain Battersea Park Tree Walk!

Stock
Manning Wardle 0-6-0ST No. 42 *Rhondda* 2010 built 1921
Ex BSC Harlaxton Ironstone Quarry, Lincolnshire, 1973.

121 Harlow Development Corporation E

Standard gauge static locomotive exhibit

Lower Meadow Play Centre, off Paringdon Road, Southern Way, Harlow, Essex
OS Ref: TL 452078

Stock
Hibberd 4WDM 3596 built 1953

122 East Anglia Transport Museum BE

Comprehensive rail and road transport museum featuring railway, tramway and trolleybus operation

Chapel Road, Carlton Colville, Lowestoft, Suffolk
Details from: the Secretary at the above address
Tel: Ubberston 398
OS Ref: TM 505903

Eastern Counties bus route Nos 631, 632, 671 and 672 from Lowestoft to Carlton Crown. No. 688 from Lowestoft Central to Carlton Church. Nearest BR stations: Lowestoft and Oulton Broad South.
Opening times: Weekends and Bank Holidays from Late Spring Bank Holiday to end of September. Also Tuesday to Friday during August, 2 pm to 4 pm.
The Museum grew from small beginnings as a result of the purchase in 1961 of a former Lowestoft tramcar which had been in retirement for many years as a summerhouse. Work started in earnest in 1966 on land kindly provided by the founder, Mr A. V. Bird. Since then buildings have been erected, track and overhead wiring constructed, and generating plant for powering the trams and trolleybuses installed. The Museum has one of the widest ranges of preserved vehicles of any museum in the country.
On Sundays during the Summer, passenger services are provided by standard gauge electric trams and the narrow gauge East Suffolk Light Railway.

Tramcar fleet list
Blackpool 'Vambac' Car No. 11 built 1939
Lowestoft No. 14 built Milnes 1904
Blackpool Standard bogie car No. 159 built 1927
Glasgow 'Coronation' car No. 1245 built 1939
LCC HR2 Class car No. 1858 built English Electric 1930
Amsterdam 4-wheel tramcar No. 474 built 1929

East Suffolk Light Railway

A 2ft gauge line of about 200 yards length commenced operation early in 1973, running along the northern side

of the museum site between two stations, Chapel Road and Woodside.
The rails and rolling stock have all served in East Anglian sites or quarries at some time and there is even a short section of original Southwold Railway track now being used in Chapel Road Station.
The signalbox at Chapel Road was formerly on the Norfolk and Suffolk Joint Railway line between Lowestoft and Yarmouth dating back to 1903; the associated signals and equipment are primarily of Great Eastern Railway parentage. Many other railway relics are in store and will be restored for use in the station buildings, which it is hoped to erect at a future date.
Near the signal box is the body of the only remaining item of Southwold Railway rolling stock, a passenger luggage van, believed to be No. 14 built in 1885 and rebuilt by English Bros of Wisbech about 1918.
Future work will entail building a locomotive shed and developing the station areas and facilities, connecting signals and points to the box and the provision of telephone communication between stations. Locomotives are being rebuilt and closed coaches may later be provided for wet weather use. A battery-powered tramcar is also under construction and will later run on the line supplementing the train service.

Stock
Motor Rail 4WDM 22212 built 1964
Motor Rail 4WPM No. 1 5902 built 1934
Motor Rail 4WPM No. 2 5912 built 1934
Ruston Hornsby 4WDM No. 4 177604 built 1936
Hudson 24-seat open bogie coach No. 10 (rebuilt 1973)
BIS tank wagon
Skip wagons

123 Rayleigh, Essex E

Standard gauge steam locomotive on static display

Sharpe Brothers, Gables Service Station, Rayleigh Spur Road, Rayleigh, Essex
OS Ref: TQ 784920

Stock
Hawthorn Leslie 0-4-0ST No. 139 *Beatty* 3240 built 1917

Ex-Dorman Long (Steel) Ltd, Dock Street Foundry, Middlesbrough, Yorkshire, 1972.

124 Kirton in Lindsey Railway Museum and Windmill E

A live railway museum where visitors are encouraged to operate the equipment and enjoy the atmosphere of bygone railways

The Mill, North Cliff Road, Kirton Lindsey, Gainsborough, Lincolnshire DN21 4NH
Owner: Mr Alan Turner
Access: The Mill and Museum are adjacent to the B1398 road from Lincoln to Scunthorpe, just to the north of Kirton Lindsey. Lincoln is 19 miles away, Scunthorpe 8 and Gainsborough 12
OS Ref: SK 939994

The museum is open on the first three Sundays from Easter through to the end of September plus Bank Holidays. Evening and other open times may be arranged for parties, societies and organisations. Normal open times are 1.30 pm to 5 pm.
Light refreshments are available but we cannot offer toilet facilities. The nearest public toilets may be found ¼ mile away in Kirton market place. There is limited parking space in the mill yard and ample parking in Kirton.
Children unaccompanied by an adult are not permitted within the grounds. No dogs allowed on the premises.
The collection herein represents a lifelong interest in the old railways, especially those of Lincolnshire (mainly the London and North Eastern, the Great Northern and the Great Central). Other companies are however represented.
Entry is by ticket from the genuine ticket window in the Booking Office, which forms one end of the Station Master's Office. The whole of the fully fitted interior may be viewed through the windows.
The first display area contains mainly small items ranging from lamps and tickets, to buttons and models. Many facets of the railways are evident here and the visitor may take a nostalgic look at photographs, printed ephemera and items from long closed lines and stations. An extra showcase has been added to display a wide variety of railway models. Model railways of yesteryear are displayed in the form of a small working layout of Hornby Dublo and Trix Twin equipment as a contrast to the more accurate models of today.
On entering the platform area, the visitor may observe the larger items and soak up the atmosphere of the old style railway station. GNR and GCR signals stand in the bay and along with ground signals are operated from the signal box. Visitors may enter the box and operate the equipment by asking whoever is on duty. Adjacent to the signal box, part of the body of a GCR coach has been restored to the most attractive teak livery.
Visitors leave by way of the steps down between the platforms into the bay, past the signals and the tablet catcher. The acquisition of another ground frame means that the GN lattice post signal in the yard may now be operated.

Stock
[1]Hudswell Clarke 0-6-0ST 1604 built 1928

[1]Ex-Bardney sugar factory, Lincs, 1973. On extended loan from the Nene Valley Railway.

125 Wolferton Station Museum E

The former railway station at Wolferton, which was the disembarking point for the Royal Family's journeys to Sandringham House, Norfolk, has been restored as a museum commemorating its many years of royal service

Wolferton, Kings Lynn, Norfolk
Access: 9 miles north east of Kings Lynn, on B1440
Tel: 0485-40674
OS Ref: TF 661286

The museum is open from April to the end of September on weekdays from 11 am to 6 pm (except Saturdays) and on Sundays from 2 pm to 6 pm.
The museum exhibits are housed in the former down side Royal building which was once used by Kings and Queens and their distinguished guests visiting Sandringham House. Built in 1898, it contains fine old panelling, original fittings (some gold plated), unusual small railway relics and Edwardian curios, including some from Royal trains and Queen Victoria's travelling bed made for her in 1828.
It is the only museum in the country whose theme is Edwardian Royal travel.

Stock
Wickham 4WPMR No. 960220 built 1933

126 Museum of Lincolnshire Life E

Static locomotive exhibits in a museum of crafts, tools and machinery evoking life in Lincolnshire in bygone times

Old Barracks, Burton Road, Lincoln LN1 3LY
Access: Bus route No. 1 from Bus station. Nearest BR station: Lincoln Central and St Marks
Tel: Lincoln 28448
OS Ref: SK 972723

The Museum of Lincolnshire Life was first opened to the public in 1969 as a private museum run by the Lincolnshire Association. Since 1974 the museum has formed part of the Lincolnshire County Council's County Museum Service and is the headquarters of the Department of Lincolnshire History.
Collections assembled over many years by members of the Lincolnshire Local History Society formed the nucleus of the museum which was set up in the gatehouse of the Old Barracks in Burton Road. Since that time the collections have expanded rapidly so that the museum now occupied the whole of the Old Barracks site including a specially constructed building over part of the courtyard. In the courtyard are two excavators made by Ruston-Bucyrus of Lincoln. One is a 4RB and is the first machine built by the joint company in 1930. The other is an unusual 17RB built in 1938 which spent all its working life at the Lincoln Brick Company's works at Waddington. Both machines were restored for the museum by the Ruston-Bucyrus apprentices. The new building at the far end of the courtyard contains displays relating to agriculture, transport, and engineering. Farming has always been the county's major industry and some of its many diverse aspects are shown here with the emphasis on locally built machinery. One section showing the development of harvesting techniques includes a combine harvester built by Marshalls of Gainsborough about 1952. There is also a set of steam threshing tackle, though the 1913 Ruston Proctor Traction Engine spends much of the summer away from the Museum appearing at shows and rallies all over the area.
A recent major acquisition is a set of steam ploughing tackle built by Fowler of Leeds in 1925 and used in Lincolnshire until the early 1960s. This was purchased with the aid of public appeal early in 1978. The two engines *John* and *Michael* will be restored over the next few years and will then give working demonstrations whenever possible.
A collection of steam, oil and gas engines built by local firms forms the basis of a growing industrial collection.
The Museum is open Monday–Saturday 10.30 am to 5.30 pm, and Sundays 2.30 pm to 6 pm. Late weekend opening until 6 pm June to August. Closed in January and December.

Stock
Ruston Hornsby 4WDM (11/13HP Class) 192888 built 1939 (2ft 3in gauge)
[1]Ruston Proctor 4WPM 52124 built 1918 (2ft 6in gauge)
[2]Ruston Proctor steam navvy built 1909 (standard gauge)

[1]This locomotive was discovered in April 1974 after being buried under a pile of scrap Army tanks in a breaker's yard for seventeen years.
[2]Acquired by the Museum in 1981 after being rescued from a flooded pit by Mr Ray Hooley who arranged for its recovery and restoration. It is believed to be the oldest working steam navvy in the country and although space at the Museum is very restricted, it will be worked from time to time.

127 Wells–Walsingham Railway A

This 4-mile 10¼in gauge passenger-carrying line is the longest of its gauge in the world and the only one operating a public service under a Light Railway Order. The course of the railway is famous for wildlife and butterflies in season

Egmere Road station, Walsingham, Norfolk. Wells station situated alongside the A149 at Wells-next-the-Sea, Norfolk
Owner & Operator: Lt Cmdr Roy Francis
The railway operates daily from Easter to the end of September
Opened 6 April, 1982

Stock
King 0-4-2WT *Edmund Hannay* built 1971
King 0-6-0T *Pilgrim* built 1981
Freelance 4WPM *Weasel* built King 1982
Four air-braked coaches
Bogie open wagon
Further bogie coaches under construction
A fund has been started to finance the construction of a Beyer Garratt locomotive

128 Carless Solvents Ltd E

Standard gauge steam locomotive on static display

Harwich Refinery, Parkeston, Essex
OS Ref: TM 232323

Stock
RSH 0-4-0F No. 35 7803 built 1954
Used on the works internal railway system until placed on display 1979.

129 Romford, Essex G

3ft 6½in gauge locomotives in store. No casual visitors please

Mr P. Elms, 73 Crow Lane, Romford, Essex
OS Ref: TQ 500878

Stock
Bagnall 0-4-0ST *Sir Tom* 2135 built 1925
Bagnall 0-4-0ST *Woto* 2133 built 1924
Both ex-BICC Ltd, Belvedere, Kent, 1969.

130 Kilverstone Wildlife Park B

Passenger-carrying 1ft 8in gauge line ½-mile in length

Near Thetford, Norfolk
OS Ref: TL 820840

Opened 1982 using stock from the former Morecambe Miniature Railway

Stock
Hudswell Clarke 4-6-4T No. 1932 *Robin Hood* D570 built 1932
Hudswell Clarke 4-6-2 4-6-2DM No. 4472 *Flying Scotsman* D582 built 1933

131 Orwell, Cambridgeshire G

Standard gauge locomotive in store. No casual visitors please

Mr C. Roads, Hillside, Orwell, Cambs
OS Ref: TL 364510

Stock
Hudswell Clarke 0-6-0ST 1208 built 1916

132 South Cambridgeshire Railway C

Short private standard gauge light railway

Mr Drage, New Buildings Farm, Heydon, near Royston, Cambs
OS Ref: TL 419409

Planning permission for this site specifically excludes public access, therefore, written permission is required before entry will be permitted. Casual visitors ignoring this stipulation have found themselves turned away at shotgun point. You have been warned!

Stock
[1]Kitson 0-6-0ST No. 44 *Conway* 5469 built 1933
[2]Manning Wardle 0-6-0ST *Newcastle* 1532 built 1901
Barclay 0-4-0ST 1219 built 1910
Wickham 4WPMR 1519 built 1934
GNR six-wheeled passenger brake van built 1888
MS & LR six-wheeled coach
Two GER six-wheeled coach bodies

[1]Ex-Stewart & Lloyds Minerals Ltd, Gretton Brook, Corby, Northants, 1969.
[2]Ex-Wissington Light Railway, Norfolk, 1973.

133 The Crofts Collection G

A collection of 10¼in gauge equipment for which an East Anglian site is being sought where a public railway can be operated. No public access

Mr Michael Crofts, Hollytrees Farm, Theberton, Suffolk

Stock
Jennings 4-4-2 No. 1430 *Lake Shore*
LNER 2-6-2 No. 4771 *Green Arrow* (V2 Class) built Scrimshaw

134 North Lincolnshire Locomotive Preservation Group C

A private collection of standard gauge steam locomotives under the care of Mr Peter Clark and friends

Fulstow, Lincolnshire

Casual callers are definitely not welcome

Stock
RSH 0-4-0ST *Agecroft No. 1* 7416 built 1948
RSH 0-4-0ST 7680 built 1950
Peckett 0-4-0ST 1749 built 1928
BR goods brake van No. 952012 built 1957

135 Bacton, Suffolk — E

Standard gauge locomotive being privately restored. It is sited alongside the road and may be viewed between 9 am and 5 pm

Mr R. Finbow, Station Road, Bacton, Suffolk
Tel: Bacton 781354
OS Ref: TM 064682

Stock

Sentinel 4WVBTG *Fry* 7492 built 1928

Ex-J. S. Fry & Sons Ltd, Somerdale, Bristol, 1964. Presented to Mr Alfred Lewis by the company in 1968 and subsequently resold to Mr Finbow.

136 Imperial War Museum — E

SG Loco on static display

Duxford Aerodrome, Cambridgeshire
Access: 2 miles west of Duxford village on A505
Tel: Cambridge 833963
OS Ref: TL 44

Open daily mid-March to end October 11 am to 5 pm (or dusk). Car parking

Stock

Motor Rail 4WPM 1364 built 1918

137 Nettleton Mines Sports Club — B

Short 2ft 6in gauge passenger-carrying line on company sports field

John Lysaghts Ltd, Holton-le-Moor, Lincs
OS Ref: TF 094973

Stock

Ruston Hornsby 4WDM *Cannonball* 175403 built 1935

138 Ickleton, Cambridgeshire — C

Short private 1ft 6in gauge line in the grounds of Caldrees Manor. No casual visitors please

Mr A. B. M. Braithwaite, Caldrees Manor, Ickleton, Cambs
Access: BR Great Chesterford Station
OS Ref: TL 493438

Stock

Regent Street Polytechnic 4-2-2 built 1896

This locomotive was constructed from a set of castings and forgings supplied by W. G. Bagnall of Stafford to give instruction on fitting and engine work to students. Amongst those who worked on the engine was Henry Greenly. The locomotive was formerly used on the Jaywick Railway. The line is being extended to 1¼ miles.

139 Holbeach St Johns — G

1ft 9in gauge locomotives in store, though it has been proposed to build a short line on the airfield for them to run on

Mr J. H. P. Wright, Fenland Airfield, Holbeach St Johns, Lincolnshire
OS Ref: TF 333179

At present, both locomotives are dumped in a compound with piles of scrap cars. No public access

Stock

Hudswell Clarke 4-6-2DM D611 built 1938 (steam outline)
Hudswell Clarke 4-6-2DM No. 6203 *Princess Elizabeth* D612 built 1938 (steam outline)

140 Yaxham Light Railway — C

Private 1ft 11½in gauge line, 300 yards in length owned by Mr M. Mayes and Mr C. Fisher, used for transporting materials about the yard. No public access, but interested enthusiasts may visit the line by prior application

Yaxham Station Goods Yard, Dereham, Norfolk
Access: 2 miles SSE of Dereham on Yaxham to Westfield road
Tel: Dereham 3509 or Norwich 407433
OS Ref: TG 003102

Construction of the railway began in January 1980 and is still proceeding.
The railway operates on Saturdays only throughout the year. Helpers would be welcome to work on the railway. Please contact M. Mayes, Station Cottage, Yaxham, Dereham, Norfolk or C. Fisher, 165 Hellesdon Road, Norwich, Norfolk.
A continuation of the line through the former BR station area is owned and operated by Mr Paul Hemnell. This line is being extended.

Stock

Potter 0-4-0VBTG No. 1 *The Coffee Pot* built 1970
[1]Lister 4WDM 50191 built 1957
Lister 4WDM No. 2 *Rusty* 32801 built 1948
Lister 4WDM No. 3 *Pest* 40011 built 1954
Ruston Hornsby 4WDM 170369 built 1934
[1]Ruston Hornsby 4WDM No. 6 202967 built 1940
Motor Rail 4WDM No. 4 *Ousel* 7153 built 1937
Orenstein and Koppel 4WDM No. 4 *Goofy* 7688 built *c*1936
Orenstein and Koppel 4WDM No. 5 7728 built 1938
Ruston Hornsby 4WDM 202969 built 1940
Three passenger coaches
Fourteen assorted goods vehicles

[1]Owned by Paul Hemnell.

141 Maldon Miniature Railway B

Passenger-carrying 10¼in gauge line, 250 yards in length

The Promenade, Maldon, Essex

This railway was originally steam-worked, but when its boiler wore out, the locomotive was converted to electric power by fitting a motor in the tender. The line is straight and the train is hauled in one direction and propelled in the other. Operates Easter–September, all Bank Holidays, school holidays, and weekends.

Stock
LMS 4-6-0E No. 4716 built Carland 1948 ('Royal Scot' type)
Three bogie open coaches

142 Butlins, Skegness B

A 2ft gauge passenger-carrying line running round the camp

Skegness Holiday Camp, Ingoldmells, Lincolnshire

Stock
Chance 4-2-4DH No. 1863 *C. P. Huntington* 64-5030-24 built 1964 (steam outline)

143 Fakenham & Dereham Railway H

Standard gauge railway preservation project aimed at restoring a short length of this former GER branch line

Hardingham station, Norfolk

Stock
Ruston Hornsby 0-4-0DH 497753 built 1963

144 Skegness Rail Services B

Passenger-carrying 10¼in gauge railway running from Tower Esplanade to Prince's Parade

Tower Esplanade, Skegness, Lincolnshire
OS Ref: TF 570627

The line operates daily in the holiday season.

Stock
Cable Bo-BoBE *Duplex 2*
Yorkshire EV Bo-BoBE No. 15577 *The Fisherman*
Cromar White 4WBE No. E7052
Two articulated 4-car sets of coaches

145 D. A. Miller, Downham Market G

Standard gauge steam locomotive in store. No public access

72 Lynn Road, Downham Market, Norfolk
OS Ref: TF 614037

Stock
Hudswell Clarke 0-6-0ST No. 38 *Rhos* 1308 built 1918

146 Mablethorpe Miniature Railway B

Passenger-carrying 7¼in gauge railway operating on a continuous circuit

Queens Park, Mablethorpe, Lincs

This short line was regauged from 10¼in in 1971 and for a short while was steam-operated.

Stock
Mawsby Bo-BoPM No. 1958 *Nottingham–Derby* built 1971

147 Mardyke Miniature Railway B

A 7¼in gauge passenger-carrying line giving a 1 mile return journey

Coalhouse Fort, East Tilbury, Essex

The railway operates on Saturdays and Sundays, and public and school holidays, May to September. 1–5 pm weekdays, 10–6 pm on Sundays and Bank Holidays.

Stock
BR 6-car HST 125 set
BR 7-car APT set
Steam locomotives work occasionally.

148 Mr L. J. Smith C

Private 2ft gauge railway running round Mr Smith's market garden. No public access

The Bungalow, Nursery Lane, Battlesbridge, Essex
OS Ref: TQ 783965

Stock
Motor Rail 4WDM *Smudge* 8729 built 1941
Ruston Hornsby 4WDM 218016 built 1943
Baguley 0-4-0DM *Hayley* 3232 built 1947
Clark Chapman 4WBE 5667 built 1969

149 Courtaulds Ltd I

Industrial steam location with locomotives in store

Courtelle Division, P.O. Box 24, Great Coates, Grimsby, Humberside
OS Ref: TA 238124

One of the Sentinels is currently being restored by apprentices.

Stock
Sentinel 4WVBTG *William* 9599 built 1956
Sentinel 4WVBTG *George* 9596 built 1955

150 Pleasurewood Hills American Theme Park ABE

A pleasure park containing a 2ft gauge passenger-carrying railway as well as a similar 7¼in gauge line. There is also a standard gauge diesel locomotive as a static exhibit

Corton Road, Lowestoft, Suffolk
OS Ref: TM 545965

Stock
Ruston Hornsby 4wDM 305315 built 1952
Chance 4w-2-4wPH *Calamity Jane* 1795016724 built 1983 (steam outline) (2ft gauge)

7¼in gauge stock
Two steam locomotives
Two petrol locomotives
4wBE locomotive

AREA D

North East

Yorkshire
Durham
Northumberland
Cleveland
Tyne & Wear
North Humberside
(Group Nos 151–200)

151 Keighley and Worth Valley Railway A

Standard gauge steam-operated passenger-carrying railway, 5 miles long from Keighley to Oxenhope

Haworth Station, Keighley, West Yorkshire BD22 8NJ
Access: By BRITISH RAIL, Keighley Station is served by local trains from Leeds, Bradford, Skipton, Morecambe, etc. Some Leeds–Carlisle expresses also stop at Keighley.
By BUS, Services from Bradford and Leeds pass Keighley Station. Other bus services operate to Keighley from Halifax, Hebden Bridge and Todmorden (for Manchester trains), Ilkley, Skipton, Colne, Nelson, Burnley, Preston, Accrington, Blackburn and Blackpool.
By ROAD, A650 road from Bradford and Leeds, A629 road from Halifax and M62, A629 road from Skipton, A6033 road from Hebden Bridge.
Tel: Haworth 43639 (Timetable enquiries)
Haworth 45214 (All other enquiries)
OS Ref: SE 034371
K&WVRPS Details from: P. Eastham, 79 Cedar Street, Skew Bridge, Blackburn, Lancs BB1 9TQ

The Keighley and Worth Valley Railway packs more into its five-mile run than practically any other preserved railway in the British Isles. For a start, it's a complete working branch line with a main line junction with BR, several small country stations, two tunnels, two level-crossings, a viaduct and a rural terminus in the shelter of Oxenhope Moor. Its scenery varies from the industrial townscape of Keighley to pleasant West Riding countryside, whilst its collection of over 30 steam locomotives is one of the largest and most varied in the country. It was built in 1867 by the Midland Railway and operated in unspectacular fashion until closed by British Railways in 1962. The K & WVRPS was formed in that year and progressed steadily until it was able to reopen the railway in 1968.

A regular steam service has operated every weekend since then with additional services midweek in summer. Diesel railbuses operate the morning services on Saturdays and Sundays. All these trains are operated by unpaid Society Member volunteers. The Society has built up a fine collection of over thirty locomotives and a similar number of carriages, which are on display at Haworth and Oxenhope.

The railway operates on every weekend throughout the year, also on Bank Holidays and every day in July and August.

Facilities for visitors include car parking, museum, railway shops, refreshments, toilet and picnic area at Oxenhope.

Keighley and Worth Valley Railway Preservation Society Membership details from Haworth Station.

Members are entitled to Concessionary fares (up to 3 days free). They also have the chance to help in the operation of the Railway and receive a free copy of the society's quarterly magazine 'Push and Pull'.

Hire a Train
Our ordinary trains can be arranged to seat up to 450 for special visits, but we can also offer a steam-hauled Pullman train (incorporating the Jubilee Bar Car) for up to 150 persons. Another speciality is a conducted tour by diesel railbus (seating 56) which can be arranged for summer evenings.

Stock
[21]SR 4-6-2 No. 34092 *City of Wells* (Bulleid West Country Class) built 1949
[16]BR 2-6-4T No. 80002 (Riddles Class 4MT) built 1952
[6]BR 4-6-0 No. 75078 (Riddles Class 4MT) built 1956
[6]BR 2-6-0 No. 78022 (Riddles Class 2MT) built 1953
[1]L & YR 'Pug' 0-4-0ST No. 19 (Aspinall Class 21) built 1910
[1]L & YR 'Pug' 0-4-0ST No. 51218 (Aspinall Class 21) built 1901
[1]L & YR 0-6-0ST No. 752 (Beyer Peacock 1989) built 1881
[3]MR 0-6-0 No. 3924 (Fowler Class 4F) built 1920
LMS 0-6-0T No. 47279 (Fowler Class 3F) built 1924
[15]LMS 2-6-2T No. 41241 (Ivatt Class 2MT) built 1949
[22]LMS 2-6-0 No. 42765 (Hughes/Fowler Class 6P5F) built 1927
[17]LMS 4-6-0 No. 45212 (Stanier Class 5MT) built 1935
[23]LMS 2-8-0 No. 8431 (Stanier Class 8F) built 1944
Swedish State Railways 2-8-0 No. 1931 (Riddles WD Class) (Vulcan Foundry 5200) built 1945
Polish State Railways 2-8-0 No. 5820 (S160 Class) Lima 8758 built 1945
[18]SR 0-6-0T No. 72 (BR No. 30072) (USA Class) (Vulcan Iron Works 4446) built 1943
[19]GWR 0-6-0PT No. L89 (Collett Class 57XX) built 1929
[14]GWR 0-6-0PT No. 4612 (57XX Class) built 1942
[20]L and YR 0-6-0 No. 52044 (Barton Wright Class 25) built 1887
TVR 0-6-2T No. 85 (Class 02) Neilson Reid 5408 built 1899 (GWR No. 426)
RSH 0-6-0ST *Fred* 7289 built 1945
RSH 0-6-0ST No. 57 7668 built 1950
RSH 0-6-0ST No. 63 *Corby* 7761 built 1954
Barclay 0-4-0ST 2226 built 1946
[2]Haydock Foundry 0-6-0WT *Bellerophon* C built 1874

[2,4]Manning Wardle 0-6-0ST *Sir Berkeley* 1210 built 1890
Hudswell Clarke 0-6-0ST *Lord Mayor* 402 built 1893
Hudswell Clarke 0-6-0T No. 31 *Hamburg* 697 built 1903
Hudswell Clarke 0-6-0T No. 67 1379 built 1919
Hudswell Clarke 0-6-0ST No. 118 *Brussells* 1782 built 1945
Barclay 0-6-0ST No. 68077 2215 built 1947
Peckett 0-4-0DM *Austins No. 1* 5003 built 1961
Hunslet 0-6-0DM No. 32 *Huskisson* 2699 built 1944
Hudswell Clarke 0-6-0DM No. D2519 D1210 built 1962
English Electric 0-6-0DE No. D0226 2345 built 1956
Hudswell Clarke 0-6-0D No. D2511 D1202 built 1961
BR Diesel railbuses Nos E79962 & M79964 (Waggon und Maschinenbau) built 1958
LMS compartment coach No. M12066M built 1938 (KWVR No. 6)
BR Mk.1 TSO coach No. E4555 (KWVR No. 31) built 1956
BR Mk.1 TSO coach No. E4588 (KWVR No. 25) (bar car) built 1956
BR compartment brake coach No. E43345 built 1955 (KWVR No. 10)
[1]L & YR Hughes brake/third coach No. M23964M built 1910 (KWVR No. 102)
[2,7]GNR six-wheeled brake/third coach No. DE940281E built 1888
[2,8]MSLR four-wheeled coach No. 103 built 1876
[2,9]MR six-wheeled coach No. DM284677 built 1886
[2,10]SR Bulleid SO bogie coach No. S1469 built 1951
[2,11]SR BSK bogie coach No. 3554 built 1924
[2,12]Metropolitan Railway brake/third bogie coach No. 427 built 1910
[2,12]Metropolitan Railway third-class bogie coach No. 465 built 1919
[2,13]Metropolitan Railway first-class bogie coach No. 509 built 1923
[5]LNER bogie saloon No. 21661 built 1871, rebuilt 1904
BR Mk.1 brake/2nd coach No. E43145 built 1955
BR Mk.1 TSO coach No. E3825 built 1954 (KWVR No. 14)
BR compartment coach No. E46145 built 1954 (KWVR No. 15)
BR compartment coach No. E46157 built 1954 (KWVR No. 16)
BR Mk.1 TSO coach No. E4840 built 1959
BR open coach No. E48011 built 1955 (KWVR No. 17)
BR open coach No. E48018 built 1955 (KWVR No. 19)
BR Mk.1 brake/2nd coach No. 43231 built 1957
BR compartment brake coach No. E43128 built 1954 (KWVR No. 20)
LNER bogie passenger brake van No. E100E built 1948 as tool van (KWVR No. 100)
LNER Thompson sleeping car No. W1770E built 1951 (KWVR No. 103)
LNER Thompson sleeping car No. W1769E built 1951 (KWVR No. 104)
LNER bogie passenger brake van No. E70442E built 1940 (KWVR No. 105)
LNER bogie passenger brake van No. E70470E built 1939 (KWVR No. 106)
BR compartment coach No. E43003 built 1954 (KWVR No. 32)
Pullman car No. 84 *Mary* built 1930
LYR inspection saloon No. 2 (Sc45038M) built 1878
NER inspection saloon No. 1173 built 1870
BR CCT-type parcels can No. E1334E built 1950 (KWVR No. 108)
BR CCT-type parcels van No. M37224 built 1956 (KWVR No. 109)
BR CCT-type parcels van No. M37311 built 1957 (KWVR No. 110)
SR PMV 4-wheel van No. S1125S built 1936 (KWVR No. 107)
LMS Stanier bogie parcels van No. M31082 built 1940
BR 'Weltrol' 20-ton wagon No. B900802 built 1950
BR plate wagon No. B931692 built 1952
BR 'Shark' brake van No. DB993889 built 1957
LMS open VB No. M401155
SR 'Walrus' ballast hopper No. DS62041 built 1936
Shell BP oil tankers Nos A5066, A5281 and A5081 built 1938
Booth Rodley 10-ton steam crane No. 5011 built 1944
Cowans Sheldon 50-ton steam crane
Five SR PMV vehicles
Grafton 10-ton steam crane
LNER 'Dolphin' rail/sleeper wagon No. DE150667 built 1940
NCB mobile workshop (ex-LMS brake van)
LNER 20-ton 'Lowmac' wagon No. 230927 built 1939
Esso tank wagon No. 1854 built 1938

[1]Owned by L & Y Saddletanks Fund (*q.v.*).
[2]Owned by Vintage Carriages Trust (*q.v.*).
[3]Withdrawn as BR No. 43924 in 1965 and sold to Woodham Brothers, Barry, for scrap. Purchased for preservation in 1968. This locomotive was the first of the many rescued from Barry scrapyard to be restored to working order and run again under its own steam. Apart from the solitary 0-10-0 Lickey banker, this class was the largest and most powerful goods engine constructed by the Midland. They can only be described as of medium size, but throughout their long and active life worked hard on all forms of freight duties. Owned by the Midland 4F Preservation Society (*q.v.*).
[4]Built in 1890 to the order of Logan and Hemingway, contractors for the MS & LR Derbyshire lines and London Extension construction, this little engine went on to a second career in the ironstone quarrying industry before being honourably retired in 1964.
[5]Built 1871 as a six-wheeled saloon for the Stockton and Darlington Railway. Became NER No. 1661 and used as Locomotive Superintendent's saloon hauled by locomotive No. 66 *Aerolite*. Rebuilt 1904 as a bogie saloon and altered to present restored condition by LNER in 1934. Owned by North Eastern Railway 1661 Coach Partnership (*q.v.*).

[6]Owned by Standard 4 Locomotive Preservation Society Ltd (*q.v.*).

[7]This is a six-wheeled brake/third built by the GNR at Doncaster in 1888. It is restored externally to its original varnished teak finish.

[8]This four-wheeled tri-composite has one first-class, one second-class, two third-class and a central luggage compartment. It was built at Dukinfield by the Manchester, Sheffield and Lincolnshire Railway in 1876. Restoration of this carriage began in 1973.

[9]A Midland Railway six-wheeled composite having two first-class, two third-class and a central baggage compartment. This carriage was built at Derby in 1886.

[10]Built by British Railways in 1951 to a Southern Railway design by O. V. Bulleid, this carriage is a gangwayed open second. It ended its BR days in 1969 on the Eastern Region. It is restored to the livery of British Railways Southern Region.

[11]An ex-Southern Railway third-class/brake end, side corridor coach, this is the last surviving example of the distinctive South Eastern and Chatham Railway designed 'Matchboards', so called because of the unusual vertical panelling below the waist. It was built by the Metropolitan Carriage, Wagon and Finance Co at Birmingham in 1924 for use on the 'continental' trains between London, Dover and Folkestone. Withdrawn from service in 1962, it was acquired by the VCT in 1972, and has since been extensively renovated and restored to its Southern Railway livery.

[12]Two of the Metropolitan Railway's high-capacity suburban coaches of the 'Dreadnought' type, familiar to commuters from Aylesbury and the north-west London suburbs until the mid-1960s, when they were withdrawn from service by London Transport. Acquired in 1975, they have been restored to their London Transport livery. No. 427 is a seven-compartment brake/third, built by the Metropolitan Carriage, Wagon and Finance Company in 1910, and No. 465 is a nine-compartment third built by the same company in 1919.

[13]Similar to Nos 427 and 465, this is a seven-compartment first-class carriage built in 1923 by the Metropolitan Carriage, Wagon and Finance Company.

[14]Withdrawn August 1965 and sent to Woodham Bros scrapyard, Barry. Purchased for preservation and moved to the K&WVR in January 1981.

[15]Withdrawn from Skipton shed December 1966 and purchased immediately for preservation. The first member of this useful class, No. 1200, emerged from Crewe works towards the end of 1946. Building continued until 1952 when a similar Standard BR type was introduced. Only four of the class still survive – a great pity, for they are ideal modern branchline engines and would be highly suitable for operating short preserved railways.

[16]Withdrawn in March 1967, but subsequently used as a stationary boiler at Cowlairs, Glasgow. Purchased for preservation in May 1969.

[17]Built by Armstrong Whitworth & Co (Works No. 1253) in December 1935. Withdrawn from Lostock Hall shed at the end of BR steam working in August 1968 and purchased for preservation in January 1969.

[18]US Army Transportation Corps No. 1973. Taken into Southern Railway stock in April 1947. Withdrawn from Guildford shed July 1967. After withdrawal this locomotive was dispatched to Salisbury, along with the remainder of the Southern's steam fleet, whence it was purchased for preservation in January 1968. No. 72 has now been converted to oil-firing and is finished in an American-style golden-brown livery.

[19]Originally GWR No. 5775 but sold to London Transport in August 1963, becoming their No. L89. Purchased for preservation in January 1970 and since fully restored to LT lined maroon livery.

[20]Originally L & YR No. 957, a '25' class freight engine. Built by Beyer Peacock (Works No. 2840) in May 1887. Rebuilt in August 1896 and March 1906. Withdrawn from Wakefield shed in July 1959. 280 locomotives of this class were constructed, but owing to the introduction of a larger 0-6-0 and an acute shortage of shunting engines, 230 members were rebuilt as 0-6-0 saddletanks, as major repairs fell due. The remaining 50 tender engines remained intact until 1930, in which year 12 were scrapped. The remaining 38 continued to work on light goods trains, being gradually withdrawn until finally No. 52044 was taken out of service in 1959 after 72 years' service.

[21]Withdrawn in November 1964 and moved to Woodham Bros scrapyard, Barry. Purchased for preservation in October 1971 and since restored to working order.

[22]Withdrawn in December 1966 and sent to Woodham Bros scrapyard, Barry. Purchased for preservation in April 1978.

[23]Withdrawn in May 1964 and sent to Woodham Bros scrapyard, Barry. Purchased for preservation in May 1972 and since restored to working order.

Vintage Carriages Trust **H**

Details from: Secretary, Vintage Carriages Trust, c/o Haworth Station, Haworth, Keighley, West Yorkshire BD22 8NJ

The Trust has broadened its interests to encompass not just vintage coaches but has now taken under its wing the two historic industrial steam locomotives, *Sir Berkeley* and *Bellerophon*.

The Trust is now a registered charity, which further safeguards the future of its historic assets.

L & Y Saddletanks Fund **H**

Secretary: G. Hallos, 9 Fairfield Close, Ossett, Yorkshire.

Midland 4F Preservation Society **H**

Details from: Ian Johnson, 13 Shepley Close, Hazel Grove, Stockport, Cheshire SK7 6JJ.

Standard 4 Locomotive Preservation Society Ltd H

Details from: T. R. England, 105 Laudsdale Road, Rotherham, South Yorkshire S65 3NT

This society owns two locomotives, both of which were rescued from that well-known establishment at Barry. Both locomotives were withdrawn in 1966 and were bought for preservation in 1972 and 1975 respectively.

North Eastern Railway 1661 Coach Partnership H

Details from: J. B. Dawson, 20 Towton Avenue, York YO2 2DW. Tel: (0904) 51458

152 Middleton Railway A

Passenger-carrying standard gauge steam railway, 1½ miles in length

Tunstall Road/Moor Road, Leeds LS11 5JY, West Yorkshire

Access: (to Tunstall Road Halt)

By car via M1 motorway from the south to Exit 45 (Beeston, Hunslet), then turn right along Tunstall Road, then right at the roundabout. The halt is on the right. Or via the A653 to Tunstall Road traffic lights, approximately one mile from the city boundary, then turn down Tunstall Road to the roundabout and proceed as above.

By public transport: bus No. 74 or 76 from Park Row (across City Square from BR City Station) to Tunstall Road roundabout, then proceed as above.

Tel: Leeds 645424

OS Ref: SE 302309

The Middleton Railway, which can claim to be the direct descendant of Branding's Railway, authorised by Act of Parliament in 1758 (the first railway legislation), which subsequently saw the first successful commercial use of steam locomotives in 1812, was also the first standard gauge railway to be taken over by a preservation society in 1960. The undertaking is now a registered charity and a limited company, and has acquired a selection of industrial locomotives and stock in keeping with its long history of service. All work is carried out by volunteers.

All enquiries to: Mrs E. M. Lee, 71 Knightsway, Whitkirk, Leeds LS15 7BL. (Please enclosed stamped addressed envelope).

Facilities for visitors include free car parking, a small museum, railway shop, refreshments and toilets a short distance away.

The Middleton Railway is run by Rail-fans as a working museum. It is the only line of its kind that carries goods for local firms during the week, and on weekends and Bank holidays a steam-hauled visitors service. Trains leave Hunslet Moor (Tunstall Road) for Middleton (Park Gates) half hourly, from 2 pm to 4.30 pm. This service runs from Easter to the end of October. It is an inexpensive and popular way of reaching one of the largest parks in Leeds. Special trains can be arranged for parties.

Train services may be altered in accordance with demand.

Stock

Peckett 0-4-0ST (Class R4 special) 2103 built 1950
[1]Peckett 0-4-0ST *John Blenkinsop* 2003 built 1941
Hudswell Clarke 0-4-0ST *Henry de Lacy II* 1309 built 1917
Borrows 0-4-0WT *Sir Windle* 53 built 1909
Bagnall 0-4-0ST *Matthew Murray* 2702 built 1943
Hawthorn Leslie 0-4-0ST No. 6 3860 built 1935
[6]Sentinel 4WVBTG No. 59 (LNER Class Y1) 8839 built 1933
[4]NER 0-4-0 No. 1310 (LNER Class Y7) built 1891
[5]DSB 0-4-0WT No. 385 (Class HS) Hartmann 2110 built 1895
Hill/Sentinel 4WDH 138c built 1964
Hudswell Clarke 0-4-0DM *Carroll* D631 built 1946
Hudswell Clarke 0-4-0DM *Mary* D577 built 1932
[2]Hudson–Hunslet 4WDM *Courage* 1786 built 1935
Fowler 4WDM 3900002 built 1945
Fowler 0-4-0DH 4220038 built 1966
Fowler 0-4-0DH 4220029 built 1964
Wickham 4WPMR No. DB 965049 7564 built 1956
LMS goods brake van No. M158760 built 1926
LMS covered wagon
LMS open wagon
[3]Middleton colliery wagon No. 350 built 1890
LNER ballast brake/riding van built 1940
GWR four-wheeled steam crane built Thomas Booth, *c*1880
5-ton diesel crane ex NCB Glasshoughton Colliery built 1954
GWR 12-ton open wagon No. 11308
Two SCR CCT vehicles, one rebuilt as coach
Several industrial wagons in original state or converted for use on the Middleton Railway

[1]Owned jointly by the MRT and one of its members.
[2]Owned by Leeds University Union Railway and Transport Society.
[3]Static exhibit.
[4]Worsdell Class H withdrawn as LNER No. 1310 in 1931 and sold to Pelaw Main Collieries Ltd. Purchased for preservation from NCB Watergate Colliery in 1965. Owned by Steam Power Trust '65 (*q.v.*).
[5]Owned by Steam Power Trust '65 (*q.v.*).
[6]Y1 class geared shunting locomotive which spent its entire working life in the Geneva PW Yard, Darlington in LNER and BR service stock until withdrawn in September 1961. Large numbers of Sentinels of this type were used by the LNER in permanent way and sleeper depots, etc. Renumbered 8153 in 1946, 68153 by BR and Departmental No. 54 in 1954, it has now reverted to its original LNER number and livery.

Steam Power Trust '65 H

Details from: A. Bowman, 'Evergreen', Durham Road, Stockton-on-Tees, Cleveland.

153 North Yorkshire Moors Railway A

Passenger-carrying standard gauge steam railway, 18 miles in length, from Pickering to Grosmont

Pickering Station, Pickering, North Yorkshire
Access: By British Rail from Darlington, Middlesbrough and Newcastle to Grosmont Station, near Whitby; by United Bus from York and Scarborough, to Pickering, from Whitby to Goathland or Pickering; by car on the A169 from York towards Whitby, on the A171 from Middlesbrough towards Whitby, turning off at Egton for Grosmont Station
Tel: Pickering 72508, Speaking timetable 73535
OS Ref: NZ 797842

The railway is open from Easter to the end of October, with reduced services in early and late season. Please consult full timetable.
Facilities: Catering. Private trains can be booked or coaches reserved on normal trains. Bar and light refreshments available on most trains from Goathland to Pickering and return. Car parks at Grosmont and Pickering Stations. Shops at Grosmont, Goathland and Pickering Stations. Locomotive shed with inspection gallery at Grosmont.
The North Yorkshire Moors Railway is of considerable historic merit. It was constructed as long ago as 1836 by George Stephenson as a horse-worked line incorporating a 1,500-yard incline on a gradient of 1 in 10 between Grosmont and Beckhole over which trains were rope-hauled. Between Ellerbeck and Pickering the line threaded its way through sinuous Newtondale, a classic Ice-Age gorge cutting through the heart of the Moors. The line was reconstructed to make it suitable for locomotive haulage and in 1865 a four-and-a-half mile deviation route on a 1 in 49 gradient replaced the old rope-hauled incline. The railway was closed by British Railways as part of the implementations of the iniquitous Beeching Plan in 1965. But two years later, a preservation society was formed which entered into an agreement to purchase the railway, initially with the intention of operating the Grosmont–Goathland section. Subsequently the remainder of the line was also bid for and, following the issuing of a Light Railway Order, the railway was re-opened by HRH The Duchess of Kent on 1 May 1973.

Stock

NER 0-6-0 No. 2392 (Raven Class P3) built 1923
[4]SR 4-6-0 No. 841 *Greene King* (Maunsell S15 Class) built 1936
[2]LNER 2-6-0 No. 2005 (Thompson Class K1) built 1949
[1]NER 0-8-0 No. 2238 (Raven Class T2) built 1918
[7]NER 0-8-0 No. 901 (Raven Class T3) built 1919
[5]LMS 4-6-0 No. 5428 *Eric Treacy* (Stanier Class 5MT) built 1937
[7]LMS 4-6-0 No. 44767 *George Stephenson* (Stanier Class 5MT) built 1947
[7]Lambton Railway 0-6-2T No. 5 *Robert Stephenson* 3377 built 1909
[8]Lambton Railway 0-6-2T No. 29 *Kitson* 4263 built 1904
NER 0-6-0T No. 69023 *Joem* (Class J72) built 1949
[3]SR 4-6-2 No. 34010 *Sidmouth* (Bulleid Rebuilt WC Class) built 1945
[9]BR 4-6-0 No. 75014 (Riddles Class 4MT) built 1951
[16]BR 2-10-0 No. 92134 (Riddles Class 9F) built 1957
[14]BR 2-6-4T No. 80135 (Riddles Class 4MT) built 1956
[15]GWR 0-6-2T No. 6619 (Collett Class 56XX) built 1928
RSH 0-6-0T No. 31 *Meteor* 7604 built 1956
Hunslet 0-6-0ST *Antwerp* 3180 built 1944
Hudswell Clarke 0-4-0ST No. 1 *Mirvale* 1882 built 1955
[18]BR Bo-BoDE No. D8568 *Clayton* 4365U/69 built 1964
[17]BR Co-CoDE No. 55009 *Alycidon* (Class 55) English Electric 2914 built 1961
[17]BR Co-CoDE No. 55019 *Royal Highland Fusilier* (Class 55) English Electric 2924 built 1961
BR Bo-BoDE No. D5032 *Helen Thompson* (Class 24) built 1959
BR/Drewry 0-6-0DM No. D2207 2482 built 1953
[18]BR Bo-BoDH No. D821 *Greyhound* built 1960
[18]BR Bo-BoDH No. D7029 *Beyer Peacock* 7923 built 1962
BR 0-6-0DH No. D9529 *Permanent Way Institution* (Class 14) built 1965
Yorkshire Engine Company 0-4-0DE *Stanton No. 44* 2622 built 1956
Fowler 0-4-0DH No. 21 4210034 built 1954
English Electric 0-6-0DE 1553 built 1948
Baguley/Drewry 0-4-0DM No. 16 2164 built 1941

BR/Gloucester DMU E50341/E56099 (two-car set, motor brake second and trailer composite) built 1957
BR/Gloucester DMU E51118/56097 (two-car set, motor brake second and trailer composite) built 1957
BR Mk.1 FK coach No. E13102 built 1957
BR Mk.1 coaches Nos E13043, E24804 and E21100 (ex-Derwent Valley Railway) built 1957
BR Mk.1 TSO coach No. E4481 built 1957
BR Mk.1 SK coach No. E25700 built 1958
BR Mk.1 TSO coach No. E4290 built 1956
BR Mk.1 TSO coach No. SC3801 built 1953
BR Mk.1 SK coach No. E24808 built 1953
BR Mk.1 TSO coach No. E3798 built 1953
BR Mk.1 BSK coach No. E35089 built 1957
BR Mk.1 CK coach No. E15709 built 1955
BR Mk.1 BSO coaches Nos E9235 and E9267 built 1955
BR Mk.1 TSO coach No. E3860 built 1953
BR Mk.1 TSO coach No. E4597 built 1956
BR first-class buffet car No. SC79443 built 1956
BR Mk.1 SK coach No. E25142 built 1954
BR XP64 SK coach No. W25508 built 1964
BR XP64 TSO coach No. W4728 built 1964
BR Mk.1 CK coach No. E15700 built 1955
BR Mk.1 BSO coach No. SC9274 built 1956
BR Mk.1 TSO coach No. SC4198 built 1956
BR Mk.1 TSO coach No. SC4252 built 1956

BR Pullman parlour car No. E327 *Opal* built Metro Cammell 1960
BR Pullman parlour car No. E328 *Garnet* built Metro Cammell 1960
BR Pullman kitchen car No. E318 *Robin* built Metro Cammell 1960
BR Mk.1 RMB coach No. E1823 built 1960
LNER Gresley sleeping car No. 1299 built 1930
LNER Thompson coach No. DE32133
LNER Gresley buffet car No. 9129 built 1937
BR Mk.1 RFK restaurant car
[17]BR Mk.1 BSK coach No. E34699 built 1955
BR Mk.1 SK coach No. E24284 built 1951
BR Mk.1 TSO coach No. E4455 built 1957
BR Mk.1 TSO coach No. SC4207 built 1956
BR Mk.1 RKB buffet car No. E1526 built Cravens 1961
[11]H & BR semi-corridor brake third No. 5 built Birmingham RC & W 1912
[11]H & BR brake third No. 40 (R. Y. Pickering & Co) built 1907
GWR officers inspection saloon No. 80974 built 1947
[12]NER clerestory bogie autocoach No. 3453 built 1904
[12]NER main line open 3rd coach No. 945 built 1924
[12]NER 6-wheel luggage composite coach No. 1111 built 1890
LNER Gresley open 3rd coach No. 24109 built 1936
LNER Gresley open 3rd coach No. 13344 built 1936
LNER Gresley brake/3rd coach No. 3641 built Clayton Wagon Co 1926
LNER Gresley BSO bogie coach No. E16547E built 1934
LNER first-class sleeping coach No. E1259E built 1949
LNER buffet car No. E9134S built 1937
LNER Gresley suburban brake/3rd No. RDE320779 built 1926
LMS Stanier corridor/3rd coach No. 1782 built 1934 (converted to sleeping coach)
LMS 1st class 12-wheel sleeping car No. 378 built 1951
LNER corridor composite coach No. 18477 built 1950
LNER composite coach No. 88339 built 1947
LNER Gresley mess and tool coach built 1924
GCR 'Barnum' brake/third-class coach No. 695 built 1911
GNR bogie brake/composite coach No. 2856 built 1898
BR DMU buffet cars Nos SC59098 and SC59099 converted to camping coaches built 1960
Six Wickham petrol rail trolleys
Seven five-plank open wagons
Pullman brake/third coach No. 79 built 1928
LNER 45-ton steam crane No. 107 Cowans Sheldon 4524 built 1926 plus runner wagon No. ADE330107
LNER CCT No. E1322 built 1950
NER 20-ton hopper wagons Nos 4503, 4551 and 4561
GNR eight-wheeled 20-ton goods brake van No. 23791 built 1914
NER LWB ballast brake van No. DE58033 built 1914
SR CCT van No. S2530 built 1955
Two 'Walrus' 40-ton bogie ballast wagons
LMS 23-ton goods brake van No. M732170 built 1946
BR plate wagon No. B932267
SR 'Borail' wagon No. DS64752
NER 12-ton goods van No. 101707 built 1911
LNER 10-ton goods van No. 632802 built 1923
GWR 10-ton open wagons Nos 77306 and A893 built 1908
Shell-Mex Ltd tank wagon No. 7285 built 1943
[11]H & BR 18ft 6in open wagon No. 3697 (C. Roberts & Co) built 1905
[11]H & BR 15ft 6in open wagon (believed to be No. 577) (Ashbury RCW) built 1886
[11]H & BR four-wheeled engineer's van No. 2 (Metropolitan RC & W) built 1885
British Molasses tank wagon
NER 10-ton wagon No. 104
LNER BZ van (used as PW tool van) No. E70687 built 1950
10-ton open wagon No. 117 (used by C & W Department)
[8]GWR long-wheelbase fruit van No. 642432 (used as Tool Van)
[11]H & BR 5-plank open wagon No. AD46025
3 BR 'Herring' hopper wagons
BR 'Plate' wagons Nos B933122, B934279 and B934386
LNER 'Weltrol' well-wagon
SR 'Walrus' 40-ton ballast wagons Nos DS62058 & DS62064 built 1947
[13]LNER vacuum-fitted goods brake van No. 246710 built 1941
[13]GCR single bolster wagon No. 14 (NYMR No. 110) built 1920
[13]NER 26-ton six-wheeled snowplough No. DE900572 built 1909
[13]GNR double bolster wagon No. 1352 (NYMR No. 111) built 1920
[13]LSWR Lowmac SB wagon No. DS63024 built 1921
[13]NER covered goods van No. 75544 built 1915
[6]LNER 10-ton tool van No. 53829 built 1923
LNER BG No. E110E built 1947
Five-ton diesel mobile crane
Three-ton Coles diesel electric mobile road crane
Dumper, air compressor and Chaseside loader for coal

[1]Withdrawn from Sunderland in 1967 as BR No. 63395 (LNER Class Q6), 2238 was one of 120 0-8-0s built by the North Eastern Railway for working heavy coal traffic. Powerful engines, built with superheated boilers and steam reversing gear, they were popular with drivers all over the region. After withdrawal was sold by BR to a scrap dealer in Blyth, but a determined effort by NELPG members raised the purchase price of £2,300 within the incredible time of only five months, enabling the engine to be purchased on 1 April 1968. The engine has now been vacuum-fitted and entered traffic on the NYMR in June 1970.

[2]Thompson Class K1 locomotive withdrawn in 1967 as BR 62005. Built by the North British Locomotive Co Ltd, Glasgow, the K1 worked its full life in the north-east and gained fame by working several 'royal' trains and

enthusiast specials. No. 62005 was donated to the NELPG by the 5428 Stanier Black Five Preservation Society Ltd in 1972. A restoration appeal raised £1,200, which enabled a major overhaul and retubing to be undertaken, including repainting in LNER apple green livery and numbered 2005. The engine entered NYMR service in June 1974.

[4]Withdrawn as BR No. 30841 in 1964 and sold to Woodham Brothers, Barry, for scrap. Purchased for preservation in 1972. Owned by the Essex Locomotive Society Ltd.

[5]No. 5428 was built by Armstrong Whitworth & Co (Works No. 1483) and was a standard member of the class with Walschaert's valve gear; withdrawn from Leeds (Holbeck) in 1967 as BR No. 45428. Owned by 45428 Stanier Blacl Five Preservation Society Ltd (*q.v.*).

[3]Withdrawn March 1965 and sent to Woodham Bros scrapyard, Barry. Purchased for preservation and moved to the NYMR in 1981.

[9]Withdrawn December 1966 and sent to Woodham Bros scrapyard, Barry. Purchased for preservation and moved to the NYMR in February 1981.

[16]Withdrawn December 1966 and sent to Woodham Bros scrapyard, Barry. Purchased for preservation and moved to the NYMR in December 1980. Moved to Brightlingsea, Essex for restoration 1984.

[6]Owned by the North Eastern Locomotive Preservation Group (*q.v.*).

[7]In the care of the North Eastern Locomotive Preservation Group (*q.v.*). On loan from the National Collection.

[8]Owned by the Lambton No. 29 Locomotive Syndicate (*q.v.*).

[11]Owned by the Hull and Barnsley Railway Stock Fund (*q.v.*).

[12]Owned by the North Eastern Railway Coach Group (*q.v.*).

[13]Owned by the Hexham Rolling Stock Group (*q.v.*).

[14]Withdrawn July 1965 and sent to Woodham Bros scrapyard, Barry. Purchased for preservation in April 1973.

[15]Withdrawn March 1963 and sent to Woodham Bros scrapyard, Barry. Purchased for preservation in October 1974.

[17]Owned by the Deltic Preservation Society.

[18]Owned by the Diesel Traction Group.

45428 Stanier Black Five Preservation Society Ltd **H**

Details from: J. B. Hollingsworth, 'Creua', Llanfrothen, Penrhyndeudraeth, Gwynedd LL48 6SH
Tel: 0766-770-534

North Eastern Locomotive Preservation Group **H**

Registered Charity No. 261122

Group members receive six technical and informative newsletters each year about NYMR locomotive news and have the opportunity to attend regular meetings in Newcastle upon Tyne to hear first-class speakers. There is a very active sales service and special opportunities to participate in the North Yorkshire Moors Railway Locomotive Department, and reduced fares to travel on the picturesque Grosmont to Pickering line.

Details from: Peter Robinson, 53 West Dene Drive, North Shields, Tyne and Wear.

Hull and Barnsley Railway Stock Fund **H**

Apart from its preservation activities, the Group specialises in collecting tools, equipment and historical data appertaining to the H & BR.

The Stock Fund was formed in March 1968 after the discovery and for the purchase of H & BR coach No. 5 at Springhead workshops. Two H & BR open wagons from the Port of Tyne Authority and coach No. 40 from York were acquired in 1969 and engineers van No. 2 in 1974. Coach No. 5 hauled by Borrows Well Tank No. 3 formed the first passenger train on the NYMR since closure of the line in 1965. No. 40 was used on members only trains in the early 1970s and as a stationary Buffet at Pickering in 1974–5. Both coaches have been subsequently used for fiction film sequences. Our latest addition is H & BR 5-plank open wagon (Army No. 46025) which we intend to dismantle for spare parts which will be used to rebuild H & BR wagon No. 577.

Details from: A. Halman, 6 Chequerfield Court, Chequerfield Avenue, Pontefract, Yorkshire WF8 2TQ.

Lambton No. 29 Locomotive Syndicate **H**

Secretary: J. M. Richardson, c/o Midland Bank Ltd, 1 Murray Street, Filey, North Yorkshire YO14 9DB

North Eastern Railway Coach Group **H**

Secretary: P. J. Brumby, 48 Laburnum Walk, Gilberdyke, Brough, North Humberside HU15 2TU

Life membership of the Group by purchase of one or more shares in any of the Group's vehicles.

Hexham Rolling Stock Group **H**

Details from: G. Hall, 24 Welton Close, Stocksfield, Northumberland NE43 7EP

Formed in 1972 as a temporary arrangement to raise funds and purchase a much needed fitted goods brake van for the NYMR. On completion of this project the Group became permanent and has since purchased further essential goods vehicles for the railway. The Group has also preserved two small industrial locomotives (RSH 0-4-0ST *Eustace Forth* and Armstrong Whitworth 0-4-0DE *Hexhamshire*), both on loan to the National Railway Museum at York.

Many items have been purchased and restored for a small museum at Wylam, Northumberland, the village now known as the 'Cradle of railways'. This museum of local history has special reference to George Stephenson,

Hedley and Hackworth and the Newcastle–Carlisle line. The Museum is located at Falcon Terrace, Wylam, Northumberland and was officially opened by Dr John Coiley, Keeper of the National Railway Museum, on 9 June 1981 to coincide with the bi-centenary of the birth of George Stephenson.
The museum is open at weekends and during afternoons and evenings on Tuesdays and Thursdays.
Tel: Wylam 3520

154 Tanfield Railway A

Passenger-carrying standard gauge steam railway, currently 1 mile in length but being extended

Headquarters: Marley Hill Engine Shed, Marley Hill, Tyne and Wear
Access: One mile south of Sunniside, off the A6076 Sunniside–Stanley road, 5 miles south-west of Gateshead. Buses Nos 701/704 connect from Marlborough Crescent Bus Station, Newcastle, alighting at Andrews House
Tel: Newcastle 742002
OS Ref: NZ 207573

The railway is in operation every Bank Holiday Sunday and Monday from Easter to August and every Sunday in July and August. Marley Hill shed is open every Sunday throughout the year from 10 am to 5 pm.
Facilities for visitors include railway shop, refreshments, car parking and toilets.
The Tanfield Waggonway, the most famous of the wooden waggonways, was opened in 1725, replacing earlier lines used by the owners, the Grand Allies, its advanced engineering features, such as the Causey Arch and Embankment, still stand today and some will be used by the Tanfield Railway. The railway is being built on a three-mile section of the waggonway between Sunniside and East Tanfield.
Thus the Tanfield Railway lays claim to being the oldest existing railway in the world. The longstanding industrial character is being retained in the railway with its resemblance to the self-contained minor and colliery railways of former years. These lines used locos from the private manufacturers and most had small, non-bogie coaches. A large collection of steam locomotives has been acquired for use on the Tanfield Railway, many of them built in Newcastle, whilst the railway is constructing its own coaches, typical of those used on the minor railways.
This is the only standard gauge railway *not* using bogie carriages, and the only one offering authentic minor railway mixed trains for discerning enthusiasts.

Stock
Black Hawthorn 0-4-0ST *Wellington* 266 built 1873
R. W. Hawthorn 0-4-0ST No. 3 *Enterprise* 2009 built 1884
Barclay 0-6-0ST *Horden* 1015 built 1906
Hawthorn Leslie 0-4-0ST *Cyclops* 2711 built 1907
Barclay 0-4-2ST No. 6 1193 built 1910
Hawthorn Leslie 0-4-0ST No. 2 2859 built 1911
Borrows 0-4-0WT No. 3 37 built 1898
Barclay 0-6-0T No. 17 1338 built 1913
Barclay 0-4-0ST No. 32 1659 built 1920
Hawthorn Leslie 0-6-0ST *Stagshaw* 3513 built 1923
Hawthorn Leslie 0-6-0ST No. 3 3575 built 1923
Hudswell Clarke 0-4-0ST *Irwell* 1672 built 1937
Bagnall 0-6-0ST *Gamma* 2779 built 1945
Barclay 0-6-0ST No. 68078 (Class J94) 2212 built 1946
RSH 0-6-0ST *Lysaght's* 7035 built 1940
RSH 0-4-0CT *Hendon* 7007 built 1940
RSH 0-4-0ST *Sir Cecil A. Cochrane* 7409 built 1948
Hudswell Clarke 0-6-0T No. 38 1823 built 1949
R. Stephenson & Hawthorns 0-6-0ST No. 49 7098 built 1943
R. Stephenson & Hawthorns 0-6-0ST No. 16 7944 built 1957
Sentinel 4WVBTG No. 4 9559 built 1953
R. Stephenson & Hawthorns 0-6-0ST No. 44 7760 built 1953
R. Stephenson & Hawthorns 0-6-0ST No. 38 7763 built 1954
R. Stephenson & Hawthorns 0-4-0ST No. 21 7796 built 1954
Black Hawthorn 0-4-0T No. 11 *Eschucha* 748 built 1883 (600mm gauge)
Hawthorn Leslie 0-6-0F *Huncoat No. 3* 3746 built 1929
Barclay 0-4-0DH *F.C.F.* 552 built 1968
Armstrong Whitworth 0-4-0DE No. 2 D22 built 1933
Joshua Wilson 10-ton steam crane *Joshua*

Working Collection
These vehicles comprise the regular working carriages and wagons on the railway. All are vacuum brake fitted, a requirement for all trains carrying passengers.
Balcony saloon carriage No. 1 built 1976
Balcony saloon carriage No. 2 built 1977
Brake saloon carriage No. 3 built 1982
Brake saloon carriage No. 4
Covered wagon No. 19
Open wagon No. 77
Open wagon No. 90
Covered wagon No. 105
Covered wagon No. 111
Covered wagon No. 115
Covered wagon No. 129
Covered wagon No. 131
Two BR ballast brake vans converted for passenger-carrying

Industrial Railway Vehicles Collection
A small collection of the various types of vehicles used on the industrial railways of the north east has been built up. They are not intended for regular working on the railway but are mainly for display, giving an insight into the appearance of colliery railways etc during the heyday of those lines.

Ashington Coal Co brake van No. 665
Bowes Railway 10-ton hopper wagon No. 608
Cowpen Coal Co 20-ton hopper wagon
Dorman Long & Co 4-wheel saloon carriage built *c*1880
Heworth Coal Co 10-ton hopper wagon No. 210
Lambton Hetton & Joicey Collieries 10-ton hopper wagon
Londonderry Railway black wagon
North-Eastern Electric Supply Co 20-ton hopper wagon No. 16 built 1921
North-Eastern Electric Supply Co 20-ton hopper wagon No. 25 built 1921
North-Eastern Electric Supply Co 20-ton hopper wagon No. 33 built 1921
Pelaw Main Collieries 10-ton hopper wagon No. 1207
Pontop & Jarrow Railway 10-ton hopper wagon No. 359
Tyne Improvement Commission bogie
Tyne Improvement Commission flat wagon
Tyne Improvement Commission flat wagon
Tyne Improvement Commission flat wagon
Tyne Improvement Commission flat wagon
Tyne Improvement Commission flat wagon

Reserve Collection
These vehicles are, in the course of time, due for restoration and return to regular working on the railway as part of the main working collection.
Great Northern Railway 5 compt 3rd carriage
Great Northern Railway 5 compt composite carriage built *c*1870
North Eastern Railway 5 compt 3rd carriage built 1882
North Eastern Railway 3 compt 3rd brake carriage
North Eastern Railway family saloon carriage
North Eastern Railway 1st saloon carriage
North Eastern brake van No. 28662 built 1894
Storage van

Tanfield Railway Co details may be obtained from Mr E. Maxwell, 33 Stocksfield Avenue, Newcastle upon Tyne NE5 2DX.

155 Beamish — ABE

Beamish is a 200-acre site housing a comprehensive reconstruction of all aspects of life in the North of England. Particular emphasis is placed on the significant industrial history of the region and so railways figure largely in the museum. There is a ¼ mile standard gauge track on which visitors can see a full-scale working replica of George Stephenson's Locomotion No. 1*, and a ½ mile standard gauge track in the railway area. Also a ½ mile electric tramway*

North of England Open-Air Museum, Stanley, Tyne & Wear
Access: A1(M) to Chester-le-Street turnoff, A693 towards Stanley. Beamish is signposted on all major surrounding roads during the summer months.
Bus route No. 704 from Marlborough Crescent, Newcastle upon Tyne, Bus route No. 775 from Market Place, Chester-le-Street and Sunderland
Tel: Stanley (0207) 31811
OS Ref: NZ 217547

The Museum is open every day April to September inclusive from 10 am to 6 pm. Closed on Mondays during the rest of the year. Last admission is always 1 hour before closing time.
Facilities for visitors include car parking, museum shop, Victorian pub, refreshments and toilets.
The Museum shows the past way of life in the North East around the early 1900s. Collecting commenced in 1958, and there was a preliminary opening in 1971 followed by an official opening in 1972. Since then a railway area with station, footbridges, goods shed, signal box and weighbridge house has been rebuilt on the site and visitors can ride behind a steam locomotive. At Home Farm visitors can see traditional northern farm animals, exhibitions and a large collection of farm implements and carts. A complete Northern colliery has been rebuilt on the site and here visitors can see an old pit cage, an 1855 steam winding engine in operation, furnished pit cottages and go down a 'drift' mine to see how coal was worked. Demonstrations of pottery throwing, hand printing, bread baking, 'proggy' mat making and smithing.
A society has been formed of those interested in the project, known as 'Friends of the North of England Open-Air Museum', and currently has a membership of 800.

Details from: The Museum Secretary.

Stock
[1]NER 0-6-0 No. 876 (BR No. 65033) (LNER Class J21) built 1889
Stephenson 0-4-0 *Locomotion* (Replica) built 1975
[4]Stephenson 0-4-0 Hetton Colliery loco built 1822
Stephenson 0-6-0T No. 3 *Twizell* 2730 built 1891
Hawthorn Leslie 0-4-0ST No. 14 3056 built 1914
[2]Stockton Ironworks 0-4-0ST *South Durham Malleable No. 5* built 1900
Head Wrightson 0-4-0VBT built 1871
Lewin 0-4-0T No. 18 built 1863
[3]Black Hawthorn 2-4-0VBCT E No. 1 897 built 1887
Ruston Hornsby 4WDM 476140 built 1963
NER luggage composite coach No. 818 built 1903
NER luggage composite coach No. 1149 built 1900
NER third-class bogie coach No. 1972 built 1911
NER third-class bogie coach No. 118 built 1913
NER snowplough No. 20 built 1909
NER stores van No. 5523 built 1902
NER 6-wheel tool van No. 92189 built 1899
NER fire engine wagon No. 03938 built 1903
NER 20-ton loco coal wagon No. 69468 built *c*1900
NER 12-ton box van No. 102833
NER 15-ton tranship van No. 8635
NER 12-ton coal wagons Nos 1077, 1285, 1319 built *c*1890
NER 20-ton coal wagon No. 46153 built 1910

NER oil tank wagon No. 8935 built c1920
GWR 10-ton 'Mink A' van No. 95861 built 1917
2500 gallon oil tank wagon No. 41 built 1915
Thrislington Colliery 8-ton coal wagon No. 81 built c1880
Ward 1-ton hand crane, with runner built 1937
3-ton side-tipping stone wagon built 1937 c1870
29 2½-ton Chaldron wagons built c1880
Smith/Rodley steam crane No. 8371 built 1913
NER 'Birdcage' goods brake van No. 44824 built 1895

[1]Two-hundred-and-one of these useful locomotives were acquired by the LNER at the grouping. Most of the class were built as Worsdell-Von Borries two-cylinder compounds, but all had been rebuilt as simple-expansion locomotives before 1923. The class were equally at home on passenger or freight trains and No. 876 must certainly be the luckiest engine to be preserved, since it survived to become the last member of its class, having been withdrawn at the outbreak of World War II but reinstated a month later. It was set aside for possible preservation by BR, but the decision was later reversed and the engine sold to a scrap merchant. In the nick of time it was purchased for the Beamish Hall collection, a fitting end for a machine that saw 73 years hard work in its native north-east.
[2]Origin not recorded, but most likely built by Stockton Ironworks.
[3]Ex Consett Iron Co Ltd.

The following standard gauge electric tramcars are maintained at Beamish for use on the Museum's passenger-carrying tramway:
Sheffield 4-wheel double deck tramcar No. 513 built 1950
Gateshead bogie single-deck tramcar No. 10 built 1925
Sheffield 4-wheel double-deck tramcar No. 342 built 1907
Newcastle and Gosforth horse tram No. 49

Also on display is a large collection of horse-drawn vehicles including trader's vans, fire engine, gypsy caravans, sleigh and fine collection of Northumbrian carts.
Visitors can also see buses, trolley bus, trams, fire engines and coal wagons.

156 Yorkshire Dales Railway — A

Passenger-carrying standard gauge steam railway, currently 1 mile in length

Embsay Station, Embsay, Skipton, North Yorkshire
Access: 2 miles from Skipton off the A59 Harrogate Road. On bus routes 75 & 76 from Skipton
Tel: Skipton 4727
OS Ref: SE 007533

Embsay station is open every weekend throughout the year. Steam trains operate on certain Sundays and Bank Holidays. Facilities for visitors include car parking, museum (open when steaming), railway shop, refreshments (summer weekends), chemical toilets, miniature steam railway (summer Sundays) and a 2ft gauge line under construction.
Founded in 1968, the YDR is based on a 1¼-mile stretch of the former Midland Railway Skipton–Ilkley line. Initial plans to operate the Grassington branch were thwarted in the early seventies, so the aim now is to relay and run the 3½ miles to Bolton Abbey.
Emphasis has been laid on establishing a collection of industrial tank locomotives, these being the most suitable for the line.
The railway is now administered by the 'Museum Trust' and is entirely run by volunteers.
Details from: Jonathan Youdan, 22 Mount Street, Oatlands, Harrogate HG2 8DQ.

Stock
[2]LMS 2-8-0 No. 48151 (Stanier Class 8F) built 1942
Hudswell Clarke 0-6-0ST *Dorothy* 1450 built 1922
Hudswell Clarke 0-6-0ST *Slough Estates Ltd No. 5* 1709 built 1939
Hunslet 0-6-0ST *Primrose No. 2* 3715 built 1951
Peckett 0-4-0ST *City of Carlisle* 2085 built 1948
Sentinel 4WVBTG *Ann* 7232 built 1927
Hunslet 0-6-0ST *Wheldale* 3168 built 1944
Hunslet 0-6-0ST *Airedale* 1440 built 1923
Hunslet 0-6-0ST *Darfield No. 1* 3783 built 1953
Yorkshire Engine Co 0-4-0ST *City Link* 2474 built 1949
Hudswell Clarke 0-6-0ST No. S140 1821 built 1948
Hunslet 0-6-0ST *Monckton No. 1* 3788 built 1952
[1]Hunslet 0-6-0ST No. 7 *Spitfire* 2414 built 1941
Hunslet 0-6-0ST *Beatrice* 2705 built 1945
Hunslet 0-6-0ST No. 69 3785 built 1953
[1]Barclay 0-4-0ST No. 22 *Defiant* 2320 built 1952
RSH 0-4-0ST *Thomas* 7661 built 1950
Peckett 0-4-0ST *Annie* 1159 built 1908
BR/Drewry 0-6-0DM No. D2203 *Hemelite* (Class 03) 2400 built 1952
Baguley/Drewry 4WDM *Bug* 2136 built 1938
Fowler 0-4-0DM *H. W. Robinson* 4100003 built 1946
Ruston Hornsby 4WDM No. 887 394009 built 1955
Ruston Hornsby 4WDM 294263 built 1950
Wickham 4WPMR No. DB965095 7610 built 1957
LNER Gresley TO bogie coach No. 43636 built 1935
LNER Gresley TO bogie coach No. 43654 built 1935
LNER Gresley TO bogie coach No. 52256 built 1935
BR Mk.1 RMB buffet car No. SC 1826 built 1960
BR Mk.1 BSK coach No. E21261 built 1963
BR Mk.1 TSO coach No. E4460 built 1957
BR Mk.1 SK coach No. E25472 built 1958
BR Mk.1 CK coach No. E15952 built 1957
BR Mk.1 sleeping car
NER 6-wheel directors' saloon No. 41 built 1896
BR compartment bogie coach No. E46235 built 1954
LNER Gresley brake/3rd coach No. ADE 320984 built 1930 (converted to riding van)

SR four-wheel PMV parcels van
LNER fruit van
WD box van No. 47729
LMS box van WD No. 47803
WD brake van No. 49007 built SR 1942
NCB steel hopper wagon No. WH10 built Metro-Cammell 1936
BEA low flat machinery wagon
LMS 4-plank open wagon No. PC197
SR 'BY' 4-wheel parcels/brake van No. S798 built 1939
BP fuel tanker wagon built Charles Roberts 1950
LNER 8-plank mineral wagon
CEGB 20-ton hopper wagon built Metro-Cammell 1947
Smith Rodley steam crane No. 11108

9½in gauge Stock
Freelance 2-4-2 *King Tut* built in 1932 by Stephen Smith
One Pullman car
Three open bogie coaches built *c*1926
One bogie wagon

2ft gauge Stock
Motor Rail 4WDM 5213 built 1930
Motor Rail 4WDM 5979 built 1946
Ruston Hornsby 4WDM No. 22 175418 built 1936
Lister 4WPM 9993 built 1938
Lister 4WPM 10225 built 1938
Skip wagons

[1]Locomotives owned by Steam Enterprises Ltd (see Group No. 254).
[2]Withdrawn in January 1968 and sent to Woodham Bros scrapyard, Barry. Purchased for preservation November 1975. Undergoing restoration elsewhere.

157 Bowes Railway ABE

Standard gauge operating industrial railway 1½ miles in length offering short steam-hauled rides, demonstrations of rope-worked inclines, historic workshops and static exhibits

The Bowes Railway Company Ltd, Springwell, near Gateshead, Tyne and Wear
Access: Adjacent to Level Crossing in Springwell Village, on B1288 road between Gateshead and the A1(M) near Washington
Buses from Newcastle leave Worswick Street bus station. Northern buses Nos 183, 188 and 189 from Newcastle, 181 from Chester-le-Street, and 188 and 638 from Sunderland all stop at the gate
Tel: Washington 461847
OS Ref: NZ 285588

Operating takes place on Bank Holiday Sundays and Mondays and the first Sunday of each month, from Easter Monday to October, plus some other dates advertised locally. The railway is open on non-operating weekends from 10.45 am to 4.30 pm. Operating days open from 12 noon to 5 pm.

Facilities for visitors include car parking, museum, refreshments, toilets, souvenir shop, exhibitions of documents, etc and historic wagons, guided tours round workshops. There are no admission or car park charges.
The Bowes Railway (called the Pontop and Jarrow Railway until 1932) was one of a number of large colliery railways developed to carry coal to the rivers of North-East England for shipment. Its oldest section, from Mount Moor Colliery via Springwell to Jarrow, was designed by George Stephenson and opened in 1826. At its fullest extent the railway, owned by John Bowes & Partners Ltd, was 15 miles long, and during its life it served 13 collieries, with another three on a section of the Pelaw Main Railway, which was linked to it in 1955. It had seven rope-worked inclines and three locomotive-worked sections, and for a time ran its own passenger service. For nearly 150 years it fulfilled its purpose without any radical alteration, but colliery closures have meant that from 1974 only the section from Monkton to Jarrow has remained in use by the NCB.
As the Railway was not only a direct link to George Stephenson but an almost unique early relic of the Industrial Revolution, Tyne and Wear County Council decided to preserve part of the line, and in March 1976 it purchased the main line between Black Fell Bank Head (near the former Mount Moor Colliery) and Springwell Bank Head, together with two electric winding engines, the lineside buildings and a large number of wagons. This section, part of the 1826 line, consists of two inclines (750 yards at 1 in 15 approx and 1170 yards at 1 in 70 approx) operated by the Blackham's Hill Engine, which are thus the only preserved rope inclines in the world. This was followed in September 1977 by the purchase of the Railway's Engineering and Wagon Shops at Springwell with much of their machinery, at the eastern end of the preserved section. The whole Railway, its buildings and machinery, is now a scheduled Ancient Monument protected by the Department of the Environment. The Tyne and Wear Industrial Monuments Trust, a registered charity set up in 1975 and run by volunteers, is the Council's agent in restoration work and in operating the Railway for the public. Public passenger operation commenced on 1 July 1979 in a provisional form, but following the granting of a Light Railway Order in 1981, an extended service now carries visitors between the workshops complex and the rope-haulage demonstrations at Blackham's Hill.

Stock
RSH 0-6-0ST No. 77 *Norwood* 7412 built 1948
[1]Barclay 0-4-0ST No. 22 2274 built 1949
Barclay 0-4-0ST *WST* 2361 built 1954
[3]Hibberd 4WDM No. 101 3922 built 1959
Smith 4-wheeled crane 18773 built 1948
Wagons – 10-ton hopper wagons
Darlington Wagon & Engineering No. 122 built 1887
Darlington Wagon & Engineering Nos 197, 202, 210

Springwell Shops Nos 6, 80, 289, 308, 364, 406, 511, 525, 572, 573, 605, 649, 701, 717, 775, 782, 788, 790, 842, 939, 971 built 1897
Ex-NER Nos 1104, 1107, 1111, 1160, 1212, 1220, 1254, 1255, 1289
Watts Hardy Nos 1611, 1615
3-plank wagons Nos B24 and B39
Flat wagons Nos B3 and B51
Local coal wagon No. 1424
Kibblesworth drift bogie (used in rope haulage shunting of sidings)
Reel wagon (used for unwinding new rope on inclines)
[2]Brake van No. 1
GER tool van
MR goods brake van No. 1872 built 1920
LMS goods brake van No. 3
LMS goods brake van No. 730202 built 1936 (converted to mobile booking office)
Two NER hopper wagons Nos 888 and 947 (for spares)
NCB side-tipping steel chaldron wagon

[1]The only steam locomotive purchased new for the Railway still surviving; acquired on loan from Thomas Ness Ltd in June 1976.
[2]Built by Lambton, Hetton & Joicey Collieries Ltd at their Philadelphia Shops in 1933 to run over LNER between Penshaw and Sunderland; acquired in March 1977.
[3]The first diesel to be purchased by NCB No. 6 Area. It worked on the now preserved line and the Pelaw Main Branch.
Details can be obtained from: Tyne and Wear Industrial Monuments Trust, Sandyford House, Archbold Terrace, Newcastle upon Tyne NE2 1ED. Tel: Newcastle (0632) 816144

158 Whorlton Lido Railway A

A 15in gauge line opened in 1971 in attractive surroundings in a popular beauty spot on the Yorkshire bank of the River Tees, offering a ride of over ½ mile in length

Whorlton Lido, Whorlton Bridge, Barnard Castle, County Durham
Access: Near to A66 and A1(M) roads
Tel: Whorlton 397
OS Ref: NZ 106146

The railway operates from Easter until the end of September every weekend. The line is also in operation on most days during the school holiday periods, subject to demand and weather conditions.
Facilities for visitors include car parking, refreshments, toilets, souvenir shop, swimming, fishing, etc.
Future developments will include signalling, other lineside equipment and possible extension of the line itself.

Stock
Bassett-Lowke 4-4-2 *King George* 21 built 1912
Severn-Lamb 2-8-0DH No. 278 R9 built 1976 (steam outline)
Coleby-Simkins Bo-BoDM *Wendy* built 1972
Four 12-seater bogie coaches
Three open bogie coaches ex-Lambton Pleasure Park Railway

It is proposed to add further items of rolling stock in due course. The management meanwhile offers facilities to any 15in gauge locomotive owner who would like to try out his locomotive on the railway.

159 Newby Hall Miniature Railway A

A 10¼in gauge line running for nearly half a mile along the wooded banks of one of the most secluded stretches of the River Ure

Newby Hall, Skelton-on-Ure, Ripon, Yorkshire HG4 5AE
Access: 4 miles south-east of Ripon, off B6265 road, 3 miles west of A1
Tel: Boroughbridge 2583
OS Ref: SE 3468

The railway crosses a lifting steel bridge over the old ferry boat shipway, runs through a deep cutting and a tunnel and then returns through the station to the garden, crossing rock pools and running through groves of bamboo.
The train operates when the house is open: 1.00 pm to 5.30 pm April, May and September on Wednesday, Thursday, Saturday and Sunday. June, July and August every day except Mondays but open Bank Holiday Mondays. Easter and Bank Holidays.
The gardens are open from 11.00 am to 5.30 pm April 1 to September 30 every day except Mondays but open Bank Holiday Mondays.
Other facilities for visitors include car parking and picnic area, late C17th house, twenty-five acres of gardens and adventure gardens for children.

Stock
LMS 4-6-0 No. 6100 *Royal Scot* built Battison 1950
Severn-Lamb Bo-BoPH *Countess de Grey* built 1973
Six open bogie coaches

160 Lightwater Valley Railway A

Passenger-carrying 15in gauge railway opened in 1979. The line is in the form of a continuous loop just over a mile in length. There are three stations serving the various amenities in the park, a long tunnel and deep cuttings

Lightwater Valley Visitor Farm and Country Park, North Stainley, near Ripon, North Yorkshire, HG4 3HT
Access: Situated on the main road to the Dales (A6108) between Ripon and Masham at North Stainley. Whether travelling from the north or the south, head for Ripon and

pick up the A6108, following the signs for Masham and Lightwater Valley
Tel: Ripon (0765) 85321/85213
OS Ref: SE 285756

A four-road engine shed built in traditional 1860's style accommodates the line's collection of historic, working 15in gauge locomotives. This building also incorporates a museum, workshop, exhibition model railway and railway shop.
Lightwater now also houses a large collection of traction engines, steam rollers, showman's engines, fairground organ and threshing machine, all in working order, and these can be seen working on most weekends. An annual Grand Steam Working is held each September.
Other steam-driven attractions are Messrs Screeton Bros 19th-century steam-worked Galloping Horses Carousel, in action at weekends and daily during the peak season.
The main attractions at Lightwater Valley include boat rides, an enormous and somewhat dangerous adventure playground, a nine hole golf course, covered golf driving range, putting greens, archery range, three restaurants, various shops, crafts, cross-country rides on 'go anywhere' amphibious vehicles, mini motorbike rides, fifty acres of self-pick fruit, a modern piggery where it is usually possible to watch piglets being born.
Open April–May weekends only plus Bank Holidays and Easter Tuesday 10.30 am–dusk. May–August 10.30 am–7 pm daily. September weekends only 11 am–6 pm. October Sundays only 11.30 am–dusk. Last entrance 1 hour prior to closing.

Stock
Bassett-Lowke 4-4-2 *Little Giant* built 1905
Craven 4-4-0 No. 111 *Yvette* (LNER D49 Class) built 1946
Bassett-Lowke 4-4-4PMT (LNER No. 1326) *Blacolvesley* built 1909 (steam outline)
LMS 4-6-0 No. 6100 *Royal Scot* built Carland
Severn-Lamb 2-8-0DH No. 278 built 1979 (steam outline)
Two semi-open covered bogie coaches
Four open bogie coaches
Steam breakdown crane *Little Titan* built Cheeseman 1975

161 South Tynedale Railway Preservation Society — F

Passenger-carrying 2ft gauge railway along part of the trackbed of the former Haltwhistle–Alston branch line

The Railway Station, Alston, Cumbria CA9 3JB (all enquiries to this address please)
Access: A686, A689 & B6277 roads
Nearest BR station – Haltwhistle (13 miles)
Buses – Ribble 681 (Haltwhistle–Alston), Wright Bros 888 (Newcastle–Alston–Keswick). Alston Station is just off the A686 (Hexham) road; five minutes walk from the town centre
Tel: (0498) 81696
OS Ref: NY 717467

Passenger trains operate on the first 1½ mile section (Alston to Gilderdale Burn) from Spring Bank Holiday to the end of September.
Negotiations are continuing with the Tourist Board and Northumberland County Council regarding an extension of the line from Gilderdale to Slaggyford.
Facilities at Alston Station: Car park, picnic area, toilets, plus bookshop and tourist information centre, railway and local interest books, maps, gifts, tourist board publications, local information and accommodation booking service. Open daily May to September; limited service for remainder of year.
Society details from: The Membership Secretary, c/o Alston Station, Cumbria, CA9 3JB.
Membership: Local groups in Sunderland, Newcastle and Carlisle.
Newsletter: Published six times per year; free to members.
Railtours: Programme of railtours organised each year, from Carlisle, Tyne Valley, Newcastle, Sunderland and Durham areas.

Stock
[1]Orenstein & Koppel 0-6-0WT *Sao Domingos* 11784 built 1925
Henschel 0-4-0T No. 32 16032 built 1918
Hudswell Clarke 0-6-0DM D819 built 1952
[1]Hunslet 4WDM *Ayle* 2607 built 1942
Motor Rail 4WDM 5880 built 1935 (rebuilt as a brake van)
Motor Rail 4WDM No. 5 11297 built 1964
Ruston Hornsby 4WDM 222101 built 1943
Hibberd 4WDM *The Phoenix* 2325 built 1941
Skip wagon
Four wagon frames
Two MOD bogie wagons, ex-RAF Fauld
Two Hudson bogie wagons being reconstructed as 32-seat passenger coaches
Lincs Coast Light Rly bogie van
Hudson four-wheel oil tank wagon
Two MOD four-wheel wagons, ex-RAF Fauld
Mine wagon ex-Haggs Mine, Nentsberry (20in gauge)

[1]Owned by the Durham Narrow Gauge Group.

A member also owns the following standard gauge locomotive, housed at Slaggyford Station. Northumberland. This is not connected with the Society's proposals for the development of the line.

Stock
Hawthorn Leslie 0-4-0ST No. 13 *The Barra* 3732 built 1928

162 Lake Shore Railroad — A

Passenger-carrying 9½in gauge railway, 500 yards in length, running round the boating lake in the park

South Marine Park, South Shields, Tyne and Wear
OS Ref: NZ 3767

The railway operates from Easter to the end of November.

Stock
Jennings 4-6-2 No. 3440 *Mountaineer* built *c*1950 (American Type)
FFCC Magdalena-Colombia 2-6-2 No. 27 built 1976 (South American Type)
Wabash RR 4-6-4 under construction by Proudlock
Open bogie coaches

163 Humberside Locomotive Preservation Group D

A steam locomotive restoration and maintenance group. No public admittance

BR Dairycoates Depot, Brighton Street, Hessle Road, Hull, North Humberside

The HLPG was formed in 1969 by three people to restore A. E. Draper's 'Black Five' No. 5305 to pristine condition for main line running in the event of the then ban on such operation being removed. In 1974, No. 5305 was moved to the former Breakdown crane shed at British Rail's Dairycoates Depot, Hull, and its restoration was completed in 1976. Since then, it has worked over 30 trains around the approved network for BR steam running in the North of England.

Stock
LMS 4-6-0 No. 5305 *Alderman A. E. Draper* (Stanier 5MT Class) Armstrong Whitworth 1360 built 1937
[1]SR 4-6-0 No. 777 *Sir Lamiel* NBL 23223 built 1925
SR 4-6-2 No. 34053 *Sir Keith Park* (Bulleid rebuilt BB Class) built 1947
Barclay 0-4-0ST No. 8 2369 built 1955
Ruston Hornsby 4WDM No. 801 275882 built 1950
BR Mk.1 BCK coach No. 21214 built 1958
LNER goods brake van

[1]Maunsell 'King Arthur' Class locomotive originally SR No. 777 and finally withdrawn from Basingstoke shed in 1961. The Maunsell N15s, or 'Scotch Arthurs' as they were known had their beginnings in R. W. Urie's LSWR N15 Class and quickly became one of the most popular Southern express engine designs. They worked over all sections of the SR being progressively displaced due to electrification schemes. Towards the end of their career many of the class were stored during the winter, only being put into traffic to assist with mixed traffic duties at busy periods in the summer. It was originally intended to put the Urie N15 *King Arthur* aside for preservation, but plans were revised at the last minute and *Sir Lamiel* was retained by BR as the official museum piece. On loan from the National Collection.

164 North Bay Railway, Scarborough B

This is the largest municipally-owned miniature railway in the country. The 20in gauge line was opened in 1931 and runs for seven-eighths-of-a-mile through the Northstead Manor Gardens from Peasholm to Scalby Mills

Northstead Manor Gardens, Scarborough, Yorkshire
OS Ref: TA 035898

The railway is single track throughout with terminal and midway loops, and though unsignalled, has a tablet control system to ensure safety of operation.
The railway operates daily from Easter until early October. A service approximately every 20 minutes operates in the early and late season, but a ten minute interval applies in the height of the season.

Stock
Hudswell Clarke 4-6-2DH No. 1931 *Neptune* D565 built 1931
Hudswell Clarke 4-6-2DH No. 1932 *Triton* D573 built 1932
Ten open toastrack bogie coaches, each seating 20 passengers
Both locomotives are of the LNER 'Pacific' steam outline.

165 Timothy Hackworth Museum E

Timothy Hackworth's house and workshop have been restored as a museum to show the life and work of one of the under-rated pioneers of railways. The 16-room house has been fully renovated and contains displays of Hackworth's papers and personal trivia as well as Stockton & Darlington Railway items and furniture from the 1830s

Sedgefield District Council, Soho Street, Shildon, County Durham
Access: By bus Nos 1, 4, 5, 91 & 92 from Bishop Auckland, No. 1 from Darlington, No. 93 from Newton Aycliffe or No. 99 from Spennymoor
BR Shildon station is served by trains from Darlington and Bishop Auckland
Tel: Shildon 2086
OS Ref: NZ 22

The renovation of Soho House and opening of the museum coincided with the 150th Anniversary Celebrations of the Stockton and Darlington Railway in 1975. The museum was officially opened by HRH The Queen Mother, on 17 July 1975, and the project received a 'Come to Britain' tourist trophy.
The museum is open from 10 am to 6 pm, Wednesday to Sunday, April to September inclusive.
The Rail Trail begins outside the Timothy Hackworth Museum complex and heads west following the line of the old Stockton and Darlington Railway to Brussleton, where can be viewed the remains of the old stationary engine engineman's house and continues on to Phoenix Row at the site near to the old Witton Park Colliery. The

total walk in one direction is approximately 3 miles, and the walker can still see in situ original S & DR stone sleepers at a number of places along the trail.
Details of the Hackworth Society can be obtained from the Chairman, 12 Queen Street, Shildon, County Durham.

Stock
[1]Hackworth 0-6-0 *Braddyll* built 1835
Hackworth 0-4-0 *Sanspareil* replica built BR Shildon Wagon Works 1980
Forcett Railway 4-wheel coach No. 179 built 1867

[1]Withdrawn 1875 and used as a snowplough at South Hetton Colliery until remains preserved 1951.

166 National Railway Museum E

The Museum's collection is an extensive one, and there are three or four times as many items as can be exhibited in the Museum at one time. Various items are loaned to other museums and preservation societies, while others are 'rotated' between the Museum and the reserve collection in the Peter Allen building

Leeman Road, York YO2 4XJ
Access: Short walk from York BR station
Tel: York (0904) 21261
OS Ref: SE 594519

Opening times: Weekdays 10 am–6 pm; Sundays 2.30 pm–6 pm; closed on some public holidays.
Admission free.
There are limited parking facilities, a museum shop and refreshment room.
Comprehensive education facilities, including an 80-seat lecture theatre, are available for school parties *by prior arrangement.*
Keeper: Dr J. A. Coiley
The National Railway Museum, which is part of the Science Museum, London, was opened by the Duke of Edinburgh on 27 September 1975.
The building is based on the old York North motive power depot, and two of the turntables, with their radial tracks, are used to house the full-size exhibits in the two-acre main hall. Two tracks connect the building with British Railways main lines, permitting locomotives and rolling stock to be exchanged with other museums and preservation societies, as well as the operation of steam specials using those of the Museum's locomotives which are passed for steaming. A balcony along one side of the hall enables visitors to view the exhibits below, as well as housing the display cases which depict the social and economic aspects of the development of the railways. Other show cases around the walls of the main hall house models showing technical features of locomotives, as well as the development of locomotives, rolling stock, signalling and permanent way.
A supporting organisation, the 'Friends of the NRM', exists and details may be obtained from Mr R. Rowntree, c/o The National Railway Museum, Leeman Road, York YO2 4XJ.

Exhibits
Locomotives
Shutt End Railway 0-4-0 *Agenoria* (Foster, Rastrick, built 1829)
Grand Junction Railway 2-2-2 (LNWR No. 1868) built 1845
Furness Railway 0-4-0 No. 3 *Coppernob* (Bury, Curtis and Kennedy, built 1846)
NER 2-2-4T No. 66 *Aerolite* built 1869
GNR 4-2-2 No. 1 built 1870
NER 2-4-0 No. 910 built 1875
LNWR 2-4-0 No. 790 *Hardwicke* built 1892
[9]LB&SCR 0-6-0T No. 82 *Boxhill* (Stroudley Class A1) built 1880
LB&SCR 0-4-2 No. 214 *Gladstone* (Stroudley Class B1) built 1882
LNWR 2-2-2 No. 3020 *Cornwall* built 1847
L&YR 0-4-0ST *Wren* Beyer Peacock 2825 built 1887 (1ft 6in gauge)
MR 4-2-2 No. 673 built 1890
[19]NER 4-4-0 No. 1621 (Worsdell Class M) built 1893
[20]LSWR 4-4-0 No. 563 (Adams Class T3) built 1893
[21]GER 2-4-0 No. 490 (Holden Class T26) built 1894
Waterloo & City Railway 4W electric No. 75S built 1898
[17]GNR 0-6-0ST No. 1247 (LNER J52 Class) built 1899
Beyer Peacock 2-4-0T IMR No. 6 *Peveril* 1524 built 1875 (3ft gauge)
GWR 4-2-2 *Iron Duke* replica built Resco 1982–83 (7ft gauge)
BR Co-CoDE No. 55002 *Kings Own Yorkshire Light Infantry* English Electric 2907 built 1961
BR Bo-BoDE No. D8000 (Class 20) English Electric 2347 built 1957
BR 2-10-0 No. 92220 *Evening Star* (Riddles 9F Class) built 1960
[28]Stephenson 0-2-2 *Rocket* replica built Locomotion Enterprises 1979
[22]GNR 4-4-2 No. 990 *Henry Oakley* built 1898
[23]SECR 4-4-0 No. 737 (BR No. 31737) (Wainwright Class D) built 1901
[24]GNR 4-4-2 No. 251 built 1902
[25]MR 4-4-0 No. 1000 (Deeley Class 4P) built 1902
[26]GER 0-6-0T No. 87 (Holden Class P57) built 1904
[27]L&YR 2-4-2T No. 1008 (BR No. 50621) built 1889
[31]LSWR 0-4-4T 245 (Drummond Class M7) (BR No. 30245) built 1897
[13]Beyer Peacock 0-6-0T *The Earl* 3496 built 1903 (2ft 6in gauge)
[3]NER Bo-BoE No. 1 (BR No. 26500) built 1904
[4]GWR 2-8-0 No. 2818 (Churchward 28XX Class) built 1905
[14]LMS 0-6-0DM No. 7401 Hunslet 1697 built 1932
[29]LNER 4-6-2 No. 4468 *Mallard* (Gresley Class A4) built 1938
NSR 4WBE No. 2 built 1917

LNWR 0-4-0ST No. 1439 built 1865
[10]LMS 2-6-0 No. 2700 (Hughes/Fowler Class 5MT) built 1926
[11]LNER 2-6-2 No. 4771 *Green Arrow* built 1936
SR 4-6-2 No. 34051 *Winston Churchill* (BB Class) built 1946
SR 4-4-0 No. 925 *Cheltenham* (Maunsell V Class) built 1934
[5]LMS 4-6-2 No. 46229 *Duchess of Hamilton* (Stanier Class 8P) built 1938
[6]SR 4-6-2 No. 35029 *Ellerman Lines* (Bulleid 'Merchant Navy' Class) built 1948 (sectioned)
[8]Hunslet 0-4-0ST *Hodbarrow* 299 built 1882
[16]RSH 0-4-0ST No. 15 *Eustace Forth* 7063 built 1942
Barclay 0-4-0F *Imperial No. 1* 2372 built 1956
BR 0-6-0 DM No. 03 090 built Doncaster 1960
[15]Tasmanian Railways 0-4-0 + 0-4-0T No. K1 (Beyer Peacock 5292 built 1909) (2ft gauge)
BR Bo-Bo Electric No. E5001 built 1959
BR 0-4-0DH No. D2860 YE 2843 built 1961
BR advanced passenger train APT-E (two power cars plus two intermediate trailers) built 1972
[16]Armstrong Whitworth 0-4-0DE No. 1421 built 1933
BR AIA-AIADE No. D5500 built Brush 1957
BR Bo-BoE No. 84001 NBL 27793 built 1960
Sentinel 4WVBTG *Frank Galbraith* 9629 built 1957
RSH 0-6-0DM No. 3 7746 built 1954
Chinese People's Republic Railways 4-8-4 No. 607 (Class KF) Vulcan Foundry 9674 built 1935
Post Office Rly AI-IAE No. 809 English Electric 809 built 1930 (2ft gauge)
Motor Rail 4WPM No. 2 1377 built 1918 (2ft gauge)
Ruston Hornsby 4w DM 187105 built 1937 (2ft gauge)
Gyro Mining Transport Bo-BoDH *Kirstin* built 1981 (2ft 6in gauge)

Rolling stock
Peak Forest Canal quarry truck built 1797
Belvoir Castle Railway truck built 1816
Cramlington Colliery chaldron wagon built 1825
Stockton & Darlington Railway horse dandy built 1828
South Hetton Colliery chaldron wagon No. 1155 built *c*1850
Londonderry Railway chaldron wagon No. 31 built *c*1870
Bodmin and Wadebridge Railway third class coach built 1834
Bodmin and Wadebridge Railway composite coach
London & Birmingham Railway Queen Adelaide's saloon built 1842
Stockton & Darlington Railway composite coach No. 59 built 1845
NBR Port Carlisle horse dandy No. 1 built 1861
LNWR Queen Victoria's saloon built 1869 as two six-wheel coaches
NLR directors' saloon No. 1032 built 1872
LNWR corridor brake/1st coach LMS No. 5154 built 1905
LNWR corridor brake/1st coach LMS No. 5155 built 1905
GWR composite dining car No. 9605 built 1930
LNER open 3rd class coaches Nos 13251 & 13254 built 1936
BR Mk.1 TSO coach No. E4286 built 1956
MR six-wheel composite coach No. 901 built 1885
WCJS dining saloon LMS No. 76 built 1900
NER dynamometer car LNER No. 902502 built 1906
ECJS royal saloon No. 395 built 1908
Pullman Car *Topaz* built 1913
LNWR 'Oerlikon' electric motor coach No. 28249 built 1915
SR '3-SUB' electric motor coach No. 8143 built 1925
LMS third class sleeping car No. 14241 built 1928
LNER buffet car No. 9135 built 1937
SR '4COR' electric motor coach No. 11179 built 1938
LMS royal salons Nos 798 and 799 built 1941
BR griddle car No. Sc1100 built 1960
BR Pullman cars *Eagle* and *Emerald* built 1960
Wagons-Lits International 'Night Ferry' sleeping car No. 3792 built 1936
MR 3rd class dining car No. 3463 built 1914
LMS brake/3rd coach No. 27093 built 1950
LMS open third coaches Nos 7828 & 7863 built 1925
GWR 'Siphon G' van No. 2798 built 1937
Liverpool & Manchester Rly first class coach *Huskisson* (reproduction built 1930)
Liverpool & Manchester Rly first class coach *Traveller* (reproduction built 1930)
Liverpool & Manchester Rly second class coach (reproduction built 1930)
Liverpool & Manchester Rly second class coach (reproduction built 1930)
Bodmin & Wadebridge Rly second class coach built 1834
GNR hand crane No. 112 with match truck No. DE 942114 built 1850
Shell Mex tank wagon No. 512 built 1889
ICI nitric acid tank wagon No. 14 built 1928
LMS 3-plank open wagon No. 472867 built 1936
BR Flatrol No. B900402 built 1949
BR Weltrol No. B900805 built 1950
BR 12-ton cattle wagon No. B892156 built 1950
BR 8-ton cattle wagon No. B893343 built 1951
ICI liquid chlorine tank wagon No. 47484 built 1951
National Benzole tank wagon No. 2022 built 1954
BR iron ore tippler wagon No. B383560 built 1954
BR banana van No. B882593 built 1960
SR bogie brake van No. 56287 built 1936
Lynton & Barnstaple Rly bogie coach No. 2 (SR No. 6992) built 1898 (1ft 11½in gauge)
BR dmu motor coach No. M51591 built 1959
BR Mk.1 BCK coach No. M21236 built 1961
BR fish van No. E7905
LMS 7-ton gunpowder van No. 288824 built 1933
LMS 6-wheel milk tank wagon No. 44057 built 1937
Glasgow Underground Railway trailer car No. 7 built Oldbury

RC&W Co 1896 (4ft gauge)
LNWR King Edward's saloon No. 800 built 1903
LNWR Queen Alexandra's saloon No. 801 built 1903
LSWR tri-composite coach No. 3598 built 1903
LNER 'Dolphin' bogie ballast wagon No. 633474 built 1939
NER steam breakdown crane No. CME13 built 1907
LNER match truck No. DE 320952 built 1926
BR Mk.1 lavatory composite coach No. E43046 built 1955
LMS mobile test unit No. 45053 built 1938
LMS/BR dynamometer car No. 45049 built 1949
WCJS travelling post office No. 186 built 1885
GNR six-wheel brake van No. 948 built 1887
Grand Junction Railway travelling post office (Replica) on wagon frame built 1838
NER snow plough No. DE900566 built 1891
ECJS third class corridor coach No. 12 built 1898
LSWR goods brake van No. 99 built 1894
LSWR open carriage truck No. 5830 built 1895
Duke of Sutherland's saloon No. 57A built 1899
GWR hand crane No. 537 built 1899
GNR loco tender No. 1002 built *c*1890
GNR goods van No. E432764
MR officers' saloon No. 2234 built 1904
ECJS passenger brake van LNER No. 109 built 1908
LBSC open wagon No. 3537 built 1912
GWR shunter's truck No. 94988 built 1914
GWR goods brake van No. 56518 built 1916
LMS vestibule third class coach No. 8207 built 1927
LNER tube wagon No. 181358
GWR 'Mink-G' goods van No. 112884 built 1931
LMS ballast plough brake van No. 197266 built 1932
GWR 'Mogo' motor car van No. 126438 built 1935
LNER Wickham petrol trolley No. 960209 built 1932
LNER goods brake van No. 187774 built 1936
LMS corridor third brake No. 5987 built 1937
LMS tube wagon No. 499254 built 1936
WD 'Warflat' BR No. 161042 built 1940
LMS 'Lowmac' No. 700728 built 1944
LNER hopper coal wagon No. 270919 built 1946
BR iron ore hopper wagon No. 436275 built 1950
BR show cattle van No. S3733S built 1951
BR bogie bolster C No. 943139 built 1952
BR horse box No. S96369 built 1957
BR Matisa tamping machine No. 74/007
Two replica Chaldron wagons
NER 20-ton wooden hopper wagon No. 4551 built 1902
LSWR gunpowder van No. KDS61209 built 1912
GER sand wagon No. DE14974
MR 8-ton open wagon
GCR box van
LNWR box van
NER box van
LMS box van
Stanton Iron Works 12-ton mineral wagon
LMS Single bolster wagon No. 722702 built 1938
GWR 13-ton open wagon No. DW143698 built 1944
SNCF 16-ton mineral wagon No. ADB192437 built 1946
BR conflat wagon No. B737725 built 1959
BR speedfreight container No. BA4324B built 1962
LMS train heating van No. DM 395939 built 1926
PLM (SNCF) 4-wheel fourgon van No. 475014 built 1935
Phillips Petroleum 100-ton bogie tank wagon
BR 16-ton mineral wagons Nos B234830 & B227009
Shell/BP rectangular tank wagon No. 3171

Other exhibits include
Weatherhill winding engine built 1833 (in operating order)
Leicester & Swannington winding engine built 1833 (in operating order)
KESR horse bus
Gaunless bridge
Euston turntable
LNER Gresley articulated carriage bogie built 1930
LNER sleeping car section (four-berth, third-class) built 1931
BR standard stock compartments built 1951
BR standard locomotive cab
MR heavy horse dray
LSWR horse ambulance
The Museum also owns a pair of newly-built 7¼in gauge live steam locomotives which may be demonstrated at intervals:
Manning Wardle 2-6-2T L & BR *Taw* built Milner Engineering 1980
Hunslet 0-4-0ST *Margaret* built NRM Workshops 1981

[3]Originally NER No. 1. Withdrawn as BR No. 26500 in 1964 and on exhibition at Leicester before the opening of the NRM.
[4]Withdrawn from Severn Tunnel Junction as BR No. 2818 in 1963 and stored until restored at Eastleigh Works in 1966–67. At the time of their introduction, Churchward's 2-8-0 mineral engines were in many ways well in advance of their time and remained the standard GWR heavy goods type for the rest of the Company's existence. They were the first 2-8-0 locomotives to be introduced in this country.
[5]Withdrawn from Liverpool (Edge Hill) as BR No. 46229 in 1964 and purchased by Butlins Ltd. Restored to LMS livery at Crewe. Put on display at Minehead later that year. The appearance of this class of locomotive in 1937 brought with it the climax of development of steam express passenger locomotives on the LMS. When new, this locomotive was fitted with streamlined casing which was removed in 1948 to ease access to the moving parts. No. 6229 was sent to America in 1938 after having exchanged numbers with No. 6220 *Coronation*, but resumed its correct identity on return. On long-term loan from Butlins Limited. Exhibited as BR No. 46229 in BR crimson lake livery. Restored to working order at the expense of the Friends of the NRM.
[6]Built by BR at Eastleigh in 1949 to a design of O. V. S. Bulleid. Rebuilt without air-smoothed casing and with

conventional Walschaert's valve gear in 1959. Withdrawn from service in 1966 and recovered from Barry in 1973. Sectioned to the requirements of the Science Museum.

[8]Ex-Millom Hematite Ore and Iron Co, Hodbarrow Mines, 1968. Preserved by the Hunslet Engine Co, it is the oldest of their make in existence. On loan from the Hunslet Engine Co.

[9]The only example of William Stroudley's famous Brighton 'Terriers' to be preserved in original form in this country. *Boxhill* was renumbered 682 by the LBSCR and subsequently placed in service stock as Brighton Works shunter, being identified as 'B'. Renumbered 380S by the Southern in their service stock list. Retired in 1946 and set aside for preservation. Repainted in Stroudley livery for the Centenary of Waterloo station.

[10]Class 5 mixed traffic locomotive built at Horwich Works in May 1926. Withdrawn from Birkenhead shed as BR No. 42700 in March 1966. The first locomotive to be built to an LMS design (though admittedly following Hughes L & YR concepts) and forerunner of a useful class of 245 engines all of which gave at least 30 years' service. Nicknamed 'Crabs' because of their high running plates, prominent cylinders and rolling gait, their main employment was on fast freight and parcels trains, especially in Scotland. Constructed as No. 13000, this locomotive was renumbered 2700 in 1934 and 42700 by BR. Selected as an official museum piece, it was stored at Hellifield for some months before being loaned to the K & WVR. It was moved to the museum in 1978.

[11]Withdrawn from King's Cross shed in 1962 as BR No. 60800 and stored until moved to Carnforth via Norwich and Tyseley in 1973. One-hundred-and-eighty-four of these highly successful locomotives were constructed principally for hauling express freight and parcels trains. However, they could often be found working alongside the LNER 'Pacifics' on express passenger turns. They were the first 2-6-2 tender engines built for use in Great Britain (with the exception of the Paget Midland Railway experimental locomotive of 1908).

[12]On loan from the Leighton Buzzard Narrow Gauge Railway (see Group No. 451).

[13]On loan from the Welshpool & Llanfair Light Railway (see Group No. 302).

[14]On loan from the Middleton Railway. Named *John Alcock* (see Group No. 152).

[15]On loan from the Ffestiniog Railway (see Group No. 301).

[16]On loan from the Hexham Rolling Stock Group (see Group No. 153).

[17]Built by Sharp Stewart & Co of Glasgow (Works No. 4492) in 1899. After 60 years' railway service, finally as shed pilot at King's Cross MPD, the locomotive was acquired by Captain W. G. Smith and restored to its original livery in April 1959. Believed to be the first privately owned locomotive permitted to work passenger trains over BR metals. It worked the first 'Bluebell' from London Bridge to Sheffield Park in April 1962.

[19]Classified D17/1 by the LNER, this locomotive was allocated No. 2108 in the 1946 scheme, but this was not actually carried as the engine had been withdrawn from Alnmouth shed in July 1945. This particular locomotive, survivor of a class of 20 with 7ft 1¼in driving wheels, took part in the 1895 railway race to the North, covering the distance from Newcastle to Edinburgh in 113 minutes, a feat which earned No. 1621 her place in the National Collection, restored to the elegant NER green livery.

[20]Originally withdrawn in March 1939, but reinstated in December as a wartime emergency, No. 563 was finally withdrawn from Basingstoke shed in August 1945. One of ten T3 Class locomotives designed by William Adams for express passenger work West of Salisbury, No. 563 is the sole survivor of the distinctive and handsome Adams outside-cylindered 4-4-0 Classes which were responsible for all LSWR main-line express work up to the turn of the Century. When No. 563 was finally withdrawn in 1945, it was laid aside for cutting up and towed to Kimbridge Junction to meet its doom. As luck would have it, a locomotive was required for an exhibition at Waterloo, and 563 was chosen, being virtually in original condition. After appearances at various exhibitions, the locomotive finally took its place in Clapham Museum in January 1961.

[21]100 of these 5ft 8in mixed traffic locomotives were built between 1891 and 1902 and proved very useful on both main and branch line work. Withdrawal of the class commenced in April 1926, but this locomotive, as LNER E4 Class No. 7490, then BR No. 62785 survived long enough to become the last 2-4-0 in service. It was withdrawn from Cambridge in December 1959 and restored to GER lined blue livery.

[22]This locomotive was the first GNR 'Atlantic', and while eclipsed by the large-boilered, superheated 'Atlantics' of four years later, when built it represented a considerable increase in power over the small 2-4-0 and 4-4-0 types that had hitherto worked the main-line expresses. *Henry Oakley* spent its last few years as LNER No. 3990 on relatively easy work before being withdrawn from Lincoln shed in October 1937. No. 990 came out of retirement in 1975 and worked for a season on the Keighley & Worth Valley Railway.

[23]No. 737 is the sole survivor not only of Class D but of all the family of SECR inside-cylinder 4-4-0s. All were highly successful designs and several were rebuilt with larger boilers between 1921 and 1927 to increase their haulage capacity. No. 737 stands in all the glory of its SECR passenger livery – Brunswick Green and Indian Red, with brass dome, copper-capped chimney and virtually every visible part fully lined out.

[24]GNR No. 251 was the first 'Large Atlantic', and when new was the largest passenger engine in the UK. For many years, members of this class worked the heaviest and fastest trains on the GN main line, and even when displaced by the Gresley 'Pacifics' from 1922 onwards, continued to do yeoman service with lighter passenger

trains until 1946, after which they were rapidly displaced by the new B1 4-6-0s. Even when the class had become extinct, it was still possible to see four of these engines supplying steam at Doncaster Works. Renumbered 2800 in 1946 and withdrawn from King's Cross shed in July 1947, following which it was restored to GNR livery for display in York Museum.

[25]Compound locomotives do not seem to have proved very successful in this country, but this class is the exception. After the Grouping, the LMS built 195 of them with 6ft 9in driving wheels to add to the 45 Midland-built locos with 7ft wheels, making them the largest class of express passenger engines on the LMS. Originally numbered 2631, it became No. 1000 in the Midland 1907 renumbering scheme. When withdrawn as BR No. 41000 in October 1951, it lay in unrestored condition in Crewe paintshop for several years before being reinstated in June 1959 for preservation. No. 1000 now carries the beautiful Midland crimson lake livery and makes occasional appearances at the head of steam specials on BR.

[26]When new, many of the 160 locomotives of this type worked the Liverpool Street suburban 'Jazz' services. Sharing such turns with 0-4-4 and 2-4-2 tanks, the little 0-6-0s had a fair turn of speed and were considerably more powerful than their appearance would suggest. Their lively performance earned them the nickname 'Buckjumpers'. Although gradually ousted from 1915 onwards by the larger N7 0-6-2 tanks, they continued to be station and carriage pilots at Liverpool Street until almost the end of GE steam, albeit in reduced numbers. The main bulk of the class were relegated to shunting and goods work. Renumbered 8633 in 1946 and 68633 by BR, this engine was withdrawn from Parkeston in November 1960 and has been restored to GER Royal Blue livery.

[27]The Lancashire & Yorkshire Railway made extensive use of 2-4-2 tanks for its lighter passenger services, building over 300 of the type in various forms, and the design proved to be a tremendous success. They handled everything from relatively light branch trains to relatively enormous excursions to Blackpool and other resorts. Withdrawal commenced in 1928 and proceeded slowly but surely until 1961, when the last two engines were broken up. No. 1008, being the first engine built at Horwich, and typical of late Victorian passenger tank engines, was selected by BR for preservation. The loco was withdrawn from Manningham in October 1954 and restored to L & YR lined black livery.

[28]The replica of 'Rocket' was built for the National Railway and Science Museums by Locomotion Enterprises of Springwell, Tyne and Wear. Since its handover in August 1979, it has been operated in numerous places, including Cannes and Sacramento, California for the opening of their State Railroad Museum, in addition to appearing in the Rainhill Cavalcade at 'Rocket 150'.

[29]The A4s were the ultimate development of Gresley's 3-cylinder Pacific design and were built at Doncaster from 1935 onwards specially for hauling new high-speed streamlined trains such as the 'Silver Jubilee'. Whilst not the most powerful of British express engines, they were generally acknowledged as the fastest. With their svelte wedge-streamlined form, their syncopated Gresley beat and distinctive chime whistles, the A4s had a special magic for enthusiasts and railwaymen alike. *Mallard* attained a speed of 126 mph whilst working a special test train in 1938, a speed unsurpassed by any other steam locomotive before or since. Withdrawn from King's Cross MPD in April 1963 as BR No. 60022, *Mallard* was restored to its original blue livery at Doncaster.

[31]One of the first batch of Dugald Drummond's very successful M7 Class which finished its days at Nine Elms shed on empty carriage workings into Waterloo in November 1962.

167 Darlington Railway Museum — E

The original station of the pioneer Stockton and Darlington Railway has become the fitting home for a splendid collection of locomotives and other railway relics with strong associations with the North-East

North Road Station, Darlington, County Durham DL3 6ST
Access: By rail direct from Darlington Main Line Station. By road, turn off A167 into Station Road, ½ mile north of town centre
Tel: Darlington (0325) 60532
OS Ref: NZ 289157

The building, with its long façade and entrance portico, dates from 1842 and was restored as a museum in 1975 as a contribution to the 150th Anniversary of the opening of the Stockton & Darlington Railway. Apart from the principal locomotive exhibits, the collection of small exhibits and models illustrates the history of the S & D and NER companies. The surrounding area still contains several buildings of railway history significance and DMUs still pass through the station.

The Museum is open from Mondays to Saturdays 10 am–5 pm and on Sundays 11 am to 4 pm from Easter to the end of September. October to Easter: Mondays to Saturdays 10 am to 3 pm, closed on Sundays.

Facilities for visitors include free car parking, museum shop, refreshments and toilets.

Stock

[1]Stephenson 0-4-0 S & DR No. 1 *Locomotion* built 1825
[2]Kitching 0-6-0 S & DR No. 25 *Derwent* built 1845
Head Wrightson 0-4-0VBT No. 17 33 built 1873
[3]NER 0-6-0 No. 1275 Dubs 708 built 1874
[3]NER 2-4-0 No. 1463 built 1885
Hawthorn Leslie 0-4-0ST *Met* 2800 built 1909
Bagnall 0-4-0F *Patons* 2898 built 1948
[4]S & DR composite carriage No. 31 built 1846

NER 20-ton mineral wagon
[4]Body of NER carriage built *c*1860 (to be restored)

[1]Hauled the first train on the Stockton and Darlington Railway. Withdrawn from regular service in 1846 but worked occasionally thereafter. Sold for scrap in 1850 but reinstated as pumping engine at Lucy Pit, Crook. Returned to the NER and restored for display in 1857. Placed on show at Darlington Bank Top Station in 1890. On loan from the National Collection.
[2]Withdrawn and sold to Joseph Pease & Co, *c*1865. Presented to the NER in 1898 and placed on display. On loan from the National Collection.
[3]On loan from the NRM.
[4]On loan from the National Collection.

The activities of the museum are supported by 'The Friends of the Museum'. Details may be obtained from the above address.

168 Tyne and Wear County Council G

Standard gauge rolling stock undergoing restoration

Tyne and Wear County Council Museums, Museum Storage, Middle Engine Lane, Wallsend, North Tyneside
Access: Off Newcastle–Tynemouth Coast Road A1058
OS Ref: NZ 323692
Details from: Mr Paul Talbot. Tel: Newcastle 326789

No public access except Open Days as advertised.
The two road depot on the former Metro Test Track in North Tyneside has been acquired by the County Council for use as a store and workshop and the Consett steam and diesel locomotives, the NER electric parcels van and the River Wear.
Commissioners side-tipping wagon were moved there from storage in Sunderland in March 1981. They were joined later by the George Stephenson 0-4-0 *Billy* from the old Museum of Science and Engineering, Newcastle.

Stock
Siemens Bo-BoE built 1909
[1]Killingworth Colliery 0-4-0 *Billy* A4 built 1826
Kitson 0-6-0PT No. A5 2509 built 1883
Consett 0-6-0DM No. 10 built 1958
NER electric parcels van No. 3267 built 1904 (on loan from National Railway Museum)
River Wear Commissioners side-tipping wagon

[1]Presented to the Corporation of Newcastle upon Tyne in 1881 to commemorate the centenary of the birth of George Stephenson. Placed on display beside the High Level Bridge until 1896, then at Newcastle Central Station until 1945, when it was put on display at the Museum of Science and Engineering. Moved to storage 1981.

169 Preston Hall Museum E

Standard gauge steam locomotive on static display included in the Museum collection

Yarm Road, Stockton, Teesside, Cleveland
Access: Eaglescliffe BR station
Bus routes Nos 54, 57 & 87, also United Bus Services Nos 80, 294 & 295. By road along the A135
Tel: 0642-602474
OS Ref: NZ 430158

The Park is open from Mondays to Saturdays 10 am–6 pm and on Sundays from 2 pm to 6 pm throughout the year.

Stock
Head Wrightson 0-4-0VBTG 21 built 1870
Chaldron wagon
Ex-Seaham Harbour Dock Co Ltd, Seaham, Co Durham, 1959

170 Leeds City Museum of Science and Industry AE

Narrow gauge locomotive exhibits in the newly-opened transport gallery at Armley Mills. A ¼-mile mixed 18in and 2ft gauge passenger-carrying demonstration track was opened in 1982

Armley Mills, Canal Road, Leeds 12, West Yorkshire
Tel: Leeds 637861
OS Ref: SE 275342

Stock
[1]Hunslet 0-4-0WT *Jack* 684 built 1898 (1ft 6in gauge)
[2]T. Green 0-6-2ST *Barber* 441 built 1908 (2ft gauge)
[3]Hudswell Clarke 0-4-0ST *Lord Granby* 633 built 1902 (3ft gauge)
Hudswell Clarke 0-4-0ST *Elizabeth* 1888 built 1958
Ruston Hornsby 4WDM 172901 built 1935 (2ft gauge)
Motor Rail 4WPM No. 1 1369 built 1918 (2ft gauge)
[4]Hudswell Clarke 4WDM D571 built 1932 (2ft 11in gauge)
Greenwood and Batley 4WBE 1210 built 1930
E. B. Wilson 0-6-0 (GWR No. 252) built 1855 (section only)
Orenstein and Koppel 4WDM *Ingrid* (2ft gauge)
Booth 4WVB steam crane 41618 built 1931
Two Hudson air-braked bogie coaches built 1982 (2ft gauge)
Steam locomotives preserved by the Narrow Gauge Railway Society

[1]Presented by John Knowles (Wooden Box) Ltd, Woodville, Leicestershire, 1958.
[2]Presented by North Eastern Gas Board, Harrogate, Yorkshire, 1957.
[3]Presented by Staveley Minerals Ltd, Eastwell Quarries, Leicestershire, 1961.
[4]Owned by Mr E. N. Redman.

171 Museum of South Yorkshire Life E

2ft gauge static locomotive exhibit at present in store but may be viewed by special arrangement

Cusworth Hall, Doncaster, South Yorkshire
Tel: Doncaster 61842
OS Ref: SE 547039

The Museum is open daily throughout the year.
Cusworth Hall house was built between 1741 and 1750 and has fine chimney pieces and a chapel in the South West wing. The Museum has sections of interest to children and features a study base with research facilities. The Museum is set in extensive grounds which are open all year round with fishing in the ponds, cricket and football pitches.

Stock
Hunslet 0-4-0DM 2008 built 1939
Two NCB man-riding cars

172 Bradford Industrial Museum E

Bradford Metropolitan Council, Moorside Mill, Eccleshill, Bradford
Access: BR Bradford Exchange Station, thence by bus to Moorside Road
Tel: Bradford 631756
OS Ref: SE 184353

The Museum is open daily except Good Fridays, Christmas and Boxing Days from 10 am to 5 pm. Closed on all Mondays except Bank Holidays. Admission free.
Facilities for visitors include car parking, a museum shop, refreshments and toilets.
The Industrial Museum in the four-storey former spinning mill at Moorside Road, Eccleshill, has proved itself to be Bradford's premier museum attraction since it opened to the public in 1974.
Part of its success is due to the genuine mill atmosphere. The machines are almost all in working order and may be seen in operation at set times daily. Another reason is the museum's variety. The transport gallery contains a colourful array of vehicles including several of the famous Bradford-made Jowett cars and the now equally famous tank engine *Nellie*. The entrance hall presents both a permanent history of Bradford, emphasising the development of its woollen industry and a series of temporary displays.
A little museum on its own is the mill owner's house, set apart off the cobbled drive. Each room has been furnished in genuine Victorian or Edwardian style and the curious bath-shower always draws surprised comments.
Those who have wondered what happened to the façade of the old Kirkgate Market will have their answer as they leave the museum. The carved masonry from the entrance to the Market is set into a grassy bank in the mill yard.

Stock
Hudswell Clarke 0-4-0ST *Nellie* 1435 built 1922
Smith Rodley four-ton steam crane No. 10302 built 1924
Hull 4-wheel double-deck tramcar No. 132 built 1910
Bradford 4-wheel double-deck tramcar No. 104 built 1925 (4ft gauge)
Other items of interest include a Bradford trolleybus, several stationary steam engines and a 10¼in gauge model of an NER 4-4-0.

173 Kingston upon Hull City Transport Museum E

36 High Street, Kingston upon Hull, North Humberside
Access: Bus routes Nos 33, 37, 40, 41C & 43
Nearest BR station: Hull Paragon
Tel: 0482-223111 Ext 2737
OS Ref: TA 102284

Open weekdays 10 am–5 pm; Sundays 2.30 pm–4.30 pm. Closed Good Friday, Christmas Day and Boxing Day. Admission free.

Stock
[1]Portstewart Tramway 0-4-0 Tram Loco No. 1 Kitson T56 built 1882 (3ft gauge)
Ryde Pier Tramway horse tram No. 3 built 1871

[1]Withdrawn 1926 on the closure of the Tramway and stored at York Road Works, Belfast. Presented for display by the LMS (NCC) in 1939.

174 Monkwearmouth Station Museum E

Standard gauge rolling stock exhibits on static display at restored historic railway station of considerable architectural note

Tyne and Wear County Council Museums, North Bridge Street, Sunderland SR5 1AP
Access: Tyne & Wear Transport and Northern buses from Sunderland Town Centre, Newcastle, South Shields, Blythe and Hartlepool. By road along the A1018, 10 minutes walk from Sunderland station
Tel: 0783 77075
OS Ref: NZ 396576

The impressive classical façade of 1848 is one of the finest station frontages in the country. The station also boasts a North Eastern Railway booking office, virtually unchanged since 1867 and restored to its 1900 condition. There is also a restored footbridge dating from 1879.
Exhibits inside the museum include models of Tynesidebuilt locomotives and material relating to George Stephenson and to George Hudson who was responsible for the station being built in its impressive style. Other displays deal with the development of municipal trans-

port in Tyne & Wear and Victorian and Edwardian bicycles.
The museum is open on weekdays and Bank Holidays throughout the year from 10 am to 6 pm and on Sundays from 2 pm to 5 pm.
Closed on Christmas Day, Boxing Day, New Year's Day and Good Friday.
Admission free.

Stock
NER goods brake van No. 20800 built 1916
LNER CCT No. 1298 built 1939
NER EMU driving car No. DE 900730

Tyne and Wear County Council Museums have moved the part of their collection of locomotives and rolling stock which is not on public view to their new stores and workshop at the two road depot at the former Metro Test Track in North Tyneside. The Consett Iron Company 0-6-0PT A5 (Kitson 1883) diesel mechanical 0-6-0 10 (Consett 1958). NER electric parcels van of 1904, and River Wear Commissioners side-tipping wagon were transported by road from the former store in Monkwearmouth goods shed in February 1981.
The Monkwearmouth Station Museum Association supports the activities of the County Council Museums on both sites. Members of the locomotive group are at present restoring the Consett boiler 0-6-0PT A5 to working order. This work has involved retyring the wheels and retubing the boiler. Details of MSMA can be obtained from the Hon Secretary, c/o Monkwearmouth Station Museum.

175 Durham County Council E

Standard gauge static locomotive exhibit

Dinsdale Park Residential School, near Darlington
OS Ref: NZ 341121

Stock
Fowler 0-4-0DM No. 4 4210087 built 1953

176 Washington Development Corporation E

2ft gauge locomotive on static display at Mining Museum

'F' Pit Museum, Washington, Tyne and Wear
OS Ref: NZ 303574

Stock
Ruston Hornsby 0-4-0DM 392157 built 1956
Four tub wagons

Also on display and worked electrically is a mines beam engine, built in 1888 by the Grange Iron Co.

177 Army Transport Museum E

Display of Army vehicles from 1890 onwards, plus amphibious craft and helicopters

Flemingate, near Beverley, Humberside

Stock
Hunslet 0-6-0ST No. 92 *Waggoner* 3792 built 1953
S&MR 0-4-2WT No. 1 *Gazelle* built Dodman 1893
Avonside 0-6-0ST *Woolmer* 1572 built 1910
LMS 0-4-0DM No. 7050 *Rorke's Drift* Drewry 2047 built 1934
'Crocodile' bogie wagon built *c*1914
German track wrecking wagon built *c*1942

60cm gauge stock:
Motor Rail 4WDM 8855 built 1943
Nocton Estates bogie ambulance wagon *c*1917
LCLR ration wagon
Two WD 4-wheel open wagons
Two WD 4-wheel skip wagons

Gazelle was originally built as a 2-2-2WT for Mr W. Burkitt who had private running powers over the GER and M & GNJR. Sold to the Shropshire and Montgomeryshire Railway in 1911 and rebuilt into its present form. Taken into BR stock in 1950 and immediately placed on loan to the Army. It is the smallest standard gauge engine in the country, and is even more unusual in combining inside cylinders with a well tank.

178 Hunday National Tractor and Farm Museum BE

Passenger-carrying 2ft 6in gauge railway, 500 yards in length, due to be extended to over 1 mile

John Moffitt, Newton, Stocksfield-upon-Tyne, Northumberland, NE43 7TW
Access: Museum signposted from A68 and A69. Bus 685 from Newcastle to Newton Road, then a 1½ mile walk. 3½ miles from Stocksfield BR station
Tel: Stocksfield 2553

The rolling stock, equipment and rails being used here are all from the former Dalmunzie Hotel Light Railway in Scotland, which was bought in its entirety by Mr Moffitt following its closure in 1978.
The museum collection is housed in original stone buildings dating from 1806. Over 250 vintage tractors and engines are on display, showing the development of agriculture from 1900 to the post-war period. The collection includes small hand tools, harness, farm and dairy equipment, an 1835 Bingfield steam engine and thresher, also a 1903 Ivel which won a first prize at the Royal Show in 1903.
Opened by HRH The Queen Mother in April 1979, the National Tractor and Farm Museum has received a further accolade. It won the '1981 Museum of the Year Award' sponsored by the *Illustrated London News* and run by the National Heritage Organisation.

The museum is open from 30 April to 30 September on weekdays (excluding Fridays) between 10 am and 6 pm, and on Sundays from 12 noon to 6 pm.
Facilities for visitors include car parking, gift shop and refreshments.

Stock
Motor Rail 4WPM *Dalmunzie* (20HP Class) 2014 built 1920
Hunslet 0-4-0DM 2250 built 1940
Open carriage
Enclosed carriage
Two four-wheel flat wagons

179 S. Harrison & Sons (Transport) Ltd G

Standard gauge locomotives undergoing restoration

310 Sheffield Road, Tinsley, Sheffield, South Yorkshire
OS Ref: SK 399910

Stock
Barclay 0-4-0ST *Henry Ellison* 2217 built 1947
Barclay 0-4-0ST *Wee Yorkie* 2360 built 1954

180 South Yorkshire Railway Preservation Society D

Standard gauge Railway Centre operating industrial steam locomotives over 200 yards of track

Newton Chambers Ltd, Chapeltown, Sheffield, South Yorks
Tel: Sheffield 20449 or 388440
OS Ref: 350977

The Centre is open every weekend and Public Holidays throughout the year.
Details from: Mr I. Williams, 114 Sheffield Road, Penistone, Sheffield.

Stock
Yorkshire Engine Co 0-4-0DE 2729 built 1958
Hudswell Clarke 0-6-0T No. S102 *Cathryn* 1884 built 1955
Hunslet 0-6-0ST 3183 built 1944
Hudswell Clarke 0-4-0ST No. 7 1689 built 1937
Hunslet 0-4-0DM 2083 built 1940
Fowler 0-4-0DH 4200019 built 1947, rebuilt 1960
Ruston Hornsby 4WDM *Ivor* 212653 built 1942
GER bogie coach
LNER 20-ton box van
Various good brake vans and wagons

181 Shipley Glen Cable Tramway B

Quarter-mile, 1ft 8in gauge double-track, cable-operated line running between Easter and 31 October each year from 11 am to dusk

Shipley Glen, Prod Lane, Baildon, Shipley, Middle Airedale, West Yorkshire
Access: Bus routes Nos 623 and 647 Bradford–Shipley Glen at approx 15 and 30 minute frequencies respectively.
Nearest BR station: Shipley (1 mile)
Tel: Bradford 592217

Maximum gradient 1 in 12; maximum speed 10 mph; journey time two minutes.
The tramway has been fully restored and is now run by the Bradford Trolleybus Association. The line has been relaid, its stock repainted and gas lighting has been installed at the top station.
The trains consist of two double-cars (one on each track) capable of seating thirty passengers each. Power is provided by a 35 hp electric motor installed in the powerhouse near the upper station where the 'motorman' controls the operation by observing the speed of the ascending car.

182 Saltburn Miniature Railway B

Passenger-carrying 15in gauge railway, ½ mile in length running from Cat Nab to Valley Gardens Station

Italian Gardens, Saltburn-by-the-Sea, Cleveland
OS Ref: NZ 666215

After many seasons out of use, during which it suffered heavily at the hands of vandals, the Saltburn Miniature Railway is being reconstructed by Mr Brian Leonard.

Stock
Barlow 0-6-2DE *Prince of Wales* built 1953 (steam outline)
Four open bogie coaches

183 Wylam Railway Museum E

Wylam, Northumberland

Local railway relics from Tyne Valley, etc, and a model of Wylam station in 1914. Open on Saturdays and Tuesday and Thursday afternoons all year round. Admission free. (Wylam was George Stephenson's birthplace).

184 Olton Hall Preservation Society G

Standard gauge steam locomotive undergoing restoration

Procor (UK) Ltd, Horbury Junction Works, Wakefield, West Yorkshire

Stock
GWR 4-6-0 No. 5972 *Olton Hall* built 1937

Withdrawn December 1963 and sent to Woodham Bros scrapyard, Barry. Purchased for preservation and moved to Wakefield, May 1981.

185 National Coal Board I

Industrial steam location

Smithywood Coking Plant, Chapeltown, South Yorkshire

No public admittance.

Stock
Hunslet 0-6-0ST No. 1 3192 built 1944

186 Yorkshire Museum of Farming E

700 yard length of former DVLR retained as museum with static exhibit of standard gauge train

Murton, near York

Stock
Fowler 0-4-0DM *Churchill* 4100005 built 1947

187 Darlington Railway Preservation Society E

Standard gauge locomotives undergoing restoration at site alongside Darlington Railway Museum in original S and DR Goods Shed built c1840

Details from: T. Eden, 75 Millbank Road, Darlington, County Durham
OS Ref: NZ 290157

Open each weekend throughout the year.

Stock
BR 2-6-0 No. 78018 (Riddles 2MT Class) built 1954
Peckett 0-4-0ST No. 12142 built 1953
GEC 4WE built *c*1928
Fowler 0-4-0DM No. 185 *David Payne* 4110006 built 1950
BR/Drewry 0-6-0DM Class 03

[1]Ex-Market Bosworth Light Railway 1981; withdrawn November 1966 and sent to Woodham Bros scrapyard, Barry. Purchased for preservation in November 1978.

188 Flamingoland Miniature Railway B

Passenger-carrying 15in gauge railway, 350 yards in length, linking the car park to the fairground

'Flamingoland' Park and Zoo, Kirby Misperton, Pickering, North Yorkshire
Tel: Kirby Misperton 287
OS Ref: SE 77

This is a simple continuous loop with no spurs or sidings, running for most of its length between two rows of trees. The park is open daily from Easter to September from 10 am to 4 pm.
Facilities for visitors include a Late 18th Century House and 350 acres of Zoo and Pleasure Park with 1,000 animals, birds and reptiles, Jungle Cruise, Children's farm, Gnomeland, fairground and caravan village.

Stock
Severn-Lamb 2-8-0DH No. 278 1/84 built 1984
BR APT-outline 4-4w-4-4wER set built Rapido Rail Systems 1983

189 Great Yorkshire Railway Preservation Society F

Standard gauge railway preservation project

Octavius Atkinson and Sons Ltd, Prospect Works, Starbeck, Harrogate, Yorks. (Site of former Starbeck MPD and Yard)
OS Ref: SE 331556

Stock
Ruston Hornsby 4WDM 417892 built 1959
Fowler 0-4-0DM *Ormsby* 22077 built 1938

190 Slaggyford Light Railway C

Private passenger-carrying 2ft gauge line, 500 yards in length, running through a small caravan park, delightfully situated in woodland by the River South Tyne with private fishing and provides bed and breakfast accommodation. The railway was opened in May 1978

Mr W. F. Horseman, The Island, Slaggyford, near Alston, Northumberland, CA6 7NJ
Tel: Alston (049-83) 422

Stock
Baguley 0-4-0DM (29HP type) 3236 built 1947 (steam outline)
[1]Baguley open bogie coaches Nos 3237 and 3239 built 1947

[1]Coach No. 3237 has now been rebuilt into a cowboy-style carriage for children or adults.

191 Westcliff Miniature Railway B

Passenger-carrying 10¼in gauge railway, 300 yards in length, laid in an irregular circle

Westcliff Sports Ground, Whitby, North Yorkshire

The line operates daily in the holiday season.

Stock
Shepperton 2-4-2DM *Meteor II* built 1969
5 articulated bogie coaches

192 Saville Bros Ltd B

Passenger-carrying 10¼in gauge railway

Garden Centre, Garforth Cliff, Leeds, West Yorkshire

The line was opened on 20 May 1978 and is an ambitious

project in an attractive setting. The track is laid out as a pair of joined balloon loops and incorporates an impressive girder bridge over an ornamental pond. As befits a railway located in a Garden Centre, the main station, Cactus Junction, is to be found *inside* a large greenhouse!

Stock
Severn-Lamb 2-8-0PH built 1978 (steam outline)
'Wild-West'-style toastrack bogie coaches

193 Spen Valley Railway F

A scheme for the establishment of a major transport museum encompassing road and rail exhibits. The emphasis on the railway operation will be on electric working of locomotive-hauled trains and tramcars

West Yorkshire Metropolitan County Council. Low Moor to Heckmondwike line

Details from: John Chilvers, County Hall, Wakefield, West Yorkshire WF1 2GW.
Tel: 0924-367111 ext 4719

The museum collection will be based at Ludham Street depot in Bradford and will include trams, trolleybuses, motor buses and electric railway vehicles.

Stock
RSH Bo-BoE No. 3 7078 built 1944
Rotterdam bogie single-deck tramcars Nos 109 and 115
Rotterdam bogie single-deck tramcar trailer No. 1033
English Electric 4wBE No. 1 905 built 1935
English Electric 4wBE No. 3 1379 built 1946

194 Abbey Light Railway B

2ft gauge light railway, 400 yards long

Mr P. N. Lowe, 10 Blackwood Avenue, Cookridge, Leeds
OS Ref: SE 262357

The Abbey Light Railway is best described as a Railway and Engineering Plant Museum.
Public services commenced June 1984.
The 2ft gauge track itself at the moment runs from the engine shed, just inside the entrance in Bridge Street, along the boundary of the Clover Warehouse car park for ⅛th of a mile where it comes to an end at the Mill Race. Work is being carried out to repair sluice gates upstream from the track where the race is diverted from the River Aire so that the water level may be lowered and the race bridged. The track will then continue for another ⅛th mile on the opposite side of the stream to within close vicinity of the Abbey itself.

Stock
Hunslet 4WDM 2463 built 1943
Lister 4WDM *Loweco* 20449 built 1942
Motor Rail 4WDM 5859 built 1934
Hunslet 4WDM 2959 built 1944
Ruston Hornsby 4WDM 235654 built 1946
Ruston Hornsby 4WDM 198287 built 1940
Four-wheeled bench-type open coaches

In addition, the collection includes a Petter-engined stone crusher used for the production of ballast for the track and a Priestman rope-operated excavator together with a variety of rolling stock and tracklaying equipment.

195 Tyne and Wear County Council E

Children's playground static exhibit

Wideopen, Newcastle-on-Tyne

Stock
Ruston Hornsby 4WDM 263000 built 1946

196 'The Carriage' Inn E

Coach in use as a restaurant

Old Station House, Jesmond, Tyneside

Stock
GNR Saloon Coach No. 397 built 1912

Constructed as a First Class Family Saloon at a cost of £1,718. In its later years it was converted for departmental use as BR No. DE 320206. Purchased for preservation at Steamtown, Carnforth, and subsequently resold for its present use.

197 'The Black Bull' E

Coach in use as a restaurant

Moulton, Yorks

Stock
SR Pullman car No. 279 *Hazel* built 1932 (ex-'Brighton Belle' Set No. 3051).

AREA E

Scotland

(Group Nos 201–250)

201 Bo'ness & Kinneil Railway A

Standard gauge, steam operated, passenger-carrying railway ½ mile in length, being extended to 1¼ miles

Scottish Railway Preservation Society, Bo'ness Station, off Union Street, Bo'ness, West Lothian, Scotland EH51
Access: ½ mile east of town centre along river frontage. Regular bus service from Edinburgh, Glasgow, etc, or train to Linlithgow and then regular local bus to Bo'ness; or via the M9 from Glasgow and Edinburgh
Tel: Bo'ness 2298
OS Ref: NT 003817

Ceremonially opened for traffic on 27 June 1981, the Bo'ness line triumphantly crowns seventeen years of achievement in the preservation business by the SRPS. At Kinneil the line will link up with an existing 1½ mile section of track recently purchased from British Rail. Beyond that, lies the task of re-laying the rest of the branch and making a connection with the Edinburgh–Glasgow main line.
Facilities: Train rides, shop, refreshments, toilets, car park.
In July 1978, Falkirk District Council granted the Scottish Railway Preservation Society planning permission for 'the formation of a railway system and the erection of an engine shed and station platform at The Foreshore, Bo'ness'. Work began in May 1979, following a grant from the Scottish Tourist Board.
In two years, a green field site alongside the dock basin was transformed into a living steam railway.
On Saturday 27 June 1981, a magnificent Festival of Transport was held at the station site at Bo'ness to open the first stage of the Bo'ness and Kinneil Railway. Vehicles of every kind, from horse drawn to hang gliders, launched the railway in grand style, with thousands of passengers carried on the trains during its first weekend of operation.
As well as the efforts of SRPS members, work has been carried out by men from a Special Temporary Employment Scheme, Community Industry, Polmont Borstal, and Royal Engineers Territorials.
Details from: SRPS Publicity Officer, Tom Noble, 35 Thrums Avenue, Bishopbriggs, Glasgow G64 1ER.
Trains run every Saturday and Sunday from Easter to the end of September between 12 noon and 5 pm plus special event weekends. Visitors are welcome every weekend all of the year, 12 noon–5 pm.

Stock
CR 0-4-4T No. 419 built 1907
SJ 4-6-0 No. 1313 (Class B) Motala 586 built 1917
Barclay 0-6-0T No. 24 2335 built 1953
Barclay 0-4-0ST No. 3 1937 built 1928
Hawthorn Leslie 0-4-0ST *Sir John King* 3640 built 1926
Hunslet 0-6-0ST No. 18 3809 built 1954
Barclay 0-4-0T *Borrowstounness* 840 built 1899 (3ft gauge)
Fowler 0-4-0DM 4210140 built 1958
Ruston Hornsby 0-4-0DE 312984 built 1951
Ruston Hornsby 4WDM No. D7 *Pioneer* 275883 built 1949
Yorkshire Engine Co 0-6-0DE No. 401 2691 built 1959
Motor Rail 4WDM 110U082 built 1970 (3ft gauge)
Wickham 4WPMR 10482 built 1970
NSB bogie saloon coach No. 663 built 1937
NSB 4-wheel passenger brake van No. 5010 built 1914
NSB bogie saloon coach No. 791 built 1923
NSB bogie saloon coach No. 645 built 1928
NSB bogie compartment brake coach No. 412 built 1930
LNER-type non-corridor brake composite coach No. 80417 built 1951
NBR bogie invalid saloon No. 461 built 1919
CR 6-wheel goods brake van No. 437 built *c*1920
William Baird & Co three plank wagon No. 7 built 1903
Two LMS short-wheelbase brake vans
MR high goods wagon No. 94 built *c*1910
Steel frame flat wagons Nos 221 & 222
CR bogie bolster wagons Nos 170 & 212 built *c*1910
NCB mineral wagon No. 4898 built *c*1930
BP tank wagon built 1894
Bogie wagon built Fairfield Shipbuilding 1939
LMS six-wheel fish van No. M40226 built 1946
GWR bogie bolster wagon No. 84115 built 1922
Matisa ballast tamping machine No. 48626 built 1957
Carron Iron Co dumb-buffered mineral wagon No. 755 built *c*1890

This is the new permanent home for the Society. Rolling stock is to be gradually transferred from Falkirk.

202 The Scottish Railway Preservation Society D

Standard gauge railway preservation depot

SRPS Depot, Springfield Yard, Wallace Street, off Grahams Road, Falkirk, Central Region, Scotland FK2 7DR
Access: ½ mile north of town centre along Grahams Road. Near BR Falkirk Grahamston Station. Regular train service from Edinburgh and Glasgow; or bus service from Edinburgh and Glasgow, etc; or by car M9.
Tel: Falkirk 20790
OS Ref: NS 891805

Falkirk depot is open to the public virtually every Saturday and Sunday in the year between 11 am and 5 pm when visitors are very welcome, subject to a nominal admission charge. A sales stand and other facilities are provided.

Special open days are held as advertised, when engines may be steamed and other attractions provided. Visitors are asked to note that the depot is not open at other times, except by prior special arrangement. Large party groups are especially welcome at weekends, but organisers are asked to give adequate prior notice when tours are planned to call at Falkirk in order that special arrangements can be made.

The Society has gained wide recognition for the comprehensive and balanced collection of locomotives, rolling stock and other equipment which it has built up to illustrate the history and development of Scottish railways and the Scottish railway industry. Many items have been restored to full working order by the Society's volunteer members and an extensive and ambitious work programme is in hand at Falkirk depot, which is best described as a workshop rather than just a museum. Several of the Society's passenger coaches have been plated by British Rail for operating over BR lines and some of the Society's steam engines have seen occasional outings onto main line, notably to Rail 150 at Shildon in 1975 and Rocket 150 at Rainhill in 1980.

The Society, which is incorporated as a company limited by guarantee, and is recognised as a charity, has a flourishing membership. A bi-monthly magazine *Blastpipe* is issued free to members.

The Society runs an enterprising sales department and an extensive programme of special excursion trains from stations in central Scotland to places of scenic or other interest, many of them composed partly or wholly of SRPS preserved coaches.

Publicity Officer: Tom Noble, 35 Thrums Avenue, Bishopbriggs, Glasgow G64 1ER

Membership Secretary: Mrs I. M. Gollan, 16 West Relugas Road, Edinburgh EH9 2PL

Stock

[1]BR 2-6-4T No. 80105 (Riddles Class 4MT) built 1955
[2]LNER 4-4-0 No. 246 *Morayshire* (Gresley Class D49) built 1928
[4]NBR 0-6-0 No. 673 *Maude* (LNER Class J36) Neilson 4392 built 1891
[5]Neilson-Reid 0-6-0T No. 1 5710 built 1902
[6]Neilson 0-4-0ST No. 13 *Kelton Fell* 2203 built 1876
[7]Hawthorn (Leith) 0-4-0WT *Ellesmere* 244 built 1861
Barclay 0-6-0ST No. 3 1458 built 1916
Barclay 0-4-0CT No. 6 2127 built 1942
Black Hawthorn 0-4-0ST *City of Aberdeen* 912 built 1887
[8]Barclay 0-6-0T No. 20 2068 built 1939
Barclay 0-6-0DM 343 built 1941
Ruston Hornsby 4WDM 262998 built 1949
Ruston Hornsby 4WDM 506500 built 1965
Ruston Hornsby 0-4-0DE No. 1 *Midden* (Class 165DE) 423658 built 1958
Ruston Hornsby 0-4-0DE 421439 built 1958
Ruston Hornsby 0-4-0DE No. 3 423662 built 1958
Baldwin 4WE *Oakbank No. 2* 20587 built 1902 (2ft 6in gauge)
BTH 4WE built 1908
English Electric A-I-A BE 701 built 1926
[9]English Electric 4WE 1131 built 1940
BR 0-6-0DH No. D9524 (Class 14) built 1964
LNER Russell 5-ton steam crane built 1938
Wickham 4WPMR 10482
Two BR Mk.1 TSO coaches
BR Mk.1 RMB buffet car
BR Mk.1 compartment coach
LMS open second coaches Nos 27389 and 27407 built 1946 and 1948
LMS design composite coach No. 24725 built 1950
CR brake composite bogie coach No. 7369 built 1921
CR corridor third bogie coach No. 1375 built 1921
CR non-corridor bogie third coach No. 426 built 1914
HR six-wheeled coupe composite coach No. 17 built 1909
GNSR non-corridor bogie saloon No. 1 built 1898
LNER Gresley buffet car No. 644 built 1937
BR Mk.1 TSO coach No. E4280 built 1956
LNER Thompson T0 No. SC13803E built 1949
LMS 2nd class sleeping car No. M622M built 1951
LNER Gresley corridor third coach No. DE320874 built 1924
GSWR corridor bogie third class coach No. 731 built 1914
GSWR six-wheeled passenger brake No. 122 built 1901
NBR brake/3rd coach No. 3467 built 1916
NBR corridor/3rd coach No. 3565 built 1921
LNER Gresley bogie pigeon van No. E7049E built 1940
CR covered goods vans Nos 73004 and 73007 built *c*1920
LNER Gresley brake/3rd corridor coach No. 62515 built 1924
NBR 6-wheel 3rd class coach built *c*1890
Cauldron wagon No. 25 built *c*1880
Covered grain hopper wagon
GSWR covered van No. 6272 built *c*1910
Two flat wagons built *c*1920
Oakbank Oil Co tank wagon No. 13 built 1894
GNSR single-plank wagon No. 1329 built *c*1880
Shell-BP oil tank wagon No. A43 built 1897
NBR 8-ton loco coal wagon No. 65013 built *c*1890
NBR goods van
LNWR goods van No. 55251 built *c*1910
LNER 36-ton steam crane No. RS1062 built Cowans Sheldon 1936 plus 6-wheel runner wagon
Briggs of Dundee tank wagons Nos 17 and 20 built 1927 and 1918
Scottish Tar Disillers tank wagon No. 78 built 1877; rebuilt
Leith General Warehouse covered grain hopper No. 120 built 1903
Robert Hutchison & Son (Kirkcaldy) covered grain hopper No. 5 built 1903
NCB mineral wagon No. 5362 built *c*1930
GNR high-sided mineral wagon No. 31 built *c*1880
Clyde Iron Works eight-ton hopper wagon (rebuilt)
GWR bogie bolster wagon No. 84974 built 1922
AEC Victor 11-ton road crane

Wickham Type 'B' 4WPM rail trolley 6049 and trailer 6050
In addition, the Society owns numerous items of plant and machinery, including the former wheel lathe from Heaton MPD, Newcastle.

[1]Withdrawn as BR No. 80105 and sold to Woodham Brothers, Barry, for scrap. Purchased for preservation in 1973 by Locomotive Owners Group (Scotland) Limited, an associated group.
[2]Withdrawn as BR No. 62712 in 1961 and purchased by Mr I. N. Fraser for private preservation. Externally restored at Inverurie Works in 1964 and presented to the Royal Scottish Museum, Edinburgh, in 1966. Restored to working order by SRPS in 1975, under loan agreement with RSM.
[4]North British Railway Class C (LNER Class J36) withdrawn by BR from Bathgate shed in 1966 as No. 65243. This locomotive was one of 25 of its class shipped to France during World War I and named on their return. One hundred and sixty-eight engines of this class were built and two of the class survived to become the final steam engines in traffic with BR Scottish Region in 1967.
[5]Outshopped as *Lord Roberts* by Neilson-Reid and Company of Glasgow in 1902 for the Coltness Iron Company Limited at Newmains, Lanarkshire, where the engine stayed until 1955. Bought by the NCB in that year upon closure of the works and sent to Bedlay Colliery, near Coatbridge. Retired in 1968 following the breakage of a cross-head. Donated to the Society by NCB.
[6]Built for William Baird and Son (Iron-founders) by Neilson of Glasgow in 1876, this engine saw service at the company's hematite mine at Lamplugh in West Cumberland, bearing the name *Kelton Fell*, the hill from which the ore was extracted. The engine returned to Scotland in 1914 to work in the Twechar area, passing into NCB stock as No. 13 in 1947. Its external appearance altered little through the years, and it received its final overhaul in 1965 at Shotts Workshops. No. 13 was withdrawn from Gartshore Colliery in1968 and donated to the Society by the NCB. Restored to full working order and original livery by the Society in 1974, and celebrated its centenary in 1976 with a special re-naming ceremony at Falkirk.
[7]The oldest Scottish-built locomotive known to be in existence. Spent all her working life at Howe Bridge Colliery, near Wigan, and withdrawn by the NCB in 1957. Privately preserved and brought to Falkirk in 1966, this engine is now owned by the Royal Scottish Museum and is intended for eventual display in Edinburgh.
[8]The largest locomotive owned by the Society, the last of five such engines delivered to the Wemyss Coal Company Limited at Fife in the 1930s. The company's own railway, the Wemyss Private Railway, escaped nationalisation, and No. 20 worked on the line until its closure in 1970 following the Michael Colliery disaster. The engine was overhauled and reboilered by the builders in 1968 and was purchased by the Society in 1970.
[9]Ex Fairfield Shipyard, Glasgow.

203 Strathspey Railway — A

5 mile passenger-carrying standard gauge steam railway between Aviemore (Speyside) and Boat of Garten, part of the Aviemore/Forres section of the original Highland Railway which opened in 1863

The Station, Boat of Garten, Inverness-shire PH24 3BH
Access: BR trains to Aviemore (direct services from London, Edinburgh, Glasgow and Inverness). Strathspey Station, 'Aviemore Speyside', is ten minutes walk – route displayed at Main Line station. Pedestrian access is by footpath at Bank of Scotland building.
By Car – Access is by Dalfaber Road, off B970 at South end of Aviemore. For Aviemore – leave A9 at B9152 exit then take B970 ('Coylumbridge'). For Boat of Garten – take A95 turn-off and follow 'Boat of Garten' and 'Strathspey Railway' route signs. Car parks at both stations.
By Bus – Highland and independent operators now have direct express services to Aviemore from Glasgow/ Edinburgh and Inverness. Local Aviemore/Grantown-on-Spey services pass through Boat of Garten.
Tel: Boat of Garten (047 983) 692
OS Ref: NH 9419

Closed completely in 1968, after withdrawal of passenger service in 1965, the line was reopened in 1978 and operates at Easter Weekend, weekends from mid-May until mid-October and also on Mondays, Tuesdays and Wednesdays from the end of June until the end of August. Dates, times and fares shown in Timetable available each March.
The line runs through moorland and woodland country and provides fine views of the Cairngorm and Monadhliath Mountains, scenes which have changed little since the line was built. The buildings forming 'Speyside' station were brought from Dalnaspidal, Kyle of Lochalsh provided the turntable, the platform is composed of materials from a number of stations while the footbridge is from Longmorn. All track leading to the engine shed and passing loops at this station have been laid by members as have the sidings at Boat of Garten. However, the station at that end of the line is much as it was during its life as the meeting point between the Highland and the Great North of Scotland.
In addition to the passenger service visitors can view items of stock displayed at Boat of Garten where there is also a museum of small relics. Aviemore loco shed is not open to visitors but some items may be seen on outside tracks which can be viewed from Speyside station.
The railway's Black 5, No. 5025, also makes occasional Main Line runs on charter to other organisations. She has operated to Kyle of Lochalsh, the first steam for 20 years, and on Perth/Aviemore trips.
Membership: Details of membership are available from the Membership Secretary. In addition to providing the entire workforce for the railway, members undertake work away from the line such as recovering materials, manning exhibition stands and publishing newsletters.

The Area Groups in Glasgow, Edinburgh and Inverness have meetings during the winter months.
Secretary: Strathspey Railway Co Ltd., D. B. Barclay, C.A., 111 Union Street, Glasgow G1 (registered office).
Membership Secretary: Strathspey Railway Association, W. Brownlie, 44 Knocklea, Biggar, Lanarkshire ML12 6EQ.
Publicity Officer: R. Black, 37 Castle Avenue, Balloch, Alexandria, Dumbartonshire G83.
Annual Subscription: Adult £5.00, Junior & O.A.P. £2.50, Family £7.50, Group £25.00.

Stock
[1]LMS 4-6-0 No. 5025 (Stanier Class 5MT) built 1934
[2]LMS 2-6-0 No. 46464 (Ivatt Class 2MT) built 1950
[3,4]LMS 2-6-0 No. 46512 (Ivatt Class 2MT) built 1952
[11]LMS 2-6-0 No. 46428 (Ivatt Class 2MT) built 1948
[12]CR 0-6-0 No. 828 built 1899
[4]Barclay 0-6-0T WPR No. 17 2017 built 1935
[4]Barclay 0-4-0ST No. 3 *Clyde* 2315 built 1951
[5]Hunslet 0-6-0ST No. 48 2864 built 1943
[5]RSH 0-6-0ST No. 9 *Cairngorm* 7097 built 1943
[6]Hunslet 0-6-0ST No. 60 3686 built 1948
[14]Barclay 0-6-0ST No. 20 *Niddrie* 1833 built 1924
[7]Barclay 0-4-0ST No. 1 *Dailuaine* 2073 built 1939
[8]Barclay 0-4-0ST No. 2 *Balmenach* 2020 built 1936
BR 1-Co-Co-1DE No. 44008 *Schiehallion* built 1959
Hudswell Clarke 0-6-0DM AMW No. 147 D613 built 1948
Ruston Hornsby 0-4-0DM No. 14 *Inveresk* (165DS Class) 260756 built 1950
[9]Motor Rail 4WDM No. 15 *Inverdon* 5763 built 1957
Ruston Hornsby 4WDM *Queen Anne* 265618 built 1948
[10]North British 0-4-0DH 27549 built 1956
Ruston Hornsby 0-4-0DM *Madalene* 304471 built 1951
BR Mk.1 restaurant cars Nos E1928 and E1936 built 1959
BR Mk.1 CK coach No. 101 (formerly E15401) built 1954
BR Mk.1 non-gangwayed corridor composite No. 102 (formerly E43024) built 1954
BR Mk.1 TSO coach No. 103 (formerly W4127) built 1955
BR Mk.1 brake/3rd coach No. 104 (formerly E43349) built 1955
BR Mk.1 buffet car *Glenfiddich* No. 105 (formerly SC79441) built 1956
BR Mk.1 BSO coach No. 106 (formerly SC9362) built 1959
BR Mk.1 2nd class coach No. E46218 built 1954
LMS 6-wheel full brake coach No. 153 (formerly M32988M) built 1938
LNWR Clerestory coach No. ADM198614
BR Pullman car *Amethyst* (formerly E325E) built 1960
LMS 3rd class sleeping car No. 621 built 1952
LMS corridor brake third No. 27043 built 1951
LMS corridor open third No. 27234 built *c*1945
LMS 'Stove R' six-wheeled full brake No. 33003 built 1939
LMS 12-wheeled first-class sleeping car No. 394 built 1952
LMS third-class sleeping car No. 14452 (latterly No. DM395778) built 1928
LMS engineer's inspection saloon No. M45021 built 1944
LNER first-class sleeping car No. 1211 built 1935
HR four-wheeled full brake No. 5 built *c*1870 (not at Aviemore)
NBR dormitory coach No. DE970012 built 1905
GNSR six-wheeled luggage van No. 68 (latterly No. DE320010) built 1898
GNSR six-wheeled composite No. 34 (latterly No. DE970204) built 1896
BR bogie bolster wagon (latterly B944445)
Three-ton diesel crane built 1951
CR five-ton hand crane built 1905
LMS crane runner built 1935
LNER bolster wagon
Two flat wagons
'SMD' tank wagons Nos 1 and 4
Jones 20-ton diesel crane
Box Van
Wickham 4WPMR *Shara* 1288 built 1933
Esso tank wagon No. 731 built 1908
Four box vans ex-Longmorn Distillery
LMS goods brake van
GNSR coach body
Two open wagons
50-ton diesel crane ex-Glengarnock Steel Works

[1]One of the first batch of the famous 'Black Fives', built at Newton-le-Willows by the Vulcan Foundry (Works No. 4570). Entered service on 2 August 1934 and allocated to Perth shed for work on the Highland line to Inverness and the Caledonian route to Aberdeen. Withdrawn from Carnforth shed in August 1968 after hauling what was at that time thought to be one of the last steam trains on BR. Overhauled first by Hunslet's at Leeds and then by Barclay at Kilmarnock, she travelled to the Strathspey Railway under her own steam on 29 May 1975.
[2]Owned by the '46464 Preservation Trust'. Purchased by the Trust for preservation following withdrawal from Dundee shed. For many years the locomotive worked the Carmyllie Branch and was known locally as 'The Carmyllie Pilot'. Stored at Dundee until moved to the Strathspey Railway in March 1975.
[3]Withdrawn in November 1966 and sold to Woodham Brothers, Barry, for scrap. Purchased by the Strathspey Railway, moved to Bewdley on the Severn Valley Railway in June 1973, subsequently to Hereford, and finally to the Strathspey Railway in 1981.
[4]Owned by the Highland Locomotive Company Ltd (*q.v.*).
[5]Purchased from the National Coal Board (ex-Backworth Colliery).
[6]Purchased from the National Coal Board (ex Dawdon Colliery, Seaham Harbour).
[7]Donated by Scottish Malt Distillers. Formerly used on the branch from Carron Station to Dialuaine Distillery. Latterly this locomotive swopped duties with *Balmenach* and before the line from Cromdale was lifted it was moved to Aviemore.
[8]Donated by Scottish Malt Distillers. Formerly used on the branch from Cromdale to Balmenach Distillery.

[9]Donated by the Scottish Gas Board, Aberdeen Gas Works.
[10]Purchased from the South of Scotland Electricity Board. Formerly used at Barony Power Station, Ayrshire.
[11]Withdrawn in November 1966 and sent to Woodham Bros scrapyard, Barry. Purchased for preservation in December 1979 to provide a replacement boiler and other spares for sister engine No. 46464.
[12]McIntosh 812 Class withdrawn from Ardrossan shed in 1963 as BR No. 57566. Purchased by the Scottish Locomotive Preservation Trust Fund in 1964 and stored until restored to CR livery at Cowlairs in 1966. At the time of their construction, the 812 Class were the largest CR goods engines; a freight counterpart of the famous 'Dunalastair' 4-4-0s. This locomotive was housed in Glasgow Museum of Transport until moved to the Strathspey Railway in 1980 where it is being prepared for return to traffic.
[14]Donated by the NCB. Undergoing restoration at Leith.

The Highland Locomotive Company Limited **H**

Registered office: The Station, Boat of Garten, Inverness-shire PH24 3BH
Secretary: D. B. Barclay, C.A., at the above address.
Tel: Bridge of Allan 3013

Company formed in 1975 to represent the original supporters of an appeal to purchase Ivatt Class 2, 46512, in 1973. Its function is to purchase, restore, maintain and supply locomotives for use on the Strathspey Railway. The Company is a subsidiary of the Strathspey Railway Co Ltd and shareholders also include the Strathspey Railway Association. In 1976 Barclay 0-4-0ST (SR No. 3) and 0-6-0T (SR No. 7) were transferred to the Company. The restored locomotives carry the Strathspey colours – an adaptation of the Highland Railway scheme, dark green with 'Strathspey Railway' – in full on the tanks or tender sides.
Enquiries regarding purchase of shares are welcome.

204 Lochty Private Railway A

One mile passenger-carrying line near Anstruther, Fife

Access: By own transport (1½ miles from nearest bus route). Off B940 Cupar–Crail Road (10 miles from Cupar and 7 miles from Crail)
Nearest BR station: Cupar (10 miles)
Tel: 0592-4587
OS Ref: NO 522080

The railway operates on Sundays from mid-June to early September between 2 pm and 5 pm.
Facilities for visitors include car parking and souvenir shop. The Lochty Private Railway forms part of the former East Fife Central Railway, closed in 1965. The Lochty–Knightsward section lies bordered by farmland owned by John B. Cameron and thus no statutory authority was necessary for services to commence in 1967. It was the first standard gauge preserved line to operate in Scotland. Operation of the railway is now undertaken by members of the Fife Railway Preservation Group. Membership of the Group is open to railway enthusiasts who are interested in helping with the operation, maintenance and development of the LPR as a working steam railway museum. The Group is engaged in acquiring items of railway equipment previously used in and around Fife for use or display at Lochty.

Stock
[1]Peckett 0-4-0ST No. 1 1376 built 1915
[2]Bagnall 0-6-0ST WPR No. 16 2759 built 1944
[3]Barclay 0-4-0ST *Forth* 1890 built 1926
[4]Barclay 0-4-0ST NCB No. 21 2292 built 1951
Yorkshire Engine Co 0-6-0DE 2603 built 1955
[5]Ruston Hornsby 4WDM (88DS Class) 421415 built 1958
LNER observation coach No. 1719 built 1937
BR Mk.1 BSO coach No. E9315 built 1956
Two 3-plank dropside wagons ex Tullis Russell of Markinch
NBR 8-ton box van built 1901
Briggs of Dundee bitumen tank wagon No. 202
5-plank open goods wagon No. 11
Three standard RCH 7-plank mineral wagons
RCH mineral converted to 5 plank
RCH mineral converted to flat wagon
Hurst Nelson coal wagon

[1]Ex-British Aluminium Co, Burntisland, 1972.
[2]Ex-Wemyss Private Railway, 1973.
[3]Ex-Scottish Gas Board, Granton Gas Works, on permanent loan from the Strathspey Railway 1981.
[4]Ex-National Coal Board 1981, on permanent loan under the terms of their Mining Relics Scheme.
[5]Donated to the Fife Railway Preservation Group by the North British Distillery Co, Edinburgh, in 1974.

Details of the FRPG may be obtained from P. M. Westwater, 48 Hendry Road, Kircaldy, Fife. Tel: 0592-4587.

205 Alford Valley Railway B

Passenger-carrying 2ft gauge railway under construction from the former GN of SR Alford Station to Bridge of Alford, a distance of 3 miles

Alford, Murray Park, Grampian
Tel: Alford 2326
OS Ref: NJ 579159

About 2¼ miles of track has been laid and services commenced in 1979. Operation from April to June at weekends and daily in July and August.
Facilities for visitors include car parking, railway shop, refreshments and toilets.
Work commenced on constructing the railway in February 1979 and the first section, from Haughton

Country Park to Murray Park, was brought into use at the end of June 1979.
The project is complementary to the proposed Grampian Region Museum of Transport which is to be sited in the area of the old station at Alford. The railway will have eight stations and passes through a recognised tourist area with popular picnic areas and caravan/camping sites. The railway traverses nature trails, woodland and a historic battlefield. The company is being closely assisted by the Alford Valley Railway Association.
Help and finance are required to assist the company in its aims and membership of the Association is open to all interested parties. Members will be entitled to free travel on the line and a regular newsletter on progress. Volunteer help is always required with track laying and train operation. The Association will be shareholders of the railway company.
Details from: Jim Gordon, Ravenswood, Alford, Grampian.

Stock
Fowler 0-4-2T *Saccharine* 13355 built 1912
Motor Rail 4WDM 22221 built 1964
Motor Rail 4WDM *The Bra' Lass* 9381 built 1948 (steam outline)
Motor Rail 4WDM 9215 built 1946
Motor Rail 4WDM 5342 built 1931
Lister 4WDM *Hamewith* 3198 built 1930
Two open 4-wheel coaches
Two closed 4-wheel coaches
Six 4-wheeled peat wagons
Two enclosed bogie coaches ex-Warwick Castle Railway
There is also to be a display of GN of SR standard gauge exhibits at Alford Station.

206 Glasgow Museum of Transport E

Standard gauge steam locomotives on static display in a large museum devoted to all aspects of Scottish, and particularly Glaswegian, transport

25 Albert Drive, Glasgow G41 2PE
Access: In easy reach of the M8 Motorway, near Eglinton Toll. Albert Drive connects with Pollokshaws Road, the A77 signposted to Kilmarnock. The nearest Subway station is West Street. By bus, going South from Renfield Street (City Centre). By train, Pollokshields East Station is adjacent to the museum with frequent electric trains from Glasgow Central Station.
Tel: 041-423-8000
OS Ref: NS 581632

The Museum is open daily from 10 am to 5 pm and on Sundays from 2 pm to 5 pm. Closed on Christmas Day and New Year's Day.
Admission Free.
Facilities for visitors include museum shop, refreshments and toilets.
Many aspects of Transport History are represented in the Museum. The horse-drawn vehicles display includes private passenger carriages, public coaches and wagons, including a Royal Mail Coach of the 1840s.
The bicycle and motor cycle collections, like other sections, include important exhibits.
The most notable is perhaps the oldest surviving pedal cycle in the world, a contemporary copy of MacMillan's of 1839. The car collection traces the fascinating history of the motor car. Amongst others can be seen an important group of Scottish built vehicles, including Argylls, Albions and Arrol-Johnstons, as well as more modern cars.
Trams are by no means forgotten – the Glaswegians' love of the 'caurs' is legendary – from the original horse-drawn tram of 1894, to the Cunarder, the story of the trams can be seen, and times-past recalled.
The development of the various Scottish railway companies can be seen with the aid of models and full-size exhibits.
The model railway is an attraction for railway enthusiasts of all ages.
Also to be seen are commercial vehicles, ranging from a steam-powered traction engine to road rollers.
On 14 December 1979, a new gallery featuring the Glasgow Underground Railway was opened. This is in the form of a reconstruction of the old Merkland Street station and includes two of the old cars:
Oldbury C & W Co Car No. 1 built 1896 (4ft gauge)
Hurst Nelson Car No. 39T built 1898 (4ft gauge)
Another recent addition to the displays in the Clyde Room exhibition of nearly 200 model ships.
Further details may be obtained from The Keeper, at the above address. (SAE with your enquiry appreciated.)

Stock
[1]CR 4-2-2 No. 123 Neilson 3553 built 1886
[2]GSWR 0-6-0T No. 9 (Class 5) NB Loco 21521 built 1917
[3]GNSR 4-4-0 No. 49 *Gordon Highlander* (Class F) NB Loco 22563 built 1920
[4]HR 4-6-0 No. 103 Sharp Stewart 4022 built 1894
[5]NBR 4-4-0 No. 256 *Glen Douglas* (Class K) built 1913
[6]Barclay 0-6-0F No. 1 1571 built 1917
[7]Chaplin 0-4-0 VBTG 2638 built 1885

Tramcar Exhibits
Glasgow Horse Tramcar No. 543 built 1894
Glasgow 'Room & Kitchen' car No. 672 built 1898
Glasgow 'Round dash' Standard car No. 779 built 1900
Glasgow 'Hex dash' Standard car No. 1088 built 1924
Glasgow single-deck bogie car No. 1089 built 1926
Glasgow double-deck 'Coronation' car No. 1173 built 1938
Glasgow double-deck 'Cunarder' car No. 1392 built 1952

[1]Built for display at the International Exhibition of Industry, Science and Art, held at Edinburgh in 1886. Taken into Caledonian Railway stock at the closure of the exhibition and worked as the Chief Mechanical Engineer's saloon engine and royal train pilot. Withdrawn as LMS No. 14010 in 1935 and restored to CR blue livery. Stored at

St Rollox Works until returned to traffic to work special excursion trains in 1958. Taken out of traffic in 1965 and moved to the Museum in 1966.

[2]Smellie Class 5 withdrawn as LMS No. 16379 in 1934 and sold to Ruabon Coal and Coke Co Ltd. Withdrawn in 1962 and presented by the NCB for display. Stored until moved to the Museum in 1966.

[3]A member of the Heywood 'F' Class (LNER Class D40), this graceful 4-4-0 was withdrawn from Keith shed in 1958 as BR No. 62277. Restored to GNSR livery and returned to traffic in 1959 to work special trains. Withdrawn in 1965 and moved to the Museum in 1966.

[4]'Jones Goods' Class withdrawn as LMS No. 17916 in 1934. Restored to Highland Railway green livery in 1935 and stored at St Rollox Works until repainted in HR yellow livery and returned to traffic in 1959. Taken out of traffic in 1965 and moved to the Museum in 1966. The 'Jones Goods' was the first 4-6-0 design to enter service in the United Kingdom.

[5]Reid 'K' Class (LNER Class D34), became BR No. 62469 and was restored to NBR livery in 1959 whilst still in service. Officially withdrawn in 1962, it was retained to work special trains along with the other preserved Scottish locomotives. Taken out of traffic in 1965 and moved to the Museum in 1966.

[6]Presented by the South of Scotland Electricity Board, Dalmarnock Power Station, Glasgow, in 1969. Originally built for the Ministry of Munitions.

[7]A small Glasgow-built locomotive with vertical boiler and geared drive. Employed at Northampton Gas Works, the locomotive was presented by Nottingham Industrial Museum in 1980. Its maker also manufactured boilers, stationary engines, steam cranes and evaporators from the 1860s until the early 1900s.

Other railway items include a collection of exhibition models of locomotives built by the North British Locomotive Co and an important collection of material illustrating the development of permanent way. There is a large '00' gauge model railway of Carlisle Station which is operated regularly.

207 Royal Scottish Museum E

Locomotive on static display in transport gallery

Chambers Street, Edinburgh EH1 1JF
Tel: 031-225-7534
OS Ref: NT 258734

The museum is open on weekdays from 10 am to 5 pm and on Sundays from 2 pm to 5 pm.
Facilities for visitors include a museum shop, refreshments and toilets.
The Royal Scottish Museum is the most comprehensive display in Britain under one roof comprising the decorative arts, natural history, geology and technology. Transport is represented, including a colliery locomotive of 1813, many scale model locomotives and models of ships.
Further details from The Keeper, Mr J. D. Storer, at the above address.

Stock
[1]William Hedley 4WVCG *Wylam Dilly* built 1813 (5ft gauge)

The following exhibits are on loan to the Scottish RPS at Bo'ness and Falkirk (see Group Nos 201 & 202):
LNER 4-4-0 No. 246 *Morayshire* (Class D49) built 1928
Hawthorn (Leith) 0-4-0WT *Ellesmere* 244 built 1861
[2]Baldwin 4WE *Oakbank No. 2* 20587 built 1902 (2ft 6in gauge)
Barclay 0-6-0T No. 24 2335 built 1953
BTH 4WE built 1908
LNER Russell 5-ton steam crane built 1938
Chaldron wagon built 1870

[1]Withdrawn in 1864 and acquired from Wylam Colliery, Northumberland, by the sons of the builder. Loaned by them for display in 1882.

[2]Ex-Scottish Oils Ltd, Winchburgh Shale Mine, Midlothian, 1961. In store at present.

208 John B. Cameron D

Steam locomotive stored in Parcels shed, Markinch Station, in between working main line railtours in Scotland

Markinch Station, Fife, Scotland
Tel: St Monans 210
OS Ref: NO 299014

No public access.

Stock
LNER 4-6-2 No. 60009 *Union of South Africa* (Class A4) built 1937

Withdrawn from Aberdeen (Ferryhill) shed as BR No. 60009 in 1966. Purchased for preservation in 1967 and moved to the Lochty Private Railway, where it was used as a tourist attraction until 1972. The following April the locomotive was returned to BR tracks to work steam-hauled excursions in Scotland.

209 Ayrshire Railway Preservation Group F

Collection of locomotives undergoing restoration by the Group on a site that was part of the former Dalmellington Iron Company's system

Minnivey, near Dalmellington, Strathclyde
OS Ref: NS 476074

Site not open to the public but facilities can be arranged for interested parties.
Details from: Norman Gee, 43 Glebe Road, Kilmarnock, Ayrshire. Tel: Kilmarnock (0563) 43428
Formed in 1974, the Group has as its aims the preservation and restoration of items of railway and associated industrial interest in South-West Scotland. Our hope for the future is to form a railway museum in which items we have preserved can be displayed to the public in a working environment.
To this end, we have obtained locomotives, rolling stock (standard and narrow gauge), station and signalling equipment, and many smaller historical items and documents. Restoration is being carried out on the above to ensure that they are in a suitable condition for working and display.
The Group is a purely voluntary organisation, all funds being raised through exhibitions, waste paper collections, donations and subscriptions.
Other Group activities include informal monthly meetings and visits. Meetings are held in the Loudoun Hall, Ayr, between September and May, and include guest speakers, slide and film shows, quiz nights, etc. The Group has organised visits to British Rail depots and works, railway museums and other preservation societies.
Members receive a regular newsletter to keep them informed of all Group activities. Membership also gives voting rights and the opportunity to help in the satisfying work of restoring and maintaining the locomotives and rolling stock.

Stock
Barclay 0-4-0ST No. 3 1889 built 1926
[1]Barclay 0-4-0ST No. 1 2368 built 1955
[1]Barclay 0-4-0ST No. 10 2244 built 1947
[2]Barclay 0-4-0ST No. 19 1614 built 1918
Barclay 0-6-0ST No. 25 2358 built 1954
Barclay 0-4-0ST No. 16 1116 built 1910
Barclay 0-4-0DM No. 7 399 built 1956
Ruston Hornsby 4WDM *Blinkin Bess* (Class 88DS) 284839 built 1950
Fowler 0-4-0DM 4200028 built 1948
Fowler 0-4-0DM *Lily of the Valley* 22888 built 1939
Wickham 4WPMR 10179 built 1968
Wickham 4WPMR No. DB965330 10180 built 1968
Ruston Hornsby 4WDM 183749 built 1937 (2ft 6in gauge)
Ruston Hornsby 4WDM 211681 built 1942 (2ft 6in gauge)
Ruston Hornsby 4WDM 210959 built 1941 (2ft 6in gauge)
G & SWR 30-cwt rail-mounted hand crane
LNER 12-ton mineral wagon No. 45406 built 1938
NCB 12-ton ballast wagon built LMS
LMS mineral wagon
Two LMS open wagons
NER Insulated van
LNER 12-ton box van built 1935
Ministry of Supply acid tank wagon No. 3 built 1940
NCB hopper wagon/snowplough
Three tipper wagons (2ft 6in gauge)
Two flat wagons (2ft 6in gauge)

[1]Both on loan from NCB via Cumnock and Doon Valley District Council and are from Dunaskin Loco shed, Waterside, being withdrawn from use in 1978.
[2]On loan to the Dalmellington Countryside Society by the NCB and in store at Minnivey prior to restoration and possible display in Dalmellington.

210 Lochranza Transport Museum E

Static 4ft gauge coach exhibit

The Piggery, Corriegills, Isle of Arran, Strathclyde

Stock
Glasgow Underground Railway Coach No. 10 built 1896 rebuilt 1935

211 Prestongrange Mining Museum E

The historic Prestongrange site has now become an industrial museum commemorating 800 years of recorded history of its use in the coal and salt industries. Incorporated in the site are the former colliery, brickworks and harbour, which was once a customs port but is now in need of restoration

Prestongrange, East Lothian
Access: On coast road, between Musselburgh and Prestonpans
OS Ref: NT 374737

The principal exhibit is the Cornish beam pumping engine built by Harvey & Co of Hayle in 1874.
The Beam Engine, now an Industrial Monument, is planned to become the centrepiece of a Historical Site for the Mining Industry. The first written record of coal mining in Britain is the Charter given to the monks of Newbattle in 1210 to work the coal in the Grange of Preston. The first coal harbour, Acheson's Haven, lay across the road and the first railway in Scotland was laid on wooden rails from Tranent to Cockenzie, some three miles down the coast.
The East Lothian District Council has acquired the site and is laying it out to show the various different stages in miners' efforts to win coal. The main display will endeavour to simulate a colliery at the beginning of the 20th century when the deeper mines were sunk. The Grant Ritchie steam winding engine 1909, dismantled from Newcraighall Colliery, is being reassembled. Other machinery is on view in the Power House. A great deal of the work has been done by a band of volunteers working under the inspiration of David Spence, the Honorary Curator, 24 Woodlands Grove, Edinburgh 15 (Tel: 031-661-2718), who will be glad to hear from anyone interested and willing to help.

The Prestongrange Mining Museum incorporates a short standard gauge line running from the colliery to the adjacent main line as well as a short length of 2ft gauge track. Steam operation of the standard gauge line takes place on the first Sunday of each month from April to October.

Stock
Barclay 0-4-0ST No. 6 2043 built 1937
Barclay 0-4-0ST Bo. 17 2219 built 1946
Grant Ritchie 0-4-2ST No. 7 *Prestongrange* 536 built 1914
Motor Rail 4WDM No. 1 9925 built 1963
Ruston Hornsby 4WDM (2ft gauge)
Hunslet 4WDM 4440 built 1952 (2ft gauge)
Kalmdo steam winch
Six open coal wagons
Whittaker steam crane No. 136
Marshall Fleming steam crane

212 Aberdeen City Council E

Locomotive and rolling stock on static display

Seaton Park Aberdeen
OS Ref: NJ 943092

Stock
[1]Barclay 0-4-0ST *Mr Therm* 2239 built 1947
Three wagons
One brake van

[1]Ex-Scottish Gas Board, Aberdeen, 1972. Depot, Aberdeen. It is intended that this locomotive will form a static display item at a children's playground in Aberdeen.

Details from: Alan Greig, Broomfold Cottage, Tornaveen, Torphins, Kincardine and Deeside.

213 Caledonian Railway (Brechin) Ltd F

A standard gauge railway preservation scheme aimed at re-opening the line from Brechin to Bridge of Dun, then possibly on to Dubton, a total distance of 7 miles. Locomotives under restoration, and 4 miles of track to Bridge of Dun now acquired

Brechin Station, 2 Park Road, Brechin, Angus DD9 7AF
Access: Just off A935 near town centre. No 44 bus from Montrose passes the station; also No 104 and 105 (Dundee to Aberdeen) to Brechin town centre. Nearest BR station, Montrose (seven miles)
OS Ref: NO 602602

The Caledonian Railway (Brechin) Limited, was formed in 1982 to become the operating Company of the Brechin Railway Preservation Society. The Company now has successfully concluded negotiations for the lease of the 4 mile Brechin to Bridge of Dun branch line, following its joint purchase by the Scottish Tourist Board, Angus District and Tayside Regional Councils from BR.
The Bridge of Dun to Brechin line was opened in 1847 by the Aberdeen Railway Company and became a busy branch of the Caledonian Railway Glasgow to Aberdeen main line through Strathmore. Passenger services to Brechin ceased in the early 1950s, although the main line was closed in 1967, final withdrawal of freight services and closure of the branch from the East Coast main line did not take place until 1981. The closure date was marked by a hugely successful 'last train' to Brechin from Edinburgh on 2 May, 1981.
The Brechin Railway Preservation Society. *Details from:* Mr P. Farquhar, 31A St David Street, Brechin, Angus, Scotland.
Plans for a volunteer-run steam railway were launched by the BRPS in February 1979, and since then locomotives, rolling stock, and other railway relics have continued to arrive at Brechin for restoration. In 1980 the lease was acquired to the large imposing station, and work has gone on to restore this listed Georgian building (probably the last Caledonian Railway branch line terminus left in existence). Sales shop and small relics museum Brechin station. Steam days during the summer months.

Stock
Bagnall 0-6-0ST No. 6 2749 built 1944
Hunslet 0-6-0ST *Diana* 2879 built 1943
Barclay 0-4-0ST *Bon Accord* 807 built 1897
Barclay 0-4-0ST No. 17 1863 built 1926
Barclay 0-4-0ST No. 4 2047 built 1937
Ruston Hornsby 0-4-0DE 449747 built 1960
Ruston Hornsby 0-4-0DM No. 6 421700 built 1959
BR 3-car DMU set No. 413 (Class 126) comprising Nos SC51017, SC59404 and SC51043 built 1959
Hibberd 4WDM 3743 built 1955
BR Mk.1 suburban 2nd class coach No. E46162 built 1953
BR Mk.1 engineers saloon coach built 1959
BR Mk.1 BSK coach No. E34539 built 1955
BR Mk.1 TSO coach No. SC4249 built 1956
BR CCT van No. M94259 built 1960
Three plank open wagon
Three ex-MOD Rectank wagons built *c*1918
Grafton 10-ton diesel crane
L & YR flat wagon built 1918
Two MR flat wagons

214 Shell UK Ltd I

Industrial steam location featuring regular steam working

North Crescent, Ardrossan, Strathclyde
OS Ref: NS 230428

No public access

Stock
Barclay 0-4-0F 1952 built 1928

215 R. B. Tennent Ltd I

Industrial steam location featuring regular steam working

Steel and Iron Roll Manufacturers, Whifflet Foundry, Coatbridge, Strathclyde
OS Ref: NS 738643

No public access.

Stock
Sentinel 4WVBTG *John* 9561 built 1953
Sentinel 4WVBTG *Ranald* 9627 built 1957
Sentinel 4WVBTG *Robin* 9628 built 1957
Sentinel 4WVBTG *Denis* 9631 built 1958

216 British Aluminium Co Ltd I

Industrial steam location with locomotive stored out of use, nominally spare to the diesels

Burntisland, Fife
OS Ref: NT 225862

No public access

Stock
Barclay 0-4-0ST *BA Co No. 3* 2046 built 1937

217 National Coal Board (Scotland) I

Industrial steam locations, many of them featuring regular steam working

No public access

Stock
Barclay 0-6-0T No. 8 1296 built 1912 (Polkemmet Colliery, Whitburn, West Lothian)
Barclay 0-6-0ST No. 12 1829 built 1924 (Polkemmet Colliery, Whitburn, West Lothian)
Hunslet 0-6-0ST No. 17 2880 built 1943 (Polkemmet Colliery, Whitburn, West Lothian)
[1]Barclay 0-6-0ST No. 8 *Dardanelles* 1175 built 1909 (Polkemmet Colliery, Whitburn, West Lothian)
Barclay 0-4-0ST No. 17 2296 built 1952 (Barony Colliery, Auchinleck)
Hunslet 0-6-0ST No. 19 3818 built 1954 (Comrie Colliery, Saline, Fife)
Hunslet 0-6-0ST No. 5 3837 built 1955 (Comrie Colliery, Saline, Fife)
Bagnall 0-6-0ST No. 7 2777 built 1945 (Comrie Collery, Saline, Fife)
Barclay 0-4-0ST No. 5 2260 built 1949 (Cardowan Colliery, Stepps, Lanarkshire)
Barclay 0-4-0ST No. 29 1996 built 1934 (Bilston Glen Colliery, Loanhead)
Barclay 0-4-0ST No. 20 2357 built 1955 (Cowdenbeath Central Workshops)

[1]Restored as a static exhibit by the gateway to Polkemmet Colliery, Whitburn, West Lothian.

218 Port Erroll Railway A

7¼in gauge passenger-carrying steam railway alongside Main street car park, Cruden Bay

Banff and Buchan, Grampian, AB4 7NF
Access: Located between the twin villages of Cruden Bay and Port Erroll, 23 miles north of Aberdeen
Bus services available. Car parking in Port Erroll village
Trains stop at Castle Woods and Burnside to pick up or set down passengers by request only. Passenger may return from Smugglers Bay to Port Erroll by any train of their choice. The railway provides public transport to a heritage coastal region and castle not served by road.
Tel: 0770-812410

Details from: Alan Sangster, 12 Station Place, Cruden Bay, Peterhead, Grampian AB4 9NF.
Operates at weekends from April to the end of September, and daily in June, July and August.
Facilities for visitors include car parking, refreshments, railway shop, picnic area and small railway museum at Smugglers Bay.

Stock
Severn Lamb 0-6-0 No. 1 *Donald* ('Romulus' Class) built 1980
Mardyke Engineering 4WDM No. 2 *Samson* built 1980

219 Dr R. P. Jack G

Private collection of 2ft gauge rolling stock in store

The Station, Eddleston, Borders

Please contact before visiting

Stock
Barclay 0-4-0T 1871 built 1925
Hunslet 4WDM 2927 built 1944

220 Gladstone Court Museum G

2ft gauge steam locomotive in store pending the construction of this long-term museum project

Biggar Gas Works (Branch of Royal Scottish Museum)

Stock
Barclay 0-4-0T No. 5 988 built 1903

221 D. Ritchie & C. Young G

A private collection of narrow gauge locomotives in store

Haddington, Lothian

No public access.

Stock
Ruston Hornsby 4WDM 189992 built 1938 (2ft 6in gauge)
Ruston Hornsby 4WDM 466591 built 1961 (3ft gauge)

Ruston Hornsby 4WDM 179005 built 1936 (2ft gauge)
Motor Rail 4WDM 7330 built 1938 (2ft gauge)
Ruston Hornsby 4WDM 249530 built 1947 (2ft gauge)
Ruston Hornsby 4WDM 242916 built 1946 (2ft 6in gauge)
Ruston Hornsby 4WDM 273843 built 1949 (3ft gauge)
Ruston Hornsby 0-4-0DM 338429 built 1955 (2ft 6in gauge)
Motor Rail 4WDM *Terras* 7189 built 1937 (2ft gauge)
Hunslet 4WDM 2654 built 1942 (2ft gauge)

222 Hardridge Grouse Railway C

Private 2ft gauge passenger-carrying grouse railway

Operated by Sir William Lithgow at Hardridge, Kilmacolm, Strathclyde
OS Ref: NS 313675

No public access.

Stock
Motor Rail 4WDM No. 2 8700 built 1941
Motor Rail 4WPM 2097 built 1922
Motor Rail 4WPM 2171 built 1922

223 Fraserburgh Mini-Railway B

2ft gauge passenger-carrying line, approx 300 yards long arranged in an oval loop

Banff and Buchan District Council, Fraserburgh, Grampian
OS Ref: NK 001659

Railway opened in 1961.
Services operate daily during the summer, weather permitting.

Stock
Lister Blackstone 4WDM No. 677 *Kessock Knight* 53541 built 1963 (steam outline)
Three 4-wheel coaches

224 Butlins Ltd B

A 2ft gauge passenger-carrying line about 1000 yards long with a return loop at either end

Heads of Ayr Holiday Camp
OS Ref: NS 299187

Stock
Chance 4-2-4DH No. 145 *C. P. Huntington* built 1976 (steam outline)
Four 14-seat bogie coaches

225 Kerrs Miniature Railway B

A 10¼in gauge line 400 yards long running from West Links Station, alongside the BR East Coast main line, to Burnside. The railway was originally opened in 1935 as 7¼in gauge, but converted to 10¼in in 1938

West Links Park, Arbroath, Angus
Access: Via the A92, 500 yards along the promenade from the Bathing pool. By rail to BR Arbroath station
Tel: Arbroath 79249

After being requisitioned during the War by the Government, the railway reopened in 1946 and was extended to almost twice its former length alongside BR's Edinburgh–Aberdeen main line, giving rise to the famous publicity photographs of East Coach Pacifics racing along behind their miniature relations on the KMR. Following a period of dieselisation and decline, the railway was revitalised in 1978 when taken over by Mr Matthew Kerr Junior. Since then, the track has been relaid and many improvements made, including the return of steam motive power. As an attraction it remains as popular as ever, carrying around twenty thousand passengers each summer – over one-third of whom are adults.
The railway operates at weekends only in April, May, June and September; daily during July and the first fortnight in August.

Stock
Jennings 4-4-2PM No. 9872 *Auld Reekie* built *c*1934 (steam outline)
BR Bo-BoPM (Class 25) No. 25081 built Eastwood 1981
Clitheroe 4-6-4BE *Prince Andrew* built 1961
Croall 4-4-0 CR No. 769 built 1906 (11in gauge)
Two open bogie coaches built 1961
Three open bogie coaches built 1981

226 Craigtoun Miniature Railway B

Passenger-carrying 15in gauge railway

North East Fife District Council, Craigtoun Park, near St Andrews, Fife
OS Ref: NO 482141

Operating from 11 am onwards on Saturdays.

Stock
Severn-Lamb 2-8-0PH No. 278 R8 built 1976 (steam outline)
Two open bogie coaches
Closed bogie coach

227 Strathan Miniature Railway B

Passenger-carrying 7¼in gauge railway, 156 yards in length laid out as a continuous circuit

George Allan Park, Strathaven, Larkhall, Lanarkshire

In operation daily during the holiday season from May to September.

Stock
Steam-outline locomotive
Three open bogie coaches

228 Ayr Miniature Railway B

Passenger-carrying 10¼in gauge railway forming a short circuit in the seafront children's playground

The Promenade, Ayr

In operation daily during June, July and August.

Stock
Severn-Lamb Co-CoPH *Ayr Princess* built 1968
Two bogie coaches built Severn-Lamb 1968

229 Thomas Muir G

A collection of industrial steam locomotives retained pending scrapping

Scrap Metal Contractor, Easter Balbeggie, near Thornton, Fife
OS Ref: NT 291962

This is the 'Woodhams of the North'!
No public access.

Stock
Barclay 0-4-0ST No. 47 2157 built 1943
Barclay 0-4-0ST No. 3 946 built 1902
Barclay 0-4-0ST No. 22 1069 built 1906
Barclay 0-6-0T No. 10 1245 built 1911
Barclay 0-4-0ST No. 7 2262 built 1949
Barclay 0-4-0ST No. 53 1807 built 1923
Barclay 0-6-0ST No. 15 2183 built 1945
Barclay 0-4-0ST No. 6 2261 built 1949
Grant Ritchie 0-4-0ST No. 61 272 built 1894
Hunslet 4wDM 3286 built 1945 (2ft gauge)

[1]Reserved for Glenrothes Council for some considerable time, though this scheme is now thought doubtful.

230 Mull and West Highland Narrow Gauge Railway A

10¼in gauge passenger-carrying railway

Isle of Mull, Argyll, Scotland
Access: Off A849 Craignure to Iona Road

Opened 22 June, 1984. It runs for just over 1½ miles from Craignure to Torosay Castle and Gardens using steam motive power. A supporters' organisation has been formed for what has been described as the remotest miniature railway in the UK.

Further details from: Mr M. R. Oliver, 32 Kilmory Road, Lochgilphead, Argyll. Tel: 0546-2509.

Stock
LMS 4-6-0 No. 5156 *Ayrshire Yeomanry* Class 5MT, built Guest 1950
Curwen 4-4-2 *Waverley* built 1948
LNER 4-6-2 No. 4472 *Flying Scotsman* built Carland 1949
[1]Marsh 2-6-4T *Lady of the Isles* built 1981
GNR 4-2-2 No. 1 under construction by Marsh
BR Bo-BoPM (Class 26 replica) No. 5330 built 1984
Three 20-seat passenger coaches

[1]On loan to Suffolk Miniature Light Railway (Group No. 119). Trains connect with Caledonian–Mac Brayne, Oban–Craignure advertised sailings, starting with the 10 am from Oban and finishing with the 1700 from Craignure.

231 Carnegie Dunfermline Trust E

Standard gauge static locomotive exhibit located just behind 'The Peacock' restaurant

Pittencrieff Park, Dunfermline, Fife KY12 8QH
Tel: 0383-29881
OS Ref: NT 086872

Stock
Gibb & Hogg 0-4-0ST No. 11 16 built 1898

Presented by National Coal Board, Cardowan Colliery, 1968. Restored by the Fife Industrial Locomotive Preservation Group.

232 William de Venney & Sons Ltd G

Standard gauge steam locomotive stored on behalf of its owner, Mr P. Fielding

Camsail Works, Rosneath, Strathclyde

No public access.

Stock
Sentinel 4WVBTG 9593 built 1954

233 East Lothian District Council E

Standard gauge steam locomotive on static display

Danderhall Children's Recreation Park, Danderhall, East Lothian
OS Ref: NT 308698

Stock
Barclay 0-4-0ST No. 29 1142 built 1908

Owned by local NUM Branch.

234 Captain J. Hay G

Private collection of narrow gauge rolling stock

Dalgettie Castle, Grampian
OS Ref: NJ 754507

Stock
Lister Blackstone 4WDM 52610 (2ft guage)
Skip wagons

235 Coatbridge Industrial Museum E

Standard gauge steam locomotive on static display

Monklands District Council, Glasgow

Stock
Hudswell Clarke 0-6-0T No. 9 895 built 1909

236 Lochore Meadows County Park E

Loco on static display alongside assembly of pit winding gear

Countryside Commission Park, Fife Regional Council

Stock
Barclay 0-4-0ST No. 30 2259 built 1949

237 Lothian Regional Council E

Standard gauge steam locomotive on static display

Rail and Mining Heritage Centre, Lady Victoria Colliery, Newtongrange
OS Ref: NT 332638

Stock
Barclay 0-4-0ST No. 21 2284 built 1949

238 J. Marshall and Son (Builders) G

Standard gauge steam locomotive undergoing restoration

Duncan Fraser, Glenfoot, Tillicoultry
OS Ref: NS 908964

Stock
Hunslet 0-6-0ST No. 18 3809 built 1954

239 West Buchan Railway A

A 15in gauge passenger-carrying line 1¾ miles long built on the trackbed of the former Banff–Tillynaught branch line

Banff Harbour Station, Banff

Services commenced in June 1984.

Stock
Heiden 0-4-0WTT *Chough* built 1962
Severn-Lamb 2-8-0 + Bo-BoDH 7218 built 1972 (steam outline)

240 Ness Islands Railway A

A 7¼in gauge passenger-carrying line ⅓-mile long

Whin Island, Bught Park, Inverness

Opened on 31 March 1984, and operates at weekends from July to September.

241 Grampian Transport Museum E

Museum of historic road and rail exhibits

Alford, Grampian, Scotland
Access: 25 miles west of Aberdeen

Open daily from 11 am to 5 pm.

Stock
Aberdeen 4-wheel double-deck horse tram No. 1 built 1896.

AREA F

North West

Cumbria
Lancashire
Cheshire
Isle of Man
Merseyside
(Group Nos 251–300)

251 Ravenglass and Eskdale Railway A

Passenger-carrying 15in gauge steam railway, 7 miles in length, running from Ravenglass to Eskdale (Dalegarth)

Ravenglass Station, Ravenglass, Cumbria CA18 1SW
Access: Ravenglass BR station. Cumberland Motor Services buses serve Ravenglass and Muncaster Mill. By road, along the A595
Tel: Ravenglass (06577) 226 & 227
OS Ref: SD 086967

The railway is in operation all year except for Christmas period and not at weekends Christmas to 21 February. Limited service in winter, trains every 30 minutes in summer.
Facilities for visitors include car parking, refreshments, toilets, a museum which traces history of R & ER and its relations with the valleys, souvenir shops, a restored watermill at Muncaster and a picnic area at Dalegath. The R & ER owns a pub at Ravenglass called the 'Ratty Arms' in the former station house of the BR main line station.
It also owns two Pullman camping coaches which are let to visitors. The Pullmans are kitchen/firsts *Elmira* and *Maid of Kent*, both built 1914 and converted 1921.
The Ravenglass and Eskdale Railway, 'T'laal Ratty' to Cumbrians, was originally opened in 1875 to bring iron ore, and later passengers, from Eskdale. A very chequered existence during which it almost died twice has brought it to the present day, when the line has to depend almost entirely on passenger traffic. Always a private company, the railway is today supported by a Preservation Society.
It is England's oldest Narrow Gauge Railway, but features train control by VHF FM radio telephone, a system unique in the United Kingdom, copied by British Rail.

R & ER Preservation Society details from: Mr J. D. Stanbra, 5 Sheriff Bank, Greenodd, Ulverston, Cumbria LA12 7RF.

Stock
[1]Clarkson 2-8-2 *River Mite* 4669 built 1966
Heywood 0-8-2 *River Irt* (built 1894 as 0-8-0T *Muriel* and rebuilt at Ravenglass in 1927)
R & ER 2-6-2 *Northern Rock* built 1976
Davey Paxman 2-8-2 *River Esk* 21104 built 1923
Curwen/Severn-Lamb 4-6-4DH *Shelagh of Eskdale* built 1969
Kerr Stuart 0-4-2T No. 15 *Bonnie Dundee* 720 built 1901
Muir-Hill 4WPM *Quarryman* built 1926
Muir-Hill 0-4-2 DM *Pretender*, converted in 1929 from 1925 Muir-Hill 0-4-0
R & ER Bo-BoD No. 8 *Lady Wakefield* built 1980
R & ER 3-car bogie diesel railcar multiple unit *Silver Jubilee* built 1977
Greenwood and Batley 4WBE 2782 built 1937
Two semi-open wheelchair passenger coaches built 1981
Eighteen open bogie coaches built 1928–73
Eighteen saloon coaches built 1972–74
Six semi-open coaches built 1972–74
Six steel drop-side granite wagons
Twelve wood-framed flat wagons
One steel tank wagon
One weed-killing wagon

The Society owns LMS brake/third coach No. M20165M (built 1927) to accommodate members wishing to work on the line.

A Museum is operated in the former Standard Gauge railway goods shed at Ravenglass by the Eskdale (Cumbria) Trust and contains the following stock:
Bassett-Lowke 4-4-2 *Synolda* 30 built 1912
R & ER 4-6-2 *Ella*
R & ER Bo-BoDM *ICL No. 1* rebuilt 1925
Muir-Hill 4WPM *Quarryman* built 1926
R & ER 2w-2PMR *Scooter* 1 built 1970
Heywood 0-4-0T *Katie* 4 built 1896 (frames only)

[1]Owned by the R & ER Preservation Society.

252 Lakeside and Haverthwaite Railway A

Passenger-carrying standard gauge steam railway from Haverthwaite to Lakeside, a distance of 3¼ miles

Haverthwaite Station, near Newby Bridge, Ulverston, Cumbria
Access: Bus routes Nos 517 and X30 Ulverston to Grange-over-Sands. Hourly frequency
Tel: 04483-594
OS Ref: SD 349843

Operated by the Lakeside and Haverthwaite Railway Co Ltd supported by the Lakeside Railway Society.
Details from: A. Middleton, at Haverthwaite Station.
Facilities for visitors include car parking, souvenir shop, refreshments and toilets.
The railway operates at Easter and on Sundays in April and October, and daily May to the end of September, 11 am to 5.30 pm. Trains run hourly and most connect with the Lake Windermere steamers at Lakeside.
The Lakeside Railway was opened by the Furness Railway

Co on 1 June 1869 and after almost 100 years of operation was closed at the end of 1965. The Lakeside Railway Society was founded in 1967 as the supporting enthusiasts body of the company, who were then proposing to purchase and reopen the Plumpton Junction to Lakeside branch in its entirety. This original proposal had to be abandoned and the Society and company subsequently gave their attention to the eventual reopening of the three-and-a-quarter mile Haverthwaite to Lakeside section. Services commenced over Easter 1973 and the railway was officially opened by the Bishop of Wakefield on 2 May 1973.

Stock
[1]LMS 2-6-4T No. 2073 (Fairburn Class 4MT) built 1950
[1]LMS 2-6-4T No. 2085 (Fairburn Class 4MT) built 1951
[3]Hudswell Clarke 0-6-0ST LHR No. 5 1631 built 1929
Hudswell Clarke 0-6-0ST LHR No. 6 1366 built 1919
Bagnall 0-6-0ST LHR No. 14 *Princess* 2682 built 1942
[2]Hunslet 0-6-0ST No. 10 *Cumbria* 3794 built 1953
Hunslet 0-6-0ST No. 11 *Repulse* 3698 built 1950
Peckett 0-4-0ST LHR No. 1 *Caliban* 1925 built 1937
Barclay 0-4-0ST No. 13 *David* 2333 built 1953
Barclay 0-4-0ST No. 12 *Alexandra* 929 built 1902
Avonside 0-4-0ST No. 15 *Askham Hall* 1772 built 1917
BR/Drewry 0-6-0DM No. 03072 built 1959
Fowler-Vanguard 0-4-0DH No. 7 22919 built 1940, rebuilt 1961
BR/Drewry 0-6-0DM LHR No. 8 (BR Class 03 No. D2117) built 1959
Motor Rail 4WPM No. 9 *Rachel* 2098 built 1924
Fowler 0-4-0DH 4220045 built 1967
Fowler 0-4-0DH 4220044 built 1967
Barclay 0-6-0F *Sir James* 1550 built 1917
Fowler 0-4-0DM 4200022 built 1948
LMS 0-6-0DE No. 601 built 1945
Fowler 0-4-0DM LHR No. 16 *Fluff* 21999 built 1937
BR Mk.1 TSO coach No. SC4255 built 1956
BR Mk.1 TSO coach No. E3962 built 1955
BR Mk.1 TSO coach No. SC4760 built 1957
BR Mk.1 TSO coach No. SC3881 built 1954
BR Mk.1 SK coach No. 25364 built 1957
BR Mk.1 RMB coach No. SC1812 built 1957
BR Mk.1 TSO coach No. E4410 built 1957
BR Mk.1 SK coach No. M25337 built 1957
BR Mk.1 SK carriages Nos E24248, 24377, 24381, 24449, 24731 and 24799 built 1953/54
BR Mk.1 BSO coach No. E9218 built 1953
BR Mk.1 BSK coach No. E34181 built 1951
LNER BG No. E70361 built 1936
Two Nitric Acid tank wagons
LNWR 6-wheel livestock van underframe No. DM 395081 built 1908
LMS 20-ton goods brake van No. M731874 built 1947
LMS bogie bolster wagon No. 319192 built 1925
LNWR 12-ton van No. AD47693 built 1924
LNWR 12-ton van No. AD47971 built 1920
GWR 12-ton box van No. 142096 built 1941
SR 12-ton box van No. 515142 built 1940
BR Conflat 'A' wagon No. B706063 built 1958
Esso oil tank wagon No. 2375 built 1942
Five-plank coal wagon (ex-Vickers Ltd, Barrow)
Wickham 4WPMR No. TP1 691 built 1932 and trailer
NLR 4-wheel coach body built *c*1890 (to be mounted on
Jones KL-100 5-ton diesel rail crane built 1952

[1]Withdrawn from Normanton shed as BR Nos 42073 and 42085 in October 1967. The LMS 2-6-4 tanks, which were developed over a number of years from the original Fowler design of 1927, proved highly successful on suburban and cross-country passenger work. As an interim measure, pending the appearance of a BR standard type, the Fairburn version of the LMS design was constructed in reasonably small numbers to replace the remaining LBSCR 4-4-2 and 4-6-2 tanks. Both engines were built at Brighton Works and worked on the Southern Region until displaced by electrification schemes.
[2]Ex MODAD, Shoeburyness Military Railway, Essex, 1973.
[3]To be rebuilt as a tender locomotive with 4-wheel tender constructed on the frames of Barclay 0-4-0DM 344 built 1941.

253 Southport Locomotive and Transport Museum (Steamport) DE

A live steam museum housing a collection of standard gauge steam locomotives based in the former LMS Southport Derby Road loco shed

Steamport Southport Ltd, Derby Road, Southport, Merseyside PR9 0TY
Access: Bus routes Nos X27, X37, X47, 100 & 102 to Ribble bus station from Liverpool and Preston. Frequent services Nos 309 and 319 from St Helens and Warrington. Local buses to Monument, then eight minutes walk via London Street. Other local services from Formby, Wigan, etc. Five minutes walk from Southport BR station. Free car park adjoining depot
Tel: Southport 30693
OS Ref: SD 341170

Regular steam open days held throughout the year when short brake van rides are available over ¼ mile of track. The depot is open every weekend afternoon, from October to April, weekends from May to September, and daily from the end of May to mid-September.
Details from: The Secretary at the Museum.

Stock
BR 2-6-0 No. 76079 (Riddles Class 4MT) built 1957
GWR 2-6-2T No. 5193 (Collett 51XX Class) built 1934
[2]Mersey Railway 0-6-0T No. 5 *Cecil Raikes* Beyer Peacock 2605 built 1885
[1]Avonside 0-6-0ST *Lucy* 1568 built 1909
[1]Barclay 0-4-0ST *Efficient* 1598 built 1918

Peckett 0-4-0ST *Hornet* 1935 built 1937
Hunslet 0-6-0ST *Fitzwilliam* 1954 built 1939
RSH 0-4-0ST *Agecroft No. 2* 7485 built 1948
Hunslet 0-6-0ST No. 9 *Glashoughton* 3855 built 1954
Peckett 0-4-0ST *Whitehead* 1163 built 1908
Peckett 0-6-0ST No. 5 2153 built 1954
Peckett 0-4-0ST *North Western Gas Board* 1999 built 1941
Hudswell Clarke 0-4-0ST *Waleswood* 750 built 1906
Sentinel 4WVBTG *St Monans* 9373 built 1947
Fowler 0-4-0DM *Persil* 4160001 built 1952
BR Bo-BoDE No. 24081 built 1960
Hill 4wDH *Sefton* 123V built 1963
Greenwood and Batley 4wBE *Greenbat* 2000 built 1945
Yorkshire Engine Co 0-4-0DH No. D2870 2677 built 1960
Yorkshire Engine Co 0-4-0DH No. DH2 2820 built 1960
BR Co-CoDH No. D1048 *Western Lady* built 1962
Ruston Hornsby 4WDM 312432
LOR trailer coach No. 7 built 1895, rebuilt 1947 (body only)
Grafton 10-ton steam crane No. 2733 built 1949
LMS 'Stove R' van No. M33007 built 1940
LMS 13-ton open wagon No. 130397
LMS goods brake No. 731733 built 1943
LMS goods brake No. 732386 built 1948
[1]MR four-wheeled goods van built *c*1922
Esso tank wagon No. 1954 built 1950
L & YR open wagons
LMS Class 502 electric trailer coach No. 29896 built 1939
LMS Class 502 electric motor coach No. 28361 built 1939
LMS inspection saloon No. M45048 built 1941
MR goods brake van
MR 3-plank open wagon built *c*1900
LMS non-corridor 3rd class coach No. M12244 built 1951
GWR box van No. DW 82917 built *c*1923
L & YR rail-mounted hand crane built *c*1865

[1]Owned by the Liverpool Locomotive Preservation Group (*q.v.*).
[2]Withdrawn in 1903 and sold to Coppice Colliery, Derbyshire. Presented by NCB to BTC in 1956. Stored until presented by BRB in 1964 and moved to Liverpool in 1967. Arrived at Steamport 1979.

Tramcar Exhibits

Body of Southport Horse tramcar No. 7 built 1873
Liverpool 'Baby Grand' double-deck electric tramcar No. 245 built 1938
Blackpool 'Coronation' single-deck electric tramcar No. 323 built 1953
Stockport open-top double-deck electric tramcar No. 5 built 1901

Liverpool Locomotive Preservation Group **H**

Hon Secretary: E. Wheelwright, 25 Glendevon Road, Childwall, Liverpool L16 6AE
Facilities: Working parties are held each weekend. A bi-monthly newsletter is produced. Bi-monthly meetings and film shows are held on alternative months to the newsletter.

254 Steamtown Railway Museum AD

Major standard gauge railway preservation centre housing a large collection of main line and industrial locomotives from Great Britain and the continent. Steam-hauled rides are available in vintage vehicles over nearly a mile of track within the boundaries of the centre. There is also a passenger-carrying 15in gauge railway

Warton Road, Carnforth, Lancashire LA5 8HX
Access: Short walk from BR Carnforth Station. By road via the M6 Junctions 35 and 35A and the A6
Bus routes Nos 553 and 554 Kendal–Lancaster, Nos 555 and 556 Keswick–Lancaster and No. 573 from Morecambe. All at half-hourly frequency.
Tel: Carnforth (052473) 4220 or 2100
OS Ref: SD 496708

Steamtown is open daily (except Christmas Day) between 9 am and 4 pm in winter and 9 am and 5 pm the remainder of the year.
Facilities for visitors include car parking, souvenir shop, refreshments, toilets, picnic area, Collectors Corner for Railway relics and model railway.
Carnforth Motive Power Depot (10A in British Railways shed classification) was one of the last in the country to retain steam locomotives. After the final withdrawal of steam motive power in 1968, a private company promoted by some steam enthusiasts leased the depot in order to house various locomotives which had been bought for preservation. The leased area covers about 20 acres and in addition to the shed, offices and workshops contains a coaling tower, ash disposal plant, water columns, a 70ft turntable and a carriage and wagon shop together with a GW signal box. From end to end the site is about a mile long and has about five miles of track. The southern end lies on the west side of the main line from London to Glasgow, now electrified. A rail connection at the northern end allows access to and from the Furness line of British Railways.
There are between 25 and 30 British and Continental main line and industrial locomotives on view. Occasionally exchanges are made with locomotives of the National Railway Museum and private owners.
In addition to restoring steam locomotives, Steamtown can undertake engineering contracts within the scope of its well-equipped workshop, which includes a 7ft wheel lathe.
Further locomotives will be added to the collection as they become available from home and abroad.
Steamtown is the operating base for many main line locomotives, principal amongst them, *Flying Scotsman, Lord Nelson* and *Sir Nigel Gresley*.

Stock

[4]SR 4-6-2 No. 35005 *Canadian Pacific* (Bulleid MN Class) built 1941
[1]LNER 4-6-2 No. 4472 *Flying Scotsman* (Gresley A3 Class) built 1923

[4]GWR 0-6-2T No. 5643 (Collett Class 56XX) built 1925
[12]GWR 0-6-0PT No. 9629 (8750 Class) built 1945
[2]SNCF 4-6-2 No. 231K22 *La France* built 1912, rebuilt 1936
[10]SR 4-6-0 No. 850 *Lord Nelson* (Maunsell LN Class) built 1926
LMS 4-6-0 No. 44871 *Sovereign* (Stanier Class 5MT) built 1945
LMS 4-6-0 No. 45407 (Stanier Class 5MT) built 1937
LMS 2-6-0 No. 6441 (BR No. 46441) (Ivatt Class 2MT) built 1950
DB 4-6-2 No. 01.1104 *Schwartzkopf* 11360 built 1940
[9]LNER 4-6-2 No. 4498 *Sir Nigel Gresley* (Gresley Class A4) built 1935
Furness Railway 0-4-0ST No. 7 *Chloe* Sharp Stewart 1435 built 1863
[3]L & YR 0-6-0 No. 1300 (Aspinall Class 27) built 1896
Hudswell Clarke 0-6-0T *Firefly* 1864 built 1952
Barclay 0-4-0ST *John Howe* 1147 built 1908
Barclay 0-4-0ST No. 1969 *Jane Darbyshire* 1969 built 1929
Barclay 0-4-0ST No. 2134 *Coronation* 2134 built 1942
Barclay 0-4-0CT No. 1 *Glenfield* 880 built 1902
Peckett 0-4-0ST *May* 1370 built 1915
Bagnall 0-6-0F *Trimpell* 3019 built 1953
Bagnall 0-6-0ST *Cranford No. 2* 2668 built 1942
[5,6]Barclay 0-4-0ST No. 1 *Hurricane* 2230 built 1947
[5,7]Barclay 0-4-0ST No. 4 *British Gypsum* 2343 built 1953
Aveling Porter 0-4-0TG *Sirapite* 6158 built 1906
Avonside 0-6-0ST *Pitsford* 1917 built 1923
Wigan Coal and Iron 0-6-0ST *Lindsay* built 1887
Sentinel 4WVBTG *Gas Bag* 8024 built 1929
General Electric Bo-BoDE *New Jersey* 30483 built 1949
BR 0-6-0DM No. D2381 (Class 03) built 1961
RSH 0-6-0T No. 39 6947 built 1938
Hunslet 0-6-0DM No. 7049 *Tom Rolt* 2697 built 1944
Ruston Hornsby 4WDM No. 5 *Flying Flea* (48DS Class) 294266 built 1951

NER clerestory bogie saloon No. 305 built 1903
GER saloon bogie coach No. 1 built 1920
GER royal saloon bogie coach No. 5 built 1898
LMS inspection saloon No. M45005 built 1942
BR Pullman Car No. 349 built Metro-Cammell 1961
BR Pullman Car No. 350 built Metro-Cammell 1961
BR Pullman Car No. 351 built Metro-Cammell 1961
BR Pullman Car No. 352 built Metro-Cammell 1961
BR Pullman Car No. 353 built Metro-Cammell 1961
BR Pullman 1st bar car *Hadrian Bar* built Metro-Cammell 1961
BR Pullman Car No. 347 built Metro-Cammell 1961
BR Pullman Car No. 348 built Metro-Cammell 1961
LMS 12-wheeled sleeping car No. M395 built 1951
GWR saloon No. 9004 built 1930
BR Mk.1 BSK coach No. E34612 built 1955
LNER 'Coronation' observation car No. 1729 built 1937
LNER buffet/lounge car No. 1706 built 1948
LNER teak control coach DE 320959
LNER SK coach No. 23890 built 1935
BR Mk.1 restaurant car No. E1949 built 1949
BR Mk.1 TSO coach No. 4328 built 1956
[9]BR Mk.1 BCK coach No. E21096 built 1956
GNR invalid saloon No. 3087 built 1909 and 807 built 1912
LNER Gresley buffet car No. 24287 built 1939
SECR 12-wheeled Pullman car *Rosalind* built 1921
BR Mk.1 FO coaches Nos 3112 and 3116 built 1962
BR Mk.1 BCK coach No. M21249 built 1962
BR kitchen/buffet cars Nos 1566 and 1569 built 1961
SR full brake No. S207 built 1939
LMS full brake No. 31129 built 1940
LMS full brake No. 31148 built 1941
LMS full brake No. 31930 built 1943
LNER BG van No. 70592 built 1945
LNER BG van No. 70630 built 1946
LNER BG van No. 70460 built 1946 (body only)
GWR Hawksworth BG van No. W295 built 1951
Two ex-WD coach underframes
Smith Rodley diesel crane 9066 built 1944
Smith Rodley diesel crane 9067 built 1946
Ransomes and Rapier steam crane built 1939
[11]LNWR match truck No. 284235 built 1907
[11]LNWR steam breakdown crane No. 2987 (30-ton capacity) built 1908
LMS 16-ton mineral wagon No. 32464 built 1948
BR 16-ton mineral wagon No. B105736 built 1951
BP tank wagon built 1932
GWR 'Toad' 20-ton brake van No. 35234 (Neath and District)
Four BR 16-ton mineral wagons
LMS open wagon
Shell/BP tank wagons Nos A56 and A350 built 1902
Two flat wagons
Twelve-wheeled heavy machinery wagon
Wickham 4WPMR No. 4153
Smith Rodley steam crane
Bogie bolster wagon

[1]Withdrawn as BR No. 60103 in 1963 and purchased for preservation by Mr Alan Pegler. Restored to LNER livery with two tenders at Doncaster Works in 1963. Toured in the United States from 1969 to 1972. Bought by Mr W. H. McAlpine and returned to this country early in 1973. *Flying Scotsman* completed over two million miles in regular express passenger service and since then has become the most famous preserved steam locomotive in the world.
[2]French National Railways four-cylinder compound 'Pacific' built by the Paris–Lyons–Mediterranean Railway and rebuilt in 1937. Used on the Calais to Amiens section of the 'Golden Arrow' service. The locomotive arrived at Steamtown in 1970.
[3]Withdrawn from Lees, Oldham, as BR No. 52322 in 1960. One of a class of 385 engines for working medium-range freight traffic throughout the L & Y system.
[4]Withdrawn and sold for scrap to Woodham Brothers, Barry. Purchased for preservation and moved to Carnforth in 1973.

[5]Owned by Steam Enterprises Ltd (*q.v.*).
[6]Ex-Cook and Nuttall Ltd, Vale Paper Works, Horwich, Lancashire, 1972.
[7]Ex-British Gypsum Ltd, Thistle Plaster Works, Kirkby Thore, Westmorland, 1971.
[9]Owned by the A4 Locomotive Society Ltd (*q.v.*).
[10]When new, the 'Lord Nelsons' were the most powerful 4-6-0s ever built in this country, an honour which lasted only a few months until snatched away by the GWR 'King' Class. For sixteen years, until sufficient 'Merchant Navy' 4-6-2s had been constructed, the 'Nelsons' worked the heaviest express passenger trains, and until the end of their days took their share of main line work, even if occasionally on parcels trains. In common with most of the preserved Southern locomotives in the National Collection, it spent many years in store following withdrawal from Eastleigh shed in August 1962 as BR No. 30850 before being allocated to Carnforth for restoration to working order. *Lord Nelson* made a triumphant return to steam in time for the 'Rocket 150' celebrations at Rainhill in 1980 and since then has been used on several main line railtour trains. On loan from the National Collection.
[11]On loan from the National Collection.
[12]Withdrawn October 1964 and sent to Woodham Bros scrapyard, Barry. Purchased for preservation by Commonwealth Holiday Inns Ltd for static display in their new Cardiff hotel. Moved to Carnforth in May 1981 for restoration as a static exhibit.

15in gauge stock
Bassett-Lowke 4-4-2 *George the Fifth* 18 built 1911
Bassett-Lowke 4-4-2 *Princess Elizabeth* 22 built 1914
Lane Bo-Bo DH *Royal Anchor* built 1956
Guest/GAS 4-6-2 No. 5751 *Prince William* 9 built 1946
Batty 2-6-4DE built *c*1955 (steam outline)
Mini-Rail Bo-BoDE *Doctor Diesel* built 1966
Open and closed bogie coaches
Eaton Hall Railway brake van

Steam Enterprises Ltd **H**

Details from: Mr M. Hanson, 35 Farnham Way, Poulton, Blackpool. Tel: Blackpool 891882

The organisation was formed in 1972 by the owners of a number of industrial steam locomotives in order to co-operate in the supply of spare parts and equipment to ensure the continued operation of steam locomotives on private railways. The group's locos are being, or have been, overhauled and vacuum-fitted.
Locomotives may be available for loan, sale or hire from time to time.
This group also owns the Hunslet 'Austerity' 0-6-0ST No. 7 and Andrew Barclay 0-4-0ST No. 22 located at Embsay. (See Group No. 156.)

A4 Locomotive Society Ltd **H**

Membership Secretary: Mrs Ruth Milson, 4 The Mirren, Wallingford, Oxon.

The A4 Locomotive Society Ltd owns ex-LNER Pacific 4498 *Sir Nigel Gresley*.
Some £15,000 has been spent in 1967 on a major overhaul at BR workshops at Crewe, where restoration to LNER garter blue took place. The aims of the Society are to continue to maintain this locomotive in main line working order and to organise whenever possible steam-hauled excursions over the main lines of British Railways with this famous engine. New members are always welcome and receive certain concessions on railtours organised by the Society.
A newsletter, *Chime*, is sent out quarterly to the members and this reports on the activities of the Society so that members can take an active interest in the progress of the Society. The locomotive is also available for charter to reputable organisations and societies.

4472 & Steamtown Club

Details from: Miss S. A. Cooke, Membership Secretary, Steamtown Railway Museum, Warton Road, Carnforth, Lancashire LA5 9HX.

255 Bury Transport Museum DE

A Museum of standard gauge steam locomotives and rolling stock and commercial road vehicles. On special open days, steam-hauled trains are demonstrated over ¼ mile of track

East Lancashire Railway Preservation Society, Castlecroft Road, Bury, Greater Manchester BL9 0LN
Access: Off Bolton Street, Bury. By road, via A56 and A58. Short walk from BR Bury Station
Tel: 061-764-7790
OS Ref: SD 803109

The Museum is open every Saturday and Sunday, Easter Monday, Spring and Late Summer Bank Holidays. Loco in steam on the last Sunday in each month from March to September and on Bank Holidays.
Facilities for visitors include car parking, museum shop, model railway, refreshments (steam days only) and toilets.
The East Lancashire Railway Preservation Society moved to Bury in 1972. Its home is a former East Lancashire Railway Goods Shed built in the mid 1840s and converted by the Society into Bury Transport Museum.
Details from: Mr H. Hatcher at Bury Transport Museum.
The Museum is adjacent to the Bury–Rawtenstall line but the ultimate aim is to operate steam-hauled passenger services, and negotiations are taking place between the East Lancashire Light Railway Co Ltd, Greater Manchester Council, Lancashire County Council, Bury Metropolitan Borough Council, Rossendale Borough Council, and British Rail to take over the line which is now closed.
The scheme already has the backing of Greater Manchester Council and the deadline for track lifting has been extended to allow negotiations to take place.

In the meantime a ¼ mile of track has been laid alongside the BR line and vacuum braking equipment has been fitted to a brake van and one loco. Permission has not yet been given to carry passengers.

Stock
LMS 4-6-0 No. 45337 (5MT Class) built 1937
SR 4-6-2 No. 34027 *Taw Valley* built 1946
[1]Hudswell Clarke 0-6-0T No. 32 *Gothenburg* 680 built 1903
[1]Hudswell Clarke 0-6-0T No. 70 *Phoenix* 1464 built 1921
[2]Barclay 0-4-0ST No. 1 1927 built 1927
[3]RSH 0-6-0T MEA No. 1 7683 built 1951
Hunslet 0-6-0ST No. 7 *Bickershaw* 3776 built 1952
Sentinel 4wDH No. C930 10175 built 1964
BR 1-Co-Co-1 DE No. 40, 145 (Class 40) English Electric 3091 built 1961
BR Bo-BoDE No. 24054 built 1959
BR 0-6-0DM No. D2587 Hunslet 5636 built 1959
BR 0-4-0DH No. D2767 NBL 28020 built 1960
BR 0-6-0DM No. D2593 Hunslet 5642 built 1959
BR Bo-BoDH No. D7076 Beyer Peacock 7980 built 1963
BR Co-CoDH No. D1041 *Western Prince* built 1962
BR Co-CoDE No. 40.145 English Electric 3091 built 1961
BR Bo-BoDH No. D832 *Onslaught* built 1961
Hibberd 4WDM No. 1 *Mr Mercury* 3438 built 1950
Motor Rail 4WDM 9009 built 1948
BR Mk.1 TSO coach No. NE 4350 built 1956
L & YR four-wheeled goods van LMS No. 149196 built 1914
L & YR brake/3rd bogie coach No. 1856 built 1910
NER hand crane No. 902135 built 1880, plus match truck No. DB 915390 built 1957
Esso 4-wheel rail tank wagon No. 2184
BR Mk.1 BSO coach No. M9356 built 1959
BR Mk.1 BG passenger brake van No. E80993 built 1956
BR Mk.1 RMB buffet car
Two BR Mk.1 TSO coaches
Cowans Sheldon 50-ton steam crane 1013 built 1950
LMS 7-plank wagon built 1946
Two BR 16-ton mineral wagons built *c*1954
LMS Stanier 50ft bogie passenger brake van No. M31402 built 1950
BR goods brake van No. B953942 built 1958

[1]Ex-Manchester Ship Canal Co, Mode Wheel Works, Old Trafford, Manchester, 1973.
[2]Ex-North Western Gas Board, Oswald Street Gasworks, Burnley, Lancashire, 1970.
[3]Ex-CEGB, Meaford Power Station, Staffordshire, 1971.

ELRPS details may be obtained from The Secretary at the Museum.

256 Isle of Man Railway A

Passenger-carrying 3ft gauge steam railway, 15½ miles in length, running from Douglas to Port Erin

Steam Railway Station, Athol Street, Harbour, Douglas, IOM
Access: Short walk from Douglas Bus Station, Harbour and Town Centre
Tel: Douglas (0624) 4549
OS Ref: SC 374754

Details from: Public Relations Dept, Terminus Building, Strathallan Crescent, Douglas, Isle of Man.
The railway operates from Sundays to Fridays mid-May to mid-September. Also on Easter Sunday and Monday. The IMR, with absorbed companies, was opened in stages between 1873 and 1886. Services were maintained on all lines until World War II when the two-and-a-half-mile Foxdale branch was closed. Complete closure of the rest of the system took place in 1965. The railway was leased in 1967, but at the end of the 1968 season the Peel and Ramsey lines were closed and have now been lifted. Eventually, the railway, now reduced to the present 15½ mile section, was purchased by the Manx Government at the end of 1977.

Stock
[1]Beyer Peacock 2-4-0T No. 4 *Loch* 1416 built 1874
[2]Beyer Peacock 2-4-0T No. 10 *G. H. Wood* 4662 built 1905
[1]Beyer Peacock 2-4-0T No. 11 *Maitland* 4663 built 1905
[1]Beyer Peacock 2-4-0T No. 12 *Hutchinson* 5126 built 1908
[1]Beyer Peacock 2-4-0T No. 13 *Kissack* 5382 built 1910
[3]Walker Brothers bogie diesel railcar No. 19 built 1950
[3]Walker Brothers bogie diesel railcar No. 20 built 1951
IMR 3rd class bogie coaches F10, F11 built 1881
IMR composite bogie coach No. F15 built 1894
IMR 3rd class bogie coach No. F18 built 1894
IMR 3rd class bogie coaches Nos F25, F26 built 1896
IMR bogie luggage vans Nos F27, F28 built 1897
IMR 3rd class saloon bogie coaches Nos F29, F30, F31, F32 built 1905
IMR composite bogie saloon coach No. F35 built 1905
MNR brake composite bogie coach No. 15 built 1886
IMR brake/3rd bogie coach No. F41 built 1905
IMR brake/3rd bogie coach No. F43 built 1906
IMR composite bogie coaches Nos F45, F46 built 1913
Eighteen wagons
Wickham 4WPMR 7442 built 1956
Wickham 4WPMR 5763 built 1950
Wickham 4WPMR 8849 built 1961
Several 4-wheel ex-freight wagons in departmental use, plus various bogie wagons using ex-coach chassis for pw duties

[1]Still operational.
[2]Dismantled pending reboilering.
[3]Ex-County Donegal Railways Joint Committee, 1961.

Two locomotives, No. 11 *Maitland* and No. 12 *Hutchinson* were rebuilt with new 3ft 7½in diameter boilers in time for the 1981 season.
The ex-CDRJC railcars received a major overhaul in 1982.

257 Manx Electric Railway B

3ft gauge electric light railway, 18 miles long, running from Derby Castle, Douglas (connects with Douglas Horse Tramway, see Group No. 259) to Ramsey. Change at Laxey for the Snaefell Mountain Railway (Group No. 258)

Isle of Man Transport, Terminus Building, Strathallan Crescent, Douglas, Isle of Man
Tel: Douglas 4549
OS Ref: SC 3977

This railway has no parallel within the British Isles, being a genuine electrically-worked light railway which formerly carried a large quantity of goods traffic but now relies mainly on tourists. It runs through magnificent scenery and no visitor should miss the opportunity of a ride on one of its trains. It was opened in stages between 1893 and 1899 and passed through the ownership of several companies before being nationalised by the Manx Parliament at the end of 1956. The line is double-track throughout and electrified at 500 volts dc, current collection from the overhead wire being by trolley pole.

Stock

Ten saloon motor cars built 1893–99
Three saloon trailer cars built 1895–1904
Fourteen semi-open motor cars built 1898–1906
Twenty-two semi-open trailer cars built 1893–1930
Five four-wheeled wagons
Five four-wheeled vans

258 Snaefell Mountain Railway B

3ft 6in gauge electric mountain railway opened in 1895, running four-and-three-quarter miles to the summit of Snaefell (2,036ft)

Laxey, Isle of Man
Tel: Douglas 4549
OS Ref: SC 433845

Operated by Isle of Man Transport.
Operates May–September.
With a ruling gradient of 1 in 12 it is the steepest line in the British Isles worked by adhesion only; but a centre rail, using the Fell system, is also installed, being used only for braking purposes on the descent.

Stock

Rolling stock consists of six 48-seat bogie electric passenger cars built by G. F. Milnes of Birkenhead for the opening of the line.
There are also two four-wheeled service wagons and a double-cab works car incorporating a six-ton wagon body. This latter vehicle borrows power bogies from one of the passenger cars when its services are required.
Wickham 4WPMR 5864 built 1951

259 Douglas Horse Tramway B

The only example of a horse tramway still operating in the British Isles

Tel: Douglas 5222

The Douglas Horse Tramway has survived changes of ownership, closure and electrification proposals and omnibus competition to remain extremely popular and carry well over a million passengers during a summer season.
Built originally by Thomas Lightfoot and Sons, services began on 7 August 1876 and have continued ever since, apart from a period during World War II when part of the Promenade became a prisoner of war camp. Douglas Corporation Transport Department acquired the tramway in 1902 and run cars daily from May to September.
The line, of 3ft gauge and now double-track throughout, runs for 1⅝ miles along the sea front, from Victoria Pier in the south to a northern terminus near the Manx Electric Railway station, and uses 31 cars of various types seating 30–40 passengers. The 60 horses, mostly from Ireland, are fine animals and are well cared for.
The tramway operates daily from 9 am to 11 pm approximately with cars every one-and-a-half minutes when traffic is heavy.
The following cars are also maintained in the Horse Tram Depot at Derby Castle:
Douglas 4-wheel double-deck car No. 14 built 1883
Upper Douglas cable tramway, bogie toastrack tram No. 72/73 built 1896.

260 Port Erin Railway Museum E

Museum of 3ft gauge locomotives and rolling stock and smaller exhibits associated with the steam railways in the Isle of Man

Strand Road, Port Erin, Isle of Man
Access: Adjacent to Port Erin Station, Isle of Man Railway
OS Ref: SC 198689

The Museum is open from May to September inclusive, Saturdays excepted. Operated by Isle of Man Railways assisted by members of the Isle of Man Railway Society (*q.v.*).
The Museum has a small souvenir shop. Refreshments and toilets are available at Port Erin Station.
The Museum was opened in 1975 in the former bus garage at Port Erin.
An extension of the museum is planned by taking over the former steam locomotive shed, the locomotive stables at Port Erin being in turn transferred to the former goods shed which has been rebuilt with an inspection pit, water tank, etc. The new display hall provided by the loco shed will be used to house additional items of rolling stock and small exhibits.

Stock
Beyer Peacock 2-4-0T IMR No. 1 *Sutherland* 1253 built 1873
Dubs 0-6-0T MNR No. 4 *Caledonia* 2178 built 1885
Beyer Peacock 2-4-0T IMR No. 16 *Mannin* 6296 built 1926
Isle of Man Railway coach No. F36 in which HM Queen Elizabeth II travelled in 1972
Isle of Man Railway coach No. F75 used in 1873 by the Duke of Sutherland
[1]Manx Northern Railway 6-wheel Cleminson coach No. 3 built 1879
There are numerous other small exhibits, ranging from documents, posters and photographs to signal windlasses, lamps and signals.

[1]Owned by the Isle of Man Railway Society.

Isle of Man Railway Society **H**

Patron: The Most Hon the Marquess of Ailsa
President: J. J. Christian, Esq, Immediate Past Chairman Manx Electric Railway Board
Chairman: Dr R. Preston Hendry
Secretary: W. A. Camwell, Esq
Details from: R. P. Hendry, 4 Clifton Road, Rugby, Warwickshire

The Society works in conjunction with IOM Railways to promote the Island's steam and electric railways, and is actively engaged in preservation. The Society had provided many exhibits for the two railway museums on the Island, the Port Erin Steam Museum, opened in 1975, and the Electric Railway Museum at Ramsey which opened on 31 May 1979. (See Group No. 271.)
With UK and Manx based members, the Society is ideally placed to stimulate interest in the Island's railways, and members have the satisfaction of being involved with an ambitious preservation programme embracing steam, electric and even horse-drawn vehicles. Funds are raised by subscriptions and a vigorous sales campaign of Manx railwayana.
The Society owns a number of items of rolling stock which are not yet on display at either of the Museums. These are listed hereunder.

Stock
[3]Beyer Peacock 2-4-0T IMR No. 5 *Mona* 1417 built 1874
Beyer Peacock 2-4-0T IMR No. 9 *Douglas* 3815 built 1896
[1]Frames of Beyer Peacock 2-4-0T OMR No. 7 *Tynwald* 2038 built 1880
[2]Beyer Peacock 2-4-0T IMR No. 8 *Fenella* 3610 built 1894
Isle of Man Railway 4-wheel Gibbins accident crane built 1893
Douglas Corporation Transport horse car No. 11. (On permanent loan from DCT)

[1]No. 7 *Tynwald* was dismantled some thirty years ago and the superstructure has been scrapped. The frame has been preserved for use as an instructional exhibit in due course.
[2]No. 8 *Fenella* of 1894 was the last small boilered IMR engine to remain in service. She was withdrawn in 1968 and is to be restored by the Society.
[3]In service until 1969, awaiting overhaul.

Other stock owned by the Society includes MER Loco 23, freight car 26 and MNR Cleminson 6-wheel carriage No. 3.

261 Ramsey Electric Railway Museum E

A Museum of electric railway rolling stock and equipment, principally tracing the history of the electrically-worked lines in the Isle of Man

Ramsey, Isle of Man
Access: Near Ramsey Station, Manx Electric Railway

The Museum is open from mid-May to late September, Saturdays excepted, from approx 11.15 am to 4.00 pm. The Museum is operated and administered by the Isle of Man Railway Society. Special opening on Saturdays may on occasion be possible for organised parties travelling by MER. Enquiries should be directed to the IOM Railways, Terminus Buildings, Douglas in writing for onward transmission to the museum.

Stock
[1]MER Bo-BoE No. 23 built Derby Castle 1900
[3]Hibberd 4WPM 2027 built 1937
[3]Hibberd-PRV Bogie 'Toastrack' passenger coach 2028 built 1937
[5]MER Royal trailer 59 built 1895 (used by King Edward VII in 1902)
[4]Douglas Corporation open toastrack car No. 11 built 1886
[4]Douglas Corporation roofed toastrack car No. 47 built 1911
[4]Douglas Corporation convertible car No. 49 built 1935
[4]Douglas Corporation horse tram transporter built *c*1930
[2]MER Bogie freight car No. 26 (ex-passenger car No. 10) built 1895
Ballijorn Quarries side-tipping wagon (2ft gauge)

[1]No. 23 of 1900 is the oldest preserved bogie locomotive in the British Isles. She was built at Derby Castle works, the only locomotive to have been built in the IOM, and is owned by the Isle of Man Railway Society.
[2]Built as a passenger car in 1895 and withdrawn in 1902 for conversion to freight use. In store since 1944 and restored by the Isle of Man Railway Society in 1979.
[3]Ex-Queens Pier Tramway 1982.
[4]In the custody of the IOM Railway Society.
[5]On loan to the museum from IOM Railways.

262 Lezayre, Isle of Man G

Privately-preserved 3ft gauge rolling stock in store awaiting restoration

Mr J. Edwards, Lezayre, Isle of Man

No public admittance.

Stock
[1]Beyer Peacock 2-4-0T MNR No. 3 *Thornhill* 2028 built 1880
MNR carriage No. 6 Swansea Wagon Co built 1879

[1]Purchased from the Isle of Man Railway as IMR No. 14 in 1978. Last in service 1963.

263 Groudle Glen Railwav B

2ft gauge passenger-carrying railway

Groudle, Isle of Man
OS Ref: SC 421783

Public services will resume on Sundays during summer 1985.
Access: Adjacent to Manx Electric Railway Groudle Station.
Details from: Groudle Glen Railway Ltd, 19 Ballabrooie Grove, Douglas, I.O.M.

Stock
Bagnall 2-4-0T *Sea Lion* 1484 built 1896
Hunslet 4WDM No. 2 4395 built 1952
Hunslet 4WDM No. 1 4394 built 1952
Three bogie coaches
Bogie wagons

264 Pleasure Beach Railway, Blackpool B

Passenger-carrying, 1ft 9in gauge line two-thirds-of-a-mile long, opened in 1934

South Shore, Blackpool, Lancashire
Access: By Blackpool trams and buses which stop directly outside the Pleasure Beach
Nearest BR station: Blackpool South
Tel: 0253-41033
OS Ref: SD 305332

The engineering works include two tunnels. All points and signals are electrically operated and it is possible for three trains to operate at once, but only two are normally in service.
A journey on our famous Pleasure Beach Express starts at the Main Station and proceeds south underneath the Cableway South Station. Turning east through the African Safari and Yellowstone Park then north to run alongside the Big Dipper. It then doubles back passing Tokaydo Express, Revolution, Tidal Wave, and back to the Main Station.
Blackpool Pleasure Beach has been operating miniature railways since 1905, the first line being 15in gauge using steam motive power. It was reconstructed as 21in gauge in 1934.
In 1970 the original station was replaced by another built in the LMS style of the 1920s. The elaborately-decorated steelwork originally formed the structure of the Pavilion on Southport Pier, whilst the booking office, ticket collectors box and other station furniture are copies of items to be found on LMS stations in the Fylde area. The LMS colour scheme is used throughout.
Dates of operation:
Open Easter and Easter Week from 11 am. Then open from 2 pm weekends only until Spring Bank Holiday. Then open from 11 am daily until the end of the illuminations in October.

Stock
Hudswell Clarke 4-6-4T No. 4473 *Carol Jean* D579 built 1933
Hudswell Clarke 4-6-2 No. 6200 *Princess Royal* D586 built 1935
Hudswell Clarke 4-6-2 No. 4472 *Mary Louise* D578 built 1933
Twelve open six-seater bogie coaches
Pullman dining car
Two fuel-oil tank wagons
Two bogie flat wagons
Two four-wheel box vans
Six tipping skips
All three locomotives are steam outline, powered by diesel engines.
Power is transmitted via Hydrostatic Drive and worm wheel.

265 Lakeside Miniature Railway B

A 15in gauge line dating from May 1911 and now extending to approximately three-quarters-of-a-mile in length

Marine Lake, Southport, Merseyside
OS Ref: SD 331174

The line opened under the auspices of the Bassett-Lowke associate company, Narrow Gauge Railways Limited, but in 1913 passed to G. V. Llewelyn and in the early 1930s was resold to H. N. Barlow. A disastrous fire in 1938 damaged the two original steam locomotives and much of the line's rolling stock.
Normally, three trains are in operation simultaneously, a 'staff' system being employed to ensure that only one occupies each single line section at a time. Operation commences at Easter, then each weekend until Spring Bank Holiday, then daily until mid-September, thereafter at weekends until the end of October, weather permitting.

Stock
Barlow 4-6-0DE *Duke of Edinburgh* built 1948 (steam outline)
Severn-Lamb Co-CoDH *Princess Anne* built 1971
Barlow 4-6-0DE *Golden Jubilee 1911–61* built 1963 (steam outline)
Barlow 4-6-0DE *Prince Charles* built 1964 (steam outline)
Eighteen bogie open coaches including vehicles from the Far Tottering & Oyster Creek Railway built 1951.

266 Southport Pier Railway B

A 900-yard, 60cm gauge passenger-carrying line on Southport Pier

Southport, Merseyside
OS Ref: SD 335176

Operated by the Sefton Metropolitan Borough Council Tourism and Attractions Department, Cambridge Arcade, Southport PR8 1AS.
Southport Pier is noteworthy as the first pier in this country to be constructed of iron, and it is also one of the longest in Great Britain, having a length of 1,211 yards. Work on the present pier commenced in August 1859 and the official opening took place in 1860.
There have been several railways and tramways on the pier during its history. The first was a cable tramway operated by a stationary engine opened as long ago as 1863. The 60cm gauge line dates from 1954 and was operated by an eight-car train, *The Silver Belle*, consisting of a diesel-powered car at each end with four open and two closed coaches between. This train was retired in 1973 and replaced by the Severn-Lamb train described below. The railway operates daily from Easter to October from 9 am.

Stock
Five-coach train built by Severn-Lamb Ltd in 1973 comprising a Bo-Bo DH locomotive, *English Rose*, permanently coupled to three open and one saloon bogie coaches. Seating capacity approximately 100.

267 West Lancashire Light Railway A

A 2ft gauge passenger-carrying line, 450 yards long. Also collection of Narrow Gauge Railway equipment

Station Road, Hesketh Bank, near Preston, Lancashire
Access: A59 Liverpool–Preston, turn off at the A565 junction for Southport at Tarleton, then unclassified road to Hesketh Bank.
Ribble bus servies Nos 100 and 102 from Southport and Preston.
OS Ref: SD 448229

The railway was constructed in 1967 by a local group of narrow gauge railway enthusiasts and runs from Becconsall (off Station Road, Hesketh Bank) via Willow Tree Halt to Asland terminus.
Steam locomotive in operation last Sunday in Month or Bank Holiday Mondays March–October. The railway is open on all Sundays and Bank Holidays from 1 to 5.30 pm.
Details from: Mr N. McMurdy, Hon Sec, 790 Ormskirk Road, Pemberton, Wigan, Lancs. Tel: (0942) 218078.

Stock
Ruston Hornsby 4WDM No. 1 *Clwyd* (13DL Class) 264251 built 1951
Orenstein & Koppel 0-4-0WT No. 21 *Utrillas* built 1913
Orenstein & Koppel 0-4-0WT No. 22 *Montalban* 6641 built 1913
Ruston Hornsby 4WDM No. 2 *Tawd* (20DL Class) 222074 built 1943
[1]Hunslet 0-4-0ST No. 3 *Irish Mail* 823 built 1903
Hibberd 4WPM No. 4 1777 built 1931
Ruston Hornsby 4WDM No. 5 (25/30 HP Class) 200478 built 1940
Motor Rail 4WDM No. 7 8992 built 1946
Hudson-Hunslet 4WDM No. 8 4480 built 1953
Kerr Stuart 0-6-0T No. 9 ('Joffre' Class) 2405 built 1915
Hibberd 4WDM No. 10 (type 39) 2555 built 1946
Motor Rail 4WDM No. 11 (32/42 HP Class) 5906 built 1934
Ruston Hornsby 4WDM No. 16 202036 built 1941
Motor Rail 4WDM No. 17 11142 built 1960
Ruston Hornsby 4WDM No. 18 *Trent* 283507 built 1949
Lister 4WPM No. 19 (RT Class) 10805 built 1939
Baguley 4WPM No. 20 3002 built 1937
Hunslet 4WDM No. 21 1963 built 1939
Ruston Hornsby 4WDM No. 22 (LAT Class) 408430 built 1957
Motor Rail 4WDM No. 30 11258 built 1964
Motor Rail 4WDM No. 26 11223 built 1963
Motor Rail 4WDM *Red Rum* No. 29 7105 built 1936
Motor Rail 4WDM *Arkle* No. 28 7108 built 1937
Motor Rail 4WDM *Mill Reef* No. 27 7371 built 1939
Motor Rail 4WDM No. 32 11246 built 1963
Baguley 4WPM 2095 built 1936
Ruston Hornsby 4WDM No. 25 (30DL Class) 297054 built 1950
Baguley 4WPM No. 26 2095 built 1937
Four 20-seat coaches, ex Southport Pier Railway built 1953
Six-seat open coach
Brake van built on chassis of Motor Rail 4WDM 7955 built 1945
Large collection of wagons and associated Railway equipment on display.

[1]Ex Dinorwic Slate Quarries Co Ltd, Llanberis, Caernarfonshire, 1969. Restored to working order 1980.

268 Blackpool and Fleetwood Tramway B

Standard gauge electric tramway operated by Blackpool Borough Council Transport Department, Blundell Street, Blackpool, Lancashire FY1 5DD
Tel: Blackpool 23931

The tramway extends just over 11 miles from Starr Gate, Blackpool, to Fleetwood Ferry. Frequent services are operated on the coastal tramway during the summer season with short journey cars increasing the frequency of the through service over parts of the route.
Stock includes single-deck railcars of several types, double-deck cars and single-deck cars hauling a trailer, all of modern design. During the summer season open 'boat' cars run on part of the system at the Blackpool end.

Special coastal, promenade and illuminations tours and tours using illuminated cars are also run.
Blackpool Transport's trams now operate about 900,000 miles each year and about 7,500,000 passengers are carried annually. Trams operate every day (except Christmas Day, Boxing Day and New Year's Day) and nine OMO cars provide the basic 15-minute winter headway; these are supplemented by three vehicles operating at peak hours for works and school traffic. The twelve-minute summer service, which operates from the Monday before the Spring Bank Holiday until the end of the Autumn Illuminations, uses 14 cars, with additional trams being operated as the traffic requires. At the height of the summer, there is a tram scheduled to operate every six minutes on the section between Starr Gate and Little Bispham, and the scheduled service takes 20 cars (eight OMO cars with 12 double-deckers), with perhaps as many again operating on unscheduled duplication.
Regular maintenance and renewal of track and overhead is carried out, principally during the winter months, and, with financial assistance from Lancashire County Council towards permanent way renewal, the system continues to provide a vital part of the public transport network along the Fylde coast.

Stock
OMO single-deck cars Nos 1–13 built Blackpool Transport 1972–76
Open boat cars Nos 600, 602–607 built English Electric 1934
Single-deck railcoaches Nos 621–627, 630–634, 636–637 built Brush 1937
Single-deck Coronation car No. 660 built Roberts 1953
Single-deck trailer set motor cars Nos 671–680 built English Electric 1935, rebuilt 1960–61
Single-deck trailer cars Nos 681–690 built MCW 1960
Double-deck cars Nos 700–704, 706–713, 715–724, 726 built English Electric 1935, rebuilt 1960–61
OMO double-deck car No. 761 built Blackpool Transport 1979
OMO double-deck car No. 762 built BCT 1982
OMO single-deck car No. 641 built BCT 1984
Blackpool double-deck bogie car No. 59 built 1902
Bolton double-deck bogie car No. 66 built 1901
Edinburgh double-deck 4-wheel car No. 35 built 1948
Glasgow bogie double-deck car No. 1297 built 1948
Illuminated 'Tramnik One' built Blackpool Transport 1960
Illuminated 'Santa Fe train' set built Blackpool Transport 1962
Illuminated 'Hovertram' built Blackpool Transport 1963
Illuminated 'HMS Prudential' built Blackpool Transport 1965
Unimog 4WDM 12/983 built 1982
Overhead tower trailer car No. 749 built 1920
Overhead reel trailer car No. 750 built 1920
Permanent way maintenance trailer car with hydraulic crane No. 751 built 1937, rebuilt 1973
Railgrinder/Snowplough No. 752 built 1928
Overhead maintenance car with diesel generator No. 753 built 1924, rebuilt 1958
Overhead maintenance car No. 754 built 1901, rebuilt 1930

Although many cars have been rebuilt and modernised in recent years, the majority of the fleet dates from 1934–7. Modifications in recent years have been the conversion of ten cars to pull specially constructed trailers (671–690, 1960), the introduction of one-man trams (1–13, 1972–6) and the production of car 761, the first of a proposed 'Jubilee' Class, which entered service on 2 July 1979.
Designed and built by Blackpool Transport, 761 features a number of technical innovations not found on the rest of the fleet, including 'chopper' control supplied by the Westinghouse Brake and Signal Co Ltd, self-adjusting brakes, and air operated sanders and lifeguard reset mechanism. The car, which is designed to be suitable for one-man operation, has seats for 100 passengers, and features a small circulating area on the upper deck to improve accessibility for the upper saloon seats.

269 Moseley Industrial Tramway and Museum B

Passenger-carrying 2ft gauge railway, ⅓ mile in length, running round the side of the school playing field

Moseley Boys School, Northdowns Road, Cheadle, near Stockport, Cheshire
Access: Short walk from BR Cheadle Hulme Station. Manchester Bus No. 157
Tel: 061-485-4372 (School)
OS Ref: SJ 864871

The railway operates on the second Sunday of every month from 10.30 am to 4.30 pm, or by appointment at any other time.
Facilities for visitors include car parking, museum and toilets.
The project began as a school activity in 1969 under the direction of Mr Colin Saxton. For two years a horse tram was operated, originally single deck but later converted to double deck. This was novel, but expensive and inconvenient to operate, so a move to new premises in 1971 coincided with a change to 1ft 8in gauge after the purchase of a railway system from a brickworks at Crowle in Lincolnshire. In 1974 the system was converted back to 2ft gauge to enable more stock to be added. The railway has been extended and developed ever since.
Further details can be obtained from: Mr C. Saxton, 60 Pingate Lane, Cheadle Hulme, Cheshire SK8 7LT.

Stock
Motor Rail 4WPM 4565 built 1928
Motor Rail 4WDM 7333 built 1938
Lister 4WDM 38296 built 1952

Motor Rail 4WDM *The Lady D* 8934 built 1944
Motor Rail 4WDM *Z. W. Wade* 8663 built 1941
Kent Construction Co 4WDM built *c*1926
Ruston Hornsby 4WDM (13HP Class) 177639 built 1936
Ruston Hornsby 4WDM 462365 built 1960
Ruston Hornsby 4WDM 229647 built 1943
Ruston Hornsby 4WDM 223667 built 1943
Motor Rail 4WDM 7191 built 1937
Lister 4WPM 4404 built 1932
Motor Rail 4WDM 8878 built 1944
Motor Rail 4WDM 8937 built 1944
Two open bogie coaches ex-Southport Pier Railway built 1953
4-seat closed coach
9-seat open coach
9-seat covered coach
Eleven wagons ex-RAF Fauld
Approx 20 wagons, from 10¼in gauge static chain haulage tubs to skips and peat wagons, etc.

270 Hadlow Road Station Museum E

This station on the former Birkenhead Railway Hooton–West Kirby line has been restored to LMS condition as part of the Wirral Country Park scheme

Willaston-in-Wirral, Cheshire
Tel: 051-648-4371

The station and park are open all year round between 9 am and 6 pm.
Details from: The Head Ranger, Wirral Country Park, Station Road, Thurstaston, Merseyside L61 0HW.
Facilities for visitors include car parking and toilets as well as the 12-mile Country Park itself.

The Character of the Park
A railway line once linked the towns of West Kirby and Hooton. It was twelve miles long and for seven of those miles it ran close to the Dee estuary before curving inland to Hooton. For nearly seventy years its cuttings echoed to the rumble of steam engines and carriages but today there are different sounds, for the abandoned railway is the backbone of a country park developed by Cheshire County Council and the Countryside Commission. A country park is a new idea. It is not a park with rose gardens, fountains and football pitches but a stretch of open countryside amid towns and farmland. It is a place to relax or take a closer look at nature. The Wirral Country Park is a place to walk, ride, picnic, camp and fish, too.
Each country park has its own personality. The Wirral Country Park is a place of contrasts. It has embankments open to the wind and sky with views across the Dee to the Welsh hills. It also has cuttings where trees form an arch overhead. It has mud flats and cliffs. This place of contrasts provides for a variety of wild life, from badgers and foxes to the wading birds of the estuary and the frogs and newts of the ponds.

271 Lytham Motive Power Museum E

Operator: J. M. Morris, Helical Springs Ltd, Dock Road, Lytham, Lancashire
Tel: Lytham 733122
OS Ref: SD 381276

Opening hours: By appointment only, 11 am to 5 pm Mon–Thurs.
The collection embraces railway locomotives, cars and road engines, gas lamps, aircraft exhibits and a vintage model railway.

Stock
[1]NBR 0-4-0ST No. 42 (LNER Class Y9) built 1887
[2]NB Locomotive Co 0-4-0ST *Gartsherrie* No. 20 18386 built 1908
[4]Neilson 0-4-0CT *Snipey* 4004 built 1890
[6]Hawthorn Leslie 0-4-0ST No. 3 *Penicuik* 3799 built 1935
[7]Hudswell Clarke 0-4-0ST *Ribble Cement No. 3* 1661 built 1936
Howard 4WPM *Hotto* 965 built 1930
LNER Pullman coach *Minerva* 1928
MR 12-ton locomotive coal wagon

1ft 10¾in gauge stock:
Hudson-Hunslet 4WDM No. LOD758049 2198 built 1940
Groudle Glen railway coach
Dinorwic Quarry slate wagons
NCB open coaches

[1]North British Railway 'G' Class withdrawn as BR No. 68095 from St Margarets shed, Edinburgh, in 1962.
[2]Owned by Bairds and Scottish Steel Ltd, Gartsherrie, near Glasgow. It has been steamed occasionally since arrival and has received a temporary repaint.
[4]Formerly Hodbarrow Mining Co No. 6 *Spinney*, where it was until moved to Lytham in 1968. Since its arrival it has been used more than any of the other locomotives. The livery is that of the North Eastern Railway.
[6]Oil-fired locomotive used by the paper manufacturing firm of Alex Cowan Ltd, at Penicuik, near Edinburgh. Its present livery is that of the London, Brighton and South Coast Railway.
[7]Previously owned by Ribble Cement Co, at Clitheroe, Lancashire. She has been steamed on a number of occasions at Lytham. The livery is after the style of the LNWR as used on the locomotive *Greater Britain*.

Road vehicle exhibits
The largest and most impressive of these is TB2847, a Burrell single-crank compound traction engine (2513) built in 1902. The car is a 1933 Austin Saloon. The Leyland engines on display were supplied by the British Leyland Motor Corporation.

Aircraft exhibits
These include a Cheetah engine; cylinders from a Hercules engine; propellers from a Britannia, Viscount and Flying Flea; wheels from a Junkers JU52; an ejector

seat and an aircraft radar unit. Several models are on display, including one of the TSR2. The fullsize glider is a Slingsby Tutor and the cockpit is from a Spitfire. Parts of the first seaplane to fly from Lytham Creek are also on view.

272 City of Liverpool Museum E

Standard gauge locomotives and rolling stock on static display

Merseyside County Museum, Land Transport Gallery, William Brown Street, Liverpool L3 8EN
Access: Served by numerous bus routes along Lime Street or Haymarket. Nearest BR station: Liverpool Lime Street (1¼ miles)
Tel: 051-207 0001
OS Ref: SJ 349908

Open: Weekdays 10 am–5 pm; Sundays 2 pm–5 pm. Admission free.
The collection includes locomotives, steam tractors, a road-roller and a steam fire-pump.

Stock
[1]L & MR 0-4-2 *Lion* Todd, Kitson and Laird built 1838
[2]Avonside 0-6-0ST *MD & HB No. 1* 1465 built 1904
LOR Bo-Bo electric coach No. 3 built 1893
[3]L & MR 1st class 4-wheel coach (replica) built 1929
[3]L & MR 3rd class 4-wheel coach (replica) built 1929
Replica of *Cycloped* 4W horse-powered locomotive of 1829 built New Heys Comprehensive School 1979/80

[1]Originally Liverpool and Manchester Railway No. 57, becoming Grand Junction Railway No. 116 in 1845. Withdrawn as LNWR No. 116 in 1859 and sold to the Mersey Docks and Harbour Board for use as a pumping engine at Princes Dock. Taken out of service in 1928 and presented to the Liverpool Engineering Society in 1929. Restored by the LMS and put on display at Liverpool (Lime Street) Station in 1931. Removed to Crewe for storage in 1939 until returned to Liverpool in 1967. The locomotive has appeared in several films, principally as the 'star' of *The Titfield Thunderbolt: Lion* was restored to working order in 1979 by Ruston Diesels Ltd and has appeared at various venues since leading the Rocket 150 Cavalcade. She is the second oldest working locomotive in the World.
[2]Ex-Mersey Docks and Harbour Board, 1969, after restoration at Brunswick Dock.
[3]On loan from the National Collection.

The museum is the home of the Merseyside County Archives, which include much to interest the transport historian and are available by appointment.

273 Delph Station E

Standard gauge static exhibits on a 75-yard length of track

Mr Alf Hall, Delph Station, Oldham, Greater Manchester
OS Ref: SD 987074

Stock
BR Mk.1 TSO bogie coach
Oil tank wagon No. 9369A built 1924
SR goods brake van No. 555170
Wickham 4wPMR 7615 built 1957

274 Skelmersdale New Town Development Corporation E

Standard gauge steam locomotives on static display

Skelmersdale, Lancashire

Stock
[1]Peckett 0-4-0ST *Daphne* 737 built 1899
[2]Avonside 0-6-0ST MDHB No. 26 1810 built 1918

[1]Presented by Pilkington Brothers Ltd, St Helens, 1966. At New Church Farm Play Area (OS Ref: SD 477061).
[2]Presented by Mersey Docks and Harbour Board, Liverpool, 1969. At Digmoor Shopping Parade Play Area (OS Ref: SD 497048).

275 Ulverston G

Standard gauge steam locomotive on static display

Cumbria Education Committee, Stone Cross Special School, Barrow Road, Cumbria. (School closed 1982. Loco for disposal)
OS Ref: SD 283783

Stock
Furness Railway 0-4-0ST No. 17 Sharp Stewart 1585 built 1865

Presented by Barrow Hematite Steel Works Ltd, 1960. Originally a Furness Railway 0-4-0 tender loco No. 25.

276 Lowther Miniature Railway B

Passenger-carrying 7¼in gauge line, 1100 yards in length

Lowther Wildlife Adventure Park, Lowther, near Penrith, Cumbria

Stock
Fifer Bo-BoPH

277 Heaton Park Tramway B

A passenger-carrying standard gauge electric tramway, 280 yards in length consisting of double track laid on a reservation alongside the carriage drive leading into Heaton Park from Middleton Road

Heaton Park, off Middleton Road, Manchester
Access: Frequent buses from City Centre on routes Nos 59, 60 & 61

The tramway is in operation on Saturdays in July and August and Sundays from Easter to October. Also on Bank Holidays.
Facilities for visitors include car parking, museum, souvenir shop, and toilets.
The Park is one of the largest in the region and covers over 600 acres. It was originally owned by the Earls of Wilton and nowadays is open throughout the year providing passive and active recreation for visitors.
The tramway is operated by Manchester Transport Museum Society and its construction was supported by grants from Greater Manchester County Council. The Heaton Park route of the Manchester Tramway system was closed in 1934, but instead of the track being lifted, it was covered in tarmac for use as a bus terminal. The tarmac covering has now been stripped away to reveal the track in good order and poles and overhead wiring replaced. Society members have laid a new siding into a storage building and restored electrical power to the system. The tramway opened for public operation on 2 September 1979. A 700 yard extension is under construction for 1985.

Stock
Manchester double-deck horse tramcar No. L53
Manchester single-deck semi-saloon bogie tramcar No. 765 built 1914
Blackpool & Fleetwood Tramway bogie saloon tramcar No. 40 built 1914
Two Oporto 4-wheel works cars

Cars can be hired outside normal opening hours, by special arrangement with the operations manager, Mr C. Taylor, 1020 Manchester Road, Castleton, Rochdale, OL11 2UB. Tel: Rochdale 43918.

278 Greater Manchester Science and Railway Museum G
Locomotives and rolling stock on static display

Liverpool Road Station, Lower Byron Street entrance, Manchester
OS Ref: SJ 831978

Open 12 noon to 4 pm at weekends.
Details from: Secretary, Liverpool Road Station Society, 276 Blackburn Road, Edgeworth, Bolton BL7 0PL.

Stock
LMS 4-6-0 No. 44806 *Magpie* (Stanier Class 5MT) built 1944
SAR 4-8-2 + 2-8-4T No. 2352 (Class GL)
Beyer Peacock 6639 built 1930 (3ft 6in gauge)
[1]Beyer Peacock 2-4-0T IMR No. 3 *Pender* 1255 built 1873 (3ft gauge)
[2]Barclay 0-4-0ST 1964 built 1929
RSH 0-4-0ST *Agecroft No. 3* 7681 built 1951
Fowler 0-4-0DM 4210074 built 1952
Hudswell Clarke 0-6-0DM D1199 built 1960
Braithwaite and Ericsson 2-2-0VBWT *Novelty* replica built 1980
Pakistan Railways 4-4-0 No. 3157 (SPS Class) Vulcan Foundry 3064 built 1911 (5ft 6in gauge)
BR Co-Co No. 27000 'Electra' built 1953
BR Co-CoE No. 27002 'Aurora' built 1954
Hawthorn Leslie Bo-BoE 3682 built 1927
English Electric 4WBE 1378 built 1944
LMS passenger brake van built 1944
BR/Metro Cammell dmu buffet car No. E59575 built 1960

[1]Ex-Isle of Man Railway 1979 (sectioned).
[2]Ex-CPC (UK) Ltd, Cornflour Manufacturers, Trafford Park, Manchester 1979.

279 CEGB North Western Area I
Standard gauge industrial steam locations, some featuring regular steam working

No public admittance

Stock
Barclay 0-6-0F No. 1 *Lancaster* 1572 built 1917 Heysham Power Station
Barclay 0-4-0F No. 2 1950 built 1928 Heysham Power Station
Barclay 0-6-0F *Lord Ashfield* 1989 built 1930 Kearsley Power Station
Bagnall 0-4-0F *Huncoat No. 1* 2989 built 1951 Huncoat Power Station
Bagnall 0-4-0F *Huncoat No. 2* 3022 built 1951 Huncoat Power Station

280 Glaxo Laboratories Ltd I
Standard gauge industrial steam location featuring regular steam working

Ulverston, Cumbria
OS Ref: SO 30677

No public admittance

Stock
Barclay 0-4-0F *Glaxo* 2268 built 1949

281 National Coal Board I
Industrial steam locations featuring occasional steam working

Bold Colliery, St Helens, Lancs

No public admittance

Stock
Hunslet 0-6-0ST *Joseph* 3163 built 1944
Hudswell Clarke 0-6-0ST *Robert* 1752 built 1943

282 British Nuclear Fuels Ltd — I

Standard gauge industrial steam location featuring occasional steam working

Sellafield Research Centre, Cumbria
OS Ref: NY 025034

No public admittance

Stock
Peckett 0-4-0ST No. 1 (Class W7) 2027 built 1942

283 Eaton Hall Railway Museum — E

15in gauge rolling stock built by Sir Arthur Heywood for the Eaton Hall Railway now undergoing restoration for static display

Eaton Hall, near Balderton, Cheshire

Stock
EHR open carriage
EHR closed carriage
EHR bogie brake van
EHR goods wagon

284 Halton Miniature Railway — A

A passenger-carrying 7¼in gauge miniature railway 1 mile in length running from Mousetrap Hall to Tower View

Halton Miniature Railway Society, Town Park, Runcorn, Cheshire
Access: By road, follow signs for Palacefields and 'squash', also engine symbol
Tel: Runcorn 74396

The line was opened in Spring 1980 and can be found in operation on Sundays from 1 pm. Please telephone to ensure that trains are running.
The railway has been built as a joint effort by the Society and Runcorn Development Corporation (who have financed its building). The line runs through a delightful setting and has a spacious engine shed and clubroom at the main station, Mousetrap Hall. It is hoped to extend by a further ½-mile to reach Norton Lane.
Details from: Mr J. Goulden, 55 Victoria Road, Runcorn, Cheshire WA7 5BE.

Stock
Freelance 0-4-0T *Valerie* built 1983
Goulden 0-4-0PM *Pixie* built 1976
Gouldon 0-4-4PH built 1980
Bimpson 0-4-0PM *Scamp* built 1979
Three open bogie coaches built Goulden
Two open wagons built Bimpson
Two open wagons built Goulden
Tipper wagons built Goulden
Tank wagon built Goulden

There are four steam locos under construction, whilst an LMS Black 5 steam loco and a BR Class 20 diesel are already for future use.
Enthusiasts with their own locomotives are welcome by invitation (ring for details). Steam locomotives must have a current boiler certificate.
The Society holds meetings on the last Sunday in the month at Mousetrap Hall station at 2 pm; visitors and prospective members are always welcome. Working nights are held every Thursday at the station, when locomotive and carriage building and track fabrication take place. All members get involved in the various operating activities such as guards, ticket collectors, signalmen, etc.
Membership details from: Mrs P. Stewart, 1 Laggan Street, Liverpool (Tel: 051-260 0954).

285 Dyke Nook Farm Museum — A

Passenger-carrying 7¼in gauge line

Dyke Nook Farm, Sandford, near Warcop, Cumbria

Operates at weekends from Easter to September and some weekdays in high season.

Stock
Clifford 2-6-0 No. 4247 *Lady Margaret* built 1981
Clifford 0-6-0PH No. 7170

286 Salford Metropolitan District Council — E

Standard gauge steam locomotive on static display

George Thorns Recreation Centre, Liverpool Road, Irlam, Greater Manchester
OS Ref: SJ 722943

Stock
Peckett 0-4-0F 2155 built 1955

Presented by CWS Ltd, Irlam Soap Works, 1969.

287 Carrex Metals — E

Standard gauge steam locomotive preserved as a static exhibit on a short length of track by the entrance to the yard

Scrap Merchants, Regent Street, Rochdale, Greater Manchester
OS Ref: SD 900140

Stock
Hawthorn Leslie 0-6-0F *Hartshead* 3805 built 1932

Ex-CEGB, Hartshead Power Station, 1976.

288 The 'Yew Tree' Inn E

Coach in use as a restaurant

Oldham Road, Rochdale, Lancashire
On the A62 between Rochdale and Oldham, immediately south of the M62 overbridge.

Stock
Pullman car *Aries* built *c*1923

Bought in 1969 and installed on site.

289 Stockport Model Engineering Society C

7¼in gauge passenger-carrying line

Royal School for the Deaf, Handforth, Wilmslow, Greater Manchester

Stock
'Romulus'-type 0-4-0T built Kay 1978
'Romulus'-type 0-4-0T built Kay 1978

290 Knowsley Hall Safari Park B

Passenger-carrying 15in gauge miniature railway, ¼ mile in length

Knowsley Hall, Prescott, Merseyside
Access: 7 miles east of Liverpool, off the A580
Tel: Prescott 9009
OS Ref: SJ 49

The park is open daily from 10.30 am to 6.30 pm (in winter 10 am to sunset).
Facilities for visitors include car parking, refreshments, Dolphinarium, amusement park and pets corner.
The railway at Knowsley Hall formerly operated at Alexandra Palace, London, until 1970. It runs from the Amusement Park in a balloon loop, passing through a wood alongside the sealion pool.

Stock
Barlow 4-6-2DE No. 4498 *Sir Nigel Gresley* built 1950 (steam outline)
Five open bogie coaches

291 Blackpool Zoo Miniature Railway B

Passenger-carrying 15in gauge miniature railway, nearly 1 mile in length

'World of Animals' Zoological Gardens, Stanley Park, Great Marton, Blackpool, Lancs
OS Ref: SD 335362

Stock
Severn-Lamb 2-8-0PM No. 279 7219 built 1972 (steam outline)
Open bogie coaches

292 Red Rose Live Steam Group E

Railway Preservation Centre

Astley Green Colliery, Higher Green Lane, Tyldesley, near Manchester
OS Ref: SJ 705998

Open on Sundays from 1.30 to 3 pm.
Details from: Roy Pinches, 71 Tintern Avenue, Astley, Manchester

Stock
[1]Avonside 0-4-0ST 1563 built 1908
[2]Ruston Hornsby 4WDM (48DS Class) 244580 built 1946
[3]Hudswell Clarke 0-6-0ST *Harry* 1776 built 1944
[3]Avonside 0-6-0ST 1600 built 1912
Ruston Hornsby 4WDM 462365 built 1960 (2ft gauge)
Motor Rail 4WDM 8937 (2ft gauge)
Motor Rail 4WDM 7497 (2ft gauge)
Ruston Hornsby 4WDM 422573 (2ft gauge)

[1]Ex-Millom Hermatite Ore and Iron Co Ltd, Hodbarrow Mine, Cumberland, 1968.
[2]Ex-Park Webb Ltd, Ince Forge, Wigan, 1974.
[3]Ex-J. K. Holt and Gordon, scrap merchants, Chequerbent, Greater Manchester.

The Group was formed in 1972 with the aim of establishing in Wigan a museum of industrial steam engines and a short light railway. Until the 1950s, Wigan was one of the main centres of coalmining and heavy industry, as well as being a major cotton town. Now there are few remains of this era when the steam engine was the chief source of power and the Group hopes to assemble a representative selection of engines and exhibits.

293 Park Hall Miniature Railway B

2ft gauge passenger-carrying railway

Charnock Richard, Chorley, Lancs

Stock
Baguley 0-4-0PM *The Lady Guinevere* 3024 built 1939 (Ex-Walton-on-the-Naze Pier Tramway)

294 The 'Brighton Belle' Inn E

Coach in use as a restaurant

Winsford, Cheshire

Stock

SR Pullman car No. 283 *Mona* (ex-'Brighton Belle' set No. 3053) built 1932

295 Stockport G

Private 15in gauge steam locomotive in store

Mr P. Blackham, Stockport, Greater Manchester

No public access.

Stock

K. L. Guinness 4-6-2 *Blue Pacific* built *c*1935

Mr Blackham proposes to built a 15in gauge railway between Stockport Sewage works and the BR line at Cheadle Heath.

296 Copeland District Council E

2ft 6in gauge stock preserved on site of Wellington Colliery

Whitehaven Docks, Cumbria
OS Ref: NX 968183

Stock

Wingrove and Rogers 0-4-0BE No. 2206/16 (Type W217) 5931
Two open wagons

297 45491 Preservation Society G

Standard gauge locomotive preservation project

c/o ICI Ltd, Hillhouse Works, Thornton, Fleetwood, Lancs
OS Ref: SD 338444

Tel: 0253-865997

Details from: C. J. Moore, Esq, 33 Cookson Road, Thornton, Blackpool F5 2RL

Stock

LMS 4-6-0 No. 45491 built 1943
LMS corridor composite coach No. 3515 built 1924 (8E Assoc Northwich BR depot)

298 Silloth Miniature Railway A

7¼in gauge passenger-carrying steam railway

Silloth, Cumbria

Stock

Freelance 0-4-2T *Valerie*
Freelance 2-6-2 (based on R & ER *Northern Rock*) under construction 1982

299 Maryport Miniature Railway B

A 10¼in gauge passenger-carrying line ½-mile long

Netherhall Park, Maryport, Cumbria

Work is progressing on an extension to the line, including a new station and passing loop.

Stock

Freelance Co-Co Gas E
Freelance 0-6-0 Gas M

300 Keswick Railway Museum E

Victorian station building, exhibition of local railway photographs, railway relics and models

Keswick Station, Keswick, Cumbria

Open on Saturdays and Sundays (daily during Cumbria school holidays) Easter–October.

AREA G

Wales

Gwynedd
Clwyd
Powys
Dyfed
Gwent
Glamorgan
Anglesey
(Group Nos 301–350)

301 Ffestiniog Railway A

Passenger-carrying 1ft 11½in gauge railway, 13 miles in length, from Porthmadog to Blaenau Ffestiniog

Porthmadog Harbour Station, Porthmadog, Gwynedd
Access: BR Stations at Porthmadog, Minffordd and Blaenau Ffestiniog
Crosville bus services operate to Porthmadog or Tanygrisiau from Blaenau Ffestiniog, Dolgellau, Caernarfon, Pwllheli and Criccieth
Tel: Porthmadog 2384
OS Ref: SH 584379

Trains run daily from March to November inclusive, plus winter weekends and Christmas.
Facilities offered – Museum at Porthmadog. Shops at Porthmadog, Tan-y-Bwlch, Tanygrisiau and Blaenau Ffestiniog. Refreshments on trains, and at Porthmadog, Tan-y-Bwlch, Tanygrisiau and Blaenau Ffestiniog. Car parks at Porthmadog, Tan-y-Bwlch, Tanygrisiau and Blaenau Ffestiniog. Toilets at Porthmadog, Tan-y-Bwlch, Tanygrisiau and Blaenau Ffestiniog. Information and Travel bureaux at Porthmadog.
Nature trail at Tan-y-Bwlch.
With so many notable 'firsts' to its credit, it's difficult to sum up the Ffestiniog Railway's special claims to fame in just a few words. However, it does operate the only spiral on a passenger-carrying railway in the UK (at Dduallt); the first bogie coaches in the UK (1872) still in service; the only known double Fairlie locomotives still in service in the world.
The historic Ffestiniog Railway was built to the plans of James Spooner, to convey slate from the mountains around Blaenau Ffestiniog to the new harbour at Porthmadog. It was opened in 1836.
The line was constructed on a continuously falling gradient from Blaenau Ffestiniog so that the laden trains of slate could run by gravity. The returning empties were hauled up the hill by horses. The Ffestiniog Railway pioneered the use of steam traction on the 2ft gauge in 1863. Three out of the four locomotives built at that time are still extant. The first double Fairlie locomotive was introduced in 1869; the outcome of ever increasing traffic. The first bogie carriages to be used in the UK were introduced on the Ffestiniog Railway in 1872. In the twentieth century the slate trade went into a decline and tourists and holiday makers began to provide the railway with an increasing amount of traffic. By the end of the last war the line was in such a dilapidated condition that the Company was unable to restore services. With the exception of a small amount of track in Blaenau Ffestiniog, used by the slate quarries, the line closed in 1946. A new administration obtained control of the Company in 1954 and the Festiniog Railway Society Ltd was formed to assist it in the formidable task of restoring and reopening the derelict railway. Passenger services between Porthmadog and Boston Lodge were resumed on 23 July 1955 and they have been progressively extended back to Blaenau Ffestiniog for 1982 after building 2½ miles of new line, opened in 1978, a major achievement of unique interest.

Festiniog Railway Society
Details from: John Manisty, 4 Kingsgate Street, Winchester, Hants SO23 9PD.

Stock
[1]George England 0-4-0STT *Princess* built 1863
[2]George England 0-4-0STT *Prince* built 1863
[3]George England 0-4-0STT *Welsh Pony* built 1867
FR 0-4-4-0T *Merddin Emrys* built 1879
[4]FR 0-4-4-0T *Livingston Thompson* built 1886
[5]Hunslet 2-4-0STT *Blanche* 589 built 1893
[5]Hunslet 2-4-0STT *Linda* 590 built 1893
[6]Hunslet 0-4-0ST *Britomart* 707 built 1899
[7]Alco 2-6-2PT *Mountaineer* 57156 built 1916
[8]Peckett 0-6-0ST *Volunteer* 2050 built 1944
[9]FR 0-4-4-0T *Earl of Merioneth/Iarll Meirionnydd* built 1979
Baldwin 2-4-0DM *Moelwyn* 49604 built 1918
Motor Rail 4WDM *Mary Ann* 596 built 1917
Hibberd 4WDM *Upnor Castle* 3687 built 1954
Ruston Hornsby 4WDM *Andrew* 193984 built 1939
Ruston Hornsby 4WDM *Alistair* 201970 built 1940
Motor Rail 4WDM *Jane* 8565 built 1940
Hunslet 4WDM *Tyke* 2290 built 1941
Hunslet 0-4-0DM *Moel Hebog* 4113 built 1955
Motor Rail 4WDM *The Lady Diana* 21579 built 1957
Hibberd 4WDM 3307 built 1948
Hibberd 4WDM 3831 built 1957
Motor Rail 4WDM 8788 built 1943
Motor Rail 4WDM 22119 built 1962
Matisa 2-2-0DH ballast tamping machine
Wickham 4WPMR PW trolley
FR 4-wheeled passenger brake van No. 1 built 1964
FR 4-wheeled goods brake van No. 2
FR 4-wheeled knifeboard coaches Nos 3, 4, 5, 6 and 7 built 1864–67
FR 4-wheeled quarrymen's coach No. 8

GWR 4-wheeled luggage/stores van No. 59 (ex-W & LLR, built 1923 for V of RR)
FR brake/third bogie coach No. 10 built 1872
FR brake/first observation coach No. 11 built 1880
FR buffet/3rd saloon No. 12 built 1880
Buffet/3rd saloon No. 14 built 1898 for Lynton & Barnstaple Railway
FR 1st/3rd composite bogie coaches Nos 15 and 16 built 1871
FR 1st/3rd composite bogie coaches Nos 17 and 18 built 1876
FR 1st/3rd composite bogie coaches Nos 19 and 20 built 1879
FR 3rd bogie coach No. 22 built 1896
3rd bogie coaches Nos 23 and 26 built 1894 for North Wales Narrow Gauge Railway
FR brake/1st observation coaches Nos 100 and 101 built 1965 and 1970
FR buffet/3rd saloon No. 103 built 1968
FR 1st/3rd composite bogie coaches Nos 104 and 106 built 1964 and 1968
FR 1st/3rd/lav composite bogie coach No. 105 built 1966
FR 3rd tourist open bogie coaches Nos 37 and 38 built 1971 and 1972
FR 3rd saloon bogie coach No. 110 built 1975 – push-pull fitted
FR 1st/3rd composite bogie coach No. 116 built 1972
FR 3rd saloon bogie coaches Nos 117 and 118 built 1977
FR 3rd saloon/lav bogie coaches Nos 119 and 120 built 1979 and 1980
FR 3rd saloon bogie coach No. 121 built 1981
Three Admiralty brake vans
Bogie flat wagon
18 side-tipping wagons

[1]On display in the museum at Porthmadog.
[2]Major overhaul and rebuild completed 1980.
[3]Awaiting restoration.
[4]Until recently known as *Earl of Merioneth/Iarll Meirionnydd*, and previously as *Taliesin*. Awaiting restoration as museum piece.
[5]Built as 0-4-0ST for the Penrhyn Quarry Railway. Purchased 1963. *Linda* previously on loan for Summer, 1962.
[6]Ex-Penyrorsedd Quarry. Privately owned.
[7]Ex-Tramway de Pithiviers a Toury (Central France) and previously War Department tramways (during First World War). Acquired 1967.
[8]Ex-Harrogate Gas Works, 1957. Name not carried. Awaiting restoration.
[9]Constructed around a new boiler built by the Hunslet Engine Co in 1969. Mainly new construction but some parts, primarily power bogie frames, from *Livingston Thompson*.

302 Welshpool and Llanfair Light Railway A

An 8-mile 2ft 6in gauge passenger-carrying line from Llanfair Caereinion to Welshpool (Raven Square)

Llanfair Caereinion Station, Powys
Access: Crosville bus services from Shrewsbury, Oswestry and Newtown. One mile from Welshpool BR station; railway runs parallel to A458
Tel: Llanfair Caereinion (0938) 810441
OS Ref: SJ 107069

The railway operates at weekends from Easter to October, daily from June to September and at Bank Holidays.
Facilities: Car parks at Welshpool, Llanfair and Castle Caereinion; refreshments and railway shop at Llanfair.
This line, authorised by a Light Railway Order granted in 1899, was opened for goods traffic on 9 March 1903. Passenger services started a month later on 4 April, when the line was officially opened. Just over nine miles in length and running for a short distance over the site of a tramway built by the then Earl of Powis as early as 1818, the line was operated in turn by the Cambrian Railways, the Great Western Railway and British Railways. Passenger services ceased as long ago as 7 February 1931 but, unlike most narrow-gauge railways, the Welshpool and Llanfair was not built to serve a specific industry and until its closure on 5 November 1956 it carried a considerable tonnage of coal and general agricultural traffic, including both sheep and cattle.
The Welshpool extension was opened on 18 July 1981. It adds 2¾ miles to the railway including the 1-mile long 1-in-29 climb up Golfa Bank. This is a very scenic part of the railway, twisting and turning to climb up the valley of the Sylfaen. It's also a testing piece of line to operate!
The railway is operated by the Welshpool and Llanfair Light Railway Preservation Co Ltd.
Details from: Mr T. White, 13 Frampton Close, Sutton, Surrey SM2 6SU.

Stock
Beyer Peacock 0-6-0T No. 1 *The Earl* 3496 built 1902
Beyer Peacock 0-6-0T No. 2 *The Countess* 3497 built 1902
Tubize 2-6-2T No. 5 2369 built 1948
Bagnall 0-4-4-0T No. 6 *Monarch* 3024 built 1953
Drewry 6WDM No. 7 *Chattenden* 2263 built 1949
Barclay 0-4-0T No. 8 *Dougal* 2207 built 1946
Franco-Belge 0-8-0T No. 10 *Sir Drefaldwyn* 2855 built 1944
Hunslet 0-4-0DM No. 11 *Ferret* 2251 built 1940
Kerr Stuart 0-6-2T No. 12 *Joan* 4404 built 1927
Hunslet 2-6-2T No. 14 3815 built 1954
Hunslet 0-4-0DM 2245 built 1940
Wickham 4WPMR 2904 built 1940
Chattenden and Upnor Railway bogie coach No. 214 built 1957
Balcony saloon 4-wheel coach No. B24 Salzkammergut Lokalbahn built 1925
Balcony saloon 4-wheel coach No. B27 ex-Zillertalbahn built 1906
Balcony saloon 4-wheeled coaches Nos B14, B16 and B17 ex-Zillertalbahn, Austria, built 1900–01

Sierra Leone Government Railway bogie coaches Nos 1040, 1048, 1066 and 1207 built 1961
Admiralty 4-wheeled brake vans Nos 210 and 211, built 1935–40
W & LIR open wagons Nos 8, 10 and 11 built 1902
W & LIR closed vans Nos 4 and 6 built 1902
W & LIR cattle wagon No. 3 built 1902
W & LIR brake vans Nos 1 and 2 built 1902
Chattenden and Upnor Railway bogie wagons Nos 32, 33, 35, 38, 41, 60 and 65 built 1942
Talyllyn Railway 4-wheel tipper wagons Nos 48 and 49
Chattenden and Upnor Railway 4-wheel riding/brake van No. 212
Chattenden and Upnor Railway 4-wheel brake van No. 213
Admiralty 5-ton flat wagons Nos 248 and 249
S & KLR bogie pulp wagons Nos 610 & 631 built Butterley Co 1951 (converted to ballast wagons)
Also BR/Thompson first-class sleeping car E1260E used for volunteer accommodation

The Welshpool and Llanfair Light Railway is notable nowadays for its international collection of narrow gauge rolling stock. Trains are composed of locomotives and carriages from as far afield as Austria, Antigua and Sierra Leone.

303 Rheiffordd Llyn Padarn (Llanberis Lake Railway) A

A two-mile 1ft 11½in gauge passenger-carrying line from Llanberis (Gilfach Ddu) to Penllyn following the trackbed of the former Padarn Railway. Opened in 1971

Padarn Country Park, Gilfach Ddu, Llanberis, Gwynedd LL55 4TY
Access: Bangor BR Station, thence by bus to Llanberis. To reach the railway leave the A4086 main road almost opposite the Snowdon Railway Station in Llanberis. Follow the signposts down the approach road to the station at Padarn Park (Gilfach Ddu)
Tel: Llanberis 870549
OS Ref: SH 586603

The railway operates daily from Easter to the first Sunday in October. Facilities for visitors include car parking, souvenir shop, picnic area at Cei Llydan, refreshments and toilets.
The Llanberis Lake Railway was the first of the new generation of 'Great Little Trains of Wales' and was constructed to very high standards of workmanship during the early part of 1971. Motive power comes from former Dinorwic slate quarry locomotives assisted by small diesels from a variety of industrial sources, but the railway had to construct all its own passenger carriages prior to the inauguration of services. Operation of the railway is interesting in that westbound trains do not stop at the intermediate station of Cei Llydan but proceed direct to Penllyn where passengers may not alight due to narrow clearances. On the return journey, the train halts at Cei Llydan where passengers may alight to make use of the lakeside picnic area. The railway runs alongside the very edge of the lake and gives unsurpassed views of the Snowdon mountain range.

Stock
Hunslet 0-4-0ST No. 1 *Elidir* 493 built 1889
Hunslet 0-4-0ST No. 2 *Wild Aster* 849 built 1904
Hunslet 0-4-0ST No. 3 *Dolbadarn* 1430 built 1922
Henschel 0-4-0T No. 5 *Helen Kathryn* 28035 built 1948
Ruston Hornsby 4WDM 198286 built 1940
Ruston Hornsby 4WDM No. 10 *Braich* 203031 built 1941
Motor Rail 4WDM No. 9 *Dolgarrog* 22154 built 1962
Ruston Hornsby 4WDM (Class 48DLZ) 441427 built 1961
Ruston Hornsby 4WDM (Class 48DLZ) 425796 built 1958
Ruston Hornsby 4WDM No. 8 *Twll Coed* (Class 48DLZ) 268878 built 1952
Motor Rail 4WDM 7927 built 1941
Ruston Hornsby 4WDM No. 19 *Llanelli* 451901 (Class 48DLG) built 1961
13 bogie coaches
Six ballast wagons
Nine bogie flat wagons
Three tipping trucks
Three FR slab trucks
Brake van rebuilt from Motor Rail 4WDM 5861 built 1934

North Wales Quarrying Museum (National Museum of Wales)

Padarn Country Park, Gilfach Ddu, Llanberis, Gwynedd
Access: Alongside Gilfach Ddu terminus of Llanberis Lake Railway
Tel: Llanberis 870630

A Museum of equipment, machinery and small exhibits tracing the history of the slate-quarrying industry in North Wales.

Stock
Hunslet 0-4-0ST *Una* 873 built 1905 (1ft 11½in gauge)
Brush 4WBE (2ft 3in gauge)
Smith Rodley 4WVB steam crane 6618
Oakeley 4WPMR

The Museum is housed in the former maintenance workshops for the Dinorwic Slate Quarry – the largest slate quarry in the world. After the quarry closed in 1969, a scheme was prepared to transform the Gilfach Ddu area into a major tourist attraction, now known as the Padarn Country Park. The workshop buildings are open to the public as a quarrying museum, and we are certain that you will find a visit most rewarding. Also in the Museum is the chimney and side tanks of Hunslet 0-6-0T *Velinheli* which used to operate on the 4ft gauge Padarn Railway, together with two manually-operated passenger vehicles from the same line.

304 Rheilffordd Llyn Tegid (Bala Lake Railway) A

A 4½ mile, 1ft 11½in gauge passenger-carrying line opened on 13 August 1972 along the trackbed of the former GWR Morfa Mawddach–Ruabon line between Llanuwchllyn and Bala

Llanuwchllyn Station, Gwynedd LL23 7DD
Access: Off the A494 from Bala to Dolgellau, 5 miles from Bala. Turn left at garage (signposted). Bus route No. D94 (Wrexham–Barmouth)
Tel: Llanuwchllyn (06784) 666
OS Ref: SH 881300

The Bala Lake Railway, one of the latest of the 'Great Little Trains of Wales', has been built solely for tourist traffic, though a pleasing development is the growing support from local residents along the lakeside, who use it as a convenient method of transport to and from Bala.
The railway operates from Easter to the end of September daily from 10 am to 6 pm, and at weekends to mid-October.
Facilities for visitors include railway shop, car parking, refreshments and toilets.
Seven years after BR closed the entire length of the Ruabon–Barmouth Jct Line (54 miles), the Bala Lake Railway started operating trains from Llanuwchllyn to Pentrepiod (1¼m), and on to Llangower (2m) within six months, and extended to Pant-yr-hen-felin (3m) in 1975, and reached Bala (Llyn Tegid) in 1976 (4½m).
Trains run daily from Easter to late September, with special Steam Gala Days in May and September.
The scenery along the route is amongst the finest in the North Wales area, and is seen to advantage along the south shore of the Lake.
Steam and Diesel hauled trains run on the line, and provide a service to the many Camping and Caravan Sites alongside the Lake, also to the small Housing Estate at Llangower.
Modern Corridor Coaching stock is used on the line, plus Open and Closed Carriages, providing a choice of comfortable travel.
Historic Wagons and items of equipment are on view at Llanuwchllyn, and the Signalling is mainly ex-L & Y; however new signals started being made to the Company's own design in 1978.
Special evening Guided Tour trips are run on summer evenings for local Caravan and Camping Site patrons, and they are well supported.
A permanent 7¼in gauge track has been laid along the boundary fence on the north side of the station site. This will ultimately be extended to about 300 yards in length.
General Manager: G. H. Barnes, 'Yr Orsaf', Llanuwchllyn, Bala, Gwynedd, LL23 7DD.
The Railway is supported by Cymdeithas Rheilffordd Llyn Tegid (Bala Lake Railway Society).
Details from: Mr C. Bie, 24 Chestnut Close, Chester.

Stock
[4]Hunslet 0-4-0ST *Holy War* 779 built 1902
[1]Hunslet 0-4-0ST *Alice* 780 built 1902
[2]Hunslet 0-4-0ST *Maid Marian* 822 built 1903
[3]Hunslet 0-4-0ST *Jonathan* 678 built 1898
Kerr Stuart 0-4-0ST *Ashover Drwfach* built 1918
Kerr Stuart 0-6-0T ('Joffre' Class) 2442 built 1915
de Winton 0-4-0VBT *Kathleen* built 1877
Lister-Blackstone 4WDM 34025 built 1949
Severn-Lamb/Leyland Bo-BoDH No. 4 *Meirion Ydd* 7322 built 1973
Ruston Hornsby 4WDM No. 2 182137 (20HP Class) built 1936
Ruston Hornsby 4WDM No. 11 *Cernyw* (33/40HP Class) 200748 built 1940
Ruston Hornsby 4WDM 189972 built 1938
Hunslet 4WDM 1974 built 1939
Ruston Hornsby 4WDM *Flaxen* 209430 built 1942
Ruston Hornsby 4WDM No. 3 *Indian Runner* 200744 built 1940
Motor Rail 4WDM 5821 built 1934
Ruston Hornsby 4WDM 283512 built 1949
Ruston Hornsby 4WDM *Chilmark* 194771 built 1939
Hibberd 4WDM 2544 built 1942
Hudson 4WDM *Goofy* 38384 built *c*1930
Lister Blackstone 4WDM No. 2 *Alister* 44052 built 1958
Ruston Hornsby 4WDM 235729 built 1944 (2ft 6in gauge)
Closed saloon coach with invalid and guard's compartments built 1981
Two semi-open saloon coaches built 1981
Two 'toastrack' covered bogie coaches built 1972
Two enclosed bogie saloon coaches built 1978
Three compartment bogie coaches built 1973–75
Eight slate wagons
Two flat wagons converted from slate trucks
FR gunpowder van

[1]Ex-Dinorwic Quarries. Purchased at the same time as *Holy War* whose first owner removed all easily-removable parts and abandoned the frames, tank and boiler at the top level of the quarry. The cylinders, wheels, motion, etc, came to Llanuwchllyn as spares with *Holy War*. The boiler, frames and tank were purchased and removed from the quarry by the West Lancashire Light Railway who used the boiler on *Irish Mail*. The frames and tank arrived at Llanuwchllyn in 1977. The rebuilding of this locomotive as an 0-4-2T with tender is a long-term project.
[2]Ex-Dinorwic Slate Quarries Co Ltd, Llanberis, Caernarfonshire, 1968. Ran on the Bressingham Narrow Gauge Railway until the end of 1971 and on the Llanberis Lake Railway until 1975. Owned by the Maid Marian Locomotive Fund (*q.v.*).
[3]Built by Hunslet in 1898 and completely restored after its purchase from Dinorwic Quarry, Caernarfonshire, who had been its sole owners and where it was named *Bernstein*. Ran on the Lythan Creek Railway until 1979.

[4]Ex-Dinorwic Slate Quarries. Withdrawn in 1968, the last working steam locomotive in a Welsh Slate Quarry. Purchased and taken to Quainton Railway Centre where it was steamed once or twice. Purchased late 1975 by Rev A. Cliff of Wrexham and brought to Llanuwchllyn. Entered service after extensive restoration at Easter 1979.

Maid Marian Locomotive Fund

Details from: Douglas C. Carrington, 223 Sunnybank Road, Unsworth, Bury, Lancashire BL9 8JU.

305 Vale of Rheidol Narrow Gauge Steam Railway — A

British Rail's only narrow gauge passenger line, 11¾ miles long, one class only, operated by steam traction

Aberystwyth, Dyfed
Access: Aberystwyth BR Station. Bus route Nos S1 & S17
Tel: Aberystwyth 612377
OS Ref: SN 587812

Facilities: Car parks and refreshments at Aberystwyth; car park, refreshments and souvenir shop at Devil's Bridge; railway letter service.
Details from: Public Relations Officer, Divisional Manager's Office, British Rail, Station Road, Stoke-on-Trent, Staffordshire ST4 2AA.
Opened for goods and mineral traffic in August 1902, passengers were first carried on 22 December of the same year. The Cambrian Railways absorbed the line in August 1913 and they in turn were incorporated within the Great Western Railway from 1 January 1923 under the Railway Act of 1921. On 1 January 1948 the line was taken over by British Railways on nationalisation and placed in the Western Region, being transferred to the London Midland Region in 1963.
The service is maintained by three specially designed locomotives variously overhauled at Swindon, Oswestry and Crewe and each capable of hauling six coaches and a brake van up the heavy gradients to Devil's Bridge, climbing to an altitude of 680ft above sea level.
Between Aberystwyth and Devil's Bridge the line passes through the magnificent scenery of the Rheidol Valley, George Borrow having described the Devil's Bridge area as 'one of the most remarkable localities in the world'.
In 1966–67 the line was diverted into the main station at Aberystwyth (Carmarthen bay platforms). En route to Devil's Bridge the single line serves seven stations and halts on the way at Llanbadarn, Glanrafon, Capel Bangor, Nantyronen, Aberffrwd, Rheidol Falls and Rhiwfron.
In 1967 engines and coaches were repainted in BR blue with arrow totem.
A decision to end the inclusion of the Vale of Rheidol within BR's corporate identity was taken in 1980 and as a first step to restoring the line's character, locomotive No. 8 *Llywelyn* has been painted in full GWR livery. Three of the line's wagons, used for engineers' trains, have been restored to 1902 V of R livery, whilst a named train, *The Welsh Dragon*, complete with headboard, runs daily. All passengers on the line are issued with souvenir tickets.

Vale of Rheidol Railway Supporters Association

The Association exists to promote development of the line under BR ownership. Its members give practical promotional support to the railway and hold periodic group and management meetings. Newsletters are issued from time to time.
Details from: Mr G. T. Jones, 5 Erw Goch, Waunfawr, Aberystwyth, Dyfed SY23 3AZ.

Stock

GWR 2-6-2T No. 7 *Owain Glyndwr* built Swindon 1923
GWR 2-6-2T No. 8 *Llywelyn* built Swindon 1923
V of R 2-6-2T No. 9 *Prince of Wales* built Davies and Metcalfe of Romiley near Manchester in 1902 for the opening of the line
Sixteen bogie coaches, including seven second-class closed coaches Nos 1 to 6 (M4143–M4148) and 10 (M4994), two brake-seconds Nos 11 and 12 (M4995–M4996) and seven open observation coaches Nos 7 to 9 (M4149–M4151) and Nos 13 to 16 (M4997–M5000) built 1923
GWR four-wheeled passenger brake van No. 19 (M137) built 1938
Wickham 4WPMR No. PWM 2214 4131 built *c*1947 (Outstationed at Nantyronen)
V of R flat wagon No. W8512 built Midland RC & W 1906
V of R side door wagons Nos DW34104, DW34108, M34110 and M34111 built Midland RC & W 1906
Hafan Tramway end door wagons Nos ADM34124, M34136 and ADM34141
Hafan Tramway bolster wagons Nos W8510 and W34106
Hafan Tramway flat wagon No. W8513

306 Snowdon Mountain Railway — A

A four-and-three-quarter miles long, 2ft 7½in gauge, passenger-carrying rack railway climbing to the summit of Snowdon (3560ft)

Llanberis, Gwynedd
Access: Bangor BR Station, thence by bus to Llanberis. By road along the A4086 from Caernarfon or Capel Curig.
Tel: Llanberis (028-682) 223
OS Ref: SH 582597

Operated by Snowdon Mountain Railway Ltd, Llanberis, Gwynedd.
Facilities: Modern shop and restaurant, snack bar and craft chalet. Parking facilities at Llanberis. Restaurant, bar and shop at the summit. Parties catered for by arrangement outside mid-summer peak period.
The railway operates from Easter to the first weekend in October.

The railway was first opened in 1896 and the ABT system in use in Switzerland was used in the construction of the line. The system involves the laying of two toothed racks laid side by side in the centre of the track and the teeth of the racks are engaged by two cogged wheels or rack pinions fitted to the locomotives.
The Company has seven steam locomotives, all built by the Swiss locomotive works at Winterthur. A train is made up of one locomotive with one coach of a passenger capacity of a maximum 60 persons. There are severe gradients on the line and in the interests of safety the speed of the locomotives is restricted to a maximum of 5 mph. It is the only rack railway in the British Isles.

Stock
0-4-2T No. 2 *Enid* 924 built 1895
0-4-2T No. 3 *Wyddfa* 925 built 1895
0-4-2T No. 4 *Snowdon* 988 built 1896
0-4-2T No. 5 *Moel Siabod* 989 built 1896
0-4-2T No. 6 *Padarn* 2838 built 1922
0-4-2T No. 7 *Ralph Sadler* 2869 built 1923
0-4-2T No. 8 *Eryri* 2870 built 1923
Seven saloon bogie coaches
Bogie works car
Four-wheeled open wagon

A train will not leave the terminus for the ascent if the Company so determines with less than forty return adult passengers or the equivalent in adult fares.
Snow and ice may prevent progress to the summit early and late in the season, and strong winds at high altitude may at any time result in the summit not being reached.
All enquiries regarding train services and applications for special party fares to: The General Manager, Snowdon Mountain Railway Ltd, Llanberis, Gwynedd.

307 Talyllyn Railway A

Passenger-carrying 2ft 3in gauge steam railway, 7¼ miles in length, running from Tywyn Wharf to Nant Gwernol

Wharf Station, Tywyn, Gwynedd LL36 9EY
Access: Tywyn BR Station, Crosville bus routes S26, S28 and S30. By roads A493 and B4405
Tel: Tywyn 710472
OS Ref: SH 590008

Facilities: Car park and restaurant facilities at or near Tywyn Wharf, Dolgoch and Abergynolwyn. Railway shop and museum at Tywyn. Special arrangements for parties of 15 and over (limited in July and August).
Trains operate from Easter to the end of October daily except during October. Also Christmas Holidays.
In 1865 an Act of Parliament gave the Talyllyn Railway Company powers to build and operate a railway from a wharf abutting the then Aberystwyth and Welsh Coast Railway at Towyn, Merioneth (now Tywyn, Gwynedd) to Abergynolwyn, a distance of 6¾ miles. From Abergynolwyn there was to be a further line for mineral traffic only to the quarries at Bryn Eglwys.
Engineer of the 2ft 3in gauge line was James Spooner, son of the man who had built the Ffestiniog Railway and brother of C. E. Spooner who introduced steam traction on the narrow gauge at Porthmadog (Portmadoc as it was then). In contrast to the Ffestiniog Railway the Talylln was intended to serve the quarry whose owners built the railway, although a secondary use of the line was to provide transport for the village of Abergynolwyn (where many of the quarry workers lived) and the valley hamlets of Rhydyronen and Pandy. The line opened to passenger traffic in 1867 and has carried passengers every year since, a record that no other narrow gauge line anywhere in the world can equal.
Two very different steam locomotives were purchased from Fletcher, Jennings & Co Ltd of Whitehaven for the opening. No. 1 *Talyllyn*, as 0-4-0ST later converted to 0-4-2ST whilst No. 2 *Dolgoch* was an 0-4-0WT with an unusually long wheelbase. Passenger stock consisted of three bowsided four-wheelers built by Brown Marshalls and a Guards Van also by Brown Marshalls. Another four-wheeler with straight sides was purchased from the Lancaster Wagon Co Ltd. For more than eighty years these two locomotives and five four-wheelers remained the sole motive power and passenger stock on the line.
And so the Talyllyn Railway ran, day in and day out carrying slates for the roofs of the industrial Midlands (and indeed further afield) and Victorian and then Edwardian families on their holiday outings on the 'Toy Railway'. History and great national events passed it by – until in 1911 the owners sold both the ailing quarry and the railway to Sir Henry Hadyn Jones, who was a local figure of note and who became MP for the County of Merioneth. With the slate revenue declining and the best veins becoming worked out the quarries struggled on and the railway ran with little or no money to spare for repairs or maintenance. After the Second World War came the news of the closure of the Ffestiniog Railway (which, after all, had served half a dozen independent quarries) and then when Bryn Eglwys quarries closed the end of the railway seemed in sight. But Sir Haydn had declared his intention of keeping the railway running during his lifetime – and although this meant sorely needed work for the remaining employees it also meant that rolling stock and track became even more run-down.
When, in 1950, Sir Haydn died, the closure of the line seemed imminent, but a group of enthusiasts had been planning ways to rescue this just-surviving example of Victorian engineering. In 1951, a society was formed to take over and operate the line and to preserve its historic stock. So there was born the world's first railway preservation society; and against tremendous odds and in spite of widespread scepticism the project succeeded. Modestly at first, but all the time with improving revenues from members' subscriptions and passengers' fares the railway has been progressively restored so that now

more than 170,000 travel on the line each year.
The railway is controlled and supported by the **Talyllyn Railway Preservation Society.**
Details from: TRPS, Wharf Station, Tywyn, Gwynedd.

Stock
Fletcher Jennings 0-4-2ST No. 1 *Talyllyn* 42 built 1865
Fletcher Jennings 0-4-0WT No. 2 *Dolgoch* 63 built 1866
Hughes 0-4-2ST No. 3 *Sir Haydn* 323 built 1878
Kerr Stuart 0-4-2ST No. 4 *Edward Thomas* 4047 built 1921
Ruston Hornsby 4WDM No. 5 *Midlander* 200792 (44/58 HP Class) built 1940
Barclay 0-4-0WT No. 6 *Douglas* 1431 built 1918
[1]Barclay 0-4-2T No. 7 *Irish Pete* 2263 built 1949
Ruston Hornsby 4WDH No. 8 *Merseysider* 476108 (LF Class) built 1964
Hunslet 0-4-0DM No. 9 *Alf* 4136 built 1950
Brown Marshalls four-wheeled coaches Nos 1 and 2 built 1867
Brown Marshalls four-wheeled coach No. 3 built 1866
Lancaster Wagon Co four-wheeled coach No. 4 built 1870
Brown Marshalls four-wheeled brake van No. 5 built 1866
Corris Railway four-wheeled brake van No. 6
Penrhyn Railway four-wheeled van No. 7 built 1963
Talyllyn Railway four-wheeled coach No. 8 built 1966
TR/W. G. Allen compartment bogie coach No. 9 built 1954
TR/W. G. Allen brake/third bogie coach No. 10 built 1954
TR four-wheeled coach No. 11 built 1955
TR four-wheeled coach No. 12 built 1956
TR four-wheeled coach No. 13 built 1957
Glyn Valley Tramway four-wheeled first-class coach No. 14 built 1892
Glyn Valley Tramway four-wheeled first-class coach No. 15 built 1901
TR/Kerr Stuart brake/third bogie coach No. 16 built 1961
Corris Railway third-class saloon bogie coach No. 17 built 1898
TR compartment bogie coach No. 18 built 1965
TR composite bogie coach No. 19
TR compartment bogie coach No. 20
TR compartment bogie coach No. 21 built 1975
TR compartment/brake bogie coach No. 22 built 1975
TR compartment coach No. 23 built 1975
Forty-four goods wagons

[1]Not yet in service. Locomotive being rebuilt from 3ft gauge 0-4-0WT.

308 Rhyl Miniature Railway — A

A passenger-carrying 15in gauge steam railway laid out as a continuous circuit

Rhyddlan Borough Council, Marine Lake, Rhyl, Clwyd
OS Ref: SJ 002806

Stock
Barnes 4-4-2 No. 2 *Joan* 101 built 1920
Barnes 4-4-2 No. 1 106 built 1934
Ford BoBoPM *Railway Queen* built 1959

309 Fairbourne Railway — A

A two mile 15in gauge line connecting Fairbourne with Barmouth Ferry

Operated by North Wales Narrow Gauge Railway Ltd, Beach Road, Fairbourne, Gwynedd LL38 2EX
Access: Fairbourne BR Station; Crosville bus service S28; A493 road
Tel: Fairbourne 250362
OS Ref: SH 616128

The line started as a 2ft gauge horse tramway in 1890 and was rebuilt as a 15in gauge railway in 1916 by Narrow Gauge Railways Ltd, a subsidiary of Bassett-Lowke Ltd. The railway was closed for the duration of the war in 1940 and was so severely damaged by the weather and the military that it seemed unlikely to reopen. It was, however, acquired by a new company after the war and reopened in stages from 1947. Since then it has been extensively developed, with new and rebuilt locomotives and rolling stock and an enlarged station and depot at Fairbourne. The railway offers panoramic views of the North Wales mountains and the renowned Mawddach estuary. Trains connect with the Barmouth ferry at Penrhyn Point.
The railway operates Easter to October daily.
Facilities: Car park, railway shop and refreshments, etc, at Fairbourne. Refreshment and sales coach at Ferry terminus. Special reduced rates for parties of ten or more. Season and weekly tickets available.
Sales and publicity: Hugh Sykes, 78 Hawthorn Road, Kingstanding, Birmingham B44 8QP.
Note: The Fairbourne Railway was acquired by a new owner at the end of 1983, and is to be relaid to 12¼in gauge with new rolling stock.

Stock
15in gauge locomotives
Bassett-Lowke 4-4-2 *Count Louis* 32 built 1924
Guest 2-4-2 *Shon* 14 built 1954 formerly *Katie*
[1]Guest 2-4-2 *Sydney* 18 built 1963 formerly *Siân*
G & S Light Engineering 0-6-0DH *Rachel* 15 built 1959, rebuilt 1972
[1]G & S Light Engineering Bo-Bo PH *Sylvia* 14A built 1961
Lister 4WPM *Gwril* 20886 built 1941

12¼in gauge locomotives are stored pending the change of gauge
Two end glass screen open bogie coaches Nos 16 and 20
Four-car articulated saloon coaches G & S built 1965
Bogie open coaches Nos 14, 15 and 17
Bogie saloon coaches Nos 18 and 19 G & S built 1960

Two three-car open articulated sets Nos 11 (ABC) and 21 (DEF)
Two bogie bolsters ex-No. 12 open coach and No. 13 ex-first class closed coach. Both converted to bogie tipper wagons
Twelve-wheeled bogie canteen coach G & S built 1969
Two four-wheeled open wagons
One four-wheeled side-tipping wagon
Six flat wagons
Rail-mounted saw
Rail-bender wagon

[1]Locomotive fitted with air-braking system.

310 Gwili Railway A

A passenger-carrying standard gauge steam railway, 1½ miles in length, running from Bronwydd Arms to Penybont

Bronwydd Arms Station, Bronwydd, near Carmarthen, Dyfed
Access: Carmarthen (BR); A484 road; Crosville bus No. S44 Carmarthen–Cardigan
Tel: Maesteg 732176
OS Ref: SN 417239

The railway operates on Bank Holidays, Mondays and Tuesdays. Saturdays and Sundays from beginning of June to end of September. Mondays, Tuesdays, Wednesdays mid July to end August. First train 11 am except Saturdays when it is 12 noon. Last train will run at 5.15 pm. Timetables are issued from the Company's Office: 51 Neath Road, Maesteg, Mid Glamorgan. Facilities for visitors include car parking, refreshments and souvenir shops.

Gwili Railway Preservation Society/Cymdeithas Gadwraeth Rheiffordd Gwili

The Society has been set up as the supporting society to the Gwili Railway Company Limited.

Secretary: Mrs H. M. Headon, 16 Church Close, Bryncoch, Neath, West Glamorgan.

Stock
RSH 0-4-0ST *Olwen* 7058 built 1942
RSH 0-6-0ST 7170 built 1944
Peckett 0-4-0ST *Merlin/Myrddin* 1967 built 1939
Peckett 0-4-0ST *Little Lady* 1903 built 1936
Hudswell Clarke 0-6-0ST No. 1 1885 built 1955
Yorkshire Engine Co 0-4-0DE 2779 built 1960
Ruston Hornsby 4WDM 207103 built 1941
BR Mk.1 buffet car No. E3060 built 1955
BR dmu trailer coach No. E56317 built 1957
BR Mk.1 griddle car No. E1106 built 1962, rebuilt 1968
BR Mk.1 2nd class compartment coach No. W46132 built 1954
BR Mk.1 brake/2nd compartment coach No. W43264 built 1955
10-ton diesel rail crane No. 19305 built Coles 1963
National Benzole tank wagon No. 2002
GWR 'Mink A' van No. W96302
GWR 'Toad' 20-ton goods brake van No. W35380 built 1949
LNER box van No. E985882
GWR 'Fruit D' van No. W92004 built 1957
GWR 'Loriot B' well wagon No. 42155 built 1909
Taff Vale Railway brake/third coach body No. 220 (GWR No. 3846) built 1891 on BSC 4-wheel wagon chassis
GWR 6-plank open wagons PBA Nos 58057 and 58093
PBA 8-plank open wagons Nos 59246 and 59260
BP wagons Nos W113386, W11313, M105114, O71884, M74831, M90810, M108025, W900872, 070688 and O71204
Wickham 4WPMR Type 17A No. B154 (PWM 2222) 4139, built 1947
Four-wheeled hand-propelled trolley

311 Llangollen Railway A

Standard gauge passenger-carrying railway 1½ miles in length from Llangollen to Berwyn, with track being laid westwards towards Corwen

Llangollen Railway Society Ltd, Llangollen Station, Llangollen, Clwyd, North Wales
Access: Via A539 Ruabon–Corwen road or via A5 Shrewsbury–Holyhead road
Hourly bus services from Chester
Tel: Llangollen (0978) 860951
OS Ref: SJ 211423

Llangollen station is open all year round with a locomotive in steam on weekends and public holidays. Opening hours 9.30 am to 5.30 pm.
Facilities for visitors include car parking, souvenir shop, museum, refreshments and toilets.
Originally started in 1972 by a group of enthusiasts in Flint, North Wales, and known as Flint and Deeside Railway Preservation Society. They began protracted negotiations with Clwyd County Council for acquisition of Llangollen Station and track bed of 10 miles of former GW Ruabon–Barmouth branch line. This was closed under Beeching in 1965 and was lifted two years later.
The Society eventually gained a lease on the property and site in 1975, and set about the task of transforming a wilderness into the semblance of a GW station again. Membership increased as people were attracted by the idea of reopening the section of line to public use again. The line runs through an area of outstanding beauty on the edge of the Snowdonia National Park, and is the only preserved standard gauge line in North Wales.
As all track and fittings were removed by BR after closure, it has meant that the Society has had to start to com-

pletely re-lay all track, etc, as it became available to them. In 1978 it was decided that the project was becoming much larger, and it was decided that in order to give financial protection to members, the Society should become a limited company. The assets of the former Flint & Deeside Society were transferred to the new body, Llangollen Railway Society Ltd.

Six years of hard work at Llangollen were crowned with achievement on 26 July 1981, when the railway ran its first steam passenger trains under special authorisation from the Railway Inspectorate, pending completion of the Light Railway Order formalities.

The railway operates on Sundays and Public Holidays from Spring Bank Holiday onwards.

Further details from: Mr A. E. Terry (Secretary), 33 Deeside, Ellesmere Port, South Wirral, Cheshire L65 6RG.

Stock

GWR 0-6-0PT No. 7754 (57XX Class) North British Loco 24042 built 1930
LMS 0-6-0T No. 7298 (Fowler Class 3F) built 1924
[1]Kitson 0-6-0ST *Burtonwood Brewer* 5459 built 1932
[2]Hudswell Clarke 0-6-0T *Richboro* 1243 built 1917
[7]Peckett 0-6-0ST *Ackton Hall No. 3* 1567 built 1920
[3]Fowler 0-4-0DM *Eliseg* 22753 built 1939
Hudswell Clarke 0-4-0DM No. D4 D1012 built 1956
North British 0-4-0DH 27734 built 1958
[4]Fowler 0-4-0DM *Burmah* 4000007 built 1947
BR Class 127 DMU DMBS coach No. M51618 built 1959
BR/Cravens DMU trailer car No. E56456 built 1959
BR Class 105 2-car dmu set built Cravens
[5]GWR 'Toad' goods brake van (20-ton) No. 17407 built 1940
GWR brake third-class coach No. 5539 built 1938
GWR brake/third coach No. 1649 built 1938
[8]BR non-corridor passenger coach No. E46130 built 1954
BR Mk.1 brake/third compartment coach No. E43182 built 1954
Shell tank wagon No. A6264 built 1947
GWR 'Siphon G' 6-wheel van No. W1037 built 1955
LNWR brake van
Lancashire Tar Distillers square tank wagon built 1926
ICI Salt wagon built *c*1890
SR 'BY' passenger van No. S931
[10]LNER 6-wheel pigeon loft van No. 70250 converted to handicapped visitors coach 1984
Smith Rodley 5-ton diesel crane No. X63486 built 1957
Goods van
Two flat wagons
BSC 20-ton hopper wagon
BSC 7-plank open wagon
Four open wagons ex-TI Chesterfield Ltd
Two Courtaulds side-tipping wagons
GWR 'Toad' 20-ton goods brake van
Low-sided wagon
[9]GWR steam crane No. RS38 built 1947 with match trucks Nos DW38 & DW39 built 1917
GWR 'Open C' tube wagon built 1922
[6]LMS registered 14-ton rail tank wagon (Castrol livery) No. 164494 built 1944

[1]Ex-British Leyland Motor Corporation, Austin-Morris Division, Longbridge, Birmingham, 1973. This locomotive was bought for the Society by Burtonwood Brewery Ltd.
[2]Ex-National Coal Board, Gresford Colliery and Ifton Colliery.
[3]Ex-Hawker Siddeley Aviation Ltd, Broughton, Clwyd, 1974.
[4]Ex-Burmah Castrol Ltd, Ellesmere Port, presented for use at Llangollen in 1975.
[5]Privately owned by the 17407 Group. On loan to the Llangollen Railway.
[6]Ex-Burmah Castrol Ltd, Ellesmere Port, presented as a gift to the Llangollen Railway Society in 1976.
[7]Ex-Keighley & Worth Valley Railway 1979.
[8]This coach was taken out of passenger carrying service on 23 August 1976 at Finsbury Park and was despatched, along with three others, to York for shop repairs. While at York it was decided that they were excess to requirements and were withdrawn and offered for sale in January 1977.
[9]Ex-Severn Valley Railway 1978.
[10]Ex-Derwent Valley Railway 1979.

Llangollen Railway Rolling Stock Group

The Llangollen Railway Rolling Stock Group was formed with the aim of acquiring suitable items of rolling stock for use on the Llangollen Railway. Membership is open to the general public and is available by purchasing one or more shares in any item of stock subsequently purchased by the Group. A number of suitable locomotives, passenger coaches and goods vehicles have been selected for possible purchase when they become available. Further particulars can be obtained from: Mr Medwyn Roberts, 3 Bryn Dyffryn, Holywell, Clwyd, Wales.

312 Caerphilly Railway Society Ltd D

Standard gauge railway preservation centre incorporating a ¼-mile demonstration line

Harold Wilson Industrial Estate, Van Road, Caerphilly, Mid-Glamorgan
Access: 1 mile from Caerphilly BR Station and bus station. Via Van Road to estate entrance
OS Ref: ST 163865

The Society was formed in 1973 and is based in the yard of the former locomotive works of the Rhymney Railway, now an industrial estate. The Society has a growing collection of locomotives in its care, six of which are part of the National Museum of Wales collection. On advertised Open Days rides are given in the GWR brake van propelled by one of the locomotives, train movements being controlled by a Brecon and Merthyr Railway signal-

box, formerly at Rhiwderin, and built by Saxby & Farmer more than 100 years ago and open to visitors. The site is also open on Sunday afternoons when members are carrying out restoration work on the site.
For Open Day dates see railway press.
Membership details from: Mr A. Smith, 51 Worcester Crescent, Newport, Gwent.
Open Day Details from: Mr M. Brown (Publicity Officer), 18 Henilys Road, Cardiff.
Facilities for visitors include souvenir shop and refreshments on Open Days only and car parking.

Stock
[5]Avonside 0-4-0ST *Desmond* 1498 built 1906
[6]Barclay 0-4-0ST *Victory* 2201 built 1945
[4]LMS 2-6-2T No. 41312 (Ivatt Class 2MT) built 1952
[1]TVR 0-6-2T No. 28 (GWR No. 450) (Class 01) built 1897
[3]Barclay 0-4-0ST *Forester* 1260 built 1911
Vulcan Foundry 0-6-0ST *Haulwen* 5272 built 1945
Yorkshire Engine Co 0-4-0DE *Caerphilly* 2731 built 1959
Shell-Mex 4-wheel tank wagon built 1948
GWR 'Toad' 20-ton goods brake van No. 35267
BR Mk.1 BSK coach No. M34460 built 1953
GWR 4-wheel 6-ton hand crane
GWR prototype ballast wagon No. 60501 built 1899
BR fruit van No. W92040
BR mess & tool van No. KDS 8

[1]Taff Vale Railway No. 28 was sold by the GWR to the Government in 1927 for use at Longmoor. After the war it was sold for use by the NCB who later presented it to BR for preservation and since 1965 it has been in the care of the National Museum of Wales. After being in store for several years, work on restoration is now being undertaken. This is the only surviving Welsh built standard gauge locomotive. On loan from the National Collection.
[3]Ex-British Steel Corporation, Ebbw Vale Steelworks, 1973.
[4]Built Crewe Works 1952, spent most of its working life on Southern Region of BR. Withdrawn 1967 and sent to Barry scrapyard. Bought by a Society member and arrived Caerphilly 1974.
[5]Ex-British Steel Corporation, Orb Works, Newport, 1977.
[6]Ex-Stewarts & Lloyds, Newport, 1975.

313 9642 Preservation Group D

NCB Workshops, Maesteg, Glamorgan
OS Ref: SS 848915

Secretary: W. T. Jones, 'Bryn-Awelon', 55 Salisbury Road, Maesteg, Glamorgan CF34 9EH.

Stock
[1]GWR 0-6-0T No. 9642 (Class 57XX) built 1946
GWR 'Toad' 20-ton goods brake van converted for passenger use
GWR covered van converted for passenger use

[1]Withdrawn in 1964 as BR No. 9642 and sold to R. S. Hayes Ltd, Bridgend, for scrap but retained for shunting purposes. Purchased for preservation in 1968. The most successful shunting engines ever built, the 5700 type could be seen almost everywhere on the GWR. These engines were equally at home on short-distance passenger trains and many of them worked such turns, especially in South Wales. Speeds up to 60 mph have been achieved at times by these remarkable machines. At the other extreme, they have been recorded working 70–80-wagon goods trains. No less than 862 of these locomotives were constructed between 1929 and 1950. As with all large classes there were variations. The earliest engines were constructed with the older flatter-roofed cab and round spectacles, whilst those built from 1932 onwards had the enlarged cab and sundry improvements. Withdrawal commenced in 1956, but three of the class lasted until November 1966 to become the last GWR engines to work on BR. A number of the earlier locomotives were sold to London Transport on withdrawal and some of these have subsequently been preserved.

314 Fort Belan Miniature Railway A

Passenger-carrying 7¼in gauge steam railway, ⅝ mile in length, running from the car park to the Fort

Fort Belan, Dinas Dinlle, near Caernarfon, North Wales
Access: Off the A499 Caernarfon–Pwllheli Road through Dinas Dinlle (about 5 miles)
Tel: Llanwnda (0286) 830220
OS Ref: SH 440609

The railway operates from 1 May to 30 September between 10 am and 5.30 pm daily.
Facilities for visitors include car parking, maritime museum, pleasure cruises to Caernarfon, pleasure flights by light aircraft, cannon firing, pottery, gift shop, refreshments and toilets.
This charming old Fort, situated in secluded and eminently picturesque surroundings, remains a singularly romantic and unspoilt place. Built some two hundred years ago on a small peninsula at the Western entrance to the Menai Straits, Belan is surrounded on three sides by the sea. The Snowdonia range of mountains in the background makes the neighbourhood one of great and varied loveliness.
Very little has changed at Belan for over 200 years, and the Fort, Docks, and cannons have all been maintained in first class working order.
The railway is laid out in a pear-shaped loop configuration running through the sand dunes. Its locomotives are ¼ full size replicas of original engines built by Bagnalls of Stafford.

Stock
[1]Bagnall 0-4-2T built 1980
[2]Bagnall 0-6-0 *El Meson* built Potts 1964–69
Five 5-seat bogie coaches
Two driving/guard trucks built 1981

[1]Modelled on Bagnall 2ft gauge locomotive built for the Rustenberg Platinum Mines, South Africa.
[2]Modelled on Bagnall locomotive built in 1910 for Mexico. Like the original, it has Bagnall-Price patented valve gear and a marine-type firebox.

315 Great Orme Tramway B

The Great Orme Tramway runs from Victoria Station, Llandudno, to just below the summit of the Great Orme headland, 679ft above sea level

Victoria Station, Church Walks, Llandudno, Gwynedd
Operated by Aberconway Borough Council, Leisure and Amenities Department, Town Hall, Llandudno
Access: Bus routes Nos 7 and 10. BR Llandudno station (½ mile)
Tel: Llandudno 76749
OS Ref: SH 7781

Authorised in 1898, this 3ft 6in gauge line is in two sections, passengers changing cars halfway. The lower section, opened on 31 July 1902, is 800 yards long (maximum gradient 1 in 4.4); the upper, opened on 8 July 1903, is 827 yards long (maximum gradient 1 in 10.3). Both are single track with a passing loop, although the lower incline has a portion of double track with a common middle rail.
Cable traction is employed, though an overhead wire is used for signalling purposes. The cable and pulleys are carried in a central conduit on the lower (paved) section and above the ground on conventional sleepers on the upper portion.
Originally steam-driven, the winding and control gear at the halfway station is now powered by electric induction motors. The line, which was taken over by Llandudno Urban District Council from the Great Orme Railway Company on 1 January 1949, opens each summer with a basic 20-minute service, extra journeys being worked during busy periods.

Stock
Four six-and-a-half-ton tramcars each seating 48 built 1902–3

316 Ceudwll Llechwedd (Llechwedd Slate Caverns) B

A 2ft gauge passenger-carrying partially underground line operated by Quarry Tours Ltd. Opened in 1972

Blaenau Ffestiniog, Gwynedd LL41 3NB
Access: Crosville bus route No. R34. Connecting service from Tan-y-Grisiau
Nearest BR station: Blaenau Ffestiniog
Tel: Blaenau Ffestiniog 306
OS Ref: SH 699468

The mine is open for visitors and the tramway operates from 10 am to 6 pm daily, 1 March to 30 October (last train into mine 5.15 pm).
The Llechwedd Slate Caverns are part of the Llechwedd Slate Mines at the northern end of Blaenau Ffestiniog in the Snowdonia National Park. The veins of slate run deeply underground and mining, rather than opencast quarrying, was found to be the most economic method of extracting the slate. These underground workings extend to a depth of 900ft and consist of some 25 miles of tunnels connecting the vast chambers from which the slate has been removed over the last 100 years or so.
Visitors to the caverns can take a half-mile return journey through the mine in specially-designed trains hauled by battery-electric locomotives. Two trains can operate simultaneously, if required by traffic, as a passing loop is provided about half-way into the mine. The train conveys visitors to a slate chamber in which the working conditions of a century ago have been recreated. Here visitors will see how the vast caverns were formed by the extraction of slate from the mountainside. A guide will demonstrate the hand tools used in bygone days. Back in the slate mill, visitors will be shown the fascinating process of slate splitting and can try cleaving a block of slate themselves. Visitors should note that the temperature underground remains fairly constant throughout the year at about 50°F (10°C) and that wearing a jacket or cardigan would be appropriate.

Stock
Wingrove and Rogers 4WBE No. 1
Wingrove and Rogers 4WBE No. 2
Wingrove and Rogers 4WBE No. 3
Wingrove and Rogers 4WBE 308 built 1921
Bagnall 0-4-0E *The Eclipse* 1445 built 1895, rebuilt Greaves 1927
Wingrove and Rogers 4WBE 323 built 1921
Wingrove and Rogers 4WBE E6807 built 1965
Wingrove and Rogers 4WBE C6766 built 1963
Logan 4WBE MBS387 1953 built 1950
Logan 4WBE MBS236 1066 built 1950
Bagnall 0-4-0E *The Coalition* 1278 built 1890, rebuilt Greaves 1930
Twelve Hudson four-seat, four-wheel carriages

The Llechwedd Slate Caverns have been a top tourist attraction ever since their opening in 1972. In that year they gained their first British Tourist Authority Award, and have received many awards and commendations since then, culminating in the 1980 Certificage of Special Commendation of the 'Come to Britain' trophy.
Opening up the Deep Mine in 1979 proved to be another

award-winning 'first' for Llechwedd Slate Caverns. Operating within the restrictions of what was originally an industrial incline, commenced in 1846, it required the construction of a special 24-seat vehicle to negotiate Britain's steepest underground passenger railway. A failsafe braking system had to be incorporated in the 3-ton car, which is cable-hauled on 3ft gauge heavy-duty track on a 1 in 1.8 gradient. Known as the Llechwedd-Tredomen system, the brakes operate automatically should the descending speed exceed 2.4 mph. The car and track were designed and made by Tredomen Engineering (a subsidiary of the National Coal Board) and the system is powered and controlled with GEC equipment – the latter incorporating another failsafe mechanical braking device in the event of power failure.

317 Welsh Highland Light Railway A

Passenger-carrying 60cm gauge railway, ¾ mile in length, from Porthmadog to Pen-y-mount

Rheilffordd Ysgafn Ucheldir Cymraeg, Gelert's Farm Works, Madoc Street West, Porthmadog, Gwynedd LL49 9DY
Access: Adjacent to BR Porthmadog station on A487 road. Crosville buses to Porthmadog
Tel: 0766-3402
OS Ref: SH 567393

Membership Secretary: Mr G. Weigh, 30 Ivory Way, St Marys, Oldham, Lancs OL1 3DX

The Welsh Highland Railway was the result of many years' endeavour to build a narrow gauge through route linking the Porthmadog terminus of the Ffestiniog Railway with the LNWR Afon Wen–Caernarfon line. When completed in 1923 it provided an unbroken 35-mile stretch of 60cm gauge track between Dinas Junction and Blaenau Ffestiniog. In actual fact, although the FR and the WHR ultimately came under the same management, the system was never worked as one line.

The expense and inconvenience of running the Welsh Highland finally proved too much for the Ffestiniog and passenger traffic ceased in 1936. The line was dismantled for scrap during the war, but miraculously the WHR locomotive *Russell* survived in industrial service and was preserved in 1955.

In 1961 – following a meeting on Crewe Station – the Welsh Highland Railway Society was formed, with the aim of rebuilding a part of the old railway. This was followed in 1964 by the registration of the present company.

Negotiations to acquire the trackbed have been repeatedly delayed. The death of the original company's liquidator, possible road widening schemes – and even the reorganisation of local government are amongst the causes for these delays.

Despite these setbacks, the present company has continued working towards its goal, and in 1973 was allowed occupation of its present site, Beddgelert Siding, Porthmadog, where slate used to be transhipped from narrow gauge to standard gauge wagons.

Passenger operation commenced on 2 August 1980. Over 7,000 passengers were carried during the ensuing short season and the railway was officially opened on 18 July 1981 by Councillor Roberts, Chairman of Gwynedd County Council.

Although some legal problems remain, the company hopes to soon start on re-building the next section of line between Pen-y-Mount and Pont Croesor – 1½ miles. Sufficient materials for a substantial portion of this distance are on hand, and the extension could be in use by 1985.

Stock

[3]Orenstein and Koppel 0-6-0WT *Pademoura* 10808 built 1924
[1]Hunslet 2-6-2T *Russell* 901 built 1906
[4]Peckett 0-4-2T *Karen* 2024 built 1942
Hunslet 0-4-0DM 2252 built 1940
[3]Orenstein and Koppel 0-6-0WT *Nantmor* 9239 built 1921
Bagnall 0-4-2T No. 3 *Snowdon Ranger* 3023 built 1948
Bagnall 0-4-2T No. 5 *Moel Tryfan* 3050 built 1953
Ruston Hornsby 4WDM 237914 built 1946
Ruston Hornsby 4WDM No. 10 191658 built 1938
Motor Rail 4WDM No. 4 60S333 built 1968
Motor Rail 4WDM No. 6 11102 built 1959
Motor Rail 4WDM *Katherine* 60S363 built 1968
Motor Rail 4WDM No. 36 *Cnicht* 8703 built 1941
Hunslet 4WDM 6285 built 1968
Ruston Hornsby 4WDM 327904 (20DL Class) built 1951
Ruston Hornsby 4WDM *Kinnerley* 354068 (40DL Class) built 1953
Ruston Hornsby 4WDM *Cilgwyn* (18/21 HP Class) 175414 built 1936
[5]Motor Rail 4WDM No. 9 9547 built 1950
Ruston Hornsby 4WDM No. 10 *Glaslyn* 297030 built 1952
DR coach No. 960–104 built 1913
Two Hudson/WHR bogie coaches
55 miscellaneous freight wagons
Snailbeach Railway wagon
Vale of Rheidol Railway four-wheeled passenger brake van
Hudson four-wheeled wagon
Several slate wagons
Hudson skips and open bogie wagons

[1]Supplied new to North Wales Narrow Gauge Railways and taken over by the Welsh Highland Railway. Sold to Brymbo Steel Co Ltd on closure of the WHR and used at Hook Norton Ironstone Mines, Oxfordshire. Sold to Pike Brothers, Fayle and Co Ltd, Norden Clay Mines, Dorset, in 1948. Preserved by the Birmingham Locomotive Club in 1955.
[2]Ex-Stewarts and Lloyds, Bilston, Staffs, in 1960. Loaned to WHLR in 1963 and at present undergoing repairs.

[3]Ex-Minas de Pejao, Portugal.
[4]Ex-Selukwe Peak Light Railway, Southern Rhodesia.
[5]On loan from West Denbighshire Light Railway.

318 Brecon Mountain Railway (Rheilffordd Mynydd Brycheiniog) A

Passenger-carrying 1ft 11¾in gauge steam railway, 2 miles in length, running from Pant to Pontsticil

Pant Station, Merthyr Tydfil, Mid-Glamorgan
Access: Bus route Merthyr Tydfil to Pant (approx ½ hour frequency). Nearest BR station: Merthyr Tydfil (3 miles)
Tel: Merthyr Tydfil (0685) 4854
OS Ref: SO 058098

The Brecon Mountain Railway is constructed almost entirely on the trackbed of the Brecon & Merthyr Railway. This railway, opened in 1859, originally ran from Newport to Brecon. Becoming part of the Great Western Railway under the Railways Act of 1921, the line continued to serve the area until closed for passenger traffic in 1962.
Re-construction of the railway between Pant and Pontsticill has involved the construction of a 600 yard deviation at Pant, necessitated by the original alignment being unobtainable. Building this deviation involved excavating 3,000 cubic metres of rock. Since closure by BR, three bridges had been removed and replacement of these has been necessary. Pontsticill station site has been cleared and landscaped and the railway buildings erected.
Services operate daily from the beginning of May to the beginning of October. Trains commence running at 11 am and continue until dusk. A weekend, Saturdays and Sundays, service will operate from October until December.
During the schools Autumn half-terms trains will operate daily between 12 noon and 3 pm.
Over the holiday period between 21 December and 3 January 1983, except Christmas Day, a service of four return trains will run, commencing at 12 noon and continuing hourly.
The return journey time is approximately ¾ hour, but why not remain at Pontsticill and enjoy the marvellous scenery or take a forest or lakeside walk, returning to Pant by a later service?
Locomotives on the railway have been collected together from three continents and some are still in the process of restoration.
Passenger coaches have been constructed on the line and have ample window area for the magnificent scenery to be appreciated to the full.
Workshop facilities at Pontsticill are open for inspection by the public on the first Sunday in October. Entrance to the workshops will be free to railway passengers.
Eventually it is intended that the railway be extended further into the Brecon Beacons National Park to a terminus at Torpantau. Completion of this section will mean the line passing through the highest railway tunnel in Great Britain.

Stock
[1]Baldwin 4-6-2 61269 built 1930
Jung 0-6-2WT *Graf Schwerin-Löwitz* 1261 built 1908
Hunslet 0-4-0ST *Sybil* 827 built 1903
Orenstein and Koppel 0-4-0T No. 9 12722 built 1936
Redstone 0-4-0VBT *Redstone* built 1905
de Winton/Hills 0-4-0VBT *Pendyffryn* built 1894
Ruston Hornsby 4WDM 425798 built 1958
Ruston Hornsby 4WDM 444207 built 1961
Motor Rail 4WDM No. 14 *Rhydychen* 11177 built 1961
Motor Rail 4WDM No. 17 *Garret* 7902 built 1939
Saloon bogie coaches Nos 1 and 2 built 1980–1
Saloon bogie coach No. 3 built 1982
Saloon bogie coach No. 4 built 1983
IMR bogie coach No. F68, rebuilt and regauged 1983
Various construction wagons and components for building verandah-end 39 seat bogie coaches
SAR bogie covered van
Nine bogie wagons
Southend Pier Railway hydraulic crane
Wickham 4wPMR inspection trolley (ex-Southend Pier)
SR CCT 4-wheel van No. S1418 built 1951
SR CCT 4-wheel van No. S2524 built 1955
SR CCT 4-wheel van No. S2504 built 1955 (all converted to provide cafeteria and toilet facilities at Pontsticill)

[1]Ex-Eastern Provinces Cement Co, South Africa, 1974.

The Brecon Mountain Railway Association has been formed to promote and support the railway. Details of the Association may be obtained from: The Membership Secretary, c/o Pontsticill Station, Merthyr Tydfil, Mid-Glamorgan, CF48 2UP.

319 Coney Beach Miniature Railway B

A 15in gauge passenger-carrying line, a quarter of a mile in length connecting Coney Beach with Porthcawl Pier

Porthcawl, Glamorgan
OS Ref: SS 821768

Operates daily during the holiday season with very frequent train service.

Stock
Freelance 4-6-4PE No. 1935 *Silver Jubilee* built 1935 (steam outline)
Freelance 4-6-4PE No. 36 *Coney Queen* built 1936 (steam outline)
Open bogie coaches (ex Festival Gardens Railway, Battersea).

320 Swansea Maritime and Industrial Museum DE

The Museum houses the Barclay 0-4-0 fireless locomotive Sir Charles *from BP Llandarcy Refinery, as well as the locomotives of Y Clwb Rheil Cymru. This Club organises occasional working days*

Swansea, West Glamorgan
Access: The Museum is fittingly situated on South Dock in the former 'Coast Lines' warehouse near the City centre, and is adjacent to the Leisure Centre
Tel: Swansea (0792) 50351
OS Ref: SS 660928

Admission free.
Open from 10.30 am until 5.30 pm Monday to Saturday (closed Christmas Day, Boxing Day and New Year's Day).
At present, the Museum houses the fully-operational Abbey Woollen Mill among its exhibits. New displays have been made on canals and plateways, and on oil refining and petrochemicals; it is hoped that suitable material on coal mining and export, and on the fishing industry will be added soon.
Two ships are also owned by the Museum: the steam tug 'Canning' and a lightship formerly on the 'Helwick' station. These are not on view to the public at present, but will be moored alongside the Museum when access can be gained to the Dock.
Although the emphasis is on local industrial and marine activity (which has been very rich and varied in the Swansea area over the past 300 years) it is felt that much of the material upon which the Museum draws can be considered to have a far wider appeal.

Stock
Barclay 0-4-0F No. 1 *Sir Charles* 1473 built 1916
RSH 0-4-0DM *Husky* 7910 built 1963
Peckett 0-6-0ST (B2 Class) 1426 built 1916
Swansea 4-wheel double-deck tramcar No. 14 built 1924
Other exhibits include a Mumbles Railway electric tram-car end (Car No. 7), a section of original Mumbles Railway track, a model of Brunel's Landore viaduct and the beam from one of the original Severn Tunnel pumping engines.

The Museum is adjacent to the operational area of Y Clwb Rheil Cymru. (*q.v.*).
Details from: The Curator, City of Swansea Maritime and Industrial Museum, c/o Glynn Vivian Art Gallery and Museum, Alexandra Road, Swansea, West Glamorgan. Tel: (0792) 55006.

The Railway Club of Wales (Y Clwb Rheil Cymru) H

Adjacent to Swansea Industrial and Maritime Museum, Coast Lines Warehouse, South Dock, Swansea, West Glamorgan
Registered Charity No. 509782
Access: A483 or A4067 to Swansea Leisure Centre, Museum is at rear of Leisure Centre. Nearest BR Station, Swansea High Street
OS Ref: SS 659927

The first steam centre in South West Wales is being established by the Club in association with the Museum. A running line 100 yards long has been laid where locomotives are steamed on Sunday afternoons from May to September.
Facilities for visitors include car parking, toilets and sales stand of railwayana on Steam Days.
The Club was formed in 1968 to provide for the varied interests of railway enthusiasts in Wales by preserving items of rolling stock, and encouraging an interest in the Principality's railways past, present and future.
Amongst the club's early achievements were the restoration of the 0-4-0 Fireless loco *Sir Charles* and the section of Mumbles railcar No. 7 at Swansea Museum. Publicity given to the latter project led to a renewal of local interest in the Mumbles Railway, and an extensive range of souvenirs appeared in local shops almost overnight.
The Club's main activity is the operation and maintenance of its rolling stock at the South Dock Railway, at the Swansea Industrial and Maritime Museum. Steam Days are held at Bank Holidays and at other times as advertised. A diesel service is run on summer Sundays when steaming is not taking place. For the remaining months of the year, members are hard at work keeping the locomotives at the highest possible standard of restoration.
The Club holds fortnightly meetings at the Clubroom in 3 Gloucester Place, Swansea. The meetings take the form of talks, slideshows, quizzes and filmshows. Visits to locations of railway interest are yet another exciting part of the club calendar.
'The Red Dragon' is the Club's own *free* quarterly magazine which takes its name from the important Paddington–South Wales express of steam days. Members may write articles on any railway topic for inclusion in the magazine.
Perhaps the most pleasing aspect of the club is that it maintains a warm, 'family atmosphere' amongst its membership. Any member is free to participate in the club's activities in any way he or she feels capable.

Details from: 14 Lon Masarn, Tycoch, Swansea SA2 9EL. The club is happy to consider special steamings for groups from recognised societies, providing reasonable notice of the visit is given, and the visiting organisation agrees to cover coal costs.

Stock
[1]Sentinel 4WVBTG *Swansea Vale No. 1* 9622 built 1958
[2]Barclay 0-4-0ST *Rosyth No. 1* 1385 built 1914
[3]North British 0-4-0DH *Dylan Thomas* 27654 built 1956
[4]Ruston Hornsby 4WDM *The Duke* (48DS Class) 3933302 built 1955
GWR 'Toad' 20-ton brake van No. 35978 built 1946

[1]Ex-Imperial Smelting Corporation, Vale Works, Llansamlet.
[2]Ex-Royal Navy Rosyth Dockyard, RAF Pembroke Dock and RAF St Athan.
[3]Ex-BSC Landore Foundry. An early example of a North British diesel-hydraulic loco, and the first diesel to be purchased by Landore Foundry when they withdrew their steam locos.
[4]Ex-Aluminium Wire & Cable Co, Port Tennant Works, Swansea.

321 Narrow Gauge Railway Museum — E

Museum established in 1956

Tywyn, Gwynedd LL36 9EY
Access: BR Tywyn Station: Crosville buses Nos 26, 28 and 30
Tel: Tywyn (0654) 710472
OS Ref: SH 586004

Managed by the Narrow Gauge Railway Museum Trust. The Museum adjoins the platform at Tywyn Wharf Station, accommodated in a modern building. Here is displayed a unique collection of equipment from narrow gauge railways all over Britain, ranging in size from steam locomotives – seven in number – wagons and signals, down to uniform buttons and tickets. Slate quarry railways predominate, but there are locomotives from a famous brewery, a gas works and from other industries. The Museum has considerable educational value and is a popular destination for school parties. Organised and managed by a charitable trust, it relies on volunteer labour for most of the restoration and display work.
Enquiries to: Narrow Gauge Railway Museum Trust, Wharf Station, Tywyn, Gwynedd LL36 9EY
Opening times: 10 am to 5 pm Easter to October (later in July and August); out of season on request.

Stock
Beyer Peacock 0-4-0ST *Dot* 2817 built 1887 (1ft 6in gauge)
[1]LNWR 0-4-0ST *Pet* built 1865 (1ft 6in gauge)
Hunslet 0-4-0ST *Rough Pup* 541 built 1891 (1ft 10¾in gauge)
Sentinel 4WVBTG *Nutty* 7701 built 1929 (2ft 6in gauge) (not on public display; can be seen by special request)
Spence 0-4-0T No. 13 built 1895 (1ft 10in gauge)
De Winton 0-4-0T *George Henry* built 1877 (1ft 10¾in gauge)
Manning Wardle 0-4-0ST *Jubilee 1897* 1382 built 1897 (1ft 10¾in gauge)
Kerr Stuart 0-4-0WT No. 2 721 built 1901 (2ft gauge)
Four four-wheeled wagons from narrow gauge industrial railways

[1]Used on the internal system at Crewe Works until withdrawn in 1929 and preserved at Crewe. On display at the Museum of British Transport, Clapham, from 1964 until presented by British Railways Board in 1967. On loan from the National Collection.

322 Welsh Industrial and Maritime Museum — E

Bute Street, Docks, Cardiff, Glamorgan CF1 6AN
Access: Bus routes Nos 8 and 9 from City Centre to Docks. Nearest BR station: Bute Road
Tel: Cardiff 371805/6
OS Ref: ST 192745

The Museum has a collection of steam, gas and oil engines some of which are operated every day. On the first Saurday of every month the engines are driven by steam and a number of films dealing with the steam scene are shown on the video units.
The Museum's four other steam locomotives are maintained and operated by the Caerphilly Railway Society (Group No. 312).
The Museum is open on weekends between 10 am and 5 pm (October to March) and 10 am to 6 pm (April to September) and on Sundays from 2.30 pm to 5 pm. Closed on Christmas Eve, Christmas Day, Boxing Day, New Year's Day, Good Friday and May Day. Admission free.
Details from: Dr E. S. Owen-Jones, Welsh Industrial and Maritime Museum, Bute Street Docks, Cardiff CF1 6AN

Stock
Hudswell Clarke 0-6-0ST No. 10 544 built 1900
Trevithick 4WG *Penydarren* replica built 1981 (4ft 4in gauge)
RSH 0-4-0ST *Thomas/Tomos* 7705 built 1952
Greenwood and Batley 4WBE No. 4 built 1962 (2ft gauge)
Ruston Hornsby 4WDM 187100 built 1937 (3ft gauge)
GWR 6-ton hand crane No. 230, plus match truck
Steam crane built Smith Rodley
TVR brake/3rd coach body No. 203 built 1912 on GER underframe No. 82667
BP & GVR inspection tricycle
TVR van body on LNER 6-wheel BZ underframe built 1950
GWR shunters truck
GKN 4-wheel tar tank wagon No. 3
GER underframe No. 82663
TVR coach body
Cardiff double-deck horse tram No. 21 built 1881

Butetown Historical Railway Society — H

Butetown Station, Cardiff, South Glamorgan
OS Ref: ST 192749

Stock
Peckett 0-6-0ST *Sir Gomer* 1859 built 1932
North British 0-6-0DH No. 107 27932 built 1959

323 Corris Railway Society E

Static exhibits (2ft 3in gauge)

The Corris Railway Museum, Corris Station Yard, near Machynlleth, Gwynedd
Access: Off A487, five miles north of Machynlleth, opposite Braich Goch Hotel
Crosville bus route No. S13 from Machynlleth and Aberystwyth to Aberllefenni and Dolgellau. Nearest BR station: Machynlleth (5½ miles)

Secretary: Mr A. H. Lawson, 165 Gynsill Lane, Anstey, Leicester LE7 7AN
The Society, founded in 1966 to preserve relics of the Corris Railway and to open a museum where they could be displayed to the public, has acquired one of the earliest buildings of this narrow gauge railway – the original motive power depot from the days before steam! This building, in the former station yard at Corris, has been renovated by members, and is in use as the museum. There is still a great deal of work to be done on the building, and new exhibits are being acquired. It is open to the public on Tuesday to Friday during July and August from 1 pm to 5.30 pm. Also on Sundays during the same period from 2 pm to 5 pm and on Bank Holiday weekends. Track is being reinstated on a short length of the old bed adjacent to the museum and a replica of an 1898 bogie coach is being built.
A company is to be formed to limit the liability of members when the demonstration track comes into operation.

Stock

Motor Rail 4WDM No. 5 *Alan Meaden* 22258 built 1965
Ruston Hornsby 4WDH No. 6 518493 built 1966
Two NCB main-rider coaches
Slate-slab wagon
Iron-bodied, side-door wagon
Skeleton of bogie coach body built 1898
Brake/tool van
Royal Navy box van
Four historical wagons in various states of repair
Three non-historical working wagons
Various minor exhibits, photographs, etc.

324 Scolton Manor Museum E

Static display of local railway rolling stock and lineside equipment

Pembrokeshire Museums, Dyfed County Council, Scolton Manor, Scolton, near Haverfordwest, Dyfed
Access: Situated on the B4329, 5½ miles north of Haverfordwest
Tel: Clarbeston 328
OS Ref: SM 991222

Facilities for visitors include: collections of natural history, geology, human social, domestic and industrial history, rural crafts and costume. Specialist rooms in the Manor House include a Local History Research Centre and Biological Records Centre.
Open 10.30–6 Tuesday to Sunday (July, August and September only). Museum shop – facilities for rest and shelter – car park.
Beautiful 40-acre grounds open all year round as Country Park with picnic sites, nature and tree trail.

Stock

Fox Walker 0-6-0ST *Margaret* 410 built 1878
Smith Rodley 5-ton steam crane No. 22936
Sarnau signal box
Locomotive supplied new to North Pembroke and Fishguard Railway, then absorbed into GWR stock as No. 1378. Later it was sold to the Gwendraeth Valleys Railway, finally passing to the Kidwelly Tinplate Co Ltd in 1923. The locomotive ceased work in 1941 and has been stored ever since.
To ensure the survival of this attractive little museum, qualified volunteers are vitally necessary to assist in the restoration and maintenance of the railway exhibits. Please contact the Curator at the Museum

325 National Trust, Penrhyn Castle Museum E

A museum devoted to the history of industrial railways containing locomotives and rolling stock of four different gauges on static display

Castell Penrhyn, Llandegai, near Bangor, Gwynedd LL57 4HN
Access: One mile east of Bangor on the A5
Nearest BR station: Bangor
Tel: Bangor (0248) 53084
OS Ref: SH 603720

Open daily from 1 April to 31 October.
Opening hours 2 pm to 5 pm in April, May and October; 11 am to 5 pm from June to September.
Facilities for visitors include car parking, refreshments and souvenir shop. There is also a small relics section with a comprehensive display of railway signs.

Stock

Stephenson 0-6-0T *Haydock* 2309 built 1879
Neilson 0-4-0WT No. 1 1561 built 1870
Hudswell Clarke 0-4-0ST *Hawarden* 526 built 1899
Hudswell Clarke 0-6-0T *Vesta* 1223 built 1916
Black Hawthorn 0-4-0ST *Kettering Furnaces No. 3* 859 built 1883 (3ft gauge)
Hunslet 0-4-0ST *Charles* 283 built 1882 (1ft 10¾in gauge)
Hunslet 0-4-0ST *Hugh Napier* 855 built 1904 (1ft 10¾in gauge)
Horlock 0-4-0 *Fire Queen* built 1848 (4ft gauge)
De Winton 0-4-0VBT *Watkin* built 1893 (3ft gauge)
Padarn Railway Velocipede *Arthur* (4ft gauge)

Ruston Hornsby 4WDM 327904
Penrhyn Railway quarryman's coach (1ft 10¾in gauge)
Penrhyn Railway, Lord Penrhyn's saloon built 1882 (1ft 10¾in gauge)
Four Penrhyn Railway open wagons (1ft 10¾in gauge)

326 Narrow Gauge Railway Centre E

The largest collection of narrow gauge locomotives in the British Isles, housed in a museum in the world's largest slate mine

Narrow Gauge Enterprises, Gloddfa Ganol Mountain Tourist Centre, Blaenau Ffestiniog, Gwynedd, North Wales LL41 3NB
Access: Off the A470 Blaenau Ffestiniog to Betws-y-Coed road ½ mile north of the town. Turn off at Loco No. 3014!
Nearest station: Blaenau Ffestiniog BR
Tel: Moelwyn (076-689) 500
OS Ref: SH 6946

The museum is open daily from Easter to October between 10 am and 5.30 pm. Facilities for visitors include car parking, licensed restaurant, snack bar and grill, toilets, children's playground and playroom, slate works, craft shops, mining museum, preserved quarrymen's cottages, slate grotto and Land Rover tours.
Coach parties especially welcome. Educational parties catered for.
The Narrow Gauge Enterprises collection of locomotives is being concentrated at Gloddfa Ganol. The first phase of the display was opened in summer 1978 and a considerable amount of work remains to be done before the museum is fully complete. Items are continually being added to the collection.
Eventual development into a major (national) NG Museum/Centre is envisaged – complementary to the nearby, established railways in the Principality and elsewhere. The first 46 locos, plus much wagonry and other miscellany, were transferred from storage in various parts of the country over the period May to September 1978. 35 locos are on public show *inside* the new Exhibition Hall recently completed for this purpose; ten others are displayed *outside* the building, plus one (Kerr Stuart 3014) at the main entrance gate. Ex-British Railways (Horwich Works) diesel locomotive 'ZM32' and others are available for work, whilst a further 22 have gone into private storage elsewhere on site.

Stock
Kerr Stuart 0-6-0T ('Joffre' Class) 3010 built 1916 (60cm gauge)
Kerr Stuart 0-6-0T ('Joffre' Class) 3014 built 1916 (60cm gauge)
de Winton 0-4-0VBT *Llanfair* built 1895 (3ft gauge)
Barclay 0-4-0T *The Wee Pug* (D Class) 984 built 1903 (2ft 6in gauge)
Bagnall 0-4-0ST 1568 built 1899 (2ft gauge)
Lister/Etherington 4WVBT *Steam Tram* 14005 built 1940 (rebuilt 1970) (2ft gauge)
Lister 4W+4WPMR *Whippit Quick* 6502 built 1935 (1ft 3in gauge)
Baguley 0-4-0PM 736 built 1918 (60cm gauge)
Baguley 0-4-0PM (10HP Class) 646 built 1917 (60cm gauge)
Baguley 0-4-0PM (10HP Class) 760 built 1918 (60cm gauge)
Baguley 0-4-0PM *Oakley* (20HP Class) 774 built 1919 (60cm gauge)
Bredbury 4WPM *Bredbury* built *c*1954 (2ft gauge)
BEV 4WBE 551 built 1924 (1ft 6in gauge)
BEV 4WE *Welsh Pony* 640 built 1926 (1ft 11½in gauge)
Deutz 0-4-0DM *Delta* 257081 built *c*1930 (2ft gauge)
Ffestiniog Rly 4WDM *Festiniog* built 1974 (1ft 11½in gauge)
Derby & Notts Electric Power Co 4WBE No. 1 *Spondon* built 1926 (2ft gauge)
Fowler 4WDM (40HP Class) 3930044 built 1950 (3ft gauge)
Hibberd 4WPM (10HP Class) 1568 built 1927 (2ft gauge)
Hibberd 4WPM (10HP Class) 1747 built 1931 (2ft gauge)
Hibberd 4WDM 2025 built 1937 (2ft gauge)
Hibberd 4WDM 2201 built 1939 (2ft gauge)
Howard 4WPM (S Class) 982 built 1931 (2ft gauge)
Hibberd 4WDM 4008
Brush 4WBE 163 built *c*1917 (2ft gauge)
Hunslet 4WDM 2577 built 1942 (2ft gauge)
Hudson 4WP/ParM (20HP Class) 45913 built 1932 (2ft 6in gauge)
Hunslet 4WDM (25/32HP Class) 2666 built 1942 (2ft gauge)
Hunslet 4WDM (21HP Class) 6018 built 1961 (2ft gauge)
Hibberd 4WPM (Y Class) 1881 built 1934 (2ft gauge)
Hibberd 4WPM (Y Class) 3424 built 1949 (2ft gauge)
Hudson 4WDM ('GoGo' type) 36863 built 1929 (2ft gauge)
Hudswell Clarke 4WDM (41HP Class) D564 built 1930 (2ft gauge)
Hunslet 4WDM (20HP Class) 1835 built 1937 (60cm gauge)
Hunslet 4WDM (20HP Class) 2024 built 1940 (60cm gauge)
Hunslet 4WDM *Dolwyddelan* (20HP Class) 2209 built 1941 (2ft 6in gauge) (At Dolwyddelan BR station)
Hudson 4WP/ParM (20HP Class) 39924 built *c*1931 (2ft gauge)
Ruston Hornsby 4WDM (10HP Class) 166028 built 1932 (2ft gauge)
Ruston Hornsby 4WDM (10HP Class) 164346 built 1932 (2ft gauge)
Ruston Hornsby 4WDM (16/20HP Class) 211647 built 1941 (60cm gauge)
Greenwood & Batley 4WBE No. 235 1840 built 1962
Motor Rail 4WDM No. 18 22128 built 1962
Ruston Hornsby 4WDM *Pen-yr-Orsedd* (20DL Class) 235711 built 1945 (2ft gauge)
Ruston Hornsby 4WDM (LBT Class) 393327 built 1956 (2ft gauge)
Ruston Hornsby 4WDM No. ZM32 (LAT Class) 416214 built 1957 (2ft gauge)

Ruston Hornsby 4WDM (LBU Class) 432664 built 1959 (2ft gauge)
Ruston Proctor 4W ParM (10HP Class) 50823 built 1915 (Metre gauge)
Ruhrthaler 0-4-0DM No. LM11 1082 built *c*1936 (3ft gauge)
Ruston Hornsby 4WDM (10HP Class) 164350 built 1932 (2ft gauge)
Wickham 4WPMR No. C13 2449 built 1938 (3ft gauge)
Wickham 4WPMR No. C18 4808 built 1948 (3ft gauge)
Wickham 4WPMR No. C20 4810 built 1948 (3ft gauge)
Wickham 4WPMR No. C23 4813 built 1948 (3ft gauge)
Wickham 4WPMR No. C26 4816 built 1948 (3ft gauge)
Wingrove & Rogers 0-4-0BE *Little George* 1298 built 1938 (2ft gauge)
Wickham 4WPMR 4091 built 1946 (3ft gauge)
Wickham 4WPMR 4092 built 1946 (3ft gauge)
Brush 4WBE 16306 built 1917 (2ft gauge)
Lister 4WPM 4 class 6299 built 1935 (2ft gauge)
Orenstein & Koppel 4WPM *Python* M Class 4470 built *c*1931 (60cm gauge)
Locospoor 4WPM No. C37 B7281E (3ft gauge)
BMW/Morris 4-2-0PMR *Rail Taxi* built 1967 (2ft gauge)
Motor Rail 4WPM No. 2182 461 built 1917 (60cm gauge)
Motor Rail 4WDM (H Class) 05H006 built 1969 (3ft gauge)
Muir Hill 4WP/ParM (A Class) 110 built 1925 (2ft gauge)
Thakeham 4WPM *Thakeham* built *c*1946 (2ft gauge)
Ruston Hornsby 4WDM 198297 built 1939 (2ft gauge)
Fowler 0-4-0DM 22900 built 1941 (Standard gauge)
Hudson-Hunslet 4WDM 2207 built 1941 (2ft gauge) (At Blaenau Ffestiniog BR station)
Wickham 4WPMR No. TR41 4168 built 1948 (Standard gauge)
Wickham 4WPMR No. TR27 4132 built 1947 (Standard gauge)
Wickham 4WPMR No. TR8 4151 built 1948 (Standard gauge)
Wickham 4WPMR No. TR10 4162 built 1948 (Standard gauge)
Wickham 4WPMR No. TR12 4165 built 1948 (Standard gauge)
Wickham 4WPMR No. TR2 6878 built 1954 (Standard gauge)
Wickham 4WPMR No. TR7 8503 built 1960 (Standard gauge)
Note: Not all items are on display at Gloddfa Ganol yet.

327 Conwy Valley Railway Museum AE

Museum of locomotives and rolling stock of various gauges. There are displays covering the whole railway scene, with special reference to standard and narrow gauge lines in North Wales. The small exhibits are in a purpose-built museum and there is a collection of standard gauge vehicles and larger exhibits on the site. 7¼in gauge miniature railway

Amgueddfa Rheilffyrdd Duffryn, Conwy, Old Goods Yard, Betws-y-Coed, Gwynedd LL24 0AL

Access: Adjacent to Betws-y-Coed BR station. Road access signed from A5
Tel: 06902 568
OS Ref: SH 796565

Details from: Colin Cartwright, 58 Charlemont Road, Walsall, West Midlands
The Museum now houses the famous L & NWR model dioramas built by the late Jack Nelson. These are quite unique and are judged by many to be in themselves well worth a visit. There is a well-appointed shop where books, souvenirs and railwayana may be purchased. The Buffet car is available for tea, coffee and light refreshments.
The Museum is open daily from Easter until the end of October between 10.30 am and 5.30 pm. Open 2 pm to 5 pm on Bank Holidays.
A passenger-carrying 7¼in gauge railway, ½ mile in length, was opened as an adjunct to the museum in 1979.

Museum exhibits
Kerr Stuart 0-6-0T *Sgt Murphy* 3117 built 1918 (60cm gauge)
GWR fitter's van No. DW14610 (converted from brake van No. 56096) built 1895
LMS 'Stove R' six-wheeled van No. 33016 built 1939
LNER CCT vehicle No. 1370 built 1950
BR Mk.1 TSO bogie coach No. 3925 built 1954
SR PMV four-wheeled utility van No. 1070
SR BY four-wheeled parcels brake van No. 407
Pullman camping coach *Emerald* built 1910
LNWR 20-ton goods brake van No. 349
Woolwich Arsenal Railway gunpowder van (1ft 6in gauge)

7¼in gauge stock
Freelance 0-4-0 *Romulus*
Freelance 0-4-0 *Bethany*
Freelance Bo-BoPM
Denver & Rio Grande 2-8-0 *Old Rube* Milner Engineering
Freelance Bo-BoBE
Eight open bogie coaches

328 Pendine Wildlife and Leisure Park G

A 2ft gauge passenger-carrying pleasure line

Pendine, Dyfed
OS Ref: SN 244083
Currently closed with rolling stock in store.

Stock
Hudson 4WDM No. 20483 LX1001 built 1968 (Steam outline)
Ex-Dredging and Construction Co Ltd, Kings Lynn, Norfolk, 1976

329 Butlins, Pwllheli B

A 2ft gauge passenger-carrying line

Pwllheli Holiday Camp, Pen-y-Chain, Gwynedd
OS Ref: SH 434363

Stock
Chance 4-2-4DM No. 157 *C. P. Huntington* built 1978 (steam outline)

330 Cefn Coed Coal and Steam Centre E

West Glamorgan County Council, Crynant
OS Ref: SN 786034
Access: South Wales bus service No. X58 from Neath

Stock
Hunslet 0-6-0ST *Cefn Coed* 3846 built 1956

331 Taff Vale Railway Preservation Society G

Standard gauge steam locomotives in store and undergoing restoration

Cae Harris Station, Dowlais, Glamorgan
Details from: Castle House, Castle Street, Merthyr Tydfil CF47 8YX
Tel: 0685-2386/7
Access: Rhymney Valley bus No. 150 from Newport and Merthyr. Also National Welsh bus No. X46
OS Ref: SO 074078

Stock
[1]Avonside 0-6-0ST *Sir John* 1680 built 1914
[1]Avonside 0-6-0ST *Lord Camrose* 2008 built 1930
[2]GWR 0-6-2T No. 5668 (56XX Class) built 1926

[1]Ex-NCB Mountain Ash colliery 1980.
[2]Withdrawn September 1964 and sent to Woodham Brothers scrapyard, Barry. Purchased for preservation 1980.

332 Woodham Brothers Limited G

Barry Scrapyard, Barry Docks, Glamorgan, South Wales
No public admittance
OS Ref: ST 111670

The following locomotives are stored pending cutting up or collection and restoration by various preservation groups. There is no guarantee that locomotives appearing in the list will, in fact, be preserved, although this is thought likely in a number of cases. A large number of engines at Barry carry painted slogans alleging they are earmarked for preservation, but it is wisest to verify individual cases with the societies involved.
Readers are asked not to trespass upon Woodham Brothers' property or interfere with the locomotive in any way.

Stock
GWR 2-8-0 No. 2859 (28XX Class) built 1918
GWR 2-8-0 No. 2861 (28XX Class) built 1918
GWR 2-8-0 No. 2873 (28XX Class) built 1918
GWR 2-8-0 No. 3814 (28XX Class) built 1940
GWR 2-8-0 No. 3845 (28XX Class) built 1942
GWR 2-8-0 No. 3855 (28XX Class) built 1942
GWR 2-8-0 No. 3862 (28XX Class) built 1942
GWR 2-8-0T No. 4247 (42XX Class) built 1916
GWR 2-8-0T No. 4248 (42XX Class) built 1916
GWR 2-8-0T No. 4253 (42XX Class) built 1917
GWR 2-8-0T No. 4277 (42XX Class) built 1920
GWR 4-6-0 No. 4979 *Wootton Hall* built 1930
GWR 2-6-2T No. 5199 (51XX Class) built 1934
GWR 2-8-0T No. 5227 (5205 Class) built 1924
GWR 2-6-2T No. 5538 (4575 Class) built 1928
GWR 2-6-2T No. 5539 (4575 Class) built 1928
GWR 2-6-2T No. 5552 (4575 Class) built 1928
GWR 2-6-2T No. 5553 (4575 Class) built 1928
GWR 4-6-0 No. 5967 *Bickmarsh Hall* built 1937
GWR 0-6-2T No. 6686 (56XX Class) built 1928
GWR 4-6-0 No. 6984 *Owsden Hall* built 1948
GWR 4-6-0 No. 7927 *Willington Hall* built 1950
SR 4-6-0 No. 30830 (S15 Class) built 1927
SR 4-6-2 No. 34028 *Eddystone* built 1946
SR 4-6-2 No. 34046 *Braunton* built 1946
SR 4-6-2 No. 34058 *Sir Frederick Pile* built 1947
SR 4-6-2 No. 35011 *General Steam Navigation* built 1944
SR 4-6-2 No. 35022 *Holland-America Line* built 1948
SR 4-6-2 No. 35025 *Brocklebank Line* built 1948
LMS 2-6-0 No. 42859 (6P/5F Class) built 1930
LMS 4-6-0 No. 44901 (5MT Class) built 1945
LMS 4-6-0 No. 45163 (5MT Class) built 1935
LMS 4-6-0 No. 45293 (5MT Class) built 1936
LMS 2-8-0 No. 48173 (8F Class) built 1943
LMS 2-8-0 No. 48305 (8F Class) built 1943
LMS 2-8-0 No. 48518 (8F Class) built 1944
BR 4-6-0 No. 73096 (5MT Class) built 1955
BR 4-6-0 No. 73156 (5MT Class) built 1956
BR 2-6-0 No. 76077 (4MT Class) built 1956
BR 2-6-4T No. 80072 (4MT Class) built 1953
BR 2-6-4T No. 80097 (4MT Class) built 1954
BR 2-6-4T No. 80098 (4MT Class) built 1954
BR 2-6-4T No. 80150 (4MT Class) built 1956
BR 2-10-0 No. 92207 (9F Class) built 1959
BR 2-10-0 No. 92245 (9F Class) built 1958

333 BP Chemical International Ltd

Industrial steam location featuring regular steam working

Sully, Penarth, Glamorgan CF6 2YU
OS Ref: ST 143683

No public access.

Stock
Barclay 0-4-0F No. 1 2238 built 1948

334 Monsanto Chemicals Ltd I

Industrial steam location featuring occasional steam working

Corporation Road, Newport, Gwent
OS Ref: ST 335855

No public access. The locomotive is normally used once every six weeks.

Stock
Barclay 0-4-0F *Monsanto* 1966 built 1929

335 Inco Europe Ltd I

Industrial steam location with locomotive in store but steamed for special occasions

Clydach-on-Tawe, West Glamorgan
OS Ref: SN 696013

No public access.

Stock
Peckett 0-4-0ST MNC No. 1 (W5 Class) 1345 built 1914

336 National Coal Board I

Industrial steam locomotives stored out of use

South Wales Area

No public access.

Stock
Peckett 0-6-0ST *Meneleaus* (B3 Class) 1889 built 1935 (Marine Washery, Cwm)
Hunslet 0-6-0ST *Pamela* 3840 built 1956. (Out of use at Maesteg depot)

337 Pontypool and Blaenavon Railway

Passenger-carrying ½ mile standard gauge railway

Big Bit, Blaenavon colliery site, Blaenavon, Gwent
OS Ref: SO 237093

The historic Blaenavon site, complete with its railway installation and locomotives, is now under the care of the Torfaen Museum Trust. The locomotives are housed in the former NCB engine shed undergoing restoration by members of the railway society.

Stock
GWR 2-8-0 No. 2874 (28XX Class) built 1918 (not yet on site)
Barclay 0-4-0ST *The Blaenavon Toto No. 6* 1619 built 1919
Barclay 0-4-0ST *The Blaenavon Nora No. 5* 1680 built 1920
RSH 0-6-0ST No. 8 7139 built 1944
Vulcan Foundry 0-6-0DM D78 built 1948
Fowler 0-4-0DM *Woodpecker* 22871 built 1939
Fowler 0-6-0DM No. 1 22497 built 1938
BR Mk.1 TSO coach No. E4677 built 1957
BR Mk.1 BSK coach No. E35494 built 1963
GWR 'Mica A' box van
Wickham 4WPMR
GWR 'Toplight' passenger luggage van
Two 10-ton diesel cranes
LNER box van
Six oil tank wagons
Eight china clay wagons
LMS 20-ton goods brake van No. B950114 built 1950

338 BSC Shotton Works Sports Club E

Locomotive on static display in corner of sports field

Rowley's Drive, Shotton, Clywd

Stock
Hudswell Clarke 0-4-0DM No. 41 D1020 built 1956

339 Rhiw Valley Light Railway A

Passenger-carrying 15in gauge line, one mile long

Mr J. Woodruffe, Lower House, Welshpool, Powys
Access: 3 miles from Berriew. Nearest BR station, Welshpool
OS Ref: SJ 143028

Open to public Thursdays and Sundays only.
Access by Crosville D75 bus, then 3-mile walk along B4390 (Manafon Road). No buses on Sunday.

Stock
Severn-Lamb 0-6-2T *Powys* 20 built 1973
Three bogie coaches
An extension to the line was under construction in 1984.

340 Croesor Junction and Pacific Railroad C

A 7¼in gauge private line under construction by Brian Hollingsworth at his home at Penrhyndeudraeth, Gwynedd

J. B. Hollingsworth, 'Cruea', Llanfrothen, Penrhydeudraeth, Gwynedd LL48 6SH
Tel: 0766-770534

There are gradients of 1 in 22 due to the terrain over

which the line is being built. The line is not open to the public and casual visitors cannot be accommodated.

Stock

East African Railways 4-8-2+2-8-4 No. 5928 *Mount Kilimanjaro* 19,340ft built Coleby-Simkins 1975
Darjeeling Himalayan Railway 0-4-0STT *Kanchenjunga* built Coleby-Simkins 1974
Rio Grande 2-8-2 No. 487 *Queen of Colorado* K36 Class built Curwen 1968
Rio Grande 2-8-0 No. 402 *Shoshone* C19 Class built Milner Engineering 1977

341 Kidwelly History Centre and Tinplate Museum — E

Kidwelly, West Glamorgan

Stock

Peckett 0-6-0ST 2114 built 1951
Barclay 0-4-0ST 1081 built 1909
Smith Rodley steam crane

342 Magic Dragon Railway — B

A passenger-carrying 10¼in gauge line, 400 yards in length

Gwrych Castle, Abergele, Clwyd

The railway operates to coincide with the Castle opening and trains run as required.

Stock

Gwrych Castle Ltd Co-BoD *The Chieftain* built 1954
Six open bogie coaches

343 Tintern Railway Station Picnic Area — E

GWR railway station restored as visitor centre

Tintern, Gwent
Access: Bus route No. 49 Chepstow–Monmouth (2-hourly frequency)
Nearest BR station: Chepstow (6 miles)
Tel: Tintern 566

Open daily April to September 10.30 am to 5.30 pm. Tintern station closed in January 1964. Today it is a very pleasant picnic site in the Wye Valley. The station building has been renovated to form an exhibition area while the signal box serves as office accommodation and as an information centre. Although not primarily conceived as a railway museum, the exhibition centre in the main station building contains several interesting GWR items as well as photographs of the station and the Wye Valley line before closure.

Facilities for visitors include car parking, refreshments, guide book and toilets.

Stock

BR Mk.1 BG No. W80797 built 1956
GWR open wagon No. 58122

344 Vale of Teifi Narrow Gauge Railway — A

½ mile long 2ft gauge passenger-carrying railway along the trackbed of the former Pencader–Newcastle Emlyn branch

Dyfed Railway Co Ltd, Henllan, Llandyssul, Dyfed
OS Ref: SN 358406

It is hoped to open the line at Easter 1985.
Details from: Mr G. Toogood, Old Coach House, Henllan, Llandyssul, Dyfed.

Stock

Hunslet 0-4-0ST *Alan George* 606 built 1894
Hunslet 4WDM *Sholto* 2433 built 1941
Motor Rail 4WDM 7215 built 1938
Motor Rail 4WDM 8683 built 1941
Motor Rail 4WDM 7126 built 1936
Three coaches built on Baguley underframes
Ten skip wagons

345 Caerleon, Gwent — G

Standard gauge private collection of rolling stock

Mr R. L. Dean, 'Glen Usk', Plas Llecha, near Caerleon, Gwent
OS Ref: ST 379935

No public access.

Stock

Manning Wardle 0-6-0ST *Aldwyth* 865 built 1882
Swansea Harbour Trust 4-wheeled inspection saloon coach built 1911 (rebuilt from MS & LR vehicle originally built *c*1850)

346 Milton — G

Standard gauge industrial steam locomotive undergoing restoration

Mr G. Davies, Stephens Green Farm, Milton, near Pembroke, Dyfed
OS Ref: SN 041019

No casual visitors please.

Stock

Bagnall 0-4-0ST 2565 built 1936

347 West Denbighshire Light Railway C

Private collection of narrow gauge locomotives and rolling stock in store and undergoing restoration. Some locomotives are stored elsewhere or operated on a line at a private location (The WDLR)

Ian Jolly, 1 Llewelyn Drive, Bryn-y-Baal, near Mold, Clwyd
Tel: Mold (0352) 57239
OS Ref: SJ 261647

Stock
[1]Motor Rail & Tramcar Co 4WPM 264 built *c*1916 (60cm gauge)
[1]Motor Rail & Tramcar Co 4WPM No. LR 2718 997 built 1918 (60cm gauge)
[1]Motor Rail & Tramcar Co 4WPM No. LR 2832 1111 built 1918 (60cm gauge)
[2]Motor Rail & Tramcar Co 4WPM built 1918 (60cm gauge)
[9]Motor Rail & Tramcar Co 4WPM 1934 built 1919 (2ft gauge)
[9]Motor Rail & Tramcar Co 4WDM 4023 built 1926 (2ft gauge)
[10]Motor Rail 4WDM LMLR No. 9 9547 built 1950 (60cm gauge)
[3]Motor Rail & Tramcar Co 4 WPM No. 21 built *c*1920 (1ft 11½in gauge)
[3]Motor Rail 4WDM No. 24 4805 built 1934 (1ft 11½in gauge)
[4]Motor Rail 4WDM *A. H. Worth* 5851 built 1933 (1ft 11½in gauge)
[5]Motor Rail & Tramcar Co 4WPM 6013 built 1931 (1ft 11½in gauge)
[3]Motor Rail 4WDM 8723 built 1941 (60cm gauge)
[6]Motor Rail 4WDM 20558 built 1955 (60cm gauge)
[7]Lister 4WPM 30233 built 1946 (1ft 11½in gauge)
[8]Wickham 2W-2PMR *Army* 9036 8196 built 1958 (60cm gauge)
[11]Wickham 2W-2PMR 3030 built 1941 (60cm gauge)
Ian has a short line near Mold where most of the locos are kept and operated. Rolling stock includes several Hudson side tipping wagons, various flats and several ex-War Department wagons of Second World War vintage. He also owns a wagon from the Duke of Westminster's former Eaton Hall Railway and several ex-WDLR first world war Class 'D' bogies to complete a trenches train.

[1]Built for War Department Light Railways for use in trenches during First World War.
[2]Rebuilt by Percy Finnie of New Pitsligo, Aberdeenshire, *c*1956 for use on his peatbog. It was built as a 20HP loco for the War Department Light Railways and was rebuilt into a much lighter loco and regauged to 2ft 8in – now regauged to 60cm.
[3]Ex-Joseph Arnold & Sons, Leighton Buzzard.
[4]Originally on A. H. Worth's 10 mile long farm railway at Fleet, Lincolnshire, one of the few farm lines in the UK.
[5]Ex-Lanarkshire County Council, Carngryffe Quarry.
[6]Originally British Waterways, later Woodside Brick Co Ltd, Croydon.
[7]Originally Western Counties Brick Co Ltd, Exeter.
[8]Ex-Army railcar, one of batch of six specially built for staff transport on military railways. Built as standard gauge but now 60cm gauge.
[9]Ex-Whixall Moss Peat Works, Clwyd.
[10]Originally Leighton Buzzard Light Railway Company's No. 9 – temporarily at Welsh Highland Railway, Porthmadog, but should be returning soon.
[11]Ex-Army target trolley for use on gun ranges.

348 Caernarfon Harbour, Gwynedd G

3ft gauge steam locomotive undergoing restoration alongside the preserved steam dredger Seiont

Stock
DeWinton 0-4-0VBT *Penmaen* built 1878

349 Lower Swansea Valley Railway Preservation Society G

A preservation scheme centred on the former MR Swansea–Brynamman line between Upper Bank junction and Six Pit Junction. Rolling stock under restoration

Six Pit Junction, Llansamlet, Glamorgan (on A4217 near junction with A48)

Stock
GWR 2-8-0T No. 4270 (Churchward 42XX Class) built 1919
Barclay 0-6-0ST *Llantarnam Abbey* 2074 built 1939
Hunslet 0-6-0ST 3829 built 1955
NBL 0-4-0DH 27941 built 1961
NBL 0-4-0DH 27939 built 1959
Fowler 0-4-0DM 22878 built 1939
Fowler 0-4-0DM 22876 built 1939
Hibberd 4WDM 3837 built 1957
Ruston Hornsby 4WDM 476143 built 1963
GWR 'Toad' 20-ton goods brake van No. 114762
GWR riding van built 1903
Three BR Mk.1 coaches
Diesel-Electric rail crane

350 P. Dobbins (Chester) Ltd G

Standard gauge steam locomotive stored in scrapyard

Scrap metal processors, Saltney Ferry Works, Clwyd
OS Ref: SJ 367652

Stock
Peckett 0-4-0ST No. 3 2084 built 1948

AREA H

West Midlands

Worcestershire
Warwickshire
Staffordshire
Herefordshire
Gloucestershire
West Midlands
Shropshire
(Group Nos 351–400)

351 Foxfield Light Railway A

A 3½ mile standard gauge line from Dilhorne Park to Blythe Bridge (Caverswall Road)

Foxfield Colliery, Dilhorne, Blythe Bridge, Stoke-on-Trent, Staffordshire
Access: Potteries Motor Traction bus service 86B from either Longton (Stoke-on-Trent) or Cheadle operates in conjunction with the trains on Sundays. A special all-inclusive fare applies; the bus ticket being exchanged for a railway ticket at the Foxfield booking office, whilst the railway ticket acts as the return bus ticket. Passengers alight from the bus at Godley Brook, approximately 200 yards from the railway station.
Tel: Stoke-on-Trent 313920
Os Ref: SJ 957421

Details from: Mr B. Allen, 25 Drubbery Lane, Dresden, Stoke-on-Trent, Staffs ST3 4BH
The railway was built in 1893 to connect Foxfield Colliery, Dilhorne, with the North Staffordshire Railway at a junction 400 yards west of Blythe Bridge Station. The colliery closed in 1965 and with it the railway, but both were purchased by Tean Minerals Ltd, who now occupy the colliery buildings.
The line starts at Dilhorne Park and runs through Dilhorne Wood, past the 17th century Stansmore Hall to circle the foot of Blakely Bank Wood and cross the Caverswall–Dilhorne road by a gated level crossing. Continuing downhill, there is a further straight section and deep cutting spanned by the Caverswall–Blythe Bridge road overbridge, and a little further on passengers get a view of the 13th century Caverswall Castle. The railway terminates at Blythe Bridge (Caverswall Road station), not from Blythe Bridge BR station.
Facilities: Train rides and refreshments.
The railway operates each Sunday between April and October inclusive. Special trains at other times by arrangement.

Stock
Hunslet 0-6-0ST *Wimblebury* 3839 built 1956
Kerr Stuart 0-4-0ST *Moss Bay* 4167 built 1920
Kerr Stuart 0-4-0ST 4388 built 1926
Peckett 0-4-0ST No. 1 *Ironbridge* (W6 Class) 1803 built 1933
Hunslet 0-6-0ST *Whiston* 3694 built 1950
Manning Wardle 0-6-0ST No. 35 *Rhiwnant* 1317 built 1895
Avonside 0-6-0ST *Robert* 2068 built 1933
Avonside 0-6-0ST *Cranford* 1919 built 1924
Bagnall 0-6-0ST *Topham* 2193 built 1922
Bagnall 0-6-0ST *Lewisham* 2221 built 1927
Bagnall 0-4-0ST *Hawarden* 2623 built 1940
Peckett 0-4-0ST *Henry Cort* 933 built 1903
Peckett 0-4-0ST No. 11 2081 built 1947
Barclay 0-4-0ST *Little Barford* 2069 built 1939
Barclay 0-4-0F No. 1 1984 built 1930
RSH 0-4-0CT *Roker* 7006 built 1940
Ruston Hornsby 4WDM 408496 built 1957
Ruston Hornsby 4WDM 408494 built 1957
English Electric 4WE No. 2 1130 built 1939
Bagnall 4wDH 3207 built 1961
Motor Rail 4WDM *Helen* 2262 built 1923
Ruston Hornsby 4WDM 395305 built 1956
Ruston Hornsby 4WDM 242915 built 1946
North British 0-4-0DH *Coronation* 27097 built 1953
Wickham 4WPMR 497 built 1932
Wickham 4WPMR 580 built 1932
Wickham 4WPMR 4121 built 1946
Wickham 4WPMR 4985 built 1949
Wickham 4WPMR 7139 built 1955
Wickham 4WPMR 8501 built 1960
LMS 60ft vestibuled corridor coach No. 27249 built 1945
GWR Hawksworth dynamometer car No. ADW 150192 built 1947
BR Mk.1 SK coach No. M25231 built 1957
Two BR Mk.1 coaches built 1957
LMS four-wheeled covered goods vans Nos 7090 and 50085
Four LMS bogie scenery vans Nos 37508, 37518, 37519 and 38268 (two converted into observation coaches and another used as refreshment van)
Shell 4-wheel rail tank wagon
NSR flat wagon No. 11995 built 1916
BR 20-ton goods brake van No. B951789
Seven NCB open coal wagon
CEGB 21-ton all-steel coal wagon built 1937
LNWR coke hopper wagon No. 17420
Tar wagon
LNER tank wagon No. 38386
Two 4-wheel box vans
7-plank coal wagon
3-plank sand wagon
Bolster flat wagon
20-ton hopper wagon
GWR wagon frame
Smith Rodley steam crane No. 12394

GWR 'Toad' 20-ton goods brake van No. 56550 built 1916
NSR third-class loop-line coach body built *c*1875
[1]MR first-class saloon coach body No. 2741 built 1884
[1]NSR 4-wheel coach body built *c*1880

Note: Some of the above items are privately-owned.

[1]To be mounted on BR CCT van underframes.

352 Severn Valley Railway **A**

One of the finest Standard Gauge Steam Railways operating in this country and running 16 miles from Bridgnorth to Kidderminster

The Railway Station, Bewdley, Worcs DY12 1BG and the Railway Station, Bridgnorth, Shropshire WV16 5DF
Access: Wolverhampton, Stourbridge or Kidderminster BR Stations. Midland Red or Whittle Bus services
Tel: Bewdley 403816 or Bridgnorth 4361

The Railway operates every Saturday and Sunday from the beginning of March until the end of October and on all Public Holidays, during weekends in December and daily from early May until early September. Comprehensive facilities for visitors including car parking on all stations, railway gift shops, full catering facilities, picnic areas and on-train catering and bar coaches.
General Manager: Mr M. J. Draper, The Railway Station, Bewdley, Worcs.
Having started to run passenger trains in 1970, the SVR is firmly established in the premier league of the Railway Preservation Movement and houses one of the finest collections of locomotives, passenger coaches and rolling stock to be found anywhere in the UK. Future plans include the development of comprehensive carriage and wagon storage facilities.
Details of membership are available from the Membership Secretary, at Bewdley. With over 11,000 members, the SVR enjoys the largest supporting society in the country, but more volunteers are always welcome.
The Severn Valley Railway from Shrewsbury to Hartlebury, 40 miles long, was opened in 1862. It became part of the Great Western Railway in 1872 and that company constructed a spur from Bewdley to Kidderminster in 1878, allowing through running from the industrial West Midlands. Under British Railways ownership, the Severn Valley line was closed to through traffic in 1963. North of Bridgnorth the line was lifted, whilst south of Alveley, coal trains used the line until 1969.
A scheme to preserve the disused but intact section from Bridgnorth to Alveley and to run passenger trains as far as Hampton Loade was first mooted in 1965. The Severn Valley Railway Society was formed in July of that year and after considerable fund-raising efforts and a legal battle with the local councils to obtain Light Railway Orders, the line reopened on 23 May 1970.
In 1972, the Severn Valley Railway (Holdings) Co was formed and £110,000 was raised by public subscription to enable the railway to be purchased from Alveley to Foley Park (Kidderminster) allowing a 12½ mile passenger run from Bridgnorth to Bewdley. This section was reopened on 18 May 1974. A further £300,000 share issue was successfully launched in 1983 to allow the purchase of the line from Foley Park to Kidderminster, where a new SVR terminal station was built in 1984.

Stock
[33]LMS 4-6-0 No. 5690 *Leander* (Class 5XP) built 1936
[6]LMS 4-6-0 No. 5000 (Stanier 5MT Class) built 1934
[3]LMS 4-6-0 No. 45110 *RAF Biggin Hill* (Stanier Class 5MT) (Vulcan Foundry 4653) built 1935
[2]LMS 2-6-0 No. 43106 (Ivatt Class 4MT) built 1951
LMS 2-6-0 No. 46443 (Ivatt Class 2MT) built 1950
[20]LMS 2-6-0 No. 46521 (Ivatt Class 2MT) built 1953
[10]LMS 2-8-0 No. 8233 (Stanier Class 8F) (North British Locomotive Co No. 24607) built 1940
[9]LMS 0-6-0T No. 47383 (Fowler Class 3F) (Vulcan Foundry 3954) built 1926
[11]LMS 2-6-0 No. 2968 (Stanier Class 5P/4F) built 1933
[1]LNER 2-6-0 No. 3442 *The Great Marquess* (Gresley Class K4) built 1938
[21]LMR 2-10-0 No. 600 *Gordon* (Riddles Class WD) North British 25437 built 1943
[22]BR 2-6-4T No. 80079 (Riddles Class 4MT) built 1954
[31]BR 2-6-0 No. 78019 (Riddles Class 2MT) built 1954
[32]BR 4-6-0 No. 75069 (Riddles Class 4MT) built 1955
GWR 0-6-0PT No. 7714 (Class 57XX) Kerr Stuart 4449 built 1930
[23]GWR 2-6-2T No. 4141 (Class 5101) built 1946
[24]GWR 2-8-0 No. 2857 (Churchward Class 28XX) built 1918
[25]GWR 4-6-0 No. 7819 *Hinton Manor* built 1939
[26]GWR 0-6-0PT No. 3612 built 1939
[15]GWR 2-6-0 No. 9303 (Class 43XX) built 1932
[8]GWR 0-6-0ST No. 813 (ex-Port Talbot Railway No. 26) Hudswell Clarke 555 built 1901
[16]GWR 4-6-0 No. 7802 *Bradley Manor* built 1938
[16]GWR 4-6-0 No. 7812 *Erlestoke Manor* built 1939
[17]GWR 2-6-2T No. 4150 (41XX Class) built 1947
[12]GWR 0-6-0PT No. 1501 (Hawksworth Class 15XX) built 1949
[35]GWR 4-4-0 No. 3440 *City of Truro* built 1903
[4]GWR 0-6-0 No. 3205 (Class 2251) built 1946
[27]GWR 2-6-2T No. 5164 (Class 5101) built 1930
[28]GWR 0-6-0PT No. 5764 (Class 57XX) built 1929
[7]GWR 4-6-0 No. 6960 *Raveningham Hall* (Hawksworth 6959 Class) built 1944
[29]GWR 2-6-2T No. 4566 (45XX Class) built 1924
[30]GWR 4-6-0 No. 4930 *Hagley Hall* built 1929
[13]Manning Wardle 0-6-0ST *Warwickshire* 2047 built 1926
[14]Hunslet 0-6-0T *The Lady Armaghdale* 686 built 1898
Peckett 0-4-0ST No. 4 1738 built 1928
BR Co-CoDH No. D1013 *Western Ranger* built 1962
BR Co-CoDG No. D1062 *Western Courier* built 1963
Ruston Hornsby 0-4-0DM (165DS Class) 319290 built 1953

Ruston Hornsby 0-4-0DM *Archibald* 418789 built 1957
Ruston Hornsby 0-4-0DM *Alan* 414304 built 1957
Ruston Hornsby 0-4-0DE 418596 built 1957
Ruston Hornsby 4WDM 281269 built 1948
BR 0-6-0DE No. D3022 built 1953
BR SK Mk.1 coach No. 24396 built 1953
BR BSK Mk.1 coach No. 34562 built 1955
BR Mk.1 CK coach No. S16202 built 1961
LMS open third bogie coach No. 9355 built 1936, rebuilt as buffet car
BR Mk.1 BSO coach No. M9220 built 1955
BR Mk.1 FO coach No. W3083 built 1957
GWS Hawksworth engineers saloon No. W80969 built 1948
LNER Gresley composite restaurant car No. 7690 built 1936
BR Mk.1 restaurant buffet car No. E1682 built 1961
[6]GWR third class restaurant cars Nos 9653 and 9654 built 1925 (originally articulated)
LNER Gresley open third coach No. 24105 built 1936
BR Mk.1 BCK coach No. 21254 built 1963
GWR tunnel inspection van No. DW150341 built 1933 (formerly brake/third corridor coach No. 5796)
BR Mk.1 TSO coach No. E4690 built 1957
BR Mk.1 TSO coach No. E4509 built 1956
BR Mk.1 SK coach
GNR BCK coach No. 229 built 1912
GWR third-class diner coach No. 9627 built 1932
GWR first-class diner coach No. 9615 built 1932
GWR corridor third bogie coach No. 1116 built 1938
GWR corridor third bogie coach No. 2119 built 1949
LNER Gresley open 3rd class coach No. 13366 built 1934
GWR corridor third-class bogie coach No. 3930 built 1915
GWR unclassed bogie saloon coach No. 9369 built 1923
LSWR bogie saloon coach No. 11 built 1910
SECR bogie saloon coach No. 177 built 1907
LNWR six-wheeled directors saloon No. 45021 built 1910
GWR corridor composite coach No. 7284 built 1941
GWR Collett third-class saloon coach No. 9103 built 1929
GWR sleeping cars Nos 9082, 9084 and 9085 built 1951
GWR corridor/composite coach No. 6045 built 1928
[17]GNR Gresley brake/composite No. 229 built 1912
[19]LMS open third coach No. 27218 built 1945
[15]GWR Churchward brake/third-class saloon No. 9055 built 1912
[15]GWR Hawksworth corridor third coach No. 829 built 1948
[15]GWR Collett corridor third bogie coach No. 1087 built 1938
[15]GWR Collett brake corridor third coach No. 5883 built 1934
[18]GWR Collett corridor third-class coach No. 1146 built 1938
GWR 'Toplight' corridor third coach No. 2426 built 1910
GWR Churchward passenger brake van No. 1145 built 1922
LMS corridor composite bogie coach No. 24617 built 1950
LMS brake/third coaches Nos 26921 and 26986 built 1950
LMS third-class open coaches Nos 27220 and 27270 built 1945
[6]GWR buffet car No. 9631 built 1934
LMS corridor third coach No. 12992 built 1949
BR Mk.1 TSO coach No. SC4054 built 1957
[15]GWR Collett brake corridor composite coach No. 6562 built 1938
[15]GWR Collett brake corridor composite coaches Nos 6912 and 6913 built 1934
LMS Stanier corridor third class coach No. W2300M built 1946
[18]GWR passenger brake van No. 98 built 1945
LNER Gresley open 3rd bogie coach No. 13547 built 1935
LNER Gresley open 3rd bogie coach No. 13354 built 1934
LNER Gresley buffet car No. 643 built 1937
LNER Gresley corridor brake composite coach No. 24068 built 1937
LMS brake/third bogie coach No. 26680 built 1950
GWR corridor/third bogie coach No. 1086 built 1938
LMS open first-class bogie coach No. 7511 built 1934
BR Pullman parlour 1st No. E331 *Topaz* built Metro-Cammell 1960
BR Pullman parlour 1st No. E324 *Amber* built Metro-Cammell 1960
BR Pullman parlour 1st No. E329 *Pearl* built Metro-Cammell 1960
BR Pullman kitchen 1st No. E313 *Finch* built Metro-Cammell 1960
BR Pullman kitchen 1st No. E317 *Raven* built Metro-Cammell 1960
BR Pullman kitchen 1st No. E319 *Snipe* built Metro-Cammell 1960
BR Mk.1 SK coach No. E24726 built 1953
GWR milk brake van No. 1399 built 1920
LMS six-wheeled 'Stove R' van No. 32919 built 1932
GWR six-wheeled tool van No. 112 built 1904
GWR four-wheeled tool van No. 141 built 1920
GWR four-wheeled riding van No. 89 built 1908
GWR four-wheeled riding van No. 118 built 1904
GWR four-wheeled tool van No. 143 built 1913
GWR 'Toad' 20-ton goods brake van No. 17410 built 1940
[15]GWR 'Siphon G' bogie van No. 1257 built 1927
GWR 10-ton banana van No. 82554 built 1927
GWR 'Loriot' 20-ton machinery wagon No. 42343 built 1944
[17]GWR 'Fruit D' van No. W92080 built 1958
[16]GWR 'Fruit D' van No. W92090 built 1958
[16]GWR breakdown tool van No. 66 built 1920
[16]GWR breakdown riding van No. 162 built 1923
[16]LNER bogie pigeon van No. 4236 built 1938
[18]GWR breakdown riding van No. 55 built 1908
[18]GWR sleeper wagon No. 40554 built 1899
[18]GWR steel tool van No. 80982 built 1913
[18]GWR 'Mink' 10-ton covered van No. 93016 built 1918
[18]GWR open wagon No. 97398 built 1921
[18]GWR signal department wagon No. 14428 built 1921

[18]GWR 'Mink' 12-ton covered van No. 104621 built 1925
[18]GWR 'Mica B' refrigerated meat van No. 105873 built 1925
[15]GWR 'Macaw B' bogie bolster wagon No. 107291 built 1935
[18]GWR 'Mogo' motor-car van No. 65801 built 1947
[18]GWR 10-ton ballast wagon No. 30903 built 1941
[18]GWR six-ton passenger fruit van No. 2303 built 1898
[18]GWR shunter's 'chariot' No. 41736 built 1913
[18]GWR 'Iron Mink' gunpowder van No. 58725 built 1890
MR tar tank wagon No. 76073 built 1914
LNWR covered combination truck No. 12220 built 1921
Cowans Sheldon 30-ton steam crane No. RS1087/30 built 1930
WD 'Warwell' well-wagon
LNER CCT vans Nos E1249 and E1296
GWR 'Snake C' Churchward brake van No. 1150 built 1922
GWR 'Fruit D' van No. 3467 built 1955
[18]GWR 20-ton 'Toad' goods brake van No. 68501 built 1925
[18]GWR china clay wagon No. 94059 built 1915
[18]GWR 'Vanfit' covered van (plywood body) No. 65620 built 1947
CR engineers wagon No. 300682 cut down from covered van built 1910
BSC 7-plank open wagon No. 16053 built 1937
LMS 10-ton open wagon No. 14188 built 1934
GWR four-wheeled riding van No. DW9 built 1912
GWR insulated fruit van A No. 134290 built 1938
GWR 'Mink A' covered van No. 101961 built 1920
LMS 12-ton open wagon No. 257632
Luggage van No. 173873 converted from BSC open wagon
Luggage van No. 151636 converted from BSC open wagon
LNER coke hopper wagon No. 274231 built 1945
LNER coke hopper wagon No. 307306 built 1948
LNER 12-ton open wagon 'Ynysarwed' No. 223162 built 1938
LNER 13-ton open wagon No. 225641 built 1938
GWR 'Gane A' bogie bolster wagon No. 60841 built 1935
GWR Ballast wagons Nos 80225 and 80603 built 1937
BR 30-ton steam crane No. ADM1091/30 built Cowans Sheldon, 1961
BR match truck No. ADB9998524 built 1961
BR 'Macaw B' bogie bolster wagon No. 943286
BR horsebox underframes Nos SV14191, 14192 and 14193
BR steam crane No. DW35 built 1949
GWR match truck No. DW75 built 1927
Field and Mackay 12-ton open wagon No. 41 built 1936
CR 10-ton covered van Nos 2080 and 4543 built 1910
Esso oil tank wagon No. 2686 built 1949
Great Western Collieries 13-ton open wagon No. 2717 built 1936
Highley Mining Co 13-ton open wagon No. 136 built 1946
Lothian Coal Co Ltd 12-ton open wagon No. 37
GWR 'Fruit D' covered van No. 3429 built 1950
LMS covered van No. 98543 built 1924
Matisa ballast tamping machine No. PWM4025
BR large tamping machine No. TT65RD
Cadbury all-steel covered van No. 8718
Goodyear Tyre Co steel mineral wagon No. 1A
Wickham 4WPMR 1580 built 1934
Wickham 4WPMR 5005 built 1949
Wickham 4WPMR 5008 built 1949
Wickham 4WPMR 5019 built 1949
Wickham 4WPMR 6653 built 1953
Wickham 4WPMR 7577 built 1957
Wickham 4WPMR 7690 built 1957
Wickham 4WPMR 8085 built 1958
Wickham 4WPMR 8200 built 1958

[1]Built at Darlington in June 1938 and withdrawn from Thornton Junction shed in December 1961 as BR No. 61994. The K4 class, of which only six were built, were the last steam locomotives to be specially designed for the West Highland line from Glasgow to Fort William. On withdrawal, *The Great Marquess* was purchased for preservation by Viscount Garnock and for several years was based in Leeds and worked enthusiasts' special trains.
[2]This design was the last to appear on the LMS prior to nationalisation. Embodying many new features and designed for maximum accessibility of working parts, the locomotives looked impressive and powerful but otherwise were not very pleasing to the eye compared with the older types they were designed to replace. Early examples of the class had double chimneys. Several of the class worked on the former M & GNJR line, in fact the entire class appears to have worked in rather exposed areas where their enclosed cabs and tender shields gave more protection to their crews. No. 43106 was withdrawn from Lostock Hall shed, Preston, in July 1968 and is the only member of the class preserved.
[3]Withdrawn from Lostock Hall shed in August 1968 after working the last steam-hauled standard-gauge BR passenger train. Purchased for preservation in 1969.
[4]Withdrawn from Templecombe (S & DJR) shed in May 1965 as BR No. 3205. The GWR never utilised 0-6-0 tender locomotives to the same extent as other railways, relying on their 2-6-0s for most mixed traffic, intermediate work. The 2251 class was designed to relieve the 'Dean Goods' locomotives of their duties on unrestricted routes in order that these older, smaller engines could be concentrated on the Cambrian section, thus replacing many of the older Cambrian types. One-hundred-and-twenty of the 2251 type were constructed and took their turn with passenger work over the longer cross-country routes, the Didcot, Newbury and Southampton line being a typical example.
[6]On loan from the National Collection.
[7]Withdrawn June 1964 and sent to Woodham Bros scrapyard, Barry. Purchased privately for preservation and moved to Steamtown Carnforth in October 1972. Moved to the Severn Valley Railway in late 1977.

[8]Sold to Backworth Colliery, Northumberland, as GWR No. 813 in 1934. Purchased for preservation 1968. During the course of overhauls at Swindon, this locomotive was fitted with various standard GWR fittings, making it a prime example of the hybrid products which appeared on the GWR following the grouping. Owned by the GWR 813 Preservation Fund (*q.v.*).

[9]Originally LMS No. 16466. Withdrawn from Westhouses shed in 1967 as BR No. 47383 and purchased for preservation. This engine worked at Williamthorpe Colliery in its later days and was first withdrawn in 1966 when diesel replacements arrived. However, due to repeated diesel failures, No. 47383 was reinstated and worked satisfactorily at the colliery until purchased for preservation. Owned by the Manchester Rail Travel Society (*q.v.*).

[10]Built for War Department service, this locomotive was briefly loaned to the LMS until 1941, after which it was sent to Iran as No. 307, later becoming Iran State Railways No. 41.109, before transfer to Egypt in 1944 as WD No. 70307. Renumbered WD No. 500, it was returned to England in 1952 and served on the Longmoor Military Railway before joining 663 sisters as British Railway No. 48773 in 1957. It was finally withdrawn from Rose Grove shed in 1968 and purchased for preservation. Owned by the Stanier 8F Locomotive Society Ltd (*q.v.*).

[11]The first design of Sir W. A. Stanier following his appointment as CME to the LMSR in 1932 was a batch of 40 2-6-0s built at Crewe Works in 1933/34. A mixed traffic design, the class were deployed and operated throughout the LMSR network and were regularly employed on fast freight and passenger duties. First numbered in the 132XX series, No. 13268 was completed on 24 January 1934 and renumbered 2968 on 20 September 1935 in LMS stock. She eventually became the last working member of the class, being withdrawn as BR No. 42968 from Springs Branch motive power depot, Wigan, on 31 December 1966 as part of the elimination of steam on BR and sold for scrap to Woodham Brothers of Barry on 8 March 1967. Owned by the Stanier Mogul Fund (*q.v.*).

[12]Ex-NCB Coventry Colliery, 1971. Owned by the Warwickshire Railway Society (*q.v.*).

[13]The very last locomotive built by Manning Wardle and Co. It was purchased from the Rugby Portland Cement Co Ltd, New Bilton Works, Rugby, in 1967 and has been immaculately restored in a fully-lined sky-blue livery and named *Warwickshire*. Owned by the Warwickshire Railway Society (*q.v.*).

[14]Ex-ICI Dyestuffs Division, Blackley Works, Manchester, 1969. The locomotive formerly worked on the Manchester Ship Canal Railway. Owned by the Warwickshire Railway Society (*q.v.*).

[15]Owned by the Great Western (SVR) Association (*q.v.*).

[16]Owned by Erlestoke Manor Fund (*q.v.*).

[17]Owned by 4150 Locomotive Fund (*q.v.*).

[18]Owned by GWR 813 Preservation Fund (*q.v.*).

[19]Owned by the Warwickshire Railway Society (*q.v.*).

[20]Withdrawn October 1966 and sent to Woodham Brothers scrapyard, Barry. Purchased for preservation and moved to the SVR in 1971. Overhauled and restored to working order July 1974.

[21]One of a class of 150 locomotives developed for wartime use over lightly laid track and one of the few WD 2-10-0s not to see service abroad. Instead, *Gordon* spent its working life on the Longmoor Military Railway and passed to the SVR in 1971.

[22]Worked from Tilbury and Croes Newydd depots until withdrawn in July 1965 and sold to Woodham Brothers, Barry, for scrap. Purchased for preservation and moved to the SVR in 1971. Subsequently restored to full working order.

[23]Withdrawn in February 1963 and sold to Woodham Brothers, Barry, for scrap. Purchased for preservation and moved to the SVR in January 1973. Restoration is being undertaken at Hampton Loade.

[24]During a working career of 45 years No. 2857 saw service over most of the GWR system, hauling South Wales coal traffic from Aberdare and Oxfordshire iron ore traffic from Banbury. Withdrawn from Neath in April 1963 and sold to Woodham Brothers, Barry, for scrap. Purchased for preservation and moved to the SVR in 1975. Restored to working order in 1979. Owned by the 2857 Society Ltd (*q.v.*).

[25]Spending almost all its working life on the Cambrian routes of the GWR, No. 7819 was once the regular engine rostered for the 'Cambrian Coast Express'. Withdrawn in November 1965 and sent to Woodham Brothers scrapyard, Barry. Purchased for preservation and moved to the SVR in January 1973. Restored to full working order in GWR livery in 1977.

[26]Withdrawn in October 1964 and sold to Woodham Brothers, Barry, for scrap. Purchased as a source of spares for the SVR's other two pannier tanks in 1978.

[27]No. 5164 worked local trains in the Birmingham and Wolverhampton areas for nearly 30 years before being transferred to Newton Abbot for West Country local traffic until withdrawn in April 1963 and was sent to Woodham Brothers scrapyard, Barry. Purchased for preservation and moved to the SVR in January 1973. Returned to steam 1979.

[28]Allocated to Old Oak Common depot until sold to London Transport in May 1960. Worked permanent way and engineers' trains as No. L95, based at Neasden and Lillie Bridge depots. Purchased for preservation and moved to the SVR in 1971. Restored to GWR livery, regaining its old No. 5764 in 1972.

[29]Withdrawn April 1962 and sent to Woodham Bros scrapyard, Barry. Purchased for preservation and moved to the Severn Valley Railway in July 1970. Subsequently fully restored and in regular use.

[30]Withdrawn December 1963 and sent to Woodham Bros scrapyard, Barry. Purchased for preservation and moved to the Severn Valley Railway in January 1973. Since restored to main line running condition and in regular use.

[31]Withdrawn November 1966 and sent to Woodham Bros scrapyard, Barry. Purchased for preservation and moved to the SVR in March 1973.
[32]Withdrawn September 1966 and sent to Woodham Bros scrapyard, Barry. Purchased for preservation and moved to the SVR in March 1973.
[33]Withdrawn March 1964 and sent to Woodham Bros scrapyard, Barry. Purchased for preservation in 1972 and overhauled at the BR workshops, Derby. *Leander* returned to steam in August 1973 and has hauled many main line specials, based first at Dinting and subsequently at Carnforth. Between August 1980 and February 1982, the locomotive underwent a major overhaul on the Severn Valley Railway and has since returned there, having been purchased by the SVR in 1983.
[35]This double-framed 4-4-0 was reconstructed at Swindon in March 1938 using frames from 'Bulldog' No. 3425 and officially replacing 'Duke' Class No. 3258 *The Lizard*. Withdrawn from Machynlleth shed in October 1960 as BR No. 9017 and purchased privately for preservation. Many of the 'Dukes' (built in 1895) spent several years working on the Cambrian section of the GWR, where they were the heaviest permitted engines. Between 1936 and 1938 the frames from newer 'Bulldogs' – these latter engines having been replaced by 'Halls' and 'Castles' – were used to rebuild 29 of the 'Dukes' in order to extend their working lives. No. 3217 was the last of its class to survive and was the last double-framed engine in regular traffic on BR.

Stanier 8F Locomotive Society Ltd **H**

Registered Charity No. 261751
Secretary: M. Shackleton, 201 Newmarket Road, Ashton-under-Lyne, Lancs OL7 9JW

The Society exists to further the continued operation and preservation of Class 8F 2-8-0 No. 8233 as a tribute to these tough and reliable machines, and to the outstanding school of design initiated by Sir William Stanier on the London Midland and Scottish Railway. Members are kept fully informed of all activities through a quarterly illustrated magazine *Black Eight*.

GWR 813 Preservation Fund **H**

Aims: (1) The permanent preservation and restoration to working order of former GWR locomotive 813; (2) the preservation and restoration of a representative collection of items of rolling stock from the former GWR with a special emphasis on goods and other non-passenger vehicles.
Membership: Currently about 200 shareholders.
Subscription: Minimum of two 50p shares (or equivalent in trading stamps), for which a share certificate is issued. No annual subscription stipulated other than a small period contribution for issue of newsletters, etc.
Secretary: P. H. Goss, 23 Hatchmere, Thornbury, near Bristol BS12 2EU

The Fund also owns rolling stock housed on the West Somerset Railway (see Group No. 4), The Bristol Suburban Railway (see Group No. 9) and GWS Didcot (see Group No. 456).

Manchester Rail Travel Society **H**

Details from: F. G. Cronin, 12 Chiltern Road, Ramsbottom, Lancashire
Aims: The preservation and restoration to working order on the SVR of LMS *Jinty* No. 47383. Steamed late in 1973 after complete overhaul. With the exception of a period in 1976 has worked ever since on the SVR with over 10,000 miles to its credit.

Erlestoke Manor Fund **H**

An independent fund, formed in March 1973, to purchase and restore to working order the former GWR 'Manor' Class 4-6-0 locomotive No. 7812 *Erlestoke Manor*.
Details from: The Secretary, Erlestoke Manor Fund, c/o Severn Valley Railway, Bewdley, Worcs DY12 1BG.
Subscription: Shares issued in £5 units.

The locomotive was purchased from Woodham Brothers within a record time of just twelve weeks, and one year later was moved by rail to temporary storage at the Dowty RPS site at Ashchurch.
In April 1976, following a share-holders' referendum, No. 7812 was transferred to Bewdley, on the Severn Valley Railway, where restoration work commenced in earnest. During the following three years, the locomotive was completely dismantled, overhauled, and rebuilt with many newly-fabricated components, finally re-entering service on 1 September 1979.
Sister engine No. 7802 *Bradley Manor* has subsequently been purchased to provide an interchangeable boiler and other 'strategic reserve' spares for No. 7812.

2857 Society Ltd **H**

The custodians of GWR 2-8-0 No. 2857
Details from: Keith Deakin, 3 Athelstone Way, Coton Green, Tamworth, Staffs. Tel: 0827-51269.

Stanier Mogul Fund **H**

Secretary: D. J. Montgomery, 23 Garth Crescent, Ermsford Grange, Coventry CV3 2PP
Subscriptions: Restoration certificates issued in £1 units (maximum 250)

Following a successful appeal, No. 42968 was purchased by the Fund in 1973. As the only survivor of her class, the engine has emerged as one of the important preservation schemes of the 1970s, representing the link between Stanier's Swindon training and subsequent LMS and BR practice up to the demise of Steam.

Great Western (SVR) Association **H**

Aims: To acquire and maintain for the Severn Valley Railway rolling stock of GWR origin. To gather under one banner all funds and societies of the SVR and GWR.
Details from: C. Howell, 63 Upper Street, Bewdley, Worcs.

Warwickshire Railway Society **H**

Details from: Pete Kennard, 145 Fulford Hall Road, Tidbury Green, Solihull, West Midlands B90 1QY

4150 Locomotive Fund **H**

Details from: D. J. Hall, 33 Gibbs Road, Newport, Gwent NPT 8AR

353 Chasewater Light Railway A

Passenger-carrying standard gauge steam railway, 2 miles in length

Chasewater Park, Brownhills, Staffordshire
Access: Off southbound carriageway of the A5 near junction with A452; entrance is signposted in Pool Road
Tel: Brownhills 5852
OS Ref: SK 034070

The Chasewater Light Railway has been closed for major reconstruction and track relaying since the end of 1982. It is hoped that some sort of service may be reinstated over part of the route in 1985.
Facilities for visitors include car parking, refreshments, railway shop and museum of small relics.
The railway is operated by members of the Railway Preservation Society.
The RPS was formed as part of a national movement to preserve historic relics from the railways of Great Britain and to restore them to original condition wherever possible. The Society originally set up a depot at Hednesford, Staffs, to accommodate its acquisitions, but by the summer of 1970 had closed this depot and transferred all the stock to Chasewater Pleasure Park, situated just off the A5 at Brownhills.
The Chasewater Light Railway was first leased by the Society from the NCB in 1965. At the time the line comprised the truncated remains of part of the former Cannock Chase and Wolverhampton Railway built in 1856 and an extension of the Midland Railway's Walsall Wood branch opened in 1884. To run the railway, a company, the Chasewater Light Railway Co Ltd, was formed and operates under a licence from the RPS. Trains normally run on Sunday afternoons between May and September with pre-grouping stock, usually with steam motive power. The role of the railway in the expanding Chasewater Pleasure Park is a prominent one. Ultimately it is envisaged that vintage steam trains will operate each weekend over the full two-mile length of the line, offering passengers a unique ride through pleasantly varied scenery, including the narrow quarter-mile causeway across the northern end of the lake. Proper station facilities are to be constructed at either end of the line and the track is being brought up to a condition whereby it will withstand heavy continuous use.
Details from: 3 Cherwell Drive, Brownhills, near Walsall, West Midlands.

Stock
Barclay 0-4-0ST *Invicta* 2220 built 1946
[1]Barclay 0-4-0ST *Colin McAndrew* 1223 built 1911
Peckett 0-4-0ST *The Colonel* 1351 built 1914
[2]Neilson 0-4-0ST No. 11 *Alfred Paget* 2937 built 1882
Peckett 0-4-0ST (R1 Class) 917 built 1902
Hudswell Clarke 0-6-0T No. 10 *Whit No. 4* 1822 built 1949
[3]Hudswell Clarke 0-6-0ST No. 15 431 built 1895
[4]Hawthorn Leslie 0-4-0ST *Asbestos* 2780 built 1909
Ruston Hornsby 0-4-0DE *Fleet No. DL7* 458641 built 1963
Hibberd 4WDM No. 1 2914 built 1944
Sentinel 4WVBTG 9632 built 1957
Kent Con/Planet 4WDM No. 21 1612 built 1929
Motor Rail 4WPM (L & YR Departmental No. 1) 1947 built 1919
MR four-wheeled full brake coach built *c*1880
M & CR six-wheeled coach No. 11 built 1879
BR Gloucester saloon DMU trailer coach No. E56301 built 1957
BR Park Royal DMU coach No. E50416 built 1957
BR Park Royal DMU coach No. E56171 built 1958
GER six-wheeled full brake coach No. 44 built 1885
MSLR six-wheeled coach built *c*1890
LNWR brake/3rd coach No. 22687 built 1917
[5]LNWR passenger brake van No. DM01836M built 1905
MR four-wheeled flat truck built *c*1890
MR four-wheeled box van built 1902
MR four-wheeled 25-cwt hand crane built 1881
L & YR four-wheeled box van built *c*1904
CCCR goods brake van built *c*1910
NER four-wheeled box van No. 100684 built *c*1910
GWR 16-ton goods brake van No. 35831 built 1888
Four-wheeled weedkilling truck built *c*1890
Two four-wheeled open wagons built *c*1897
Four-wheeled pump-handle trolley (ex-BR)
Smith Rodley 24-ton diesel rail crane
Wickham 4WPMR No. DB 975005
Wickham 4WPMR No. DB 975006

[1]Ex-N. Greening (Warrington) Ltd, Warrington, Lancs, 1966.
[2]Ex-Bairds and Scottish Steels Ltd, Gartsherrie Ironworks, Lanarkshire, 1968.
[3]Ex-Staveley Minerals Ltd, Desborough Quarry, Northants, 1967.

[4]Presented by Turners Asbestos Cement Co Ltd, Trafford Park, Manchester, 1968.
[5]Owned by the London and North Western Society (*q.v.*).

London and North Western Society **H**

Details from: J. C. James, 4 Longview Drive, Huyton, Liverpool L36 6EE

Formed in January 1974 as a registered charity to preserve and exhibit for the benefit of the public, items of London and North Western Railway origin. In furtherance of the above but not otherwise:

(*a*) The acquisition of historic relics from the London and North Western Railway together with associated research.
(*b*) Restoration to original condition of such historic relics wherever possible and their display to the public in suitable museums in Great Britain.
(*c*) Modelling of items of London and North Western Railway origin for display in suitable museums in Great Britain.

354 Birmingham Railway Museum D

Standard gauge steam railway centre and workshops, featuring steam-hauled rides over ¼ mile of track

670 Warwick Road, Tyseley, Birmingham B11 2HL
Access: By rail to Tyseley Station (note: this station is closed on Sundays when the Museum is open). By bus routes 37 and 44 from City Centre. By car along the Warwick Road adjacent to the BR depot
Tel: 021-707 4696
OS Ref: SP 105841

The museum is open daily throughout the year from 10 am to 5 pm. Steam days on the first Sunday of each month from April to December, plus Bank Holiday Mondays.
Facilities for visitors include car parking, museum and workshop, railway shop, refreshments including Pullman meal service by arrangement.
The Birmingham Railway Museum was formed in 1969 to cater for the increasing need for a specialised steam workshop and in 1975 the West Midlands County Council became a one-third partner in the project. Now, this appropriately located museum is one of the best equipped steam restoration and maintenance workshops in Britain, with many unique pieces of machinery of considerable industrial archaeological interest.
The museum also has a collection of historically important rolling stock, encompassing all the 'Big Four' pre-nationalisation railways.
A ¼-mile steam-hauled passenger shuttle service starting from a GWR-style wooden platform was inaugurated on 1 May 1983.
An additional four acres of land was acquired for the Museum in 1984, allowing future development to include re-erection of the locomotive roundhouse and a considerable extension of the running track.
Workshop equipment: Noble & Lund wheel lathe built 1947, Ransome & Rapier wheel drop (ex-Ipswich), 6ft 6in double head planing machine, special purpose running shed combination machine, Lang centre lathe, Short bed Dean Smith & Grace centre lathe, Hendy Norton centre lathe, No. 4 Herbert capstan lathe, Cincinnati No. 2 vertical drilling machine, Herbert drilling machine (all in machine shop) and various other lathes, milling and drilling machines in tool room.

Stock
[5]GWR 4-6-0 No. 4983 *Albert Hall* built 1931
[10]GWR 4-6-0 No. 5043 *Earl of Mount Edgcumbe* built 1936
GWR 4-6-0 No. 5080 *Defiant* built 1939
[4]GWR 4-6-0 No. 7027 *Thornbury Castle* built 1949
[2]GWR 4-6-0 No. 7029 *Clun Castle* built 1950
[7]GWR 0-6-0PT No. 7752 (LT No. L94) (57XX Class) NBL 24040 built 1930
[8]GWR 0-6-0PT No. 7760 (LT No. L90) (57XX Class) NBL 24048 built 1930
[9]GWR 0-6-0PT No. 9600 (57XX Class) built 1945
[3]LMS 4-6-0 No. 5593 *Kolhapur* (Stanier 5XP Class) NBL 24151 built 1934
Peckett 0-4-0ST *Rocket* 1722 built 1926
Peckett 0-4-0ST No. 1 2004 built 1941
[6]Baguley 0-4-0PM 800 built 1920
Pullman bar car *Pegasus* built 1951
GWR Hawksworth engineers saloon No. W80972 built 1948
LNWR royal saloon No. M806 built 1903
GWR semi-royal saloon coach No. 9001 built 1940
LNER Gresley buffet car No. 24279 built 1937
LNWR bogie TPO No. 20 built 1908
[11]LMS TPO coach No. 30272 built 1950
GWR corridor brake composite coach No. 6515 built 1926 (in use as staff mess van)
BR Mk.1 TSO coach No. M3736 built 1953
LMS Stanier 50ft bogie parcels van No. M31244 built 1944
LNWR six-wheeled goods brake van built *c*1900
GWR 6-wheel mess and tool van built 1904
GWR 10-ton ballast wagon No. 60911
BR 21-ton steel-bogied coal wagon No. B281137 built 1954
BR bogie well wagon No. B949578 built 1962
GWR shunters truck No. DW 43958
GWR 'Mogo' van built 1934
GWR match truck No. TDW 438
SR PMV 4-wheel van No. S1367 built 1939
Shell tank wagon No. 47757 built Charles Roberts 1963
Two GWR standard 5-plank wagons
GWR standard box van No. DW 126348 built 1934
Pensnett Railway 7-plank wagon
GWR bogie riding and tool van No. ADW 174 built 1908
GWR 'Fruit D' vans Nos W2342W and W92076
Shell oil tank wagon (ex-GER) No. A498 built 1902

Cowans-Sheldon 30-ton steam crane No. 139 built 1960
GWR 'Toad' 20-ton goods brake van No. 35938 built 1943
GWR 6-ton hand crane No. 438 built 1888
Fifteen-ton match trucks Nos ADW 42194 and ADB 998526
Leamington and Warwick horse tram No. 1 built 1881
Leamington and Warwick horse tram No. 8 built 1899

[2]One of the final batch of 'Castles' (7028–37) built at Swindon under BR auspices in May 1950. Withdrawn from Gloucester shed on 31 December 1965 as BR No. 7029 and purchased for preservation by 7029 Clun Castle Limited. In common with a number of its class, 7029 was later fitted with a double chimney and in this condition worked the last steam train out of Paddington. The engine finished its days in BR service as Gloucester station pilot.
[3]'Jubilee' Class three-cylinder 4-6-0 built by the North British Locomotive Co Ltd (Works No. 24151). Withdrawn from Leeds (Holbeck) in November 1967 as BR No. 45593 and purchased for preservation. First introduced in May 1934, all the 191 locomotives comprising the class were in traffic by the end of 1936. Many of the class worked on the Midland section of the LMS, most of which was banned to larger locomotives.
[4]No. 7027 was built by British Railways in 1949, although originally scheduled for construction in 1939 by the GWR. Unlike No. 7029, she retains the single chimney and blast-pipe, so that Tyseley now has a representative engine of both types. No. 7027 was purchased from Woodham Brothers at Barry in August 1972 as a source of spares for No. 7029. However, preliminary examination has proved she is in sound mechanical order and that the tolerances are on the top size. In due course – when time and finances permit – she will be restored to become a working companion to No. 7029. *Thornbury Castle* spent a large part of her working life running between Worcester and London, and, like No. 7029 *Clun Castle*, often worked the crack train over that section – the 'Cathedrals Express'.
[5]The Great Western 'Hall' Class was developed from the earlier two-cylinder 'Saints' designed by G. J. Churchward in the early part of the century. In 1931, No. 4983 was one of the first batches of engines, originally built with a 3,500 gallon tender, which she now carries. 'Halls' ran over most of the Great Western system, and were 'the maids of all work', being used on any job from an express to a freight train. No. 4983 spent a large part of her working life in South Devon and South Wales where she ended her active days. She carries a standard boiler which received a heavy repair shortly before withdrawal, but it is interesting to note that this boiler once adorned a 'Saint' giving No. 4983 a true link with Churchward.
[6]Owned by Staffordshire County Council and formerly housed at Shugborough. Ex-London Brick Company Ltd, Gildenburgh Works, Cambridgeshire, 1968. The locomotive is painted in a rather startling white livery!
[7]No. 7752 spent most of her working life in South Wales. She was withdrawn from Tondu and sold to London Transport in 1959. She had the distinction of working the last steam train on LT lines and arrived at Tyseley during the summer of 1971.
[8]No. 7760 was withdrawn from Oxford and sold to London Transport in 1961. Ten years later it was sold to a London scrap merchant from whom it was purchased for Tyseley. Neither of these engines was used for passenger traffic on London Transport, but were acquired solely for goods and maintenance trains. Both were built by the North British Locomotive Company on the instruction of the GWR.
[9]No. 9600 is a later design of pannier tank, being constructed at Swindon in 1945. She was purchased from the National Coal Board in South Wales and is at present undergoing a complete overhaul.
[10]Retained for spares only.
[11]On loan from the National Collection.

355 Bulmer Railway Centre D

Standard gauge steam railway preservation centre

H. P. Bulmer Ltd (Cider Makers), Whitecross Road, Hereford
Access: ½ mile from city centre on A438 Brecon road. Nearest BR station Hereford
Tel: Hereford 760787 or 4376
OS Ref: SO 505406

The Bulmer Railway Centre is operated by the 6000 Locomotive Association (Steam in Hereford Ltd) in conjunction with the Merchant Navy Locomotive Preservation Society and the Princess Elizabeth Locomotive Society on behalf of Bulmers, the Hereford Cider Makers.
The Centre was opened in 1968 to house the ex-GWR Locomotive 6000 *King George V* (which had been restored by Bulmers Cider) and the Bulmer Cider Train. Following a highly successful week-long 'Return to Steam' tour by the 'King' and the Cider Train in 1971, the BR ban on steam haulage was lifted and the Centre became the working depot for steam trains on the 'North and West' route between Newport and Shrewsbury (and later, Chester). Other preservation societies, notably the MNLPS and PELS, have brought their locomotives to use the facilities and participate in the activities at the Centre and on the main line.
The centre is open for static display every weekend from April to September inclusive. Steam days on the last Sunday in each month; also Easter, Spring and Summer Bank Holidays.
Facilities for visitors include car parking, souvenir shop, refreshments and toilets.

Stock
[1]GWR 4-6-0 No. 6000 *King George V* built 1927
[2]SR 4-6-2 No. 35028 *Clan Line* (Bulleid MN Class) built 1948

[4]LMS 4-6-2 No. 6201 *Princess Elizabeth* (Stanier Class 8P) built 1933
[5]GWR 0-6-0PT No. 5786 (57XX Class) built 1930
[6]Kitson 0-6-0ST No. 47 *Carnarvon* 5474 built 1934
[7]Peckett 0-4-0ST *Pectin* 1579 built 1921
[8]Hunslet 0-6-0DM No. 2 *Cider Queen* 5460 built 1958 (BR No. D2578)
[8]Pullman FK coach *Aquila* built 1951
[8]Pullman brake parlour third *Morella* built 1926 (originally car 36)
[8]Pullman parlour third *Christine* built 1928 (originally car 64)
[8]Pullman parlour third *Eve* built 1928 (originally car 76)
[8]Pullman parlour third *Prinia* built 1930 (originally car 83)
[7]SR Pullman car *Ruth* (refitted as members clubroom); formerly a kitchen composite car (ex-6PUL) built 1932
[3]LNER Gresley pigeon van No. 4268 built 1940
[7]BR Mk.1 BSK coach No. 35219 built 1958
[3]BR Mk.1 BSK coach No. S35028 (originally E35270) built 1959
[7]BR Mk.1 CK coach No. 15879 built 1957 (now SHL 99205)
BR Mk.1 BSK coach (used as dining trailer)
[7]LNER Gresley buffet coach No. E9115 built 1937
[7]GWR 20-ton PW brake van No. 40732 built 1893
[7]GWR 'Toad' 20-ton goods brake van No. 35923
[7]PO 12-ton flat wagon
[10]GWR covered goods van No. W96835 built 1921
[9]LMS 'Stove R' six-wheeled van No. 32918 built 1932

[1]Withdrawn from Old Oak Common shed in 1962 as BR No. 6000 and stored until presented to Swindon Borough Council and moved to Swindon in 1966. Loaned to H. P. Bulmer Ltd and restored to BR livery by A. R. Adams Ltd, Newport, in 1968. *King George V* was the first locomotive to inaugurate a 'Return to Steam' on BR tracks in October 1971.
Designed specifically for hauling the very heaviest express passenger trains, the 'Kings' were the largest and most powerful 4-6-0s ever built. No. 6000 visited America in 1927 for the Baltimore and Ohio Railroad Centenary celebrations and has carried its presentation plaque and bell ever since. On loan from the National Collection.
[2]Bulleid 'Merchant Navy' Class locomotive, the most powerful class ever built for the Southern Railway. As constructed, they incorporated many of Oliver Bulleid's unorthodox features such as the 'air-smoothed' streamline casing, chain-driven valve gear working in an enclosed oilbath and BFB cast steel wheel centres. From 1956 onwards the entire class was rebuilt by BR with outside Walschaert's valve gear and with the air-smoothed casing removed. In their new guise the class did much excellent work, recording speeds in excess of 100 mph on several occasions. *Clan Line* was so rebuilt in 1959 and withdrawn from Nine Elms shed on the last day of Southern steam, 9 July 1967. Owned by the Merchant Navy Locomotive Preservation Society Ltd (*q.v.*).
[3]Owned by the Merchant Navy Locomotive Preservation Society Ltd (*q.v.*).
[4]Nos 6200 and 6201 were the first 'Pacifics' built for the LMS and the first major Stanier design. During the course of a test run on the 16/17 November 1936, *Princess Elizabeth* hauled a load averaging 240 tons from Euston to Glasgow and return, a distance of 802.8 miles, at an average speed of 69 mph. This remains a world record for continuous high-speed travel with steam traction. The locomotive was finally withdrawn from Carlisle Kingmoor shed in 1962 as BR No. 46201 and purchased for preservation. It has been painted in LMS livery, the boiler completely retubed, plus other work, and attended the S & D 150th Anniversary Celebrations at Shildon in 1975. Owned by the Princess Elizabeth Locomotive Society (*q.v.*).
[5]Sold to London Transport in 1958, becoming No. L92. Purchased for preservation 1969 and restored to GWR livery at Bewdley. Moved to Hereford in 1970. Owned by the Worcester Locomotive Society Ltd (*q.v.*).
[6]Ex-Stewarts and Lloyds Minerals Ltd, Gretton Brook, Corby, Northants, 1969. Owned by the Worcester Locomotive Society Ltd (*q.v.*).
[7]Owned by Steam in Hereford Ltd (*q.v.*).
[8]Owned by H. P. Bulmer Ltd.
[9]Owned by the Princess Elizabeth Locomotives Society (*q.v.*).
[10]Owned by the Worcester Locomotive Society Ltd (*q.v.*).

Steam in Hereford Ltd **H**

The 6000 Locomotive Association
(stewards to GWR locomotive 6000 *King George V* restored by Bulmers Cider)
Details from: J. Loynes, 31 Ecroyd Park, Credenhill, Hereford HR4 7EL

Steam enthusiasts in Hereford were particularly fortunate when 6000, the GWR 'King' Class locomotive *King George V*, arrived in Hereford through the good offices of Bulmers Cider. Some thirty of these enthusiasts got together and the 6000 Locomotive Association was founded with the prime object of stewardship of the great locomotive. Membership has risen steadily and now numbers about 300. Steam in Hereford Ltd was formed for the sole purpose of protecting the members by limiting liability (the amount members would have to pay if the company went into liquidation). The Company continues to trade as the 6000 Locomotive Association, has the same spirit and objectives, and membership of Steam in Hereford Ltd automatically constitutes membership of the 6000 Locomotive Association.
The major activities of the Association are centred upon the 'stewardship' duties with 'KGV' and maintenance of the Association's locomotives and rolling stock. These activities require a lot of effort but the Association is run by steam enthusiasts for steam enthusiasts and the Association's success is reward enough. Regular working parties are held and it is from these working members that the 'Return to Steam' loco parties are recruited.

Merchant Navy Locomotive Preservation Society Ltd **H**

Registered as a charity.
Details from: John Harvey, a Ponsonby Road, Roehampton, London SW15

The MNLPS was formed in 1965 and purchased *Clan Line* for £2200. Initially the Society stored the loco on the Longmoor Military Railway. From August 1971 the loco was resident at Ashford, Kent, and it was during this period that she worked her first 'Return to Steam' Special, between Basingstoke, Salisbury and Westbury. In April 1975 she moved to the Bulmer Steam Centre at Hereford, her present home. *Clan Line* is the fastest 'Merchant Navy' pacific with an authenticated speed of 104 mph at Axminster on the ACE. It is also one of the most consistent locomotives now in service and has never failed on a tour of any kind since its return to traffic in 1974.
Clan Line took part in the Rocket 150 celebrations in May 1980. It was withdrawn from active service at the end of that year for extensive overhaul prior to returning to the main lines in 1982.
No society can exist without its members. This Society is unusual in that it is not backed by big names, or sponsored by big money. It is a grouping of enthusiasts who, together with professional railwaymen, carry out the essential tasks of maintenance and coachwork. The Society maintains its links with members via its quarterly magazine (produced in association with the Bulleid Society), Hereford Open Days, Railtours and social evenings.

Princess Elizabeth Locomotive Society **H**

General Secretary: V. Smart, 7 Pine Close, Thornbury, Avon
Membership Secretary: Mrs J. Allen, 56 Springfields Avenue, Sandiacre, Nottingham

Worcester Locomotive Society Ltd **H**

General Secretary: David R. G. Nowell, 1 Ranelagh Street, Hereford
Facilities: Meetings and film shows in Worcester, Gloucester, Cheltenham and occasionally in other towns. Coach and Rail tours to BR installations and preservation locations. Work on Society's locomotives and rolling stock at weekends at Bulmer Railway Centre in Hereford.

The WLS also owns the following rolling stock:
Motor Rail 4WPM 4217 built 1931
GWR covered goods van No. W95750
GWR covered goods van No. W16295
Wickham 4WPMR 6645 built 1956
Wickham 4WPMR No. TR22 7515 built 1956
Wickham 4WPMR No. TR40 7517 built 1956

356 Dean Forest Railway **DF**

A small railway station and half a mile of railway track where steam train rides are operated on certain days through the summer months. There is also a collection of smaller items, signs, signals, photographs, drawings, telling the story of the railways formerly serving the industries of the Forest of Dean

Dean Forest Railway Society Ltd, Norchard, near Lydney, Forest of Dean, Gloucestershire
Access: Norchard is half mile off A48 at Lydney. BR Gloucester–Newport service to Lydney. National Welsh bus No. 40 passes the site
Tel: Dean (0594) 43423
OS Ref: SO 629044
Details from: Mr C. A. Bladon, Laurel Cottage, Northwood Green, Westbury-on-Severn, Gloucs.

The Society operates Norchard Steam Centre, which is situated ½ mile north of Lydney, in the Forest of Dean, Gloucestershire, alongside the Lydney to Parkend branch railway and with road access from B4234.
There is a shop selling souvenirs, railway books and models and a refreshment counter serving hot and cold drinks and snacks. The centre welcomes visitors every Saturday and Sunday (11 am to 5 pm) and the shop is open every Sunday afternoon and Saturday afternoons also in summer. Steam train rides are normally operated on Bank Holiday Sundays and Mondays and on Sundays mid-July to the first Sunday in September.
The Dean Forest Railway Society Ltd was formed in 1970 when the goods-only branch railway from Lydney Junction to Parkend, in the Forest of Dean, first came under threat of closure. The Society has built up a collection of railway equipment close to this line and is in a position to operate steam passenger trains now that British Rail have decided to dispose of it.
All the work has been done on a voluntary basis by the railway enthusiast members of the Society. Fund raising, particularly sales and operation of steam rides, has allowed them to purchase a number of locomotives and items of rolling stock and they have worked to restore these to working order. They are also developing the amenities of the site, clearing viewing and picnic areas. Visitors can see the results of these labours at Norchard and there is rewarding work for all those sufficiently interested to join the Society and help.
The long term object is the operation of the 3½ mile branch railway line between Lydney and Parkend as a tourist attraction using steam trains.
Terms for purchase have been agreed with BR.
The line climbs from the Cardiff–Gloucester line at Lydney, on the Severn Estuary, through a wooded valley, passing Norchard and the village of Whitecroft, into the Dean National Forest Park, terminating at Parkend.
The Society is restoring stock and equipment to the former GWR/LMS (MR) condition, preserving the history of the original Severn and Wye Railway where appropriate.

Stock
[5]GWR 2-6-2T No. 5521 (Class 4575) built 1927
[4]GWR 2-6-2T No. 5532 (Class 4575) built 1928
[1]GWR 2-6-2T No. 5541 (Class 4575) built 1928
[3]GWR 2-6-2T No. 4121 (Class 41XX) built 1937
[2]GWR 0-6-0PT No. 9681 (Class 8750) built 1949
GWR 4-6-0 No. 4953 *Pitchford Hall* built 1929
Hunslet 0-6-0ST *Warrior* 3823 built 1954
[3]Hunslet 0-6-0ST No. 18 *Jessie* 1873 built 1937
Hunslet 0-6-0ST *G. B. Keeling* 3806 built 1953
[3]Peckett 0-4-0ST *Uskmouth 1* 2147 built 1952
Hibberd 4WDM 3947 built 1960
Sentinel/Rolls-Royce 0-6-0DH PBA No. 39 10218 built 1965
BR/Drewry 0-6-0DM No. 03.062 (Class 03) built 1959
Fowler 0-4-0DM 4210127 built 1957
Fowler 0-4-0DM 4210101 built 1955
Hunslet 0-4-0DM 2145 built 1940
GWR auto-trailer No. 167 built 1929
[3]GWR auto-trailer No. 178 built 1930
[3]GWR Hawksworth engineers saloon No. 80943 built 1948
[3]GWR corridor 3rd class coaches Nos 5813, 5848 & 5863 built 1934
[3]GWR corridor 3rd class coach No. 5929 built 1935
BR Mk.1 TSO coach No. SC4218 built 1956
BR Mk.1 restaurant car No. W1917
BR Mk.1 CK coach No. E15849 built 1956
BR Mk.1 SK coach No. E24918 built 1955
BR Mk.1 BCK coach No. W21129 built 1956
BR XP64 TSO coach No. 4729 built 1964
BR XP64 SK coach No. W25509 built 1964
BR XP64 FK coach No. 13407 built 1964
LMS sleeping car No. W617 built 1952
GWR brake/3rd corridor coach No. 1645 built 1938
BR 'Low mac' wagon No. 904050
GWR 'Siphon G' No. 2988 built 1945
LMS BG van No. M31406 built 1950
SR PMV van No. S1227 built 1936
GWR 'Toad' brake van No. 56769
SR bogie parcels van
GWR 'Mica B' insulated meat van No. 79636 built 1913
GWR 'Toad' 20-ton goods brake van No. 56835 built 1906
[3]LMS 'Stove R' 6-wheel passenger brake van No. 32978 built 1938
GWR 'Prawn' bogie steel-carrying wagon
GWR 'Toad' 24-ton goods brake van No. 17294 built 1943
[2]GWR shunter's truck No. 41152 built 1942
[3]GWR breakdown train van No. 161 built 1923
GWR 'Mica B' wagon underframe No. 105928 used as a flat wagon
GWR 'Fruit D' van No. W3411 built 1950
GWR Smith Rodley 10-ton steam crane No. TS 5027 built 1953
Shell tank wagon No. A88 built 1889
Shell tank wagon No. A100 built 1890
BR 'Low fit' wagon No. 457627 built 1951
GWR 5-plank wagon built *c*1915
GWR box van built 1919
GWR 5-plank wagon No. 130554
MR open wagon built *c*1900
GWR sleeper wagon
Six GWR steel-bodied engineering dept wagons
Two LMS 3-plank wooden-bodied wagons
LMS vans PBA Nos 32, 34, 38 built 1938
PMA flat wagons Nos 125, 138, 149 and 154
Wickham 4WPMR 8774 built 1961 (WD No. 9045)
Wickham 4WPMR 4254 built 1947 (SR No. DS 3057)
Two þitumen tank wagons
Two GWR hand cranes and runner wagons

Signal boxes
GWR 13-lever, formerly at Mileage Yard, Gloucester
LMS (Midland Railway) 30-lever, formerly at Charfield
LMS (MR), formerly at Barnwood (building only)

[1]Withdrawn as BR No. 5541 in July 1962 and sold to Woodham Brothers, Barry, for scrap. Purchased for preservation and moved to Parkend in 1972. Owned by the Forest Prairie Fund (*q.v.*).
[2]Owned by the Forest Pannier Tank Fund (*q.v.*).
[3]Owned by individual members or groups of members.
[4]Withdrawn July 1962 and sold to Woodham Bros, Barry for scrap. Purchased for preservation by the Forest Prairie Fund and moved to Norchard in April 1981.
[5]Withdrawn April 1962 and sold to Woodham Bros, Barry for scrap. Purchased for preservation by the West Somerset Railway in September 1975 and subsequently re-sold to the Dean Forest Railway.

Forest Prairie Fund H

Details from: John Harris, 21 Chandos Street, Hereford

No. 5541 returned to service in November 1975 and has since been regularly used at Dean Forest Railway Society steam days. Restoration has been made possible by a loan, still partly outstanding, and shares at £1 are still available in the locomotive.
The Fund has purchased No. 5532, ex-Woodham Brothers, Barry, for spares.

The Forest Pannier Tank Fund H

Details from: J. Hatton, 23 Robinson Road, Gloucester GL1 5DL

Stock
LMS 12-ton goods van No. 507190 built 1935
LMS 12-ton goods van No. 514262 built 1940

357 Gloucester–Warwickshire Railway and Cotswold Narrow Gauge Railway A

An ambitious railway preservation scheme aimed at reviving the former GWR Stratford-on-Avon to Cheltenham line using steam motive power

Toddington Station, Gloucestershire

OS Ref: SP 0627
Access: Toddington is 11 miles north east of Cheltenham. Marchant and Castleway coaches from Cheltenham; Cresswell coaches from Evesham and Blockley

Operates on Saturdays, Sundays and Bank Holidays when standard and narrow gauge rides are available over ⅓-mile runs.
Facilities for visitors include car parking, railway shop and refreshments. The station is open at weekends and Bank Holidays from 10 am to 5 pm.

Stock
Avonside 0-4-0T *Cadbury No. 1* 1977 built 1925
Barclay 0-4-0ST No. 2 2221 built 1946
Barclay 0-4-0F 2126 built 1942
Barclay 0-4-0ST *Drake* 2086 built 1940
SR 4-6-2 No. 35006 *Peninsular and Oriental S.N. Co* built 1941
GWR 2-6-2T No. 4115 (41XX Class) built 1936
GWR 2-6-2T No. 5526 (4575 Class) built 1928
[1]GWR 2-8-0 No. 2807 (28XX Class) built 1905
GWR 4-6-0 No. 4936 *Kinlet Hall* built 1929
[2]GWR 4-6-0 No. 5952 *Cogan Hall* built 1935
[3]GWR 4-6-0 No. 7821 *Ditcheat Manor* built 1950
[4]GWR 4-6-0 No. 7828 *Odney Manor* built 1950
Hunslet 0-6-0ST *King George* 2409 built 1942
Peckett 0-4-0ST 1976 built 1939
Hudswell Clarke 0-6-0DM No. D1 D615 built 1938
BR 0-6-0DE No. 08.118 (Class 08) built 1955
BR 0-6-0DH No. D9539 (Class 14) built 1965
BR 0-6-0DH No. D9553 (Class 14) built 1965
BR 0-6-0DH No. D9537 (Class 14) built 1965
Fowler 0-4-0DM No. 21 4210130 built 1957
Fowler 0-6-0DH No. 19 4240016 built 1964
Hibberd 4WDM 2893 built 1944
BR Mk.1 RMB coach No. SC 1811 built 1957
LMS inspection saloon No. M45048 built 1941
BR Mk.1 SK coach No. E25020 built 1955
BR Mk.1 BCK coach No. W21187 built 1958
BR Mk.1 BSK coach No. W34929 built 1956
BR Mk.1 suburban 2nd class coach No. E461116 built 1951
GWR auto-trailer coach No. 169 built 1929
GWR corridor third coach No. 2447 built 1911
GWR corridor third coach No. 3665 built 1921
GWR corridor third coach No. 3898 built 1920
GWR corridor third coach No. 3917 built 1915
GWR corridor third coach No. 3963 built 1919
GWR brake/third corridor coach No. 2370 built 1911
GWR restaurant car No. 9635 built 1935
GWR special saloon carriage No. 9044 built 1881
L & YR covered van built 1894
MR six-wheeled brake van No. 1060 built 1904
GWR three-ton manual crane No. 538 built 1903
LMS 20-ton goods brake van built 1948
Pensnett Railway open wagon
LMS 20-ton goods brake van
GWR 'Toad' 20-ton goods brake DW 35959 built 1945
GWR tool van
GWR 16-ton hand crane built 1908
GWR 'Siphon G' van No. 2983 built 1945
GWR 10-ton open wagon No. 10445W built 1940
GWR 'Fruit D' van No. W204W built 1940
GWR 'Fruit D' van No. W92110W built 1925
Two LMS 14-ton tank wagons
LNER 12-ton box van
GWR 'Siphon G' van No. W1019 built 1951
SR PMV vehicle No. S1863 built 1940
BR 12-ton ventilated vans Nos B783898 and B7834496
BR 21-ton hopper wagon No. B346194
45-ton steam crane plus match truck
GWR 'Mink C' 4-wheeled van No. DW 79412 built 1906
LNER 12-ton box van
Two LMS tank wagons
GWR 'Fruit D' van No. W92110W built 1940
GWR 'Fruit D' van No. W204W built 1940
GWR 10-ton open wagon No. W10445W built 1940
Wickham 4WPM inspection trolley 7516
Wickham 4WPMR No. TR23

Narrow gauge stock
Hunslet 0-4-0ST *George B* 680 built 1898
Jung 0-4-0WT *Justine* 939 built 1906
Bagnall 4-4-0T No. 5 *Isibutu* 2820 built 1946
Kerr Stuart 0-4-0ST *Peter Pan* 4256 built 1922
Hunslet 0-4-2ST *Chaka* 2075 built 1940
Lister 4WDM No. 2 34523 built 1949
Lister 4WDM No. 8 28039 built 1945
Motor Rail 4WPM No. 3 4565 built 1928
Motor Rail 4WPM *Spitfire* 7053 built 1937
Ruston Hornsby 4WDM No. 802 221645 built 1944
Ruston Hornsby 4WDM No. L5 181820 built 1936
Ruston Hornsby 4WDM No. 1 166010 built 1932
Ruston Hornsby 4WDM 354028 built 1953
Hunslet 4WDM 5258 built 1957
Ruston Hornsby 4WDM 213834 built 1942
Lister 4WDM No. 3 *Goat* 8022 built 1936
Motor Rail 4WDM 26007 built 1964 and bogie open coach
Two Hudson bogie gondolas
MOD brake van
Two Hudson bogie carriages
Hudson all-steel bogie wagon
Hudson wooden-bodied drop-side four-wheeled wagon
Three Hudson tipping skips
Two four-wheeled coaches on skip chassis
Four unsprung four-wheeled flat wagons
One tipping skip (continental origin)
Also a comprehensive collection of signalling, station and lineside equipment

[1]Withdrawn March 1963 and sent to Woodham Bros scrapyard, Barry. Purchased for preservation and moved to Toddington in June 1981.
[2]Withdrawn June 1964 and sent to Woodham Bros scrapyard, Barry. Purchased for preservation 1981.
[3]Withdrawn November 1965 and sent to Woodham Bros

scrapyard, Barry. Purchased for preservation and moved to Toddington in June 1981.
[4]Withdrawn October 1965 and sent to Woodham Bros scrapyard, Barry. Purchased for preservation and moved to Toddington in June 1981.

Dowty Railway Preservation Society **H**

The Dowty Railway Preservation Society was formed in 1962 to cater for the needs of railway enthusiast members of the Dowty Sports and Social Society – the sports and social club of the Dowty Group of engineering companies (based in Gloucestershire).
Non-employees may join as associate members.

Details from: Mr R. H. Wales, 7 Lypiatt Street, Cheltenham, Glos.

358 North Staffordshire Steam Railway Centre DF

Standard gauge railway preservation centre which is the first phase of the scheme to reopen a passenger railway in the Churnet Valley

North Staffordshire Railway Co (1978) Ltd, Cheddleton Station, Station Road, Cheddleton, near Leek, Staffordshire
Access: Off the A520 Leek–Stone road at Cheddleton, then follow signposts. Berrisford's buses operate to Cheddleton from Leek and Hanley (bus routed via Cheddleton station on weekends).
By rail via 'Churnetrail' scenic cruise trains on limited summer weekends from Chester, Crewe and all stations to Stoke-on-Trent direct to Cheddleton. Coach parties and charter railtours welcome by prior arrangement.
Nearest BR station Stoke-on-Trent.
Tel: Churnet Side 360522
OS Ref: SJ 983519

The station buildings have been converted into a museum reflecting the original North Staffordshire Railway Company, 'Owd Knotty'. Short train rides are available at the museum on Sundays and Bank Holidays hauled by steam or diesel locomotives.
Facilities for visitors include souvenir shop, refreshments, museum and toilets.
The museum is open daily from May to September and on Sundays only from October to April.
The Churnet Valley is renowned for its natural beauty and visitors to the station can readily sample the pleasant scenery and places of interest within a short radius of the museum. In fact the picturesque Cauldon Canal runs parallel to the railway and is only a short walk away from the station. The passenger carrying narrow boat 'Royal Jubilee' operates along the Cauldon Canal throughout the Summer Season – enquiries re booking should be made at Cheddleton Station. A well restored flint mill and church (St Edward's) are located in Cheddleton village, with Coombes Valley nature reserve nearby; the area is honeycombed with pleasant walkways and the station is situated on the Staffordshire County Council leisure drive. The well-known tourist attractions of Alton Towers and Rudyard Lake are within easy driving distance of the museum.
The station building at Cheddleton is both beautiful and imposing, built in the Jacobean style, reputedly by the famous architect Pugin and is protected as a listed building (grade 2) by the Department of the Environment. An attractive souvenir shop and museum rooms are situated at platform level in the main building with the railway offices above. Light refreshments are available from either the shop or one of the carriages located in the bay-platform area. Snacks are provided at the nearby 'Boat Inn' and hot meals are available at the station. Cheddleton is being restored to represent a typical country station of the old 'Knotty' railway and the museum contains authentic relics and items of interest from the original North Staffordshire Railway.

Details from: Mr I. J. Bowland, 78 Park Lane, Sandbach, Cheshire.

Stock

BR 2-6-4T No. 80136 (Riddles Class 4MT) built 1956
[1]LMS 0-6-0 No. 4422 (Fowler Class 4F) built 1927
Hunslet 0-6-0ST *Josiah Wedgewood* 3777 built 1952
BR 0-6-0DE No. 08.350 built 1957
BR 0-6-0DE No. 08.359 built 1958
RSH 0-4-0DM No. D2982 *Camel* 6980 built 1940
BR Mk.1 coaches Nos M15207 and M15208 built Metro-Cammell 1953
BR Mk.1 brake/2nd compartment coaches Nos M43275 and M43300 built 1955
BR brake/3rd compartment coaches Nos M42375 and M43300 built 1955
Esso tank wagon No. 2305 built Charles Roberts 1944
BR fitted freight van No. B763092 built 1954
BR fitted freight van No. B764459 built 1955
Smith Rodley 7-ton diesel crane built 1972
Esso tank wagon No. 2305
LMS 12-ton box van No. M155046 built 1926
LMS 12-ton box van No. M269460 built 1929
Two Esso tank wagons
Smith Rodley self-propelled 7-ton diesel crane built 1972
BR fitted freight vans Nos B73059 and B75443
BSC 21-ton hopper wagon
Two BSC coke wagons
Two NSR coach bodies
LMS 4-wheel horse dray built 1929

[1]No. 4422 was completed at Derby in October 1927 and spent much of her working life in the Midlands and later the south-west of England.
During her time with the London, Midland and Scottish Railway she was shedded at Leicester, Wigston, Bristol and Bath. She later worked from Penzance during BR

days and was often seen on the Somerset and Dorset line before her withdrawal in June 1965 as BR No. 44422. Sent to Woodham Bros scrapyard, Barry, and purchased for preservation in April 1977.

359 Walsall Steam Railway — A

Passenger-carrying, 7¼in gauge steam railway, ¾ mile in length featuring double-track running

Arboretum Park, Walsall, West Midlands
Access: Off Broadway North, double gates by Grange Playhouse. AA signed on approaching roads.
15 minutes walk from Walsall BR Station
Tel: Walsall 30078 or 22544
OS Ref: SP 0298

The railway operates every Saturday, Sunday and Bank Holiday from Easter to October from 2 pm to dusk.
Facilities for visitors include car parking, refreshments, toilets, putting greens and boating on the lake.
Walsall Arboretum Railway was opened Easter 1976 with single track and passing loops at each end. Loco power was provided by the 4-6-2 Steam Loco *Princess Elizabeth* together with two Cromar White Battery Electric Locos. The following year saw double track installed throughout, loco shed erected, and two new system locos, *A. H. Peppercon* and *Duchess of Buccleugh*, together with a Bo-Bo battery Electric Railcar. For the 1979 season the track was extended a further 200 yards and a new Terminal Station with 3 bays built.
The Walsall Steam Railway is now the longest 7¼in double-track system in the country using scale steam locomotives.

Details from: C. M. Cartwright, 58 Charlemont Road, Walsall, West Midlands.

Stock
LMS 4-6-2 No. 6201 *Princess Elizabeth* built Glaze
LMS 4-6-2 No. 6230 *Duchess of Buccleugh* built Monk 1978
LNER 4-6-2 No. 525 *A. H. Peppercorn* built Glaze 1977
BR 2-10-0 No. 92220 *Evening Star* built Pownall 1980
BR 2-10-0 No. 92203 *Black Prince* built 1979
LMS 4-6-0 No. 5000 *Sister Dora* (Stanier Class 5MT) built Glaze 1980
LMS 2-8-0 under construction by Cartwright/Milner Eng 1984
LMS 4-6-0 (Fowler large-boilered 'Royal Scot') built Glaze 1982
BR Bo-BoDH Hymek built Glaze and Mills
Cromar White Bo-BoBER No. E7051 built 1977
Denver & Rio Grande 2-8-0 built 1982
12 'Sit-astride' bogie coaches
2 works mineral wagons

360 Weston Park Railway — A

Passenger-carrying 7¼in gauge steam railway

Weston Park, Weston-under-Lizard, Shropshire
Access: With the growing network of motorways Weston Park is well situated for easy access from a great number of the English counties. The Park is seven miles west from the M6/A5 interchange (Junction 12) on the A5 at Weston-under-Lizard. The nearest railway station is at Shifnal and public bus services run to Tong and Weston-under-Lizard
Tel: Weston-under-Lizard 207 or 385
OS Ref: SJ 807106

Railway details from: Hilton Valley Railway Ltd, Hern Manor, Shifnal, Shropshire TF11 9PT.

This extensive and well-known 7¼in gauge system was moved in its entirety from its original site at Hilton, near Bridgnorth, during the winter of 1979/80. Advantage is being taken of the new location to lay the line out with future development in mind. Existing operational features are retained, such as crossing loops controlled by colour light signals, interlocked with the train 'staff' system.
Weston Park is open at the following times:
Mid-April–31 July: Daily, except for Mondays and Fridays, open Bank Holidays. Additionally open Mondays in May, June and July for school parties only.
August: Daily. September: Weekends only. Closed on 30 September.
The Park is open from 11 am to 7.30 pm, and the House from 2 pm to 6 pm. Last admissions 5.30 pm.
There is ample free parking space for cars and coaches. Particular arrangements are made to ensure comfort for the aged and physically handicapped, including the provision of special lavatory facilities.
A cafeteria and restaurant offer excellent catering facilities from snacks to full meals. The emphasis is on home-baking, estate produce and additional fare.
Prior booking for large parties wishing to have meals is essential.
Fully licensed catering facilities for special events, conferences, promotional events etc in The Old Stables, the House or the Temple of Diana throughout the year.
Every year more and more coach parties find Weston Park an enjoyable venue. Around 30% reduction available on coach parties. These terms apply for parties of 20 or more in coaches only. Special evening visits can be made on the first and last Wednesday of every open month, and every Wednesday in June. Prior booking is essential.
Full details of all party booking arrangements are available on request.
Other facilities for visitors include Woodland Adventure Playground, British Wildlife collection, Aquarium and pottery.

Stock
Shaw 4-6-2 No. 1 *Lorna Doone* built 1925, rebuilt 1969
Liversage 2-6-0 No. 2 *Hilton Queen* built 1950, rebuilt 1968

Guest/Lloyd 4-8-4 No. 3 *Francis Henry Lloyd* built 1959, rebuilt 1970
Freelance Bo+2 BE No. 4 built 1958
Freelance 4WBE No. 5 built 1960
Freelance Bo+2 PE No. 6 built 1965, rebuilt 1971
GWR/Freelance 2-6-2 No. 7 built by Monk, rebuilt Glaze 1969
Cromo Bo+2 DM No. 8 rebuilt 1970
Glaze 2-8-0 No. 9 *Michael Charles Lloyd MBE* built 1975
Two enclosed bogie saloon coaches built 1972
Thirteen open bogie coaches
Open bogie wagon
Open four-wheeled wagon built 1968

361 Cambrian Railways Society Ltd F

This Society is promoting a scheme for the formation of a living museum of Cambrian Railways relics centred on Oswestry, Shropshire

Railway Depot, Oswald Road, Oswestry, Shropshire
Access: Crosville bus route Nos D2, D59, D63, D64, D65, D66 and D68 Gobowen–Oswestry. Nearest BR station: Gobowen (2½ miles)
OS Ref: SJ 294297

Details from: Mr J. L. D. Price, 9 Liverpool Road West, Oswestry, Shropshire SY1 1NZ

The Society aims to be a major participant in the restoration of the Oswestry station building from its present dilapidated state. The building, an imposing Victorian structure, was the administrative headquarters of the Cambrian Railways until the Grouping, and a divisional HQ for GWR and BR after that. The Society is negotiating for the purchase of the depot area to enable trains to be operated in the sidings at Oswestry.
The site is open every Sunday from March to October from 11 am to 5 pm. Occasional steaming days are held.

Stock
[3]GWR 4-6-0 No. 7822 *Foxcote Manor* built 1950
Hunslet 0-6-0ST *Norma* 3770 built 1952
Peckett 0-4-0ST *Adam* 1430 built 1916
Peckett 0-4-0ST No. 6 *Oliver Veltom* 2131 built 1951
[1]Beyer Peacock 0-4-0ST 1827 built 1879
Barclay 0-6-0ST No. 8 885 built 1900
Hunslet 0-6-0DM No. 3 3526 built 1947
Hudswell Clarke 0-4-0DM No. 1 D843 built 1954
[2]Hibberd 4WDM No. 322 3541 built 1952
GWR auto-trailer coach No. 163 built 1928
Burmah-Castrol oil tank wagons Nos 101 and 115 built 1932 and 1942
Port of Sunderland Authority 3-plank open wagon
LMS 20-ton goods brake van

[1]Ex-Beyer Peacock and Co Ltd, Gorton Foundry, Manchester, 1966.
[2]Ex-Fletcher and Stewart Ltd, Masson Works, Derby, 1973.
[3]Owned by the Foxcote Manor Society (*q.v.*).

Foxcote Manor Society

Details from: Ian Travers, 5 Marlow Avenue, Upton-by-Chester CH2 1NQ.

362 Echills Wood Railway A

A 7¼in gauge passenger-carrying railway on the National Agricultural Centre, Stoneleigh, Warwickshire

OS Ref: SP 3372

The NAC is the headquarters of the Royal Agricultural Society of England and the permanent home of the Royal Show. Through the Royal Show and various competitions associated with it, the RASE played a leading role in the development of steam power during the last century. The first public showing of the Decauville portable railway system took place at the 1877 show and in 1881 Sir Arthur Heywood gave the first public demonstration of his 15in gauge line at Duffield Bank at the request of the RASE, coinciding with the Royal Show which was held in Derby that year. The Echills Wood Railway perpetuates the Heywood tradition, having from its inception been laid out as a minimum gauge, high density railway in its own right with no pretensions whatsoever of being a model of anything that had gone before.
The line is operated by a group of local enthusiasts. Construction started in 1975 and although the track plan reached its final form by 1978, development has continued to bring the whole railway up to the standards demanded by its creators. The line comprises a single-track main line running from Harvesters station to a continuous circuit laid in Echills Wood itself, making possible both out-and-back or continuous running as desired. The circuit is approximately 830ft, an out-and-back run using most of the circuit as a return loop is just over 2000ft. Harvesters station has two platforms, arrival and departure functions being separate, a turntable, locomotive servicing bay and purpose-built station buildings and furniture. At the approach to Echills Wood is a level crossing over the perimeter road, claimed to be the busiest steam-worked level crossing in the world on the basis of 38 crossings/hr during the 1981 Royal Show. The line is operated by magnetic train staff and colour-light signals, the crossing being protected by correct road signals operated from track circuits.
The railway operates public services during the Royal Show (early July), the Town & Country Festival (late Summer Bank Holiday) and certain other events on the showground. At other times access to the site is restricted as it is on private property but visitors can be accommodated by prior arrangement. Locomotives and other stock are usually removed from site between major events.

Publicity Officer: Mr K. Blackham, 'Blaken Knob', Fosse Way, Harbury, Leamington Spa, Warwickshire.

Stock

As locomotives are the personal property of individual members, the roster on any given day will vary. Representatives of the following 7¼in gauge designs are usually present on running days:
Marsh 4-4-0 based on Beira Rly Falcon design
Marsh 0-4-0ST based on Hunslet quarry design
Marsh 0-4-0 tank 'Romulus' design (freelance)
Marsh 0-4-2T 'Tinkerbell' design
Passenger stock consists of nine bogie wagons designed and built by the EWR.

363 Trentham Gardens Miniature Railway B

2ft gauge passenger-carrying railway

Trentham Gardens, a few miles south of Stoke-on-Trent and formerly owned by the Dukes of Sutherland, have long been a favourite resort of the inhabitants of the Potteries. They are administered by a limited company, of which the present Duke is chairman.
A 2ft gauge line was added to the attractions in 1935. Built under the supervision of the engineer to the Stafford Coal and Iron Co Ltd, it runs for about a mile through woodland scenery alongside the lake. The station and engine shed are situated in the children's playground on the west side of the lake. The passenger service begins daily at 2 pm, a four-coach train being normally run. On Sundays and Bank Holidays two six-coach trains depart at seven-minute intervals, if required.
OS Ref: SJ 864406

Stock

Baguley 0-4-0PM *Brora* 1797 built 1930
Baguley 0-4-0DM *Golspie* 2085 built 1934
Baguley 0-6-0DM *Dunrobin* 3014 built 1938
Twelve open 'Toastrack' 12-seat coaches

All locomotives have steam outline.

364 Alton Towers Railway B

In the grounds of Alton Towers, long noted for their beauty, runs a 2ft gauge passenger-carrying line, some 750 yards long

Alton Towers, near Leek, Staffordshire
Tel: Oakamoor 702449
OS Ref: SK 075437

Operates from Easter to mid-October from 9.30 am to dusk.
Alton Towers is a ruined early 19th-century mansion, former home of Charles, Earl of Shrewsbury, set in beautiful grounds. Numerous lakes and fountains are to be found, the foremost being the Chinese Pagoda fountain. Facilities for visitors include car parking, cable cars, boating lake, refreshments, amusement park, planetarium and pottery studio. A large touring caravan park is available.

Stock

Baguley 0-4-0DM *Altonia* 1769 built 1929 (steam outline)
Six 4-wheel open coaches
Also on view is a 15in gauge steam locomotive on static display
[1]Barnes 4-4-2 *John* 103 built 1924

[1]Ex-Marine Lake Miniature Railway, Rhyl.

365 Telford Horsehay Steam Trust A

Standard gauge passenger-carrying line ½-mile long from Horsehay to Heath Hill tunnel

The Old Loco Shed, Horsehay, Telford, Shropshire TF4 2LT
Access: 1 mile from Dawley on Dawley to Horsehay Road
Tel: Telford 503880
OS Ref: SJ 675073

The centre is open to visitors on Saturdays from 10 am to 5 pm and on Tuesday and Thursday evenings from 7 pm to 10 pm. Parties may be accommodated at other times by arrangement with the secretary.
Steam trains operate on one weekend each month.
The Trust was formed in 1976 with the purpose of restoring, and eventually running, steam locomotives and rolling stock that had local connections with the East Shropshire Branch lines.
Acting Secretary: 173 Sundorne Road, Shrewsbury, Shropshire.

The Loco Shed was originally part of the Horsehay Company railway system (now Adamson Butterley Limited) who made the plates for the SS *Great Britain*, and also were responsible for the manufacture of many railway bridges within the UK. The location of the Trust is ideally suited to blend in with several other recreational amenities within the Telford New Town Boundaries. At the Lightmoor end of the line, 'park and ride' operations are planned to link the railway with the Ironbridge Gorge Museum Trust, a nationally famous museum complex, again interlinked with 'park and ride' facilities.
The potential for the Steam Trust is enormous and it is envisaged that with the acquisition of further locomotives and rolling stock, and the completion of purchase of the line from Horsehay to Lightmoor, steam hauled passenger services will become an integral part of the recreational facilities of the New Town, providing visitors and residents alike the opportunity for relaxation and education in an area now famous as the 'Birthplace of Industry'. Further details of the Trust are obtainable from the Secretary, or details of membership, which is open to anyone over 16 years of age, from the Membership

Secretary at the Old Loco Shed, Horsehay, Telford, Shropshire.

Stock

[1]GWR 0-6-2T No. 5619 (Class 56XX) built 1925
Peckett 0-4-0ST No. 3 (W7 Class) 1990 built 1940
Ruston Hornsby 0-4-0WDM No. D2959 382824 built 1955
Barclay 0-6-0ST *Peter* 782 built 1896
Sentinel 4WVBTG *F. T. Clamp* 9535 built 1952
North British 0-4-0DH *Tom* 27414 built 1954
GWR Auto-Trailer Coach No. 38 built 1902
Two NCB brake vans
LMS 6-wheel scenery van
Four MOD flat wagons
SR five-plank wagon
Wickham 4WPMR No. TR36 6885 built 1954
BR Mk.1 lounge corridor 1st class coach No. SC14901
Telford Town Tramway Loco (2ft gauge) built 1962

[1]Withdrawn from service as BR No. 5619 and sold for scrap to Woodham Brothers, Barry. Purchased for preservation and moved to its present location in 1973.

366 Bromyard and Linton Light Railway C

A 2ft gauge line constructed along the track-bed of the former GWR Worcester–Bromyard branch, half-a-mile long, to be extended to one mile

Bromyard GWR station site, Herefordshire
OS Ref: SO 657548

Details from: R. F. Walland, 42 West Malvern Road, Malvern, Worcs.

Stock

Peckett 0-6-0ST *Mesozoic* 1327 built 1913
Ruston Hornsby 4WDM (16/20 Class) 213848 built 1942
Ruston Hornsby 4WDM (30DL Class) 246793 built 1947
Ruston Hornsby 4WDM 229656 built 1944
Ruston Hornsby 4WDM No. 6 *Princess* (20DL Class) 229655 built 1944
Ruston Hornsby 4WDM 437367 built 1959
Ruston Hornsby 4WDM No. 3 *Nell Gwynne* (20DL Class) 229648 built 1944
Ruston Hornsby 4WDM No. L10 (25/30HP Class) 198241 built 1939
Ruston Hornsby 4WDM (16/20 Class) 187101 built 1937
Ruston Hornsby 4WDM 195849 built 1939
Motor Rail 4WDM 102G038 built 1972
Motor Rail 4WDM No. 7 20082 built 1953
Motor Rail 4WDM 9676 built 1952
Motor Rail 4WDM 9677 built 1952
Motor Rail 4WDM 9382 built 1948
Baguley 4WDM 3406 built 1953 (2ft 6in gauge)
Wickham 4WPM 3034
Six MOD 4-wheel wagons
Four MOD bogie wagons
MOD crane (2ft 6in gauge)

367 Herefordshire Waterworks Museum B

A 300-yard, 2ft gauge passenger-carrying railway

Broomy Hill Waterworks Museum, Hereford
Tel: Hereford 4101
OS Ref: SO 497394

Leaving a shed/workshop via a curve, in which the inner rail has a radius of only about 7ft, the line crosses a short section which is only laid on running days, being normally removed for the passage of contractor's vehicles, and then enters the meadows rising at about 1 in 30. Steepening to less than 1 in 20 the railway reaches a summit and then falls until the end of the line is reached after about 100 yards.
The Museum is housed in a Victorian pumping station of 1856, near the banks of the River Wye. The first phase of the Museum was opened in April 1975 and contains two steam pumping engines built in 1895 and 1906 which have now been restored to working order.
The rest of the Museum is expected to be ready within the next 2–3 years, when a number of very old pumping engines and other waterworks equipment from Herefordshire will be displayed.
Open on the first Sunday in each month from April to September and also Saturdays in July and August between 1 pm and 5 pm.
Details from: Mr H. R. Penhale, 87 Ledbury Road, Hereford HR1 2TR.

Stock

Lister-Blackstone 4WDM 52886 built 1962
Motor Rail 4WPM 1381 built 1918
Three coaches
Tipper wagons
The Museum itself has two vertical steam engines as well as many small exhibits and displays, including a special section on waterworks railways.

368 Aerospace Museum, Cosford E

60cm gauge diesel locomotive on static display

RAF Cosford, Wolverhampton, West Midlands WV7 3EX
Access: Infrequent bus services from Wolverhampton
Nearest BR station: Cosford (¼ mile). No trains on Sundays
Tel: Albrighton (090722-4872)
OS Ref: SJ 789051

The Museum contains a superb collection of over forty famous and rare aircraft of British, American, German and Japanese origin. The range includes military, civil and research aircraft, a number of which are unique. The

Museum houses the finest display of German wartime rockets and missiles in Europe.
Also shown are aircraft engines, models and aerospace equipment including the Moon Buggy.
The Museum is open from Easter to the end of October on every Saturday, Sunday and Bank Holiday between 10 am and 5 pm. Coach parties during the week by arrangement. Facilities for visitors include car parking, refreshments and toilets.

Stock
Ruston Hornsby 4WDM (48DL Class) 370571 built 1954

Formerly operated on the service railway at RAF Masirah in the Middle East. Flown back to England in February 1977 for restoration for museum display.

369 The Black Country Museum BE

3ft 6in gauge electric tramway in Museum of Regional Heritage

Tipton Road, Dudley, West Midlands DY1 4SQ
Access: On A459 near junction with A4123 Birmingham–Wolverhampton road. Bus route No. 125 Wolverhampton–Dudley–Birmingham. Nearest BR station: Tipton (3/4 mile)
Tel: 021-557 9643
OS Ref: SO 948917

The Museum strives to capture and preserve the special cultural character of the area by means of a careful selection of preserved buildings and equipment to illustrate the traditional crafts and social activities of Black Country Communities.
The Museum is open daily except Saturdays from April to November between 10 am and 5 pm.
The Museum is being built on a triangular site of 26 acres, near Dudley Castle Hill.
This land has been an area of intensive limestone and coal mining activity. Landscaping work is still being undertaken on parts of the site, which will later be incorporated into the Museum.
The first stage, which opened to the public in 1979, will represent a typical Black Country village at the end of the 19th century. Domestic and industrial activity is crowded together on an island site bordered by the Dudley Canal on the far side, and by a canal arm which brought boats to the lime kilns which dominate the site.
The Museum has a planned growth for several years ahead, and gradually the whole area will be covered with items of industrial and social interest, until the site has become a complete representation of local life and achievement – waterways, tramways, road, coal and clay pits, furnaces and forges interlaced with the homes, pubs, and places of worship to provide a complete insight into the life of the region. This will not be a static museum – wherever possible, homes will be furnished, fires will burn and craftsmen will demonstrate the trades practised by their forefathers. Throughout the year, various events will take place, to stimulate interest in particular aspects of the Museum's work, and involve visitors in the history of the Black Country.
Running within the Museum is a 3ft 6in gauge electric tramway, 1/3 mile in length, which carries visitors the length of the site. This is the only rebuilt electric tramway of this gauge in the country.

Stock
Dudley, Stourbridge & District 4WE tramcar No. 5 built 1920
Dudley, Stourbridge and District tramcar No. 75 built 1919
Birmingham Central Tramways cable car built 1888
Wolverhampton 4-wheel double-deck car No. 23 built 1892
Wolverhampton 4-wheel double-deck car No. 49 built 1909

Details of the Black Country Museum Transport Group can be obtained from: Dr E. R. Clarke, 122 Coniston Road, Wolverhampton.

370 Ironbridge Gorge Museum E

Standard gauge steam locomotive and rolling stock on static display

Ironbridge Gorge Museum Trust Ltd, Blists Hill Industrial Museum, Ironbridge, Telford, Shropshire TF8 7AW
Access: Ironbridge stands on the River Severn in Telford, Shropshire, south of the A5, west of the A442, thirty minutes from the M6. Visitors should follow signposts leading to Telford.
Nearest BR stations Wellington and Shifnal. Buses thence to Ironbridge.
OS Ref: SJ 694033

Facilities for visitors include car parking, museum shop, refreshments and toilets.
The Ironbridge Gorge was the scene of the remarkable breakthrough which led Britain to become the first industrial nation and the workshop of the world. The area still retains much of the atmosphere of those momentous times.
Here, the ironmaster Abraham Darby first smelted iron, using coke as fuel. This paved the way for the first iron rails, iron bridge, iron boat, iron aqueduct and iron-framed building. In tribute to these achievements the Ironbridge Gorge Museum is being created around a unique series of industrial monuments spread over three miles of the Severn Valley.
At Blists Hill Open Air Museum stand steam engines and pitheads, with examples of clay-working, iron-making and early transport methods, all on a 42-acre woodland site.

Ironbridge lies in the heart of England, an hour's drive from Birmingham, two from Manchester and three from London.
On sale at our three main locations are a wide variety of museum publications and products. At Blists Hill you may also visit a working pottery.
The Museum Site is open daily from 10 am to 6 pm April to October inclusive, 10 am to 5 pm November to March inclusive. Closed Christmas Day.
For further information on the Museum and its activities contact: The Ironbridge Gorge Museum Trust, Ironbridge, Telford, Shropshire TF8 7AW.
Tel: Ironbridge (095-245) 3522 (weekdays); Ironbridge (095-245) 3418 (weekends).

Stock
[1]LNWR 0-8-0 No. 9395 (BR No. 49395) built 1921
Motor Rail 4WPM 6031 built 1936 (2ft gauge)
MR goods brake van (ex-Cannock Wood Colliery)
Five mineral wagons painted in various private owners liveries

[1]On loan from the National Collection.

371 Coalbrookdale Works Museum E

Standard gauge steam locomotives on static display

Ironbridge Gorge Museum Trust Ltd, Coalbrookdale, Shropshire
Access: Ironbridge stands on the River Severn in Telford, Shropshire, south of the A5, west of the A442, thirty minutes from the M6. Visitors should follow signposts leading to Telford
OS Ref: SJ 668044

Here, in 1709 the Quaker ironmaster Abraham Darby first smelted iron using coke as a fuel instead of the traditional charcoal. This was a major breakthrough in ironmaking and one of the most significant events in Britain's early progress towards industrialisation. In the succeeding century the Coalbrookdale Company which Darby established was in the forefront of iron technology, producing in the 1720s the first iron steam engine cylinders, in 1767 the first iron rails on which iron wheels ran and in 1779 the world's first iron bridge.
In 1959 the original Darby furnaces, excavated and restored, was opened to the public by its then owners Allied Ironfounders together with a museum of ironfounding.
The furnace and museum are now administered by the Ironbridge Gorge Museum Trust which was set up in 1968 to conserve for all time the unique range of industrial monuments in the Ironbridge Gorge.
Opening times: The Furnace Site and Museum are open daily from 10 am to 6 pm April to October inclusive, 10 am to 5 pm November to March inclusive. Closed Christmas Day.
For further information on the Museum and its activities contact: The Ironbridge Gorge Museum Trust, Ironbridge, Telford, Shropshire TF8 7AW
Tel: Ironbridge (095-245) 3522 (weekdays); Ironbridge (095-245) 3418 (weekends).

Stock
[1]Coalbrookdale 0-4-0ST No. 5 built *c*1865
[2]Coalbrookdale 0-4-0VBTG built 1865
[3]Sentinel 0-4-0VBTG 6155 built 1925

[1]Presented by Bardon Hill Quarries (Ellis and Everard Ltd), Coalville, Leicestershire, 1959.
[2]Rebuilt by Sentinel as their 6185 of 1925 from a Coalbrookdale 0-4-0ST of 1865.
[3]Awaiting removal for restoration. Rebuilt from a Manning Wardle 0-4-0ST.

A supporting organisation for all the Ironbridge Gorge Museum Sites is known as the Friends of Ironbridge Gorge Museum Trust. Details are available from all museum sites and from the address above.

372 Birmingham Museum of Science and Industry E

Steam locomotives on static display

Newhall Street, Birmingham B3 1RZ
Access: Nearest BR station: Birmingham New Street (10 minutes' walk). 'Centrebus' from Stephenson Place to Newhall Street (frequency approx 10 minutes)
Tel: 021-236 1022
OS Ref: SP 064874

Open Monday–Friday 10 am–5 pm; Saturdays 10 am–5.30 pm, Sundays from 2 pm to 5.30 pm.
Closed Good Friday, Christmas Day and Boxing Day.
Admission free.
The Museum also houses a collection of road locomotives, cars, bicycles, steam-engines and other transport items. Live steam events take place periodically.
Facilities for visitors include museum shop, refreshments and toilets. Car parking nearby.

Stock
[1]LMS 4-6-2 No. 46235 *City of Birmingham* (Stanier Class 8P) built 1939
Bagnall 0-4-0ST No. 1 *Leonard* 2087 built 1918 (2ft gauge)
Kerr Stuart 0-4-0ST No. 56 *Lorna Doone* 4250 built 1922 (2ft gauge)
[2]Bellis and Seekings 0-6-0WT *Secundus* built 1874 (2ft 8½in gauge)
Birmingham Corporation 4-wheel electric tramcar No. 395 built 1911 (3ft 6in gauge)

[1]Capable of being moved by external power unit along a short length of track. *City of Birmingham* was built as a streamlined 'Coronation' Class Pacific to Sir William

Stanier's design at Crewe. In 1946, the streamline casing was removed and the class performed well in their unstreamlined form at the head of the heaviest Anglo-Scottish expresses. From 1960, the introduction of diesel locomotives meant the 'Coronation' Pacifics being relegated to parcels and secondary duties. All were withdrawn by the end of 1964 and No. 46235 gained a well-earned retirement in the city whose name it carries.
[2]Ex-Pike Brothers, Fayle and Co Ltd, Furzebrook, Dorset. Purchased and presented by Abelson and Co (Engineers) Ltd and the Birmingham Locomotive Club in 1955.

373 The Bass Museum E

Standard gauge static locomotive and carriage exhibits

Horninglow Street, Burton-upon-Trent, Staffordshire
OS Ref: SK 248234

Details from: The Bass Museum, c/o Bass Production, High Street, Burton-upon-Trent, Staffs. Tel: 0283 42031 (office hours) 0283 45707 (all other times).
Opening times: Weekdays 10.30 am to 4.30 pm. Saturday, Sunday and Bank Holidays 11 am to 5 pm.
Refreshments: Snacks and light meals always available, party lunches by arrangement.
Shop: Reprints of early accounts of the brewery and its railway system; general industrial archaeological literature; brewery advertising material.
The Museum is situated at the entrance to Bass's Brewery and is housed in what was formerly the company's joiners shop and its surrounding buildings.
Bass's fleet of 11 locomotives once operated over 26 miles of track and much emphasis is given in the exhibition to Burton's Victorian railway boom.
On display is Bass No. 9 – an 0-4-0 saddle tank locomotive built in Glasgow in 1901 – and the directors coach built in 1889 by the Ashby Railway Carriage and Iron Co Ltd, Manchester.
A recent addition is a Worthington petrol engined shunting engine of 1926. A new exhibition at the Museum traces the development of brewery transport and includes a major exhibition on the railway system including an audio-visual presentation and many photographs of early Bass and Worthington locomotives at work.
Also on display are a Robey horizontal compound engine and a late 19th-century experimental brewery.

Stock
Neilson Reid 0-4-0ST No. 9 5907 built 1901
Kent Construction Co 4WDM No. 20 built 1926
Burton Brewery Rly 4-wheel saloon coach built 1889

374 Winchcombe Railway Museum E

The Winchcombe Railway Museum specialises not in locomotives and rolling stock but in other delights, such as signalling equipment, lineside fixtures, horse-drawn road vehicles, tickets and all kinds of paperwork, lamps and even a couple of railway gas meters! There are indoor and outdoor displays in pleasant garden surroundings

23 Gloucester Street, Winchcombe, Gloucestershire
Operated by Mr T. R. Petchey
Access: On the A46, near the church
Tel: Winchcombe 602257
OS Ref: SP 023283

Opening dates: Easter, Spring and Summer Bank Holidays, Sunday and Monday; Sundays in June, July and August. Daily during the first week in August. Open 2.30 pm until 6 pm.
A replica of a small booking office has been built in one corner of the Museum complete with ticket racks and ticket dating machines. The booking office also contains such domestic items as a GWR slow combustion stove, LMS kettle and GNR fender. Also in this department is the Museum's collection of tickets and other paperwork which may be inspected on application to the curator.

Stock
MR horse dray

375 LCP Holdings Ltd E

Standard gauge locomotives on static display on Industrial Trading Estate

Stock
Manning Wardle 0-6-0ST *Winston Churchill* 2025 built 1923
Ruston Hornsby 4WDM 215755 built 1942

376 Stafford G

2ft gauge steam locomotive not at present on static display, but removed for restoration

Victoria Gardens (outside Stafford BR Station)
OS Ref: SJ 919229

Stock
Bagnall 0-4-0ST *Isabel* 1491 built 1898

Presented by English Electric Co Ltd, for display, 1963.

377 Birmingham City Council E

Standard gauge steam locomotive on static display

Hindlow Close Playground, Duddeston, Birmingham
Access: BR Duddeston Station
OS Ref: SP 087877

Stock
Manning Wardle 0-6-0ST *Abernant* 2015 built 1921
Ex-Austin Motor Co Ltd, Longbridge, Birmingham, 1964.

378 Redditch Steam Locomotive Preservation Society F

Standard gauge railway preservation group with rolling stock on static display

Dixon's Siding, Redditch, Worcs.
OS Ref: SP 039682

Stock
Fowler 0-4-0DM 4100013 built 1948
Box van

379 Lichfield District Council E

Standard gauge locomotive on static display

Beacon Park, Lichfield, Staffordshire
OS Ref: SK 110097

Stock
Hibberd 4WDM 3809 built 1963
Ex-Rom River Reinforcements Co Ltd, Lichfield 1973.

380 Rocester E

Standard gauge steam locomotive on static display in children's playground at Rocester, Staffordshire

OS Ref: SK 108394

Stock
Barclay 0-4-0ST No. 67 *Hong Kong Flyer* 2352 built 1954
Ex-CEGB, Goldington Power Station, Bedford, 1973.
This locomotive is also variously (and just as spuriously) labelled *Eastern Promise* and *Kowloon and Canton Railway*!

381 Warwick District Council E

Standard gauge steam locomotive on static display

Newbold Comyn Park, Leamington, Warwickshire
OS Ref: SP 333657

Stock
Bagnall 0-6-0ST No. 75170 2758 built 1944

382 Branston UDC E

Standard gauge diesel locomotive on static display

Branston Playing Fields, near Burton-on-Trent, Staffs
OS Ref: SK 218227

Stock
Hunslet 0-4-0DM No. 4 5389 *The Branston Belle* built 1960

383 Dudley Zoo Miniature Railway A

A passenger-carrying 15in gauge line running through the grounds of Dudley Zoo

Dudley, West Midlands
OS Ref: SO 947911

The line was opened in 1938 on the 10¼in gauge and converted to 15in gauge after World War II. For many years, the line's motive power was provided by G & S Light Engineering of Stourbridge with steam locomotives of Trevor Guest's design. These were ultimately sold to various miniature lines, notably the Fairbourne Railway, and the Dudley line was acquired by new owners using new stock.
The railway closed in 1979, but following the change of ownership of the Zoo itself, was reopened in 1981.

Stock
Barnes 4-4-2 *Billie* 104 built 1928
Barnes 4-4-2 *Michael* 105 built 1930
Guest/G&S 0-4-2DM *Clara* built 1961 (steam outline)
Twelve open bogie coaches

384 Courtaulds Ltd G

Standard gauge steam locomotive in store pending display in Museum of British Road Transport, Coventry

Coventry, West Midlands
OS Ref: SP 336808

Stock
Hawthorn Leslie 0-4-0ST *Henry* 2491 built 1901

385 Synthetic Chemicals Ltd I

Industrial steam location featuring occasional steam working

Four Ashes, Staffordshire
OS Ref: SJ 917085

No public access.

Stock
Barclay 0-4-0F 1944 built 1927

386 MODAD, Long Marston I

Industrial steam location featuring occasional steam working

Ministry of Defence Central Engineering Park, Long Marston, Warwickshire
OS Ref: SP 153473

No public access.

Stock
Hunslet 0-6-0ST No. 98 *Royal Engineer* 3798 built 1953
SR Bulleid BSK coach No. 4367 built 1948
SR Bulleid coach
LMS Stanier coach

387 North Warwickshire Railway Society F

2ft gauge line being planned near Nuneaton

Stock
Motor Rail 4WDM 8739
Motor Rail 4WDM 5881 built 1935
Motor Rail 4WDM *Thunderbird II* 9411 built 1948

Details from: Peter Lee, 116 Abbey Street, Nuneaton CV11 5BX.

388 J. and H. B. Jackson Ltd E

Standard gauge industrial locomotive preserved as a static exhibit on a short length of track by the entrance to the yard

Scrap Merchants, Coventry, West Midlands
OS Ref: SP 343804

Stock
Hudswell Clarke 0-4-0DM *Southam* D604 built 1936

389 Birds Commercial Motors Ltd G

Standard gauge steam locomotive in storage pending scrapping

Scrap Merchants, Long Marston, Warwickshire
OS Ref: SP 154458

No public access.

Stock
Barclay 0-4-0F No. 1 1772 built 1922

390 Minsterley, Shropshire G

1ft 11½in gauge steam locomotive in private storage

Mr D. L. Walker, The Firs, Hope Park, Minsterley, Shropshire
OS Ref: SJ 329008

No public admittance.

Stock
Hunslet 0-4-0ST *Dorothea* 763 built 1901

391 Umberslade Light Railway C

Private 2ft gauge light railway

J. Marshall, 38 Spring Lane, Hockley Heath, Warwickshire
OS Ref: SP 152725

Occasional open days are organised. No casual visitors please.

Stock
Marshall 4WVBTG No. 1 *Oddson* built 1970
Hunslet 4WDM No. PWG 5 2207 built 1941

392 Oldberrow Light Railway G

2ft gauge locomotive dumped out of use

A. D. Smith, Oldberrow House, Henley-in-Arden, Warwickshire
OS Ref: SP 121659

No casual visitors please.

Stock
Bagnall 0-4-0ST *Lady Luxborough* 2088 built 1918

Ex-Birmingham Tame and Rea District Drainage Board, Minworth, 1961.

393 Woolhope Light Railway B

1ft 3in gauge portable light railway

P. J. Fortey, The Hornets Nest, Checkley, Mordiford, near Hereford
OS Ref: SO 608378

Stock
Taylor 0-6-0PM No. 202 built *c*1974
4-wheel open coaches

394 Gloucester Railway Carriage and Wagon Company G

Standard gauge vehicle preserved in works

Bristol Road, Gloucester
OS Ref: SO 827175

No public admittance.

Stock
London Transport 'G'-Class third-class motor car No. 4184 built 1923

395 'The Spot Gate' E

Ind Coope Restaurant, Hilderstone, Staffordshire

Stock
Pullman Car No. 75 built 1928
Pullman Car *Ursula* built 1928

Vehicles in use as a 'Pullman steak bar'.

396 Drayton Manor Park Miniature Railway B

A 10¼in gauge line comprising almost a mile of track running round the main lake in this well-appointed inland pleasure resort of 160 acres

Drayton Manor Park, Fazeley, near Tamworth, Staffordshire
Access: Drayton Manor Park is located on the A4091, 1 mile south of the A5/A4091 junction at Fazeley. It is 2½ miles from Tamworth and approximately 10 miles north from Intersection No. 4 near Coleshill on the M6–M1 link motorway and 12 miles N.E. from Spaghetti Junction. Intersection 6. A.A. signposted.
Tel: Tamworth (0827) 68481
OS Ref: SK 197012

Apart from the miniature railway, its attractions include alpine aerial cars, an amusement park, fleets of boats, a sternwheeler paddle boat seating 36 and a well-known zoo. The railway was opened to traffic in 1950.
The park is open daily from Easter to October between 10.30 am and 6 pm. The railway operates daily during this period from 2 pm to 6.30 pm.

Stock
Severn Lamb 2-8-0 Bo-Bo PH No. 278 *Drayton Queen* built 1970 (steam outline)
Three open bogie coaches
Three closed bogie coaches

397 Ledbury and District Light Railway C

Private 7¼in gauge passenger-carrying line, ½ mile in length running round the school grounds. Plans exist to extend the line to 1 mile

John Masefield High School, Mabels Furlong, Ledbury, Herefordshire
Tel: Ledbury 2717 or 3677

This little railway was built as a school project, mainly during lunch hours, and opened to traffic in 1977. Trains run from Mabels Furlong to Cuckoo's Nest station and beyond to a turning circle under construction at Orchard. Operation takes place on every schoolday throughout the year, but visitors can be accommodated by invitation only.

Stock
Freelance 4WPM *Primus* built 1979
Freelance 4WBE *Triumph* built 1980
Petrol-Electric 'Autorail' built 1981
Two four-seat bogie coaches
4-wheel brake van
4-wheel open wagon
Bogie wagon
A steam 4-4-0 is under construction

This is the only miniature railway built by a state school in the country. Many prototype features such as signalling and telephone circuits between stations are featured.

398 Hunt Bros (Oldbury) Ltd G

15in gauge locomotives and rolling stock from the former Sutton Park Miniature Railway stored in factory

West Bromwich Lane, Oldbury, Warley, West Midlands
OS Ref: SO 9889

Not available for inspection. No public admittance

Stock
Cannon 4-4-2 No. 1 *Sutton Belle* built 1933, rebuilt 1953
Cannon 4-4-2 No. 2 *Sutton Flyer* built 1939
Bassett Lowke 4-4-2 No. 3 *Prince of Wales* 11 built 1908
Guest Bo-BoPMR (GWR diesel railcar design) built 1936

399 West Midland Safari and Leisure Park B

Passenger-carrying 15in gauge railway

Spring Grove, Bewdley, Worcs
Access:On A456 Kidderminster to Bewdley road
Nearest railway stations: Kidderminster (BR) or Bewdley (SVR)
Tel: 0299-402114
OS Ref: SO 805755

In 200 acres of beautiful parkland, animals of three continents roam almost unhindered in surroundings often close to those of their natural habitat. Study them, photograph them or simply enjoy their natural grace and beauty.
A tour of the game reserves is only the beginning of your day out.
When you leave the Safari Park why not enjoy a picnic or barbecue in one of the shady picnic areas before moving on to the Animal Nursery/Pets' Corner and the breathtaking Sea Lion Show. The youngsters won't want to miss the Amusement Park, one of the biggest and most diverse in the country.
There really is something for everyone at the West Midlands Safari and Leisure Park. And it's all in for one price. Open daily from mid-March to early November.

Stock
Severn Lamb 2-8-0DH No. 278 15-2-79 built 1979 (steam outline)
Four covered toastrack bogie coaches

The line was built in 1979 to provide an additional recreational attraction to the many others offered at the park. The railway takes visitors from the car parks to the main amusements area.

400 Chatterley Whitfield Mining Museum C

Standard gauge steam locomotives on static display

Tunstall, Staffs

Stock

NSR 0-6-0ST No. 2 built 1922
R Heath 0-4-0ST No. 6 built 1896

AREA I

East Midlands

Leicestershire
Derbyshire
Nottinghamshire
Northamptonshire
(Group Nos 401–450)

401 Cadeby Light Railway A

2ft gauge passenger-carrying line

Access: On the A447, one mile south of Market Bosworth. Bus routes Nos 687, 697 and 731 from Hinckley and Market Bosworth. Infrequent service. Nearest BR station: Hinckley (5 miles)
OS Ref: SK 426024

Details from: The Rev E. R. Boston, Cadeby Rectory, Cadeby, Hinckley, Leicestershire

The railway is in operation on the second Sunday of each month from April to November and an advertised timetable is operated, though of necessity trains run with a wide recovery margin.

The Cadeby Light Railway is probably the smallest steam-worked narrow gauge railway in the world. The line exists because of people who are fascinated by steam locomotives and the complications of a railway system and who thoroughly enjoy themselves working out the problems involved. Largely, it is the brainchild of the well-known steam enthusiast and Rector of Cadeby, the Rev 'Teddy' Boston, who bought *Pixie* from Cranford Ironstone Quarry, Northants, in 1962 and laid about 400 yards of 2ft gauge track round the perimeter of the Rectory garden on which to run her.

The railway has stations at each end of the line known as Sutton Lane and Cadeby respectively. At a point about half-way along the route, where the line runs in the trees parallel to the main A447, is Hinckley Road Halt. At Cadeby there are sidings leading to the motive power sheds and to the road transfer dock near the church.

The motive power is predominantly steam, though both petrol and diesel locomotives are used on works trains and the winter services.

A collection box is available to cover fuel costs and for local church restoration. At the Cadeby end of the line there is a small steam roller and a 1927 Foster traction engine. There is also a 4mm scale model Great Western Railway layout measuring 20ft by 40ft with about 50 representative locomotives.

Interested persons are welcome at any time, but are advised to telephone Market Bosworth 290462 before 9 am any morning to ascertain whether the line is open.

Stock
[1]Bagnall 0-4-0ST No. 1 *Pixie* 2090 built 1919
[2]Hunslet 0-4-0ST *Margaret* 605 built 1894
Orenstein & Koppel 0-4-0WT No. 2 7529 built 1914
Orenstein & Koppel 4WPM 4588 built 1932
[3]Baguley 0-4-0PM 1695 built 1928
Lister 4WPM *New Star* 4088 built 1931
Motor Rail 4WDM 4572 built 1929
Ruston Hornsby 4WDM 179870 built 1936
Motor Rail 4WDM No. 20 8748 built 1942
Motor Rail 4WDM No. 42 7710 built 1939
Motor Rail 4WDM 3874 built 1929
Motor Rail 4WDM No. 24 5853 built 1934
Hudswell Clarke 4WDM D558 built 1930
Penrhyn Quarries coach 'O'
Two wooden-sided wagons
Four Fullersite wagons
Two flat trucks
Three open trucks
Platelayers trolley

Standard gauge static exhibit:
Peckett 0-4-0ST *Herbert* 2012 built 1942

[1]Ex-Staveley Minerals Ltd, Cranford Quarries, Northants, 1962.
[2]Ex-Penrhyn Quarries Ltd, Bethesda, Caernarfonshire, 1968. (In store).
[3]Ex-Lilleshall Abbey and Woodland Railway, Shropshire, 1967 (steam outline).

402 Market Bosworth Light Railway A

Passenger-carrying standard gauge steam railway, 2¾ miles in length, running from Shackerstone to Market Bosworth

Shackerstone Station, near Market Bosworth, Leicestershire
Access: Turn right at Twycross on the A444 Nuneaton–Burton road, then take unclassified road through Congerstone. B585 to Market Bosworth from A444 or A447. Gibson Bros buses from Leicester Bowling Green Street
Tel: Atherstone 3966
OS Ref: SK 379066

The railway operates on Sundays and Bank Holidays from Easter to November.

Facilities for visitors include car parking, museum, shop, refreshments and toilets.

The line runs alongside the Ashby Canal through rural shires countryside. The southernmost station, still to be rail-connected, is Shenton, which lies in the middle of the Battlefield of Bosworth now being developed by the County Council as a tourist centre. The line is intended to connect the Battlefield with the Museum at Shackerstone.

Stock

[1]Borrows 0-4-0WT *The King* 48 built 1906
Hunslet 0-4-0ST *NCB No. 11* 1493 built 1925
[5]Bagnall 0-6-0ST *Lamport No. 3* 2670 built 1942
Bagnall 0-6-0ST No. 2 3059 built 1953
Peckett 0-4-0ST *Dunlop No. 7* (W6 Class) 2130 built 1951
[2]RSH 0-6-0T No. 3 7537 built 1949
[2]RSH 0-6-0T No. 4 7684 built 1951
Bagnall 0-4-0ST 2648 built 1941
BR/Drewry 0-6-0DM DVLR No. 2 (BR No. D2245) 2577 built 1956
RSH 0-6-0DM No. 48 7697 built 1953
Ruston Hornsby 4WDM 393304 built 1956
Ruston Hornsby 4WDM No. 2 *Nancy* (88DS Class) 263001 built 1949
Ruston Hornsby 0-4-0DE 423657 built 1958
Ruston Hornsby 4WVBTG 235513 (48DS Class) built 1945 (rebuilt from 4WDM as self-propelled carriage heater in 1903)
Ruston Hornsby 0-6-0DM *The 1211 Squadron* 347747 built 1957
BR Mk.1 griddle car No. SC1104 built 1952
BR Mk.1 BCK coach No. E21031 built 1954
BR Mk.1 FK coach No. 13125 built 1954
BR/Park Royal observation car No. M50397 built 1957
BR/Park Royal observation car No. M56160 built 1957
BR Mk.1 TSO bogie coach No. E3785 built 1953
SR PMV vehicles Nos S1258 and S1333 built 1938
SR PMV 4-wheel van No. S1563 built 1950
RCT mobile workshop US Army 20570 built 1942
[3]BR 16-ton mineral wagon No. B276232 built 1956
[4]Shell/BP tank wagon No. 5029 built 1938
LMS flat wagon No. M45605 built 1926
LMS brake van No. M732195 built 1946
LMS 13-ton open wagon
Smith 6-ton steam crane No. 21058 built 1953
GWR banana van on LMS underframe
GWR banana van body
21-ton mineral wagon
LNER fruit van No. 186635 built 1938 (body only)
BR 12-ton van No. B759106
Wickham 4WPMR No. 9024 7090 built 1955
Wickham 4WPMR No. 9033 6857 built 1954
SECR Grafton steam crane 1618 built 1917
Jones 4WDM 6-ton shunting crane
Flat wagon (cut down from LMS 13-ton mineral wagon)

[1]Ex-United Glass (England) Ltd, Charlton, London, 1967. Purchased for preservation by the Industrial Locomotive Preservation Group and stored at Robertsbridge, K & ESR, until 1969 when it was resold to the Shackerstone Railway Society.
[2]Ex-CEGB, Nechells Power Station, Birmingham, 1972.
[3]Presented by Cravens of Sheffield.
[4]Donated by Shell-Mex BP.
[5]Ex-Staveley Minerals Ltd, Lamport, Northants 1969. Housed at Loughborough Great Central Railway until 1979.

The Supporters' Association for the Market Bosworth Light Railway is the Shackerstone Railway Society.

403 Great Central Railway A

Passenger-carrying standard gauge steam railway, 5½ miles in length running from Loughborough Central to Rothley Station

Loughborough Central Station, Great Central Road, Loughborough, Leicestershire LE11 1RW
Access: Bus routes Nos 625 and 626 from St Margarets bus station, Leicester to Leicester Road, Loughborough. Bus route No. 624 to Quorn & Woodhouse station
Tel: Loughborough 216433 or 30726
OS Ref: SK 543194

The railway operates at weekends and Bank Holidays throughout the year. Also Wednesdays in June, July and August. Facilities for visitors include car parking, museum, souvenir shop, refreshments and toilets.

Stock

[1]LMS 4-6-0 No. 5231 *3rd Volunteer Battalion, The Worcestershire and Sherwood Foresters Regiment* (Stanier Class 5MT) Armstrong Whitworth 1286 built 1936
[2]SR 4-6-2 No. 34039 *Boscastle* (Bulleid Rebuilt WC Class) built 1946
[3]GWR 4-6-0 No. 6990 *Witherslack Hall* (Hawksworth 6959 Class) built 1948
[4]LNER 4-6-0 No. 1264 (Thompson Class B1) built 1947
LNER 4-6-0 No. 1306 *Mayflower* (Thompson Class B1) built 1948
[9]LNER 0-6-2T No. 4744 (Gresley Class N2) NB Locomotive 22600 built 1921
GWR 2-8-0T No. 5224 (5205 Class) built 1924
BR 2-10-0 No. 92212 (Riddles Class 9F) built 1959
[10]BR 4-6-2 No. 71000 *Duke of Gloucester* (Riddles Class 8P) built 1954
[5]GCR 4-4-0 No. 506 *Butler Henderson* (Robinson Class 11F) built 1919
Hunslet 0-6-0ST No. 1 3887 built 1964
Hunslet 0-6-0ST No. 9 3825 built 1954
[11]RSH 0-6-0T No. 7597 built 1949
Hunslet 0-6-0ST *Robert Nelson No. 4* 1800 built 1936
[7]NER 0-4-0T No. 68088 (LNER Class Y7) built 1923
[8]Hawthorn Leslie 0-4-0ST *Marston No. 3* 3581 built 1924
Peckett 0-4-0ST *Hilda* 1963 built 1938
BR 1-Co-Co-1DE No. 40.106 *Atlantic Conveyor* (Class 40) English Electric 2726 built 1960
BR 0-6-0DH No. D9516 (Class 14) built 1964
BR 0-6-0DH No. D9523 (Class 14) built 1964
Ruston Hornsby 4WDM *Qwag* 371971 built 1954
BR 0-6-0DE No. D4067 (Class 10) built 1961
Hill 4WDH No. 11 *Alen Grice* 134C built 1964
Wickham 4WPM rail inspection trolley 693 built 1932
Fowler 0-4-0DM No. D4279 *Arthur Wright* 4210079 built 1952

GCR 'Barnum' open end third-class coach No. 5664 built 1910
BR Mk.1 FO coach No. M3042 built 1953
BR Mk.1 CK coaches Nos W15096 and W15611 built 1953 and 1955
BR CK coach No. E15296 built Craven 1952
BR CK coach No. E15514 built Metro-Cammell 1954
BR SK coach No. Sc24656 built BC & W Co 1953
BR Mk.1 TSO coach No. S4914 built 1961
BR Mk.1 BSK coaches Nos M34393 and E34738 built 1954 and 1955
BR Mk.1 suburban coach No. E46139 built 1954
LNER Post Office tender 70268 built 1931
LNER Post Office sorter 70294 built 1937
LNER composite coach 1st/3rd 18033 built 1924
LNER Gresley buffet car No. 1852 built 1938
LNER buffet car 9122 built 1937
LNER brake/3rd 62565 built 1927
LNER fullbrake (pigeon) 70427 built 1941
LNER Gresley buffet car No. 9124 built 1937
LNER Gresley brake/3rd coach No. 16520 built 1939
LNER non-gangwayed 6-wheel full brake No. 70654 built 1951
BR dmu buffet car No. M59276 built 1958
BR 2-car dmu set (Class 127) comprising motor coaches Nos M51616 and M51622 built 1959
BR Mk.1 RMB coach No. 1852 built 1960
BR Mk.1 RKB coach No. 1525 built 1961
BR Mk.1 TSO coach No. 4630 built 1957
BR Mk.1 griddle car No. SC1102 built 1961
BR Mk.1 SLO coach No. E48001 built 1955
BR Mk.1 CL coach No. E43043 built 1955
BR Mk.1 FO coach No. E3126 built 1963
BR 12-wheeled sleeping car No. DB975183
BR Mk.1 BSO coach No. E9316 built 1956 (invalid coach)
BR Mk.1 SK coach No. E25312 built 1957
BR Mk.1 TSO coach No. E4662 built 1957
[12]GCR 'Barnum' 2nd class saloon coach No. 666 built 1910
LMS 20-ton goods brake van No. 2 built 1924
Esso tank wagon (LMS No. 162740) built 1941
Rail-carrying flat wagon converted from NSB Konductorvogn No. 547 built 1912
SR 'Walrus' ballast hopper wagon No. DS62067 built 1947
[6]BR 'Catfish' ballast hopper wagon No. DB983393 built 1956
Shell/BP tank wagon (LMS No. 164253) in 'Vickers Oils' livery built 1943
Three NCB wooden coal wagons
[6]LMS 12-ton open wagon No. DM742591
BR train heating and generator van No. TDE 321099
[11]Two BR CCT vans
BR 'Dolphin' rail wagon No. DE 470809
GWR Ransomes & Rapier 45-ton steam crane No. RS 1097 built 1939 plus runner wagons
NLR coach body built *c*1870

[1]LMS Stanier *Black Five* withdrawn from Carnforth shed in 1968 as BR No. 45231 and kept at Steamtown, Carnforth, following preservation until moved to Loughborough in 1973.

[2]Withdrawn from service as BR No. 34039 in 1965 and sold to Woodham Brothers, Barry, for scrap. Purchased for preservation and moved to Loughborough in 1973.

[3]Withdrawn from service in November 1965 and sold to Woodham Brothers, Barry, for scrap. Purchased for preservation by the Witherslack Hall Society and moved to Loughborough in 1975.

[4]Withdrawn from service as BR Eastern Region Departmental Locomotive No. 29 in November 1965 and sold to Woodham Brothers of Barry for scrap. Purchased for preservation by the Thompson B1 Locomotive Society in 1975.

[5]Robinson 'Director' Class locomotive withdrawn from Sheffield (Darnall) as BR No. 62660 in 1960. This fine locomotive is the sole survivor of the GCR passenger classes and was housed in Clapham Museum until its closure in 1973. On loan from the National Collection.

[7]Formerly BR No. 68088. Withdrawn as Departmental Locomotive No. 34 in 1952. Sold to NCB and purchased for preservation in 1964. Twenty-two of these locomotives were built, many being sold for further work after withdrawal. No. 985 worked at Tyne Dock until June 1948, after which it was sent to Stratford as works shunter.

[8]Ex-Marston, Thompson and Evershed Ltd, Burton-on-Trent, Staffs, 1967. This locomotive was housed on the Foxfield Light Railway until the end of 1972.

[9]Originally GNR No. 1744 and withdrawn from Peterborough shed in 1962 as BR No. 69523. Purchased for preservation in 1963 and moved to the Keighley and Worth Valley Railway in 1965. One hundred and seven of these locomotives were constructed and were principally used on the Kings Cross suburban services. For working in the Metropolitan tunnels, these engines were fitted with condensing gear consisting of large diameter pipes for carrying exhaust steam from the smokebox to the top of the side tanks. Owned by the Gresley Society (*q.v.*).

[10]No. 71000 *Duke of Gloucester* was Britain's last Class 8 'Pacific' locomotive. Built in 1954 at Crewe Works, it hauled express trains on the London Midland Region until 1962, when it was withdrawn for preservation by British Rail, probably because of its unique cylinders and valve gear (the latter being an improvement of the British Caprotti type) which were the most efficient on any simple expansion steam locomotive in history. However, after some considerable time, British Rail changed their mind and decided to scrap the locomotive, but on doing this in 1967, removed one of the outside cylinders, complete with valve gear, and placed it (sectioned) on display in the Science Museum at Kensington. Eventually the locomotive appeared in the scrapyard at Barry, South Wales, minus the other outside cylinder. It remained there until 1973, when it was purchased by members of the present Trust who then took it to Main Line Steam Trust at

Loughborough, Leicestershire. The locomotive is now being restored to its former condition. Owned by the Duke of Gloucester Steam Locomotive Trust Ltd (*q.v.*).
[11]Owned by Railway Vehicle Preservations Ltd (*q.v.*).
[12]On loan from the National Collection.

The Gresley Society

Details from: Mr P. Holmes, Argyll Cottage, Thurgarton Quarters, Oxton Road, Southwell, Notts NG25 0RW

Duke of Gloucester Steam Locomotive Trust Limited (formerly the 71000 Preservation Society) **H**

At present the Trust has approximately 180 members and membership is now available on a two-tier system; full membership at £3 per annum, which gives all privileges and benefits available from the Trust; and associate membership at £1.50 per annum, which is really only intended for those who wish to keep informed of the events within the Trust. Further membership details are available from Mr C. Hazlehurst, 138 Fernhill, Harlow, Essex.

Main Line Steam Trust **H**

The Great Central's supporting educational and charitable organisation is the Main Line Steam Trust. Details of membership may be obtained from: The Membership Secretary, Main Line Steam Trust, PO Box 33, Loughborough, Leics LE11 1SS.

Thompson B1 Locomotive Society

Details from: Mr J. G. Gwnett, 11 Valance End, Dunstable, Bedfordshire LU6 3LR

Railway Vehicle Preservations Ltd

Details from: Mr D. Pearce, 77 Gosling House, Sutton Street, Shadwell, London E1.

404 Dinting Railway Centre D

Standard gauge steam railway centre, featuring short steam-hauled train rides over ¼ mile of track

Dinting Lane, Glossop, Derbyshire
Access: Dinting Lane, off A57 road, 1 mile from Glossop. Dinting BR station. Bus routes Nos 125, 236 and 237 Manchester–Dinting
Tel: Glossop 5596
OS Ref: SK 021946

Dinting Railway Centre is open daily except Christmas and Boxing Days from 10.30 am to 5 pm. Locomotives in steam each Sunday from March to October inclusive. Facilities for visitors include car parking, museum, shop, refreshments, toilets, picnic area and miniature steam railway.

In 1968 the Committee of the Bahamas Locomotive Society began to search for a home for their newly restored locomotive *Bahamas*. Dinting was ideal and with generous assistance from a Society member and encouragement from Glossop Council the site was purchased from British Rail. Since that time a great deal of work has been undertaken to improve the services offered. An Exhibition Hall, capable of housing up to nine main line locomotives has been constructed, a picnic area created, road access, car park facilities, refreshment and shop areas built. There is also an extensive steam operated miniature railway which has been constructed by members of the Buxton Model Engineering Society.

Details from: Mr K. J. Tait, 73 Derby Road, Heaton Mersey, Stockport, Cheshire

Stock
[1]LMS 4-6-0 No. 5596 *Bahamas* (Stanier Class 5XP) built 1935
[9]LNER 4-6-2 No. 532 *Blue Peter* (Peppercorn A2/3 Class) built 1948
[10]LNER 4-6-2 No. 19 *Bittern* (Gresley A4 Class) built 1937
[2]LMS 4-6-0 No. 6115 *Scots Guardsman* (Stanier Class 7P) built 1927
[8]GCR 2-8-0 No. 102 (BR No. 63601) (Robinson 04 Class) built 1911
[4]LNWR 0-6-2T No. 1054 (Webb 'Coal Tank') built 1888
RSH 0-4-0CT *Southwick* 7069 built 1942
RSH 0-6-0ST No. 150 *Warrington* 7136 built 1944
Hudswell Clarke 0-6-0T *Nunlow* 1704 built 1938
Avonside 0-6-0ST 1883 built 1923
Barclay 0-4-0ST *Tiny* 2258 built 1949
[8]BR Bo-BoE No. 26020 Metrovick 1027 built 1951
[5]Beyer Peacock 0-4-0VB tram locomotive 2734 built 1886
Cravens 50-ton steam breakdown crane No. 1015
[6]Baguley (McEwan Pratt) 0-4-0PM *Jacob* 680 built 1916
[7]Avonside/Rolls Royce 0-4-0DH No. RS8 1913 built 1923
LMS medical officer's saloon 45017 built 1923
LNER Thompson brake/3rd corridor coach No. E1866 built 1950
MSCR open wagon No. 6115
SR bogie brake van No. S56287 built 1936
BR brake van No. B950690 built 1950

[1]'Jubilee' Class locomotive built by the North British Locomotive Co Ltd (Works No. 24154). Withdrawn from Stockport shed as BR No. 45596 in August 1966. This locomotive was fitted with a double chimney during the course of its career, apart from which it is identical with No. 5593 at Tyseley and its shed mate No. 5690. Given a complete overhaul by the Hunslet Engine Co Ltd, Leeds, during 1968 and repainted in original LMS maroon, *Bahamas* has since taken part in many 'Return to Steam' rail tours. The locomotive is at present undergoing extensive repairs, for which purposes a special appeal fund has been launched.
[2]Three-cylinder 'Royal Scot' Class locomotive built by the

North British Locomotive Co Ltd (Works No. 23610). Rebuilt with taper boiler at Crewe in 1947 and withdrawn from Carlisle (Kingmoor) as BR No. 46115 in December 1965. *Scots Guardsman* was the last of its class in service and made a number of excursions with enthusiasts' special trains immediately prior to its withdrawal. The locomotive was preserved privately and housed initially on the K & WVR before moving on to Dinting.

[4]On loan from The National Trust, Penrhyn Castle Museum (Group No. 325). Formerly BR No. 58926.

[5]On loan from the National Collection.

[6]On loan from the North of England Open Air Museum (Group No. 155).

[7]Rebuilt from 0-4-0ST in 1957 by ICI Ltd at Tunstead, near Buxton, Derbyshire, from whom the engine was purchased in 1974.

[8]On loan from the National Railway Museum.

[9]Built as BR No. 60532 and withdrawn from Dundee shed in 1966. Purchased for preservation in 1968 and restored in LNER livery in 1969. *Blue Peter* was, in fact, the first new locomotive built at Doncaster Works to bear a number in the BR series. In view of its LNER lineage, its new owners have restored it as No. 532.

[10]Originally LNER No. 4464. Withdrawn from Aberdeen (Ferryhill) shed in 1966 as BR No. 60019 and restored for working special trains.

405 Midland Railway Centre A

Standard gauge steam railway whose operation is based on that of the Midland Railway and its successors. Trains run over 3½ miles of track between Hammersmith and Ironville

Butterley Station, near Ripley, Derbyshire
Access: On A61 road, 1½ miles north of Ripley
Bus routes Nos 243, 244 & 245 from Alfreton to Derby. Frequency approx 20 minutes.
Tel: Ripley 44920
OS Ref: SK 403520

Facilities for visitors include car parking, souvenir shop and refreshments.

The Midland Railway project historically portrays the Midland Railway and early LMS by means of a static museum and a working length of line. This is on part of the ex-Midland line from Ambergate to Pye Bridge, in particular the section from Hammersmith to Pye Bridge, a distance of 3 miles 22 chains. The main museum exhibits and amenities area is incorporated, along with the main station, locomotive workshops, carriage sidings, etc, at Butterley.

At Swanwick Junction, a 65-acre museum site with sidings etc, provides a major public amenity. The main museum building of 42,000 square feet is currently being erected. Also to be provided will be a turntable and other facilities.

The basic operating railway will consist initially of a single track main line with availability to double track throughout. The main station is Swanwick Junction where two short branch lines join the main line, one to the former Swanwick colliery and the other serving Adamson-Butterley Co's works, whose traffic is worked by the Midland Railway Trust.

A full timetable of passenger trains operates on Saturdays and Sundays and Bank Holiday Mondays from Easter to the end of September. Eventually, trains will serve six stations, all built by the Trust.

Stock

[5]S & DJR 2-8-0 No. 13809 *Beaumont* (S & D No. 89) Stephenson 3895 built 1925
BR 4-6-0 No. 73129 (Riddles Class 5MT Caprotti) built 1956
[1]LMS 4-6-2 No. 6203 *Princess Margaret Rose* (Stanier Class 8P) built 1935
[2]MR 2-4-0 No. 158A built 1866
[6]LMS 0-6-0 No. 4027 (Fowler Class 4F) built 1924
LMS 0-6-0T No. 47564 (Fowler Class 3F) Hunslet 1580 built 1928
LMS 0-6-0 No. 47327 (Fowler Class 3F) NB Loco 23406 built 1926
LMS 0-6-0T No. 16440 (BR No. 47357) (Fowler Class 3F) NB Loco 23436 built 1926
LMS 0-6-0T No. 47445 (Fowler Class 3F) Hunslet 1529 built 1927
[4]MR 0-6-0T No. 1708 (Johnson Class 1F) built 1880
LMS 4-6-0 No. 44932 (Stanier Class 5MT) built 1945
BR 2-6-4T No. 80080 (Riddles Class 4MT) built 1954
Hunslet 0-6-0ST No. 68012 3193 built 1944
Markham 0-4-0ST *Gladys* 109 built 1894
Peckett 0-4-0ST *Victory* 1547 built 1919
Nasmyth Wilson 0-4-0ST No. 4 built 1894
Barclay 0-4-0CT *Stanton No. 24* 1875 built 1925
Barclay 0-4-0F No. 2 2008 built 1935
Sentinel 4WVBTG 9370 built 1947
BR 1-Co-Co-1DE No. D4 *Great Gable* built 1959
Motor Rail 4WPM No. 1 1930 built 1919
Ruston Hornsby 0-4-0DE 384139 built 1955
BR 0-6-0DE No. D3014 built English Electric 1952
BR Co-CoDE No. D9015 *Tulyar* (Class 55) English Electric 2920 built 1961
Hudswell Clarke 0-6-0DM D1114 built 1958
Mercury 2W-2DM No. 1311-G 5337 built 1927
LMS 0-6-0DE No. 12077 built 1950
Motor Rail 4WDM No. RS9 2024 built 1921
Motor Rail 4WDM No. RS12 460 built 1917
Fowler 0-4-0DM *Andy* 16038 built 1923
Deutz 4WDM 10249 built 1932 (2ft gauge)
BR compartment bogie coach No. E46097 built 1954
BR brake/second compartment coach No. E43186 built 1954
BR Mk.1 compartment coach No. M46140 built 1954
BR Mk.1 compartment coach No. M46213 built 1954
BR Mk.1 SK coach No. E26025 built 1962

BR Mk.1 SK coach No. E26043 built 1962
BR Mk.1 SK coach No. E26049 built 1962
BR Mk.1 SK coach No. E26157 built 1962
BR Mk.1 TSO coach No. E5045 built 1963
BR Mk.1 BCK coach No. E21256 built 1963
BR Mk.1 BSK coach No. E21232 built 1960
BR Mk.1 SK coach No. M24886 built 1955
LMS vestibule 3rd class coach No. 5861
MR royal saloon coach No. 1910 built 1912
LMS full brake No. 31299 built 1941
L & YR first-class family saloon coach No. 995 built 1911
LMS third-class sleeping car No. M612 built 1952
LMS dynamometer car No. 1 (BR No. M45050) built 1913
MSJ & AR composite coach No. 29663 built 1931
LMS inspection saloon No. DM395222 built 1930
LD & ECR staff van No. DE950249 built 1898
MR bogie composite coach No. DM195955 built 1910
MR six-wheeled passenger brake van No. DM198587 built 1902
MSJ & AR compartment composite coaches Nos 29666 and 29670 (117 & 121) built 1931
MR six-wheeled third/brake coach No. 7243 built 1884
MR clerestory passenger brake van built 1902
MR clerestory brake/composite No. 198829 built 1905
LMS travelling post office No. M30225M built 1939
BR Mk.1 SLO coach No. M48004 built 1955
BR Mk.1 RMB coach No. M1802 built 1957
BR Mk.1 BSO coach No. M9281 built 1955
BR Mk.1 BCK coach No. E21059 built 1954
MR Pullman 1st/2nd composite coach body built 1874
MR Pullman 3rd/baggage coach body built 1874
MR Pullman car body *Midland* built 1874
MR third-class composite brake coach No. DM395525 built 1921
LMS open 3rd coach No. 7991 built 1926
Two MR general user wagons built 1920
MR hand crane and match trucks built 1880
MR six-wheeled brake van built *c*1900
Two LMS box vans built 1939
Two BR bulk grain wagons built 1958–60
Stanton & Staveley 4-plank wagon No. 1485
Stanton & Staveley 5-plank wagon No. 660
Cowans Sheldon 50-ton steam crane No. RS1001 built 1930 plus match wagon No. DS3105
AD flat truck No. 60007 built 1901
Twelve-ton low-sided wagon No. 11 built 1926
LNWR three-ton hand crane built 1897
MR four-wheeled motor car van No. 8272 built 1916
MR six-wheeled ballast brake van No. 291 built 1916
MR 10-ton covered goods van No. WD47135 built 1915
MR 20-ton goods brake van No. 11 built 1921
MR bogie tool van No. DM198715 built 1905
MR 10-ton covered goods van No. WD47872 built 1915
MR 10-ton covered goods van No. WD47961 built 1915
BR four-wheeled horsebox No. M42608 built 1949
NCB square-tank tar wagon No. 72110 built 1913
NCB gas tar tank wagon No. 18712 built 1895
MR 20-ton brake van 1253 built 1921
Private owner bow-ended wagon No. 9655 built Charles Roberts 1881
LMS fish van No. ADM 40252 built 1949
LMS 10-ton stores van
Wickham 4WPMR No. TR19 7505 built 1956
Taylor & Hubbard 10-ton steam crane No. 57 1694 built 1956 plus runner wagon
Private owner round-topped square tank wagon No. 10867 built Charles Roberts 1888
Clay Cross Co 8-ton open wagons Nos 1136 and 1153
Fourteen 8-ton coal wagons ex-NCB built 1900
Hudswell Clarke 0-4-0ST *Handyman* 573 built 1900 (3ft gauge)
Fowler 2-4-0DM No. 2 20685 built 1935 (3ft gauge)

[1]Withdrawn from Carlisle (Upperby) in 1962 as BR No. 46203. Restored to LMS livery at Crewe and placed on display in 1963. The class worked Anglo-Scottish expresses until 1937–8, after which they were favourites on the Liverpool–London trains for a number of years.
[2]This locomotive survived successive renumberings and reboilerings to enjoy an exceptionally long life in service, not being withdrawn until 1947. This is all the more remarkable since the rest of its class became extinct in the 1930s. Originally used on express passenger work, it is almost certain that its declining years would have been spent on station or shed pilot work, with maybe the odd excursion now and then. On withdrawal, the LMS restored it to its pre-1923 condition as No. 158A. On loan from the National Collection.
[4]Withdrawn as BR No. 41708 in 1966. This engine, together with four other members of its class, was retained for shunting duties at Staveley Ironworks under the terms of a 100-year agreement entered into by the Midland Railway in 1866. All five engines were withdrawn immediately the agreement expired and No. 41708, being in the best condition, was purchased for preservation in 1967. A total of 240 of these locomotives were built between 1878 and 1899 and from the design was developed the standard LMS shunting type. Owned by the 1708 Locomotive Preservation Trust Ltd (*q.v.*).
[5]Fowler Class 7F heavy freight design for the Somerset and Dorset Railway. Withdrawn in May 1964 and sent to Woodham Brothers scrapyard, Barry. Purchased for preservation in December 1975.
[6]On loan from the National Collection.

1708 Locomotive Preservation Trust Ltd — H

Details from: G. S. Mimms, 64 Elmwood Crescent, Luton, Bedfordshire.
The Trust also owns the following locomotive, currently on loan to the Swanage Railway.

Hunslet 0-6-0ST *Cunarder* 1690 built 1931
Ex-APCM Ltd, Harbury, Warwickshire, 1969.

Altrincham Electric Railway Preservation Society

Details from: Jonathan Rowse, 26 Ashlands Road, Timperley, Altrincham, Cheshire.

406 Northamptonshire Ironstone Railway Trust Limited BE

Operating museum of Ironstone Railway equipment

Hunsbury Hill Museum and Country Park, Hunsbury Hill Road, Camp Hill, Northampton
Nearest BR station: Northampton
OS Ref: SP 735584

Passenger trains operate on late Spring Bank Holiday Sunday and Monday and on the second and last Sundays in each month until the end of September.
The Trust was formed to put together a museum of ironstone relics in order to preserve something of the county's heritage. The Trust is also committed to the permanent preservation, display and demonstration of steam and other railway locomotives, rolling stock, equipment, machinery and relics of general, historical and educational interest.
Trust members are now engaged in consolidating the work already done at the Hunsbury Hill Industrial Museum, on the outskirts of Northampton, where a railway is being built on the site of former ironstone workings. Several engines have already been acquired, along with rolling stock and equipment. A temporary Museum building exists, pending the acquisition of a larger, permanent structure, and a wide variety of exhibits are to be seen, along with many explanatory diagrams. Visitors are always made most welcome during the hours of opening, from 10 am until 4 pm, every Sunday throughout the year.
The Trust is a voluntary organisation, being a registered charity, and can only continue if the initial interest is maintained at its present level. We are always happy to have new members, whether they join because they wish to join in the work, or simply because they feel the Trust is filling a gap in the preservation and recording of a most important aspect of the Social and Economic history of Northamptonshire.
Details from: The Membership Secretary, 5 Forest Road, Delapre, Northampton NN4 9NZ.

Stock
Manning Wardle 0-4-0ST No. 14 *Brill* 1795 built 1912
Sentinel 4WVBTG *Musketeer* 9365 built 1946
Sentinel 4WVBTG *Belvedere* 9369 built 1946
Hunslet 0-4-0DM No. 16 2087 built 1940
Ruston Hornsby 4WDM *Express* 235511 built 1945
Ruston Hornsby 4WDM 299100 built 1950
Ruston Hornsby 4WDM 386875 built 1955
Hibberd 4WDM 4WDH *Ely* 3967 built 1961
[1]Peckett 0-6-0ST No. 86 1871 built 1934 (metre gauge)
[1]Peckett 0-6-0ST No. 87 2029 built 1942 (metre gauge)
Lister 4WPM 14006 built 1940 (2ft gauge)
Motor Rail 4WDM 9711 built 1952 (2ft gauge)
Motor Rail 4WDM 8969 built 1945 (2ft gauge)
Motor Rail 4WDM 8731 built 1941 (2ft gauge)
Wickham 4WPMR 6887 built 1954 (metre gauge)
Motor Rail 4WDM 8756 built 1941 (2ft gauge)
Two LMS brake vans
Also the station buildings from Yelvertoft and Lilbourne

[1]Ex-Stewarts and Lloyds Minerals Ltd, Wellingborough Quarries, 1967.

407 Papplewick Pumping Station A

Passenger-carrying 7¼in gauge steam railway, 800ft in length

Longdale Lane, Ravenshead, Nottinghamshire NG15 9AJ
Access: 7 miles north of Nottingham. Signposted East opposite the Seven Mile House on the A60
OS Ref: SK 584522

The railway is in operation when the pumping engines are steamed, i.e. Bank Holidays, etc.
The pumping station is open for visitors on Sundays from April to October between 2 pm and 5 pm, though the beam engines are static on these occasions.
Private parties by arrangement.
For further information contact: The Custodian, The Deputy's House, Papplewick Pumping Station, Longdale Lane, Ravenshead, Notts. Tel: Nottingham 632938.
The railway was opened at Easter 1978 and is operated by members of the Chesterfield and District Model Engineering Society.

Stock
CMES 0-4-0WTT *Percy* ('Romulus' type) built 1978
Two open bogie coaches

Papplewick is worthy of a visit in its own right. There is preserved a complete Victorian steam pumping station complete with working beam engines. The elegant pumping station building is set in attractively landscaped grounds with ornamental lakes.

409 Thoresby Hall Miniature Railway A

A 10¼in gauge line, 750 yards long, opened in 1969 and still being developed

Thoresby Park, Ollerton, Newark, Notts
OS Ref: SK 6371

It runs alongside the River Medan and the smaller of two lakes in the park, which is in the centre of Sherwood Forest. A locomotive shed is at one end of the line and a temporary platform is situated at the other, so present operation is 'push-pull'. Further extensions of track are planned for both ends of the route.

Operation is on Sunday afternoons and Bank Holidays from Easter until September.

Stock
LNER 4-6-2 No. 4498 *Sir Nigel Gresley* (A4 Class) built Kirkland 1967
Three articulated bogie coaches

410 Hall Leys Miniature Railway A

A 9½in gauge passenger-carrying line, 220 yards in length, originally opened in 1947

Hall Leys Pleasure Gardens, Matlock, Derbyshire. Operated by L & S Miniature Railway Co Ltd
Tel: Matlock 55976

Facilities for visitors include car parking, refreshments and toilets.
The railway operates from Easter to the end of September (weather permitting).

Stock
Batteson 4-6-2 (LNER Pacific type) built 1948
Allcock/Coleby-Simkins 0-6-0DH built 1975
Two 'sit-astride' bogie coaches
Children's open bogie coach

411 Manor Park Miniature Railway A

A 7¼in gauge passenger-carrying line, 600 yards in length, opened in 1970. The line forms a circuit round a wooded park, crossing a stream in two places

Manor Park, Glossop, Derbyshire
Access: Manor Park is situated on Manor Road, just off the A57 road through Glossop in Derbyshire. Apart from the railway there are games and facilities for all the family together with extensive gardens which are as well kept as any in the region. There are also some of the fattest ducks in Derbyshire which nevertheless make every attempt to eat all the bread fed to them.
By public transport, the Park is a short walk from Glossop railway station and Norfolk Square bus terminus
Tel: 061-430 7092

From Easter to September trains run on Saturday afternoons and Sundays from mid-morning. During school summer holidays trains operate on Wednesday afternoons and other day and evening operation takes place as circumstances require. Special services run on Bank and Public Holidays. From October to Easter, trains run on Sunday mornings when possible. We expect Father Christmas to visit us on Boxing Day. Adults are as welcome to ride on the trains as children and a single flat fare applies to all passengers.
Services are operated on a generally regular pattern; for details of specific days, party bookings or special trains please telephone us at the number given above.

At the start of the 1981 season, a group of model engineers specialising in 7¼in gauge miniature railway operation negotiated a lease of the line with the Local Authority. The Manor Park Miniature Railway Company Limited was formed with the three aims of operating, maintaining and developing the line. The company is non-profit making, all proceeds being devoted to the railway and all the staff are volunteers. A policy of charging the lowest fare possible compatible with covering costs is operated.
The company are steadily improving the railway. A variety of steam, diesel and electric locomotives are now available together with four additional new coaches of modern design.
The steam locomotives are based on narrow gauge prototypes and are therefore large models. Double heading by steam locomotives of heavy trains is a regular operating feature.
New locomotives will be brought into service at intervals during the next few years.
Automatic colour light signals are now in use at times when more than one train is in operation. A new locomotive shed and station are being progressed together with general improvements to the overall environment.
All correspondence to: The Secretary, 10 Bredbury Green, Romiley, Stockport, Cheshire SK6 3DN.

Stock
Cromar White Bo-BoPM No. 7001 *Galahad*
A selection of six miniature steam locomotives with a further five anticipated to enter service 1982–83
Three sit-astride bogie coaches
Four open bogie coaches built 1981

412 Wicksteed Park Lakeside Railway BE

A 2ft gauge passenger-carrying line, one-and-a-half miles long laid out in a circuit of the park

Wicksteed Park, Kettering, Northants
Tel: Kettering 2475
OS Ref: SP 883770

The railway operates from Easter to the end of September.

Stock
Baguley 0-4-0DM *King Arthur* 2042 built 1931
Baguley 0-4-0DM *Lady of the Lake* 2043 built 1931
Motor Rail 4WDM *Cheyenne* 22224 built 1966
Ten open four-wheeled coaches with rustic-type garden seats built 1931
Four covered toastrack bogie coaches built 1966
All the locomotives have a steam outline.

Also at Wicksteed Park
Standard gauge steam locomotive on static display
OS Ref: SP 879773

Barclay 0-4-0ST No. 9 2323 built 1952
Presented by South Durham Steel and Iron Co Ltd, Irchester Quarry, 1969. On display at Wollaston Road recreation ground, Irchester, until 1979

Wicksteed Park is an attractive expanse of over 150 acres bordering the main A6 road between Kettering and Barton Seagrave. The park was created for the public by the late Charles Wicksteed who was a pioneer of the steam plough. This enterprising engineer first visited Kettering in 1871 and established the engineering works which bears his name. The miniature railway was the last of Wicksteed's enterprises before his death in 1931.
Entrance to the park is free.
Facilities for visitors include a souvenir shop, car parking, refreshments, toilets, 30 major rides, mini racecars, bumper boats, model railway exhibition and railway video show.

413 Billing Miniature Railway B

A 2ft gauge passenger-carrying line three-quarters-of-a-mile long around the Willow Lake and fishing area

Billing Aquadrome, Billing, Northampton
Tel: Northampton 890849
OS Ref: SP 808615

Billing Aquadrome is a 350-acre expanse of lakes, lawns, woods and parkland set in the rich Northamptonshire countryside. Besides providing caravan and camping sites, the Aquadrome is an attractive resort for the day visitor and with its railway is open from March to October each year.

Stock
Motor Rail 4WDM *Oliver* 9869 built 1954 (steam outline)
Ruston Hornsby 4WDM 242887 built 1946
Five articulated open bogie coaches

414 Overstone Solarium Light Railway B

A 60cm gauge passenger-carrying line 1,300 yards long

Overstone Park, Sywell, Northamptonshire NN6 0BD
Tel: Northampton 42241
OS Ref: SP 819654

The railway operates (weather permitting) on Saturdays, Sundays and Bank Holidays from April to September. Also on weekdays in July and August.

Stock
Motor Rail 4WDM No. 22 8727 built 1941
Three bogie coaches

The trackage of the railway totals some 800 yards, laid as a single main line from the station (which is near the swimming pool and funfair) along the edge of the park and then into the wood. In the woods, the line is looped to return trains to the station, giving a total run of some 1,300 yards. Every effort has been made to capture the narrow-gauge image on this railway, which opened in 1969.

415 The National Tramway Museum B

One mile long standard gauge electric tramway

Crich, near Matlock and Ambergate, Derbyshire DE4 5DP
Access: Trent bus 240 from Matlock, Alfreton, Alfreton & Mansfield Parkway. BR ½-hour uphill walk from Whatstandwell (BR)
Tel: 077-385-2565
OS Ref: SK 345549

Open Saturdays, Sundays and Bank Holidays, April–October, 10.30 am to 5 pm; Tuesdays, Wednesdays and Thursdays, May, June, July and August only, 10 am to 4.30 pm. Also Mondays in August.
A regular service is operated on these dates by the largest collection of tramcars in Europe. The Museum has a unique collection of over 40 trams, of which the majority are in working order. Apart from British vehicles, the collection includes examples from Czechoslovakia, Portugal and South Africa, as well as a former New York streetcar which last ran in Vienna.
Other special features of the Museum include Edwardian street project; façade of Assembly Rooms – Ancient Monument from Derby re-erected at Museum. Lead Mining display by Peak District Mines Historical Society. Tramway power station, exhibition of early horse and electric cars.
Amenities: Car and coach park; museum shop for tramway and light railway books, films and souvenirs; cafe, toilets and picnic area.
Details from: The Museum.

The National Tramway Museum was established in 1955 to preserve and operate a representative collection of trams and tramway equipment. In 1959 the Museum was established in part of a limestone quarry which had been served by a narrow gauge mineral railway built by George Stephenson. Depots and workshops have been built and the electric tramway has been progressively extended to give visitors scenic views over the Derwent Valley. Over 40 trams have been collected and many restored to their original condition and full working order. The collection includes horse and electric cars and a steam tramway locomotive.

Stock
Beyer Peacock 0-4-0VB Tram No. 2 2464 built 1885
English Electric 4WE 717 built 1927
Ruston Hornsby 4WDM *Rupert* (20DL Class) 223741; built 1944, rebuilt TMS 1964
Ruston Hornsby 4WDM *GMJ* (48DL Class) 326058 built 1952, rebuilt RMS 1969

Ruston Hornsby 4WDM (48DL Class) 373363 built 1954 (metre gauge)

Tramcar Fleet List
Blackpool No. 1 built 1884
Derby No. 1 built 1903
Douglas Southern Electric Tramways No. 1 built 1896
London Transport No. 1 built 1932
Blackpool & Fleetwood No. 2 built 1898
Gateshead & District No. 5 built 1927
Oporto No. 9 built 1873
Hill of Howth (Dublin) No. 10 built 1902 (5ft 3in gauge)
Grimsby & Immingham No. 14 built 1915
Sheffield No. 15 built 1874
Glasgow No. 22 built 1922
Blackpool No. 40 built 1926
Southampton No. 45 built 1903
Sheffield No. 46 built 1899
Blackpool No. 49 built 1926
Gateshead & District No. 52 built 1901
[1]Blackpool No. 59 built 1902
Johannesburg No. 60 built 1905
Paisley District No. 68 built 1919
Leicester No. 76 built 1904
Newcastle No. 102 built 1901
Hull No. 132 built 1910
Blackpool No. 166 built 1927
Blackpool No. 167 built 1928
Leeds No. 180 built 1931
Prague No. 180 built 1908
Sheffield No. 189 built 1934
LCC No. 106 built Dick Kerr 1903
Blackpool No. 710 built English Electric 1934
Dundee steam tram trailer No. 21 built 1894
London County Council No. 106 built 1903
Sheffield No. 264 built 1937
Metropolitan Electric Tramways (London) No. 331 built 1929
Leeds No. 345 built 1921
Leeds No. 399 built 1925
Sheffield No. 510 built 1950
Leeds No. 600 built 1931, rebuilt 1954
Leeds No. 602 built 1953
Glasgow No. 812 built 1900
Liverpool No. 869 built 1936
Glasgow No. 1100 built 1928
Glasgow No. 1115 built 1929
Glasgow No. 1282 built 1940
[2]New York No. 674 built 1939
Leeds No. 2 (Tower Car) built 1932
Sheffield No. 330 (Rail Grinder) built 1920
Glasgow No. 1 (Cable Layer) built 1905
Glasgow No. 21 (Tool Van)
Blackpool No. 2 (Generator) built 1927
Cardiff No. 131 (Water Car) built 1905

[1]Currently on loan to Blackpool Corporation.
[2]Purchased for preservation as Vienna No. 4225.

416 National Mining Museum BE

Standard gauge steam locomotives on static display. Also a 2ft 3in gauge demonstration railway, including a continuous cable-haulage section

National Coal Board, Lound Hall, Haughton, Bevercotes, near Retford, Nottinghamshire
Access: On B6387 Retford–New Ollerton Road
Bus routes Nos 15, 102, 103 and 162
Tel: 0623-860728
OS Ref: SK 700728

Museum open 10.30 am to 5.30 pm on Tuesdays; and 2 pm to 5.30 pm on Saturdays and Sundays.
Enquiries to: Industrial Relations Officer, National Coal Board, Edwinstowe, Mansfield, Nottinghamshire

Stock
Manning Wardle 0-6-0ST *The Welshman* 1207 built 1890
Yorkshire Engine Co 0-6-0ST No. 9 2521 built 1952
Ruston Hornsby 4WDM (LAT Class) 375347 built 1954
NCB 4-wheel manriding coach
Wentworth Silkstone wooden tub wagon (1ft 2½in gauge)
Little Eaton tramroad wagon (3ft 6in gauge)
Blaenant Iron tub wagon built *c*1840 (2ft 5in guage)

The collection also includes a rail-mounted steam crane which may be seen in operation from time to time.

417 Peak Rail Operations Ltd A

Standard gauge railway preservation project based on two centres. On 21 April 1984, a steam-hauled passenger service commenced at the Buxton Centre, operating over 150 yards of track. Further extension of the operating line towards Ashwood Dale is dependent on the reinstatement of the Bridge Street railway overbridge in Buxton for which an appeal fund has been started

Buxton Railway Station, Buxton, Derbyshire. Matlock Railway Station, Matlock, Derbyshire
Access: (Buxton) On the A6, 20 miles south of Manchester. (Matlock) On A6, 18 miles north of Derby
BR from Derby (Monday to Saturday)
Tel: Derby 558197
OS Ref: SK 296603

Shop and Office open every weekend and public holiday 10.30 am–5.30 pm.
Facilities for visitors include car parking, shop and toilets.
The 20 mile railway line between Matlock and Buxton closed down in 1968. Seven years later, Peak Railway Society Ltd was formed to measure the possible support for reopening of the route. The organisation grew to over 2,000 members in four years and is still growing at an impressive rate.
In 1978 Peak Rail Operations Ltd came into existence. This company intends to control the organisation of the rail-

way, proposing to run daily passenger services along the whole route, and also freight services, providing a considerable benefit to local industry and affording an alternative to road transport for heavy goods along the main route through the Peak District. The railway would provide connections with established British Railways services at Matlock and at Buxton, with the potential of through trains to towns and cities beyond the Peak Rail route.

Finance for the project is being raised through a public share issue, and substantial amounts of money have also been promised by commercial sponsorship.

Peak Rail services would be manned by a combination of paid full-time staff and volunteer Society members. Locomotives and rolling stock would be owned either by the Company or by private individuals; members have already organised the rescue of six large steam locomotives which are now undergoing restoration by their new owners.

Details from: A. Royle, 17 Hamblin Crescent, Sinfin, Derby.

Stock

LMS 0-6-0T No. 47406 (3F Class) built 1926
[1]SR 4-6-2 No. 34101 *Hartland* (Bulleid WC Class) built 1947
LMS 2-8-0 No. 48624 (Stanier 8F Class) built 1944
BR 2-10-0 No. 92214 (Riddles 9F Class) built 1959
BR 2-10-0 No. 92219 (Riddles 9F Class) built 1960
BR 2-6-0 No. 76084 (Riddles 4MT Class) built 1957
Bagnall 0-6-0ST 2746 built 1944
RSH 0-4-0ST *George* 7214 built 1945
Hunslet 0-6-0ST *Brookes No. 1* 2387 built 1941
Hunslet 0-6-0ST No. 193 *Shropshire* 3793 built 1953
Peckett 0-4-0ST *Lytham No. 1* 2111 built 1949
Vulcan Foundry 0-4-0ST *Vulcan* 1828 built 1902
Barclay 0-4-0ST *Harry* 1823 built 1924
Hudswell Clarke 0-6-0DM *Engineers E1* D1199 built 1960
Barclay 0-4-0DH 499 built 1965
Ruston Hornsby 0-4-0DH 504565 built 1965
Ruston Hornsby 4WDM 305306 built 1952
Wickham 4WPMR 6901 built 1954
BR Mk.1 coach
Esso tank wagon
LNWR 6-wheel CCT van No. 395273
LMS 14-ton van No. 98542

[1]In store at Derby undergoing renovation.

418 Rutland Railway Museum DE

Standard gauge industrial railway preservation centre, where a growing collection of steam locomotives and industrial rolling stock is displayed. The line runs from Cottesmore Sidings to Ashwell Junction – a distance of 1 mile

Cottesmore Ironstone Mines Sidings, Ashwell Road, Cottesmore, Rutland
Tel: Stamford 62384
OS Ref: SK 886137

The future aim of the group is to recreate a living example of bygone iron ore mining operation. A collection of rolling stock and former ironstone mining equipment gives the museum a truly industrial atmosphere. Open days are advertised.

Details from: The Membership Secretary, Friends of Rutland Railway Museum, 4 Highgate Avenue, Birstall, Leicester LE4 8JJ.

Stock

Peckett 0-4-0ST No. 8 2110 built 1950
Avonside 0-4-0ST No. 2 *Dora* 1973 built 1927
Barclay 0-4-0ST 1931 built 1927
Barclay 0-6-0ST *Salmon* 2139 built 1942
Peckett 0-4-0ST *Elizabeth* 1759 built 1928
Peckett 0-4-0ST *Uppingham* 1257 built 1912
Hawthorn Leslie 0-4-0ST *Singapore* 3865 built 1936
Hunslet 0-6-0ST No. 24 2411 built 1941
Barclay 0-4-0ST *Sir Thomas Royden* 2088 built 1940
Hunslet 0-6-0ST *Coal Products No. 6* 3883 built 1963
Peckett 0-4-0ST *James* 2129 built 1952
BR 0-6-0DH No. D9520 (Class 14) built 1964
Ruston Hornsby 4WDM Class 88DS 306092 built 1950
Yorkshire Engine Co 0-6-0DE No. 28 2594 built 1956
Barclay 0-4-0DH No. 219001 499 built 1965
Ruston Hornsby 0-4-0DH No. 21 90 02 504565 built 1965
Barclay 0-4-0DM No. 3 352 built 1941
Yorkshire Engine Co 0-6-0DE 2872 built 1962
Ruston Hornsby 4WDM 305302 built 1951
Hibberd 4WDM *Phoenix* 3887 built 1958
Wickham 4WPMR No. DB 965072 7587 built 1957
Wisbech & Upwell Tramway saloon 3rd bogie coach body No. 7 built 1884
LMS (LNWR pattern) 10-ton van body No. 276945 built *c*1923
LNER 12-ton box van (ex-BSC Scunthorpe) CR box van No. 907
GWR 'Mink A' 10-ton box van No. 95353
ICI Salt division 12-ton box van No. 2317 built General Wagon Co
GER 6-wheel 3rd class coach No. 60741 built 1887 (body)
GER 6-wheel chief engineer's saloon No. 14 built 1889
MR 20-ton goods brake van No. M1090 built *c*1923
GWR 20-ton goods brake van MSC No. 6374 built 1923
MR goods van S&L No. 1147
S&L (LMS pattern) quarry mess van No. 4
S&L quarry platelayers van No. 2
S&L quarry tool van
LMS 6-wheel CCT van No. SW2 built *c*1926
Ketton Portland Cement Co wooden side-tipping wagon No. 30

Ketton Portland Cement Co wooden 10-ton wagon built *c*1900
James Pain 3-plank wooden dropside wagon No. 546 built *c*1900
Holwell Ironworks 3-plank wooden 10-ton wagon No. 267
Newstead Coal Co 8-plank 12-ton wagon No. 31 built 1938
5-plank wooden 10-ton wagons Nos 344 and 357
4-plank wooden 10-ton wagon No. 624
S&L 8-plank 13-ton wagon built Cambrian Wagon Co 1942
Stanton Ironworks 12-ton open wagons Nos 849, 860, 1117, 1131 and 5818
S&L 4-plank 12-ton open wagons Nos 3017, 3046, 3049, 3142 and 3153
S&L steel-bodies ironstone dumpcars Nos 76, 97, 125, 141, 144 and 148 built 1939–40
S&L Ironstone skip wagons Nos 1 and 4 built G. R. Turner 1942
BSC 27-ton iron ore tippler wagon No. 25197 built *c*1972
Appleby-Frodingham 21-ton iron ore hopper wagon No. 147590 built 1938
LMS 20-ton iron ore hopper wagons Nos 19 and 20 built 1936–38
LMS 13-ton mineral wagons Nos 21 and 24 built 1936–43
BR bogie well wagon ex-BSC, Corby
GWR bogie bolster 'C' wagon BSC No. MBW1
LMS 3-plank dropside wagon No. 3001
BSC wooden flat wagons Nos 54 and 184
S&L steel flat wagons Nos 64 and 65
Ketton Portland Cement Co tipper wagons Nos K1 and K39 built 1961
Esso oil tank wagon No. 44355 built Charles Roberts 1962
Smith Rodley 5-ton steam crane
Smith Rodley 5-ton diesel crane built 1964

419 Leicestershire Museum of Technology E

Abbey Lane Pumping Station, Corporation Road, Leicester LE4 5PX
Access: Bus routes Nos 54 or 76 from Leicester City Centre (Charles Street) to Beaumont Leys Lane. Outer circle bus services Nos 90/91 also pass nearby
Tel: Leicester 61330
OS Ref: SK 589067

Opening times: Monday to Thursday and Saturday 10 am to 5.30 pm Sundays and Steam Days 2 pm to 5.30 pm. Closed on Fridays and Christmas Day.
Special event days are held at regular intervals throughout the year when the stationary steam engines can be seen working.
The museum building itself was built in 1890–1 as a sewage pumping station for the City of Leicester. The original pump-house with four large Woolf Compound beam engines is now the centrepiece of the Museum. The engines were built by Gimsons of Leicester and used from 1891 to 1965. Leicester City Museums took over in 1968 and the site was opened in 1972. Now Leicestershire County Museums owned, the Museum of Technology houses a representative collection of items from Leicestershire's industrial past, from stationary steam engines to knitting machines.
Interesting exhibits include a 1935 Ruston Bucyrus steam shovel, an 1826 'A' frame beam engine and an 1844 Stephenson lifting bridge from the Leicester & Swannington Railway.
Facilities for visitors include car parking, toilets, refreshments on Special Event days and museum shop.

Stock
[2]RSH 0-4-0ST *Mars II* 7493 built 1948
[1]Brush 0-4-0ST No. 6 314 built 1906
Barclay 0-4-0F No. 2 1815 built 1924
Motor Rail 4WPM 52600 built 1931 (2ft gauge)
Two Hudson skip wagons (2ft gauge)
FR slate wagon (2ft gauge)
Flat wagons (2ft gauge)
Tub wagon (18in gauge)

[1]Originally Powlesland and Mason No. 6. Taken over by the GWR in 1924, becoming No. 921. Sold to Sugar Beet and Crop Driers Ltd, Eynsham, in 1928 and resold to Berry Wiggins and Co Ltd, Kingsnorth, Kent, in 1931. Purchased for preservation 1968.
[2]Ex-East Midlands Gas Board, Aylestone Road Gasworks, Leicester, 1970. Adopted by the Leicester Railway Society for restoration as a working exhibit.

Long-term plans for the development of the museum include the laying of a 2ft gauge works railway over the next five years, whilst a standard gauge line is projected within ten years.

420 Daventry Borough Council E

Standard gauge steam locomotive on static display

New Street Children's Playground, Daventry, Northants
Access: No. 311 bus from Northampton. BR Station
OS Ref: SP 574624

Stock
Bagnall 0-6-0ST *Cherwell* 2654 built 1942

Ex-Byfield Ironstone Co Ltd, Byfield, Northants, 1966.

421 Welland Valley Vintage Traction Club G

Three-foot gauge static exhibits stored pending restoration

Glebe Road, Market Harborough, Leicestershire
OS Ref: SP 742868

Stock
Manning Wardle 0-6-0ST *Kettering Furnaces No. 8* 1675 built 1906
[1]Scaldwell Quarries side-tipping wagon

[1]On loan from Kettering Borough Council.

Access to these items is only possible if the premises are manned.

422 Mr M. A. G. Jacob G

2ft gauge locomotive in store

Long Eaton, Nottinghamshire

No public access.

Stock
Lister 4WPM 3916 built 1931

423 Corby District Council E

Standard gauge industrial steam locomotive on static display

West Glebe Park, Cottingham Road, Corby, Northants
OS Ref: SP 886890

Stock
Hawthorn Leslie 0-6-0ST No. 14 3827 built 1934

Ex-British Steel Corporation, Corby Works, 1971. Preserved by Corby District Council.

424 Riber Castle Wild Life Park E

Standard gauge steam locomotive on static display

Near Matlock, Derbyshire DE4 5JU
Tel: Matlock 2073
OS Ref: SK 308590

Open daily throughout the year between 10 am and 7 pm in summer and 10 am to 4 pm in winter.
Riber Castle dates from 1862 and its grounds now contain a fauna reserve covering more than 20 acres.
Facilities for visitors include car parking, refreshments, model railway, vintage cars, children's playground and butterfly exhibition.

Stock
Peckett 0-4-0ST 1555 built 1920

Ex-Derbyshire Stone Quarries Ltd, Cawdor Limestone Quarries, Matlock, Derbyshire, 1971.

Also on display is the following 9½in gauge steam locomotive: Battison 4-6-2 *Lady Joyce*

425 Northamptonshire Locomotive Group G

Metre gauge locomotives undergoing restoration

MR Goods Shed, Irchester, Northants
OS Ref: 933660

Details from: Keith Adams. Tel: 0604-844763

Stock
Peckett 0-6-0ST *Banshee* 1870 built 1934
Hunslet 0-4-0DM *The Rock* 2419 built 1941
Corpet 0-6-0T *Cambrai* 493 built 1888

426 Millgate Museum of Social and Folk Life G

Standard gauge steam locomotive on static display

Newark, Nottinghamshire
OS Ref: SK 794537

Stock
Hudswell Clarke 0-6-0ST No. 54 *Julie* 1682 built 1937

Ex-British Sugar Corporation, Kelkham Factory, Newark, 1979.

427 Klondyke Steam Museum E

The Klondyke Mill narrow gauge railway is a 1ft 11½in gauge line being developed subject to planning permission

Klondyke Mill Recreation Centre, Draycott-in-the-Clay, Sudbury, Derbyshire DE6 5GX. (Situated in Staffordshire with Derbyshire postal address)
Access: On the A515 road, 2 miles from the A50 Sudbury–Derby road. Nearest BR station: Uttoxeter (7 miles)
Tel: Burton-on-Trent 820302
OS Ref: SK 156289

The museum and the railway are run by the North Staffordshire and Cheshire Traction Engine Club. The steam collection at Klondyke Mill comprises a large number of traction engines, road rollers, vintage agricultural tractors and associated equipment.
1ft 11½in gauge locomotive undergoing restoration.

Stock
FR/George England 0-4-0STT *Palmerston* built 1864

In 1968 a group of steam traction engine enthusiasts got together and took out a lease for 21 years from the Duchy of Lancaster on the site of the old Klondyke brick and plaster mill at Draycott-in-the-Clay. Permission was granted for change of use from plaster mill to a centre for the storage and restoration of old vehicles and subsequently their operation and exhibition. Another group of preservationists purchased the Ffestiniog Railway locomotive *Palmerston*. During 1980, fund-raising took place in order to develop a 1ft 11½in gauge railway at Klondyke. Planning permission was applied for to reinstate the old tramway which existed in the past to haul minerals across the Saltbrook Valley.

428 Newbold Verdon C

Short 1ft 10¾in gauge line running from the farmyard out into the fields

Mr J. Vernon, Church Farm, Newbold Verdon, Leicestershire
OS Ref: SK 442038

No public access.

Stock
Hunslet 0-4-0ST *Pamela* 920 built 1906
Hunslet 0-4-0ST *Sybil Mary* 921 built 1906
Vernon 4WBE built 1972

Both ex-Penrhyn Quarries Ltd, Bethesda, Caernarfonshire, 1966.

429 National Coal Board I

Standard gauge industrial steam location featuring occasional steam working

Cadley Hill Colliery, Church Gresley, near Burton-on-Trent
OS Ref: SK 279193

Stock
RSH 0-6-0ST *Progress* 7298 built 1946
Bagnall 0-6-0ST *Empress* 3061 built 1954
Hunslet 0-6-0ST *Cadley Hill No. 1* 3851 built 1962
Hunslet 0-6-0ST *Swiftsure* 2857 built 1943

430 CEGB, Castle Donington Power Station I

Standard gauge industrial steam location with locomotives stored in the shed

Castle Donington, Leicestershire
OS Ref: SK 433284

No public access.

Stock
RSH 0-4-0ST No. 1 7817 built 1954
RSH 0-4-0ST No. 2 7818 built 1954

431 Buxton Miniature Railway B

Passenger-carrying 10¼in gauge railway, ¼ mile in length, running round a small lake

Pavilion Gardens, Buxton, Derbyshire

Stock
Fenlow Bo-BoDM *Borough of Buxton* built *c*1972
Three articulated bogie coaches

432 Hunt & Co (Hinckley) Ltd G

Standard gauge steam locomotive in store

London Road Works, Hinckley, Leicestershire
OS Ref: SP 437937

No public access.

Stock
[1]Bagnall 0-6-0ST *Huntsman* 2655 built 1942 (Sold)

[1]Ex-Staveley Minerals Ltd, Cranford Ironstone Quarries, Northamptonshire 1970. Formerly named *Loddington No. 2.*

433 Queens Park Miniature Railway B

A 10¼in gauge passenger-carrying line situated on the trackbed of a former BR line and extending for a quarter of a mile

Queens Park, Chesterfield, Derbyshire

Stock
Shepperton Bo-BoPM
Three bogie coaches built by Cromar-White

434 Melton Mowbray Miniature Railway B

Passenger-carrying 10¼in gauge railway, ¼ mile in length

Sports Ground, Leicester Road, Melton Mowbray, Leicestershire

Open weekends and Bank Holidays April–September according to weather conditions.

Stock
Wilcox 4WPM
Ex-Hamworthy Miniature Railway

435 Derwent Gardens Miniature Railway B

Passenger-carrying 10¼in gauge railway, 75 yards in length, laid out in a horseshoe pattern

South Parade, Matlock Bath, Derbyshire

Stock
Freelance 4WBE
Two 4-wheel passenger coaches

436 Brian Roberts G

Short private standard gauge line

Hill Farm, Tollerton, Nottinghamshire

No public access

Stock
Peckett 0-4-0ST No. 60130 *Kestrel* 2129 built 1952
BR goods brake van

437 'Nags Head' E

Coach in use as a restaurant

Mickleover, Derbyshire

Stock
SR Pullman car No. 285 built 1932
(Ex-'Brighton Belle' set No. 3053)

438 Northampton Steam Railway F

A scheme to revive the Northampton–Market Harborough line

Lamport Station, Northants

Northampton Steam Railway applied for LRO from Kingsthorpe to Lamport (8¼ miles)

Stock
Ruston Hornsby 0-4-0DM 319286 built 1953
BR Pullman kitchen/dining car (Type R2A)
SR Bulleid double-deck EMU motor coaches Nos S13003S and S13004S (Unit No. 4002) built 1949
SR ventilated van built 1931

439 Mr J. Craven C

Private garden railway of mixed 2ft and 3ft gauge

Main Street, Walesby, Leicestershire

Stock
Motor Rail 4WDM 9673 (3ft gauge)
House 4WDM built 1974 (2ft gauge)
Ruston Hornsby 4WPM 441944 (2ft gauge)
A number of skip wagons and skip chassis used as flat wagons

440 Mr K. Woolmer G

2ft gauge locomotive undergoing restoration

15 Bakers Lane, Woodford, Kettering, Northants
OS Ref: SP 969769

Stock
Lister 4WDM 36743 built 1951

441 Mr F. R. Coombes G

Standard gauge petrol locomotive in store

Wash Lane, Ravenstone, near Coalville, Leics

Stock
Hibberd 4WPM 2895 built 1944

442 Peak District Museum E

1ft 5in gauge locomotive on static display

The Pavilion, Matlock Bath, Derbyshire

Stock
Greenwood & Batley 4WBE 1446

443 Dunkley's E

The former LNWR station goods shed at Castle Ashby, Northants, built in 1850, has been converted into a restaurant. It incorporates a bogie coach adapted as a cocktail lounge.
Details from: Mr John Dunkley

Stock
LMS 1st class coach built 1926

AREA J

Home Counties

Oxfordshire
Berkshire
Hertfordshire
Buckinghamshire
Bedfordshire
Greater London
(Group Nos 451–500)

451 Leighton Buzzard Narrow Gauge Railway — A

Passenger-carrying 2ft gauge railway, 1¾ miles in length from Pages Park to Vandyke Road over the tracks of the former Leighton Buzzard Light Railway. The overall length of line is 3½ miles

Pages Park Station, Billington Road, Leighton Buzzard, Bedfordshire LU7 8TN
Access: From M1, follow the signs from junction 11 or 13 to the A5 and follows signs on the A5 for Leighton Buzzard which is well signposted. From Leighton Buzzard follow 'Narrow Gauge Railway' signs from Town Centre. The railway lies on the east of Billington Road, the A4146 to Hemel Hempstead
Tel: Leighton Buzzard (0525) 373888
OS Ref: SP 941275

The railway operates on Sundays from the end of March to the end of September from 11 am to 5 pm, also on Bank Holidays and Saturdays (at Bank Holiday periods) from 2 pm to 5 pm.
Facilities for visitors include car parking, railway shop, refreshments and toilets (200 yds).
Operational dates: Sundays end March to end September, Good Friday, Bank Holiday Mondays and Saturdays. 1st train 11 am; last train 5 pm.
The Leighton Buzzard Light Railway was opened in 1919 to carry sand quarried in the north-east of the town to exchange sidings on the LNWR Luton–Dunstable line in the south. It was built without statutory powers by two of the principal companies of sand merchants. In 1963 the railway came under the sole ownership of its principal user, sand merchants Joseph Arnold and Sons Ltd, and until 1978 the northern end of the line was still used for sand traffic using small internal combustion locomotives. The LBNGRS reached agreement with Arnolds to use the southern portion of the line and its first train ran in March 1968.
The railway is operated by members of the Leighton Buzzard Narrow Gauge Railway Society Ltd.

Details from: LBNGRS Ltd, Pages Park Station, Billington Road, Leighton Buzzard, Bedfordshire LU7 8TN

Stock
Avonside 0-4-0T *Sezela No. 4* 1738 built 1916
[1]De Winton 0-4-0VBT No. 1 *Chaloner* built 1877
[2]Kerr Stuart 0-4-0ST No. 2 *Pixie* 4260 built 1922
[5]Baguley 0-4-0T No. 3 *Rishra* 2007 built 1921
[3]Barclay 0-6-0T No. 4 *The Doll* 1641 built 1919
[4]Orenstein and Koppel 0-6-0WT No. 5 *Elf* 12740 built 1936
Motor Rail 4WDM No. 6 *Caravan* 7129 built 1936
Orenstein and Koppel 4WDM No. 7 *Falcon* 8986 built 1929
Ruston Hornsby 4WDM No. 8 *Gollum* 217999 built 1942
Motor Rail 4WDM No. 10 *Haydn Taylor* 7956 built 1945
Orenstein and Koppel 0-4-0WT No. 11 *P. C. Allen* 5834 built 1912
Motor Rail 4WPM No. 12 *Carbon* 6012 built 1930
Hunslet 4WDM No. 14 3646 built 1946
Hibberd 4WDM No. 15 *Tom Bombadil* 2514 built 1941
Lister 4WDM No. 16 *Thor in Oakenshield* 11221 built 1939
Motor Rail 4WDM 7214 built 1938
Motor Rail 4WDM No. 18 *Feanor* 11003 built 1954
Motor Rail 4WDM No. 23 11298 built 1965
Motor Rail 4WDM No. 17 *Damredub* 7036 built 1936
Motor Rail 4WPM No. 21 *Festoon* 4570 built 1929
Motor Rail 4WDM 4805 built 1936
Motor Rail 4WDM No. 25 60S317 built 1966
Motor Rail 4WDM No. 26 11164 built 1966
Motor Rail 4WDM No. 43 10409 built 1954
Motor Rail 4WDM No. 44 *Kestrel* 7933 built 1941
Motor Rail 4WDM No. 131 5613 built 1931 (rebuilt as mobile hedge-cutter)
Five passenger coaches
Two passenger brake-coaches
Three bogie flat trucks
Several 1½ and 1 cu yd skips
Several assorted permanent way vehicles
Four-wheel tank wagon
Four-wheel steel dropside wagon
Nine four-wheel wooden dropside wagons
Two four-wheel wagon chassis
Three bogie wagons

[1]Ex-Penyrorsedd Slate Quarry Co Ltd, Nantille, Caernarfonshire, 1960. Loaned to the LBNGRS in 1968 by its owner, Mr A. Fisher, and at present on display in the National Railway Museum.
[2]Ex-Devon County Council, Wilmanstone Quarry, Tavistock, 1957, for preservation by the Industrial Locomotive Society. Loaned to the LBNGRS in 1968.
[3]Ex-Stewarts and Lloyds Ltd, Bilston, Staffordshire, 1960. Sold to Alan Bloom for use at Bressingham in 1966 and resold to LBNGRS Ltd in 1969. Undergoing extensive rebuild at present.
[4]This wood-burning locomotive is owned by A. Fisher, who rescued it from darkest Africa in 1973.
[5]Owned by Mr M. G. Satow.

452 Whipsnade and Umfolozi Railway A

Passenger-carrying 2ft 6in gauge line through the animal paddocks at Whipsnade Zoo Park, Dunstable, Beds.

Tel: Whipsnade 872995 (Zoo: 872171)
OS Ref: TL 004172

Operated by Pleasure Rail Ltd, Buchanan House, 24/30 Holborn, London EC1
Facilities: Car parking and refreshments.
The railway was opened on 26 August 1970 as a public attraction and a means of seeing some of the larger species of animals at close quarters. Much of the line's equipment and rolling stock came from the Bowaters Railway at Sittingbourne. The line forms a continuous two-mile circuit incorporating several sharp gradients, a number of bridges and a short tunnel. In this form, the line was officially opened by Princess Margaret on 2 August 1973.
The railway operates daily from Easter to the end of September and is normally steam worked.
Visitors should note that a diesel pay-train may operate before 1 pm.

Stock
Manning Wardle 0-6-2T No. 1 *Chevallier* 1877 built 1915
Kerr Stuart 0-4-2ST No. 2 *Excelsior* 1049 built 1908
Bagnall 0-6-2T No. 3 *Conqueror* 2192 built 1922
Kerr Stuart 0-6-2T No. 4 *Superior* 4034 built 1920
[1]Fowler 0-6-0DM No. 9 *Victor* 4160005 built 1951
Fowler 0-6-0DM 4160006 built 1951
Ten 30-seat passenger bogie coaches rebuilt from Bowater bogie pulp wagons in 1970

[1]Ex-Welshpool and Llanfair Light Railway 1972.

3ft 6in gauge static exhibits
Zambesi Sawmills Railway 4-8-0 No. 390 Sharp Stewart 4150 built 1896
Rhodesia Railways balcony-ended clerestory first/second-class sleeping car No. 1808 Gloucester Carriage and Wagon Co Ltd built 1927
Ford 8 motor car mounted on rail wheels for use as an inspection trolley built 1938

Historical note
In 1973, David Shepherd was presented by the Government of Zambia with two steam locomotives and a coach, and the 12,000 mile journey of one engine and the coach from Zambia to Whipsnade was the subject of the BBC TV film *Last Train to Mulobezi*. The rolling stock has now been given a home at Whipsnade, courtesy the Zoological Society of London and Pleasurerail, until such time as funds and space permit transfer to the East Somerset Railway at Cranmore. The second locomotive, ex-Rhodesia Railways Class 10 4-8-2 (Sharp Stewart 1922), remains in Bulawayo until funds are available for her return home. The Class 7 has reverted to her original number of 390, with new brass cabside plates. This was her number when exported in 1896 to the Cape Government Railway. She was renumbered 993 when taken into South African Railways stock, and she was the last Class 7 in their lists, working as Johannesburg station pilot, when purchased for work on the Zambesi Sawmills Railway in Zambia in 1971. When this system was taken over by Zambia Railways, the rolling stock became redundant and the coach and engines were given to David Shepherd.
On 6 August 1976 an exhibition of early photographs recording the 78 years of life in Africa of No. 390 was opened in the coach by Zambia's High Commissioner to London. On this occasion also, the Chairman of Ford, Great Britain, presented to David Shepherd a 1938 Ford 8, in working order – an exact replica of the cars used as inspection trolleys on the Zambesi Sawmills Railway in the 1930s. The car has been adapted for railway operation by 27 Command Workshops, REME.

453 Knebworth West Park and Winter Green Railway A

A one-and-a-quarter mile, 1ft 11½in gauge passenger-carrying line in the grounds of Knebworth House near Stevenage, Herts

Access: Knebworth House is permanently signposted on all major surrounding roads. Nearest BR station: Knebworth. Special bus service operates from BR Stevenage station on certain dates.
Direct access from A1(M) at Stevenage (South) roundabout
Tel: Stevenage 812661 Ext 12
OS Ref: TL 228208

The railway operates on Sundays from Easter to the end of September, on Tuesdays until mid-September and on Bank Holidays. Steam operation on Sundays and Bank Holidays, otherwise a diesel service is run.
Facilities for visitors include country park, skate park, picnicking, riding, refreshments and spectacular children's adventure playground.
The railway environment was enhanced during 1980 by the addition of many of the items formerly on show at the Great Molewood Railway Museum, near Hertford. These include two signal boxes, a wide variety of signs and notices and a number of signals of various patterns.

Stock
Peckett 0-6-0ST *Triassic* 1270 built 1911
Hunslet 0-4-0ST *Lilla* 554 built 1891
Motor Rail 4WDM No. 2 8993 built 1946 (steam outline)
Motor Rail 4WDM 40s273 built 1966
Ruston Hornsby 4WDM 354043 built 1953
Ruston Hornsby 4WDM *Horatio* 217967 built 1942 (steam outline)
Ruston Hornsby 4WDM No. 12 *Mor Leidr* (Class 40DL) 375315 built 1954
Ruston Hornsby 4WDM 373359 built 1958

Nine bogie coaches
Two four-wheeled brake vans

Also the following standard gauge static exhibits:
Wickham 4WPMR No. 900338 + Wickham trailer car
GNR 6-wheel compartment coach built *c*1890 (on loan from Tanfield Rly)

454 Blenheim Park Railway B

15in gauge passenger-carrying line ½ mile in length running through the grounds of Blenheim Palace

Woodstock, Oxfordshire

Trains operate daily from Easter to the end of September

Stock
Freelance 4WPM No. 15
Open bogie passenger coaches

455 Quainton Railway Centre D

Standard gauge steam railway preservation centre, featuring steam-hauled rides in vintage coaching stock over ⅓ mile of track

Quainton Railway Society Ltd, The Railway Station, Quainton, near Aylesbury, Bucks HP22 4BY
Registered Charity No. 263669
Access: By road – take A41 from Aylesbury, turn off after 6 miles at Waddesdon. Follow Quainton signs. No buses or rail access, but chartered dmu trains run from Aylesbury on Bank Holiday Mondays
Tel: 029675-450
OS Ref: SP 739190

The centre is open on Easter Monday, Spring and August Bank Holidays, on the last Sunday of every month, every Sunday in July and August between 10 am and 6 pm.
Facilities for visitors include free car parking, museum, shop, refreshments and toilets.
The Quainton Railway Centre, run by volunteers from the Quainton Railway Society Limited, was formed in 1969 to house the relics collected by the original society – the London Railway Preservation Society formed in 1962. Since then the collection has been considerably expanded to its present size. Together they form one of the country's most comprehensive collections of railway vehicles covering the complete spectrum of standard gauge railways, whether it be industrial or main line, large or small, unusual or common, revolutionary or traditional.
Quainton is of interest as being the place where the Great Central Railway and Metropolitan met, and is the reason for the extensive sidings on both sides of the line, which is now used by BR for freight only; the Society using the sidings. There are some 40 locomotives and interesting rolling stock, some owned by the Society and some privately. Many of the engines and rolling stock reflect the Great Central and Metropolitan interest, but there are also other main line and industrial engines, it being the aim to make the collection as comprehensive as possible.
Membership details from: Hon Membership Secretary, The Station, Quainton, Aylesbury, Bucks HP22 4BY.
The Vale of Aylesbury Model Engineering Society operates a 300-yard miniature passenger-carrying line alongside the Quainton site.

Stock
GWR 2-8-2T No. 7200 (72XX Class) built as 5277 in 1930, rebuilt 1934
[1]GWR 0-6-0PT No. 7715 (LT No. L99) (Class 57XX) Kerr Stuart 4450 built 1930
GWR 0-6-0PT No. 9466 (Hawksworth 94XX Class) RSH 7617 built 1952
[5]GWR 4-6-0 No. 6024 *King Edward I* built 1930
GWR 4-6-0 No. 6989 *Wightwick Hall* (Hawksworth 6959 Class) built 1949
[3]LSWR 2-4-0WT No. 0314 (BR No. 30585) Beyer Peacock 1414 built 1874
[4]Metropolitan Railway 0-4-4T No. 1 (LT No. L44) built 1896
[7]LMS 2-6-0 No. 46447 (Ivatt Class 2MT) built 1950
[8]LMS 2-6-2T No. 41298 (Ivatt Class 2MT) built 1951
[10]LMS 2-6-2T No. 41313 (Ivatt Class 2MT) built 1952
[9]Hunslet 0-6-0ST *Juno* 3850 built 1958
Yorkshire Engine Co 0-6-0ST *Chislet* 2498 built 1951
Barclay 0-6-0ST *Swordfish* 2138 built 1941
Hunslet 0-6-0ST *Arthur* 3782 built 1953
Hunslet 0-6-0ST *Spartacus* 3890 built 1964
Hunslet 0-6-0ST No. 65 3889 built 1964
Hudswell Clarke 0-6-0T *Sir Thomas* 1334 built 1918
Hudswell Clarke 0-4-0ST *Millom* 1742 built 1946
Hawthorn Leslie 0-4-0ST No. 3 3717 built 1928
Hunslet 0-4-0ST *Trym* 287 built 1883
Peckett 0-4-0ST *Hornpipe* 1756 built 1928
Peckett 0-4-0T *Jill* 1900 built 1936
Peckett 0-4-0ST (Class R4 Special) 2104 built 1948
Peckett 0-4-0ST (Class R4 Special) 2105 built 1948
Bagnall 0-4-0ST *Scott* 2469 built 1932
NB Locomotive Co 0-6-0T *Coventry No. 1* 24564 built 1939
Barclay 0-4-0ST *Swanscombe* 699 built 1891
Barclay 0-4-0ST *Punch Hull* 776 built 1896
Barclay 0-4-0ST *Alexander* 1865 built 1926
Barclay 0-4-0ST *Tom Parry* 2015 built 1935
Barclay 0-4-0F No. GF3 1477 built 1916
Barclay 0-4-0F 2243 built 1948
Peckett 0-4-0ST No. 2 *Miranda* 2087 built 1948
Aveling Porter 0-4-0TG *Sydenham* 3567 built 1895
Sentinel 4WVBTG No. 2 *Isebrook* (GWR No. 12) 6515 built 1926
Sentinel 4WVBTG No. 7 9376 built 1947
Sentinel 4WVBTG No. 11 9366 built 1945
BR/Drewry 0-6-0DM No. D2298 *Lord Wenlock* 2679 built 1960
[12]Sentinel 4WVBTG No. 7 *Susan* 9537 built 1951
Baguley/Drewry 0-4-0DM 2161 built 1941
English Electric 2W-2-2-2WE 803 built 1930 (2ft gauge)
Hunslet 0-4-0DM 2067 built 1940

Kerr Stuart 4WDM *Redland* 4428 built 1929
Fowler 0-4-0DM *Osram* 20067 built 1933
Hibberd 4WDM *Tarmac* 3765 built 1955
Hibberd 4WDM No. T1 2102 built 1937
BR Mk.1 BSK coach No. S34947 built 1956
BR Mk.1 CK coach No. M15319 built 1953
BR Mk.1 SK coach No. E24993 built 1956
LMS Stove R six-wheeled passenger brake van No. M33014 built 1939
LNWR 12-wheeled sleeping car (now cinema coach) No. 115 built 1907, rebuilt 1937
LNWR first-class kitchen/dining car No. 77 built 1901
LNWR six-wheeled passenger full brake No. DM279982 built 1891
LCDR first-class four-wheeled coach No. 9 built 1880
[11]LNWR bogie brake second coach No. 22736 built 1921
[11]LMS bogie third-class sleeper No. 592 built 1933
[11]LNWR six-wheeled CCT No. 580 built 1912
[11]MSLR six-wheeled third class coach No. 1076 built 1890
[11]GCR first-class bogie coach No. 957 built 1906
[11]GCR third-class bogie coach No. 652 built 1912
[11]GCR 'Barnum' bogie coach
[11]GCR suburban bogie coach No. 779
GWR Hawksworth brake/3rd coach No. 2242 built 1950
LNER Gresley BSK coach No. 41384 built 1936
LNER Gresley SK bogie coach No. Sc12934E built 1934
LMS SO bogie coach No. 7820 built 1924
LNWR inspection saloon No. 68 built 1874
GWR BG No. W64 built 1947 (In use as refreshment coach)
[11]LNWR corridor composite coach No. 2997 built 1920
[11]LMS open third-class coach No. 27162 built 1945
GNR six-wheeled brake/third coach No. 1470 built 1895
GNR six-compartment third-class coach No. 459 built ????
GWR 'Toad' 20-ton goods brake van No. 68624 built 1923
BR four-wheeled horsebox No. S96403 built 1958
LNWR saloon coach No. 119 built 1874
LNER non-corridor 3rd class coach No. 82145 built 1925
LNER corridor 3rd coach No. 3188
LPTB bogie electric motor coach No. 53028 built Birmingham RC&W 1937
LPTB district line bogie motor coach No. 54233 built Gloucester RC&W 1939
LNWR 6-wheel picnic saloon coach body built 1892
LPTB goods brake van No. B557 built 1935
Esso tank wagon No. 1869 built 1940
Shell tank wagon
GWR 11-ton gunpowder van No. W105777 built 1939
LNER 4-wheel 'Flatrol' wagon No. B900103 built 1953
SR 25-ton goods brake van No. 49014 built for Army 1942
MR box van No. 34676 built 1922
MR brake van No. 1692 built 1923
MR open wagon No. M18300 built 1912
LBSCR 10-ton open wagon No. AD46054
LSWR box van No. 47253
MR eight-ton box vans Nos 47251 and 47271
[2]SR four-wheeled PMV No. S1108S built 1947
[6]GWR six-wheeled milk tank wagon No. W2536
LMS box van Admiralty No. 837 built 1942
LSWR luggage van No. 5024 built 1917
[10]SR 25-ton goods brake van WD No. 49014 built 1941
[10]BR Flatrol wagon No. B900103 built 1953
[10]GWR gunpowder van No. 105777 built 1939
H & BR open wagon No. 85 built 1885
GWR open wagon rebuilt as van by the Army
Beckton Gas Works wagon No. 92 built *c*1880
LNER 10-ton five-plank wagons Nos AD46021 & AD46378
GWR 'Toad' 20-ton goods brake van No. 68766 built 1939
LMS box van No. 327466 built 1922
'Laporte' open industrial wagon
GWR 30-ton bogie bolster wagons, BSC Nos 64, 66, 97, 98 & 99
Cowans Sheldon hand-operated rail crane built 1944
Met & GCR hand crane No. 1 Cowans Sheldon 3282 built 1914 plus match truck
Wickham 4WPM rail inspection car No. 9037 8197 built 1958
Wickham 4WPM railcar No. 9040 6963 built 1955
Wickham 4WPM rail trolley No. TP53P 8263 built 1959
MR road crane built 1890
3-wheeled inspection tricycle Sheffield Car Co 50517
Signal box – ex-Harlington LMR

[1]Collett 57XX Class pannier tank sold to London Transport in 1963, becoming No. L99. Purchased for preservation in 1970.
[2]Owned by the 6024 Preservation Society Ltd (*q.v.*).
[3]Beattie well tank, originally LSWR No. 0314. Successively rebuilt throughout its long active life, it was one of three survivors of its class retained for working the Wenford Bridge mineral branch in Cornwall. Withdrawn in 1962, it was purchased for preservation in 1964 and stored at Bishop's Stortford until 1969.
[4]Metropolitan Railway 'E' Class locomotive built at Neasden to haul Aylesbury line passenger trains. The class were confined to freight work after 1937 and this particular locomotive was renumbered L44 in the following year. Withdrawn in 1964 after taking part in the Metropolitan centenary parade at Neasden. Stored at Luton until 1968.
[5]Withdrawn as BR No. 6024 in 1962 and sold to Woodham Brothers, Barry, for scrap. Purchased for preservation and moved to Quainton Road in 1973. Owned by the 6024 Preservation Society Ltd (*q.v.*).
[6]Donated by Unigate Dairies Limited 1973 and moved to Quainton Road. Owned by the 6024 Preservation Society Ltd (*q.v.*).
[7]Withdrawn as BR No. 46447 and sold to Woodham Brothers, Barry, for scrap. Purchased for preservation in 1972. Owned by the Ivatt Locomotive Trust (*q.v.*).
[8]Withdrawn as BR No. 41298 from Nine Elms shed on the last day of Southern steam, 9 July 1967. One of a batch of 30 locomotives built at Crewe Works to Ivatt's LMS design for use on the Southern Region to replace older 0-4-4T types.

[12]A Sentinel steam locomotive with a vertical boiler inside the cab. It has been steamed several times and has received no alterations since arrival from the Chesterfield Tube Co, apart from the addition of a number and a whistle from a BR Stanier 8F.
These locomotives differed from the rest of their class by having taller, tapered chimneys. Owned by the Ivatt Locomotive Trust (*q.v.*).
[9]Ex-Stewarts and Lloyds Minerals Ltd, Buckminster Ironstone Quarries, Lincolnshire, 1969. Owned by the Ivatt Locomotive Trust (*q.v.*).
[10]Owned by the Ivatt Locomotive Trust (*q.v.*).
[11]Owned by the Great Central Railway Coach Group (*q.v.*).

6024 Preservation Society Ltd H

Details from: W. A. Wilkinson (Secretary), 12 Tudor Square, Hayes End, Middlesex UB3 2QT

The Society purchased *King Edward I* No. 6024 in January 1973 from Barry, where she had lain since 1962, being the best of the two Kings there, for restoration to full running order. Removal took place in the last few days of March 1973 to Quainton Road Museum, arriving there on 1 April 1973. The Society was registered as a Charity in 1976 and became a registered Society on 30 September 1976 (No. 21746R – London). An appeal has been launched for the raising of £25,000, to be raised hopefully by fund raising. A group has been formed and it is hoped through the sale of shares, increased membership and general sales that this figure is reached.

Ivatt Locomotive Trust H

Registered Charity No. 262075
Trustees: P. I. Clarke and R. B. Miller, 'Ducal', 25 Loudham Road, Little Chalfont, Amersham, Bucks

Great Central Railway Coach Group H

Secretary: J. S. Parsons, 8 Grendon Way, Bierton, Aylesbury, Bucks HP22 5DD
The Group was formed in 1971 to purchase, finance and promote interest in coaches of GCR origin and to ensure where possible that they would return to former GCR lines. The Group's interest has changed to include other coaches of historical interest. To date 6-wheeled 1057 is carrying passengers at Quainton Road after a 30 year retirement.
Restoration continues at Quainton Road and it is hoped that GCR No. 957 will be the next coach to be completed.

456 Great Western Society Ltd D

Standard gauge steam railway preservation centre devoted specifically to the Great Western Railway. Steam-hauled rides are available on steaming days

Didcot Railway Centre, Didcot, Oxfordshire OX11 7NJ
Access: Through Didcot BR station. Bus routes Nos 302 and 306 Oxford–Wantage
Tel: Maidenhead 31767
OS Ref: SU 524906

Formed in 1961 with the aim of preserving a typical Great Western Railway branch line auto-train, the Society has now assembled a large collection of GWR locomotives and rolling stock at Didcot Railway Centre which lies in the triangle formed by the original GWR Paddington–Bristol main line and includes the original engine shed and depot. A typical GWR station has been created using the ticket office from Welford Park and 'pagoda' waiting shelter from Stockcross and Bagnor, both on the Lambourn branch, and signal box from Radstock on the North Somerset line. There are now two demonstration lines on which GWR trains operate at Steaming Days, giving rides to visitors.
Didcot Railway Centre is open Saturdays, Sundays and Bank Holidays from March to October. Steaming Days are held on the first and last Sunday of each month. Bank Holidays and all August Sundays as well as daily during the school holidays.
Santa Steamings are held at Christmas time.
Membership details from: Secretary, Great Western Society Ltd, Didcot, Oxfordshire.

Stock
[17]GWR 4-6-0 No. 5029 *Nunney Castle* built 1934
[18]GWR 2-8-0 No. 3822 (2884 Class) built 1940
[1]GWR 4-6-0 No. 5051 *Earl Bathurst/Drysllwyn Castle* built 1936
[2]GWR 4-6-0 No. 4942 *Maindy Hall* built 1929
[19]GWR 4-6-0 No. 5900 *Hinderton Hall* built 1931
[3]GWR 4-6-0 No. 6998 *Burton Agnes Hall* built 1949
[4]GWR 4-6-0 No. 7808 *Cookham Manor* built 1938
[5]GWR 2-6-0 No. 5322 (Class 43XX) built 1917
[20]GWR 2-8-2T No. 7202 (Class 72XX) built as 5275 in 1930, rebuilt 1935
[21]GWR 2-6-2T No. 4144 (Class 51XX) built 1946
[22]GWR 2-6-2T No. 5572 (Class 4575) built 1927
[6]GWR 2-6-2T No. 6106 (Class 61XX) built 1931
[7]GWR 0-6-2T No. 6697 (Class 56XX) Armstrong Whitworth 985 built 1928
GWR 0-6-0PT No. 3650 (Class 57XX) built 1939
GWR 0-6-0PT No. 3738 (Class 57XX) built 1937
[12]GWR 0-6-0ST No. 1363 (Class 1361) built 1910
GWR 0-4-2T No. 1466 (Class 48XX) built 1936
[8]GWR 0-4-0ST No. 1340 *Trojan* (ex-Alexandra Docks and Railway) Avonside 1386 built 1897
Wantage Tramway 0-4-0WT No. 5 *Shannon* George England built 1857
[10]BPGVR 0-6-0ST No. 2 *Pontyberem* Avonside 1421 built 1900
GWR diesel railcar No. 22 built 1940
Derby C & W 0-4-0PH built 1897, rebuilt 1960 and 1981

[11]RSH 0-4-0ST *Bonnie Prince Charlie* (7544) built 1949
[11]RSH 0-6-0ST No. 47 7800 built 1954
Hunslet 0-6-0DM No. DL26 5238 built 1957
[13]BR Bo-Bo DH No. D7018 (Beyer Peacock 7912) built 1962
GWR Collett full brake No. 111 built 1934
GWR auto-trailer No. 92 built 1912
GWR auto-trailer No. 190 built 1933
GWR auto-trailer No. 212 built 1936
GWR auto-trailer No. 231 built 1951
GWR four-wheeled composite No. 290 built 1902
GWR four-wheeled brake third No. 416 built 1891
GWR all-third corridor No. 536 built 1940
GWR TPO sorting van No. 814 built 1940
GWR full brake No. 933 built 1898
GWR corridor brake/third No. 2202 built 1950
GWR compartment brake/third Nos 3755 and 3756 built 1921
GWR corridor brake/third No. 5787 built 1933
GWR six-wheeled tri-composite No. 6824 built 1887
GWR corridor composite No. 7285 built 1941
GWR corridor brake/composite No. 7976 built 1924
GWR four-wheeled all-third No. 975 built 1902
GWR all-third corridor No. 1111 built 1938
GWR bow-ended full brake No. 1184 built 1930
GWR excursion third No. 1289 built 1937
GWR clerestory third No. 1357 built 1903
GWR Dean composite clerestory dining car No. 1580 built 1903
GWR clerestory third No. 1941 built 1901
GWR six-wheeled family saloon No. 2511 built 1894
GWR 'Siphon G' No. 2796 built 1937
GWR all-third 'Dreadnought' No. 3299 built 1905
GWR bow-ended corridor third No. 4553 built 1925
GWR bow-ended corridor third No. 5085 built 1928
GWR corridor third No. 5952 built 1935
GWR corridor composite No. 7313 built 1940
GWR corridor brake/composite No. 7362 built 1941
GWR corridor brake/composite No. 7371 built 1941
GWR corridor brake/composite No. 7372 built 1948
GWR Dean composite diner clerestory built 1903
GWR medical officers saloon No. 1159 built 1925
GWR special saloon No. 9002 built 1940
GWR special saloon No. 9005 built 1930
GWR first-class sleeping car No. 9083 built 1951
GWR 'Ocean' saloon No. 9112 *Queen Mary* built 1932
GWR 'Ocean' saloon No. 9113 *Prince of Wales* built 1932
GWR 'Ocean' saloon No. 9118 *Princess Elizabeth* built 1932
GWR 'Toplight' brake tri-composite (now staff van) No. 7538 built 1907
Cambrian Railways tri-composite coach No. 238 built 1895
BR composites S15565 and S15577 built 1955 (used as dormitory coaches)
GWR mess and tool vans Nos 47 and 135 built 1908
GWR sleeping car No. 243 built 1897
GWR 6-wheel water tank wagon No. 101 built 1948
LMS 6-wheel full brake No. 33002 built 1940 (body only)
GWR 12-ton hand crane and match truck No. 205 built 1894
GWR five-plank end-door china clay wagon No. 92943 built 1913
SR 'Express Dairy' six-wheeled milk tank built 1931, rebuilt 1938
GWR five-plank open wagon No. 553
GWR mess van No. 263 rebuilt 1952
GWR motor-car van *Python* (565) built 1914
GWR special cattle truck No. 752 built 1952
GWR six-wheeled 'Ro-tank' No. 3030 built 1947
GWR open wagon No. 24203 built 1915
GWR 'Crocodile F' well wagon No. 41934 built 1909
[9]GWR well wagon 'Hydra D' No. 42193 built 1917
GWR locomotive coal wagon No. 63066 built 1946
GWR tea van No. 79933 rebuilt 1938
Charles Roberts tar wagon No. 1 (adapted for weedkilling)
GWR 'Bloater' fish van No. 2671 built 1925
GWR 'Grano' grain van No. 42239 built 1927
GWR 'Toad' 16-ton brake van No. 56100 built 1895
GWR 'Toad' 20-ton brake van No. 68684 built 1924
[14]GWR 'Toad' 20-ton goods brake van No. 58092 built 1948
GWR banana van No. 105599 built 1930
[14]GWR tool van No. 1 built 1908
[14]GWR riding van No. 56 built 1912
GWR iron 'Mink' van No. 11152 built 1900
GWR water tank wagon No. DW101
Smith, Rodley 5-ton shunting steam crane No. 23059 built 1954
GWR 'Loriot L' well wagon No. 42271 built 1934
Smith, Rodley 5-ton shunting diesel crane No. CD24 built 1949 rebuilt 1967
[16]GWR 'Monster' bogie scenery vans Nos 484 & 485 built 1913
GWR 'Grampus' sleeper wagon No. 80668 built 1937
GWR shunters truck No. 100377 built 1921
GWR 10-ton van 'Mink A' No. 101720 built 1926
GWR insulated van 'Mica B' No. 105860 built 1926
GWR 20-ton van 'Mink G' No. 112843 built 1931
GWR motor-car van 'Asmo' No. 116954 built 1930
GWR ten-ton van 'Fruit B' No. 2356 built 1925
FR Esso 'Royal Daylight' tank wagon No. 745 built 1912
TVR seven-plank end-door open wagon No. 10153
Three-wheeled 'Velocipede'

[1]Withdrawn as BR No. 5051 in 1963 and sold to Woodham Brothers, Barry, for scrap. Purchased for the Great Western Society and moved to Didcot in February 1970. Restoration was completed in 1980 and it represented the GWS at the 'Rocket 150' parade at Rainhill.
[2]Withdrawn as BR No. 4942 and sold to Woodham Brothers, Barry, for scrap. Purchased for conversion into a 'Saint' class 29XX series 4-6-0 in 1973.
[3]6959 or 'Modified Hall' Class built at Swindon under BR auspices. Withdrawn from Oxford shed on 31 December

1965 and purchased by the GWS. The 'Halls' had their beginning in 1925 when a 'Saint' 4-6-0 was rebuilt with smaller driving wheels. Commencing in 1928, some were built in practically every year until 1952. The modified type appeared in 1944 and was a much superior machine. Altogether 330 of the class were constructed, the second largest class on the GWR. They worked on express passenger and ordinary freight work as required and many of the class were still in service when steam finished on GWR lines on the last day of 1965.

[4]Withdrawn from Gloucester shed in December 1965 and purchased for preservation. The 'Manors' were the smallest of the GWR 4-6-0s. Only 30 were built and they operated over the most severely restricted routes. Many were used on the former Cambrian main line between Shrewsbury and Aberystwyth, mainly on passenger work. They were the last GWR class to remain intact.

[5]No. 5322 has had a varied career, having worked in France during World War I and subsequently over most of the GWR system. It was withdrawn from Pontypool Road in 1964 and rescued from Barry scrapyard in 1969. It was the first Society engine purchased from Barry to be steamed.

[6]Withdrawn from Southall shed in December 1965 as BR No. 6106. There were several GWR classes of large 2-6-2T built for suburban passenger work, the 6100 Class being the final development and most powerful of its type. For many years the whole class of 70 engines worked entirely in the London division, the vast majority of them from Southall, Slough and Paddington sheds. Introduced to replace the ageing 4-4-2 and 2-4-0 tanks, the 6100 engines proved highly successful and several of the class survived until the last day of steam traction on the Western Region.

[7]Withdrawn from Croes Newydd shed, Wrexham, in May 1966 and purchased for preservation by the GWS, being stored initially at the Dowty RPS depot at Ashchurch. The GWR inherited a miscellany of 0-6-2 tanks at the grouping, mostly from the South Wales railways. Many of these were due for replacement and the 56XX Class was introduced in 1924 as a result. A total of 200 were built by the end of 1928 and the class remained intact until 1962. Most spent their entire working lives in the South Wales valleys where they handled both passenger and coal trains with ease.

[8]This diminutive engine was built for Messrs Dunn and Shute Ltd, the shunting contractors at Newport Docks. It was purchased by the Alexandra Docks and Railway Co in April 1903 and absorbed by the GWR in 1922, becoming No. 1340 and retaining its name. It was withdrawn from traffic in July 1932 and stood outside Swindon Works until sold to the Victoria Colliery Co of Wellington, Shropshire, in June 1934. It was hired to the Netherseal Colliery, Burton-on-Trent, and in 1947 was sold to Alders Paper Mill, Tamworth, where it worked until purchased for preservation and moved to Didcot.

[9]On loan from National Collection.

[10]The only surviving ex-Burry Port and Gwendraeth Valley Railway engine. Sold out of service in 1914 to Llewellyn (Nixon) Ltd (later Mountain Ash Colliery) before the BPGVR was absorbed into the GWR in 1923. Purchased for preservation from NCB, Penrikyber, 1972.

[11]Owned by the Salisbury Steam Locomotive Preservation Trust (*q.v.*).

[12]No. 1363 is one of five saddletanks of the 1361 Class, a modernised version of a Cornwall Mineral Railway design; the class spent their whole lives in the West Country on dock shunting and similar duties. They were the last saddletanks built for the GWR.

[13]Owned by the Diesel and Electric Group (see Group No. 4).

[14]Located at GWS Taunton Group Depot, Taunton, Somerset.

[16]Preserved by GWS South Wales Group.

[17]Withdrawn December 1963 and sent to Woodham Bros scrapyard, Barry. Purchased for preservation and moved to Didcot in May 1976.

[18]Withdrawn January 1964 and sent to Woodham Bros scrapyard, Barry. Purchased for preservation and moved to Didcot in May 1976.

[19]Withdrawn December 1963 and sent to Woodham Bros scrapyard, Barry. Purchased for preservation and moved to Didcot in June 1971. Restored to full working order for use on main line special trains.

[20]Withdrawn June 1964 and sent to Woodham Bros scrapyard, Barry. Purchased for preservation and moved by rail to Didcot in April 1974.

[21]Withdrawn June 1965 and sent to Woodham Bros scrapyard, Barry. Purchased for preservation and moved by rail to Didcot in April 1974.

[22]Withdrawn April 1962 and sent to Woodham Bros scrapyard, Barry. Purchased for preservation and moved to GWS Taunton depot in August 1971. Subsequently transferred to Didcot.

Salisbury Steam Locomotive Preservation Trust **H**

Details from: E. J. Roper, 33 Victoria Road, Wilton, near Salisbury, Wilts SP2 0OZ

457 King's Arms Miniature Railway A

A 9½in gauge passenger-carrying miniature railway in the garden of the King's Arms public house, Cardington, Bedfordshire. The line, which opened in 1962, is a quarter-of-a-mile in length and services run on Sundays only throughout the season

Operator: Mr C. Surridge

Stock

Bassett-Lowke 4-4-2 *Ruby* built *c*1914
Three 'sit-astride' bogie coaches

458 RESCO (Railways) Ltd G

Locomotive and rolling stock restoration specialists

Nathan Way, Woolwich Industrial Estate, London SE28 0AE

No public access

Stock
Hunslet 0-6-0ST *Hastings* 469 built 1888
Hunslet 0-6-0ST 3696 built 1950
RSH 0-6-0ST 7135 built 1944
RSH 0-4-0DH *Hengist* 8367 built 1962
English Electric 0-4-0DH No. 2 D1122 built 1966
Rolls Royce 4WDH No. D25 10195 built 1964
Hunslet 0-6-0DH No. 1 6973 built 1969
Rolls Royce 4WDH No. 2034 10197 built 1965
Met/District Railway coach body
LNWR kitchen diner No. 5159 (on LMS underframe)
LNWR sleeper No. 2112A body
GER luggage composite No. 197 (on LMS underframe)
GNR brake composite No. 127 (body only)
GNR first class saloon No. 807 built 1912
GNR corridor brake No. 1798
ECJS sleeper No. 107 (body only)
LNER pantry car No. 9066 built 1928
LNER Gresley TO No. 12190 built 1931
LNER Gresley TO No. 13577 built 1938
LNER Gresley TK No. 12481 built 1930
LNER Gresley TK No. 12328 built 1935

459 East Herts Miniature Railway A

Passenger-carrying 7¼in gauge steam railway, 500 yards in length

Van Hage Garden Centre, Great Amwell, near Ware, Herts
Access: On A1170 road about ½ mile north of the junction with the A414 between Hoddesdon and Ware, Herts
Tel: 01-504 2897
OS Ref: TL 368124

The railway operates every Sunday from Easter to the last Sunday in October from 11 am to 5 pm. Also runs every Saturday from 2 pm to 5 pm and every Thursday in the school holidays.
Facilities for visitors include car parking, toilets and the Garden Centre which incorporates a mini-farm.
The East Herts Miniature Railway came into being when a number of members of another East Herts Railway Club became tired of the miniature track at that club being a constant target for local vandals. After negotiations with the proprietor of the Van Hage Garden Centre, building commenced on the first Sunday in March 1978. The initial circuit of 670ft, complete with tunnel (35ft), station and workshop (Terrapin hut) was opened to the public on 30 July 1978. By the last Sunday in October, 12,811 passengers had been carried.
The railway conveyed 37,400 fare-paying passengers in 1979 since when a second circuit has been added giving almost ¼ mile run for which a 10p fare is charged.
The Van Hage Garden Centre is a very go-ahead concern, much larger than average with a 'mini-farm' which is free to visitors where many animals and birds can be seen. There is a permanent camping exhibition and a number of other attractions.
Details from: T. Miller, 70 Monkhams Avenue, Woodford Green Essex IG8 0ET

Stock
Various 7¼in gauge steam locomotives owned by members and one petrol-powered loco.

460 Cotswold Wild Life Park B

A 2ft gauge passenger-carrying line, 1 mile in length, operated by Leisuretrack Ltd

Burford, Oxfordshire
OS Ref: SP 237084

Stock
Motor Rail 4WDM *Adam* 9978 built 1954 (steam outline)
Ruston Hornsby 4WDM (20DL Class) 229631 built 1944
Motor Rail 4WDM 9976 built 1954
Six enclosed bogie coaches

461 Woburn Abbey Railway B

A 2ft gauge passenger-carrying line opened in 1973 by Track Supplies and Services Ltd, Wolverton, Bucks

Woburn Abbey, Bedfordshire
OS Ref: SP 968328

Stock
Ruston Hornsby 4WDM *Jodie II* (20DL Class) 223749 built 1944 (steam outline)
Ruston Hornsby 4WDM (40DL Class) 239381 built 1946 (steam outline)
Four open coaches

462 London Transport Museum E

London Transport has set up a permanent home for road and rail vehicles spanning nearly 200 years of public transport in the London area. Most of the exhibits were previously at the Museum of British Transport, Clapham, and then at Syon Park, Brentford, Middlesex

Old Flower Market Hall, Covent Garden, London WC2E 7BB
Access: Nearest Underground station: Covent Garden, Leicester Square or Charing Cross. Buses to Strand or Aldwych
Tel: 01-379 6344
OS Ref: TQ 303809

The Museum is open daily from 10 am to 6 pm throughout the year. Closed on Christmas Day and Boxing Day. Facilities for visitors include a coffee bar, lecture room, souvenir shop, weekend film shows, children's activity sheets, research library, refreshments and toilets.
Admission: £1.60 (adult). Handicapped visitors admitted free.
Visitors can operate the controls of a tram, an Underground train, signals and points. In addition to the vehicles and rolling stock there are models, signs, posters, paintings, audio-visual displays and a 1906 Otis lift car. A growing reserve collection of exhibits is being amassed.
The Covent Garden Museum is claimed to be the only one in Britain to cover the complete history of transport in one city.

Stock
[1]Metropolitan Railway 4-4-0T No. 23 ('A' Class) (Beyer Peacock 710) built 1866
Metropolitan Railway Bo-Bo E No. 5 *John Hampden* built 1922
Wotton Tramway 0-4-0TG (Aveling Porter 807) built 1872
District Railway Q23 stock motor coach No. 4248 built 1923
Metropolitan Railway milk van No. 3 built 1896
C & SLR underground coach No. 30 built 1890
Metropolitan Railway auto-train control trailer No. 400 built 1899
LPTB 1938 stock motor coach No. 11182 Metro-Cammell built 1938
Section of Great Northern, Piccadilly & Brompton Railway Gate stock tube car built 1906
LCC E1-type double-deck bogie electric tramcar No. 1025 built 1907
West Ham 4-wheeled double-deck electric tramcar LT No. 290 built 1910
Metropolitan Electric Tramways 'Feltham'-type double-deck tramcar No. 355 built 1931
London Tramways Co double-deck horse tram No. 284
Also London buses, trolleybuses, posters, signs, tickets and other exhibits.

[1]One of the Metropolitan 'A' Class tanks which used to work the Inner Circle line before electrification in 1905. No. 23 was rebuilt several times and in its final guise was the regular passenger engine on the rustic Brill branch in Buckinghamshire. When finally withdrawn as LTE No. L45, the engine was restored to its 1903 condition at Neasden and moved to Clapham Museum in 1961. On the closure of Clapham Museum in 1973, No. 23 was moved to Syon Park and thence to Covent Garden.

463 Science Museum — E

Historic locomotives and other transport exhibits on static display

Exhibition Road, South Kensington, London SW7 2DD
Access: LT Underground, South Kensington Station. Parking is metered. Bus routes Nos 9, 14, 30, 45, 49, 52, 73 and 74
Tel: 01-589 3456 Ext 562
OS Ref: TQ 368793

Facilities for visitors include museum shop, refreshments and toilets.
Open weekdays 10 am–6 pm, Sundays 2.30 pm–6 pm. Closed on 1 January, Good Friday, May Day Monday, 24, 25 and 26 December.
Admission free.

Stock
Wylam Colliery 4WVCG *Puffing Billy* built 1813 (5ft gauge)
L & MR 0-2-2 *Rocket* Stephenson 19 built 1829
L & MR 0-4-0 *Sanspareil* built Hackworth 1829
St Helens Railway 2-2-0 VBWT *Novelty* (replica built 1929)
C & SLR 4WE No. 1 (Mather and Platt/Beyer Peacock) built 1890
GWR 4-6-0 No. 4073 *Caerphilly Castle* built 1923
Parts of Trevithick 4WG loco built *c*1804
[1]Stephenson 0-2-2 *Rocket* 4089 built 1934
English Electric Co-Co DE *Deltic* 2007 built 1955
Black Hawthorn 0-4-0ST *Bauxite No. 2* 305 built 1874
LPTB underground coach No. 3327 built 1927
Glasgow 4-wheel double-deck tramcar No. 585 built 1901

[1]Replica of locomotive in original condition as built in 1829.

464 Southall Railway Centre — D

Standard gauge working steam railway museum

GWR Preservation Group, Bridge Road, Southall, Middlesex
OS Ref: TQ 130798

Facilities for visitors include a small relics museum, souvenir shop, refreshments and car park.
Regular open days are held at intervals throughout the year as advertised.
Details from: R. A. Gorringe, 16 Grange Close, Heston, Middlesex TW5 0HW

Stock
[4]GWR 2-8-0 No. 2885 (2884 Class) built 1938
[3]GWR 2-6-2T No. 4110 (41XX Class) built 1936
GWR 0-6-0PT No. 9682 (8750 Class) built 1949
[1]RSH 0-4-0ST *Birkenhead* 7386 built 1948
Peckett 0-4-0ST No. 2 2100 built 1949
Ruston Hornsby 0-4-0DM No. AD 251 *Francis Baily of Thatcham* 390776 built 1956
[2]AEC 4WDM No. 1 built 1938
GWR 'Toad' 20-ton goods brake van No. 17488
NER flat wagon
GCR flat wagon

[1]Ex-CEGB, Acton Lane Power Station, 1981.
[2]Ex-British Leyland, Southall, 1979.
[3]Withdrawn June 1965 and sent to Woodham Brothers scrapyard, Barry. Purchased for preservation and moved to Southall, 1979.
[4]Withdrawn January 1964 and sent to Woodham Bros scrapyard, Barry. Purchased for preservation and moved to Southall March 1981.

465 Buscot Light Railway C

Private 11½in gauge light railway 101 yards long built and operated by Mr Peacock

Mr K. Peacock, 28 Dale Cottages, Buscot, Oxfordshire

The railway is used for hauling logs from a dump to the house. Visitors are welcome, but a maximum of 6 to 8 is recommended, the land being under the care of the National Trust.
The Buscot Light Railway is quite unique in this country, being a practical working line built entirely from scrap materials and used to convey concrete blocks, logs and building materials. The railway had its beginnings 20 years ago when Mr Peacock's first two wagons ran on T-section rail over a distance of 30 yards. The line was subsequently extended and locomotives were built to increase its usefulness.
To inspect the railway, please send a note to Mr Peacock enclosing sae.
Suggested visiting hours: Saturdays 2 pm to 6 pm; Sundays 9 am to 4 pm.

Stock
Two 4WBE locomotives built 1963
Three wagons each convertible 3 ways (open, flat, bolster, etc)
Tram-type car (not in use).

466 Fancott Railway B

Passenger-carrying 10¼in gauge railway, 150 yards in length opened in 1975

Fancott Arms Public House, Fancott, near Toddington, Bedfordshire
Access: On B579 road south of Toddington
OS Ref: TL 022278

The line operates on Sundays throughout the year

Stock
Harper 0-4-0PM (steam outline)
Two covered 4-wheel coaches

467 Windsor & Eton Central Station E

GWR Victorian railway tableau featured as part of the 'Royalty and Railways' exhibition

Madame Tussaud's Ltd, Windsor, Berks

Exhibition opened Easter 1983

Stock
GWR 4-2-2 No. 3041 *The Queen* replica built 1982
GWR Queen Victoria's day saloon replica built Resco 1982
GWR royal saloon coach No. 233 built 1897, rebuilt Resco on new frame 1982

468 Fawley Hill Railway C

Private standard-gauge line owned by Mr W. H. McAlpine, Dobson's Farm, Fawley, near Henley-on-Thames, Bucks.
OS Ref: SU 755861

This line is not open to the general public and casual visitors will not be admitted. Please respect the owner's wishes and keep away.

Stock
[1]Aveling Porter 0-4-0TG *Sirapite* 6158 built 1906
[2]Avonside 0-4-0ST *Elizabeth* 1865 built 1922
Hudswell Clarke 0-6-0ST No. 31 1026 built 1913
Sentinel 4WVBTG *Joyce* 7109 built 1927
Baguley 0-4-0DM No. 5 3027 built 1939
GWR 'Toad' 20-ton brake van
GWR shunters 'chariot'

[1]Ex-Richard Garrett Engineering Works Ltd, Leiston, Suffolk, 1966. Restored at McAlpine's Duston-on-Tyne yard and moved to present site in 1970.
[2]Ex-South Eastern Gas Board, Waddon Marsh Gasworks, Croydon. Purchased for preservation by Mr J. B. Latham in 1969 and moved to Fawley Hill.

469 Goodman Brothers G

Standard gauge steam locomotive stored in scrapyard

Scrap Dealers, New Bradwell, Wolverton, Bucks
OS Ref: SP 832413

Stock
Hawthorn Leslie 0-6-0ST 3138 built 1915

470 Ware, Hertfordshire G

Standard gauge steam locomotive in store beneath a corrugated iron canopy in an orchard

Mr Malcolm Saul, Wengeo Lane, Ware, Herts
OS Ref: TL 346153

Stock
Hunslet 0-6-0ST *Newstead* 1589 built 1929

Ex-NCB, Woolley Colliery, Darton, Yorkshire, 1973.

471 Pendon Museum E

Pendon Museum of Miniature Landscape and Transport, Long Wittenham, Abingdon, Oxfordshire
Access: By road: Abingdon 5 miles, Wallingford 6 miles, Oxford 10 miles, London 55 miles. By rail: Didcot Station 3½ miles (no buses), Appleford Halt 1½ miles (footpath in summer).
Tel: Clifton Hampden 7365 (weekends only)
OS Ref: SU 543935

Open March to October on Saturdays, Sundays and Bank Holidays from 2 pm to 6 pm; November to February on Saturdays and Sundays from 2 pm to 5 pm (closed at Christmas).
Light refreshments, books and modelling items are on sale in the small shop.
At Pendon Museum, detailed and colourful model landscapes recapture the beauty of the English countryside of the early 1930s. Exquisitely modelled cottages, farms, fields and lanes recall the quiet charm of the Vale of the White Horse and country ways of half a century ago. In another scene, a cavalcade of trains moving across a long viaduct set in the wilds of Dartmoor provides a fascinating record of the Great Western Railway of that period.
Besides these unique creations, Pendon Museum presents John Ahern's famous Madder Valley layout, a tribute to the modeller's art in its own right. There is also a small collection of interesting transport relics.
Pendon is the Museum with a difference, full of absorbing details, an attraction for the enthusiast and general visitor alike. If you wear reading glasses, you should bring them – the detail work is very fine.

472 Didcot G

Narrow gauge locomotives in store

Mr R. Hilton, 'Poplars', North Moreton, Didcot, Oxfordshire
OS Ref: SU 552904

No public access.

Stock
[1]Bagnall 0-4-0ST No. ED10 1889 built 1911 (3ft gauge)
[2]Bagnall 0-4-0ST *Kidbrooke* 2043 built 1917 (1ft 11½in gauge)

[1]Ex-BR, Beeston Sleeper Works, Nottinghamshire, 1962.
[2]Ex-Oakeley Slate Quarries Co Ltd, Blaenau Ffestiniog, 1961. Stored at Minffordd on the Ffestiniog Railway until 1971.

473 Wellington Country Park A

Passenger-carrying 7¼in gauge line running through the Country Park

Near Reading, Berkshire

Operates on Saturday and Sunday afternoons and public holidays.

Stock
LMS 4-6-0 No. 6100 *Royal Scot*
Freelance 0-6-0T *Wendy*
Hammond 0-4-0T *Phoenix* built 1977
Freelance 2-6-0 No. 1320 *Iron Duke*
Freelance 0-6-0
GWR 0-6-0PT built Gibbs 1981
GNSR 4-4-0 *Gordon Highlander* built Wheeler 1981

474 Bletchley G

2ft gauge locomotive owned by Mr J. Thomas

40 Wye Close, Bletchley, Buckinghamshire

Stock
Lister 4WDM 4228 built 1931
Ex-Oxted Greystone Lime Co Ltd

475 Watford Miniature Railway B

A 10¼in gauge miniature railway approximately one-third-of-a-mile in length laid out in oval formation and situated alongside the River Gade

Cassiobury Park, Watford, Herts

The line is in operation every weekend and daily during school holidays from Easter until the end of September. The line was opened at Easter 1957

Stock
BR 0-6-0PM (08 Class) built C. Reed 1956
Shepperton 2-4-2PM built 1972 ('Meteor' Class)
Four open articulated bogie coaches

476 Bedfordshire County Council E

2ft gauge locomotive on static display

Dovery Down County Primary School, Heath Road, Leighton Buzzard, Beds
OS Ref: SP 923267

Stock
Motor Rail 4WDM No. 30 8695 built 1941
Ex-Joseph Arnold, Leighton Buzzard.

477 Windsor Safari Park E

Pullman car on static display

Windsor, Berkshire

Stock
SR Pullman coach No. 289 built 1932 (ex-Set No. 3051)

Ex-'Brighton Belle'. Formerly sited at the Little Mill Inn, Rowarth, Stockport, Cheshire, where it was known as 'The Derbyshire Belle'.

478 London Underground Railway Society G

Rolling stock undergoing restoration

West Ruislip Depot, Middlesex

Stock
C & SLR coach body No. 163 built 1907
LPTB 'Q35' stock underground trailer car No. 08063 built 1935

479 The 'Denham Express' Inn E

Ind Coope Limited. Coach used as a restaurant on the North Orbital Road, Denham, Bucks

Stock
Italian wagon-lit coach No. 2757 built Reggio, Emilia, 1926

480 Ian Allan Limited G

Pullman car in use as conference room

Shepperton, Middlesex

Stock
Pullman kitchen/first *Malaga* built 1921

481 Thames Water Authority C

Passenger-carrying 2ft gauge portable railway 100 yards in length which makes public appearances, usually at waterworks open days in the TWA area, throughout the year

Metropolitan Water Division, Charlton Road Depot, Shepperton, Middlesex
OS Ref: TQ 083694

Stock
Hibberd 4WPM *Ivan* 3317 built 1957
Two 4-wheel passenger coaches

482 Ruislip Lido Miniature Railway B

12in gauge passenger-carrying railway

The Lido, Reservoir Road, Ruislip, Middlesex
Tel: Ruislip 34081

Operates on weekends and Public Holidays from Easter until the end of September. Also runs daily throughout the School Summer Holidays.
The line is 1,000 yards long and runs from a station at Woody Bay alongside the lake to return via a loop to the starting point. Ruislip Lido is a family resort with a 40-acre lake for water sports and also beaches, woodland and children's amusements. Easily reached by bus and Underground services, the Lido is operated by the London Borough of Hillingdon.
The railway is operated by the Ruislip Lido Railway Society. The Society took over operation of the line in 1981 and a total of nearly 30,000 passengers were carried. Many members played a part in operating the service which attracted much favourable comment on availability of the amenity and on our standard of operation.
Society details from: Mr D. C. Parker, 8 Brendon Gardens, South Harrow, Middlesex HA2 8NE. Tel: 01-422 5631

Stock
Freelance Bo-BoPE *Robert*
Freelance 0-4-0DM
Four open coaches

483 Kings College, Stroud E

15in gauge steam locomotive on static display on first floor landing

OS Ref: TQ 308808

Stock
Brotherhood 2-2-2WT *Pearl* built 1860

484 C. and D. Lawson G

Private collection of narrow gauge locomotives

11 Okeley Lane, Highfield Estate, Tring, Herts
OS Ref: SP 913114

No public access. All locomotives are currently stored elsewhere.

Stock
Ruston Hornsby 4WDM No. 3 297066 built 1950 (2ft 6in gauge)
Ruston Hornsby 4WDM No. 4 402439 built 1957 (2ft 6in gauge)
Ruston Hornsby 4WDM No. 5 432654 built 1959 (2ft 6in gauge)
Ruston Hornsby 4WDM No. 6 224315 built 1944 (2ft 6in gauge)
Ruston Hornsby 4WDM No. 7 *Ellen* 200069 built 1939 (2ft 6in gauge)
Ruston Hornsby 4WDM No. 8 244559 built 1946 (2ft 6in gauge)
Lister 4WPM 34652 built 1949 (2ft 6in gauge)
Wickham 4WPMR 3431 built 1943 (2ft 6in gauge)
Wickham 4WPMR 3578 built 1944 (2ft 6in gauge)
Ruston Hornsby 4WDM 166045 built 1933 (2ft 1½in gauge)
Ruston Hornsby 4WDM 247178 built 1947 (2ft 1½in gauge)
Ruston Hornsby 4WDM 229657 built 1945 (1ft 8in gauge)
Ruston Hornsby 4WDM 441944 built 1960 (2ft gauge)

485 Alan Keef Ltd G
Locomotives undergoing restoration

Cote Farm, Cote, Near Bampton, Oxfordshire

Stock
Kerr Stuart 0-4-2ST No. 1 *Lady Morrison* 3024 built 1916 (3ft gauge) + i/c locos for rebuild, resale and hire

486 C.I.L. Storefitters Ltd G
Pullman car in use as office accommodation

Finsbury Park Station, North London

No public access

Stock
SR Pullman car No. 282 *Doris* built 1932
Ex-'Brighton Belle' set No. 3051

487 Walnut Lodge Sawmills G
1ft 8in gauge locomotive on static display

Mr P. J. Mackinnon, 36 Luton Road, Wilstead, Beds
OS Ref: TL 063433

Stock
Orenstein & Koppel 4WDM 6703

488 Tottenham E
2ft gauge vehicle on static display

Haringay Libraries, Museum & Arts Service, Bruce Castle Park, Tottenham
OS Ref: TQ 335907

Stock
4-wheel atmospheric car built *c*1865

489 Museum of London E
2ft gauge vehicle on static display

London Wall EC2
OS Ref: TQ 322816

Stock
4-wheel atmospheric car built *c*1865

490 Richard Moore G
Standard gauge steam locomotive being restored

Enfield, Middlesex

No public access

Stock
Bagnall 0-6-0PT 2613 built 1940

491 London Transport G
Electric locomotive retained as working museum piece. Occasionally used for hauling special trains

Stock
Metropolitan Railway Bo-BoE No. 12 *Sarah Siddons* built Vickers 1922

492 North Woolwich Station Museum E
A brand new museum housed in the beautifully restored North Woolwich station building

Pier Road, North Woolwich, London E16 2JJ
Access: Adjacent to Woolwich Free Ferry. Direct services by BR trains from Stratford (Mon-Fri, tubes link Stratford and West Ham). LT buses 69 and 101, plus 58 at peak periods

The museum contains three galleries of photographs, models, relics, etc to bring to life the story of the Great Eastern Railway. There is a fully-restored and furnished Edwardian period booking office open to the public and a standard gauge steam locomotive on static display.
For future development, there is a four acre goods yard and the possibility of laying a 1¼-mile demonstration track.
Facilities for visitors include a souvenir shop and bookstall.
The museum is open daily: Mon–Sat 10 am–5 pm, Sun 2–5 pm. Admission free.

Stock
GER 0-4-0ST No. 229 Neilson 2119 built 1876
SR 4-6-2 No. 35010 *Blue Star* built 1942

493 Cholsey & Wallingford Railway Preservation Society F
Standard gauge railway preservation group working towards acquiring and restoring the remains of the Cholsey–Wallingford branch, Oxfordshire

Stock
GWR auto-trailer coach No. 174 built 1930
Esso 4-wheel tank wagon

494 A.R.C. Conbloc Ltd G
2ft gauge steam locomotive in store pending restoration

Stanton Harcourt, near Witney, Oxfordshire

Stock
Freudenstein 0-4-0WT *Penlee* 73 built 1901

Ireland

(Group Nos 501–550)

501 Railway Preservation Society of Ireland AD

Whitehead Excursion Station, Co Antrim
Access: Ulsterbus Belfast–Whitehead route
Nearest NIR station: Whitehead (trains from Belfast (York Road) or Larne Harbour)
Tel: Whitehead (096 033) 78567

Operations Officer: Denis Grimshaw, 14 Craigdarragh Park East, Craigavad, Co Down. Tel: Holywood 3816.
Secretary: Robin Morton, 79 Shannon Road, Belfast 9
The RPSI was formed in 1964 to obtain some examples of Ireland's steam locomotives and to restore and maintain them in working order. The Society's base is at Whitehead Excursion Station, built by the LMS (NCC) in 1903 to cope with the day trip traffic from Belfast. The facilities include a long platform and water tower, together with the original two-road engine shed and the recently added three-road extension built by the members. The Society carries out its own minor repairs, painting and cleaning. Each year the Society operates several main line railtours over the NIR and CIE systems. RPSI tours are designed for the enthusiast with plenty of photographic and tape-recording opportunities with special stops, runpasts, line-side buses and train-splitting on two-engine tours.
Facilities for visitors include souvenir shop, refreshments in dining car and car parking.

Stock
[1]GNR (I) 4-4-0 No. 171 *Slieve Gullion* (Class S) built 1913
[2]LMS (NCC) 2-6-4T No. 4 (Class WT) built 1947
[3]GS & WR 0-6-0 No. 186 (Class J15) built 1879
[4]GSWR 0-6-0 No. 184 (Class J15) built 1899
[5]GNR (I) 4-4-0 No. 85 *Merlin* Beyer Peacock 6733 built 1932
DSER 2-6-0 No. 15 Beyer Peacock 6112 built 1922
[6]SL & NCR 0-6-4T *Lough Erne* Beyer Peacock 7242 built 1949
[7]Hudswell Clarke 0-4-0ST No. 3 *Guinness* 1152 built 1919
[8]Avonside 0-6-0ST LP & HC No. 3 *R. H. Smyth* 2021 built 1928
Ruston Hornsby 4WDM 382827 built 1955
[9]Hibberd 4WDM No. 23 3509 built 1951
GSWR 12-wheeled 'Rosslare Express' brake/composite coach No. 861 built 1906
GNR (I) directors' saloon No. 50 built 1911
GSR Bredin corridor third class coaches Nos 1327 and 1328 built 1935
GNR (I) dining car No. 88 built 1938
GSWR corridor second class coach No. 4012 built 1914
LMS-NCC 3rd class corridor coach No. 243 built for LMS 1924 sent to Ireland 1942
GSR Bredin third class corridor coach No. 1335 built 1937
GSR Bredin third class open coach No. 1333 built 1936
GNR (I) first class corridor coach No. 227 built 1947
GNR (I) third class open coach No. 176 built 1941
GNR (I) third class open coach No. 9 rebuilt as AEC non-powered driving trailer coach No. 586 built 1954
GNR (I) brake first open coach No. 231 rebuilt as BUT rail-car brake/first No. 562 built 1948
GNR (I) corridor brake third coach No. 175 rebuilt as BUT railcar brake/third No. 594 built 1946
GNR (I) 3rd class open coach No. 98 built 1941
LMS-NCC 3rd class corridor coaches Nos 238 & 241 built for MR 1921, sent to Ireland 1942
NIR dining car No. 550 built 1950
NIR corridor composite coach No. 274 built by MR 1922
Dormitory coach
LMS-NCC 'North Atlantic' brake/3rd No. 91 built 1934
B&CDR 3rd class 6-wheel coach body No. 182 built 1922
MGWR 6-wheel coach built 1897
GSWR first class coach No. 1142 built 1921
[10]Hibberd 4WDM 3719 built 1954 (3ft gauge)
[10]Schottler 4WDM 1727 built 1955 (3ft gauge)
[10]Stored on behalf of DoE for N. Ireland
Two GNR (I) bogie grain wagons
Irish Shell tank wagon
GNR (I) six-wheeled goods brake van
Inglis bread container and wagon

[1]Clifford 'S' Class rebuilt in 1938 by Glover. This locomotive is the last example of the five 'Mountain' Class 4-4-0s and is a typical Edwardian express engine. These locomotives pulled the principal trains on the Belfast to Dublin and Londonderry lines. Restored in Great Northern sky blue livery. Owned by the Northern Ireland Transport Holding Company and leased to the RPSI.
[2]No. 4 was one of 18 Class WT engines which were used extensively by the Ulster Transport Authority, later Northern Ireland Railways. Their last task was the hauling of the 20-wagon two-engine spoil trains on the Belfast–Larne line, and when No. 4 was bought by the Society in 1971 for £1,275 she was the last steam engine still in company service in the British Isles.
[3]This engine is an example of Ireland's largest class of locomotives. In all 111 of this type were built from 1866 onwards at Inchicore to the design of MacDonnell. These locomotives were typical examples of the Ramsbottom/Webb Crewe tradition and were to be found throughout the Great Southern system. They were very successful machines and were mainly used for freight and local passenger workings, with a top speed in the low 60s. Built in 1879 by Sharp Stewart principally for goods trains, 186 is now the oldest working steam engine in Ireland. Livery is unlined black.

[4]A sister engine of No. 186, this engine is the saturated steam version of the J15 Class. Until the 1940s this locomotive was fitted with the old type of double smokebox doors. Some years ago No. 184 was used in the making of the film *Darling Lili*. Both J15s have since had starring roles in the Michael Crichton film *The First Great Train Robbery*.

[5]The handsome 'V' Class 4-4-0s were the ultimate development of the Smith/Deeley Midland compound. Designed by G. T. Glover, five locomotives were built and it was possible to accelerate the Belfast to Dublin expresses immediately they entered traffic. They became well-known in the post-war years for their haulage of the 'Enterprise' express. *Merlin* passed to the CIE in 1958 on the dissolution of the GNR (I) and was withdrawn in 1963.

[6]The last surviving locomotive of the Sligo, Leitrim and Northern Counties Railway, which had been operated principally by 0-6-4Ts since 1882. It was the last conventional steam locomotive built for any Irish railway and passed to the UTA on closure of the Sligo line. It was purchased privately for preservation in 1970.

[7]No. 3 was used by the brewery of Arthur Guinness, Son and Co, for short workings between the brewery in Dublin, along streets to Kingsbridge goods yard. She became redundant in 1965 and was presented to the Society, along with spare parts, by Guinness's. Formerly she carried no nameplate, but this was added by the Society as thanks to the brewery. She is the favourite engine for the Sunday afternoon steam train rides at Whitehead during the summer.

[8]The Society's latest steam acquisition worked with the Londonderry Port and Harbour Commissioners until the late 1950s when she became redundant and was bought by a clergyman. He sold her to the Society for a penny in 1972 and since then the Whitehead locomotive maintenance team have been working hard on overhauling her.

[9]Presented to the Society via the Irish Steam Preservation Society from Irish Shell and BP in 1973. Reckoned to be the smallest standard-gauge engine ever used in Ireland.

The engines, except Nos 85, 184 and 186, are all kept at Whitehead, the base for all the tours and scene of the Sunday afternoon steam train rides in June, July and August.

Activities

The Society is the only body in Ireland operating main line steam engines, and enjoys close co-operation with the Irish railway companies CIE and NIR. No restrictions are placed on routes over which steam can run, and the Society's tours are exclusively steam-hauled. The annual tour programme usually comprises one-day outings from Dublin and then Belfast in the spring, followed by the big one – a two-day two-engine all steam tour from Dublin over part of the CIE system.

The summer is the time for the season of four 'Portrush Flyer' steam excursion trains – an accurate recreation of the Ulster excursion train to the seaside. Then, to round things off, another one-day tour is operated in Northern Ireland in September.

Steam train rides are operated at Whitehead on Sunday afternoons in June, July and August. Work goes on there every weekend.

The Society runs a number of film shows and meetings in Belfast during the winter.

Details of membership are available from Mervyn Darragh, 35 Dermott Walk, Comber, Co Down.

502 Irish Steam Preservation Society Limited — A

This Society operates a 3ft gauge railway ¾ mile in length in the grounds of Stadbally Hall, Stradbally, Co Laois, by kind permission of Mr A. P. S. A. Cosby

Stradbally, Co Laois, Ireland

Access: Stradbally is eight miles from Athy, Co Kildare, and six miles from Portlaoise, Co Laois, the nearest CIE rail stations

Certain buses on the CIE Dublin–Kilkenny route serve Stradbally, but this service is unsuitable for day visits, except on Sundays. Intending visitors should contact the Society's Secretary, Mrs Olive Condell, Main Street, Stradbally, Co Laois (Telephone 0502/25136), for appointments to visit the museum and for details of other operating dates for the railway. Work parties are there on certain Saturdays each month, when visitors would be specially welcome.

In addition to the railway, the Society has a steam museum in the town of Stradbally, which is opened on request at any time, by prior appointment. Each year, the railway is a major attraction during the National Traction Engine Rally held in the grounds of Stradbally Hall at the beginning of August. It is also hoped to operate the line for open days on other days, particularly if there are any other suitable functions in the town and on Easter Sunday and Monday and the last weekend in October.

Details from: The Secretary as above.

Workable Stock

Barclay 0-4-0WT No. 2 2264 built 1949
Hunslet 4WDM No. 1 2280 built 1941
Wickham 4WPM railcar No. C39 6861 built *c*1955
One bogie toastrack coach, 45 seats
Ballast wagon

Other Stock

Drewry 4WPM railcar No. 5 1495 built 1927 (5ft 3in gauge)
Spence 0-4-0T No. 15 built 1895 (1ft 10in gauge)

The Society was founded in 1965 by some local traction engine enthusiasts. The present 3ft gauge railway was started in 1969 and has been gradually extended since then as far as limited finance and voluntary labour has allowed. The Society organises the National Traction Engine Rally each year and the railway represents the only steam ride available to the public.

503 Shane's Castle Railway

One-and-a-half mile, 3ft gauge passenger-carrying line operated by The Lord O'Neill

Shane's Castle, Antrim, Northern Ireland
Access: On the A6 Antrim–Randalstown road, 1 mile out of Antrim. Bus route No. 110 Belfast–Antrim
Tel: Antrim 3380 or 2216
OS Ref: 136874

Facilities for visitors include car parking, railway shop, catering to a notable standard, toilets and nature reserve. The Shane's Castle Light Railway opened in May 1971 and is currently the only narrow gauge steam operated railway in regular use anywhere in Ireland. The railway runs from the terminus on the edge of Antrim through a largely wooded setting to the ruins of Old Shane's Castle. The area is also a nature reserve, which is jointly managed with the Royal Society for the Protection of Birds. The system operates on Sundays and Bank Holidays in April and May, on Saturdays, Sundays and Bank Holidays in June, on Wednesdays, Saturdays and Sundays in July plus the Northern Ireland July Holiday fortnight and August and on Sundays in September. Opening hours, 12 noon to 6 pm.

Stock
Peckett 0-4-0T No. 1 *Tyrone* 1026 built 1904
Motor Rail 4WDM No. 2 *Rory* 11039 built 1956
Barclay 0-4-0WT No. 3 *Shane* 2265 built 1949
Hibberd 4WDM No. 4 *Nippy* 2014 built 1936
Avonside 0-6-0T *Nancy* 1547 built 1908
Wickham 4WPMR 7441 built 1956
Three Charleroi Tramway trailer cars
Seven four-wheeled covered coaches
Four four-wheeled open coaches
Four-wheeled brake/saloon coach
B & NCR coal wagon
BAC (Larne) open wagon converted into a spray truck
L & LSR three-plank open wagon
L & LSR mobile crane truck
Twelve BAC (Fort William) wagons

Static Exhibits in the care of the North West of Ireland Railway Society by arrangement with Dr Ralph Cox
Nasmyth Wilson 2-6-4T No. 6 *Columbkille* 830 built 1907
CDRJC 0-4-0+4WDMR No. 12 built Walker Brothers 1934
CDRJC 0-4-0+4WDMR No. 18 built Walker Brothers 1940
CDRJC bogie composite coach No. 14 built 1893
CDRJC railcar wagon
Five CDRJC bogie coach underframes

The Shane's Castle Railway was conceived in the late sixties and opened to the public in May 1971. Essentially a tourist attraction, it complements the other points of interest at Shane's Castle. However, it is currently the only place in Ireland where 3ft gauge steam locomotives can be seen in regular use during the summer months. Recently, the stock of the North West of Ireland Railway Society has moved on to the system and plans are under discussion about future developments which could lead to a more ambitious 3ft gauge museum arising.

504 Coras Iompair Eireann E

Static exhibits on display at locations named

Stock
[1]GSWR 2-2-2 No. 36 Bury Curtis and Kennedy built 1846: Cork (Kent)
[3]GSWR 0-6-0T No. 90 built 1880: Mallow
[4]West Clare Railway 0-6-2T No. 5 Dubs 2890 built 1892 (3ft gauge): Ennis

[1]This locomotive is a passenger version of the Bury design with 5ft 8in wheels and bar frames. It is worthy of comparison with the ex-Furness Railway 0-4-0 *Coppernob*. There were 20 of these engines on the Great Southern and Western and this was the last in service in 1881.
[3]This is one of three similar engines built to the design of J. A. F. Aspinall for light lines in Ireland. They ran on the Castletown and Mitchelstown to Fermoy branches, though No. 90 ended its days on the Timoleague and Courtmacsherry Light Railway. In working order it weighed a mere 22 tons and had a tractive effort of 5,160lb.
[4]Originally named *Slieve Callan* and withdrawn as CIE (West Clare Section) Class INI No. 5C in 1959. Used during filming of *The Rising of the Moon* then stored at Inchicore Works, Dublin, until restored in 1961. This engine has been kept not only for its interest as a West Clare locomotive but as a memorial to the late Percy French who immortalised the idiosyncrasies of the line in his song, 'Are ye right there, Michael?'

505 Belfast Transport Museum E

The museum houses part of the Ulster Folk Museum collection and covers all aspects of transport. Over 100 vehicles, including railway and tramway examples, also models, equipment and records

Witham Street, Belfast, Northern Ireland BT4 1HP
Access: City bus services via Albert Bridge or Newtonards Road, 8 minutes from City Centre
Tel: Belfast 51519

Static exhibits
Open: Weekdays 10 am–6 pm (9 pm on Wednesdays). Closed on Sundays

Stock

5ft 3in gauge

[1]B & CDR 4-4-2T No. 30 Beyer Peacock 4231 built 1901
[2]GNR (I) 2-4-2T No. 93 built 1895
[3]GNR (I) 4W diesel railcar 'E' built 1934
[4]NCC 4-4-0 No. 74 *Dunluce Castle* (Fowler Class U2) NB Loco 23096 built 1924
[5]GSR 4-6-0T No. 800 *Maeve* (Bredin Class B1A) built 1939
Stephenson 0-6-0T No. 1 2738 built 1891
[6]GNR (I) Fintona horse tram No. 381
William Dargan's 6-wheel saloon coach (M & GWR No. 47) built *c*1844
Dublin, Wickham & Wexford Rly 3rd class coach No. 48 built *c*1844
Dundalk, Newry & Greenore Rly composite coupé 6-wheel coach No. 1 built 1901

3ft gauge

CDRJC 2-6-4T No. 2 *Blanche* Nasmyth Wilson 956 built 1912
CDRJC Drewry petrol railcar No. 3 built 1926
CDRJC Ford petrol railcar No. 1 built 1906
CDRJC 0-4-0D No. 11 *Phoenix* Atkinson Walker 114 built 1928
Clogher Valley Railway diesel railcar No. 1 built 1932
Cavan and Leitrim Railway 4-4-0T No. 3 *Kathleen* Stephenson 2613 built 1887
Peckett 0-4-0T No. 2 1097 built 1906
Portstewart Tramway 0-4-0 tram locomotive No. 2 Kitson T84 built 1883
Cavan & Leittim Rly clerestory bogie saloon coach No. 6 built 1887

1ft 10in gauge

Spence 0-4-0T No. 20 built 1905

[1]This is a typical Beyer Peacock design developed from earlier 2-4-2T engines. The class was responsible for the bulk of B & CDR passenger train haulage. This locomotive became UTA No. 30 and was stored from 1956 to 1961, when it was restored to its original livery and placed on display. Officially withdrawn in 1962.
[2]Clifford Class JT. Restored and presented by the GNR (I) board in 1955. Originally named *Sutton*.
[3]Originally known as 'Railcar E'. Withdrawn by the UTA in 1966.
[4]Designed by Sir Henry Fowler, this locomotive can be described as an Irish version of his LMS Class 2P 4-4-0s. Withdrawn as UTA No. 74 in 1961 and restored to NCC livery in 1962. Placed on display in 1963.
[5]Bredin Class BIA locomotive withdrawn as CIE No. 800 in 1957. This locomotive and its two sisters were the crack locomotives of Ireland. Apart from the GWR 'King' Class they were probably the most powerful 4-6-0s in Western Europe and were introduced with a view to speeding up the Dublin–Cork services. The magnificent bronze nameplates were inscribed in Erse after ancient queens of Ireland, and the spelling 'Maeve' is the English rendering. Restored at Inchicore Works, Dublin, in 1963 and presented for display in the following year by the CIE.
[6]This vehicle became a celebrity in its own right and ran on the half-mile Fintona Junction to Fintona Town branch in connection with the main line trains. It was withdrawn (and the horse retired) when the main line service ceased. The tram carried first, second and third class passengers, though these distinctions were largely ignored!

506 Arthur Guinness Son and Company (Dublin) Limited E

1ft 10in gauge steam locomotive on static display

St James Gate Brewery, Dublin 8
Access: Bus routes Nos 21, 21A and 78
Nearest CIE station: Dublin Heuston
Tel: 756701

Open daily 11 am–4.15 pm (excluding Bank and Public Holidays); admission free

Stock

Spence 0-4-0T No. 17 built 1902

507 Ulster Folk Museum BE

The theme of the Museum's displays is that of the advance of transport from bog sledges and traditional carts to fine horse carriages and thence via the bicycle and automotive vehicles to a special display illustrating significant advances in technology including the world's first VTOL aircraft, the Short SC1.
A passenger-carrying 2ft gauge railway was opened in 1976 featuring gradients up to 1 in 30

Cultra Manor, Craigavad, County Down BT18 0EU
Access: Belfast–Bangor bus service from Oxford Street depot
Tel: Holywood 5411

The Museum is open from May to September on weekdays from 11 am to 7 pm and on Sundays from 2 pm to 7 pm. May and June late closing on Tuesdays and Wednesdays. October to April open on weekdays from 11 am to 5 pm and on Sundays from 2 pm to 5 pm.
The 2ft railway is not currently operating as major improvements were necessary on the trackbed due to subsidence of made-up ground. This work is now well advanced and operation can recommence as soon as it is complete. Severe financial stringencies with consequent lack of staff are the governing factors. We cannot therefore commit ourselves to a fixed date for re-opening.
On the other hand, we have a relationship of close co-operation with the Railway Preservation Society of Ireland and GNR (I) No. 85 *Merlin* is currently being overhauled at the Belfast works of Harland & Wolff (under private sponsorship). No. 85 will then go out on loan to

RPSI and participate in their regular live steam excursions.

With Aerolite and MR 1000, No. 85 represents all that is preserved of the British compound locomotive and was in fact one of the last batch of 5 to be built (1932).

However, visitors can still ride behind a steam engine at the Museum. Perhaps uniquely among British Museums, the Model Engineers' Society Northern Ireland have built and are regularly operating a 1700ft raised level outdoor track within the Museum grounds and rides on their trains are provided during their weekend operations.

The track is equipped with automatic signalling and up to 6 trains can operate at any one time.

Stock

Motor Rail 4WDM 9202 built 1946
Hunslet 4WDM 3127 built 1943
Motor Rail 4WPM 246 built 1916
Hibberd 4WDM built 1948
Four 12-seat passenger coaches on Cravens underframes
Giant's Causeway Tramway trailer car No. 2 (3ft gauge) static exhibit
Body of Castlederg & Victoria Bridge Tramway saloon coach built 1883 (3ft gauge)
Hudson 4-wheel open wagon
Fowler steamroller as a play exhibit

508 Galway Miniature Railway B

A 10¼in gauge passenger-carrying line

Galway, Eire

Stock

Severn-Lamb 2-8-0PH No. 278 *Rio Grande* built 1975 (steam outline)

509 Doctor Ralph Cox G

3ft gauge former County Donegal Railways rolling stock in store at Strabane. The future of these acquisitions is unknown, but since much of the collection has been heavily vandalised and now lies derelict, it is doubtful whether it will remain in existence for much longer

Strabane Station, County Tyrone

Stock

Nasmyth Wilson 2-6-4T No. 4 *Meenglas* 828 built 1907
Nasmyth Wilson 2-6-4T No. 5 *Drumboe* 829 built 1907
CDRJC bogie composite coaches Nos 12, 15, 16 and 17 built 1893
CDRJC passenger van No. 23 built 1893
All the above coaches have been reduced to underframes and bogie only.

510 Belfast and County Down Railway Museum Trust F

Ballynahinch Junction Station, County Down
Access: Off main Saintfield to Downpatrick road at Junction Road

The Belfast and County Down Railway Museum Trust was established in 1972 with the aim of setting up a railway museum where relics and photographs of the Belfast and County Down and other Irish railways might be preserved. Such has been the interest in the project that the original plans have been considerably enlarged, and it is now our intention to reopen a portion of the railway as a Working Railway Museum.

This will probably be the most ambitious railway preservation project yet undertaken in Ireland. It will be the first time an attempt has been made to reopen a closed section of railway using Irish standard gauge track and it is hoped that the end product will be a working railway museum similar in proportions to the famous Bluebell Railway in England or the Strathspey Railway in the Highlands of Scotland.

The portion of line involved will include 2 miles of the old Belfast and County Down Railway main line between Rowallane Gardens, the National Trust property at Saintfield, and Ballynahinch Junction, and the 3½ miles of the branch line from there to Ballynahinch Town.

Secretary of the Trust is Mr R. J. Pue, 8 Woburn Drive, Millisle, County Down BT22 2HU.

Stock

Orenstein & Koppel 0-4-0T 12475 built 1934
Orenstein & Koppel 0-4-0T 12662 built 1935
CIE 6-wheeled passenger brake van
B & CDR 6-wheeled family saloon coach body
B & CDR 6-wheeled 3rd class coach body

511 Tramore Miniature Railway B

A 15in gauge passenger-carrying line

Tramore, County Waterford, Eire

Stock

Severn-Lamb 2-8-0PH No. 278 *Rio Grande* (22) built 1973 (steam outline)

512 Rosminian Fathers B

A 2ft gauge passenger-carrying line formerly operated by the St John of God Brothers at Drumcar, County Louth

Upton, Innishannon, County Cork

Stock

Ruston & Hornsby 4WDM (Class 13DL) 264244 built 1949

513 Great Southern Railway Preservation Society — F

The society has the long-term objective of reopening the abandoned but intact 9-mile Tralee–Fenit branch

Stock

GNR 4-4-0 No. 131 Q Class built 1899
GSR Bredin bogie coach built 1935
Four CIE side corridor coaches

514 Martin O'Keeffe — G

Petrol railcar undergoing restoration

Rostellan, near Middleton, Cork

Stock

Wickham 4WPMR No. C42 7129 built 1955 (3ft gauge)

515 Winn Technology Ltd — E

Steam locomotive on static display

Kilbrittain, Cork

Stock

Spence 0-4-0T built 1912 (1ft 10in gauge)

516 Trinity College, Dublin — E

Steam locomotive on static display

Stock

Kennon 0-6-0 built 1855 (1ft 9in gauge)

APPENDIX 1 FORMER BR AND PRE-NATIONALISATION STEAM LOCOMOTIVES

No.	*Group*	*No.*	*Group*	*No.*	*Group*	*No.*	*Group*	*No.*	*Group*	*No.*	*Group*	*No.*	*Group*
7	305	4248	332	6634	3	30841	153	35025	332	46447	455	65894	153
8	305	4253	332	6686	332	30847	52	35027	35	46464	203	68077	151
9	305	4270	349	6695	23	30850	254	35028	355	46512	203	68088	403
12	455	4277	332	6697	456	30925	166	35029	166	46521	352	68095	271
252	170	4555	1	6960	352	30928	52	W24	56	47279	151	68153	152
426	151	4561	4	6984	332	31027	52	41000	166	47298	311	68633	166
450	312	4566	352	6989	455	31065	94	41241	151	47324	55	68846	166
813	352	4588	2	6990	403	31178	52	41298	455	47327	405	69023	153
822	302	4612	151	6998	456	31263	52	41312	312	47357	405	69523	403
823	302	4920	1	7027	354	31323	52	41313	455	47383	352	69621	104
921	419	4930	352	7029	354	31556	53	41708	405	47406	417	70000	103
1338	19	4936	357	7200	455	31592	52	41966	101	47445	405	70013	101
1340	456	4942	456	7202	456	31618	52	42073	252	47493	3	71000	403
1363	456	4953	356	7229	332	31625	55	42085	252	47564	405	73050	103
1369	1	4979	332	7714	352	31638	52	42500	101	48151	156	73082	52
1378	324	4983	354	7715	455	31737	166	42700	166	48173	332	73096	332
1420	1	5029	456	7752	354	31806	55	42765	151	48305	332	73129	405
1442	27	5043	354	7754	311	31874	55	42859	332	48431	151	73156	332
1450	1	5051	456	7760	354	32110	3	42968	352	48518	332	75014	153
1466	456	5080	354	7802	352	32473	52	43106	352	48624	417	75027	52
1501	352	5164	352	7808	456	32636	52	43924	151	48773	352	75029	3
1638	1	5193	253	7812	352	32640	56	44027	405	49395	370	75069	352
2180	1	5199	332	7819	352	32646	56	44123	55	50621	166	75078	151
2516	20	5224	403	7820	310	32650	53	44422	358	51218	151	75079	49
2807	357	5227	332	7821	357	32655	52	44767	153	52044	151	76017	55
2818	166	5239	2	7822	361	32662	101	44806	278	52322	254	76077	332
2857	352	5322	456	7827	2	32670	53	44871	254	53808	4	76079	253
2859	332	5521	356	7828	357	32678	79	44901	332	53809	405	76084	417
2861	332	5526	357	7903	35	33001	52	44932	254	55189	201	78018	187
2873	332	5532	356	7927	332	34007	49	45000	352	57566	203	78019	352
2874	337	5538	332	9303	352	34010	153	45025	203	58850	52	78022	151
2885	464	5539	332	9400	20	34016	55	45110	352	58926	404	78059	52
3205	352	5541	356	9466	455	34023	52	45163	332	60007	254	80002	151
3217	52	5542	4	9600	354	34027	163	45212	151	60009	208	80064	52
3612	352	5552	332	9629	254	34028	332	45231	403	60019	404	80072	332
3650	456	5553	332	9642	313	34039	403	45293	332	60022	166	80078	23
3717	20	5572	456	9681	356	34046	332	45305	163	60103	254	80079	352
3738	456	5619	365	9682	464	34051	166	45337	332	60532	404	80080	405
3802	49	5637	35	30064	52	34053	163	45379	9	60800	166	80097	332
3803	1	5643	254	30065	53	34058	332	45407	254	61264	403	80098	332
3814	332	5668	331	30070	53	34059	52	45428	153	61306	403	80100	52
3822	456	5764	352	30072	151	34067	55	45491	297	61572	102	80104	23
3845	332	5775	151	30096	52	34070	96	45593	354	61994	352	80105	202
3850	332	5786	355	30102	101	34072	332	45596	404	62005	153	80135	153
3855	332	5900	456	30120	55	34073	332	45690	352	62277	206	80136	358
3862	332	5952	357	30245	166	34081	103	45699	254	62469	206	80150	332
4003	20	5967	332	30499	55	34092	151	46100	101	62260	403	80151	104
4073	463	5972	184	30506	55	34101	417	46115	404	62712	202	92134	153
4110	464	6000	355	30541	52	34105	55	46201	355	62785	166	92203	3
4115	357	6023		30583	52	35005	254	46203	405	63395	153	92207	332
4121	356	6024	455	30585	455	35006	357	46229	166	63460	153	92212	403
4141	352	6106	456	30587	1	35009	332	46233	101	63601	404	92214	417
4144	456	6412	4	30777	163	35010	492	46235	372	65033	155	92219	332
4150	352	6430	1	30825	332	35011	332	46428	203	65243	202	92220	166
4160	49	6435	1	30828	89	35018	55	46441	254	65462	102	92240	52
4247	332	6619	153	30830	332	35022	332	46443	352	65567	101	92245	332

APPENDIX 2 FORMER BR DIESEL AND ELECTRIC LOCOMOTIVES AND RAILCARS

No.	*Group*	*No.*	*Group*	*No.*	*Group*
GWR Railcar No. 4	20	D4067	403	E56301	353
GWR Railcar No. 20	53	D5032	153	Sc59404	213
GWR Railcar No. 22	456	D5054	255	E56456	311
DS75	166	D5081	253	M59003	2
12077	405	D5500	166	M59004	2
12131	102	D5705	38	E79960	102
15224	72	D7017	4	E79962	151
26020	404	D7018	456	E79963	102
26500	166	D7029	153	W79964	151
D4	405	D7076	255	W79976	19
D8	203	D8000	166	W79978	105
D306	403	D8568	153		
D345	255	D9002	166		
D818	38	D9009	153		
D821	153	D9015	405		
D832	255	D9016	103		
D1010	24	D9019	153		
D1013	352	D9516	403		
D1015	38	D9520	418		
D1023	2	D9523	403		
D1041	255	D9524	202		
D1048	253	D9526	4		
D1062	352	D9529	153		
D2022	35	D9537	357		
D2023	53	D9539	357		
D2024	53	D9551	4		
D2041	105	D9553	357		
D2062	356	D0226	151		
D2072	252	ZM32	326		
D2090	166	E3036	166		
D2117	252	E5001	166		
D2192	2	S13003	438		
D2203	156	S13004	438		
D2205	53	E50341	153		
D2207	153	M50397	402		
D2245	402	W50413	4		
D2271	4	W50414	4		
D2279	104	E50416	353		
D2298	455	Sc51017	213		
D2381	254	Sc51043	213		
D2511	151	E51118	153		
D2519	151	M51592	2		
D2554	56	M51604	2		
D2578	355	M51616	403		
D2587	255	M51618	311		
D2593	255	M51622	403		
D2767	255	E56097	153		
D2860	166	E56099	153		
D2994	4	M56160	402		
D3002	49	W56168	4		
D3003	33	W56169	4		
D3022	352	E56171	353		

INDEX OF LOCATIONS